Women in Southeast Asia

a bibliography

A
Reference
Publication
in
Asian
Studies

Frank Joseph Shulman
Editor

Women in Southeast Asia

a bibliography

FAN KOK SIM

G.K.HALL &CO.

70 LINCOLN STREET, BOSTON, MASS.

Library of Congress Cataloging in Publication Data

Fan, Kok-sim.
  Women in Southeast Asia.

  Includes index.
  1. Women—Asia, Southeastern—Bibliography.
I. Title.
Z7961.F35 [HQ1745.8] 016.3054′2′0959   81-6642
ISBN 0-8161-8407-0   AACR2

This publication is printed on permanent/durable acid-free paper
MANUFACTURED IN THE UNITED STATES OF AMERICA

Contents

Contents

Contents

The Author

Mrs. Fan Kok Sim graduated from the University of Malaya with Second Class Honours in Economics. She was formerly Reference Librarian at the University of Malaya Library and is now Librarian of the newly-established Institute of Advanced Studies, University of Malaya. Mrs. Fan has written articles on librarianship as well as on labour economics in Malaysia, and has compiled two editions of Dissertation Materials in the University of Malaya Library.

Preface

The stirrings of the Women's Liberation Movement, which originated in the United States in the 60s, radiated outwards to awaken the rest of the world to the problems encountered by women. Thus was generated a renewed interest and more serious study in the subject of women. The dramatic and sensationalist facets of the feminist movement have demonstrated their transiency and are now relegated as a relatively unimportant part of history, while the more essential issues concerning women have surfaced and remained. Besides striving to achieve a greater equilibrium between the role of women and that of men, ways for the betterment of womenfolk must be sought. Global acknowledgment that the progress of women is inextricably linked to the progress of mankind was accorded when the International Women's Decade was launched in 1975 by the United Nations.

Spearheading the universal drive for the progress and development of women, the International Women's Year of 1975 emphasized the new role for women everywhere in the world, including, particularly, the women of the developing countries. In Southeast Asia, encouraging strides have already been made in the improvement of the status of women. There is now better access to secondary and tertiary education; more protective and fairer laws have been legislated; the right to vote and the right to equal pay are entrenched in most Southeast Asian countries, and employment opportunities are widening. However, much more can and must be done to enhance the status and realize the full potential of women, be they housewives, mothers, rural family help, or career women.

Study and research are the twin prerequisites, not only for further enriching the wealth of human knowledge per se, but also for forming the basis on which policies and programs are to be formulated. This bibliography was conceived with the sincere desire that it will positively assist, stimulate, and intensify study and research on all aspects of women in a region which is not only fast developing, but also emerging in international importance--Southeast Asia. It is also the cherished hope of the author that these studies and researches, whether undertaken by nationals or foreigners, besides leading to a better comprehension of women will eventually find their way to the drawing-boards of concerned authorities and organizations at national, regional, and international levels and be implemented in progressive plans for the women of Southeast Asia.

Scope

Work on collecting entries for the bibliography began in late 1977 and stopped in September 1980. Altogether, a total of 3,865 entries was recorded. The bibliography aims at being broadly comprehensive in its coverage of subject, types of materials, and time. However, the ambition to achieve exhaustiveness is a compiler's elusive dream. For example, the section on Family Planning and Fertility could very well be the subject of another separate bibliographical compilation. Lest the entries on family planning and fertility overwhelm the rest of the bibliography, the author, aware of the avalanche of writings on this very popular and important subject, decided to resist the urge to go on amassing more references here. Notwithstanding this, every attempt has been made to ensure that the more significant studies on birth control and fertility have been included.

On the other hand, not very many entries could be located for subjects like literature and psychology and for countries like Brunei, Burma, and Indochina. Bibliographical sources consulted yielded disappointing results. The paucity of information on women in these subject areas and for the countries of Brunei and Burma may perhaps be attributed to the fact that relatively little has been written about them. Moreover, the compiler's own linguistic limitations closed to her sources in certain vernacular languages like Burmese, Filipino, Thai, and Vietnamese. Constraints of work, time, and manpower did not allow the compiler to personally exploit the resources of libraries outside of Malaysia and Singapore. Nonetheless, a determined effort has been made to bring into the bibliographical net all relevant entries fished out from library catalogs, bibliographies, indexes, authors' reference lists, etc. In fact, every possible trail which might lead to a storehouse of information, be it big or small, was followed zealously. Thus, newspaper articles, footnotes, and references in books and articles, and people and organizations involved with issues on women were tapped for relevant information.

The items in this listing are predominantly in English, Malay, and Indonesian, with a fair inclusion of materials in Dutch and French. Works in the non-roman alphabet are excluded. The entries collected consist of both published and unpublished studies, ranging from monographs, documents, government publications, pamphlets, reports, mimeographed papers, theses, and academic exercises to periodical articles, chapters from books, and papers from conferences. Generally, one-page items, writings which appear to be ephemeral, trivial, or popular, and newspaper articles have been omitted; however, this compilation makes no claims to be truly selective of nota-

Preface

ble materials. It was not possible to make an evaluation with regard
to the intrinsic quality of every single work as the compiler, in
many instances, had no access to it. Nonetheless, for a pioneering
effort, it can be assumed that a very large majority of significant
works on women in Southeast Asia have been identified within these
pages.

Arrangement

The entries, which have been numbered consecutively, are grouped
by subject as shown in the Table of Contents. For several subject
categories, subdivisions by country have been made whenever the number of entries warranted this. Under each heading, the items are
arranged alphabetically by author's name. The following details are
provided for monographic publications:

1. Author's name
2. Title of work, including subtitle
3. Translation of title (for non-English works)
4. Imprint
5. Pagination
6. Series (if any)

In the imprint, names of cities have been standardized, for example,
Jakarta (Batavia, Djakarta); Jogjakarta (Yogyakarta); and the Hague
(Den Haag, s'Gravenhage). For other types of materials, bibliographical details furnished vary. For example, a citation for a
journal article includes the title of the source journal together
with the volume and issue number, the year of publication, and
inclusive pagination. The designation "1 vol. (various pagings)" is
used when a work consists of articles, papers, or chapters paginated
separately rather than continuously.

Works that are jointly written by three persons or fewer are
entered under the names of all the authors. For works written by
more than three authors, only the first-named writer is cited followed by "et al." Generally, edited materials are listed under the
name of the editor. A work is cited under its title only in cases
where the author or editor cannot be determined. In a very small
number of entries, particularly for academic exercises, the pagination is lacking, but despite this, these entries have been included
in the bibliography; completeness in citation was overlooked for the
advantage of comprehensiveness in coverage.

To effect some economy, wherever it is appropriate and will not
subject the user to any great inconvenience, works that reflect two
subjects are entered under one subject field and a general reference
is made in the subject category under which they will not be listed.
For example, items which deal with the legal aspects of marriage or
divorce appear under the heading Legal Status; Laws, etc. and a general reference under the heading Marriage and Divorce is made--"For
legal aspects see Legal Status, Laws, etc." However, where it is not

convenient or expedient to do so, an item which deals with more than
one topic is placed under each of the relevant subject headings.
Thus, a work on the socioeconomic status of women appears under both
headings--<u>Economic Conditions and Status</u> . . . and <u>Social Conditions
and Status</u>. The entries have been arranged to ensure that the user
will not miss relevant entries in the subject area in which they are
interested. Nevertheless, the user is urged to pay attention to the
notes under the various subject headings and to invest a bit more
time to search under related subjects.

Personal names

When addressing an Asian by name, Westerners, and even Asians--if
they come from a different national or cultural background--may en-
counter a problem. It would be inappropriate to explain the complexities of Asian names and the various rules governing the headings
for the names here; the user is advised to consult the <u>Anglo-American
Cataloguing Rules</u> (2d ed.) to obtain a fuller explanation. However,
in this compilation, because of various constraints, it was not possible to adopt the Anglo-American Rules in toto. As a general rule,
Burmese, Chinese, Indochinese, Malay, and Thai authors are cited in
direct order of their name, that is, under the first element in
their name. In the case of a Chinese who does not have a non-Chinese
given name, the first element of the name is the surname. On the
other hand, an Indonesian name is normally entered under the last
element of the name, whilst Filipino names, which are Westernized,
are entered under their surnames. However, when the first element of
the name is a title of nobility or a term of address or honor, it is
transposed to the end. Examples:

Burmese name:	Mya Sein, Daw
Chinese name:	Chen, Peter Shou Jen Saw, Swee Hock
Malay name:	Abdul Hadi bin Zakaria Jasma Othman, Siti
Thai name:	Visid Prachuahmoh
Vietnamese name:	Tran Van Trai
Indonesian name:	Notopuro, Hardjito

The reader is requested to take special note of Indonesian names
with the variant spelling, "u" and "oe." The letter "u" is inter-
changeable with the letters "oe" (as in Dutch) and for listing purposes, "oe" is regarded as "u." Thus, Subandrio, Hurustiati is filed
before Soebekti, Tobias in the Author Index. Ample cross-references
will be provided in the Author Index for Asian authors who do not have
surnames or are addressed by their given names, so that the user who
is unfamiliar with them will not be left to grope around. Similarly,

cross-references will be made for corporate bodies with variant names, for personal authors with compound or variant names, and names with prefixes.

Data collection

The work of collecting entries was undertaken mainly in the University of Malaya Library, whose collection of nearly 800,000 volumes is strong in Southeast Asian materials. In addition, the resources of the libraries of the Institute of Southeast Asian Studies, Singapore; Universiti Kebangsaan Malaysia; the National Library of Malaysia; Singapore National Library; the University of Singapore (now known as the National University of Singapore); and MARA Institute of Technology were tapped.

As a considerable number of entries was extracted from secondary sources of varying quality and reliability, some inaccuracies in bibliographical details may have crept into this listing. To minimize these inaccuracies at least one more source has been counter-checked, wherever possible, to verify items of dubious citation. Another problem encountered relates to the difficulty of assigning appropriate subject headings for some items, in particular for references derived from secondary sources which have not been categorized into subjects. To facilitate access to articles from Asian serials, a list of Asian serials cited, together with their places of publication, has been included in this work.

The author recognizes that a bibliography without annotated entries or a subject index will be less complete; however, the major constraint--difficulty in gaining access to a considerable percentage of materials--has precluded the feasibility of such a compilation. The bibliography, albeit with imperfections, has been compiled as meticulously as possible so that, as a reference tool, it will serve to further enrich the bibliographical resources necessary for studies on women and the Southeast Asian region.

Acknowledgments

In a bibliographical compilation of this size, the saying "many hands make light work" rings true and I am pleased to be able to express my heartfelt thanks to the people who have contributed to this work. The help which I received from Professor Frank Joseph Shulman, Director of the East Asia Collection, McKeldin Library, University of Maryland, throughout the progress of the book is immeasurable. Besides providing me with constructive comments, helpful suggestions, and steering me to important sources of information, his contribution of several hundred entries has enriched the bibliography considerably.

I am deeply indebted to Datin Patricia Lim Pui Huen, Librarian of the Institute of Southeast Asian Studies, Singapore, and her staff, for alerting me to many relevant materials and for kindly putting the resources of their collection at my disposal. Mrs. Ng Swee Hua, formerly of the Population Studies Unit, Faculty of Economics and Administration, University of Malaya, brought to my attention several pertinent bibliographies and works. My workload has been greatly lightened by Mr. M. Rajoo of the University of Malaya Library, who assisted in scanning bibliographies and in recording entries.

The burden of translating non-English titles into English was placed on the shoulders of my colleagues at the University of Malaya. Puan Shaikha Zakaria, Puan Zaiton Osman, and Puan Mazidah Zakaria carefully combed through the numerous Indonesian and Malay titles; Mrs. Holy Pasaribu tackled the Dutch items, while Dr. Laurent Metzger dealt with the French titles.

I am very appreciative of the painstaking efforts that Mrs. Loh Yoon Phooi, Tengku Norazam, and Cik Rodziah Mohd Yusof put into the typing of several drafts of the manuscript. My sincere thanks go to those libraries in Malaysia and Singapore for permitting me to tap their resources and also to those libraries in the Philippines, Thailand, Australia, U.S.A., and elsewhere for having responded to my requests for assistance by verifying bibliographical details or furnishing me with the required information. To Ms. Jennefer Sebstad, who kindly made available to me her unpublished bibliography on women in Southeast Asia, to my publishers, G.K. Hall & Co., and all those,

Acknowledgments

too numerous to mention on this page but not forgotten, I would like to place on record my appreciation for their cooperation and help. However, the responsibility for any errors or imperfections in this bibliography rests solely with the compiler.

Finally, a special acknowledgment of thanks to my husband, Yew Seng, for his continuous encouragement and moral support--and for bearing with me on the several occasions when I worked into the wee hours of the morning.

K.S. Fan

Main Published Sources Consulted

For serial publications, the years
scanned are noted in parentheses.

ABC POL SCI: Advance Bibliography of Contents: Political Science & Government. Santa Barbara, Calif.: American Bibliographical Center-Clio Press. (1969-1979)

Association for Asian Studies. Bibliography of Asian Studies. New Haven, Conn.: Association for Asian Studies. (1970-1976)

_____. Cumulative Bibliography of Asian Studies, 1941-1965; 1966-1970. Boston, Mass.: G.K. Hall, 1970-1972.

Bibliografi Negara Malaysia. Malaysian National Bibliography. Kuala Lumpur: Perpustakaan Negara Malayasia. (1967-1977)

Bloomfield, Barry C. Theses on Asia Accepted by Universities in the United Kingdom and Ireland, 1877-1964. London: F. Cass, 1967.

Books on Demand and Doctoral Dissertations on Feminism and Women's Studies. Ann Arbor, Mich.: University Microfilms International, 1979.

Buvinić, Mayra et al. Women and World Development: An Annotated Bibliography. Washington, D.C.: Overseas Development Council, 1976.

Chen, Peter Shou Jen, and Tai, Ching Ling. Social Development in Singapore: A Select Bibliography. Singapore: Chopmen Enterprises, 1976.

Chety, Sida. Research on Thailand in the Philippines: An Annotated Bibliography of Theses, Dissertations and Investigation Papers. Ithaca, N.Y.: Department of Asian Studies, Cornell University, 1977.

Main Published Sources Consulted

Chung, Betty Jaime. The Status of Women and Fertility in South-east and East Asia: A Bibliography with Selected Annotations. Singapore: Institute of Southeast Asian Studies, 1976.

Comprehensive Dissertation Index, 1861-1972. Ann Arbor, Mich., Xerox University Microfilms, 1973.

Ee, George Cheng Hoe. Bibliomed-SM: A Comprehensive Bibliography of Medicine and Related Sciences in Singapore and Malaysia. Tokyo: Southeast Asian Medical Information Center, 1976.

Fan, Kok Sim. Dissertation Materials in the University of Malaya Library. Rev. ed. Kuala Lumpur: University of Malaya Library, 1977.

Freedman, Ronald. The Sociology of Human Fertility: An Annotated Bibliography. New York: Irvington Publishers, 1975.

Goil, N.K. Asian Social Science Bibliography: With Annotations and Abstracts. Delhi: Hindustan Publishing Corp., 1977.

Hobbs, Cecil Carlton. Indochina: A Bibliography of the Land and People. New York: Greenwood Press, 1969.

Indeks Majalah Malaysia. Malaysian Periodicals Index. Kuala Lumpur: Perpustakaan Negara Malaysia. (1973-1979)

Index of Indonesian Learned Periodicals. Indeks Majalah Ilmiah. Jakarta: Indonesian Institute of Sciences. (1961-1974)

Index to Philippine Periodicals. Quezon City: University of the Philippines Library. (1959-1977)

Indonesia, Projek Perpustakaan Nasional. Bibliografi Nasional Indonesia, Kumulasi 1945-1963. Jakarta: P.N. Balai Pustaka, 1965.

Institute of Southeast Asian Studies, Library. Library Accessions List. Singapore: Institute of Southeast Asian Studies.

Jacobs, Sue-Ellen. Women in Perspective: A Guide for Cross-Cultural Studies. Urbana: University of Illinois Press, 1974.

Johnson, Donald Clay. Index to Southeast Asian Journals, 1960-1974: A Guide to Articles, Book Reviews and Composite Works. Boston, Mass.: G.K. Hall, 1977.

Keyes, Jane Godfrey. A Bibliography of North Vietnamese Publications in the Cornell University Library. Ithaca, N.Y.: Southeast Asia Program, Department of Asian Studies, Cornell University, 1962.

Main Published Sources Consulted

_____. A Bibliography of Western-Language Publications Concerning North Vietnam in the Cornell University Library. Ithaca, N.Y.: Southeast Asia Program, Department of Asian Studies, Cornell University, 1966.

Koentjaraningrat, Raden Mas. Anthropology in Indonesia: A Bibliographical Review. The Hague: Martinus Nijhoff, 1975.

Kusbandarrumsamsi, Hendrarta. Selected Indonesia Periodical Articles on Women and Womanhood. Karangan-karangan dalam Majalah Ilmiah Indoneisa tentang Wanita dan Kewanitaan, 1952-1976. Jakarta: Indonesian Institute of Sciences, Project for the Development of a Social Sciences Documentation and Information Center, 1979.

Lian The, and Van der Veur, Paul W. Treasures and Trivia: Doctoral Dissertations on Southeast Asia Accepted by Universities in the United States. Athens, Ohio: Southeast Asian Program, Center for International Studies, Ohio University, 1968.

London School of Oriental and African Studies. Library Catalogue, V. 20, Subject Catalogue: Southeast Asia and Pacific Islands. Boston, Mass.: G.K. Hall, 1963.

Nemenzo, Catalina A. Graduate Theses in Philippine Universities and Colleges--1908-1969: An Annotated Bibliography. Quezon City: Philippine Center for Advanced Studies, University of the Philippines System, 1974.

Ng, Swee Hua. A Bibliography of Demography in Malaysia. Kuala Lumpur: Faculty of Economics and Administration, University of Malaya, 1977.

Pelzer, Karl J. West Malaysia and Singapore: A Selected Bibliography. New Haven, Conn.: Human Relations Area Files Press, 1971.

Philippine National Bibliography. Manila: National Library of the Philippines. (1964-1977)

Population Index. Princeton, N.J.: Princeton University for the Population Association of America. (1955-1977)

Public Affairs Information Service Bulletin. New York: Public Affairs Information Service, Inc. (1950-1979)

Saito, Shiro. Philippine Ethnography: A Critically Annotated and Selected Bibliography. Honolulu: University Press of Hawaii, 1972.

Main Published Sources Consulted

Sardesai, D.R., and Sardesai, Bhanu D. Theses and Dissertations on Southeast Asia: An International Bibliography in Social Sciences, Education and Fine Arts. Zug, Switzerland: Inter-Documentation Co., 1970.

Saw, Swee Hock, and Cheng, Siok Hwa. A Bibliography of the Demography of Malaysia and Brunei. Singapore: University Education Press, 1975.

_____. A Bibliography of the Demography of Singapore. Singapore: University Education Press, 1975.

Shulman, Frank Joseph. Doctoral Dissertations on Asia: An Annotated Bibliographical Journal of Current International Research. Ann Arbor, Mich.: Association for Asian Studies.

_____. "Doctoral Research on Malaya and Malaysia, 1895-1977: A Comprehensive Bibliography and Statistical Overview." In Malaysian Studies: Present Knowledge and Research Trends. Edited by John A. Lent. De Kalb, Ill.: Center for Southeast Asian Studies, Northern Illinois University, 1979, pp. 251-436.

Sebstad, Jennefer. "Women in Southeast Asia: An Annotated Bibliography." Ann Arbor, Mich., 1974. (Prepared for a course on development in Southeast Asia at the Department of Geography, University of Michigan.)

Singapore National Bibliography. Singapore: National Library. (1967-1977)

Singapore Periodicals Index. Singapore: National Library. (1969-1976)

Singapore University, Library, Reference Department. Dissertations, Theses and Academic Exercises, 1947-1976. Singapore: University of Singapore Library, 1977.

Singarimbun, Masri. The Population of Indonesia: A Bibliography (1930-1972). Jogjakarta: Institute of Population Studies, 1974.

Social Sciences Index. New York: H.W. Wilson. (1965-1979)

Stucki, Curtis W. American Doctoral Dissertations on Asia 1933-June 1966, including Appendix of Master's Theses at Cornell University. Ithaca, N.Y.: Southeast Asia Program, Department of Asian Studies, Cornell University, 1968.

Trager, Frank N. Burma: A Selected and Annotated Bibliography. New Haven, Conn.: Human Relations Area Files Press, 1973.

United Nations, Asian and Pacific Centre for Women and Development. A Selective List of Documents on Women in Development in the ESCAP Region. Bangkok: Asian and Pacific Centre for Women and Development, 1980.

United Nations, Economic Commission for Asia and the Pacific. Reading Profile on the Status of Women. New York: United Nations, 1980.

U.S. Library of Congress. Library of Congress Catalogs. Subject Catalog. Washington, D.C.: Library of Congress. 1970-Sept. 1979.

_____, Orientalia Division. Southeast Asia Subject Catalog. Boston, Mass.: G.K. Hall, 1972.

U.S. Library of Congress Office (Jakarta). Accessions List: Southeast Asia. Jakarta: Library of Congress Office. (1977-1979)

Universiti Kebangsaan Malaysia, Library. Bibliografi Kebudayaan Melayu. Kuala Lumpur: Perpustakaan Universiti Kebangsaan Malaysia, 1977.

Velez, Maria Cristina. Images of the Filipina: A Bibliography. Manila: Ala-Ala Foundation, in cooperation with the UNESCO National Commission of the Philippines and Yutivo Foundation, 1975.

Women Studies Abstracts. Rush, N.Y.: Rush Publishing Co. (1973-1978)

Asian Serials Cited

Academy of Medicine, Singapore, Annals. (Singapore)

Agricultural, Commercial and Industrial Life. (Manila)

Akademika; Jernal Ilmu Kemanusiaan dan Sains Kemasyarakatan.
Journal of Humanities and Social Sciences. (Kuala Lumpur)

Aktual. (Kuala Lumpur)

Analisa. (Jakarta)

Archipelago; the International Magazine of the Philippines.
(Manila)

ASEAN Journal. (Singapore)

ASEAN Review. (Kuala Lumpur)

Asia; Asian Quarterly of Culture and Synthesis. (Saigon)

Asia Magazine. (Hong Kong)

Asian & Pacific Quarterly of Cultural and Social Affairs.
(Seoul)

Asian Business. (Hong Kong)

Asian Culture. (Saigon)

Asian Culture Quarterly. (Taipei)

Asian Journal of Medicine. (Hong Kong)

Asian Profile. (Hong Kong)

Asian Studies. (Quezon City, Philippines)

Asian Trade and Industry. (Kuala Lumpur)

Bahana. (Brunei)

Bahasa dan Budaya. (Jakarta)

Bahasa dan Sastra. (Jakarta)

Bangkok Bank Monthly Review. (Bangkok)

Basis; Majalah Kebudayaan Umum. (Jogjakarta, Indonesia)

Berita MMA; Newsletter of the Malaysian Medical Association. (Kuala Lumpur)

Berita Perpustakaan Sekolah. (Jakarta)

Berkala Pembangunan. (Bandjermasin, Indonesia)

Bingkisan Pertiwi. (Kuala Lumpur)

Bintang Merah; Madjalah Teori dan Politik Marxisme-Leninisme. (Jakarta)

Black Gold. (Philippines)

Boletín eclesiástico de Filipínas. (Manila)

British Medical Association, Malaya Branch, Journal. (Singapore)

Brunei Museum Journal. (Kota Batu, Brunei)

Budaya Jaya; Madjalah Kebudajaan Umum. (Jakarta)

Buddhism. (Rangoon)

Buku Kita. (Jakarta)

Bulletin de liaison des étudiants en droit. (Phnom Penh)

Bulletin des Amis du Royaume Lao. (Vientiane)

Bulletin Forum Studi. (Bandung, Indonesia)

Bulletin YAPERNA. (Jakarta)

Bureau of Public Schools, Memorandum. (Manila)

Bureau of Women and Minors, Digest. (Manila)

Burma Research Society, Journal. (Rangoon)

CLSU Scientific Journal, (Nueva Ecija, Philippines)

Cakrawala; Majalah Penelitian Sosial. (Salatiga, Indonesia)

Centro Escolar University, Manila, Graduate and Faculty Studies.
(Manila)

Chorus; Journal of the Singapore Teachers' Association.
(Singapore)

Chronicle Magazine. (Manila)

College Folio. (Quezon City, Philippines)

Commerce Journal. (Manila)

Commonwealth Advocate. (Manila)

Contemporary Southeast Asia. (Singapore)

Contemporary Studies. (Makati, Rizal, Philippines)

Dakwah. (Kuala Lumpur)

Daya Sosial; Madjalah Ilmiah Populer. (Jakarta)

Dewan Bahasa. (Kuala Lumpur)

Dewan Masyarakat. (Kuala Lumpur)

Dewan Sastera. (Kuala Lumpur)

Dialogue. (Manila)

Dian; Madjalah Industri. (Jakarta)

Diliman Review. (Quezon City, Philippines)

Dinamika Mahasiswa. (Malang, Indonesia)

Dokumentasi LEKNAS. (Jakarta)

Dokumentasi Tenaga Kerdja. (Indonesia)

East Asian Cultural Studies. (Tokyo)

Eastern Horizon. (Hong Kong)

Ecole Française d'Extreme-Orient, Bulletin. (Hanoi)

Economica; Majalah Mahasiswa Ekonomi. (Jakarta)

Economic and Political Weekly. (Bombay)

Economic Bulletin. (Kuala Lumpur)

Economic Bulletin for Asia and the Pacific. (Bangkok)

Economic Research Journal. (Manila)

Education. (Saigon)

Education Quarterly. (Quezon City, Philippines)

Ekonomi. (Jakarta)

Ekonomi. (Kuala Lumpur)

Examiner. (Quezon City, Philippines)

Excelsior; Majalah Bulanan Majelis Pusat Pendidekan Kristen.
(Salatiga, Indonesia)

Expressweek. (Manila)

Fajar Islam. (Singapore)

Far East Medical Journal. (Hong Kong)

Far Eastern Economic Review. (Hong Kong)

Far Eastern Law Review. (Manila)

Federation Museums Journal. (Kuala Lumpur)

Feminist Japan. (Tokyo)

Filipina. (Manila)

Filipiana Review. (Manila?)

Focus. (Manila)

Fookien Times Philippines Yearbook. Formerly Fookien Times
Yearbook. (Manila)

Foreign Affairs Bulletin. (Bangkok)

Forward. (Rangoon)

France-Asie. (Tokyo)

Freedom. (Manila)

Gapura. (Surabaya, Indonesia)

Gema Islam. (Jakarta)

Geneeskundig tijdschrift voor Nederlandsch-Indie. (Jakarta)

General Education Journal. (Quezon City, Philippines)

Geographica. (Kuala Lumpur)

Graduate Forum. (Legaspi City, Philippines)

Guardian. (Rangoon)

Hikmah. (Kota Kinabalu, Sabah)

Horizons. (Saigon)

Hukum. (Jakarta)

Hukum dan Keadilan; Majalah Persatuan Advokat Indonesia.
(Jakarta)

Hukum dan Masyarakat. (Jakarta)

Hukum Nasional; Majalah Badan Pembinaan Hukum Nasional.
(Jakarta)

Human Resource Development Journal. (Quezon City, Philippines)

Ilmu Alam. (Kuala Lumpur)

Impact. (Pasay City, Philippines)

Indian Antiquary. (Bombay)

Indian Journal of Adult Education. (New Delhi)

Indisch vrouwen jaarboek. (Jogjakarta, Indonesia)

Indochine, sud-est asiatique. (Saigon)

Indonesia. (Jakarta)

Indonesia Magazine. (Jakarta)

Indonesian Affairs. (Jakarta)

Indonesian Journal of Geography. Madjalah Geografi Indonesia. (Jogjakarta, Indonesia)

Indonesian Spectator; the Magazine of Indonesian Affairs. (Jakarta)

Integrated Bar of the Philippines, Journal. (Quezon City, Philippines)

International Journal of Sociology of the Family. (Delhi, India)

Intisari; the Research Quarterly of Malaysia. (Singapore)

Irian; Bulletin of Irian Jaya Development. (Jayapura)

al-Islam. (Singapore)

al-Jami'ah; Majalah Ilmu Pengetahuan Agama Islam. (Jogjakarta, Indonesia)

Jernal Anthropologi dan Sosiologi. (Kuala Lumpur)

Jernal Sejarah. (Kuala Lumpur)

Jiwa; Majalah Psikiatri. (Jakarta)

Jiwa Baru; Majalah Pendidikan. (Jogjakarta, Indonesia)

Journal of East Asiatic Studies. (Manila)

Journal of Economic Development and Social Change in Asia and the Pacific. (Singapore)

Journal of Family Welfare. (Bombay)

Journal of Malaysian and Comparative Law. Jernal Undang-undang. (Kuala Lumpur)

Journal of Public Administration. (Manila)

Journal of Social Sciences. (Bangkok)

Journal of Sociology and Psychology. (Singapore)

Journal of Southeast Asian Studies. (Singapore)

Journal of the Indian Archipelago and Eastern Asia. (Singapore)

Jurnal Pendidikan. (Kuala Lumpur)

Jurnal Penelitian Sosial. (Jakarta)

Kajian Ekonomi Malaysia. (Kuala Lumpur)

Kancil. (Shah Alam, Malaysia)

Karya Wira Jati. (Bandung, Indonesia)

Keluarga. (Kuala Lumpur)

Keluarga Berentjana. (Jakarta)

Keluarga Sejahtera. (Jakarta)

Kemajuan Ilmu, Teknik dan Hidup. (Jakarta)

Kesehatan Masyarakat. (Jakarta)

Komentar. (Kuala Lumpur)

Labor Review. (Quezon City, Philippines)

Law Review. (Cebu City, Philippines)

Lembaran Ilmu Pengetahuan IKIP Semarang. (Indonesia)

Liwayway. (Manila)

Luat Hoc Kinh-Te. (Saigon)

MD Journal. (Rizal, Philippines)

MLQU Graduate Journal. (Manila)

Majalah Administrasi Negara. (Jakarta)

Majalah Berkala Pertanian. (Jakarta)

Majalah Berkala Peternakan. (Indonesia)

Majalah Demografi Indonesia. Journal of Indonesian Demography.
(Jakarta)

Majalah Fakultas Hukum (Universitas Indonesia). (Jakarta)

Majallah Guru. (Kuala Lumpur)

Majalah Hygiene Perusahaan Kesehatan Keselamatan Kerja dan
Jaminan Sosial. (Jakarta)

Majalah Ilmu Bahasa, Ilmu Bumi dan Kebudayaan Indonesia.
(Jakarta)

Majalah Ilmu-ilmu Sastra Indonesia. Indonesian Journal of
Cultural Studies. (Jakarta)

Majalah Kedokteraan Diponegoro. (Semarang, Indonesia)

Majalah Kedokteran Indonesia; the Journal of the Indonesian
Medical Association. (Jakarta)

Majalah Kedokteran Surabaya. (Surabaya, Indonesia)

Majalah Kelantan. (Kota Bahru, Malaysia)

Majalah Kesehatan. (Jakarta)

Majalah Kesehatan ABRI. Medical Journal of the Indonesian Armed
Forces. (Jakarta)

Majalah Kesehatan Angkatan Perang. (Jakarta)

Majalah Kesehatan Jiwa. (Indonesia)

Majalah Obstetri dan Ginekologi Indonesia. Indonesian Journal of
Obstetrics and Gynecology. (Jakarta)

Majalah Penyuluh Sosial; Ilmiah, Ringan Kemasyarakatan. (Jakarta)

Majalah Perpajakan Indonesia. (Jakarta)

Majalah Pertanian. (Jakarta)

Madjalah Sejarah Militer Angkatan Darat. (Bandung, Indonesia)

Majalah Universitas Hasanuddin. (Makassar, Indonesia)

Malacca Guardian Wangkang Memento. (Malacca, Malaysia)

Malaya Law Review. (Singapore)

Malayan Economic Review. (Singapore)

Malayan Educator. (Penang, Malaysia)

Malayan Law Journal. (Singapore)

Malayan Medical Journal. (Singapore)

Malaysia, Ministry of Education, Journal. (Kuala Lumpur)

Malaysia dari Segi Sejarah. (Kuala Lumpur)

Malaysia in History; the Journal of the Malaysian Historical
Society. (Kuala Lumpur)

Malaysian Business. (Kuala Lumpur)

Manpower Philippines. (Manila)

Manusia dan Masyarakat. (Kuala Lumpur)

Manusia Indonesia. (Jakarta)

Masalah Bangunan. (Bandung, Indonesia)

Mastika. (Kuala Lumpur)

Masyarakat Indonesia. Indonesian Community. (Jakarta)

Mawas Diri. (Jakarta)

Medan Bahasa; Madjallah Hemuat Hal-Ihwal Bahasa Indonesia dan Bahasa Daerah di Indonesia. (Jakarta)

Medan Ilmu Pengetahuan. (Jakarta)

Media Ikatan Keberabatan Antropologi. (Jakarta)

Medical Association of Thailand, Journal. (Bangkok)

Medical Journal of Malaysia. (Kuala Lumpur)

Menara. (Kuala Lumpur)

Mimbar Hukum. (Jogjakarta, Indonesia)

Mimbar Indonesia. (Jakarta)

Mimbar Islam. (Kuala Lumpur)

Mimbar Kekarya ABRI. (Jakarta)

Mimbar Ulama. (Jakarta)

Mindanao Historical Journal. (Philippines)

Mirror Magazine. (Manila)

Modern Review. (Calcutta)

Moniteur d'Indochine. (Hanoi)

Nation. (Manila)

National Security Review. (Rizal, Philippines)

National Review. (Manila)

Asian Serials Cited

National Youth Leadership Training Institute, Singapore, Journal. (Singapore)

Nederlandsch-Indische Juristan-Vereeniging. Handelingen. (Jakarta)

New Directions. (Singapore)

New Philippines. (Manila)

New Straits Times Annual. (Kuala Lumpur)

Northwestern Mindanao Research Journal. (Ozamiz City, Philippines)

Notes and Queries on China and Japan. (Hong Kong)

Obstetrical and Gynaecological Society, Proceedings. (Singapore)

Ons nageslacht. (Indonesia)

Onze stem. (Jakarta)

Opinion. (Kuala Lumpur)

Options for Policy and Practice. (Manila)

Orient. (Quezon City)

Oriza. (Mataram, Indonesia)

PAFTE Review. (Manila)

PSSC Social Science Information. (Quezon City, Philippines)

Paediatrica Indonesiana. (Jakarta)

Panorama. (Manila)

Pandji Islam. (Indonesia)

Panji Masyarakat. (Kuala Lumpur)

Pedoman dan Berita Department Kesehatan. (Jakarta)

Pekerjasama Malaysia. The Malaysian Co-operator. (Kuala Lumpur)

Pemimpin. (Kuala Lumpur)

Penelitian Gizi dan Makanan. (Bogor, Indonesia)

Pengaman. (Kuala Lumpur)

Asian Serials Cited

Phap-Ly Tap-San. (Hanoi, then Saigon)

Phu nu Viet-Nam. (Hanoi)

Philippine Christian Advance. (Manila)

Philippine Economic Journal. (Manila)

Philippine Economy and Industrial Journal. (Manila)

Philippine Economy Review. (Manila)

Philippine Education. (Manila)

Philippine Educational Forum. (Manila)

Philippine Educational Quarterly. (Manila)

Philippine Extension Worker. (Manila)

Philippine Federation of Private Medical Practitioners, Journal.
(Manila)

Philippine Industry. (Manila)

Philippine Journal of Communications Studies. (Quezon City,
Philippines)

Philippine Journal of Education. (Manila)

Philippine Journal of Home Economics. (Manila)

Philippine Journal of Nursing. (Manila)

Philippine Journal of Pediatrics. (Manila)

Philippine Journal of Philately. (Manila)

Philippine Journal of Psychology. (Quezon City, Philippines)

Philippine Journal of Public Administration. (Manila)

Philippine Labor. (Manila)

Philippine Law Journal. (Quezon City, Philippines)

Philippine Magazine. (Manila)

Philippine Medical Association, Journal. (Quezon City,
Philippines)

Philippine Medical Women's Association, Journal. (Manila)

Philippine Panorama. (Manila)

Philippine Priests' Forum. (Manila)

Philippine Quarterly of Culture and Society. (Cebu City, Philippines)

Philippine Review. (Manila)

Philippine Social Sciences and Humanities Review. (Quezon City, Philippines)

Philippine Social Security Bulletin. (Manila)

Philippine Sociological Review. (Quezon City, Philippines)

Philippine Statistician. (Manila)

Philippine Studies. (Manila)

Philippines Free Press. (Manila)

Philippines Herald Magazine. (Manila)

Philippines Quarterly. (Manila)

Philippines Today. (Manila)

Philippines Yearbook. (Manila)

Philippiniana Sacra. (Manila)

Phu-nu Viet-Nam. (Hanoi)

Power and Industry. (Manila)

Prisma. (Jakarta)

Profil Saraf Jiwa. (Jogjakarta, Indonesia)

Publico; Majalah Hukum dan Pengetahuan Masyarakat. (Malang, Indonesia)

Pudjangga Baru; Madjalah Kebudajaan. (Jakarta)

Pulse. (Quezon City, Philippines)

Pusara; Majalah Pendidikan, Ilmu dan Kebudayaan. (Jogjakarta, Indonesia)

Asian Serials Cited

Puspaniaga. (Kuala Lumpur)

Que Huong. (Saigon)

The Quill. (Chicago)

Review of Southeast Asian Studies. (Singapore)

Revista Filipina de medicina y farmacia. (Manila)

Revue indochinoise. (Hanoi)

Roh Islam. (Petaling Jaya, Malaysia)

Royal Asiatic Society of Great Britain and Ireland, Malaysian Branch, Journal. (Kuala Lumpur)

Royal Asiatic Society of Great Britain and Ireland, Straits Branch, Journal. (Singapore)

Sabah College Borneo Society, Journal. (Jesselton, Sabah)

Saint Louis University Research Journal. (Baguio City, Philippines)

Salam. (Manila)

Sana Budaya. (Jogjakarta, Indonesia)

Santajiwa. (Kota Bahru, Malaysia)

Santo Tomas Journal of Medicine. (Manila)

Sarawak Gazette. (Kuching, Sarawak)

Sarawak Museum Journal. (Kuching, Sarawak)

Sarina. (Kuala Lumpur)

Saripati. (Kuala Lumpur)

Science Bulletin. (Manila)

Science Review. (Manila)

Sedar; Journal of the Muslim Society, University of Singapore. (Singapore)

Siam Repository. (Bangkok)

Siam Society, Journal. (Bangkok)

Siasat. (Jakarta)

Silliman Journal. (Dumaguete City, Philippines)

Sinar Darussalam. (Banda Aceh, Indonesia)

Singapore Medical Journal. (Singapore)

Singapore Paediatric Society, Journal. (Singapore)

Singapore Police Journal. (Singapore)

Singapore Public Health Bulletin. (Singapore)

Singapore Statistical Bulletin. (Singapore)

Singapore Trade and Industry. (Singapore)

Social Work. (Manila)

Société des études indo-chinoises de Saigon, Bulletin. (Saigon)

Solidarity. (Manila)

Sosiografi Indonesia. (Jogjakarta, Indonesia)

Sound and Sense. (Baguio City, Philippines)

South Seas Society, Journal. (Singapore)

Southeast Asia Journal. (Iloilo City, Philippines)

Southeast Asian Affairs. (Singapore)

Southeast Asian Journal of Social Science. (Singapore)

South-east Asian Journal of Sociology. (Singapore)

Southeast Asian Journal of Tropical Medicine and Public Health. (Bangkok)

Southeast Asian Studies. (Kyoto, Japan)

Sriwijaya. (Palembang, Indonesia)

Standard. (Bangkok)

Stannia. (Jakarta)

Statistical Reporter. (Manila)

Straits Chinese Magazine. (Singapore)

Asian Serials Cited

Straits Times Annual. (Singapore)

Suara Ekonomi. (Jakarta)

Suara Guru. (Jakarta)

Suara Majlis Ugama Islam Kedah. (Kedah, Malaysia)

Sulu Studies. (Jakarta)

Suara Taqwa. (Shah Alam, Malaysia)

Sunburst. (Makati, Philippines)

Sunday Times Magazine. (Manila)

Teachers College Journal. (Manila)

Technical Association of Malaysia, Journal. (Kuala Lumpur)

Thai Journal of Development Administration. Warasan phattahana-borihansat. (Bangkok)

Tijdschrift voor Nederlandsch-Indië. (Jakarta)

Times Journal. (Rizal, Philippines)

Trisakti. (Jakarta)

Trubus. (Jakarta)

UST Journal of Education. (Manila)

UST Law Review. (Manila)

Unesco Philippines. (Manila)

Union Herald. (Petaling Jaya, Malaysia)

Union of Burma Journal of Science and Technology. (Rangoon)

Unitas; a Quarterly Review of the Arts and Science. (Manila)

United Asia; International Magazine of Afro-Asian Affairs. (Bombay)

University of the East Law Journal. (Manila)

University of the Philippines Anthropology Bulletin. (Quezon City, Philippines)

University of the Philippines Economic Bulletin. (Quezon City, Philippines)

Vietnam Magazine. (Saigon)

Vietnamese Studies. (Hanoi)

Wahida. (Kuala Lumpur)

Wanita. (Kuala Lumpur)

Warta Demografi. (Jakarta)

Warta Kejuruan. (Jakarta)

Warta ZPG; Journal of the Student Movement for Zero Population Growth. (Jogjakarta, Indonesia)

Weekly Graphic. (Manila)

Weekly Nation. (Quezon City, Philippines)

Widya. (Kuala Lumpur)

Woman's World. (Manila)

Women of Viet Nam. (Hanoi)

World Muslim League Monthly Magazine. (Singapore)

Women in Southeast Asia

BIBLIOGRAPHIES

1   AAAS SEMINAR ON WOMEN IN DEVELOPMENT, Mexico, 1975. Women and
    World Development: With an Annotated Bibliography. Edited
    by Irene Tinker, Michele Bo Bramsen, and Mayra Buvinić.
    New York: Praeger, in cooperation with the Overseas Devel-
    opment Council, 1976, vii, 382 pp.

2   ANANDA, PETER, comp. "Women in the Philippines: A Prelimi-
    nary Bibliography." Addendum compiled by Lydia Colina.
    CORMOSEA Newsletter 7 (1973/74):18-21; 8 (1974/75):10-11.

3   BUVINIĆ, MAYRA; ADAMS, CHERI STORTON; and EDGCOMB, GABRIELLE
    SIMON. Women in Development: Preliminary Annotated Bib-
    liography, 1975. Washington, D.C.: American Association
    for the Advancement of Science, 1975, 63 pp.

4   BUVINIĆ, MAYRA et al. Women and World Development: An Anno-
    tated Bibliography. Washington, D.C.: Overseas Develop-
    ment Council, 1976, ix, 162 pp.

5   CHAO, BETTY, comp. Women: A Booklist. Singapore: National
    Library, 1975, 21 pp.

6   CHUNG, BETTY JAMIE. The Status of Women and Fertility in
    Southeast and East Asia: A Bibliography with Selected
    Annotations. Singapore: Institute of Southeast Asian
    Studies, 1978, 167 pp.

7   EVIOTA, ELIZABETH U. "Philippine Women and Development: An
    Annotated Bibliography." Completed research project.
    Quezon City: Institute of Philippine Culture, Ateneo de
    Manila University, 1978, 26 pp.

8   JACOBS, SUE-ELLEN. Women in Perspective: A Guide for Cross-
    cultural Studies. Urbana: University of Illinois Press,
    1974, xvi, 299 pp.

9   KUSBANDARRUMSAMSI, HENDRARTA, comp. Selected Indonesian
    Periodical Articles on Women and Womanhood. Karangan-
    karangan dalam Majalah Ilmiah Indonesia Tentang Wanita dan
    Kewanitaan, 1952-1976. Jakarta: Indonesian Institute of
    Sciences, Project for the Development of a Social Sciences
    Documentation and Information Center, 1978, vi, 38 pp.

10 MATRO, ROSITA, comp. The Filipino Woman: A Preliminary
    Bibliography. Manila: Population Institute Library,
    University of the Philippines, 1975, 34 pp. UPPI Bibliog-
    raphy Series, no. 2.

11 PERPUSTAKAAN NEGARA, Singapore. Wanita: Senarai Buku-buku
    yang Dikarang oleh Wanita atau Mengenai Wanita [Women: a
    list of books written by women or about women]. Disusun
    sempena dengan Wanita Antarabangsa 1975 oleh Perkhidmatan
    Muda-Mudi, Perpustakaan Negara. Singapore: Perpustakaan
    Negara, 1975, 10 pp.

12 RIHANI, MAY. Development as if Women Mattered: An Annotated
    Bibliography with a Third World Focus. Prepared under the
    auspices of the Secretariat for Women in Development of the
    New TransCentury Foundation. Washington, D.C.: Overseas
    Development Council, 1978, vi, 137 pp.

13 SALMON, CLAUDINE. "Essai de bibliographie sur la question
    féminine en Indonésie" [A bibliographical essay on the
    feminine problem in Indonesia]. Archipel, no. 13 (1977):
    23-36.

14 SEBSTAD, JENNEFER. "Women in Southeast Asia: An Annotated
    Bibliography." Ann Arbor, Mich., 1974, 47 pp. (Prepared
    for a course on development in Southeast Asia at the De-
    partment of Geography, University of Michigan.)

15 SHARMA, PRAKASH C. Female Working Role and Economic Develop-
    ment: A Selected Research Bibliography. Monticello, Ill.:
    Council of Planning Librarians, 1974, 16 pp. Council of
    Planning Librarians, Exchange Bibliography, 663.

16 SMITHSONIAN INSTITUTION, Interdisciplinary Communications
    Program, International Program for Population Analysis.
    An Introduction to the Social Science Literature on
    'Woman's Place' and Fertility in the Developing World.
    Nancy Birdsall, compiler. Washington, D.C.: Smithsonian
    Institution, 1974, 39 pp. Annotated Bibliography 2, no. 1.

17 Status of Women: A Select Bibliography, 1965-1975. New York:
     UNIFO Publishers, 1976, 121 pp.

18 UNESCO, Regional Office for Education in Asia, Bangkok.
     Documents on Women's Education and Women in Public Life
     (Representing Documents in the Library of the Regional
     Office). Rev. ed. Bangkok: Unesco Regional Office for
     Education in Asia, 1970, 20 pp.

19 UNITED NATIONS, Asian and Pacific Development Institute.
     Special Bibliography on Development Planning for Women.
     Issued in connection with the Training Seminar on Develop-
     ment Planning for Women, Bangkok, 14 September-25 October,
     1978. Bangkok: Asian and Pacific Development Institute,
     1978, 18 pp.

20 _____. Special Bibliography on Techniques of Participation
     for Women. Bangkok: APDI Library and Documentation
     Centre, 1978, 22 pp.

21 UNITED NATIONS, Economic and Social Commission for Asia and
     the Pacific. Reading Profile on the Status of Women. New
     York: United Nations, 1980, vii, 161 pp. United Nations
     Document ST/ESCAP/112.

22 VELEZ, MARIA CRISTINA, ed. Images of the Filipina: A Bibli-
     ography. Manila: Ala-Ala Foundation, in cooperation with
     the UNESCO National Commission of the Philippines and
     Yutivo Foundation, 1975, 219 pp.

23 WORLD CONFERENCE OF THE INTERNATIONAL WOMEN'S YEAR, Mexico
     City, 1975. International Women's Year World Conference
     Documents. Index. New York: UNIFO Publishers, 1976, vi,
     65 pp.

BIOGRAPHIES

(For women writers see Literary Aspects;
Literary Collections; Women in Literature)

General

24 ABDULGANI, RUSLAN, Hadji. Dua Sambutan tentang Tuanku Imam
     Bondjol dan Ibu Raden Dewi Sartika [Two opinions about
     Tuanku Imam Bondjol and Ibu Raden Dewi Sartika]. Jakarta:
     B.P.U. Perusahaan-perusahaan Pertjetakan dan Penerbitan
     Negara, Departemen Penerangan R.I., 1964, 36 pp.

25 ALAM, SYAMSUL. "Opu Daeng Risadju, Wanita Alim Yang Jadi Kaum
Pergerakan" [Opu Daeng Risadju, a female Muslim scholar who
became an activist]. Mimbar Ulama 1, no. 4 (1976):76-80.

26 ALFREDSON. "Thailand: A Very Special Kind of Artist."
Asian & Pacific Quarterly of Cultural and Social Affairs
6, no. 1 (Summer 1974):69-71. (On the sculptress Khun
Misiem Yip-InTsoi. This was apparently taken from/
reprinted from the Bangkok Post [no date given] and was
written by a person named Alfredson for whom no first name
is provided in this journal.)

27 ALZONA, ENCARNACIÓN. Librada Avelino: A Biography. Manila:
Centro Escolar University, 1974, vi, 193 pp.

28 _____. María Paz Mendoza-Guazón: A Biography. Quezon City:
Capitol Publishing House, 1967, ix, 293 pp.

29 BADAN PEMBINA PAHLAWAN PUSAT. Sri Kandi Bangsaku. Heroines
of Indonesian History. Jakarta: Central Board for National Heroes Affairs, 1974, 51 pp. (Contents: Marta
Christina Tijahahu [. . .-1818]--Tjut Nja Dien [1850-1908]
--Tjut Nja Mentia [1870-1910]--Raden Adjeng Kartini [1879-
1904]--Maria Walanda Maramis [1872-1924]--Raden Dewi
Sartika [1884-1947].)

30 BARR, PAT. A Curious Life for a Lady: The Story of Isabella
Bird. London: Macmillan and J. Murray, 1970, 347 pp.

31 BIRD, ISABELLA LUCY. The Golden Chersonese and the Way
Thither. Kuala Lumpur: Oxford University Press, 1967, ix,
xvi, 384 pp. Book published earlier in 1883 by J. Murray,
London. (Recollections of the author's life in Malaya.)

32 BROOKE, SYLVIA LEONORA (BRETT). Lady Rani of Sarawak, Queen
of the Head Hunters: The Autobiography of H.H. the Hon.
Sylvia Lady Brooke. New York: Morrow, 1970, 10, 194 pp.

33 CAMERON, DANIEL. "V.N's [Vietnam's] Best Known Woman Painter."
Vietnamese Magazine 7, no. 8 (1974):18-19.

34 CARTER, R.R. LANGHAM. "Queen Me Nu and Her Family at
Palangon." Burma Research Society. Journal 19 (1929):
31-35.

35 CHOY, ELIZABETH SUMAI. "The Autobiography of Elizabeth Choy
SuMei, as Told to Shirle Gordon." Intisari 4, no. 1.
9-66.

36   COLLIS, MAURICE. She Was a Queen. New York: Criterion
      Books, 1960, 250 pp. (On Queen Saw of Burma, fl. 1287.)

37   DANKER, MILLICENT. "Illustrious Roots." New Straits Times
      Annual (1980):54-58. (On Hajjah Tom binti Abdul Razak,
      Malaysian educationist.)

38   de VEYRA, ROSARIO AVILA. "Faith, Work, Success: An Appraisal
      of the Life and Work of Sofia Reyes de Veyra." Master's
      thesis, University of San Carlos [Cebu City, Philippines],
      1959, vii, 218 pp.

39   DUMLAO, MARIA S. "A Filipino Scientist: Magdalena Alde
      Templa." Master's thesis, Ortañez University [Manila],
      1974, ix, 163 pp.

40   FARIDAH IDRIS. "Wanita Berjasa" [Meritorious women].
      Mastika 37, no. 5 (May 1977):80-85. (On Hajjah Tom binti
      Abdul Razak, Dr. Soo Kim Lan and Sister A. Mangalam, all
      of Malaysia.)

41   FERRIOLS, MARIA LEOCADIA EJERCITO. "Heroines of Philippine
      Freedom." Master's thesis, Philippine Women's University
      [Manila], 1956, 232 pp.

42   FRANQUELLI, ANGELICA ROSARIO. "Lucrecia R. Kasilag: The
      Western and Oriental Influences in Her Compositions."
      D.M.A. dissertation, Peabody Institute of the Johns Hopkins
      University, Peabody Conservatory of Music, 1979, 227 pp.
      Abstracted in Dissertation Abstracts International 40,
      no. 4 (October 1979):1942-A. University Microfilms inter-
      national order no. 7921360. (Filipino musician and music
      educator.)

43   GULLICK, J.M. "Isabella Bird's Visit to Malaya: A Centenary
      Tribute." Royal Asiatic Society of Great Britain and
      Ireland, Malaysian Branch, Journal 52, pt. 2 (1979):113-19.

44   GWEKOH, SOL H. Aurora A. Quezon, Her Life and Deeds. Manila:
      Fortune Publishers, 1950, 139 pp.

45   _____. Josefa Llanes Escoda, A Life Dedicated to Humanitarian
      Service: A Biography. Manila: Fortune, 1952, 54 pp.

46   _____. Stars of Baler. Manila: Apo Book Co., 1939, 116 pp.
      (Deals in part with Aurora A. Quezon.)

47   HALILI, BENVENUTO R., Jr. "Women of the Revolution." Special
      Features Bulletin, series of 1959 (7 Dec. 1959):1-3.
      Reproduced from the Manila Times of 30 Nov. 1959. (On
      Filipino women--Trinidad Tecson, Tandang Sora, Teresa

5

Magbanua, Marina Josefa Gabriella, Marina Dizon, Josephine
Bracken, Gregoria de Jesus, Hilaria de Agauinaldo,
Cresencia San Agustin de Santos.)

48   HALL, GORDON LANGLEY. Golden Boats from Burma. Philadelphia:
     Macrae Smith Co., 1961, 255 pp. (On the life of Ann
     Hasseltine Judson, the first American woman in Burma.)

49   HAMILTON-MERRITT, JANE. A Meditaator's Diary: A Western
     Woman's Unique Experience in Thailand Monasteries.
     Harmondsworth, Middlesex: Penguin Books, 1979, 155 pp.

50   IBRAHIM, MUCHTARUDDIN. Cut Nyak Dien: Pahlawan Nasional
     [Cut Nyak Dien: national heroine]. Jakarta: Proyek
     Biografi Pahlawan Nasional, Departemen Pendidikan dan
     Kebudayaan, 1979, 1, 101 pp. (On Cut Nyak Dien, died 1908,
     an Indonesian patriot and her struggle against the Dutch.)

51   INNES, EMILY. The Chersonese with the Gilding Off. 2 vols.
     Kuala Lumpur: Oxford University Press, 1974. Published
     earlier in 1885 by R. Bentley, London. (Recollections of
     the author's life in Malaya.)

52   JUNUS, ANIS H.M. Riwajat Hidup Njai Ahmad Dahlan, Ibu Muham-
     madijah dan 'Aisjijah, Pelopor Pergerakan Indonesia [The
     biography of Njai Ahmad Dahlan, mother of Muhammadijah
     and 'Aisjijah, the pioneer of the Indonesian movement].
     Jogjakarta, 1968.

53   "Kartini Ketjil dari Minangkabau: Sitti Rohana" [Small Kar-
     tini from Minangkabau: Sitti Rohana]. Pandji Islam
     (1940):9054-80.

54   KASSIM, M. Kisah-kisah Keperwiraan Wanita Atjeh dalam Perang
     Gerilja Melawan Belanda [Accounts of Achinese female war-
     riors in the guerilla war against the Dutch]. (Dipungut
     dari tulisan H.C. Zentgraff) Medan: Pandaraman, 1960,
     60 pp.

55   KHADIJAH binti MOHAMED SIDEK. "Riwayat Hidup Saya: My Life."
     by Ardjasani, pseud. Eastern Horizon 2, no. 1 (Jan. 1962):
     11-17; 2, no. 2 (Feb. 1962):16-23; 2, no. 3 (Mar. 1962):
     39-50; 2, no. 4 (Apr. 1962):37-46; 2, no. 5 (May 1962):
     47-52; 2, no. 6 (June 1962):39-47; 2, no. 7 (July 1962):
     49-57; 2, no. 8 (Aug. 1962):47-51; 3, no. 1 (Jan. 1964):
     55-61; 3, no. 2 (Feb. 1964):54-60; 3, no. 3 (Mar. 1964):
     58-63; 3, no. 4 (Apr. 1964):53-58; 3, no. 5 (May 1964):
     56-58. (Malaysian female politician.)

56   MANDERSON, LENORE. "Aspects of the Leadership of the
        Pergerakan Kaum Ibu UMNO Malaysia: The Sumatran Connec-
        tion." RIMA; Review of Indonesian and Malay Affairs 12,
        no. 2 (Dec. 1978);17-42. (About half of the article is a
        biography of Khadijah Mohamed Sidek, one of Malaysia's
        women leaders of the United Malays National Organization.)

57   MANUS, M.P.B. Maria Walanda Maramis: Pahlawan Nasional
        [Maria Walanda Maramis: national heroine]. Jakarta:
        Departemen Pendidikan dan Kebudayaan, 1976, iii, 35 pp.

58   MASSON, MADELEINE. Edwina: The Biography of the Countess
        Mountbatten of Burma. London: R. Hale, 1958, 261 pp.

59   "Mengenang Pahlawan Kemerdekaan Nasional, Ibu Dewi Sartika,
        1884-1947" [Remembering the national independence heroine,
        Ibu Dewi Sartika]. Jakarta: Panitia Peringatan, 1967,
        14 pp.

60   MIDDLETON, DOROTHY. "Victorian Lady Travellers in Asia."
        Asian Affairs 11 [o. ser. 67], pt. 1, (Feb. 1980):18-26.
        (Includes Isabella Lucy Bird and Marianne North.)

61   MILLER, BASIL. Ann Judson, Heroine of Burma. Grand Rapids,
        Mich.: Zondervan, 1947, 131 pp.

62   MUIS, A. Hikajat Pahlawan Puteri Atjeh (Tjut Nja Din) [The
        story of a princess-warrior, Tjut Nja Din]. Jakarta:
        Chailan Sjamsoe, 1954, 211 pp.

63   NGUYEN THI DINH. Khong con duong nao, khac; hoi ky. Tran
        Huong Nam ghi. Tai ban. Hanoi: Phu Nu, 1968, 104 pp.

64   _____. No Other Road to Take: Memoir of Mrs. Nguyen Thi
        Dinh. Translated by Mai Elliot. Ithaca, N.Y.: Southeast
        Asia Program, Department of Asian Studies, Cornell Univer-
        sity, 1976, viii, 77 pp. Data Paper, no. 102. (Transla-
        tion of Khong con duong nao khac.)

65   NINNONG, H. ANDI'. "Une princesse bugis dan la Révolution:
        pages autobiographiques" [A Bugis princess in the revolu-
        tion: autobiography]. Traduit et annoté par Ch. Pelras.
        Archipel, no. 13 (1977):137-56.

66   PHILIPPINES (REPUBLIC), Bureau of Public Libraries. Some
        Outstanding Filipino Women: Short Biographies. Manila:
        Bureau of Public Libraries, 1955, 58 pp.

67   PHUONG, LAN. Anh thu nuoc Viet tu lap quoc den hien dai.
        Saigon: Kahi-Tri, 1969, 288 pp.

68   PITMAN, EMMA RAYMOND. Ann H. Judson, Missionary Heroine of
     Burma. London: Pickering and Inglis, 1948, 96 pp.

69   "Puan Rafidah Aziz: Economics Lecturer and Youngest Member of
     the Dewan Negara: An Interview." Malaysian Business (June
     1975):30-33, 35, 37.

70   PURADIREDJA, R. EMMA. "Raden Dewi Sartika." Keoetamaan Istri
     4, no. 4 (1940):19-20.

71   RAFIDAH AZIZ, Datin Paduka. "As a Politician, as Deputy
     Finance Minister, as a Career Woman. . . ." Malaysian
     Business, (Apr. 1979):20-21. (An interview with Datin
     Paduka Aziz).

72   SANTILLAN, HEDY B. "The First Feminists--Ladies of the Revo-
     lution." Fookien Times Philippines Yearbook (1979):356-57,
     384. (Short sketches on Ma. Josefa Gabriela Silang,
     Teresa Magbanua, Trinidad Tecson, Melchora Aquino, Gregoria
     de Jesus, Marcela Agoncillo, Teodora Alonza, Eugenia
     Tanchangco Reyes, Agueda Kahabagan.)

73   SANTOS, ALFONSO P., ed. Heroic Virgins and Women Patriots:
     Female Patriotism during the Japanese Occupation. Retold
     and edited by Alfonso P. Santos. Manila: National Book
     Store, 1977, x, 158 pp. (Biographies.)

74   SHEEHAN, J.J. "Installation of Tengku Kurshiah as Tengku
     Ampuan, Negri Sembilan." Royal Asiatic Society of Great
     Britain and Ireland, Malaysian Branch, Journal 14, pt. 3
     (1936):243-46.

75   SHUNK, CAROLINE SAXE (MERILL). An Army Woman in the
     Philippines: Extracts from Letters of an Army Officer's
     Wife, Describing Her Personal Experiences in the Philippine
     Islands. Kansas City, Mo.: Franklin Hudson, 1914, 183 pp.

76   SIANU [pseud.]. "Pantun: An English Woman's Life in Malaya."
     Blackwood's Magazine 260 (July):34-44. (Early 1940s.)

77   SONZA, DEMY P., and SONZA, GLORIA. "Josefa Abiertas, 1894-
     1922. The First Filipino Woman Baptist to Gain National
     Renown." Southeast Asia Journal [Iloilo City, Philippines]
     11, no. 1 (1979):26-34.

78   STODDART, ANNA M. The Life of Isabella Bird (Mrs. Bishop)
     Hon. Member of the Oriental Society of Pekin, F.R.G.S.,
     F.R.S.G.S. 3d ed. London, J. Murray, 1908, xii, 416 pp.

79   SOEKARNO, FATMAWATI. Catatan Kecil bersama Bung Karno
      [Sketches of my life with Bung Karno]. Jakarta: Dela
      Rohita, 1978. (Published in volumes. Autobiography of
      Fatmawati Sukarno, wife of the first president of
      Indonesia.)

80   SURATNIN. Nya Ahmad Dahlan: Pahlawan Nasional [Nya Ahmad
      Dahlan: National Heroine]. Jakarta: Departemen Pendidi-
      kan dan Kebudayaan, 1977, iii, 100 pp.

81   SURIPTO. Ibu Tien Soeharto: Ibu Negara jang Rumah Tamah (the
      charming and smiling first lady). Surabaya: Pantja Pudji-
      bangun, 1971, 142 pp. (On Siti Hartinah Soeharto.)

82   SZÉKELY-LULOFS, MAGDALENA MADELON HERMINE. Tjoet Nja Din:
      de geschiedenis van een Atjehse vorstin [Tjoet Nja Din:
      the history of an Achinese queen]. Amsterdam: Moussautt's,
      1948, 219 pp.

83   _____. Tjoet Nja Din: Riwajat Hidup Seorang Puteri Atjeh
      [Tjoet Nja Din: the life history of an Achinese queen].
      Terdjemahan dan saduran Adoel Moeis. Jakarta: Chailan
      Sjamsoe, 1954, 211 pp.

84   TAMAR DJAJA. "Sitti Rohana." Buku Kita 1 (9 Sept. 1955):
      387-90.

85   TANZIL, HAZIL. Teuku Umar dan Tjut Nja Din: Sepasang
      Pahlawan Perang Atjeh [Teuku Umar and Tjut Nja Din: a
      pair of Achinese warriors]. Jakarta: Djambatan, 1952,
      viii, 167 pp. Tjermin Kehidupan, 11.

86   TASKER, RODNEY. "A Marcos Dynasty? Imee Joins the First
      Couple." Far Eastern Economic Review 102, no. 46 (Nov.
      1978):44-45. (On Imee Marcos, daughter of President
      Marcos of the Philippines.)

87   TAUFIK EFFENDY. Asmara Sukarno-Dewi [The Romance of Sukarno-
      Dewi]. Petaling Jaya, Malaysia: Penerbitan Pustaka Sari,
      1968, 83 pp.

88   THATCHER, DOROTHY. "The Baroness Angela Burdett-Coutts, One-
      time Heir to the Raj of Sarawak." Malaya (Dec. 1958):
      38-39.

89   TRAN QUOC VUONG. Truyen thong phu nu Viet-Nam. Hanoi: Phu
      Nu, 1972, 97 pp.

90   TREGONNING, KENNEDY G. "A Kedah Heroine." Malaysia in His-
      tory 4, no. 2 (1958):48-49.

91   TREMBLY, DIANE L. Petticoat Medic in Vietnam: Adventures of
      a Woman Doctor. New York: Vantage Press, 1976, 275 pp.

92   USMAN, K. Wanita Indonesia Yang Merintis Kemajuan [Indonesian
      women who paved the way for progress]. Jakarta: Aries
      Lima, 1979, 67 pp. (Biographical sketches of some Indo-
      nesian women, prominent in their struggle for independence
      and women's rights.)

93   VALENZUELA, WILFREDO P., comp. and ed. Know Them: A Book of
      Biographies. Manila: Dotela Publications, 1966, 236 pp.
      (Includes biographies on a number of Filipino women, e.g.,
      Imelda R. Marcos, Helena Z. Benitez, Teodora C. Garcia, and
      Basilia A. Fittstvedt.)

94   VARONA, FRANCISCO, and de la LLANA, PEDRO. Ada: The Life of
      Librada Avelino, or The Development of a Soul. Manila:
      P. Vera, 1935, 288 pp.

95   VETH, PIETER JOHANNES. "De vrouwenregeeringen in den
      Indischen arhipel" [Women government leaders in the East
      Indian Archipelago]. Tijdschrift voor Nederlandsch-Indië
      4, pt. 2 (1870):354-69.

96   VIET-NAM WOMEN'S UNION. Some Best Daughters of Viet-Nam.
      Saigon(?), 1953, 39 pp.

97   VORAVAN, RUDI. The Treasured One: The Story of Rudivoravan,
      Princess of Siam, as told by her to Ruth Adams Knight. New
      York: Dutton, 1957, 249 pp.

98   WERMINE, WILLIAM R. "Actress Kim Vui: Goodbye to the Cinema
      World." Vietnam Magazine 7, no. 8 (1974):5-6.

99   WIHARJA, YATI MARYATI. Ni Pollok, Model dari Desa Kelandis
      [Ni Pollok, model from the village of Kelandis]. Jakarta:
      Gramedia, 1976, 158 pp.

100   WIRIAATMADJA, ROCHIATI. Pahlawan Nasional: Dewi Sartika
      [National heroine: Dewi Sartika]. Jakarta: Proyek
      Biografi Pahlawan Nasional, Departemen Pendidikan dan
      Kebudayaan, 1977, iii, 116 pp.

101   Women of Distinction: Biographical Essays on Outstanding
      Filipino Women of the Past and the Present. Editorial
      Board: Jovita Varias-de Guzman et al. Manila: Bukang
      Liwayway(?), 1967, xiii, 243 pp.

102   WONG, JADE SNOW. Fifth Chinese Daughter. London: Hurst &
      Blackett, 1952, 256 pp. (Autobiography.)

Kartini, Raden Adjeng

103   ABENDANON, JACQUES HENRY. "Les idées d'une jeune Javanaise
      (Kartini)" [The ideas of a young Javanese girl: Kartini].
      Asie Française (Jan. 1913):28-30.

104   ABU HANIFAH. "Raden Adjeng Kartini." Cultureel nieuws
      Indonesië (Apr. 1951):6-10.

105   ADIWILAGA, AMINULLAH. "Beberapa Catatan Baru tentang Kartini"
      [Several new notes about Kartini]. Budaya Jaya 9, no. 96,
      (May 1967):257-65.

106   BADAN PEMBINA PAHLAWAN PUSAT. Sri Kandi Bangsaku. Heroines
      of Indonesian History. Jakarta: Central Board for Na-
      tional Heroes Affairs, 1974, 51 pp. (Contents: Marta
      Christina Tijahahu [1818]; Tjut Nja Dien [1850-1908]; Tjut
      Nja Mentia [1870-1910]; Raden Adjeng Kartini [1879-1904];
      Maria Walanda Maramis [1872-1924]; and Raden Dewi Sartika
      [1884-1947].)

107   BOUMAN, HENDRIK. Meer licht over Kartini [More light on
      Kartini]. Amsterdam: H.J. Paris, 1954, 72 pp.

108   CUISINIER, JEANNE. "Kartini, 'Mère des indonésiennes' (1879-
      1904)" [Kartini, 'Mother of Indonesian women' 1879-1904].
      France-Asie 17, no. 169 (1961):2475-78.

109   "Une femme d'Indonésie: Raden Adjeng Kartini" [A woman of
      Indonesia: Raden Adjeng Kartini]. Informations Indoné-
      siennes [Brussels], éd. spéciale, (21 Apr. 1954):1-7.

110   FRANS, C. "Peringatan Hari Maulid Jang Kelima Poeloeh dan
      Hari Wafat Jang Kedoea Poeloeh Lima dari Almarhoem R.A.
      Kartini, Pendekar Associatie Politiek" [Remembering the
      fiftieth birthday and the twenty-fifth anniversary of the
      death of R.A. Kartini, champion of political associations].
      Oedaya, no. 76 (Sept. 1929):140-45.

111   KADARJONO, S. Ibu Kita: Kartini [Our mother: Kartini].
      Surabaya: Penjebar Semangat, n.d., 32 pp. Watjan Rakyat,
      no. 8.

112   KARDINAH, REKSONEGORO. "Kartini: de feiten" [Kartini: the
      facts]. Bijdragen tot de taal-, land- en volkenkunde 22
      (1966):283-87.

113   KARTINI, Raden Adjeng. Door duisternis tot licht [Light after
      dark]. Gedachten over en voor het Javaansche volk van
      wijlen Raden Adjeng Kartini. Bijeengegaard en uitgegeven
      door J.H. Abendanon. 4 druk. The Hague: Luctor et
      Emergo, 1923, xxi, 410, vi pp.

114 _____. Door duisternis tot licht [Light after dark].
Gedachten over en voor het Javaansche volk. 5 druk.
Amsterdam: Gé Nabrink en Zn, 1976, 468 pp.

115 _____. Habis Gelap Terbitlah Terang [Light after dark].
Diterjemahkan oleh Armijn Pané. Jakarta: Balai Poestaka,
1938, 206 pp. (Translation of Door duisternis tot licht.)

116 _____. Habis Gelap Terbitlah Terang [Light after dark].
Terdjemahan: Armijn Pané. Tjet 7. Jakarta: P.N. Balai
Pustaka, 1972, 247 pp.

117 _____. Letters of a Javanese Princess. Translated from the
original Dutch by Agnes Louise Symmers. 4th ed. London:
Oxford University Press (E. Asia), 1976, 340 pp.

118 _____. Letters of a Javanese Princess. Translated from the
Dutch by Agnes Louise Symmers. Edited and with an introduction by Hildred Geertz. Hong Kong: Heinemann Educational Books (Asia), 1976, 246 pp.

119 _____. Lettres de Raden Adjeng Kartini: Java en 1900 [Let-
ters of Raden Adjeng Kartini: Java in 1900]. Choisies et
traduites par Louis Charles Damais. Introduction et notes
de Jeanne Cuisinier. Paris: Mouton, 1960, 149 pp. Paris.
École Pratique des Hautes Études; Le monde d'outre-mer,
passé et présent. 2d. ser. Documents, 4.

120 _____. R.A. Kartini Mboekak Pepeteng. Isi Pethikan Saking
Serat-seratipoen Radèn Adjeng Kartini, Ingkang Kagijaraken
Dhateng Pandjenenganipoen J.H. Abendanon [R.A. Kartini
'opens' the darkness. Extracts of letters of Raden Adjeng
Kartini, taken from the original work of J.H. Abendanon].
Ingkang methik R. Sasrasoegonda. Surabaya: Panitya Fonds
Kartini Djawa, 1938[?], 178 pp. (Extract from Door
duisternis tot licht.)

121 _____. Surat-surat Kartini: Renungan tentang dan untuk
Bangsanya [Letter of Kartini: reflections about and for
her nation]. Penterjemah: Sulastin Sutrisno. Jakarta:
Djambatan, atas kerjasama dengan Pemerintah Kerajaan
Belanda, 1979, 409 pp.

122 "Kartini nummer. (Contient une liste de 32 études sur
Kartini, dressé par Armijn Pané)" [Kartini number. In-
cludes a list of 32 studies on Kartini, compiled by Armijn
Pané]. Keoetamaan Istri 3, no. 4 (1939).

123   Kartini nummer, ter gelegenheid van de viering van R.A.
       Kartini's geboortedag op 21 April 1937 [Kartini number,
       in honor of the celebration of R.A. Kartini's birthday on
       21 April 1937]. Uitgegeven door de Vereeniging der Indo-
       nesische studeerenden Roeken peladjar Indonesia. Leiden,
       1937, 32 pp.

124   MIHARDJA, ACHDIAT K. "Raden Adjeng Kartini." Dewan Masyara-
       kat 11, no. 3 (Mar. 1973):26-29, 47.

125   NIEUWENHUIJS, ROBERT. "Kartini: legende en werkelijkheid"
       [Kartini: legend and reality]. In Tussen twee vader-
       landen by Robert Nieuwenhuijs, pp. 198-222. Amsterdam:
       G.A. Oorschcot, 1959.

126   NOTO SOEROTO, Raden Mas. "De gedachten van R.A. Kartini, als
       richtsnoer voor alle Indonesische nationale strevingen"
       [The thoughts of R.A. Kartini as guidelines for all Indo-
       nesian national ideals]. Oedaya, no. 79 (Dec. 1929):
       184-87.

127   _____. De gedachten van Raden Adjeng Kartini als richtsnoer
       voor de Indische Vereeniging [The thoughts of Raden Adjeng
       Kartini as guidelines for organizations]. Met inleidende
       brieven van C.Th. van Deventer en J.H. Abendanon. The
       Hague: Indische Vereeniging, 1911, 25 pp. Indische Ver-
       eeniging. Uitgave, no. 1.

128   "Raden Adjeng Kartini: (21st April 1879-17th April 1904), The
       First Woman Pioneer in the Movement for the Emancipation of
       Indonesian Women." Islamic Review 41, no. 6 (June 1953):
       30-31.

129   SALAM, SOLICHIN. R.A. Kartini Seratus Tahun, 1879-1979
       [R.A. Kartini, a hundred years, 1879-1979]. Jakarta:
       Penerbit Gunung Muria, 1979, 96 pp.

130   Satu Abad Kartini, 1879-1979: Bunga Rampai Karangan mengenai
       Kartini [A century of Kartini, 1879-1979: an anthology of
       writings on Kartini]. Jakarta: Sinar Harapan, 1979[?],
       175 pp. (Volume commemorating the centenary of Raden
       Adjeng Kartini, 1879-1979.)

131   SUBANDRIO, HURUSTIATI. Kartini: Wanita Indonesia [Kartini:
       an Indonesian woman]. Tjet. ke-6. Jakarta: Djambatan,
       1955. viii, 50 pp. Seri Tjermin Kehidupan, 1.

132   UROTO, A. Raden Adjeng Kartini: Pendekar Wanita Indonesia
       [Raden Adjeng Kartini: champion of Indonesian women].
       Jakarta: Djambatan, 1974, 33 pp.

133   SOEROTO, SITISOEMANDARI. Kartini: Sebuah Biografi [Kartini: a biography]. Jakarta: Gunung Agung, 1977, xvi, 447 pp.

134   TASHADI. R.A. Kartini: Pahlawan Nasional [R.A. Kartini: national heroine]. Jakarta: Proyek Biografi Pahlawan Nasional, Departemen Pendidikan dan Kebudayaan, 1975, iii, 120 pp.

135   TAYLOR, JEAN STEWART. "Raden Adjeng Kartini." Signs 1, no. 3, (Spring 1976):639-62.

136   TOER, PRAMOEDYA ANANTA. Panggil Aku Kartini Sadja, Djepara, 25 Mei 1899. Sebuah Pengantar pada Kartini [Just call me Kartini Japara, 25 May 1899: An introduction to Kartini], 2 vols. Jakarta: Nusantara, 1962.

137   van DEVENTER, C. Th. "Onder de hoede van Kartini's naam: inleiding woord bij de oprichting van de Vereniging Kartini-fonds" [Under the protection of Kartini's name: introduction to the establishment of the Kartini Foundation]. The Hague, 1913.

138   van ZEGGELEN, MARIE CHRISTINE. Kartini: een baandbreekster voor haar volk: roman [Kartini: a pioneer of the people: a story]. Amsterdam: J.M. Meulenhoff, 1945, 259 pp.

139   VIERHOUT, M. Raden Adjeng Kartini, 1879-1904: een Javaansche over de nooden en behoeften van haar volk [Raden Adjeng Kartini, 1879-1904: a Javanese on the needs of her people]. 2. druk. The Hague: Oceanus, 1944, 191 pp. Door alle eeuwen, 5.

140   VREEDE-DE STUERS, CORA. "Een nationale heldin: R.A. Kartini" [A national heroine: R.A. Kartini]. Bijdragen tot de taal-, land- en volkenkunde 124 (1968):386-93.

141   _____. "Kartini en de Hollandsche Lelie: emancipatie-idealen in Nederlands-Indie" [Kartini and the Dutch Lely: emancipation ideals in the Netherlands Indies]. Sociologische gids, no. 2 (Mar./Apr. 1976):70-77.

142   _____. "Kartini: feiten en ficties" [Kartini: fact and fiction]. Bijdragen tot de taal-, land- en volkenkunde 121 (1965):233-44.

143   _____. "Kartini, petit 'cheval sauvage' devenu héroïne de l'indépendance Indonésienne" [Kartini, small 'wild horse' who became the heroine of Indonesian independence]. Archipel, no. 13 (1977):105-118.

Marcos, Imelda Romualdez

144 AGUILA, DANI DUMUK, comp. and ed. Apo Ferdi and Inday Meldy:
      the Philippines First Couple. Quezon City: SPIC; Printed
      by the University of the Philippines Press, 1966, x,
      149 pp. (On Ferdinand and Imelda Marcos.)

145 ALCUAZ, F.A. "3 Images of Imelda." Philippines Free Press
      62, no. 50 (13 Dec. 1969):92-94.

146 BUCKLEY, W.F. "Marcos and the Philippines." National Review
      29 (Dec. 1977):1512-13.

147 COSETENG, ALICE M.L. "Imelda Marcos: Portrait of a Lady."
      Weekly Graphic 32 (24 Nov. 1965):9-11.

148 CRISOSTOMO, I.T. "Imelda for President?" Philippines Free
      Press 63, no. 50 (12 Dec. 1970):18-19; 141-42; 144.

149 DAY, BETH. "The First Lady: See for Yourself What We Are."
      Archipelago 1, no. 4 (Apr. 1974):17-20.

150 DAZA, J.Y. "The Heart of the First Lady." Weekly Graphic 35,
      no. 19 (30 Oct. 1968):17-19.

151 _____. "The Magnificent Politician." Sunday Times Magazine
      [Manila], (19 Oct. 1969):26-29.

152 "First Lady Drafted as 1st Governor of Metro Manila." New
      Philippines 35, no. 2 (Nov. 1975):4-5.

153 "The First Lady in Indonesia." Salam 2 (May/June 1975):36-38.
      (English and Arabic.)

154 "The First Lady's Total Love." Focus 4 (3 July 1976):34-35.

155 "Government Responds to Popular Will." New Philippines 35,
      no. 2 (Nov. 1975):6-10.

156 "Highlights of the First Lady's Visit to the Middle East."
      Salam 2 (Mar./Apr. 1975):30-38. (English and Arabic.)

157 HUFANA, ALEJANDRINO G. Imelda Romualdez Marcos: A Tonal
      Epic. Manila: Konsensus, 1975, 219 pp.

158 Imelda Romualdez Marcos: The New Filipina. Manila[?], 1969,
      26 pp. (A commemorative edition on the awarding of the
      honorary degree of Doctor of Humanities to the First Lady,
      Imelda Romualdez Marcos, by the Philippine Women's Univer-
      sity, 20 Feb. 1969.)

159   JOAQUIN, MICK. "Roman Holy Day." Philippines Free Press 62,
          no. 21 (24 May 1969):2-3, 67-69.

160   _____. "Woman of the Year." Philippines Free Press 62,
          no. 2 (11 Jan. 1969):32-37, 54-55.

161   KALAW, L.M. "Our Lady of the Jet Set." Philippines Free
          Press 63, no. 41 (10 Oct. 1970):10-11, 62, 64-65.

162   MANIQUIS, E.M. "Prospects for Posterity." Philippines Today,
          (Dec. 1970):10-15.

163   MANUEL, M.T. "The First Lady as Diplomat." Fookien Times
          Philippines Yearbook (1975):40-47.

164   MARAMAG, ILEANA. "Imelda's Vision: A Grand Design for Metro
          Manila." Philippine Panorama 5 (7 Nov. 1976):6-9.

165   MARCIAL, GENE. "Grant Me the Right to Love and Help My Hus-
          band." Weekly Graphic 35, no. 36 (26 Feb. 1969):12-16, 25.

166   _____. "Pope Paul and the First Lady." Weekly Graphic 35,
          no. 50 (4 June 1969):36-37.

167   MARCOS, IMELDA ROMUALDEZ. "A Call from Alexandria: World
          Awaits the Steadying Hand of Women." New Philippines 28
          (Apr. 1975):22-24. (Speech, n.d.)

168   _____. "First Lady Rallies RP Women during IWY Inaugural."
          New Philippines 26 (Feb. 1975):18-19. (Speech, 6 January
          1975.)

169   _____. "Role of Women in UNESCO." New Philippines 33, no. 2,
          (Sept. 1975):22-23. (Speech delivered at the 9th biennial
          conference of UNESCO, 8 Sept. 1975.)

170   _____. "The Social Development of Afro-Asian Women." Salam
          2 (Mar./Apr. 1975):26-29. (Address delivered before the
          Afro-Asian symposium on social development of women at
          Alexandria, Egypt, on 8 Mar. 1975. In English and Arabic.)

171   _____. "Toward the Rebirth of Humanity." Focus 3 (5 Apr.
          1975):4-5. (Speech delivered before more than 100 women
          leaders from Asia and Africa in Alexandria, Egypt, 8 Mar.
          1975.)

172   _____. "Women's World Hears of RP's 'Si Malakas at Si
          Maganda.'" New Philippines 31 (July 1975):32-33.

173   MELLA, CESAR T. Poems for Imelda. Makati, Rizal: Printed
          by Buendia Commercial Press, 1969, 64 pp.

174 MIJARES, PRIMITIVO. The Conjugal Dictatorship of Ferdinand
     and Imelda Marcos. San Francisco: Union Square Publica-
     tions, 1976, ix, 499 pp.

175 "Mrs. Imelda Romualdez Marcos: A New Kind of First Lady."
     Salam 1, no. 1 (Mar. 1974):17, 24.

176 MORAES, DOM. "The Cool Couple." Asia Magazine 11, no. 37
     (Sept. 1971):3-4, 6-8.

177 NAVARRO-PEDROSA, CARMEN. The Untold Story of Imelda Marcos.
     Rizal, Philippines: Tandem, 1969, xx, 231 pp.

178 PHILIPPINES (REPUBLIC), National Media Production Center.
     Imelda Romualdez Marcos: Seven Tasks. Manila: National
     Media Production Center, 1974, 92 pp.

179 _____, Office of the First Lady. Compassion and Commitment:
     Action Programmes of the First Lady, Imelda Romualdez
     Marcos. Edited by Ileana Maramag. Manila: Office of the
     First Lady, 1975, 89 pp.

180 POLICARPIO, ALFONSO P. "A Portrait Study." Philippines
     Herald Magazine (27 Nov. 1965):10-13.

181 POLOTAN, KERIMA. Imelda Romualdez Marcos: A Biography of the
     First Lady of the Philippines. Manila: Printed by Regal
     Printing Co., 1970, vi, 213 pp.

182 _____. "The Rose of Tacloban." Sunburst 1, no. 8 (Dec.
     1973):17-22.

183 PUYAT, M.C.G. "The First Lady's Christmas Wish." Philippine
     Panorama 4 (21 Dec. 1975):18-19.

184 RAMA, N.G. "Imelda, the Presidency, the Nacionalistas and
     the People." Philippines Free Press 63, no. 51 (19 Dec.
     1970):4-5, 52.

185 RIVERA, V.J., Jr. "Again . . . a Special Mission for the
     First Lady." Focus 3 (18 Jan. 1975):4-5.

186 _____. "Filipina Exemplar." Focus 3 (28 June 1975):4-8.

187 ROSCA, NINOTCHKA. "Madame la president?" Weekly Graphic 37,
     no. 29 (23 Dec. 1970):8-9, 52.

188 ROWAN, ROY. "The High-flying First Lady of the Philippines."
     Fortune (July 1979):93-96.

189 _____. "Many Sides of Imelda M. Special from Fortune Magazine." Asian Business 15, no. 9 (Sept. 1979):78-81, 83.

190 RUFIN, B.T. "Is Imelda Running for President in 1973?"
Philippines Free Press 63, no. 51 (19 Dec. 1970):12, 42-44.

191 SIACO, E.E. "Imelda's New Image: Mature Mind in a Young
Body." Weekly Graphic 36, no. 28 (17 Dec. 1969):20-25.

192 "Somebody Tell the First Lady to Refrain from Such Madness."
Weekly Graphic 37, no. 28 (16 Dec. 1970):2. (Editorial.)

193 TORRES, J.S. "The First Lady and the Black Gold." Black
Gold 1 (Mar. 1975):4-5.

194 TUPAS, R.G. "The Big Show in Osaka." Sunday Times Magazine
[Manila] (2 Aug. 1970):20, 23-24, 26-27.

195 VELOSOYAP, VERONICA. "Imelda Romualdez Marcos' thoughts on
the Philippines and the World." Fookien Times Philippines
Yearbook (1979):54-56.

196 WIDEMAN, BERNARD. "First Lady, Faults and All." Far Eastern
Economic Review 93 (6 Aug. 1976):24-25.

197 _____. "Imelda: Queen of All She Surveys." Far Eastern
Economic Review 94 (21 Nov. 1976):33-34.

CLOTHING AND DRESS

198 ACHJADI, JUDI. Pakaian Daerah Wanita Indonesia. Indonesian
Women's Costumes. Jakarta: Djambatan, 1976, x, 114 pp.

199 AZAH AZIZ. "Pakaian Tradisional yang Penuh Warna, Penuh
Budaya" [Traditional clothes which are full of color and
culture]. Wanita [Kuala Lumpur], no. 81, (Apr. 1976):4-5.
(On Indonesian clothes.)

200 "Baju Kurong: The Dress from Teluk Belanda." ASEAN Review 1,
no. 20 (July 1976):24.

201 "Dari Hal: Pakaian Wanita Islam Putusan Tardjih" [All about
the Muslim women's attire]. Jogjakarta: Muhamadijah
Madjlis Tabligh, 1953, 12 pp.

202   FATIMAH HASHIMAH binte ABDUL AZIZ. "Pakaian Perempuan Melayu
      di-Kajang" [Attire of Malay women in Kajang]. B.A. aca-
      demic exercise, University of Singapore, 1959, iv, 48,
      v-xvi pp.

203   HAWA HAJI HASSAN, Siti. "Masaalah Pendedahan Pakaian Wanita
      Islam" [The problem of exposure in the attire of Muslim
      women]. Wanita [Kuala Lumpur] no. 86 (Sept. 1976):52-53.

204   "Indonesian Women and Their National Dress." Indonesian
      Spectator 3, no. 17 (July 1959):16-17.

205   ISIDRO, JULITA ALARCON. "A Comparative Study of the Clothing
      Habits of the Grade Six Girls of Supervisory Districts II
      and VI of the City Schools, Manila." Master's thesis,
      Centro Escolar University [Manila], 1967, viii, 168 pp.

206   LOGAN, J.R. "Manners and Customs of the Malays: Dress."
      Journal of the Indian Archipelago and Eastern Asia 3:
      274-84. (On the attire of women and children.)

207   MING DANG KHANK. "Ao dai." Vietnam Magazine 3, no. 5 (July/
      Aug. 1972):15-17.

208   "Pakaian bagi Wanita Islam di dalam dan di luar Rumah"
      [Clothes for Muslim women in and outside the house].
      Saripati 3, no. 27 (June 1979):60-67.

209   SUPRAPTO. "Pakaian Wanita Indonesia" [Indonesian women's
      attire]. Dian 9, no. 1 (1961):26-32; 9, no. 2 (1961):
      28-32; 9, no. 3 (1961):27-32; 9, no. 4 (1961):27-32; 9,
      no. 5 (1961):27-32; 9, no. 6 (1961):28-32.

COOPERATIVE SOCIETIES

210   AHMAD SARJI bin ABDUL HAMID. "Peranan Wanita dalam Pembang-
      unan Koperasi Peladang" [The role of women in the develop-
      ment of farmers' cooperatives]. Kuala Lumpur: Lembaga
      Pertubuhan Peladang, 1975, 12 pp.

211   INTERNATIONAL LABOUR OFFICE. Report to the Government of the
      Federation of Malaya on the Promotion and Organisation of
      Co-operatives among Women. Geneva: International Labour
      Office, 1963, 36 pp. ILO/TAP/Malaya/R.17.

212   "Koperasi Jayanita: Pimpin Wanita dalam Ekonomi" [Jayanita
       co-operative: woman leadership in the economy]. Komentar,
       no. 6 (Apr./May 1977):12-13.

213   "Pergerakan Wanita UMNO Melahirkan Koperasi Dermajaya Wanita"
       [UMNO Women's movement in the establishment of the Derma-
       jaya Women's Cooperative]. Puspaniaga 3, no. 1 (Feb./Mar.
       1976):32-33.

214   REGIONAL CONFERENCE ON THE ROLE OF WOMEN IN COOPERATIVE
       DEVELOPMENT, Kuala Lumpur, 1975. Report. New Delhi:
       International Cooperative Alliance, 1975, 28 pp.

215   SEMINAR/KURSUS ASAS KEBANGSAAN KOPERASI-KOPERASI WANITA,
       Petaling Jaya, Malaysia, 1977. Kertaskerja-kertaskerja
       [National Seminar/Course on Cooperatives for Women,
       Petaling Jaya, Malaysia, 1977. Papers]. Petaling Jaya:
       Angkatan Kerjasama Kebangsaan Malaysia, 1977, 1 vol.
       (various pagings).

216   SEMINAR PERANAN WANITA DALAM KOPERASI, Tjipajung, Indonesia,
       1971. "Perumusan Keputusan Seminar Peranan Wanita dalam
       Koperasi" [Proceedings of the Seminar on the Role of Women
       in Co-operatives. Summary of Proceedings]. Diseleng-
       garakan pada tanggal 14 s/d 16 Jan 1971 di Cipayung-Bogor.
       Jakarta: Direktorat Jenderal Koperasi, 1971, 8 pp.

217   _____. Rumusan, Prasaran, Pembahasan [Seminar on the Role of
       Women in Co-operatives, Tjipajung, Indonesia, 1971. Pro-
       ceedings]. Jakarta: Direktorat Jenderal Koperasi, 1971,
       1 vol. (various pagings).

218   SEMINAR TENTANG PENINGKATAN PERANAN WANITA DALAM PENGEMBANGAN
       EKONOMI, KHUSUSNYA MELALUI KOPERASI, Jakarta, 1974.
       Keputusan [Seminar on Increasing the Role of Women in
       Economic Development, Especially through Co-operatives,
       Jakarta, 1974. Report]. Jakarta: Kongress Wanita
       Indonesia, Departemen Tenaga Kerja, Transmigrasi dan
       Koperasi, Direktorat Jeneral Koperasi, 1974[?], 20 pp.

219   ZAHRAH binte MOKHTAR. "Wanita dalam Gerakkan Kerjasama"
       [Women in the co-operative movement]. Pekerjasama
       Malaysia 1, no. 4 (Apr. 1967):17-19.

CRIME AND DELINQUENCY

220   ABAYA, ROSALIA M. "Female Criminality in the Philippines."
       LL.M. thesis, University of Manila [Manila], 1952, 178 pp.

221   ABDUL AHMAD. "Wanita Rosak Akhlak Perlu Dipulih dan Didi-
      siplinkan" [Immoral women should be rehabilitated and
      disciplined]. Dewan Masyarakat 16, no. 6 (June 1978):
      22-23.

222   ABDUL HADI bin ZAKARIA. "Beberapa Aspek Tentang Kewujudan
      Pelacuran di Kalangan Wanita dan Gadis" [Several aspects
      regarding the existence of prostitution among women and
      girls]. 26 pp. Paper presented at the Seminar 'Wanita
      Malaysia Masa Kini' Bangi, Selangor, 1979, organized by
      the Faculty of Social Sciences and Humanities, Universiti
      Kebangsaan Malaysia.

223   _____. "Keadaan Sosial dan Pelacur Sukarela Harga Mahal"
      [Social status and high-class prostitutes]. Widya no. 22
      (June 1979):2-9.

224   _____. "Pelacuran Sukarela sebagai Women's Liberation"
      [Voluntary prostitution as women's liberation]. Manusia
      dan Masyarakat, 1, (1978):43-46.

225   _____. "Some Patterns in High-class Prostitution in Kuala
      Lumpur and Petaling Jaya." Master's thesis, University of
      Malaya, 1975, x, 142 pp.

226   _____. "Some Problems of the Control of Prostitution in
      Malaysia." 10 pp. Paper presented at the National Work-
      shop on STD [Sexually Transmitted Diseases] Control in
      Peninsular Malaysia, Kuala Lumpur, 1980, organized by the
      Ministry of Health, Malaysia.

227   ADIKUSUMO, ARMAN. "Prevensi Pelacuran Dipandang dari Segi
      Usaha Kesehatan Djiwa" [Prevention of prostitution from
      the viewpoint of mental health]. Jiwa 1, no. 4 (1968):
      94-110.

228   AGUILAR, HELEN. "Traffic in Women in the Philippines."
      Master's thesis, University of Santo Tomas [Manila], 1960,
      181 pp.

229   AHMAD bin SAAD. Sex dan Pelacuran [Sex and Prostitution].
      Ipoh, Malaysia: Penerbitan Pustaka Muda, 1973, 112 pp.

230   AHMAD HUSSEIN S. "Prostitution as a Form of Deviant Be-
      haviour: A Case Study of 14 Prostitutes in Batu Pahat
      Town." Penang: School of Social Sciences, Universiti
      Sains Malaysia, 1972. Term paper presented to the School
      of Social Sciences, Universiti Sains Malaysia.

231   ALDABA-LIM, ESTEFANIA J. "Girls' Juvenile Delinquency in the
      Philippines." Master's thesis, University of the
      Philippines [Quezon City], 1938, 296 pp.

232 AMALI, I. <u>Wanita Tunasusila dan Germo: Penelitian tentang Kesejahteraan wts di Kramat Tunggak-Jakarta Utara</u> [Immoral women: an investigation of prostitutes in Kramat Tunggak, North Jakarta]. Jakarta: Pusat Latihan Penelitian Ilmu-Ilmu Sosial, Fakultas Ilmu-Ilmu Sosial, Universitas Indonesia, 1978, 97 pp.

233 ANGELES, SIXTO de LOS. "El problem de la prostitución en Filipinas" [The problem of prostitution in the Philippines]. <u>Revista Filipina de medicina y farmacia</u> 12, no. 4 (Apr. 1921):97-103.

234 BARRIOS, TERESITA M. "A Study of the Factors Which Contribute to Juvenile Delinquency among the Minors Committed to the Philippine Training Center for Boys and Girls from 1958-1960." Master's thesis, Davao College [Davao City, Philippines], 1960, 132 pp.

235 BILLAH, M.M. "Yang Terlibat, dan Antar Hubungannja dalam Dunia Pertunasusilaan" [Those who are involved and their interrelationship in prostitution]. <u>Cakrawala</u> 4, no. 6 (1972):9-16, 19-44.

236 BULOS, ALICIA PEÑA. "A Study of Women Criminality." Master's thesis, University of Santo Tomas [Manila], 1963, x, 124 pp.

237 CALDWELL, JOHN COPE. <u>Message Girl: A View of Siam</u>. London: Robert Hale, 1968, 173 pp.

238 "Call Girls on the Campus." <u>Orient</u> 6 (Jan. 1964):9-12. (On the Philippines.)

239 CHABOT, HENDRIK TH. "Jonge vrouwen in conflict" [Young women in conflict]. Indonesië 8 (1955):40-47.

240 CHENG, JACINTO. "Why Girls Enter into a Life of Shame." <u>Philippines Free Press</u> 54 (22 July 1961):6-7.

241 CHEOW, JOSEPHINE LI YING. "The Delinquent Girl in Singapore." Thesis for the Diploma in Social Science, University of Singapore, 1960, 64 pp.

242 COPPIN, H. <u>La Prostitution, la police des moeurs et la dispensaire municipal à Hanoi</u> [Prostitution, regulation of morals and the municipal dispensary in Hanoi]. Hanoi: Imprimerie d'Extrême-Orient, 1925. Also: Société Médico-Chirurgicale de l'Indochine. Bulletin [Hanoi] (1925): 243-72.

243   DIRDJOSISWORO, SUDJONO. Pelacuran Ditinjau dari Segi Hukum
       dan Kenyataan dalam Masyarakat [Prostitution: legal
       aspects and public opinion]. Bandung: Karya Nusantara,
       1977, iii, 200 pp.

244   Frauen in Vietnam [Women in Vietnam]. Prepared under the
       direction of Margret Peters. 2. aufl. Cologne: Initia-
       tivkomitee für Deutsch-Vietnamesische Kulturbeziehungen,
       1976, 107 pp.

245   GAMA, LEONOR G. "A Study of Offenses Committed by Young Boys
       and Girls in the City of Manila for 1960-1961." Master's
       thesis, Arellano University [Manila], 1962, 158 pp.

246   GAMBOA, VICTOR, and FEENSTRA, HENRY J. "Deviant Stereotypes:
       Call Girls, Male Homosexuals, and Lesbians." Philippine
       Sociological Review 17, nos. 3/4 (July/Oct. 1969):136-48.
       (On people in Baguio and the University of the Philippines.)

247   GAWAT, ASUNCION R. "A Study of the Correctional Institution
       for Women: Needs of Inmates and Services Rendered by the
       Socio-Civic and Religious Organization." Centro Escolar
       University, Manila, Graduate and Faculty Studies 19
       (1967):222-32.

248   _____. "A Study of the Correctional Institution for Women:
       Needs of Inmates and Services Rendered by the Socio-Civic
       and Religious Organization." Master's thesis, Centro
       Escolar University [Manila], 1968, 156 pp.

249   GO, HIANG KING. "Beberapa Catatan Tambahan mengenai Rehabili-
       tasi Pelacuran" [Some additional notes on the rehabilita-
       tion of prostitutes]. Daya Sosial 3, nos. 7/8 (1960):
       61-68.

250   HOLMES, WALTER. "A Survey of Coffee Shop Prostitutes in
       Kuala Trengganu." Medical Journal of Malaysia 10 (1955):
       178-80.

251   INDONESIA, Direktorat Rehabilitasi Tuna Sosial. "Kebijak-
       sanaan Operasional Rehabilitasi Tuna Susila: Naskah Kerja
       Direktur Direktorat Rehabilitasi Tuna Sosial dalam Hearing
       dengan Komisi VIII DRP RI, Jakarta, Nopember, 1975" [The
       wisdom of the operational rehabilitation of prostitutes:
       working paper of the Director, Tuna Social Rehabilitation
       Directorate in its hearing with the Commission VIII DRP RI,
       Jakarta, November 1975]. Jakarta: Direktorat Rehabilitasi
       Tuna Sosial, Direktorat Jenderal Rehabilitasi dan Pelayanan
       Sosial, Departemen Sosial R.I., 1975, 8 pp.

252 _____. "Penyelenggaraan Rehabilitasi Tuna Susila" [The re-habilitation of prostitutes]. Jakarta: Direktorat Rehabilitasi Tuna Sosial, Direktorat Jenderal Rehabilitasi dan Pelayanan Sosial, Departemen Sosial R.I., 1975, 18 pp.

253 JOCANO, F. LANDA. "The Slum and Female Deviant Behavior." Solidarity 6, no. 6 (June 1971):28-41.

254 JONO JOYO, Raden. "Pelacur Kelas Menengah Tidak Semua Berpunca dari Desakan Ekonomi" [The emergence of middle-class prostitutes cannot be solely attributed to economic pressure]. Wahida 1, no. 2 (Mar. 1979):115-19.

255 KALAW-LINAW, VICTORIA. "A Study of the Causes of Waywardness among Filipino Women and Girls as Observed in Welfare Home, Quezon City, and the Philippine Training School for Girls, Welfareville, Mandaluyong, Rizal." Master's thesis, Centro Escolar University [Manila], 1958, viii, 124 pp.

256 _____. "A Study of the Causes of Waywardness among Filipino Women and Girls." Centro Escolar University, Manila, Graduate and Faculty Studies 9 (1958):199-230.

257 KOHLBRUGGE, J.F.M. "Prostitutie in Nederlandsch Indië" [Prostitution in the Netherlands Indies]. (Notulen) Indisch genootschap (1901):17-36.

258 KONG, LAN LEE. "The Ones Who Stray." ASEAN Review 1, no. 6 (Mar. 1976):8-9.

259 KUSUMANTO. "Beberapa Pokok Rehabilitasi Prostitusi Ditinjau dari Sudut Psychopathologi" [Some basic aspects of the re-habilitation of prostitutes as seen from the psychopatho-logical viewpoint]. Daya Sosial 3, nos. 7/8 (1960):7-19.

260 KWA, KIM HWA, and PURUSHOTAM, NIRMALA SRIKEKAM. "Female Delinquency in the Light of the Quality of the Adolescent's Home Background: A Comparison between Delinquents and Non-Delinquents." B.A. academic exercise, University of Singapore, 1974, 74 pp.

261 LAUREL, CONSUELO T. "A Study of Female Wards Presenting Behaviour Problems Confined in Two Government Welfare Institutions." Master's thesis, Far Eastern University [Manila], 1953, viii, 110 pp.

262 MALAYSIA, Kementerian Kebajikan Am. Pusat Perlindungan Wanita dan Gadis. Women and Girls Protection Centre. Kuala Lumpur: Kementerian Kebajikan Am, 1978. 24 pp.

263 _____. Kementerian Kebajikan Am, Bahagian Penyelidikan, Perancangan dan Penilaian. <u>Laporan Kajian Penghuni-penghuni Pusat Pemulihan Wanita dan Gadis yang Ditadbirkan oleh Kementerian Kebajikan Am. Report of Survey on Inmates of Rehabilitation Centres for Women and Girls Administered by the Ministry of Welfare Services</u>. Kuala Lumpur: Bahagian Penyelidikan, Perancangan dan Penilaian, Kementerian Kebajikan Am, 1974, ii, 62 pp.

264 MUHAMMAD bin MUHAMMAD SAHED, Shaikh. "Pelacuran: Kawalan Sosial dan Undang-undang di Malaysia (Dengan Rujukan di Pulau Pinang)" [Prostitution: social control and law in Malaysia--with reference to Penang]. LL.B. academic exercise, University of Malaya, 1976, iv, 117 pp.

265 MOELIONO, PAUL MOEDIKDO. "Beberapa Catatan mengenai Pencegahan Pelacuran" [Some notes on the prevention of prostitution]. <u>Daya sosial</u> 3, nos. 7/8 (1960):43-68.

266 NEUMANN, A. LIN. "'Hospitality Girls' in the Philippines." In "Changing Role of S.E. Asian Women"--a special joint issue of <u>Southeast Asia Chronicle</u>, no. 66 (Jan./Feb. 1979) and <u>Pacific Research Bulletin</u> 9, nos. 5/6 (July/Oct. 1978): 18-23.

267 NG, KAM CHEUNG. "The Anti-Vice Squad and the Welfare Agency on the Problem of Prostitution." B.A. academic exercise, University of Malaya, 1973, ix, 76 pp.

268 NICOLL-JONES, S.C. et al. "Discussion of Prostitution in Singapore." <u>British Medical Association, Malaya Branch, Journal</u> 5 (1941):64-69.

269 ORTEGA, PETRA MONZON. "Case Studies of Inmates of Correctional Institutions for Women." Master's thesis, University of the Philippines [Quezon City], 1938, 260 pp.

270 PARUNGAO, MIGUEL D. "The Wayward Women." <u>Chronicle Magazine</u> 16 (19 Feb. 1961):14-16; (26 Feb. 1961):18-19.

271 PRAWIRODIHARDJO, TARTIB. "Pencegahan Pelacuran Ditinjau dari Pendidikan Masyarakat" [The prevention of prostitution from the viewpoint of community education]. <u>Daya Sosial</u> 3, nos. 7/8 (1960):78-84.

272 RACHMAT, ISMAIL. "Prostitusi di Kotamadya Bandung dan Sekitarnya" [Prostitution in Bandung and its surrounding area]. <u>Majalah Kesehatan ABRI</u> 4, no. 11 (1973):51-57; 4, no. 12 (1973):34-35.

273 ROMUALDEZ, ESTELA ZIALCITA. "The Woman Delinquent." LL.M. thesis, University of the Philippines [Quezon City], 1925.

274 ROMUALDEZ, VICTORIA A. "The Role of a Homemaking Course at High School Level in the Moral Rehabilitation of Women in Postwar Philippines." Master's thesis, University of Manila, 1948.

275 ROUX, J.B. "La prostituée japonaise au Tonkin" [The Japanese prostitute in Tonkin]. Société d'anthropologie de Paris. Bulletins et mémoires. 5th ser., 6 (1905):203-10.

276 RUSLAN bin KHATIB. "Pelachoran Melayu di-Kuala Lumpur: Suatu Kajian Kecil tentang Kehidupan Pelachor dan Beberapa Kepinchangan Masharakat Yang Melahirkan Golongan Ini" [Malay prostitutes in Kuala Lumpur: a survey of the life of the prostitutes and the various social imbalances that give rise to this group]. B.A. academic exercise, University of Malaya, 1966, ii, 99 pp.

277 SHAMSIAH ABDULLAH. "Keruntuhan Akhlak di Kalangan Budak-budak Perempuan" [Delinquency among girls]. B.A. academic exercise, University of Malaya, 1977, vii, 100 pp.

278 SIE, BOEN LIEP. "Pelacuran: Soal Dasar atau Sosial" [Prostitution: a basic or social issue]. Daya Sosial 2, no. 7 (1959):34-36.

279 SULEIMAN MOHAMED. "Pelacuran" [Prostitution]. Wanita [Kuala Lumpur], no. 155 (Feb. 1979):68, 85.

280 SUMINTO, HUSNUL AKIB. "Masalah Wanita Tuna Susila Ditinjau dari Segi Agama Islam" [The problem of prostitution as seen from the Islamic viewpoint]. Mimbar Ulama 1, no. 4 (1976): 57-60.

281 SUSANTO, PARIMAN EDDY. "Masalah Prostitusi (Pelatjuran)" [Problems of prostitution]. Majalah Penyuluh Sosial, no. 14 (1972):34-36.

282 _____. Usaha2 Mengatasi Masalah Pelatjuran" [Efforts to overcome the problem of prostitution]. Majalah Penyuluh Sosial, no. 15 (1972):34-36.

283 SUSILO. "Sedikit mengenai Wanita Tunasusila" [A brief discussion on prostitutes]. Cakrawala 4, no. 6 (1972):69-83.

284 SOETARDJO, IBNU. "Penanggulangan Masalah Pelatjuran di Indonesia" [Overcoming the problem of prostitution in Indonesia]. Majalah Penyuluh Sosial, no. 14 (1972):30-31.

285 WOON, CHU MENG. "Drug Abuse among Female Addicts." B.A.
     academic exercise, University of Singapore, 1976, 83 pp.

286 Thailand correspondez [journal], nos. 7/8 (1979). (Contents:
     1. Ilse Lenz, "Prostitutionstourismus in Asien" [Prostitu-
     tion/tourism in Asia]. 2. Gisela Straatmann, "Massen-
     tourismus/Prostitutionstourismus in der dritten Welt--
     Beispiel Thailand" [Mass tourism/prostitution in the Third
     World--example: Thailand]. 3. Ilse Lenz, "Frauen--
     kolonien--neokolonien. Ein Beitrag zur Theorie über die
     Frauen in der dritten Welt." [Women--colonial--neocolonial.
     A contribution on the theory of women in the Third World].
     4. Lore Henke and Gisela Pachwitz. "Frauen in Thailand:
     eine Bildserie als allgemeine Einführung" [Women in Thai-
     land: a general introduction]. 5. Marie Fua and Ruang
     Pamonsai. "Thai Frauen: ein weiter Weg zur Freiheit"
     [Thai women: a long way to freedom]. 6. Bernard Frikke,
     "Gleich den Hinterbeinen eines Elefanten: Frauen in Thai-
     land (Gespräch)" [Like the hind leg of an elephant: women
     in Thailand (discussion)].)

287 ZAKARIA ISMAIL. "Pelacuran di Bandaraya Pulau Pinang: Satu
     Kajian ke atas Pelacur-pelacur yang Terdiri Daripada
     Pelayan-pelayan Bar" [Prostitution in Penang: a study of
     prostitutes who are bar waitresses]. B.A. academic exer-
     cise, University of Malaya, 1976, ix, 197 pp.

DIRECTORIES

288 ASSOCIATION FOR ASIAN STUDIES, Ad Hoc Committee on the Role
     of Women in Asian Studies, comp. Directory of Women in
     Asian Studies. Ann Arbor, Mich.: AAS Secretariat, Uni-
     versity of Michigan, 1974, 64 pp.

289 HOSKEN, FRANZISKA P., ed. International Directory of Women's
     Development Organizations. Washington, D.C.: Agency for
     International Development, 1977, ix, 311 pp.

290 NEW TRANSCENTURY FOUNDATION, Secretariat for Women in Develop-
     ment. Directory of Projects Involving Women. Washington,
     D.C.: Secretariat for Women in Development, New Trans-
     Century Foundation, 1980[?]. (Vols. 1, 2, and 3 contain
     a collection of information on projects involving women in
     the Third World.)

291 UNITED NATIONS, Asian and Pacific Centre for Women and Devel-
     opment. APCWD Women's Resource Book, 1979. Produced by
     International Women's Tribune Centre, New York, for Asian &

Pacific Centre for Women and Development, Kuala Lumpur,
New York: International Women's Tribune Centre, 1980,
1 vol. (various pagings).

292 _____ . Directory of Fellows and Consultants 1977-1980.
Bangkok: APCWD, 1980, 71 pp.

293 WOMEN LAWYERS' ASSOCIATION OF THE PHILIPPINES, Manila.
National Directory of Women Lawyers of the Philippines.
Manila: Women Lawyers' Association of the Philippines,
1975. 156 pp.

ECONOMIC CONDITIONS AND STATUS; EMPLOYMENT; OCCUPATIONS; ROLE IN DEVELOPMENT

(On legal aspects see Legal Status, Laws, etc.
On married women see Married Women and Mothers.)

Southeast Asia

294 AAAS SEMINAR ON WOMEN IN DEVELOPMENT, Mexico, 1975. Women and
World Development: With an Annotated Bibliography. Edited by Irene Tinker, Michèle Bo Bramsen, and Mayra Buvinić.
New York: Praeger, in cooperation with the Overseas Development Council, 1976, vii, 382 pp.

295 ASEAN SEMINAR ON INTEGRATION OF WOMEN IN DEVELOPMENT,
Jakarta, 1975. Proceedings. Sponsored by the Indonesian
Human Resources Development Foundation et al. Jakarta,
1975, 180 pp.

296 ASEAN SEMINAR ON WOMEN AND EMPLOYMENT, Kuala Lumpur, 1976.
Proceedings. Kuala Lumpur: National Advisory Council on
the Integration of Women in Development, 1976, 1 vol.
(various pagings).

297 AWE, BONANLE. "Reflections on the Conference on Women and
Development (held in Wellesley College, Mass., 1976)."
Signs 3, no. 2 (Winter 1977):314-419.

298 BHARADWAJ, GEETA R., and SRIVASTAVA, SUMAN. The Special
Needs of Women; a Plea for an Integrated Approach and Some
Programme Proposals. Bangkok: Asian and Pacific Centre
for Women and Development, 1980, 35 pp.

299   BILSBORROW, R.E. "Effects of Economic Dependency on Labour
      Force Participation Rates in Less Developed Countries."
      Oxford Economic Papers (29 Mar. 1977):61-83. (Includes
      discussion about the female labour force in Thailand, etc.)

300   BLITZ, R.C. "An International Comparison of Women's Partici-
      pation in the Professions." Journal of Developing Areas
      9, no. 4 (July 1975):499-510.

301   BOSERUP, ESTER. "Employment of Women in Developing Countries."
      In Population Growth and Economic Development in the Third
      World. Vol. 1. Edited by Léon Tabah, Dolhain, Belgium:
      Ordina Editions, 1975[?], pp. 79-107.

302   _____. Women's Role in Economic Development. London: Allen
      and Unwin; New York: St. Martin's Press, 1970, 283 pp.

303   BOSERUP, ESTER, and LILJENCRANTZ, CHRISTINA. Integration of
      Women in Development: Why? When? How? New York: United
      Nations Development Programme, 1975, 42 pp.

304   "The Changing Role of SE Asian Women." Special joint issue of
      Southeast Asia Chronicle, no. 66 (Jan./Feb. 1979) and
      Pacific Research Bulletin, nos. 5/6 (July/Oct. 1978),
      27 pp.

305   CONCEPCIÓN, MERCEDES B. "Female Labour Force Participation
      and Fertility." International Labour Review 109, nos. 5/6
      (May/June 1974):503-57. (Covers various Asian countries.)

306   "Conditions of Employment of Women Workers in Asia: Problems
      Raised by the Regulation of Their Conditions of Employ-
      ment." International Labour Review 70 (Dec. 1954):542-56.

307   EXPERT GROUP MEETING ON THE IDENTIFICATION OF THE BASIC NEEDS
      OF WOMEN OF ASIA AND THE PACIFIC AND ON THE FORMULATION OF
      A PROGRAMME OF WORK, Teheran, 1977. Report. Bangkok:
      Asian and Pacific Centre for Women and Development,
      1980[?], iv, 67 pp.

308   FERNANDO, SYLVIA. "Women and Economic Development in Asia."
      Eastern World 16, no. 8 (Aug. 1962):27-28.

309   FRIEDRICH-EBERT-STIFTUNG, Bangkok. The Role of Women in Con-
      tributing to Family Income. Proceedings of the Regional
      Workshop in Bangkok, 19-23 July, 1976. Bangkok:
      Friedrich-Ebert-Stiftung, 1977, 321 pp.

310   HOLLNSTEINER, MARY RACELIS. "Rural Women Workers in Asia."
      Impact 11, no. 7 (July 1976):237-44.

311 HULL, VALERIE J. "Fertility, Women's Work and Economic Class:
     A Case Study from Southeast Asia." In The Fertility of
     Working Women: A Synthesis of International Research.
     Edited by Stanley Kupinsky. New York: Praeger, 1977,
     pp. 35-80.

312 IFFTU-UNESCO ASEAN SEMINAR ON EQUAL OPPORTUNITIES FOR WOMEN IN
     EDUCATION AND EMPLOYMENT, Kuala Lumpur, 1977. Report of
     Proceedings. Sponsored and organised by International
     Federation of Free Teachers Unions in co-operation with
     National Union of the Teaching Profession, Malaysia and the
     assistance of Unesco and Unctad. Kuala Lumpur, 1980,
     74 pp.

313 ILO REGIONAL SEMINAR ON WOMEN PARTICIPATION IN TRADE UNION
     ACTIVITIES, Kuala Lumpur, 1979. Papers. Sponsored by the
     International Labour Organization and Malaysian Trades
     Union Congress. Kuala Lumpur, 1979, 1 vol. (various
     pagings).

314 INTERNATIONAL BANK FOR RECONSTRUCTION AND DEVELOPMENT. Inte-
     grating Women into Development. Washington, D.C.: World
     Bank, 1975, 29 pp.

315 INTERNATIONAL FEDERATION OF COMMERCIAL, CLERICAL AND TECHNICAL
     EMPLOYEES, Asian Regional Organisation, comp. Equality for
     Women, Penang-Malaysia, 12-16 February 1979. Singapore[?]
     Asia-FIET, 1980, 138 pp. (Proceedings of the First Asia-
     FIET Regional Women Conference held in Penang. Includes
     country reports of Indonesia, Malaysia, Philippines, and
     Singapore.)

316 INTERNATIONAL INSTITUTE OF DIFFERING CIVILIZATIONS. Women's
     Rôle in the Development of Tropical and Subtropical Coun-
     tries: Report of the XXXIth Meeting, Held in Brussels on
     17th, 18th 19th and 20th September 1958. Brussels:
     International Institute of Differing Civilizations, 1959,
     543 pp.

317 INTERNATIONAL LABOUR OFFICE. Report on the ILO/SIDA Asian
     Regional Seminar on Labour Inspection in Relation to the
     Employment of Women and Protection of Children, Singapore,
     28 November-13 December, 1972. Geneva: ILO, 1973, iii,
     90 pp. ILO/TF/AFE/R.21.

318 INTERNATIONAL LABOUR OFFICE, and CLEARING HOUSE FOR SOCIAL
     DEVELOPMENT IN ASIA. The Role of Women in Contributing to
     Family Income: Proceedings of the Regional Workshop,
     Bangkok, Thailand, 19-23 July 1976. Bangkok: Friedrich-
     Ebert-Stiftung, 1977, 321 pp.

319   INTERNATIONAL LABOUR ORGANIZATION. The Role of Women in Con-
      tributing to Family Income. Proceedings of the regional
      workshop in Bangkok from 19 to 23 July 1976, organised by
      the International Labour Organization, Regional Office and
      the Clearing House for Social Development in Asia, ESCAP,
      and Friedrich-Ebert-Stiftung, 1977. Bangkok: Inter-
      national Labour Organization, 1977, 321 pp.

320   JAHAN, ROUNAQ, and PAPANEK, HANNA, eds. Women and Develop-
      ment: Perspectives from South and Southeast Asia.   Dacca:
      Bangladesh Institute of Law and International Affairs,
      1979, 439 pp.

321   KALLGREN, JOYCE K. "Enhancing the Role of Women in Developing
      Countries." Washington, D.C.: Agency for International
      Development, 1973.

322   LEGASPI, LEONARDO Z., ed. The Role of Women in Development:
      Seminar Papers and Statement. Manila: University of Santo
      Tomas Press, 1976.

323   LILY binti ABDUL MAJEED. "Women in Development in the ASEAN
      Region." 17 pp. Paper presented at the 15th World Con-
      ference of the Society of International Development,
      Amsterdam, 28 November-3 December 1976.

324   McCABE, JAMES, and ROSENZWEIG, MARK RICHARD. Female Labor-
      Force Participation and Fertility in Developing Countries.
      New Haven, Conn.: Yale University, 1974. Yale University.
      Economic Growth Center, Discussion Paper, no. 216.

325   MANDERSON, LENORE. "Women and Work: Continuities of the Past
      and Present." Asia Teachers' Association, Bulletin 6,
      no. 2 (June 1978):6-24.

326   MANGAHAS, MAHAR, and JAYME-HO, TERESA. "The Economic Status
      of Women: An Analytical Framework." Economic Bulletin for
      Asia and the Pacific 27, no. 1 (June 1976):62-72.

327   MULIAKOESUMA, SUTARSIH. "Partisipasi Wanita dalam Angkatan
      Kerja di Negara Sedang dan di Negara Maju" [The participa-
      tion of women in work in developing and developed coun-
      tries]. Warta Demografi [Universitas Indonesia] 5, no. 8
      (1975):1-6.

328   NEW TRANSCENTURY FOUNDATION, Secretariat for Women in Develop-
      ment. Directory of Projects Involving Women. Washington,
      D.C.: Secretariat for Women in Development, New Trans-
      Century Foundation, 1980[?]. (Vols. 1, 2, and 3 contain
      a collection of information on projects involving women in
      the Third World.)

329   REGIONAL CONSULTATION FOR ASIA AND THE FAR EAST ON INTEGRATION
       OF WOMEN IN DEVELOPMENT WITH SPECIAL REFERENCE TO POPULA-
       TION FACTORS, Bangkok, 1974. Plan of Action. Report.
       Bangkok, 1974, 14 pp. United Nations Document ST/ESA/
       Ser. B/5/Add.1.

330   RICAFRENTE, CHERRY-LYNN S. "International Labor Standards for
       Working Women." Philippine Law Journal 50, no. 1 (Feb.
       1975):55-79.

331   SANTILLAN-CASTRENCE, PURA. "The Role of Asian Women in Devel-
       opment." Impact 6, no. 6 (June 1971):18-23.

332   SEMINAR ON ASEAN WOMEN IN MASS MEDIA, Kuala Lumpur, 1979.
       Working Papers. Organised by PERTAMA (Malaysian Women
       Journalist Association). Kuala Lumpur, 1979, 1 vol.
       (various pagings).

333   SEMINAR ON LABOR SUPPLY, Makati, Rizal, Philippines, 1976.
       Papers. Jointly sponsored by the Council for Asian Man-
       power Studies and the Organization of Demographic Asso-
       ciates. Manila, 1976.

334   SHAHANI, LETICIA RAMOS. "The Status of Women in Asia and
       National Development Programs." Asian & Pacific Quarterly
       of Cultural and Social Affairs 5, no. 2 (Autumn 1973):
       60-67.

335   SOON, YOUNG YOON. "The Halfway House: MNCS, Industries, and
       Asian Factory Girls (Selected Countries of the ESCAP Re-
       gion)." Bangkok: United Nations Asian and Pacific Devel-
       opment Institute, 1979, 49 pp.

336   THADANI, VEENA N., and TODARO, MICHAEL P. Female Migration in
       Developing Countries: A Framework for Analysis. New York:
       Center for Policy Studies, Population Council, 1979,
       48 pp. Population Council, Center for Policy Studies.
       Working Papers, no. 47.

337   TWARO ASEAN AND OCEANIC WOMEN SEMINAR, Singapore, 1978.
       Lectures and Country Reports. Jointly sponsored by the
       International Textile Garment and Leather Workers' Federa-
       tion and Asian American Free Labor Institute. Singapore,
       1978, 311 pp.

338   UNITED NATIONS, Asian and Pacific Centre for Women and
       Development. Participation of Women in Decision-
       making . . . Some Guidelines. Bangkok: Asian and
       Pacific Centre for Women and Development, 1980, v, 50 pp.

339   , Economic Commission for Asia and the Far East. <u>Learning from Rural Women: Village Level Success Cases of Rural Women's Group Income-raising Activities</u>. ESCAP/FAO Inter-Country Project for the Promotion and Training of Rural Women in Income-raising Group Activities. Bangkok: ECAFE, 1979, 140 pp.

340   . <u>Report on the ESCAP/FAO Inter-Country Project for the Promotion and Training of Rural Women in Income-raising Group Activities in Nine Asian Countries, February 1978-1979</u>. Bangkok: ECAFE, 1979, 19 pp.

341 UNITED NATIONS, Secretary-General 1961-1971 (Thant). <u>Participation of Women in the Economic and Social Development of Their Countries</u>. New York: United Nations, 1970, iv, 104 pp. United Nations Document E/CN.6/513/Rev.1.

342 van HAEFTEN, ROBERTA K., and CATON, DOUGLAS D. "A Strategy Paper for Integrating LDC Rural Women into Their National Economies." Washington, D.C.: Department of State, Agency for International Development, 1974.

343 WARD, BARBARA E. "Women and Technology in Developing Countries." <u>Impact of Science on Society</u> 20, no. 1 (1970): 93-101.

344 WELLESLEY EDITORIAL COMMITTEE, ed. <u>Women and National Development: The Complexities of Change</u>. Chicago: University of Chicago Press, 1977, xiv, 346 pp. (Based on a conference on women and development held 2-6 June 1976, sponsored by the Center for Research on Women in Higher Education and the Professions, Wellesley College; the African Studies Association; the Association for Asian Studies; and the Latin American Studies Association.)

345 WHYTE, ROBERT ORR, and WHYTE, PAULINE. <u>Rural Asian Women: Status and Environment</u>. Singapore: Institute of Southeast Asian Studies, 1978, 34 pp. Institute of Southeast Asian Studies, Singapore, Research Notes and Discussion Paper, no. 9.

346 "The Women of ASEAN." <u>Asian Trade and Industry</u> 8, no. 2 (1976):58-59.

347 <u>Women Workers and Society: International Perspectives</u>. Geneva: International Labour Office, 1976, vii, 211 pp.

348 "Women's Employment in Asian Countries." <u>International Labour Review</u> 68 (Sept. 1953):303-18.

349 YOUSSEF, NADIA HAGGAG. "Women and Agricultural Production in Moslem Societies." Paper presented at the Seminar on Prospects for Growth in Rural Societies: With or Without the Active Participation of Women, sponsored by the Agricultural Development Council, Princeton, New Jersey, 1974.

Brunei

350 ABDUL LATIF HAJI IBRAHIM. "Padian, Its Market and the Women Vendors." Brunei Museum Journal 2, pt. 1 (1970):39-51.

Burma

351 PURCELL, VICTOR. "Burma, Thailand and Malaya." In Women's Rôle in the Development of Tropical and Sub-Tropical Countries, by International Institute of Differing Civilizations. Brussels: International Institute of Differing Civilizations, 1959, pp. 291-300.

Indochina

352 BROWN, JAMES A., and SALKIN, JAY S. "Underemployment in Rural South Vietnam: A Comment and a Discussion of Family Labor." Economic Development and Cultural Change 23 (Oct. 1974): 151-62.

353 BUI THU. "Assigning Labor on the Basis of Women's Physical Conditions." U.S. JPRS. Translations on North Vietnam, no. 146 (13 Apr. 1967): 40, 620.

354 LE PHOUNG HANG. "Utilizing Women in Agriculture." U.S. JPRS. Translations on North Vietnam, no. 144 (12 Apr. 1967): 40,604.

355 PHUNG THI HANH. South Vietnam's Women in Uniform. Saigon: Vietnam Council on Foreign Relations, 1970[?], 18 pp.

356 SWEDISH INTERNATIONAL DEVELOPMENT AUTHORITY, Research Division. Women in Developing Countries: Case Studies of Six Countries. Stockholm: Swedish International Development Authority, 1974, 98 pp. (Includes North Vietnam.)

Indonesia

357 BOOMGAARD, PETER. "Female Labour and Population Growth in Nineteenth Century Java." 27 pp. Paper presented at the Eighth Conference of the International Association of Historians of Asia, Kuala Lumpur, August 1980.

358 "Corps Wanita Angkatan Darat" [Women's Army Corps]. Madjalah Sedjarah Militer Angkatan Darat 10 (1962):62-66.

359   DAUMONT, VÉRONIQUE. "Un monopole féminin menacé: le commerce des jamu" [A threatened feminine monopoly: the 'jamu' trade]. Archipel no. 13 (1977):265-66.

360   DIAH, HERAWATI. "Women in Modern Indonesia." Philippine Review 4 (Sept./Oct. 1955):34-36.

361   DJALAL, DJANIZAR. Wanita dan Pembangunan di Indonesia [Women and development in Indonesia]. Padang: Proyek Penerangan, Bimbingan dan Dakwah Agama Islam Prop, Sumatera Barat, 1972, 45 pp.

362   GERMAIN, ADRIENNE; JONES, SIDNEY; and BOOZ, ELIZABETH. "Food, Employment and the Role of Women in Indonesia. A Consultant Report." Jakarta: Ford Foundation, 1979.

363   HOLLNSTEINER, MARY RACELIS. "Enhancing the Participation of Indonesian Women in Development: A Consultant's Report to the United Nation's Children's Fund, 1975." Bangkok: United Nations Children's Fund, East Asia and Pakistan Regional Office, 1975, 10 pp.

364   HULL, VALERIE J. "Fertility, Socioeconomic Status and the Position of Women in a Javanese Village." Ph.D. dissertation, Australian National University, 1975, ix, 447 pp.

365   _____. Fertility, Socioeconomic Status and the Position of Women in a Javanese Village. Canberra: Australian National University, 1975, ix, 584 pp.

366   "Ibu Emmy." ISIS International Bulletin, no. 8 (Summer 1978): 10-11. (On employment in Indonesia.)

367   INDONESIA, Departemen Pertahanan-Keamanan. Mengenai Korps Wanita Angkatan Bersenjata Republik Indonesia [On the Indonesian women's armed forces corps]. Jakarta: Biro Wanita ABRI, Dep. Hankam, 1976, 29 pp.

368   _____, Departemen Tenaga Kerja Transmigrasi dan Koperasi, Direktorat Jenderal Koperasi. "Approach of Developing the Role of Indonesian Women in Rural Economic Development." Jakarta, 197[?], 5 pp.

369   _____, Sekretariat Menteri Muda Urusan Peranan Wanita. "Rancangan Repelita III: Kebijaksanaan dan Program-program Peranan Wanita dalam Pembangunan dan Pembinaan Bangsa" [Proposal for the third five-year development plan pertaining to the role of women in national development]. Jakarta: Sekretariat Menteri Muda Urusan Peranan Wanita, Republik Indonesia, 1979, 15 pp.

370   ISMAN, SUNTORO. "Peningkatan Pendidikan dan Partisipasi
      Kerja Wanita dalam Usaha Penurunan Fertilitas: Sebuah
      Tinjauan Peranan Pendidikan dan Peranan Wanita dalam
      Masyarakat yang Sedang Berkembang" [Upgrading educational
      levels and female employment in the effort to reduce fer-
      tility: a survey of the role of education and women in a
      developing society]. Jakarta: Fakultas Ekonomi, Univer-
      sitas Indonesia, 1975, 13 pp.

371   JONES, GAVIN WALLIS. "Factors Affecting Labour Force Partici-
      pation of Females in Jakarta." Kajian Ekonomi Malaysia 14,
      no. 2 (Dec. 1977):71-93.

372   KOMISI NASIONAL KEDUDUKAN WANITA INDONESIA. Pelaksanaan
      tentang Penghapusan Diskriminasi terhadap Wanita di
      Indonesia: Sebuah Laporan [The implementation of the
      (plan) to abolish discrimination against women in
      Indonesia: a report]. Jakarta: Komisi Nasional Kedudukan
      Wanita Indoensia, 1973, 38 pp.

373   Kursus Peserta Seminar Wanita se Jawa, Jakarta, 1977 [Course
      for Participants of the All-Java Women's Seminar, Jakarta,
      1977]. Sponsors, Yayasan Tenaga Kerja Indonesia and
      Friedrich-Ebert-Stiftung. Jakarta: Pusat Pembinaan Sumber
      Daya Manusia, 1977, 350 pp.

374   LOKAKARYA KERAJINAN MELALUI PENINGKATAN KERAJINAN DAN KEWIRAS-
      WASTAAN MEMANTAPKAN PARTISIPASI WANITA DALAM PEMBANGUNAN,
      Jakarta, 1977. Hasil-hasil [Workshop on Upgrading the
      Skills and Entrepreneurship of Women in Development,
      Jakarta, 1977. Report]. Jakarta: Kongres Wanita
      Indonesia, 1977[?], 24 pp.

375   LOKAKARYA PERANAN WANITA DESA SEBAGAI TENAGA PRODUKTIF DALAM
      PEMBANGUNAN PEDESAAN, Jakarta, 1976. Hasil [Workshop on
      the Role of Rural Women as Productive Force in Rural Devel-
      opment, Jakarta, 1976. Report]. Jakarta: Kowani beker-
      jasama dengan Y.T.K.I. dan F.E.S., 1977, 12 pp.

376   MILONE, PAULINE. A Preliminary Study in Three Countries:
      Indonesia Report. Washington, D.C.: Office of Women in
      Development, Agency for International Development, 1978.

377   NOOR, YETTY RIZALI. "Indonesian Women's Participation in
      Development." Indonesia Magazine, no. 31 (1975):4-14.

378   _____. "Women's Role in Society and Development in
      Indonesia." Impact 10, no. 4 (Apr. 1975):130-32.

379   OEY, MAYLING. "Some demographic notes on the progress of
      Indonesian Women." Prisma 1, no. 2 (Nov. 1975):74-80.
      (Indonesian version published in Prisma [Indonesian ed.]
      4, no. 2 [Oct. 1975]:11-18.)

380   PANJAITAN, KARTINI. "Kegiatan Dagang Inang-inang" [Activities
      of women traders]. Masyarakat Indonesia 4, no. 1 (1977):
      111-24.

381   PAPANEK, HANNA. Implications of Development for Women in
      Indonesia: Selected Research and Policy Issues. Boston:
      Center for Asian Development Studies, Boston University,
      1979, 40 pp. Boston University, Center for Asian Develop-
      ment Studies. Discussion Paper Series, no. 8. Paper pre-
      sented at the Conference on Indonesian Political Economy
      Eighth Annual Conference on Indonesian Studies, University
      of California, Berkeley, August, 1979.

382   _____. "Jakarta Middle Class Women: Modernization, Employ-
      ment and Family Life." In What is Modern Indonesian Cul-
      ture?. Edited by Gloria Davis. Athens: Ohio University
      Center for International Studies, Southeast Asia Program,
      1979, pp. 108-134.

383   PELUSO, NANCY LEE. "Collecting Data on Women's Employment in
      Rural Java." Studies in Family Planning 10, nos. 11/12
      (Nov./Dec. 1979):374-78.

384   Peranan Wanita Indonesia dalam Pembangunan [The role of Indo-
      nesian women in development]. Jakarta: Norindo Pratama,
      1975, 973 pp.

385   PERSATUAN WANITA DEPARTEMEN PENERANGAN "DIAN EKAWATI."
      Laporan Singkat Pembukaan Musjawarah Kerja Nasional keII
      Persatuan Wanita Departemen Penerangan "Dian Ekawati"
      [Short report on the opening of the Second National Labour
      Conference of the Women's Association, Department of In-
      formation]. Jakarta: Persatuan Wanita Departemen
      Penerangan "Dian Ekawati," 1973, 1 vol. (various pagings).

386   PIET, NANCY. "A glimpse of the Indonesian Woman." World
      Education Reports, no. 11 (Apr. 1976):1-5.

387   PROBONEGERO, NINUK IRAWATI. "Suka Duka Field Worker Wanita"
      [The everyday experiences of a woman field worker]. Media
      Ikatan Kekerabatan Antropologi 2, no. 2 (1974):25-29.

388   RAHARDJO, YULFITA. "Beberapa Dilemma Wanita Bekerja" [Some
      dilemmas of working women]. Prisma 4, no. 5 (Oct. 1975):
      45-51.

389   RINI. "Wanita dalam Pertanian" [Women in farming]. Majalah
      Berkala Pertanian 4, no. 4 (1953):5-9.

390   RUSDY, TAUFIQ. "Pekan Nasional: Pertemuan Wanita Tani"
      [National fair: women farmers' meeting]. Majalah
      Pertanian 19, nos. 5/6 (1971):34-41.

391   SAID, MUHAMMAD. "Peranan dan Tugas Wanita dalam Pembinaan
      Kepribadian Nasional" [The role and the task of women in
      national character development]. Pusara 22, no. 3 (1961):
      11-14.

392   SARDJONO, H. ROESIAH. "Funksi dan Peranan Tenaga Kerja Wanita
      di dalam Pembangunan" [The function and role of the female
      labor force in development]. Majalah Kesehatan 5, no. 34
      (1972):27-29, 68-69.

393   SCHILLER, B.M. "Women, Work and Status in Rural Java."
      Master's thesis, Ohio University, 1978, 163 pp.

394   SEMINAR NASIONAL BURUH WANITA, Jakarta, 1961. Peranan Buruh
      Wanita dalam Pembangunan [National Seminar on Female La-
      borers, Jakarta, 1961. Role of female laborers in devel-
      opment]. Diselenggarakan oleh D.N. SOBSI, tgl. 11-14 Mei
      1961 di Djakarta. Jakarta: Jajasan Karya Bakti, 1961,
      87 pp.

395   SEMINAR NASIONAL WANITA TANI, Jakarta, 1961. Papers [National
      Seminar of Women Farmers, Jakarta, 1961]. Jakarta:
      Jajasan Pembaruan, 1962, 92 pp.

396   SEMINAR PERWARI TENTANG PARTISIPASI WANITA DALAM PEMBANGUNAN
      MASYARAKAT DESA, Jakarta, 1971. Prasaran2, Pembahasan2
      dan Kesimpulan [Seminar on the Participation of Women in
      the Development of Rural Society, Jakarta, 1971. Proceed-
      ings]. Jakarta: Persatuan Wanita Republic Indonesia,
      1971, 1 vol. (various pagings).

397   SEMINAR TENAGA KERDJA WANITA, Tijiloto, Indonesia, 1971.
      Prasaran2 Kesimpulan2, Hasil [Seminar on the Female Labor
      Force, Tijiloto, Indonesia, 1971. Proceedings]. Jakarta,
      1971, 83 pp.

398   SEMINAR TENTANG INTEGRASI WANITA DALAM PEMBANGUNAN, Jakarta,
      1975. Hasil-hasil [Seminar on the Integration of Women in
      Development, Jakarta, 1975. Proceedings]. Sponsors:
      Yayasan Tenaga Kerja Indonesia, Komisi Nasional Kedudukan
      Wanita Indonesia, Friedrich-Ebert-Stiftung. Jakarta YTKI,
      1975, 100 pp.

399   SEMINAR TENTANG KEDUDUKAN DAN FUNGSI TENAGA KERJA WANITA
      DALAM MASYARAKAT, Bandungan-Ambarawa, Indonesia, 1975.
      Risalah [Seminar on the Status and Function of Female
      Labor Force in Society, Bandungan-Ambarawa, Indonesia,
      1975. Proceedings]. Sponsors: Yayasan Tenaga Kerja
      Indonesia, Friedrich-Ebert-Stiftung, Badan Kontak Tenaga
      Kerja Indonesia. Jakarta: YTKI, 1975[?], 51 pp.

400   SEMINAR TENTANG MENINGKATKAN KESADARAN BERORGANISASI DAN
      PENGETAHUAN UNDANG-UNDANG PERBURUHAN BAGI TENAGA KERJA
      WANITA DALAM PEMBANGUNAN, Denpasar, Indonesia, 1976.
      Risalah [Seminar on Increasing the Awareness of the
      Organization and Knowledge of Labor Laws for the Female
      Labor Force in Development, Denpasar, 1976. Proceedings].
      Diselenggarakan atas kerja sama Yayasan Tenaga Kerja
      Indonesia, Kantor Daerah Tenaga Kerja Bali, Badan Kontak
      Tenaga Kerja Wanita Indonesia dan Friedrich-Ebert-
      Stiftung, dari tgl. 22-25 Apr. 1976. Denpasar, 1976,
      119 pp.

401   SEMINAR TENTANG MENINGKATKAN KESADARAN BERORGANISASI DAN
      PENGETAHUAN UNDANG-UNDANG PERBURUHAN BAGI TENAGA KERJA
      WANITA DALAM PEMBANGUNAN, Ujung Pandang, Indonesia, 1976.
      Risalah [Seminar on Increasing the Awareness of the
      Organization and Knowledge of Labor Laws for the Female
      Labor Force in Development, Ujung Pandang, Indonesia, 1976.
      Proceedings]. Diselenggarakan oleh Yayasan Tenaga Kerja
      Indonesia, Friedrich-Ebert-Stiftung, Kantor Daerah Tenaga
      Kerja Sulawesi Selatan dan Tenggara, dari tgl. Juli-
      1 Agustus 1976. Ujung Pandang, 1976, 71 pp.

402   SEMINAR TENTANG PENDIDIKAN TENAGA KERJA WANITA DALAM PEM-
      BANGUNAN, Bandung, Indonesia, 1975. Risalah [Seminar on
      Educating the Female Labor Force in Development, Bandung,
      Indonesia, 1975. Proceedings]. Di-sponsori oleh Yayasan
      Tenaga Kerja Indonesia, Friedrich-Ebert-Stiftung, Panitia
      Daerah Tahun Wanita Internasional Jabar dan Badan Kontak
      Tenaga Kerja Wanita Indonesia, 27 s/d 30 Agustus 1975.
      Bandung, 1975, 50 pp.

403   SEMINAR TENTANG PENYUSUNAN KEBIJAKSANAAN KEARAH PENINGKATAN
      PARTISIPASI WANITA DALAM PEKERJAAN YANG BERUPAH, Jakarta,
      1976. Seminar tentang Penyusunan Kebijaksanaan Kearah
      Peningkatan Partisipasi Wanita Dalam Pekerjaan yang
      Berupah, Jakarta 3-6 Nopember 1976 [Seminar on Guidelines
      to Increase the Participation of Women in Paid Employment,
      Jakarta, 1976]. Sponsors, Direktorat Jenderal Perlin-
      dungan dan Perawatan Tenaga Kerja, Departemen Tenaga
      Kerja Transkop, Yayasan Tenaga Kerja Indonesia (YTKI),
      Friedrich-Ebert-Stiftung (FES). Jakarta, 1976, 112 pp.

404   SEMINAR WANITA DALAM PERS YANG MEMBANGUN, Jakarta, 1974.
      Kumpulan Bahan dan Hasil [Seminar on Women Working in
      Presses that are Progressive, Jakarta, 1974. A compila-
      tion]. Diselenggarakan bersama oleh Yayasan Penabur dan
      Majalah Wanita Mutiara. Jakarta: Biro Penerangan dan
      Motivasi BKKB, 1975, 141 pp.

405   SEMINAR WANITA TENTANG TENAGA KERDJA WANITA INDONESIA DALAM
      PEMBANGUNAN, Tjiloto, Indonesia, 1971. Hasil Seminar
      Wanita dengan Thema Meningkatkan Appresiasi dan Effisiensi
      Terhadap dari Tenaga Kerdja Wanita Indonesia di Tjiloto,
      24-29 September 1971 [Proceedings of the Women's Seminar on
      the Indonesian Female Labor Force in Development: With the
      aim of increasing the appreciation and efficiency of the
      Indonesian female labor force, Tjiloto, 24-29 September
      1971]. Jakarta: Jajasan Tenaga Kerdja Indonesia bersama-
      sama Friedrich-Ebert-Stiftung, 1971, 1 vol. (various
      pagings).

406   SISWORAHARDJO, S. "Case Study on Social Welfare Strategies
      to Enhance Women's Roles in Socio-Economic Development and
      Leadership in the Rural Areas, Suradita, Subdistrict of
      Serpong, Tangerang." Jakarta, 1979, viii, 35 pp. Paper
      presented at the Workshop on Social Welfare Strategies to
      Enhance Women's Roles in Economic Development Activities
      and Leadership, Jakarta, 1979.

407   SOEBEKTI, TOBIAS. "Sekitar Pendapatan Wanita Kawin" [The in-
      come of married women]. Majalah Perpajakan Indonesia 1,
      no. 3 (1969):13-15.

408   SUJATI. "Wanita sebagai Dokter" [Women as doctors]. Basis 5,
      no. 7 (Apr. 1956):231-35.

409   SULEIMAN, IBU. Pekerjaan Wanita di Rumah [Women's work at
      home]. Jakarta: Mahabharata, n.d., 32 pp.

410   SURYOCHONDRO, SUKANTI. "The Status, Roles and Achievement of
      Women in Indonesia." In The Role of Women in Development:
      Seminar Papers and Statements. Edited by Leonardo Z.
      Legaspi. Manila: University of Santo Tomas Press, 1976,
      pp. 82-96.

411   SUSANTO, ASTRID S. "Wanita Desa dan Pembangunan" [Rural
      women and development]. Prisma 4, no. 5 (Oct. 1975):25-32.

412   SOEWITO, AGUSTINAH. "Metodik Penyuluhan pada Wanita Tani"
      [Method of disseminating information to women farmers].
      Majalah Pertanian 17, no. 3 (1969):32-44.

413   TRIMURTI, S.K. "Masalah Jam Kerja pada Tenaga Kerja Wanita"
      [Problems of working hours for women workers]. Majalah
      Hygiene Perusahaan, Kesehatan Keselamatan Kerja dan
      Jaminan Sosial 5, no. 3 (1972):6-7.

414   _____ et al. Wartawan Wanita Berkisah [Accounts of
      women journalists]. Jakarta: Badan Penerbit Indonesia
      Raya, 1974, 155 pp.

415   TURBITT, CORALIE. A Preliminary Study in Three Countries:
      Indonesia Report. Executive summary. Washington, D.C.:
      Office of Women in Development, Agency for International
      Development, 1978.

416   WARIHKOESOMO, SOEWANDHI. "Peranan Metoda Partisipasi Penuh
      dalam Latihan Kepemimpin Kelompok Wanita Tani" [The role of
      the full-participation method in the leadership training of
      a group of women farmers]. Majalah Pertanian 23, no. 4
      (1975/76):36-37, 40.

417   _____. "Peranan Wanita Tani" [The role of women farmers].
      Trubus 6, no. 73 (1975):357-58.

418   WARTOMO, YOYOH (Mrs.). "Masalah Pendayagunaan Tenaga Kerja
      Wanita dalam Pembangunan" [Problem of productivity of women
      workers in development]. Majalah Kesehatan 48 (1975):22-25.

419   "Women at Work in Indonesia." Free Labour World, no. 153
      (Mar. 1963):12-13.

420   "Women Workers in Asia." ISIS International Bulletin, no. 10
      (Winter 1978/79):4-5. (Deals in part with Indonesia and
      the Philippines.)

Malaysia

421   ABDUL AHMAD. "Peranan Wanita dalam Ranchangan Malaysia Kedua"
      [The role of women in the Second Malaysia Plan]. Pemimpin,
      no. 1 (Jan. 1972):29-31.

422   ABDUL RAHMAN HAJI ABDULLAH. "Kerja untuk Wanita Islam:
      Sejauh Mana Hak Mereka?" [Employment for Muslim women:
      to what extent do they have rights?]. Dewan Masyarakat 14,
      no. 7 (July 1976):17-19.

423   ACKERMAN, SUSAN ELLEN. "Cultural Process in Malaysian Indus-
      trialization: A Study of Malay Women Factory Workers."
      Ph.D. dissertation, University of California, San Diego,
      1980, xiv, 292 pp.

424   AMINAH binti ABU BAKAR. "Peranan Peniaga-peniaga Wanita
       Melayu di Kuala Lumpur" [The role of Malay businesswomen
       in Kuala Lumpur]. B.A. academic exercise, Universiti
       Kebangsaan Malaysia, 1975, ix, 73 pp.

425   ANIS binti SABIRIN. "Wanita dan Ekonomi" [Women and the
       Economy]. Dewan Masyarakat 4 (May 1966):17-20.

426   AZIZ MUHAMMAD. "Penyertaan Wanita di dalam Pembangunan Tanah
       di Rancangan Tanah Beliawanis Bukit Mambai Segamat, Johor"
       [The participation of women in the youth land development
       scheme in Bukit Mambai, Segamat, Johore]. B.A. academic
       exercise, University of Malaya, 1977, xi, 123 pp.

427   AZIZAH KASSIM. "Diskriminasi terhadap Wanita dalam Bidang
       Pekerjaan" [Discrimination against women workers]. Wanita
       [Kuala Lumpur], no. 118 (May 1979):38-39.

428   _____. "Masalah Pekerja Wanita dan Penyelesaiannya" [The
       problems of women workers and their solutions]. Wanita
       [Kuala Lumpur], no. 109 (Aug. 1978):22-23, 85.

429   BEBE AZMAN. "Equal Pay for Equal Work." Ekonomi [Kuala
       Lumpur] 3, no. 1 (Dec. 1962):38-48.

430   CHEW, KEE MOI. "Some Aspects of Women in Employment in West
       Malaysia, with Particular Reference to the Government and
       Estate Sectors." B.Ec. academic exercise, University of
       Malaya, 1970, viii, 118 pp.

431   CONGRESS OF UNIONS OF EMPLOYEES IN THE PUBLIC AND CIVIL
       SERVICES. International Labour Organisation Conventions
       and Recommendations of Special Concern to Women. Kuala
       Lumpur: Dewan Bahasa dan Pustaka, 1973, 62 pp.

432   CUEPACS CONVENTION, 12th, Kuala Lumpur, 1973. Problems of
       Women Workers. Kuala Lumpur: Congress of Unions of
       Employees in the Public and Civil Services, 1973, 1 vol.
       (various pagings).

433   FATIMAH DAUD. "Penyertaan Wanita Bumiputra dalam Bidang
       Perniagaan dan Perusahaan di Kuala Lumpur" [The participa-
       tion of Malay women in business and industry in Kuala
       Lumpur]. Master's thesis, University of Malaya, 1975,
       xxvii, 276 pp.

434   FATIMAH HAMID-DON. "The Status, Roles and Achievements of
       Women in Malaysia." In The Role of Women in Development:
       Seminar Papers and Statements. Edited by Leonardo Z.
       Legaspi. Manila: University of Santo Tomas Press, 1976,
       pp. 23-38.

435   FOCKE, KATHARINA. "Integrating Women in Society Remains a
       Worldwide Problem." Union Herald 55, no. 204 (June 1975):
       13-17.

436   FONG, MONICA SKANTZE. Female Labor Force Participation in a
       Modernizing Society (Malaya and Singapore, 1921-1957).
       Honolulu: East-West Population Institute, 1975, vii,
       39 pp. Hawaii University, East-West Population Institute.
       Papers, no. 34.

437   _____. "Social and Economic Correlates of Female Labor Force
       Participation in West Malaysia." Ph.D. dissertation,
       University of Hawaii, 1974. Abstracted in Dissertation
       Abstracts International 35, no. 6 (Dec. 1974):3911-A.
       University Microfilms International, order no. 74-27,679.

438   GROSSMAN, RACHAEL. "Women's Place in the Integrated Circuit."
       In "Changing Role of S.E. Asian Women"--special joint issue
       of Southeast Asia Chronicle, no. 66 (Jan./Feb. 1979) and
       Pacific Research Bulletin 9, nos. 5/6 (July/Oct. 1978):
       2-17. (On the work of women in multinational semiconductor
       firms in Malaysia and the Philippines.)

439   HAMIDAH binti HUSSAIN. "Kedudukan dan Peranan Wanita di
       Malaysia (Tumpuan pada Wanita Profesional)" [The status
       and role of women in Malaysia: with special reference to
       professional women]. B.A. academic exercise, Universiti
       Kebangsaan Malaysia, 1974.

440   HAMIMA DONA MUSTAFA. "Sensitization and Mobilization of
       Resources for Wider Involvement of Women." In Women and
       Media in Asia. Edited by Timothy Yu and Leonord Chu.
       Hong Kong: Center for Communication Studies, Chinese
       University of Hong Kong, 1977, pp. 231-36.

441   HIRSCHMAN, CHARLES, and AGHAJANIAN, AKBAR. "Women's Labour
       Force Participation and Socioeconomic Development in
       Peninsular Malaysia, 1957-70." Journal of Southeast Asian
       Studies 11, no. 1 (Mar. 1980):30-49.

442   HUSSEIN ONN, Datuk. "Wanita dalam Pembangunan" [Women in
       development]. Disunting oleh Paris M. Kilau. Kuala
       Lumpur: Jabatan Penerangan Malaysia, 1976, 12 pp.

443   "Income and Labour Market Participation of Women in Malaysia."
       Prepared by EMAS (Kuala Lumpur) in collaboration with B.A.
       Perez of the ILO Regional Office for Asia. Bangkok, 1976.

444   JAAFAR bin HARUN. "Keadaan Sosial dan Ekonomi Pelajar-pelajar
       Perempuan Alor Setar, Kedah" [The socioeconomic status of
       female university students in Alor Setar, Kedah]. B.A.
       academic exercise, University of Malaya, 1978, xii, 205 pp.

445   JAMILAH ARIFFIN. "Industrial Development in Peninsular
       Malaysia and Rural-Urban Migration of Women Workers:
       Impact and Implications." Bangi, Selangor: Department
       of Economic Development and Planning, Faculty of Economics,
       Universiti Kebangsaan Malaysia, 1978[?], 21, 6 pp.

446   _____. "Penghijrahan Buruh Wanita Melayu ke Sektor Perki-
       langan: Suantu Masalah Ekonomi Bumiputra?" [The migration
       of Malay women laborers to the manufacturing sector: an
       economic 'bumiputra' problem?]. 28 pp. Paper presented
       at Konvensyen Ekonomi Bumiputra, Kuala Lumpur, March 1978,
       organized by Universiti Kebangsaan Malaysia.

447   _____. "Penghijrahan Wanita ke Bandar dan Penyertaan dalam
       Pembangunan Perindustrian Malaysia. Adakah Ini Satu
       Eksploitasi?" [The migration of women to the towns and
       participation in the industrial development of Malaysia.
       Is this exploitation?]. 30 pp. Paper presented at the
       Seminar 'Wanita Malaysia Masakini,' Bangi, Selangor, 1979,
       organized by the Faculty of Social Sciences and Humanities,
       Universiti Kebangsaan Malaysia.

448   _____. "Rural-Urban Migration and the Status of Factory Women
       Workers in a Developing Society: A Case Study of Peninsu-
       lar Malaysia." Paper presented at the Conference of the
       Sociological Association of Australia and New Zealand,
       Brisbane, 1978.

449   JONES, GAVIN WALLIS. "Female Participation in the Labour
       Force in a Plural Economy: The Malayan Example." *Malayan
       Economic Review* 10, no. 2 (Oct. 1965):61-82.

450   KALSUM binti WAN CHIK BAKAR. "Participation of Women and
       Their Emancipation through the Application of Science and
       Technology to Development. Status Paper on Malaysia pre-
       sented at the Round Table Seminar on Participation of Women
       and Their Emancipation through the Application of Science
       and Technology to Development, Bangalore, India, July
       1979." 22 pp. Organized by the Economic and Social Com-
       mission for Asia and the Pacific, the Asia and Pacific
       Centre for Women and Development and the Regional Centre
       for Technology Transfer, Bangalore.

451 KARIMAH ZAINAB. "Wanita Melayu dalam Konteks Perubahan Ekonomi dan Politik: Satu Studi di Kota Bharu" [Malay women in the context of economic and political change: a case study of Kota Bharu]. Master's thesis, University of Malaya, 1975, ix, 279 pp.

452 KHADIJAH binti HAJI MOHAMMAD. "Wanita Melayu dan Pekerjaan" [Malay women and employment]. Master's thesis, University of Malaya, 1969, xii, 286 pp.

453 KHADIJAH binti IBRAHIM. "Pekerja Wanita dalam Satu Rancangan Getah LKTP: Kajian Kes Sendayan" [Women workers in a LKTP rubber scheme: a case study of Sendayan]. B.A. academic exercise, Universiti Kebangsaan Malaysia, 1976, 70 pp.

454 LATIFAH HASSAN. "Peniaga-peniaga Wanita Melayu, Kampung Baharu, Kuala Lumpur" [Malay businesswomen, Kampung Baharu, Kuala Lumpur]. B.A. academic exercise, University of Malaya, 1974, x, 87 pp.

455 LAU, HELENA. "Employers Cannot Deny Women Workers Their Rights." Union Herald, no. 53 (Oct. 1962):475-78.

456 LIM, LINDA YUEN CHING. "Women Workers in Multinational Corporations: The Case of the Electronics Industry in Malaysia and Singapore." 60 pp. Ann Arbor: Michigan University, 1978. Michigan Occasional Papers, no. 9 (Fall 1978).

457 LOKE, SU ENG. "The Participation of Women and Their Emancipation in the Application of Science and Technology to Development. Malaysian Country Position Paper Presented at the Round Table Seminar on Participation of Women and Their Emancipation through the Application of Science and Technology to Development, Bangalore, India, July 1979." 18 pp. Organized by the Economic and Social Commission for Asia and the Pacific, the Asia and Pacific Centre for Women and Development and the Regional Centre for Technology Transfer, Bangalore.

458 LUKMAN MUDA. "Penyertaan Wanita dalam Lapangan Perniagaan di Pasir Mas, Kelantan" [The participation of women in business in Pasir Mas, Kelantan]. B.A. academic exercise, University of Malaya, 1977, vii, 65, xv pp.

459 MAIMUNAH YUSOFF. "Keluhan Gadis-gadis Kilang" [Problems of female factory workers]. Mastika 36, no. 12 (Dec. 1976): 80-84.

460 MANDERSON, LENORE. "Malay Women and Development in Peninsular Malaysia. Some Preliminary Notes." Kabar Seberang, no. 2, (June 1977):61-84.

461   _____. "A Woman's Place: Malay Women and Development in
         Peninsular Malaysia." In Issues in Malaysian Development.
         Edited by James C. Jackson and Martin Rudner. Singapore:
         Published for the Asian Studies Association of Australia
         by Heinemann Educational Books (Asia), 1979, pp. 233-71.

462   MAZIDAH binti HAJI ZAKARIA, and SAFIAH KARIM, Nik. "Women in
         Development: The Case of an All-Girls Youth Land Develop-
         ment Scheme in Malaysia." 32 pp. Paper presented at the
         10th International Congress of Anthropological and Ethno-
         logical Sciences, New Delhi, December 1978.

463   MUHAMMAD ZIN bin ABD. AZIZ. "Kajian mengenai Sikap terhadap
         Pekerjaan, Nilai, Aspirasi, Alienation dan Relative Depri-
         vation Pekerja-pekerja Wanita Kilang Letronik" [A study of
         the attitude of women workers in electronic factories to-
         wards work, values, aspirations, alienation, and relative
         deprivation]. B.A. academic exercise, University of
         Malaya, 1976, v, 80 pp.

464   MUHIBBAH MUHAMMAD ALI. "Wanita dan Perniagaan di Kampung
         Baru, Dahulu dan Sekarang" [Women and business in Kampung
         Baru, past and present]. B.A. academic exercise, Univer-
         sity of Malaya, 1974, vi, 114, vii-xxvi pp.

465   NAIR, GIRIJA. "Malaysia: A Review and Appraisal of Progress
         Made in Attaining the Objectives of the United Nations
         Decade for Women." Kuala Lumpur: National Advisory Coun-
         cil on Integration of Women in Development (NACIWID),
         197-[?], 20 pp.

466   NARAYANAN, P.P. "The Integration of Women in the Economic and
         Social Life: General Situation, Difficulties, Obstacles to
         Be Overcome." Union Herald 55, no. 208 (Oct. 1975):6-15.

467   NATIONAL ADVISORY COUNCIL ON THE INTEGRATION OF WOMEN IN
         DEVELOPMENT, Malaysia. Income-generating Skills for Women:
         Malaysia; Interim Report. Kuala Lumpur: National Advisory
         Council on the Integration of Women in Development (NACIWID)
         Malaysia, 1978, 148 pp. (This study represents part of an
         ILO comparative regional study of income-generating skills
         for women in Bangladesh, India, Japan, Philippines, Sri
         Lanka, Thailand, and Malaysia.)

468   NATIONAL UNION OF TEACHERS, MALAYSIA. "Memorandum on the
         Implications of the Claim of Equal Pay for Equal Work."
         Malayan Educator 9, no. 1 (Apr. 1962):1-6.

469   NORAINI ABDUL GHANI. "Penyertaan Wanita dalam Pekerjaan:
      Satu Kajian Kes Pekerja-pekerja Wanita di Universiti
      Kebangsaan Malaysia" [Women in employment: a case study
      of women workers in Universiti Kebangsaan Malaysia]. B.A.
      academic exercise, Universiti Kebangsaan Malaysia, 1978,
      145 pp.

470   O'BRIEN, LESLIE NOLA. "Class, Sex and Ethnic Stratification
      in West Malaysia, with Particular Reference to Women in
      the Professions." 2 vols. Ph.D. dissertation, Monash
      University, 1979, xix, 743 pp.

471   _____. "Sex, Ethnicity and the Professions in West Malaysia:
      Some Preliminary Considerations." Akademika, no. 14
      (Jan. 1979):31-42.

472   OOI, CHENG BEE. "Everything Being Equal, Female Worker Merits
      Equal Pay. There Should Be No Disparity in Wages." Union
      Herald, no. 51 (Aug. 1962):358-60.

473   OTHMAN ABDUL. "Penyertaan Wanita-wanita Melayu dalam Bidang
      Pekerjaan di Kilang Perusahaan: Satu Kajian Kes di Kilang
      Sharp Roxy, Sg. Petani, Kedah" [Malay women workers in
      factories: a case study of Sharp Roxy Factory, Sg. Petani,
      Kedah]. B.A. academic exercise, Universiti Kebangsaan
      Malaysia, 1979, 171 pp.

474   PEREZ, B.A. "Women Labour-Force Participation and Incomes in
      Three Asian Countries." Economic Bulletin for Asia and the
      Pacific 27, no. 1 (June 1976):73-81. (Countries are India,
      Malaysia, and the Philippines.)

475   PONNIAH, VIVIEN JOY. "Opportunities and Treatment of Women
      Workers in Malaya." B.Ec. academic exercise, University of
      Malaya, 1968, 74 pp.

476   "Problems of Working Women Occupy Increasingly Important
      Place in Trade Union Activity." Union Herald 55, no. 206
      (Aug. 1975):8-9.

477   PURCELL, VICTOR. "Burma, Thailand and Malaya." In Women's
      Rôle in the Development of Tropical and Subtropical Coun-
      tries, by International Institute of Differing Civiliza-
      tions. Brussels: International Institute of Differing
      Civilizations, 1959, pp. 291-300.

478   PUTHUCHEARY, MAVIS COLEEN. "Women in Employment." Union
      Herald 55, no. 202 (Apr. 1975):9-16.

479   RAFIDAH AZIZ, Datin Paduka. "Wanita dalam Zaman Pembangunan"
       [Women in the era of development]. Wanita [Kuala Lumpur],
       no. 85 (Aug. 1976):24-25.

480   _____. "Women Workers in the Rural Areas of Malaysia."
       Ekonomi [Kuala Lumpur] 5, no. 1 (Dec. 1974):39-42.

481   RAMLAH binti JANTAN. "Perubahan Sosio-ekonomi yang Dialami
       oleh Gadis-gadis yang Bekerja Dikilang Letronik" [The
       socioeconomic changes experienced by female workers in
       electronics factories]. B.A. academic exercise, University
       of Malaya, 1976, iv, 74 pp.

482   Report on Seminars for Women Trade Unionists, Penang,
       Malaysia, 1973-1974. Petaling Jaya, Malaysia: Friedrich-
       Naumann-Stiftung, 1975[?], 62 pp. (Seminars jointly
       organized with the FIET affiliates of Malaysia and
       Singapore and sponsored by Friedrich-Naumann-Stiftung in
       December 1973 and 1974.)

483   ROHANA ARIFFIN. "Exploitation of Women." 20 pp. Paper pre-
       sented at the Seminar 'Wanita Malaysia Masakini,' Bangi,
       Selangor, 1979, organized by the Faculty of Social Sciences
       and Humanities, Universiti Kebangsaan Malaysia.

484   _____. "The Political Economy of the Kitchen: Women's Ex-
       perience in Development." 5 pp. Paper presented at the
       Third Malaysian Economic Convention, Penang, August 1976.

485   "Role of Women in the National Economy." Economic Bulletin
       [Kuala Lumpur] 1, no. 3 (Nov. 1975):32-34.

486   SAROJINI DEVI APPUTHURAI. "Socio-Economic Aspects of Women
       Plantation Workers: A Case Study of the Indian Women
       Workers of Ladang Tengah." B.A. academic exercise,
       University of Malaya, 1971, viii, 102 pp.

487   SEMINAR KEARAH MEMBENTUK KUMPULAN USAHAWAN DI KALANGAN KAUM
       WANITA SEKTOR PEKEBUN KECIL, Kuala Lumpur, 1979, and
       SEMINAR ON THE ROLE OF WOMEN AS SMALLHOLDERS, Kuala
       Lumpur, 1979. Papers. Organized by the Rubber Industry
       Smallholders Development Authority. Kuala Lumpur, 1979,
       1 vol. (various pagings).

488   SEMINAR RANCANGAN MALAYSIA KEDUA: GERAKAN PEMBAHARUAN DAN
       PERANAN-PERANAN PERTUBOHAN-PERTUBOHAN WANITA, Kuala
       Lumpur, 1972. Kertaskerja-kertaskerja [Seminar on the
       Second Malaysia Plan: Innovative Moves and the Role of
       Women's Organizations, Kuala Lumpur, 1972. Working
       papers]. Kuala Lumpur: Majlis Kebangsaan Pertubohan-
       Pertubohan Wanita Malaysia, 1972, 1 vol. (various pagings.)

489 SHARIFAH binti HAMID. "Kesedaran dan Penyertaan Buruh Wanita
     Melayu dalam Kesatuan Sekerja: Satu Kajian Kes atas 50
     Orang Pekerja Wanita dari Kelas Bawahan" [The awareness and
     participation of Malay women workers in trade unions: a
     case study of fifty women workers from the lower class].
     B.A. academic exercise, Universiti Kebangsaan Malaysia,
     1975.

490 SHARIFAH MARIA MALEK. "Women: A Competitor or a Complement."
     9 pp. Paper presented at the Seminar on Malaysian Manage-
     ment, Shah Alam, Malaysia, April, 1979, organized by MARA
     Institute of Technology and Ohio University.

491 SPEEDEN, MURIEL. "Petticoat Pioneers of Johore. Malaysia's
     First All-Girls' Land Scheme in Bukit Mambai, Johore." New
     Straits Times Annual (1977):94-95, 97-100.

492 STRANGE, HEATHER. "Education and Employment Patterns of Rural
     Malay Women, 1965-1975." Journal of Asian and African
     Studies 13, nos. 1/2, (Jan./Apr. 1978):50-64.

493 TANG, YANG MOY. "The Position of Women and Their Contribution
     to Rural Productive Efforts: A Case Study in Kedah,
     Malaysia." Master's [?] thesis, Asian Institute of Tech-
     nology [Bangkok], 1976, 86 pp.

494 TEH, LULU PAIK GUAT. "The Employment of Women in Government
     Service in the Federation of Malaya." B.A. academic exer-
     cise, University of Singapore, 1959, 46 pp.

495 VASANTHA MALLIHA, NARENDRAN. "The Women of Perupuk: An Eco-
     nomic Study." Master's thesis, Universiti Sains Malaysia,
     1975, 1 vol. (various pagings).

496 VÁVRA, ZDENĚK. Labour Force Projections by Race, Sex, and
     Age for West Malaysia, 1970-1995. Bergen, Norway: Chr.
     Michelsen Institute, 1972, 141 pp.

497 VENGADASALAM, ALFRED. "Young Women Workers of Bayan Lepas
     Industrial Complex." 6 pp. Paper presented at the Inter-
     national Symposium on Local Level Development Alternatives,
     Universiti Sains Malaysia, Penang, 1979.

498 WEEKES-VAGLIANI, WINIFRED. "Malaysia (Based on the Family
     Life Survey of the Rand Corporation)--Case Studies." In
     Women in Development at the Right Time for the Right
     Reasons. Paris: Development Centre, Organisation for
     Economic Co-operation and Development, 1980, pp. 58-149.

499   "Women in the Army." Economic Bulletin [Kuala Lumpur] 2,
      no. 1 (Jan. 1976):43-45.

500   "Women Workers and Male Prejudice." Union Herald 50, no. 149
      (Nov. 1970):2-3.

501   ZAINAB HAJI ABDUL KARIM, Nik. "Sumbangan Wanita Melayu
      Kelantan dalam Pelajaran, Ekonomi dan Politik ke Arah
      Pembangunan Negara" [The contribution of Malay women from
      Kelantan in the fields of education, economics, and poli-
      tics to national development]. 13 pp. Paper presented at
      the Seminar 'Wanita Malaysia Masakini,' Bangi, Selangor,
      1979, organized by the Faculty of Social Sciences and
      Humanities, Universiti Kebangsaan Malaysia.

502   ZAKIAH LAIDIN. "Polis Wanita; Bergerak dan Bertindak"
      [Police women: mobile and active]. Pengaman 31, no. 1
      (1979):15-17.

503   ZULKURNAIN HAJI AWANG. "Peranan Wanita Melayu di dalam
      Masyarakat Petani: Satu Kajian Mengenai Peranan Socio-
      ekonomi Wanita di dalam Masyarakat Penanam Padi Kampong
      Gong Kala, Pasir Puteh, Kelantan" [The role of Malay women
      in agricultural society: a study of the socioeconomic role
      of women in the rice-growing community in Kampong Gong
      Kala, Pasir Puteh, Kelantan]. B.A. academic exercise,
      University of Malaya, 1974, xi, 85 pp.

Philippines

504   AGCAOILI, GAVINA. "An Analysis of the Principal Occupations
      of Interest to Women in the Philippines." Master's thesis,
      University of San Carlos [Cebu City, Philippines], 1952,
      ix, 147 pp.

505   ALDABA-LIM, ESTEFANIA J. "Women, Population and Employment in
      the Philippines." Philippine Historical Association, His-
      torical Bulletin 19, nos. 1/4 (June/Dec. 1975):88-91.

506   ALDAY, L.C. "Labor Standards in the Philippines and the Women
      and Young Workers." Bureau of Women and Minors, Digest
      (Mar. 1972):11-25.

507   ALVAREZ, J. BENJAMIN C., and ALVAREZ, PATRICIA M. "The
      Filipino Family-owned Business: A Matriarchal Model."
      Philippine Studies 20 (1972):547-61.

508   ALZONA, ENCARNACIÓN. The Social and Economic Status of
      Filipino Women, 1565-1932. Manila: University of
      Philippines Press, 1933, 33 pp. Institute of Pacific
      Relations, 5th Biennial Conference, Banff, 1933. Data
      Papers.

509   APOSTOL, E.D., and NUYDA, D.G. "9 Successful Women in Busi-
       ness." Orient 9 (Aug. 1967):21-27.

510   ARCEO-ORTEGA, ANGELINA. "A Career-Housewife in Philippines."
       In Women in the New Asia. Edited by Barbara E. Ward.
       Paris: Unesco, 1963, pp. 265-373.

511   ARQUISOLA, SIMPLICIO. "Women in Philippine Economy."
       Quarterly Labor Statistics 1 (Apr. 1957):6-13.

512   ASPERILLA, PURITA FALGUI. "The Mobility of Filipino Nurses."
       Ed.D. dissertation, Columbia University Teachers College,
       1971, 208 pp. Abstracted in Dissertation Abstracts Inter-
       national 32, no. 10 (Apr. 1972):5464-A. University Micro-
       films International, order no. 72-12,796.

513   _____. "Problems of Foreign Educated Nurses and Job Satis-
       faction of Filipino Nurses." 5, 36 pp. Paper presented
       at the Conference on International Migration from the
       Philippines, June, 1975, East-West Center, Honolulu,
       Hawaii.

514   BELMONTE-CUYUGAN, CARMELITA. "Women in Medicine." Santo
       Tomas Journal of Medicine 20, no. 6 (Nov./Dec. 1965):
       507-10.

515   BENITO, GREGORIO S. "Women in Industry in the Philippines."
       Quezon City: College of Business Administration, Univer-
       sity of the Philippines, 1951, 44 pp.

516   BERTHELSEN, NITA UMALI. "Filipino Women's Business Sense."
       Nation [Manila] 2 (7 Aug. 1967):35-37.

517   BOULIER, B.L., and PINEDA, L.P. "Male-Female Wage Differen-
       tials in a Philippine Government Agency." Philippine
       Economic Journal 14, no. 4 (1975):436-48.

518   CANLAS, DANTE B. "Income, Education, Fertility and Labor
       Force Participation: Philippines, 1973." 28 pp. Paper
       presented at the Seminar on Labor Supply, under the joint
       sponsorship of the Council for Asian Manpower Studies and
       the Organization of Demographic Associates held in Makati,
       Rizal, Philippines, June 1976.

519   CANLAS, DANTE B., and ENCARNACIÓN, JOSÉ. Income, Education,
       Fertility and Employment: Philippines 1973. Diliman,
       Quezon City: Council for Manpower Studies, University of
       the Philippines, 1977, 48 pp.

520   CARMEN, AUREA JOVER. "Women at Work: A Survey of Women
        Textile Workers of the National Development Company."
        Master's thesis, Philippine Women's University [Manila],
        1951, 56 pp.

521   CASEBIER, ELEANOR. "Managing Women Employees in Small Busi-
        ness." Philippine Industry 8, no. 19 (Mar. 1962):5-8.

522   CASTAÑEDA, LETICIA E. "Women and Children in Industry in the
        Philippines." Quezon City: College of Business Adminis-
        tration, University of the Philippines, 1953, 7 pp.

523   CASTILLO, GELIA TAGUMPAY. "The Filipino Woman as Manpower:
        The Image and the Empirical Reality." Human Resource
        Development Journal 1, nos. 3/4 (1978):177-88.

524   CASTILLO, GELIA TAGUMPAY, and HILOMEN-GUERRERO, SYLVIA. "The
        Filipino Woman: A Study in Multiple Roles." Journal of
        Asian and African Studies 4, no. 1 (Jan. 1969):18-29.

525   CONCEPCIÓN, MERCEDES B. "Female Employment and Fertility in
        the Philippines." Philippine Economic Journal 12, no. 23
        (1973):524-35.

526   _____. "Female Labour Force Participation and Fertility."
        International Labour Review 109, nos. 5/6 (May/June 1974):
        503-17.

527   "Decree Ensures Filipino Women Equal Opportunities in Area of
        Employment." New Philippines 36, no. 1 (Dec. 1975):46-50.

528   DEL MUNDO, FE. "Women in Medicine." Philippine Federation of
        Private Medical Practitioners, Journal 13, no. 5 (May
        1964):300-304.

529   DEL RIO, ANGELA. "Filipina Domestic Workers in Italy." ISIS
        International Bulletin, no. 10 (Winter 1978/79):19-20.

530   DIGNADICE, M.V. "The Employment of Women in Certain Financial
        Institutions in the City of Iloilo." Southeast Asia Jour-
        nal [Iloilo City, Philippines] 7, no. 2 (1974):33-37.

531   "Employment of Women and Minors in the Philippines." Labor
        Review [Quezon City] 1, no. 4 (Apr. 1965):33-50.

532   "Employment Opportunities for Women." Bureau of Women and
        Minors, Digest 1 (June 1972):17-20.

533 ENCARNACIÓN, JOSÉ. "Family Income, Education, Labour Force Participation and Fertility." In A Demographic Path to Modernity: Patterns of Early Transition in the Philippines. Edited by Wilhelm Flieger and Peter Colin Smith. Quezon City: University of the Philippines Press, 1975, pp. 190-200.

534 _____. "Family Income, Educational Level, Labor Force Participation and Fertility." Philippine Economic Journal 12, nos. 1/2 (1973):536-49.

535 _____. Fertility and Labor Force Participation: Philippines, 1968. Quezon City: Institute of Economic Development and Research, University of the Philippines, 1973, 39 pp. IEDR Discussion Paper, no. 73-13.

536 ENRILE-GUTIERREZ, BELEN. "The Role of Women . . . in the Economic Development of the Philippines." University of the Philippines Economic Bulletin (1960/1961):21-22.

537 ESPINOSA, GREGORIA I. "Filipino Nurses in Bataan and Corregidor." American Journal of Nursing 46 (Feb.):97-98.

538 EVANGELISTA, SUSAN P. "Massage Attendants in the Philippines: A Case Study of the Role of Women in Economic Development." Master's thesis, University of the Philippines [Quezon City], 1974.

539 _____. "Massage Attendants: Mainstream or Deviant?" Philippine Sociological Review 25, nos. 3/4 (July/Oct. 1977):105-12.

540 FAJARDO, IRENE S. "Occupational Practices in Some of the Women's Apparel Industry in Manila and Environs." Master's thesis, Philippine Women's University [Manila], 1959, xiii, 115 pp.

541 "Female Employment in the Local Government: July-December 1969." Bureau of Women and Minors, Digest 1 (June 1972): 21-29.

542 FERNANDEZ, LUCIA NATIVIDAD E. PANDY. "Participation of the Nursing Service Personnel in Four Selected Hospitals during the Clinical Experience of PWU Nursing Students." Master's thesis, Philippine Women's University [Manila], 1974, 204 pp.

543 FIDELINO, RACHEL. "Facts and Figures on Women Workers." Manpower Philippines 1, no. 4 (June 1971):25-28.

544　FLORES, PURA M. "Career Women and Motherhood in a Changing
　　　Society." Philippine Educational Forum 14, no. 1 (Mar.
　　　1965):50-56.

545　GONZALEZ, ANNA MIREN. "Filipino Women in Development: The
　　　Impact of Poverty." Paper presented at the National Con-
　　　vention of the Philippine Sociological Society on Poverty:
　　　The Illusion and the Reality, Quezon City, 23-25 January
　　　1976.

546　_____. "Filipino Women in Development: The Impact of Pov-
　　　erty." Philippine Sociological Review 25, nos. 3/4
　　　(July/Oct. 1977):97-104.

547　GONZALEZ, ANNA MIREN, and HOLLNSTEINER, MARY RACELIS.
　　　Filipino Women as Partners of Men in Progress and Develop-
　　　ment: A Survey of Empirical Data and Statement of Goals
　　　Fostering Male-Female Partnership. Quezon City: Ateneo de
　　　Manila University, Institute of Philippine Culture, 1976,
　　　v, 156 pp.

548　GRACIA, PABLO P. de. "The Problem of Employment among Women
　　　Office Workers." Philippine Journal of Public Administra-
　　　tion 9 (Apr. 1965):145-52.

549　GROSSMAN, RACHAEL. "Women's Place in the Integrated Circuit."
　　　In "Changing Role of S.E. Asian Women"--special joint issue
　　　of Southeast Asia Chronicle, no. 66 (Jan./Feb. 1979) and
　　　Pacific Research Bulletin 9, nos. 5/6 (July/Oct. 1978):
　　　2-17. (On the work of women in multinational semiconductor
　　　firms in Malaysia and the Philippines.)

550　GUILLERGAN, PERLA JAMAYA. "Patterns of Female Participation
　　　in the Labor Force: Mandaluyong and Quiapo-San Miguel."
　　　Master's thesis, University of the Philippines [Quezon
　　　City], 1969, 126 pp.

551　HACKENBERG, BEVERLY H., and HACKENBERG, ROBERT A. "Social
　　　Indicators of Premarital and Postmarital Labor Force Par-
　　　ticipation among Women in Region XI: Southeast Mindanao."
　　　Manila: WID Special Studies Program, Institute of Philip-
　　　pine Culture, Ateneo de Manila University, 1979, 15 pp.

552　HILLIARD, MILDRED. Orientation and Evaluation of the Profes-
　　　sional Nurse. Manila: Reprinted by Webster School and
　　　Office Supplies, 1975, ix, 168 pp.

553　HUNT, CHESTER L. "Female Occupational Roles and Urban Sex
　　　Ratios in the U.S., Japan and the Philippines." Social
　　　Forces 43, no. 3 (Mar. 1965):407-17.

554   ILLO, JEANNE FRANCES I. Involvement by Choice: The Role of
       Women in Development. Quezon City: Institute of Philip-
       pine Culture, Ateneo de Manila University, 1977, 207 pp.

555   ILUSTRE, M.L. "Do Women Make Better Executives?" Examiner
       14 (Dec. 1976):22-25.

556   INTERNATIONAL LABOUR OFFICE. Report to the Government of the
       Philippines on the Employment of Women and Minors. Geneva:
       International Labour Office, 1962, 31 pp. ILO/TPA/
       Philippines/R.7.

557   INTERNATIONAL LABOUR ORGANIZATION. "Employment of Women and
       Minors in the Philippines. Report." Labor Review [Quezon
       City] (Apr. 1965):33-50.

558   "The Katiwalas." ISIS International Bulletin, no. 8 (Summer
       1978):14-16. (On women involved in health and medical work
       in the Philippines.)

559   LACSON, LOLITA L. "Filipinos at Work: A Regular Feature:
       The Lady is a Dentist." Ningas-Cogon 4, no. 5 (Jan. 1975):
       19, 27.

560   LAPUZ, L.V. "The Filipino Woman Who Is a Professional."
       Philippine Medical Women's Association, Journal 13
       (July/Sept. 1975):81-88.

561   LEGARDA, TRINIDAD F. "The Role of the Filipino Woman in
       Nation Building." Fookien Times Philippines Yearbook
       (1962):239-40.

562   LLADOC, ANTONIA, and BRUNNER, PAUL. "Young Filipino Nurses in
       West Germany." Migration News (Mar./Apr. 1972):8-10.

563   LOPEZ, LYDIA H. Women in the Philippines Labour Force.
       Quezon City: College of Business Administration, Univer-
       sity of the Philippines, 1957, 85 pp.

564   LU, N.T. "The Female Boss and the Male Subordinate." Focus
       5, (24 Sept. 1977):20-21.

565   MAGNO, C.M. "Nightlife and the Working Woman." Focus 3
       (8 Nov. 1975):24-25.

566   MAGSAYSAY, RAMON. "Women in the Philippines." Philippine
       Journal of Home Economics 6, no. 4 (Apr./June 1955):3-4.

567   MANALO, ROSARIO G. "Strengthening the Social Infrastructure: Employment and Family Responsibilities." Speech delivered at the Seminar/Workshop on Women Workers, Population Center, 12 February 1976.

568   MANGAHAS, MAHAR, and JAYME-HO, TERESA. "Income and Labor Force Participation Rates of Women in the Philippines." Paper presented at the Seminar on Labor Supply, under the joint sponsorship of the Council for Asian Manpower Studies and the Organization of Demographic Associates held in Makati, Rizal, Philippines, June 1976.

569   MANZANO, FLORINDA T. "A Study of Nurses' Reasons for Resignations." Master's thesis, University of the Philippines [Quezon City], 1974, 62 pp.

570   MARQUEZ, ASUNCION J. "Why Women Work in the Philippines: A Study of Three Companies." Master's thesis, Ateneo de Manila University [Manila], 1959, 141 pp.

571   MARQUEZ, NELIA R. "Women Professionals in the Philippines." Philippine Statistician 24, nos. 1/2 (Jan./June 1975): 11-24.

572   MARTINEZ, B. "Women Executives." Focus 3 (8 Nov. 1975): 10-15.

573   _____. "Women in Business." Focus 3 (15 Nov. 1975):14-17.

574   MENDOZA, E.R. "The Nursing Service in the AFP." National Security Review 3 (June 1975):30-47.

575   MIJARES, TITO A. "Women in RP's Labor Force." Fookien Times Philippines Yearbook (1978):332-37, 359.

576   MILAN, PRIMITIVO C. "She's in the Army Now." Sunday Times Magazine [Manila] (14 July 1963):28-31.

577   NATIONAL TRIPARTITE CONFERENCE ON THE STATUS OF THE FILIPINO WOMEN WORKERS, Manila, 1975. Papers. Sponsored by the Department of Labor. Manila, 1975.

578   OBLEPIAS-RAMOS, LILIA, and SUAREZ, D. TORREVILLAS. Hanap-Buhay. Manila: Manila Community Services, 1978. 82 pp. (On the Filipino woman's role in family and work.)

579   ORENDAIN, LOUISE. "The Role of Women as Professionals." Panorama 18 (May 1966):24-25.

580 PAREDES, TERESITA S. "The Woman Elementary School Principal:
     Perception of Her Feminine and Community Roles." Master's
     thesis, University of the Philippines [Quezon City], 1974,
     105 pp.

581 PELAEZ, EMMANUEL. "The Role of Women in Rural Development."
     Philippines Today 10, no. 4 (Sept. 1963):4-8.

582 PENNELL, MARYLAND YOUNG, and SHOWELL, SHIRLENE. Women in
     Health Careers: Status of Women in Health Careers in the
     United States and Other Selected Countries. Washington,
     D.C.: American Public Health Association, 1975, xi, 147 pp.
     DHEW Publication; no. (HRA) 76-55. (Includes the
     Philippines.)

583 PEREZ, B.A. "Women Labour-Force Participation and Incomes in
     Three Asian Countries." Economic Bulletin for Asia and the
     Pacific 27, no. 1 (June 1976):73-81. (Countries are India,
     Malaysia, and the Philippines.)

584 PEREZ, BERNARDINO. "Problems of Women Workers in the
     Philippines." Labor (ICFTU) 5 (1967):172-73.

585 PEREZ, PRESENTACION T. "Problems of Employed Women in Certain
     Professional Groups in the Philippines and Their Educa-
     tional Implications." Ph.D. dissertation, University of
     Minnesota, 1954, x, 287 pp. Abstracted in Dissertation
     Abstracts 15, no. 3 (1955):359-60. University Microfilms
     International, order no. 11,113.

586 PHILIPPINES (REPUBLIC), Bureau of Women and Minors. The
     Bureau of Women and Minors Manual. Manila: Bureau of
     Women and Minors, 1973, 25 pp.

587 _____. Filipino Women as Workers: A Statistical Guide.
     Manila: Bureau of Women and Minors, 1974, 40 pp.

588 _____. "Mga kaalamang mahalaga sa mga manggagawang babae at
     sa mga may-ari ng mga pagawaang pangindustriya, pang-
     komersiyo at pang-agrikultura." Manila, 1970, 19 pp.
     (On employment of women and children.)

589 _____. Women in the Labour Force: Facts and Figures.
     Manila: Bureau of Women and Minors, 1977, 15 pp.

590 _____. Status of Working Women in the Philippines. Manila:
     Bureau of Women and Minors, 1975, 53 pp.

591   PHILIPPINES (REPUBLIC), National Census and Statistics Office.
       Working Life Tables for Males and Females in the
       Philippines, 1977. Manila: National Census and Statistics
       Office, 1977, 44 pp. UNFPA-NCSO Population Research Proj-
       ect Monograph, no. 7.

592   PHILIPPINES (REPUBLIC), National Commission for Unesco.
       Final Report. Theme: Participation of Rural Women in
       National Development. Manila: Unesco National Commission
       of the Philippines, 1975, 1 vol. (various pagings).

593   PHILIPPINES (REPUBLIC), National Media Production Center. The
       Filipina: A Humanizing Force in Philippine Development.
       Manila: National Media Production Center, 1975, 56 pp.

594   "The Protection of Working Women and Minors in the
       Philippines." Philippine Labor 1, no. 1 (May 1962):35-36.

595   QUISUMBING, P.V. "Working Women: Opportunities and Prob-
       lems." National Security Review 3 (June 1975):7-11.

596   RAMOS, MARIA DOLORES V. "The Woman School Teacher: An Ex-
       ploration of Her Concepts of the Feminine Roles, Profes-
       sional Membership Role and Professional Self-Image."
       Master's thesis, University of the Philippines [Quezon
       City], 1969, 124 pp.

597   RASALAN, GREGARIO. "Maternity Leave Privileges of Teachers in
       the Bureau of Public Schools." Philippine Education 14,
       no. 10 (Mar. 1960):620-22.

598   REYES, TEOFILO. "The Role of Women in Socio-Economic Develop-
       ment." Philippine Educational Forum 14, no. 1 (Mar. 1965):
       45-49.

599   RIVERA, VICTORIANO. "These Women are Pioneer Farmers."
       Philippines Free Press 49 (3 May 1958):18-19.

600   ROBLE, M.C.M. "A Study on the Professional Performances of
       Silliman University Nursing Graduates." Silliman Journal
       23 (2d Quarter, 1976):153-57.

601   RODRIGUEZ, FILEMON C. "Women and the Socio-Economic Develop-
       ment." Power and Industry 10, no. 4 (Apr. 1963):8-10, 12,
       26.

602   ROMERO, FLERIDA RUTH P. "Is the Economic Emancipation of the
       Filipino Working Woman at Hand?" Social Work 20, nos. 1/3
       (Jan./Sept. 1975):10-13.

603   _____. "Is the Economic Emancipation of the Filipino Working
       Woman at Hand?" Paper presented at the Seminar/Workshop on
       Women Workers, Population Center, Makati, Rizal, 12-14
       February 1976.

604   ROSENZWEIG, MARK RICHARD. "Female Work Experience, Employment
       Status, and Birth Expectation: Sequential Decision-
       making in the Philippines." Demography 13, no. 3 (Aug.
       1976):339-56.

605   SEMINAR ON WOMEN WORKERS, Makati, Rizal, 1976. Strategy for
       Change. Sponsored by Department of Labor, Personnel Man-
       agement Association of the Philippines, Philippine Associa-
       tion of Secretaries, Philippine Association of Trade Union
       Women, and the Manila Community Services. Manila, 1976[?],
       110 pp.

606   SESE, LUZ B. "A New Role for Farm Women." Philippines Herald
       Magazine (15 June 1963):10-13.

607   SIRON, FELIPE. "Soldiers in Skirts." Chronicle Magazine 22
       (17 June 1967):4-8.

608   SISON, P.S. "La place des femmes dans la vue économique aux
       Philippines" [The position of women in the economic life
       of the Philippines]. Revue international du travail 87
       (Feb. 1963):133-49.

609   _____. "The Role of Women in Business and Industry in the
       Philippines." International Labour Review 87 (Feb. 1963):
       118-32.

610   SMITH, PETER COLIN. "Demographic Profiles of the Filipina:
       An Approach to the Analysis of Life Cycles." Manila:
       Population Institute, University of the Philippines System,
       1974, 9 pp.

611   SOLOMON, PILAR D. "A Study of the Deficiencies of Secretaries
       on the Job in Private Offices in Greater Manila." Master's
       thesis, University of the East [Manila], 1974, viii, 190 pp.

612   "A Study of the Occupational Opportunities for Girls Enrolled
       in Trade and Agricultural Schools." Bureau of Public
       Schools, Memorandum, no. 5 (Feb. 1960):1-34.

613   TEMPLA, M.A. "Women Technologists: Their Role in Indus-
       trialization." Science Bulletin [Manila] 8, no. 3
       (Mar. 1964):13-16.

614   TUPAS, ANASTACIA GIRÓN. History of Nursing in the
       Philippines. Rev. ed. Manila, 1960, 107 pp.

615   UNITED NATIONS, Social Welfare and Development Centre for
       Asia and the Pacific. <u>City Camp/Rock Quarry Handicraft</u>
       <u>Association: A Case Study on Rural Women's Role in Socio-</u>
       <u>Economic Activities and Community Leadership within a</u>
       <u>Poverty Context</u>. Prepared by Philippines Business for
       Social Progress, 1978. Bangkok[?] United Nations Social
       Welfare and Development Centre for Asia and the Pacific,
       1978, 50 pp.

616   U.S. AGENCY FOR INTERNATIONAL DEVELOPMENT (Manila). "The
       Filipino Woman: Her Role and Status in Philippine
       Society." Annex K of USAID project paper on rural elec-
       trification, Manila. Manila: Agency for International
       Development, 1976, 32 pp.

617   WILLIAMS, GEORGE. "Filipino Exchange Nurses in Minnesota,
       U.S.A." <u>Chronicle Magazine</u> 19 (Jan. 1964):20-21.

618   "Women Workers in Asia." <u>ISIS International Bulletin</u>, no. 10
       (Winter 1978/79):4-5. (Deals in part with Indonesia and
       the Philippines.)

619   "Young Filipino Nurses in Germany." <u>Weekly Graphic</u> 32
       (July 1964):34-35.

Singapore

620   CHAN, HENG CHEE. "Notes on the Mobilization of Women into the
       Economy and Politics of Singapore." In <u>Political and</u>
       <u>Social Change in Singapore</u>. Edited by Wu Teh Yao.
       Singapore: Institute of Southeast Asian Studies, 1975,
       pp. 13-35. Southeast Asian Perspectives, no. 3.

621   CHAN, HOW FANG. "Work Commitment among Female Industrial
       Workers in Singapore." Singapore: University of
       Singapore, 1976, 62 pp.

622   CHANG, CHEN TUNG. "Female Employment and Fertility Be-
       haviour." In <u>Public Policy and Population Change in</u>
       <u>Singapore</u>. Edited by Peter S.J. Chen and James T. Fawcett.
       New York: Population Council, 1979, pp. 167-86.

623   CHEE, YOK CHIN. "Young Women Car Park Attendants in
       Singapore." Thesis for the Diploma in Social Science,
       University of Singapore, 1968, 99 pp.

624   CHENG, SIOK HWA. "Female Labour Force in Singapore, 1947-
       1975." Paper presented at the Seventh Conference of the
       International Association of Historians of Asia, August
       1977, Bangkok, Thailand.

625   _____. "Singapore Women: Legal Status, Educational Attain-
       ment, and Employment Patterns." Asian Survey 17, no. 4
       (Apr. 1977):358-74.

626   _____. "The Status, Roles and Achievements of Women in
       Singapore." In The Role of Women in Development: Seminar
       Papers and Statements. Edited by Leonardo Z. Legaspi.
       Manila: University of Santo Tomas Press, 1976, pp. 57-77.

627   _____. Women in Singapore: Legal, Educational and Economic
       Aspects. Singapore: Nanyang University, 1976, 32 pp.
       Nanyang University, College of Graduate Studies, Institute
       of Humanities and Social Science. Occasional Paper
       Studies.

628   CHEW, BENG LAN. "The Young Woman Worker at Jurong." B.A.
       academic exercise, University of Singapore, 1969, 81 pp.

629   CHEW, DAVID C.E. "Wastage Patterns in the Nursing Profession
       in Singapore: A Study of Manpower Utilisation." Inter-
       national Labour Review 100, no. 6 (1969):583-94.

630   CHIEW, SEEN KONG. Educational and Occupational Attainment of
       Singapore's Chinese Women and Men. Singapore: Chopmen
       Enterprises, 1977, 23 pp. University of Singapore, Depart-
       ment of Sociology. Sociology Working Paper, no. 59.

631   DEYO, FREDERIC C. Marital Status, Job Orientation, and Work
       Commitment among Semi-skilled Female Workers in Singapore.
       Singapore: Chopman Enterprises, 1976, 18 pp. University
       of Singapore, Department of Sociology. Sociology Working
       Paper, no. 54.

632   DEYO, FREDERIC C., and CHEN, PETER SHOU JEN. "Changing Female
       Employment Patterns in Singapore." Southeast Asian Journal
       of Social Science 4, no. 1 (1975):29-51.

633   _____. Female Labour Force Participation and Earnings in
       Singapore. Bangkok: Clearing House for Social Development
       in Asia, 1976, 31 pp. Also published in Economic Bulletin
       for Asia and the Pacific 27, no. 1 (June 1976):82-99.

634   FONG, MONICA SKANTZE. Female Labor Force Participation in a
       Modernizing Society (Malaya and Singapore, 1921-1957).
       Honolulu: East-West Population Institute, 1975, vii,
       39 pp. Hawaii University, East-West Population Institute.
       Papers, no. 34.

635   GAN, SOON BEE. "Post-War Labour Supply in Singapore and the
       Determinants of Female Workforce Participation." B.A.
       academic exercise, University of Singapore, 1975, 69 pp.

636   HEYZER, NOELEEN. "Young Women and Migrant Workers in
       Singapore's Labour Intensive Industries." Singapore:
       University of Singapore, 197-.

637   HO, GEOK LOON. "History of the Women Police in the
       Singapore Police Force." Singapore Police Journal 5,
       no. 1 (Jan. 1974):48-52.

638   HO, IT CHONG. "The Cantonese Domestic Amahs: A Study of a
       Small Occupational Group of Chinese Women." B.A. academic
       exercise, University of Singapore, 1959, 162 pp.

639   LAW, SIEW HONG. "Role of Women in Trade Unions." In Tomorrow
       --the Peril and the Promise: Report by the Secretary Gen-
       eral to the 2nd Triennial Delegates Conference, 1976. Ed-
       ited by C.V. Devan Nair. Singapore: Singapore National
       Trades Union Congress, 1976, pp. 132-37.

640   LEE, POLLY POH CHUN. "The Present Status of Women in
       Singapore: Economic Aspects." B.A. academic exercise,
       University of Singapore, 1973, 46 pp.

641   LIM, LINDA YUEN CHING. "Women Workers in Multinational Cor-
       porations: The Case of the Electronics Industry in
       Malaysia and Singapore." Ann Arbor: Michigan University,
       1978, 60 pp. Michigan Occasional Papers, no. 9, Fall 1978.

642   LIN, JING MIN. The Incentive Aspects of Enlarged Child
       Reliefs for Specially Qualified Women in Singapore Personal
       Income Tax. Singapore: Institute of Economics and Busi-
       ness Studies, College of Graduate Studies, Nanyang Univer-
       sity, 1977, 10 pp. Occasional Paper/Technical Report
       Series, no. 22.

643   LOONG, VIVIEN MAY CHI. "The Effect of Job Orientation Train-
       ing on the Job Performance of Female Employees." B.A.
       academic exercise, University of Singapore, 1970, 92 pp.

644   NATIONAL SEMINAR ON WOMEN IN A TECHNOLOGICAL SOCIETY,
       Singapore, 1973. Women in a Technological Society.
       Singapore: Singapore Teachers Union, 1974, 40 pp.

645   NEO, KIM NEO. "Woman White-Collar Workers in Singapore,
       1975." Suara Ekonomi 2 (1963):24-29.

646   PILLAY, MANON MANI. "The Employment Pattern of a Group of
       Women Residing in the Singapore Improvement Trust Flats,
       Alexandra North, Queenstown." B.A. academic exercise,
       University of Singapore, 1960, 51 pp.

647 REGIONAL BPW SEMINAR, Singapore, 1975. Papers. Singapore: Singapore Business and Professional Women's Association, 1975, 1 vol. (various pagings).

648 "Role of Women in the National Economy." Economic Bulletin [Kuala Lumpur] 1, no. 3 (Nov. 1975):32-34.

649 SALAFF, JANET WEITZNER, and WONG, ALINE K. "Women's Work in Singapore: A Handle for Smaller Family Size." Wellesley, Mass.: Wellesley College, Center for Research on Women, 1976, 54 pp.

650 SEMINAR PENYERTAAN WANITA MELAYU DALAM PEMBANGUNAN MASYARAKAT, Singapore, 1974. Laporan [Seminar on the Participation of Malay Women in Community Development, Singapore, 1974. Report]. Singapore: Majelis Pusat Pertubuhan-Pertubuhan Budaya Melayu, Singapore, 1975, 34 pp.

651 SHARP, ILSA. "Woman Power in Singapore." Singapore Trade and Industry (May 1972):9-23.

652 SHU, CHEN LIN. "Young Women in Heavy Manual Work: A Study of the Local-born Young Women Currently Employed in Building and Road Maintenance Work." Thesis for the Diploma in Social Science, University of Singapore, 1967, 97 pp.

653 SINGAPORE MINISTRY OF LABOUR, and SINGAPORE NATIONAL STATISTICAL COMMISSION. Report on the Survey on Non-Working Women in Singapore, 1974. Singapore: Ministry of Labour and the National Statistical Commission, 1974, 76 pp.

654 SOON, YOUNG YOON. Study on the Role of Young Women in the Development Process, Especially in Industry, in Selected Countries of the ESCAP Region. Bangkok: United Nations Economic and Social Commission for Asia and the Pacific, 1979, 43 pp. (Countries surveyed are Hong Kong, Korea, Singapore, and Thailand.)

655 TAN, KENG SOOI. "The Role of Young Women in the Development Process, Especially in Industries in Singapore." Singapore: Department of Sociology, University of Singapore, 1978, 31 pp.

656 TAN, NALLA. "The Impact of Modernization on Women." Paper presented at the Seminar on Modernization, organized by the Singapore National Academy of Science, Singapore, June 1972.

657   _____. "Laws and Practice on Status of Working Women and
        Protection of Motherhood in Singapore." 13 pp. Paper
        presented at the TWARO ASEAN and Oceanic Women Seminar,
        Singapore, 1978.

658   THISAINAYAGAN, AURORA. "Women in a Technological Society:
        Opportunities, Aspirations and Expectations." National
        Youth Leadership Training Institute, Singapore, Journal,
        no. 9 (Mar. 1974):77-82.

659   TING, GRACE. "Young Women and Girls in a Technological
        Society: An Overview." National Youth Leadership Training
        Institute, Singapore, Journal, no. 9 (Mar. 1974):65-76.

660   TOH, THIAN SER. Increasing Singapore's Effective Supply of
        Labour. Singapore: Research Unit, National Productivity
        Centre, 1971, iv, 24 pp. National Productivity Centre,
        Singapore. General Circulation Papers, G/1/71. (Includes
        employment of women.)

661   Towards Greater Participation and Contribution of Women in
        National Development: Papers Presented at the National
        Trades Union Congress International Women's Year Committee
        Seminar, 1st-4th September 1975. Singapore: International
        Women's Year Committee, National Trades Union Congress,
        1975, 1 vol. (various pagings).

662   WONG, ALINE K. "Maternal Employment, Education and Changing
        Family Values in Singapore." Journal of Economic Develop-
        ment and Social Change in Asia and the Pacific 1, no. 1
        (1976):23-40.

663   YU, YEE SHOON. "The Singapore Woman." In Socialism That
        Works . . . the Singapore Way. Compiled and edited by C.V.
        Devan Nair. Singapore: Federal Publications, 1976,
        pp. 114-22.

Thailand

664   AMARA PONGSAPICH. "Job Opportunities and Social Mobility of
        Young Labour Force in Chonburi Town: A Case Study."
        34 pp. Paper presented at the Seminar on Women Wage
        Earners in Thailand, Pattaya, 18-20 April 1975.

665   COOK, MICHAEL JOHN. Female Labour Force Participation and
        Fertility in Rural Thailand: Some Preliminary Findings.
        Bangkok: Institute of Population and Social Research,
        Mahidol University, 1975, 26 pp.

666   _____. "Female Labor Force Participation, Modernity and Fertility in Rural Thailand." Ph.D. dissertation, Brown University, 1977. 299 pp. Abstracted in Dissertation Abstracts International 38, no. 12 (June 1978):7586-A. University Microfilms International, order no. 7809045.

667   COOK, MICHAEL JOHN, and BOONLERT LEOPRAPAI. Labor Force Participation, Village Characteristics and Modernism and Their Influence on Fertility among Rural Thai Women. Bangkok: Institute of Population and Social Research, Mahidol University, 1977, 164 pp. Part 2 published in 1978, 29 pp.

668   DUANGDUEN BISALPUTRA. "The Status, Roles and Achievements of Women in Thailand." In The Role of Women in Development: Seminar Papers and Statements. Edited by Leonardo Z. Legaspi. Manila: University of Santo Tomas Press, 1976, pp. 15-22.

669   GOLDSTEIN, SIDNEY. "The Influence of Labour Force Participation and Education on Fertility in Thailand." Population Studies 26, no. 3 (Nov. 1972):419-36. Also published separately as Chulalongkorn University, Institute of Population Studies. Research Report, no. 9, 1972, iv, 28 pp.

670   KATTIYA KARNASUTA. "Development Planning for Women in Thailand." Thai Journal of Development Administration 18, no. 4 (Oct. 1978):679-704.

671   MAURER, KENNETH; RATAJCZAK, ROSALINDA; and SCHULTZ, T. PAUL. Marriage, Fertility and Labor Force Participation of Thai Women: An Econometric Study. Santa Monica, Calif.: Rand Corp., 1973, 54 pp. Rand Report, R-829.

672   NATIONAL WORKSHOP ON THE ROLE OF SOUTHERN THAI WOMEN IN CONTRIBUTING TO FAMILY INCOME, Bangkok, 1976. The Role of Southern Thai Women in Contributing to Family Income. Edited by Suebsaeng Promboon. Bangkok: Clearing House for Social Development in Asia, 1976, 178 pp.

673   NIBHON DEBAVALYA. Female Employment and Fertility: Cross-Sectional and Longitudinal Relationships from a National Sample of Married Thai Women. Bangkok: Institute of Population Studies, Chulalongkorn University, 1977, 88 pp. Chulalongkorn University, Institute of Population Studies. Working Paper, no. 24.

674   _____. "A Study of Female Labor Force Participation and Fertility in Thailand." Ph.D. dissertation, University of Pennsylvania, 1975. 271 pp. Abstracted in Dissertation Abstracts International 36, no. 12 (June 1976):8328-A. University Microfilms International, order no. 76-12,267.

675   _____. "A Study of Female Labor Force Participation and Fer-
       tility in Thailand." 65 pp. Paper presented at the Semi-
       nar on Labour Supply, under the joint sponsorship of the
       Council for Asian Manpower Studies and the Organization of
       Demographic Associates held in Makati, Rizal, Philippines,
       June 1976.

676   OEY, ASTRA MEESOOK. "Working Women in Thailand." 24 pp.
       Paper presented at the Conference on Women and Development,
       Wellesley College, Mass., June 1976.

677   PEERASIT KAMNUANSILPA. Socio-Economic and Demographic Analy-
       sis of Female Labour Force Participation. Bangkok:
       National Institute of Development Administration, 1977,
       66 pp.

678   PURCELL, VICTOR. "Burma, Thailand and Malaya." In Women's
       Rôle in the Development of Tropical and Sub-Tropical Coun-
       tries. By International Institute of Differing Civiliza-
       tions. Brussels: International Institute of Differing
       Civilizations, 1959, pp. 291-300.

679   "Ramai Wanita Thai Bekerja di luar Bandar" [Many Thai women
       work in rural areas]. Wanita [Kuala Lumpur], no. 93
       (Apr. 1977):64-65.

680   SEMINAR ON WOMEN WAGE EARNERS IN THAILAND, Pattaya, Thailand,
       1975. Summary Report. Organized by U.N. Asian Institute
       for Economic Development and Planning, jointly with the
       Thai Committee for International Women's Year and Southeast
       Asia Development Advisory Group of the Asia Society, New
       York, April 1975. Pattaya, 1975.

681   _____. Report of Meeting. New York, SEADAG, Asia Society,
       1975, 16 pp. SEADAG Reports.

682   SOON, YOUNG YOON. Study on the Role of Young Women in the
       Development Process, Especially in Industry, in Selected
       Countries of the ESCAP Region. Bangkok: United Nations
       Economic and Social Commission for Asia and the Pacific,
       1979, 43 pp. (Countries surveyed are Hong Kong, Korea,
       Singapore, and Thailand.)

683   SUCHART PRASITHRATHSIN. "Female Labor Force Participation and
       Fertility Behaviour in Rural Thailand." Journal of Social
       Sciences [Bangkok] 8, no. 4 (Oct. 1971):34-48.

684   SUVANNEE CHITRANUKROH-VATTANGCHIT. "The Female Labor Force
       Participation Rate in Thailand." Master's thesis, Univer-
       sity of the Philippines [Quezon City], 1975, xxi, 323 pp.

685 _____ . Female Labor Force Participation Rate in Thailand.
      Diliman, Quezon City: Council for Asian Manpower Studies,
      University of the Philippines, 1972, 323 pp. University
      of the Philippines, Council for Asian Manpower Studies.
      Discussion Paper Series, no. 77-08.

686 _____ . "Female Labor Force Participation Rate in Thailand."
      36 pp. Paper presented at the Seminar on Labor Supply,
      under the joint sponsorship of the Council for Asian
      Manpower Studies and the Organization of Demographic Asso-
      ciates held in Makati, Rizal, Philippines, June 1976.

687 THAILAND, Department of Public Welfare, Labour Division.
      Women and Employment. Bangkok: Department of Public
      Welfare, 1960, 13 pp.

688 THAILAND, National Statistical Office. Working Women in
      Bangkok-Thonburi Area: From Result of the Household Expen-
      diture Survey B.E. 2505 and Labor Force Survey, Round 1,
      B.E. 2506. Special report prepared by Phensri Pitaksakorn,
      Yupin Tuangtong and A. Hurwitz. Bangkok: National Statis-
      tical Office, 1964, 10 pp. Thailand National Statistical
      Office. Special family expenditure survey report.

689 TILAK, V.R.K. "Women Workers in Asian Countries." Geneva:
      International Labour Organization, 1974, 22 pp. (Part 3
      is a case study of Thailand.)

690 VICHITR RAVIWONGSE. "The Role of Young Women in the Devel-
      opment Process, Especially in Industries in Thailand."
      Bangkok: Faculty of Social Administration, Thammasat
      University, 1978, 47 pp.

EDUCATION

(On educational psychology see Psychology and Psychiatry)

Southeast Asia

691 ASAIHL SEMINAR-WORKSHOP ON THE ROLE OF WOMEN IN DEVELOPMENT:
      IMPLICATIONS FOR HIGHER EDUCATION IN SOUTHEAST ASIA,
      Manila, 1975. Papers. Organized by the Association of
      Southeast Asian Institutions of Higher Learning. Manila,
      1975, 1 vol. (various pagings).

692 CALIXTO, JULIA. "Education of Women in Developing Countries
      and Population Avalanche." Science Review 10, no. 2
      (Feb. 1969):20-26.

693   CHINTANA YOSSUNDARA. "Viable Programs in Higher Education for
      Women in Development in Southeast Asia." In The Role of
      Women in Development: Seminar Papers and Statements. Ed-
      ited by Leonardo Z. Legaspi. Manila: University of Santo
      Tomas Press, 1976, pp. 182-86.

694   EELS, WALTER CROSBY. "Women in the Universities of the World."
      Higher Education 9, no. 6 (15 Nov. 1952):61-65. (Number
      and percentage data for students and staff members in
      seventy-six countries.)

695   FISHER, MARGUERITE J. "Higher Education of Women and National
      Development in Asia." Asian Survey 8, no. 4 (Apr. 1968):
      263-69.

696   IFFTU-UNESCO ASEAN SEMINAR ON EQUAL OPPORTUNITIES FOR WOMEN IN
      EDUCATION AND EMPLOYMENT, Kuala Lumpur, 1977. Report of
      Proceedings. Sponsored and organized by International
      Federation of Free Teachers Unions in co-operation with
      National Union of the Teaching Profession, Malaysia and the
      assistance of Unesco and Unctad. Kuala Lumpur, 1980,
      74 pp.

697   INTERNATIONAL SEMINAR ON LONG-TERM EDUCATIONAL AND TRAINING
      PROGRAMMES FOR THE ADVANCEMENT OF WOMEN IN ASIA, Bombay,
      1967. Proceedings. Paris: International Council of
      Women, 1967, 66 pp.

698   JESUS-VIARDO, ALMA de, ed. The Educational Dilemma of Women
      in Asia. Manila: Philippine Women's University, 1970,
      xix, 509 pp. (Selected papers from the Golden anniversary
      conference of Philippine Women's University on the educa-
      tion of women in developing countries held at the National
      Science Board Pavilion, Manila, Philippines, 15-20 February
      1969.)

699   MEETING OF EXPERTS ON THE ACCESS OF GIRLS AND WOMEN IN EDUCA-
      TION IN RURAL AREAS IN ASIA, Bangkok, 1962. Papers.
      Bangkok: UNESCO Regional Office for Education in Asia,
      1962.

700   SEMINAR PERANAN WANITA DALAM BIDANG-BIDANG PELAJARAN TINGGI
      DAN IMPLIKASINYA, Kuala Lumpur, 1975. The Role of Women in
      Higher Education in Southeast Asia. Sponsored by Majlis
      Penasihat Pelajaran Tinggi, Kementerian Pelajaran Malaysia.
      Kuala Lumpur, 1975, 1 vol. (various pagings).

701   "System Analysis of Higher Education for Women in Southeast
      Asia: Focus on Its Relevance to Their Present and Expected
      Roles." In The Role of Women in Development: Seminar Pa-
      pers and Statements. Edited by Leonardo Z. Legaspi.
      Manila: University of Santo Tomas Press, 1976, pp. 162-80.

Burma

702 BURMA EDUCATIONAL RESEARCH BUREAU, and BURMA, Ministry of
Education, Department of Basic Education. <u>Case Studies on
Dropout among School-Age Girls: Country Report</u>. Rangoon,
1979, 56, 77 pp. (This study was carried out in 1979,
under contract with Unesco in a joint effort by the Burma
Educational Research Bureau and the Department of Basic
Education, under the Ministry of Education.)

Indochina

703 HOÀNG VAN CO. "La femme au Viet Nam" [Women in Viet Nam].
<u>Education</u> [Saigon] (Mar. 1948):13-26.

Indonesia

704 "AKAWI: Mendidik Wanita Akademi" [AKAWI: educating academic
women]. <u>Gapura</u> 5, no. 1 (1972):21-22.

705 "Aktivita Dewan Mahasiswa, Bakodma IAIN al-Djami'ah"
[Student council activities, Coordinating Body of Student
Councils of Higher Education State Islamic Religious Insti-
tutes]. <u>al Jami'ah</u> 9, no. 2 (Mar. 1970):23-58. (Student
councils' constitution and reports of second national conference in Malang, July 1968, in regard to a general program, girls' organizations, and higher education activities.)

706 AZIZ, MUCHTAR. "Perkembangan Madrasah Muslimat di Indonesia,
1908-1942" [The development of women's religious schools
in Indonesia, 1908-1942]. B.A. academic exercise,
Universitas Gadja Mada [Jogjakarta], 1966, 34 pp.

707 CABATON, ANTOINE. "Indes neerlandaises (deux notes brèves
sur le progrès de l'éducation féminine à Java)" [Dutch
East Indies: two brief notes on the progress of female
education in Java]. <u>Revue du monde musulman</u> 10 (Jan.
1910):131-32.

708 CHIJS, JACOBUS ANNE van der. <u>Het middlebaar school-onderwijs
te Batavia gedurende de eerste van de 19e eeuw volgens
officieele bescheiden</u> [Secondary education in Batavia during the first half of the nineteenth century according to
official documents]. Batavia: G. Kolff, 1902, 108 pp.
(Deals in part with secondary education for girls.)

709 CUISINIER, JEANNE. "Les madrasah féminines de Minangkabau"
[Koranic schools for Minangkabau women]. <u>Revue des études
islamiques</u> (1955):107-19.

710   DARDUELLA, RIZA. "Bangkitnya Kaum Hawa" [The rise of women].
      Dinamika Mahasiswa 4, no. 6 (1973):13-16.

711   DEWANTARA, KI HADJAR. Soal Wanita [Women's issues]. 2d ed.
      Jogjakarta: Madjelis Luhur Taman Siswa, 1961, 20 pp.

712   _____. "Soal Wanita" [Women's issues]. Pusara 15, no. 9
      (1953):135-38; 15, no. 10 (1953):151-54.

713   HAMIDJOJO-MUNAR, SUNDARI. Ibu dan Pendidikan [Mother and ed-
      ucation]. 5th ed. Medan: Pustaka Andalas, 1955, 68 pp.

714   "Home Economics Yang Diselenggarakan oleh Inspeksi Pusat
      Pendidikan Wanita" [Home economics organized by the
      Inspectorate of the Women's Educational Center]. Warta
      Kejuruan 1, no. 2 (1958):30-38.

715   ISMAN, SUNTORO. "Peningkatan Pendidikan dan Partisipasi Kerja
      Wanita dalam Usaha Penurunan Fertilitas: Sebuah Tinjauan
      Peranan Pendidikan dan Peranan Wanita dalam Masyarakat yang
      Sedang Berkembang" [Upgrading educational levels and female
      employment in the effort to reduce fertility: a survey of
      the role of education and women in a developing society].
      Jakarta: Fakultas Ekonomi, Universitas Indonesia, 1975,
      13 pp.

716   KADARMARWANI. "Pekerjaan Penyuluhan dengan Wanita Desa"
      [Extension work for rural women]. Majalah Berkala Peter-
      nakan 7, no. 3 (1956):96-103.

717   Kartini-Fonds (vereeniging)-Jubileum-Verslag uitgegeven ter
      gelegenheid v.h. 25 jarig bestaan der Vereeniging, 1913-
      1938 [Kartini-Fund Organisation Anniversary edition pub-
      lished in honor of the 25th anniversary of the organization,
      1913-1938]. The Hague, 1938, 115 pp.

718   LEGOWO, S.A. Kursus Kader Perwib ke 1 Tanggal 15 Desember
      1964-Tanggal 28 Maret 1965, di Djakarta [First course for
      cadres of Perwib, 15 December 1964-28 March 1965, in
      Jakarta]. Jakarta: Projek Penerbitan Sekretariat Ko-
      ordinator Urusan Irian Barat, 1965, 71 pp.

719   LEKKERKERKER, CORNELIS. "Meisjesonderwijs coeducatie en
      meisjesscholen voor de Inlandsche bevolking in Ned-Indië"
      [Girls' education, co-education, and girls' schools for the
      native people in the Netherlands Indies]. Koloniaal tijd-
      schrift 3, no. 2 (1914):865-84.

720   LOKAKARYA PELAKSANAAN PROGRAM PENDIDIKAN LUAR SEKOLAH BAGI
      WANITA, Ciloto, Indonesia, 1975. Laporan [Workshop on the
      Implementation of Educational Programs for Women, Ciloto,
      Indonesia, 1975. Report]. Diselenggarakan oleh KOWANI,

Dharma Wanita, Dharma Pertiwi bekerjasama dengan Departemen P. and K. Jakarta, 1975, 120 pp.

721 MELAJOE, S. SOETAN. "Apa Jang Perempoean Haroes Tahoe. Dan 'Koloniale School voor Meisjes en Vrouwen' di den Haag" [What ladies should know. And 'the Colonial School for Girls and Women' in the Hague]. Oedaya 3, no. 31 (Dec. 1925):82-83.

722 OEY, MAYLING. "Some Demographic Notes on the Progress of Indonesian Women." Prisma 1, no. 2 (Nov. 1975):74-80. (Indonesian version published in Prisma [Indonesian ed.] 4, no. 2 [Oct. 1975]:11-18.)

723 PADMODISASTRO, SOEDARINAH. The Women's Movement: Non-formal Education in Indonesia. Jakarta: Ministry of Education and Culture, Office of Education Development, 1975, 19 pp.

724 "Pendidikan Wanita bagian Kejuruan" [Vocational education for women]. Warta Kejuruan 1, no. 1 (1958):18-21.

725 Peranan Wanita dalam Pendidikan di Masa Kini dan di Masa Akan Datang [The present and future role of women in education]. Risalah Seminar Pengurus Besar PGRI dan IKIP Negeri Jakarta. Jakarta: Pengurus Besar Guru Republik Indonesia, 1977, 93 pp.

726 PERGURUAN DINIYAH PUTRI PADANG PANJANG. Peringatan 55 Tahun Diniyah Putri Padang Panjang [Commemorative volume of the 55th anniversary of Perguruan Diniyah Putri Padang Pan-jang]. n.p.: Ghalia Indonesia, 1979[?], 416 pp. (An Islamic girls' school in Sumatra.)

727 PRATOMO. Pantja Marga Pendidikan Masjarakat Tuntunan bagi Kursus Kader Pembangunan Masjarakat [Five aspects of mass education: a guide for cadre courses in community develop-ment]. Jakarta: Vita Vera, 1963. (One of the "five aspects" is women's education.)

728 PRAWIRODIHARDJO, TARTIB. Women and Their Families in Com-munity Education. Jakarta: Ministry of Education, 1960.

729 PROBOPRANOWO, MAOEDJONO. "Pendidikan Kewanitaan" [Girls' (vocational) education]. Pusara 23, nos. 1/2 (1962):22-25.

730 _____. "Peranan Wanita dalam Melaksanakan Sistem Life-long Education" [The role of women in the implementation of the life-long education system]. Pusara 41, no. 1 (1972): 17-20.

731   RAHARDJO, F.O. "Sekolah Kepandaian Putri" [Home economics
       school]. Jiwa Baru 8, no. 8 (1960):19-23.

732   RUMTIAH. Pedoman untuk Guru2 PBH Wanita [Teacher's guidebook
       for the women's literacy campaign]. Jakarta: Kementerian
       P.P. dan K., 1955, 72 pp. (Information about practical
       home economics.)

733   SEMINAR AKHIR PEKAN TENTANG PENDIDIKAN PERBURUHAN BAGI TENAGA
       KERJA WANITA DI PERUSAHAAN SWASTA, Jakarta, 1974. Kesim-
       pulan dan Prasaran [Seminar on Labor Education for the
       Female Labor Force in Private Industries, Jakarta, 1974.
       Proceedings]. Sponsors, Yayasan Tenaga Kerja Indonesia,
       Badan Kontak Tenaga Kerja Wanita Indonesia, Friedrich-
       Ebert-Stiftung. Jakarta, 1974, 47 pp.

734   SEMINAR TENTANG PENDIDIKAN TENAGA KERJA WANITA DALAM PEM-
       BANGUNAN, Bandung, Indonesia, 1975. Risalah [Seminar on
       the Education of the Female Labor Force in Development,
       Bandung, Indonesia, 1975. Proceedings]. Di-sponsori oleh
       Yayasan Tenaga Kerja Indonesia, Friedrich-Ebert-Stiftung,
       Panitia Daerah Tahun Wanita International Jabar dan Badan
       Kontak Tenaga Kerja Wanita Indonesia, 27 s/d 30 Agustus
       1975. Bandung, 1975, 50 pp.

735   Statistik tentang Wanita dalam Pendidikan Formil di Indonesia
       1971 [Statistics on women in formal education in Indonesia,
       1971]. Jakarta: Komisi Nasional Kedudukan Wanita
       Indonesia, 1973, ii, 52 pp.

736   Statistik tentang Wanita dalam Pendidikan Tinggi di Indonesia
       1972 [Statistics on women in higher education in Indonesia
       1972]. Jakarta: Komisi Nasional Kedudukan Wanita
       Indonesia, 1973, 20 pp.

737   SUHARSO. "Tingkat Pendidikan dan Kesuburan Ibu" [Educational
       level and fertility]. Dokumentasi LEKNAS 3 (1970):28-33.

738   SULIANTI. "Mempertinggi Pendidikan Kaum Ibu Menuju Kese-
       jahteraan Keluarga" [Upgrading the education of mothers for
       family welfare]. Majalah Administrasi Negara 3, no. 3
       (1961):89-92.

739   SUNARDI, S. "Kemana Perginja Anak Gadis Kita setelah
       Sekolah Landjutan?" [Where do our girls go after high
       school?]. Suara Guru 22, no. 22 (Aug. 1968):26-27.
       (Describes opportunities for women in army education.)

740   WAHJUDI, M. "Pendidikan Non-formil untuk dan oleh Wanita: Sumbangan Fikiran untuk Kongress Kowani ke-13 di Jakarta, Tg. 14-19 Mar 1974" [Nonformal education for and by women: contributions to the 13th Kowani Congress in Jakarta, 14-19 March 1974]. Jakarta: Komisi Nasional Kedudukan Wanita Indonesia (KNKWI), 1974, 16 pp.

741   WARNAEN, MIEN SOEWARNI. "Partisipasi Wanita dalam Pengembangan Pendidikan" [The participation of women in the development of education]. Suara Guru 25, no. 5 (1975):47-50.

742   _____. "Peranan Anggota Wanita di dalam PGRI sebagai Suatu Organisasi Profesi: Suatu Analisa" [The role of women members in PGRI as a professional organization: an analysis]. Suara Guru 25, no. 6 (1975):45-47; 25, no. 7 (1975):41-44.

743   WIROWIDJOJO, R. SOETJIPTO. "Pendidikan Kewanitaan dalam Konteks Persekolahan Kristen pada Umumnya" [Female education in the context of Christianity in general]. Excelsior 4, no. 7 (1974):248-59.

744   YASSIN, M. "Perkembangan Pendidikan Wanita Indonesia" [The growth of women's education in Indonesia]. Warta Demografi 5, no. 3 (1975):1-3.

Malaysia

745   ADIBAH AMIN. "Ahmad Luthfi on the Education and Freedom of Women: A Critical Examination of His Views on the Education and Freedom of Muslim Women in Malaya as Stated and Implied in His Novels," by Khalidah Adibah binti Haji Amin. B.A. academic exercise, University of Singapore, 1957, iv, 39 pp.

746   AINON MUHAMMAD. "Pengaruh Pendidikan Tinggi terhadap Nilai dan Kebebasan Wanita" [The influence of higher education on the values and freedom of women]. Dewan Masyarakat 13, no. 8 (Aug. 1975):43-45.

747   AISHA HANUN binti DALAMEAH. "Malay Women's Training College, Malacca." Chorus (1940).

748   AMPALAVANAR RAJESWARY. "Female Education." In "Social and Political Developments in the Indian Community of Malaya 1920-41." Master's thesis, University of Malaya, 1969, pp. 284-92.

749   BRYSON, HUGH. "The Education of Girls in the Nineteenth Century." Malaysia [London] (Nov. 1970):11-14.

750   CANLAS, DANTE B., and MUHAMMAD RAZAK. Education and Labor
       Force Participation of Married Women: West Malaysia 1970.
       Quezon City:. School of Economics, University of the
       Philippines, 1979, 22 pp. Philippines University, School
       of Economics. Discussion Paper, 7910.

751   CHANG, PAUL. "Limitations Set by Physical Conditions, Health,
       Race and Sex." Malaysia, Ministry of Education, Journal
       (Dec. 1964):118-22.

752   DHALIWAL, JASBIR KAUR. "Differences in Educational Oppor-
       tunity between the Sexes." In "Equality of Educational
       Opportunity in the Federation of Malaya." B.Ed. academic
       exercise, University of Malaya, 1967, pp. 62-77.

753   DUSUKI HAJI AHMAD, Haji. "Wanita, Karya dan Pendidikan"
       [Women, work, and education]. Dakwah 1, no. 5 (July 1977):
       27-28.

754   GERHOLD, CAROLINE ROSE. "Factors Relating to Educational
       Opportunity for Women Residents of the Malay Peninsula."
       Ph.D. dissertation, Cornell University, 1971, vii, 129 pp.
       Abstracted in Dissertation Abstracts International 32,
       no. 10 (Apr. 1972):5468-A. University Microfilms Inter-
       national, order no. 72-13,157.

755   GOON, CECILIA AI CHIN. "A Study of the Pattern of Vocational
       Preference of Form Five Girls in Selected English-medium
       Schools in Selangor." Master's thesis, University of
       Malaya, 1975, xix, 206 pp.

756   KALSUM binti WAN CHIK BAKAR. "Participation of Women and
       Their Emancipation through the Application of Science and
       Technology to Development. Status Paper on Malaysia pre-
       sented at the Round Table Seminar on Participation of
       Women and Their Emancipation through the Application of
       Science and Technology to Development, Bangalore, India,
       July 1979." 22 pp. Organized by the Economic and Social
       Commission for Asia and the Pacific, the Asia and Pacific
       Centre for Women and Development, and the Regional Centre
       for Technology Transfer, Bangalore.

757   KUK, MAY. "Facts about Female Illiteracy." Union Herald 55,
       no. 200 (Feb. 1975):10-12.

758   LOKE, SU ENG. "The Participation of Women and Their Emanci-
       pation in the Application of Science and Technology to
       Development. Malaysian Country Position Paper Presented
       at the Round Table Seminar on Participation of Women and
       Their Emancipation through the Application of Science and
       Technology to Development, Bangalore, India, July 1979."

18 pp. Organized by the Economic and Social Commission for Asia and the Pacific, the Asia and Pacific Centre for Women and Development, and the Regional Centre for Technology Transfer, Bangalore.

759 MANDERSON, LENORE. "The Development and Direction of Female Education in Peninsular Malaysia." Royal Asiatic Society of Great Britain and Ireland, Malaysian Branch, Journal 51, pt. 2 (Dec. 1978):100-122.

760 MERIYAM ABDUL MAJID. "Pendidikan Tinggi Merobah Peranan" [Higher education changes the role]. Dewan Masyarakat 14, no. 4 (Apr. 1976):37-38.

761 O'BRIEN, LESLIE NOLA. "Class, Sex and Ethnic Stratification in West Malaysia, with Particular Reference to Women in the Professions." 2 vols. Ph.D. dissertation, Monash University, 1979, xix, 743 pp.

762 _____. "Sex, Ethnicity and the Professions in West Malaysia: Some Preliminary Considerations." Akademika, no. 14 (Jan. 1979):31-42.

763 PURVIS, BARBARA MARGARET. "Development of Extension Programmes for Rural Women in S.E. Asia: West Malaysia as a Case." Master's thesis, University of Malaya, 1974, iv, 169 pp.

764 RAHIMAH AZIZ. "Sikap Mahasiswa Terhadap Pelajaran Tinggi" [The attitude of undergraduates towards higher education]. Jernal Antropoloji dan Sosioloji 2 (1973):36-44.

765 SABIHAH binte OSMAN. "Pelajaran bagi Anak-anak Perempuan Bumiputra di Sekolah-sekolah Melayu Kerajaan di Sabah dan Sarawak pada Zaman Kompeni Berpiagam dan Rejim Brooke: Satu Tinjauan" [Education for indigenous girls in government Malay schools in Sabah and Sarawak during the period of the Chartered Company and the Brooke regime: a survey]. Malaysia in History 18 (Dec. 1975):1-8.

766 SARAWAK FEDERATION OF WOMEN'S INSTITUTES AND OVERSEAS EDUCATION FUND FOLLOW-UP SEMINAR, Kuching, 1976. Working Papers. Kuching: Sarawak Federation of Women's Institutes, 1976, 1 vol. (various pagings).

767 SIRAJ, ZAIBUN NISSA. "The Role of a Voluntary Women's Organisation in Adult Education." Jurnal Pendidikan 6, (Oct. 1976):113-22.

768 _____. "Women and Adult Education: A Case Study of the Women's Institute Movement in Peninsula Malaysia, 1952-1974." Master's thesis, University of Malaya, 1975, ix, 232 pp.

769 STRANGE, HEATHER. "Education and Employment Patterns of Rural Malay Women, 1965-1975." Journal of Asian and African Studies 13, nos. 1/2 (Jan./Apr. 1978):50-64.

770 TAYLOR, M.C. "Domestic Science in Malay Girls' Schools of Perak." Oversea Education 10, no. 4 (July 1959):177.

771 ZAIN binti SULEIMAN, Hajjah. "Wanita dan Pelajaran" [Women and education]. Majallah Guru, no. 1 (Jan. 1950):15-16.

772 ZAINAB HAJI ABDUL KARIM, Nik. "Sumbangan Wanita Melayu Kelantan dalam Bidang Pelajaran, Ekonomi dan Politik ke Arah Pembangunan Negara" [The contribution of Malay women from Kelantan in the fields of education, economics, and politics to national development]. 13 pp. Paper presented at the Seminar 'Wanita Malaysia Masakini', Bangi, Selangor, 1979, organized by the Faculty of Social Sciences and Humanities, Universiti Kebangsaan Malaysia.

Philippines

773 ADRIANO, CARMEN. "Home Extension Work, Its Place in Adult Education." Philippine Journal of Education 35, no. 2 (1956):126-27, 134.

774 ADRIANO, PAZ V. "A Study of the Conditions Affecting the Interests, Attitudes, Ideals and Problems of Adolescent Girls in Catholic and Public Schools in the Philippines." Ph.D. dissertation, Fordham University, 1956, vi, 341 pp.

775 AGUILA, CONCEPCION A. "Women in a Challenging World." Centro Escolar University, Manila, Graduate and Faculty Studies 7 (1956):1-6.

776 ALZONA, ENCARNACIÓN. "The Development of the School Education of Women in the Philippines." Master's thesis, University of the Philippines [Quezon City], 1918.

777 _____. Education of Women. Manila: University of the Philippines Press, 1939, 10 pp.

778 _____. "Higher Education and the Filipino Woman." Teachers College Journal (Jan./Mar. 1941):255-56.

779 ANCHETA, AGUSTINA T. "The Homemaking Activities of Elementary School Girls in Rural Tarlac." Master's thesis, National Teachers College [Manila], 1952.

780   ANTONIO, BENJAMIN MENDOZA. "The Interests and Participation
      of Third and Fourth Year Boys and Girls in Out-of-School
      Recreation." Master's thesis, Arellano University
      [Manila], 1952, xv, 273 pp.

781   AQUINO, LETICIA S. "Sorority Organizations, Their Activities
      and Member Attitudes." Master's thesis, University of the
      Philippines [Quezon City], 1961, xii, 314 pp.

782   ARCE-MOHAMMAD, FELICIDED. "An Appraisal of the Education of
      the Moro Women of Sulu." Master's thesis, Union College
      of Manila, 1950, v, 49 pp.

783   ATIENZA, MARIA FE G. "The Philippine Women's University and
      Extra-mural Education for Women." Indian Journal of Adult
      Education 27, no. 7 (July 1966):11-16.

784   BALILI, AMPARO G. "A Study of the Professional Motivations
      of Nursing Students in Cebu." Master's thesis, Southwest-
      ern University [Cebu City, Philippines], 1969.

785   BENGZON, SOLEDAD. "A Descriptive Study of Sixteen Sororities
      in Three Manila Universities." Master's thesis, Ateneo de
      Manila University [Manila], 1959, iii, 65 pp.

786   BENITEZ, HELENA Z. "Education of Filipino Women for Partici-
      pation in Economic and Social Life." Philippine Educa-
      tional Forum 7, no. 1 (July 1957):16-20.

787   BERAN, JANICE ANN. "Growth and Development of Physical Edu-
      cation for Women in the Philippines." Silliman Journal
      14, no. 3 (1968):427-38.

788   BERGAMINI, MARIE CARMEN. "An Assessment of International
      Nursing Students in the United States: A Case Study of
      Philippine Experience." Ph.D. dissertation, University
      of California, Berkeley, 1964, 36 pp.

789   BIOCOS, BENITA B. "A Comparative Study of the Reading
      Achievement of Fourth Grade Boys and Girls." Master's
      thesis, Central Philippine University [Iloilo City,
      Philippines], 1966, xii, 189 pp.

790   BOCOBO, JORGE C. "Education of Women." Teachers College
      Journal 1 (June/July 1939):18-21.

791   BRIONES, J. M. "Female Teachers: Where do You Belong?"
      Philippine Journal of Education 54 (July 1975):59-61.

792   CABOTAJE, ARSENIA ABELLERA. "A Comparative Study of the
Qualifications for Deans of Women in Institutions of Higher
Education in the United States and in the Republic of the
Philippines." Ed.D. dissertation, American University,
1962, 216 pp. Abstracted in Dissertation Abstracts 23,
no. 9 (March 1963):3185. University Microfilms International, order no. 62-4523.

793   CABRERA, REDENTA T. "A Study of the Needs and Interests of
the Public Elementary School Girls Taking Home Economics
and the Members of Their Families in Northern Isabela."
Master's thesis, National Teachers College [Manila], 1968.

794   CAGAMPANG, F.A. Manual for Training Rural Women. Los Baños,
Philippines: Social Laboratory Training Project for Rural
Women, SEARCA, 1973, 102 pp.

795   CAHILL, ANNE PATRICE, Sister. A Study of the Educational
Ideals and Achievements of the Sisters of St. Paul de
Chatres in the Philippines." Master's thesis, University
of Santo Tomas [Manila], 1938, 101 pp.

796   CALDERON-ANCHETA, GERONIMA. "A Study of the Education of
Filipino Women." Master's thesis, Adamson University
[Manila], 1952, vii, 94 pp.

797   CANLAS, DANTE B. "Income, Education, Fertility and Labor
Force Participation: Philippines, 1973." 28 pp. Paper
presented at the Seminar on Labor Supply, under the joint
sponsorship of the Council for Asian Manpower Studies and
the Organization of Demographic Associates held in Makati,
Rizal, Philippines, June 1976.

798   CANLAS, DANTE B., and ENCARNACIÓN, JOSÉ. Income, Education,
Fertility and Employment: Philippines 1973. Diliman,
Quezon City: Council for Manpower Studies, University of
the Philippines, 1977, 84 pp.

799   CARMEN, MARIA. "The Superior Normal School for Women
Teachers in Manila, 1893-1898." Philippine Studies 2
(1954):217-29.

800   CENDAÑA, PLACIDA N. "University Education Affords Special
Opportunities to Women in the Philippines." Master's
thesis, University of Santo Tomas [Manila], 1950, 196 pp.

801   CLEMENTE, URSULA UICHANCO. "Trends of Enrollment of U.P.
[University of the Philippines] Women Students." Education
Quarterly 5:242-53.

802   CONCUERA, MAGDALENA Y. "Some out of School Homemaking Activi-
          ties of Grade Six Girls in Eight Selected Public Elementary
          Schools of Manila during a Certain Period of Time." Mas-
          ter's thesis, Philippine Women's University [Manila], 1962,
          152 pp.

803   CONSING, Ma. ROSA V. "A Study of the Interest in Home Eco-
          nomics of the Girls in the Public General Secondary of
          Manila." Master's thesis, National Teachers College
          [Manila], 1957, 113 pp.

804   CORDETA, REMEDIOS S. "The Filipino Women Educators: Factors
          Associated with the Attainment and Use of Their Careers
          (Case Studies)." Ph.D. dissertation, Centro Escolar
          University [Manila], 1974, 18, 255 pp.

805   CRISOLOGO, THERESE, Sister. "The Leisure Time Activities of
          Adolescent Girls in Selected High Schools in Manila."
          Master's thesis, Ateneo de Manila University [Manila],
          1959, 157 pp.

806   de JESUS, ANITA V. "Certain Selected Factors Underlying the
          Choice of Teaching as a Profession by the Students in the
          PWU Junior Normal College School." Master's thesis,
          Philippine Women's University [Manila], 1951, 84 pp.

807   DIAMANTE, ROSARIO S. "Baccalaureate Basic Programs in
          Nursing in the Philippines: A Critical Study." Ed.D.
          dissertation, Philippine Women's University [Manila], 1972,
          448 pp.

808   DIAZ, VINCENTE. "The Filipino Woman and Her Intellectual
          Development." Filipiniana Review (July 1957):25-32.

809   DIMAYA, VENIDA C. "A Survey of the Home Activities of Sec-
          ondary Girls in Negros Oriental." Master's thesis, St.
          Paul's College [Dumaguete City, Philippines], 1962, v,
          79 pp.

810   ENCARNACIÓN, JOSÉ. "Family Income, Education, Labor Force
          Participation and Fertility." In A Demographic Path to
          Modernity: Patterns of Early Transition in the Philippines.
          Edited by Wilhelm Flieger and Peter C. Smith. Quezon City:
          University of the Philippines Press, 1975, pp. 190-200.

811   _____. "Family Income, Educational Level, Labor Force Par-
          ticipation and Fertility." Philippine Economic Journal
          12, nos. 1/2 (1973):536-49.

812   EPIE, FE de la CERNA. "A Survey of the High School Physical
        Education Program of Selected Private Girls Colleges in
        Quezon City." Master's thesis, Far Eastern University
        [Manila], 1974, 13, 185 pp.

813   ESCOBAR, PURITA R. "Re-organization of a Diploma Nursing
        Program to a Baccalaureate Degree Program." Master's
        thesis, Philippine Women's University [Manila], 1975, 9,
        226 pp.

814   ESPERANZA, MARIA, Sister. "A Feminine Education in the
        Philippines." Master's thesis, University of Santo Tomas
        [Manila], 1949, 107 pp.

815   EUGENIO, ELENA PRADO. "The Educational Values of the Youth
        Program of the Young Women's Christian Association of the
        Philippines." Master's thesis, University of Manila
        [Manila], 1967, 173 pp.

816   FABELLA, VIRGINIA P. "Relationship between the Vocational
        Interests and Aptitudes of One Hundred Freshmen in a Col-
        lege for Women." Master's thesis, Ateneo de Manila Uni-
        versity [Manila], 1963, v, 122 pp.

817   "15 Visayan Girls Study Nursing in West Germany." Mirror
        Magazine [Manila] (June 1964):26-27.

818   FLORES, PURA M. "The Education of Women in Asia, with Empha-
        sis on the Philippines." 11 pp. Background paper for the
        Fiftieth Anniversary Conference on the Education of Women
        in Developing Countries, Manila, February 1969.

819   FLORES-GANZON, GUADALUPE. "Education as an Aspect of Training
        for Womanhood." Education Quarterly 7 (Jan. 1960):17-21.

820   FLORO, TEODORA L. "The Boy-Girl Relation Problems of Ado-
        lescence: Its Implications to the Proposed Guidance Pro-
        gram of St. Mary's Academy (Meycavayan)." Master's thesis,
        De la Salle College [Manila], 1967.

821   FULO, AVELINA G., Sister. "A Study of the Problems of Ado-
        lescent Girls in the Philippine Secondary Schools Run by
        the Daughters of Charity." Master's thesis, University of
        Santo Tomas [Manila], 1962, 175 pp.

822   GALINDEZ, ANITA RAZON. "A Study of Living Women Leaders in
        Education in the Philippines." Master's thesis, Philippine
        Christian College, 1952, iii, 79 pp.

823 GARCIA, CONSOLACION G., Sister. "The Guidance and Counselling
     Programs in the Philippine Catholic Secondary Schools for
     Girls: A Survey and Critical Study." Master's thesis,
     University of Santo Tomas [Manila], 1955, 170 pp.

824 GOMEZ, RUTH QUEBRAL. "An Evaluation of the Educational Activ-
     ities of the Y.W.C.A. of the Philippines." Master's thesis,
     Philippine Christian College, 1952, viii, 140 pp.

825 GONZALES, FRATERNIDAD J. "The Rise of Women's Education in
     the Philippines." Master's thesis, Philippine Women's
     University [Manila], 1938.

826 GONZALEZ, ANNA MIREN, and HOLLNSTEINER, MARY RACELIS.
     Filipino Women as Partners of Men in Progress and Develop-
     ment: A Survey of Empirical Data and a Statement of Basic
     Goals Fostering Male-Female Partnership. Quezon City:
     Institute of Philippine Culture, Ateneo de Manila Univer-
     sity, 1976, v, 156 pp.

827 HILADO, M. SOLEDAD, Sister. "Contributions of the Benedictine
     Missionary Sisters to Education in the Philippines." Mas-
     ter's thesis, University of Santo Tomas [Manila], 1954,
     322 pp.

828 "Home, School, and Women's Education." Education Quarterly
     9 (Apr. 1962):40-44.

829 INCIONG, E.M. "The University Women in Culture." Philippine
     Educational Quarterly 7 (Dec. 1975):45-48.

830 ISHIWATA, THELMA F. "A Comparative Study of Married and
     Single Women Public Secondary School Teachers in Negros
     Occidental." Master's thesis, University of Santo Tomas
     [Manila], 1960, viii, 141 pp.

831 JARDIN, Ma. RUFITA, R.V.M. "Problems of College Women
     Boarders in Dormitories Run by RVM Sisters and Their Impli-
     cations for a Proposed Guidance Program." Master's thesis,
     University of San Carlos [Cebu City, Philippines], 1972.

832 JAVIER, MERCEDES S. "A Study of Present-Day Problems Affect-
     ing Girl Students of the Laguna High School." Master's
     thesis, Arellano University [Manila], 1956, xi, 150 pp.

833 JIMINEZ, CARMEN. "A Proposed Student Personnel Program for
     the Philippine Women's College." Ph.D. dissertation,
     Columbia University, 1952, 283 pp.

834   KALAW-KATIGBAK, MARIA. "Academic Excellence and Education
      for Dynamic Citizenship in a Democracy." Philippine Edu-
      cational Forum 13, no. 1 (Apr. 1964):6-12.

835   LABRADOR, AURORA M. "The Program Activity Interests of the
      Intermediate Girl Scouts in the Fourth, Fifth and Sixth
      Grades in the City of Manila." Master's thesis, University
      of the Philippines [Quezon City], 1962, xiii, 130 pp.

836   LAFORTEZA, BIBIANA T. "Homemaking Activities Performed in
      School and at Home by Second Year High School Girls En-
      rolled in Home Economics." Master's thesis, Arellano
      University [Manila], 1963, 117 pp.

837   LAGRADA, HERACLEO D. "The Filipino Women and the Doctorate
      Degree: Factors Associated with the Attainment and the
      Use of the Degree." Ph.D. dissertation, Centro Escolar
      University [Manila], 1973, 370 pp.

838   _____. "The Filipino Women and the Doctorate Degree: Factors
      Associated with the Attainment and Use of the Degree."
      Centro Escolar University, Manila, Graduate and Faculty
      Studies 24 (1973):41-53.

839   LASAP, S.L. Human Resource Development: The Social Labora-
      tory Experience. Los Baños, Philippines: JEACCA Rural
      Training Programme, 1974, 60 pp. (Extension teaching and
      planning for adult farmers, women and youth.)

840   LAURETA, ELIZABETH G. "A Comparison of Our Women in Education
      Today to That of Yesterday." Master's thesis, Adamson
      University [Manila], 1951, iii, 72 pp.

841   LEOGARDO, FELICITAS T. "A Study of the Problems of Adolescent
      Girls in High Schools." Master's thesis, Ateneo de Manila
      University [Manila], 1956, 151 pp.

842   LEON, AMPARO de. "A Follow-up Study of the Occupational
      Activities of the Girl Graduates of Tarlac School."
      Master's thesis, National Teachers College [Manila], 1959,
      vi, 109 pp.

843   LIM, PILAR H. "Education of Our Daughters." Centro Escolar
      University, Manila, Graduate and Faculty Studies 18
      (1967):1-7.

844   MA SHENG JING HENG. "A Proposed Curriculum in Homemaking for
      the Third Year Girls of the Chinese High Schools in Manila."
      Master's thesis, Philippine Women's University [Manila],
      1963, 181 pp.

845 MAGLANGIT, VIRGINIA R. "The Maranao Woman: Growing Up, Education, Courtship and Marriage." Solidarity 9, no. 7 (Sept./Oct. 1975):36-42.

846 MANILA. CENTRO ESCOLAR UNIVERSITY. Then and Now. Published by the Centro Escolar University on the occasion of her golden jubilee. Manila: Centro Escolar University, 1957, 281 pp.

847 MARTÍN-VALDÉS, MATILDE. "An Exploratory Study of Reported Personal Problems of a Group of Women Students in the College of Education, University of the Philippines." Ph.D. dissertation, University of Buffalo, 1954, iii, 222 pp.

848 MASCAREÑAS, JOSEFINA B. "Predominant Home Problems Encountered by Selected Adolescent Boys and Girls with Working Mothers." Master's thesis, Philippine Women's University [Manila], 1968, 130 pp.

849 MENDOÑEZ, BELEN C. "An Appraisal of the Services Rendered to the Wards of the Philippine Training School for Girls from June 1959 to May 1961." Master's thesis, Philippine Women's University [Manila], 1962, 99 pp.

850 MIRAFLOR, CLARITA GO. "The Philippine Nurse: Implications for Orientation and In-Service Education for Foreign Nurses in the United States." Ph.D. dissertation, Loyola University of Chicago, 1976. 202 pp. Abstracted in Dissertation Abstracts International 36, no. 11 (May 1976): 5515-B. University Microfilms International, order no. 76-11,719.

851 MORALES, ALFREDO T. "Education for Democratic Filipinism: Home, School, and Women's Education." Education Quarterly, Supplement 9, no. 4 (Apr. 1962):1-50.

852 MORALES, ROSARIO DURAN. "The Education of Women in the Philippines: A Comparative Study." Master's thesis, National University [Manila], 1952, 147 pp.

853 NAVARRETE, CATALINA ROSAL. "Homemaking Activities of Girls Enrolled in Two Secondary Schools in Vigan, Ilocos Sur." Master's thesis, University of the Philippines [Quezon City], 1961, xviii, 124 pp.

854 NOGUERA, REMEDIOS. "A Proposal for a Student Personnel Program for the Philippine Women's University." Ed.D. dissertation, Indiana University, 1954, 242 pp. Abstracted in Dissertation Abstracts 14, no. 4 (1954):618-19. University Microfilms International, order no. 7908.

855   NORA, LIWAYWAY C. "Modern Trends in a Filipino Woman's
       World." Master's thesis, Far Eastern University [Manila],
       1947, vi, 176 pp.

856   OANES, CONSTANCIA V. "The Development of Filipino Norms for
       the Vocational Interests Blank for Women." Master's thesis,
       National Teachers College [Manila], 1956, vii, 97 pp.

857   OBLIGACION, LUZ ORO. "A Study of the Home and School Problems
       of the High School Girls of the Far Eastern University."
       Master's thesis, Far Eastern University [Manila], 1952,
       x, 158 pp.

858   ORATA, PEDRO T. "Trends in Educational Opportunities for
       Women." Philippine Educational Forum 4 (2d quarter 1953):
       23-32.

859   OYSON, BONIFACIA N. "A Study of the Purposes, Field of Activ-
       ities, and Accomplishments of the Girl Scout Movement in
       Cebu." Master's thesis, University of San Carlos [Cebu
       City, Philippines], 1954, xiii, 301 pp.

860   PADERNILLA, EVANGELICA DIESTO. "An Analysis of Certain Dif-
       ficulties Met by Women Students in Their Student Teaching."
       Master's thesis, Central Philippine University [Iloilo
       City, Philippines], 1965, vi, 110 pp.

861   PANDY, ENRICA L. "A Survey of Physically Exceptional College
       Female Students in Selected Private Colleges and Universi-
       ties in Manila and Their Physical Education Activities."
       Master's thesis, National Teachers College [Manila], 1957,
       vi, 114 pp.

862   PAREDES, TERESITA S. "The Woman Elementary School Principal:
       Perception of Her Feminine and Community Roles." Master's
       thesis, University of the Philippines [Quezon City], 1974,
       105 pp.

863   PECSON, GERONIMA T. "Functional Literacy and the Role of
       Women Today." Weekly Nation 5, no. 48 (July 1970):23, 25.

864   PERALTA, MARIA CID. "Problems of Higher Education for Women."
       Philippine Educational Forum 8 (Mar. 1959):52-55; 9 (July
       1959):53-54.

865   PERALTA, ROSA LUZ. "A Study of the Pedagogical Principles of
       Father Poveda regarding the Education of Future Women Edu-
       cators." Master's thesis, University of San Agustin
       [Iloilo City, Philippines], 1974, 5, 214 pp.

866 PEREZ, PRESENTACION T. "The Filipino Woman and Her Education
     before the Twentieth Century." Home Economics 1 (Oct.
     1963):2-23.

867 _____. "Problems of Employed Women in Certain Professional
     Groups in the Philippines and Their Educational Implica-
     tions." Ph.D. dissertation, University of Minnesota, 1954,
     x, 287 pp. Abstracted in Dissertation Abstracts 15, no. 3,
     1955:359-60. University Microfilms International, order
     no. 11,113.

868 PEREZ, SOLEDAD C. "Homemaking Activities of Women Graduates
     of the University of the Philippines." Master's thesis,
     University of the Philippines [Quezon City], 1948, 158 pp.

869 PHILIPPINE ASSOCIATION OF UNIVERSITY WOMEN. Talking Things
     Over with the Growing Filipina: A Project of the Philip-
     pine University Women. Edited by Pura Santillan-
     Castrence. Manila: Bardavan Book Co., 1951, 192 pp.

870 PHILIPPINES. University, College of Education, Department of
     Home Economics. "Towards an Educated Filipino Womahood."
     Education Quarterly 6, nos. 1/2 (June/Sept. 1958):71-79.

871 PHILIPPINES (REPUBLIC), Department of Education. "Access of
     Women to Education." Geneva: UNESCO, 1953. (Brochure
     prepared for the 15th International Conference on Public
     Education.)

872 POLOTAN, KERIMA. "The Education of a Woman." Philippines
     Free Press 61, no. 35 (Aug. 1968):42, 137-39.

873 POSADAS, SALUD VIDUYA. "A Survey of the Existing Guidance
     Practices in the Catholic High School for Girls in Manila."
     Master's thesis, Ateneo de Manila University [Manila],
     1954, 94 pp.

874 QUILANG, BENJAMIN L. "Leisure-Time Activities of Selected
     High School Girls in Manila." Master's thesis, Philippine
     College of Commerce, 1967, ix, 121 pp.

875 QUITO, EMERITA S. "The Role of the University in Changing
     Women's Consciousness." Dialogue [Manila] 14, no. 1
     (Dec. 1978):21-37.

876 RAMOS, MARIA DOLORES V. "The Woman School Teacher: An Ex-
     ploration of Her Concepts of the Feminine Roles, Profes-
     sional Membership Role and Professional Self-Image."
     Master's thesis, University of the Philippines [Quezon
     City], 1969, 124 pp.

877   REMIGIO, PRIMITIVA. "History of Education of the Filipino
      Women." Master's thesis, Centro Escolar University
      [Manila], 1936.

878   REYES, MARIE CARMEN. "A Historical Study of the Superior
      Normal School for Women Teachers in Manila 1893-98."
      Master's thesis, Ateneo de Manila University [Manila],
      1953, 120 pp.

879   REYES-SISON, ALICIA. "A Study of the Fundamental Aspects of
      the Art of Home Making as Practiced by Some Representative
      Women Educators of the Department of Education." Master's
      thesis, Adamson University [Manila], 1966, 210 pp.

880   ROCES, ALFREDO R. "Strengthening Women's Education in the
      Philippines." Science Review 3, no. 5 (May 1962):15-17.

881   RODIL, CARMEN F. "A Survey of the Work-Study Type Silent
      Reading Achievements, Silent Reading Habits, Reading
      Preferences and Reading Attitudes of High School Girls,
      St. Theresa's College, Manila." Ph.D. dissertation,
      University of Santo Tomas [Manila], 1959, xiv, 149 pp.

882   ROMUALDEZ, VICTORIA A. "The Role of Homemaking Course at
      High School Level in the Moral Rehabilitation of Women in
      Postwar Philippines." Master's thesis, University of
      Manila [Manila], 1948, 87 pp.

883   RUIZ, NAOMI R. "Some Determining Factors in the Vocational
      Choices of College Students in a Select School for Women."
      Master's thesis, Ateneo de Manila University [Manila],
      1959.

884   SAINGAN, PURITA M. "Status of the Girl Scout Movement in the
      Public Schools of Pangasinan and Dagupan City 1964-1965."
      Master's thesis, Northwestern Educational Institution
      [Dagupan City], 1964.

885   SALAS, RAFAEL. "A Filipina's New Role in Her Growing Coun-
      try." PAFTE Review 2, no. 2 (Dec. 1969):182-86.

886   SAMANO, ALMA. "A Study of the Expressed Occupational Choices
      of Third and Fourth Year Girls in a Rural Parochial High
      School in Relation to Their Occupational Interests and
      Scholastic Aptitudes." Master's thesis, Ateneo de Manila
      University [Manila], 1974, ix, 117 pp.

887   SAN AGUSTÍN ZAMORA, ELENA. "Las etapas de la educación feme-
       nina en Filipinas" [The stages of .female education in the
       Philippines]. Ph.D. dissertation, Universidad de Madrid,
       1972. Abstracted in Revista de la Universidad Complutense.
       Tesis doctorales, cursos 1972-1973 II 22, no. 88-II
       (Madrid, 1973):165-67.

888   SANCHEZ, REGINA V. "The Development of Education for Women
       Since 1898." Master's thesis, Arellano University
       [Manila], 1968.

889   SARMIENTO, TOMOSA QUEBRAL. "A Study of the Problems of the
       Co-Eds of Zamboanga A.E. College." Master's thesis,
       Zamboanga A.E. College [Philippines], 1974, xiv, 142 pp.

890   SEVILLA, CONSUELO G. "The Pollyana Hypothesis among Selected
       13 to 16 Years Old Filipino High School Boys and Girls
       across Five Philippine Languages of Luzon." Ed.D. dis-
       sertation, Centro Escolar University [Manila], 1973,
       269 pp.

891   SISON, CARIDAD T. "A Study of the Adjustment Problems of the
       Students of the Girls High School, Far Eastern University."
       Master's thesis, Far Eastern University [Manila], 1952,
       xxvii, 300 pp.

892   SORIANO, LICERIA BRILLANTES. "Women and Education."
       Philippine Law Journal 50, no. 1 (Feb. 1975):88-102.

893   TEVES, MARUJA E. "A Survey of Reading Interest of High
       School Girls." Master's thesis, St. Paul's College
       [Manila], 1958, 160 pp.

874   TIRONA, RAMONA S. "Whither Art Thou Going, Woman?"
       Philippine Education Forum 11, no. 1 (Mar. 1962):22-29.

895   TORIBIO, PATERNA A. "A Study of the Leisure-Time Activities
       of Female Students in the Government Vocational of Bohol."
       Master's thesis, Rafael Palma College [Tagbilaran, Bohol,
       Philippines], 1968, 266 pp.

896   TORRALBA, AIDA G. "Physical Education and Personality Devel-
       opment of Female Students in Six Selected Colleges and
       Universities in Manila." Master's thesis, National Uni-
       versity [Manila], 1961, v, 103 pp.

897   VERGARA, EKIZA Z. "A Survey of Attitudes, Awareness and
       Knowledge about Sex among 1,000 Female College Students in
       Two Universities." Centro Escolar University, Manila,
       Graduate and Faculty Studies 20 (1960):144-62.

898   VERORA, REBECCA P. "Stressful Situations in Clinical Practice
        Met by Nursing Students of Quezon Memorial Hospital School
        of Nursing during the School Year 1973-1974." Master's
        thesis, Luzonian University [Lucena City, Philippines],
        1974, xi, 115 pp.

899   VETTER, CAROLINE (Sister Paolomaria). "Ideas on Woman Forma-
        tion as a Future Basis for Completing the Professional
        Training of Women in College." Master's thesis, University
        of San Carlos [Cebu City, Philippines], 1969, 80 pp.

900   VIDAL, Ma. NATIVIDAD, Sister. "Educational Guidance Problems
        and the Graduating High School Girl." Master's thesis,
        University of Santo Tomas [Manila], 1950, 107 pp.

901   YUSON, BONIFACIA F. "History, Organization and Status of the
        Philippine Association of University Women, Far Eastern
        University Chapter." Master's thesis, Far Eastern Univer-
        sity [Manila], 1974, xiv, 136 pp.

Singapore

902   CHENG, SIOK HWA. "Singapore Women: Legal Status, Educational
        Attainment, and Employment Patterns." Asian Survey 17,
        no. 4 (Apr. 1977):358-74.

903   _____. Women in Singapore: Legal, Educational and Economic
        Aspects. Singapore: Nanyang University, 1976, 32 pp.
        Nanyang University, College of Graduate Studies, Institute
        of Humanities and Social Science. Occasional Paper
        Studies.

904   CHIEW, SEEN KONG. Educational and Occupational Attainment of
        Singapore's Chinese Women and Men. Singapore: Chopmen
        Enterprises, 1977, 23 pp. Singapore. University, Depart-
        ment of Sociology. Working Paper, no. 59.

905   WONG, ALINE K. "Maternal Employment, Education and Changing
        Family Values in Singapore." Journal of Economic Develop-
        ment and Social Change in Asia and the Pacific 1, no. 1
        (1976):23-40.

Thailand

906   AMBHORN MEESOK, KHUNYING. "Education and the Poor." Paper
        presented at the Seminar on Women Wage Earners in Thailand,
        Bangkok, April 1975.

907   AROM TANPRAPHAT. "A Study of the Relationship between Crea-
         tivity, Academic Achievement, Scholastic Aptitude, Sex, and
         Vocational Interests of Tenth Grade Thai Students." Ed.D.
         dissertation, University of Northern Colorado, 1976,
         100 pp. Abstracted in Dissertation Abstracts International
         37, no. 1 (July 1976):119-20-A. University Microfilms
         International, order no. 76-16,300.

908   CHIRAPHAN KANCHANACHITRA. "Some Factors Related to Leadership
         Participation of Men and Women in a New York State Com-
         munity and Their Implications for Community Development in
         Thailand." Ph.D. dissertation, Cornell University, 1976,
         257 pp. Abstracted in Dissertation Abstracts International
         37, no. 10 (Apr. 1977):6226-A. University Microfilms
         International, order no. 77-8440.

909   GOLDSTEIN, SIDNEY. "The Influence of Labour Force Participa-
         tion and Education on Fertility in Thailand." Population
         Studies 26, no. 3 (Nov. 1972):419-36. Also published
         separately as Chulalongkorn University, Institute of Popu-
         lation Studies. Research Report, no. 9, 1972, iv, 28 pp.

910   NARTSIRI VIMOLCHALAO. "Higher Education of Women in
         Thailand." Paper presented at the Seventh Conference of
         the International Association of Historians of Asia,
         Bangkok, August 1977.

911   OONTA NOPAKAM. "Non-Formal Education and the Development of
         Thai Women." Paper presented at the Seventh Conference of
         the International Association of Historians of Asia,
         Bangkok, August 1977.

912   PANIT MONGKOL. "A Study of the Thirty-five Girls' Vocational
         Schools under the UNICEF Development Project in Thailand."
         Master's thesis, Adamson University [Manila], 1970.

913   PAWTHIP CHAMPATHES. "Opinions of Some Occupational Groups
         towards the Roles of Women in Thailand." Master's thesis,
         Chulalongkorn University, 1973.

914   PINDIP BORIBOONSACK. "The Role of Women in Rural Development
         in Education in Thailand." Bangkok: Ministry of Educa-
         tion, n.d.

915   PREEJA DHUNMA. "A Study of Moral Values of Two Age Groups of
         Farm and Nonfarm Adolescent Boys and Girls in Three Geo-
         graphical Regions of Thailand." Ed.D. dissertation,
         University of Maryland, 1966, 191 pp. Abstracted in
         Dissertation Abstracts 27, no. 9 (Mar. 1967):2872-73-A.
         University Microfilms International, order no. 67-2001.

916   WORLD EDUCATION, INC. The Thailand Project: An Innovative
      Program in Functional Literacy and Family Life Planning.
      New York: World Education, 1973, 16 pp.

FAMILY PLANNING AND FERTILITY

Southeast Asia

917   ASIAN REGIONAL SEMINAR ON MANAGEMENT OF FAMILY PLANNING PRO-
      GRAMMES, Singapore, 1974. Report. Bangkok: International
      Labour Office, Regional Office for Asia, 1974, 41, 186 pp.

918   BRENNER, WILLIAM E. et al. "Abortion in Four Asian Countries:
      Patient Characteristics, Morbidity and Contraception Accep-
      tance." Majalah Obstetri dan Ginekologi Indonesia 1,
      no. 2 (1974):120-41.

919   BULATAO, RODOLFO A. On the Nature of the Transition in the
      Value of Children. Honolulu: East-West Population Insti-
      tute, 1979. 104 pp. East-West Population Institute.
      Papers, no. 60-A.

920   BUTZ, WILLIAM P. Puzzles in the Demographic and Economic Be-
      haviour of Rural Southeast Asians: An Economist's View.
      Santa Monica, Calif.: Rand Corp., 1972, 12 pp. Rand Cor-
      poration Paper, P-4903.

921   CADBURY, BARBARA. "Family Planning in South and South-East
      Asia." In Women in the New Asia. Edited by Barbara E.
      Ward. Paris: Unesco, 1963, pp. 523-26.

922   CHANDRASEKARAN, C. "ECAFE Programme to Assist Fertility Con-
      trol." Demography 5, no. 2 (1968):651-53.

923   COMBINED CONFERENCE ON EVALUATION OF MALAYSIA NATIONAL FAMILY
      PLANNING PROGRAMME AND EAST ASIA POPULATION PROGRAMMES,
      Kuala Lumpur, 1970. Proceedings. Organized by National
      Family Planning Board, Malaysia. Kuala Lumpur: National
      Family Planning Board, 1970, iv, 470 pp.

924   CONCEPCIÓN, MERCEDES B. "Female Labour Force Participation
      and Fertility." International Labour Review 109, nos. 5/6
      (May/June 1974):503-57. (Covers various Asian countries.)

925   COOK, REBECCA J. "Legal and Policy Aspects of Community
      Based Distribution of Oral Contraceptives in South East
      Asia." In SOUTHEAST ASIAN REGIONAL SEMINAR ON LAW AND
      POPULATION, Jakarta, 1975. Law and Population. Edited by

Teuku Mohamed Radhie et al. Jakarta: Yayasan Penelitian dan Pengembangun Hukum, 1976, pp. 284-93.

926 CORTES, IRENE R. "Legal Aspects of World Population: Southeast Asia." Philippine Law Journal 53 (Mar. 1978):41-53.

927 DAVID, HENRY PHILIP, and LEE, SUNG JIN, eds. Social and Psychological Aspects of Fertility in Asia: Proceedings of the Technical Seminar, Choonchun, Korea, 7-9 November 1973. Washington: Transnational Family Research Institute; Seoul: Korean Institute for Research and Behavioral Sciences, 1974, 128 pp.

928 DURDIN, TILLMAN. "Masalah Kelahiran di Asia Semakin Mendesak" [The birth problem in Asia is becoming more urgent]. Siasat 14 (1960):17-19.

929 EXPERT GROUP MEETING ON ORGANIZATIONAL ASPECTS OF INTEGRATING FAMILY PLANNING WITH DEVELOPMENT PROGRAMMES, Bangkok, 1976. Report and Selected Papers. Bangkok: ESCAP, 1977, 46 pp. Asian Population Studies Series, no. 36.

930 EXPERT GROUP MEETING ON SOCIAL AND PSYCHOLOGICAL ASPECTS OF FERTILITY BEHAVIOUR, Bangkok, 1974. Report and Papers. Bangkok: ESCAP, 1974, 90 pp. Asian Population Studies Series, no. 26. United Nations Document E/CN.11/1231.

931 EXPERT GROUP MEETING ON SOCIO-ECONOMIC MEASURES AFFECTING FERTILITY BEHAVIOUR WITH SPECIAL EMPHASIS ON ACTIONABLE PROGRAMMES, Bangkok, 1977. Report. Bangkok: ESCAP, 1978, 33 pp. Asian Population Studies Series, no. 41.

932 EXPERT GROUP MEETING ON SOCIO-ECONOMIC RETURNS OF FAMILY PLANNING PROGRAMMES, Bangkok, 1972. Report of the Expert Group Meeting on Socio-Economic Returns of Family Planning Programmes: Cost-Benefit and Cost-Effectiveness Analysis: Held at Bangkok, Thailand, 19-30 June 1972. Bangkok: Economic Commission for Asia and the Far East, 1973, ii, 40 pp. Asian Population Studies Series, no. 12. United Nations Document E/CN.11/1070.

933 EXPERT GROUP MEETING ON THE ROLE OF VOLUNTARY ORGANIZATIONS IN NATIONAL FAMILY PLANNING PROGRAMMES, Bangkok, 1972. The Role of Voluntary Organizations in National Family Planning Programmes: Report and Selected Documents. Bangkok: Economic Commission for Asia and the Far East, 1973, 39 pp. Asian Population Studies Series, no. 13.

934 GLASS, DAVID VICTOR. "Fertility and Birth Control in Developed Societies and for Less Developed Societies." Malayan Economic Review 8, no. 1 (1963):29-39.

935   HULL, VALERIE J. "Fertility, Women's Work and Economic Class:
      A Case Study from Southeast Asia." In The Fertility of
      Working Women: A Synthesis of International Research.
      Edited by Stanley Kupinsky. New York: Praeger, 1977,
      pp. 35-80.

936   INTER-GOVERNMENTAL COORDINATING COMMITTEE, Regional Organiza-
      tion for Inter-governmental Cooperation and Coordination in
      Population and Family Planning in Southeast Asia. Inte-
      grated Approach at Grassroots Level towards Family Planning
      and Health Programme with Particular Emphasis on Nutrition
      and Parasite Control: A Report on the Joint JOICFP/IGCC
      Workshop Held in Genting Highlands and Kuala Lumpur,
      Malaysia, 23-25 March 1977. Kuala Lumpur: IGCC Secre-
      tariat, 1977, 127 pp.

937   _____. Joint IGCC/IFRP East and South East Asia Seminar on
      Regional Fertility Research. A Report on the Joint IGCC/
      IFRP Seminar on Regional Fertility Research Held in
      Bangkok, Thailand, 18-20 July, 1979. Edited by J.Y. Peng.
      Kuala Lumpur: IBCC Secretariat, 1979, 215 pp.

938   _____. Joint IGCC/IPPF Workshop on the Exchange of Experience
      Through Encouragement, Identification and Extension of In-
      novations in Family Planning Programmes, Jakarta, 1978. A
      Report on the Joint IGCC/IPPF Workshop on the Exchange of
      Experience through Encouragement, Identification and Ex-
      tension of Innovations in Family Planning Programmes.
      Kuala Lumpur: IGCC Secretariat, 1979, 146 pp.

939   _____. Joint IGCC/IPPF Workshop on the Policies and Pro-
      grammes for the Utilization of Non-Physicians in the
      Delivery of Family Planning Services, Pattaya, 1978. A
      Report on the Joint IGCC/IPPF Workshop on the Policies and
      Programmes for the Utilization of Non-Physicians in the
      Delivery of Family Planning Services. Edited by John M.
      Paxman. Kuala Lumpur: IGCC Secretariat, 1978, 129 pp.

940   _____. Proceedings of the Expert Meeting on Comparative Fer-
      tility Research, Sterilization and Post-Conceptive Regula-
      tion held in Pattaya, Thailand, November 1977. Sponsored
      by the Regional Organization for Inter-governmental Co-
      operation and Coordination in Population and Family Plan-
      ning in South East Asia and the International Fertility
      Research Programme. Kuala Lumpur: IGCC, 1978, 64 pp.

941   _____. Project Identification Meeting: Lactation and Fer-
      tility. A Report on the Project Identification Meeting:
      Lactation and Fertility Held in Kuala Lumpur, Malaysia,
      23-24 February 1978. Kuala Lumpur: IGCC Secretariat,
      1979[?], 57 pp.

942   . Symposium on Methodologies for Evaluation of National Family Planning Programmes in its Various Stages of Development: A Report on the Joint JOICFP/IGCC Symposium Held in Tokyo, October 1977. Kuala Lumpur: IGCC, 1977, 145 pp.

943   . Workshop/Seminar for More Effective Promotion and Management of Integrated Projects (Family Planning and Parasite Control). A Report on the Joint IGCC/JOICFP/NFPB Malaysian Workshop/Seminar for More Effective Promotion and Management of Integrated Projects held in Kuala Lumpur, 18-23 February 1979. Kuala Lumpur: IGCC Secretariat, 1978, 161 pp.

944 INTER-GOVERNMENTAL COORDINATING COMMITTEE, Southeast Asia Regional Cooperation in Family and Population Planning. Population and Development Planning: A Report on the IGCC Regional Workshop on Population and Development Planning, Held in Penang, Malaysia, September 27-29, 1973. Kuala Lumpur: Inter-governmental Coordinating Committee, Southeast Asia Regional Cooperation in Family and Population Planning, 1974[?], 42 pp.

945   . Proceedings of the Expert Meeting on Comparative Fertility Research, Sterilization and Post-Conceptive Regulation Held in Nepal, March 1975. Sponsored by the Inter-governmental Coordinating Committee and the International Fertility Research Programme. Kuala Lumpur: IGCC, 1975, 38 pp.

946   . Proceedings of the Expert Meeting on Comparative Fertility Research, Sterlization and Post-Conceptive Regulation Held in Kuala Lumpur, January 1976. Sponsored by the Inter-governmental Coordinating Committee and the International Fertility Research Programme. Kuala Lumpur: IGCC, 1976, 86 pp.

947   . Proceedings of the Expert Meeting on Comparative Fertility Research, Sterilization and Post-Conceptive Regulations Held in Bali, January 1977. Sponsored by the Inter-governmental Coordinating Committee and the International Fertility Research Programme. Kuala Lumpur: IGCC, 1977, 83 pp.

948   . Reducing Fertility through beyond Family Planning Measures: A Report on the IGCC Regional Workshop on Reducing Fertility through beyond Family Planning Measures Held in Penang, Malaysia, 26-29 January 1976. Kuala Lumpur: IGCC Secretariat, 1977[?], 137 pp.

949 _____. Regional Workshop on Adult Education and Family Planning, Singapore, 1973: Report. Kuala Lumpur: IGCC Secretariat, 1973, 312 pp.

950 _____. Report of Second Ministerial Conference and Third
Official Meeting of the Inter-governmental Coordinating
Committee of Southeast Asia Regional Cooperation in Family
and Population Planning, Venue, Rincome Hotel, Chiengmai,
Thailand, 14-16 May 1973. Kuala Lumpur: IGCC, 1973[?],
90 pp.

951 _____. Report of the First Regional Training Workshop of the
Inter-governmental Coordinating Committee, Southeast Asia
Regional Cooperation in Family and Population Planning,
Jakarta, 11-15 December, 1972. Kuala Lumpur: Jenson
Press, 1972[?], 134 pp.

952 _____. Sterilization and Abortion Procedures: Proceedings of
the First Meeting of the IGCC Expert Group Working Committee on Sterilization and Abortion Held in Penang,
Malaysia, during 3-5 January 1973. Kuala Lumpur: IGCC,
1973, vii, 59 pp.

953 INTERNATIONAL LABOUR OFFICE, Regional Office for Asia,
Bangkok. Family Planning in Industry in the Asian Region.
2 vols. Bangkok: ILO, 1974, 42, 145 pp.

954 INTERNATIONAL PLANNED PARENTHOOD FEDERATION. Facts and Fig-
ures on Family Planning in South East Asia and Oceania
Region (IPPF) IPPR-SEAOR Fact Booklet. Kuala Lumpur:
East Asia and Oceania Region, IPPF, 1972, 36 pp.

955 _____, South East Asia and Oceania Region. Accelerating
Family Planning: Problems and Approaches. Quezon City:
Institute of Mass Communication, University of the
Philippines, 1971, iv, 425 pp.

956 _____. Clinical Proceedings of the First International
Planned Parenthood Federation, South-East Asia and Oceania
Regional Medical and Scientific Congress, Sydney, 14 to 18
August 1972. Sponsored by the Family Planning Association
of Australia. Chippendale, N.S.W.: Australian and New
Zealand Journal of Obstetrics and Gynecology, 1972, 250 pp.

957 _____. Family Planning and National Development. Proceedings
of the Conference of the International Planned Parenthood
Federation, Southeast Asia and Oceania Regional Conference
held in Bandung, 1969. Edited by R.K.B. Hankinson and
Nani Soewondo. London: International Planned Parenthood
Federation, 1969, xi, 260 pp. Also published in Indonesia
under the title Keluarga Berentjana dan Pembangunan

Nasional: Hasil Konperensi I.P.P.F. di Bandung, Djuni 1969, by Perkumpulan Keluarga Berentjana Indonesia, 1969, xi, 466 pp.

958 JONES, GAVIN WALLIS. "Social Science Research on Population and Development in East and South-East Asia: A Review and a Search for Directions. Draft Report." Prepared for the International Review Group of Social Science Research on Population Development (IRG), Mexico City, 1978, 120 pp.

959 KANTER, JOHN F., and McCAFFREY, LEE, eds. Population and Development in Southeast Asia. Lexington, Mass.: Lexington Books, 1975, xv, 323 pp.

960 KEENY, S.M., ed. "East Asia Review, 1976-77." Studies in Family Planning 9, no. 9 (Sept. 1978):233-56. (Reports include Indonesia, Malaysia, the Philippines, Singapore, and Thailand.)

961 KELLOGG, EDMUND H.; KLINE, DAVID K.; and ŠTEPÁN, Jan. The World's Laws and Practices on Population and Sexuality Education. Medford, Mass.: Law and Population Programmes, Fletcher School of Law and Diplomacy, Tufts University, 1975, vi, 127 pp. Law and Population Monograph Series, no. 25.

962 KOCHER, JAMES E. "Rural Socio-Economic Stratification and Fertility Decline in Developing Countries." Paper presented at the Social Science Council Conference, University of East Africa, Nairobi, December 1972.

963 MARCOS, IMELDA ROMUALDEZ. "The Moral Dimensions of Family Planning: Keynote Speech to the First Asian Regional Conference on Family Planning." Manila: Malacanang, 1974.

964 PASTRANA, GAGRIEL B. "Abortions in the Religions of Southeast Asia." Unitas 48, no. 4 (Dec. 1975):639-54.

965 PENG, JUI YUN; SRISOMANG KEOVICHIT; and MacINTYRE, REGINALD, eds. Role of Traditional Birth Attendants in Family Planning: Proceedings of an International Seminar Held in Bangkok and Kuala Lumpur, 19-26 July, 1974. Ottawa: International Development Research Centre, 1974, 107 pp.

966 REGIONAL SEMINAR ON THE STATUS OF WOMEN AND FAMILY PLANNING FOR COUNTRIES WITHIN THE ECONOMIC COMMISSION FOR ASIA AND THE FAR EAST REGION, Jogjakarta, Indonesia, 1973. Papers. Organized by the United Nations in cooperation with the Government of Indonesia. New York: United Nations, 1974, i, 31 pp. United Nations Document ST/ESA/Ser.B2.

967 ROGERS, EVERETT M., and SOLOMON, S. "Traditional Midwives
     and Family Planning in Asia." Studies in Family Planning
     6, no. 5 (May 1975):126-33. (Countries covered are India,
     Pakistan, Indonesia, Malaysia, the Philippines, and
     Thailand.)

968 SANYAL, RANJIT K., and GOUR, MUKTA. Studies in Family Plan-
     ning: South East Asian Countries. New Delhi: National
     Institute of Family Planning, 1975, 19 pp. Bibliography
     Series, no. 2.

969 SEMINAR-WORKSHOP ON THE ROLE OF FPA CLINICS IN RELATION TO
     COMMUNITY-BASED FAMILY PLANNING SERVICES, Manila, 1975.
     Seminar-Workshop on the Role of FPA Clinics in Relation to
     Community-Based Family Planning Services, Manila,
     Philippines, 6-11 February 1975. Sponsored by Regional
     Medical Committee, International Planned Parenthood Federa-
     tion, East and South East Asia and Oceania Region in co-
     operation with the Family Planning Organization of the
     Philippines. Kuala Lumpur: Printed by Economy Printers,
     1976[?], 112 pp.

970 SEMLER, VICKI JANE. "A Study of Third World Family Planners'
     Views towards Women's Role in Society: A Communications
     Perspective." Ph.D. dissertation, Indiana University,
     1977, 348 pp. Abstracted in Dissertation Abstracts Inter-
     national 38, no. 4 (Oct. 1977):1721-A. University Micro-
     films International, order no. 77-22,636. (Based on a
     study of seventy-one family planners, among them individ-
     uals from Indonesia, Malaysia, Philippines, Singapore, and
     Thailand.)

971 SMITH, THOMAS EDWARD. "Population Characteristics of South
     and South-East Asia." In Women in the New Asia. Edited
     by Barbara E. Ward. Paris: Unesco, 1963, pp. 500-522.

972 _____, ed. The Politics of Family Planning in the Third
     World. London: G. Allen & Unwin, 1973, 352 pp.

973 SOUTHEAST ASIA MINISTERIAL CONFERENCE ON FAMILY AND POPULATION
     PLANNING, Kuala Lumpur, 1970. Report. Kuala Lumpur, 1973,
     ii, 104 pp.

974 SOUTHEAST ASIAN REGIONAL SEMINAR ON LAW AND POPULATION,
     Jakarta, 1975. Law and Population. Edited by Teuku
     Mohamed Radhie et al. Jakarta: Yayasan Penelitian dan
     Pengembangan Hukum, 1976, 299 pp.

975   STELLA, RISSA M. Increasing Youth Programmes in Family Plan-
          ning. Kuala Lumpur: International Planned Parenthood
          Federation East and South East Asia and Oceania Region,
          1975, 23 pp. IPPF-ESEAOR Monograph, no. 5.

976   ŠTĚPÁN, JAN, and KELLOGG, EDMUND H. The World's Laws on
          Contraceptives. Medford, Mass.: Law and Population Pro-
          gramme, Fletcher School of Law and Diplomacy, Tufts Univer-
          sity, 1974, vii, 105 pp. Law and Population Monograph
          Series, no. 17.

977   _____. The World's Laws on Voluntary Sterilization for Family
          Planning Purposes. Medford, Mass.: Law and Population
          Programme, Fletcher School of Law and Diplomacy, Tufts Uni-
          versity, 1972, 69 pp. Law and Population Monograph Series,
          no. 8.

978   UNITED NATIONS, Department of Economic and Social Affairs.
          Status of Women and Family Planning: Report of the Special
          Rapporteur Appointed by the Economic and Social Council
          under Resolution 1326 (XLIV). New York: United Nations,
          1975, vi, 148 pp. United Nations Document E/CN.6/575/
          Rev.1.

979   UNITED NATIONS, ECAFE Working Group on Communications Aspects
          of Family Planning Programmes. Report and Selected Papers.
          New York: United Nations, 1968, 164 pp.

980   UNITED NATIONS, Economic and Social Commission for Asia and
          the Pacific. Husband-Wife Communication and Practice of
          Family Planning. Bangkok: ECAFE, 1974, 203 pp. Asian
          Population Studies Series, no. 16.

981   _____. Report of a Comparative Study on the Administration
          of Family Planning Programmes in the ESCAP Region: Orga-
          nizational Determinants of Performance in Family Planning
          Services. Bangkok: ESCAP, 1977, 46 pp. Asian Population
          Studies Series, no. 29.

982   _____. Report of the Multinational Study in Methodologies
          for Setting Family Planning Targets in the ESCAP Region.
          Bangkok: ESCAP, 1976, 136 pp. Asian Population Studies
          Series, no. 31.

983   UNITED NATIONS, Working Group on Administrative Aspects of
          Family Planning Programmes. Administrative Aspects of
          Family Planning Programmes: Report. New York: United
          Nations, 1966, vi, 64 pp. Asian Population Studies Series,
          no. 1.

984 UNITED NATIONS FUND FOR POPULATION ACTIVITIES. Inventory of
     Population Projects in Developing Countries around the
     World, 1976/77: Multilateral Assistance, Bilateral As-
     sistance, Non-Governmental Organization Assistance. New
     York: U.N. Fund for Population Activities, 1978, xii,
     687 pp. Population Programmes and Projects, vol. 2.

985   _____. Women, Population, and Development. New York: United
     Nations Fund for Population Activities, 1977, 47 pp.
     Population Profiles, 7.

986 WATSON, WALTER B., ed. Family Planning in the Developing
     World: Review of Programs. Regional editors: S. M.
     Keeny et al. New York: Population Council, 1977, ix,
     77 pp.

987 WESTOFF, CHARLES F. "The Unmet Need for Birth Control in Five
     Asian Countries." International Family Planning Perspec-
     tives and Digest 4, no. 1 (1978):9-18.

988 WHANG, IN JOUNG. Management of Family Planning Programs in
     Asia: Concepts, Issues and Approaches. Kuala Lumpur:
     Asian Centre for Development Administration, 1976, v,
     423 pp.

989 WORLD FERTILITY SURVEY. The World Fertility Survey Inventory,
     Major Fertility and Related Surveys Conducted in Asia 1960-
     1973. Prepared by Samuel Baum et al. Voorburg: Inter-
     national Statistical Institute; London: World Fertility
     Survey, 1974, 48 pp. World Fertility Survey. Occasional
     Papers, no. 3.

990 ZATUCHNI, GERALD I., ed. Post-Partum Family Planning: A
     Report on the International Program. New York: McGraw-
     Hill, 1970, xxxii, 477 pp.

Burma

991 KYI, THIN, and AUNG, U. HIA TUNG. "A Study on the Population
     Problem of the Families in Greater Rangoon Area." Union
     of Burma Journal of Science and Technology 3, no. 2, 1971.

992 MAUNG, M. ISMAIL KHIN. "Differential Fertility in Burma,
     1953." Master's thesis, University of Chicago, 1961,
     85 pp.

993 RILEY, JAMES NELSON. "Cohabitation, Natality, and Mortality
     in Rural Thailand and Burma." In Culture, Natality, and
     Family Planning. Edited by John F. Marshall and Steven
     Polgar. Chapel Hill, N.C.: Carolina Population Centre,
     University of North Carolina, 1976, pp. 24-49.

Indochina

994   DO THI MAN.   "Birth Control Helped Me Advance."   <u>U.S. JPRS.</u>
      <u>Translations of Political and Sociological Information on</u>
      <u>North Vietnam</u> (Dec. 1964):24-26.

995   FRASER, STEWART.   "Vietnam: Special Report."   <u>People</u> 5, no. 2
      (1978):22-27.   (First comprehensive review of family plan-
      ning after the thirty-year war.)

996   HOANG THIEU SON.   "Planned Parenthood for Population Control."
      <u>U.S. JPRS.   Translations of Political and Sociological In-</u>
      <u>formation on North Vietnam</u> (May 1964):17-20.

997   KHAMPHAI ABHAY.   "Laos."   <u>Studies in Family Planning</u> 6, no. 8
      (Aug. 1975):229-30.   (On family planning programs in 1974.)

998   "Khmer Republic: Country Paper and EIC Activities for the
      ASOFA."   n.p., 1972, 8 pp.   (Khmer Association for Welfare
      of the Family.)

999   NGUYEN VAN BONG.   "Family Planning.   Do We Need It?"   <u>Vietnam</u>
      <u>Magazine</u> 6, no. 11 (1973):22-23.

1000   "Population Problems and Family Planning of Khmer Republic."
       <u>Obstetrical and Gynaecological Society, Proceedings</u>
       [Singapore] 3 (Mar. 1972):263-66.

1001   SOCIAL SCIENCE STUDY ASSOCIATION, Saigon.   <u>Study concerning</u>
       <u>the Knowledge, Attitude and Practice of Family Planning in</u>
       <u>Saigon and Gradinh</u>.   Saigon: Social Science Study Asso-
       ciation, 1973, 66 pp.

1002   TRUONG MINH CAC, and NGUYEN TUAN PHONG.   "Vietnam (South)."
       <u>Studies in Family Planning</u> 6, no. 8 (Aug. 1975):244.   (On
       family planning programs in 1974.)

Indonesia

1003   ABEDIN, SALEHA MAHMOOD.   "Islam and Muslim Fertility: Socio-
       logical Dimensions of a Demographic Dilemma."   Ph.D. dis-
       sertation, University of Pennsylvania, 1977, 261 pp.
       Abstracted in <u>Dissertation Abstracts International</u> 38,
       no. 8 (Feb. 1978):5066-67-A.   University Microfilms Inter-
       national, order no. 7730174.   (Includes some information
       relating to Indonesia and Malaysia.)

1004   "Abortus sebagai Usaha Mengatasi Jumlah Penduduk" [Abortion
       as a means of overcoming population growth].   <u>Kemajuan Ilmu</u>
       <u>Teknik dan Hidup</u> 8, no. 1 (1956):12-4.

99

1005   ADHIKARYA, R. "Communication Support for Family Planning
       Programs: The Potentialities for Folk Media in Indonesia
       and the Problems Involved in Pretesting and Evaluation."
       Honolulu: East-West Communication Institute, 1974, 37 pp.

1006   ADIWIKARTA, R.S. Membina Keluarga Menurut Rentjana:
       Berdasarkan Kemandjuran Berkala dari Wanita. Ulasan
       Keilmuan Populer tentang Azas dan Pelakuan dari "Istibra
       Berkala." [Building a family according to planning. A
       review of popular knowledge of the principle and practice
       of the "istibra berkala"]. Jakarta: Djambatan, 1955,
       viii, 36 pp.

1007   AKBAR, ALI. "Birth Control in Indonesia." Majalah Kedokteran
       Indonesia 9, no. 4 (1959):198-215.

1008   ASTAWA, IDA BAGUS; WALOEYO, SOEJENG; and LAING, JOHN E.
       "Family Planning in Bali." Studies in Family Planning 6,
       no. 4 (Apr. 1975):86-101.

1009   BADAN KOORDINASI KELUARGA BERENCANA NASIONAL, Jakarta. The
       Background of National Family Planning Program in Indonesia.
       Suwardjono Surjaningrat, chairman. Jakarta: Bureau of
       Information and Motivation, National Family Planning Co-
       ordinating Board, 1971, 19 pp.

1010   _____. Family Planning Service Statistics System: The Indo-
       nesian Experience. Jakarta: National Family Planning Co-
       ordinating Board, 1975, 32 pp. Technical Report Series;
       Monograph, no. 11.

1011   _____. Government Policy on Family Planning in Indonesia,
       1970. Jakarta: Bureau of Information and Motivation,
       National Family Planning Coordinating Board, 1971, 51 pp.

1012   _____. The Indonesian Family Planning Program: Basic Strate-
       gies. Jakarta: Bureau of Information and Motivation,
       National Family Planning Coordinating Board, 1976, 39 pp.

1013   _____. Kebidjaksanaan Pemerintah mengenai Masalah Keluarga
       Berentjana di Indonesia, 1970 [The government's solutions
       regarding family planning problems in Indonesia, 1970].
       Tjet. ke-2. Jakarta: Badan Koordinasi Keluarga Berencana
       Nasional, 1970, 50 pp.

1014   _____. Kumpulan Ichtisar Hasil-hasil Penelitian Keluarga
       Berentjana, Tahun 1961-1972 [Summary of the results of the
       study on family planning, 1961-1972]. Jakarta: Badan
       Koordinasi Keluarga Berencana Nasional, 1972, iv, 101 pp.

1015 _____. Rapat Kerja Program Nasional Keluarga Berencana Tahun
1976 [Working committee of the national family planning
programme 1976], 2 vols. Jakarta: Badan Koordinasi
Keluarga Berencana Nasional, 1976.

1016 BADAN PENELITIAN DAN PENINDJAUAN SOSIAL, Jogjakarta. Fertil-
ity Levels of Women from a Variety of Personal, Social,
Economical and Educational Conditions. Jogjakarta: Badan
Penelitian dan Penindjauan Sosial, 1971, 84 pp.

1017 BALDWIN, GEORGE B.; ZAIDAN, GEORGE C.; and MUNCIE, PETER C.
"The Population Work of the World Bank." Studies in Family
Planning 4, no. 11 (Nov. 1973):293-304. (Includes a de-
tailed review of the bank-assisted population projects in
Indonesia and India.)

1018 BARTEN, J. "Screening for Infertility in Indonesia: Results
of Examination of 863 Infertile Couples." Andrologia 10,
no. 5 (Sept./Oct. 1978):405-12.

1019 BHATTA, JITANDRA NATH. "Beberapa Aspek Kesuburan Wanita di
Djawa Timur" [Several aspects regarding fertility of women
in East Java]. Keluarga Berentjana, no. 4 (Mar. 1968):
26-30; no. 5 (June 1968):27-30.

1020 _____. An Estimate of Fertility Level of the Population of
Djakarta by Polynomial Function (Problem No. 16). Jakarta:
Dinas Geografi, Direktorat Topografi, Department Angkatan,
1966, 19 pp.

1021 BISRI, CIK HASAN. "Undang-undang Perkawinan dan Masalah
Kependudukan di Indoensia" [The marriage laws and population problems in Indonesia]. Bulletin Forum Studi 2, no. 2
(1976):9-15.

1022 BOGUE, DONALD J. "Perubahan Sikap dan Adopsi Tingkah-laku
untuk Keluarga Berentjana" [Attitude change and adoption
of new behavior in family planning]. Majalah Penyuluh
Sosial, no. 17 (1972):9-11.

1023 CHAPON, DIANA. Divorce and Fertility: A Study in Rural Java.
Jogjakarta: Population Institute, Gadjah Mada University,
1976, x, 115 pp.

1024 DARMAPUTERA, EKA. Keluarga Berentjana dalam Rangka Keluarga
Bertanggung Djawab [Family planning in a responsible family
structure]. Jakarta: Dewan Geredja-Geredja di Indonesia,
Subkomisi Keluarga Bertanggung Djawab, 1972, 20 pp. Seri
MR-7/1972.

1025   DAVIS, KINGSLEY, and BLAKE, JUDITH. Struktur Sosial dan Fer-
        tilitas: Suatu Kerangka Analitis [Social structure and
        fertility: an analytical framework]. Diterjemahkan oleh
        Hans Daen. Jogjakarta: Lembaga Kependudukan, Universitas
        Gadjah Mada, 1974, 43 pp.

1026   DJOJOSUGITO, WIRJAIWAN. "Pendidikan Tenaga Perawat, Bidan dan
        PKE dalam Rangka Perkembangan Program Keluarga Berencana"
        [The education of nursing personnel, midwives in the devel-
        opment of the family planning program]. Pedoman dan Berita
        Departemen Kesehatan, no. 4 (1970):21-25.

1027   GORDON, PERKIN W. "Pencegahan Kehamilan pada Wanita dengan
        Resiko Berat: Suatu Strategi untuk Program Nasional
        Keluarga Berencana Nasional yang Baru" [Contraception in-
        volves serious risks for women: a new strategy for a na-
        tional family planning program]. Keluarga Sejahtera 1,
        no. 3 (1969):113-26.

1028   GUNAWAN, KARTONO. "Population Growth and Its Control, Food
        Requirements and Food Production." NAS-LIPI Workshop on
        Food, Jakarta, 27 May-1 June 1968, 24, 2 pp.

1029   HAGUL, PETER. Kondom melalui Pos: Laporan Setengah Tahun.
        Mail Order Condoms: Half-Year Report. Jogjakarta:
        Lembaga Kependudukan, Universitas Gadjah Mada, 1976, iv,
        81 pp. Universitas Gadjah Mada, Lembaga Kependudukan.
        Seri Laporan, no. 4.

1030   HAMZAH, UNUS A. "Hasil Survey tentang Kedudukan Wanita dan
        Keluarga Berencana di Acheh" [Results of the survey re-
        garding the status of women and family planning in Acheh].
        Sinar Darussalam 7, no. 52 (1974):22-26; 7, no. 53 (1974):
        40-44; 7, no. 54 (1974):44-48; 7, no. 55 (1974):53-58; 8,
        no. 60 (1975):57-63; 8, no. 62 (1975):64-65.

1031   HELMY, MASDAR H. Islam dan Keluarga Berentjana [Islam and
        family planning]. Semarang: Tohaputra, 1969, 92 pp.

1032   HOEVEN, J.A. van der. "De invloed van wati-gebruik op de
        vruchtbaarheid van de vrouw" [The influence of 'wati-use'
        on the fertility of the woman]. Mededeelingen van de
        Dienst van Gezondheidszorg in Nederlands-Nieuw-Guinea 6,
        no. 1 (Mar. 1959):41-61.

1033   HULL, TERENCE H. "Each Child Brings Its Own Fortune: An
        Inquiry into the Value of Children." Ph.D. dissertation,
        Australian National University, 1975, xi, 475 pp.

1034   _____. Masalah Komunikasi Keluarga Berencana di Kodya Yogyakarta. Communication of Family Planning Information in Yogyakarta City. Ditulis dalam Bahasa Inggeris oleh Terence Hull dan kemudian diterjemahkan ke dalam bahasa Indonesia oleh Peter Hagul. Jogjakarta: Cabang Kotamadya Yogjakarta, Perkumpulan Keluarga Berencana Indoensia, 1976, iv, 50 pp.

1035   _____. "Population Control in a Village, Java: The Case of Maguwohardjo." Clayton, Victoria: Centre of Southeast Asian Studies, Monash University, 1974, 17 pp.

1036   _____. Prospect for Rapid Fertility Decline in Indonesia. Jogjakarta: Population Institute, Gadjah Mada University, 1976, 13 pp. Universitas Gadjah Mada, Lembaga Kependudukan. Working Paper Series, no. 2.

1037   _____. "Rapid Fertility Decline: A Comment." Bulletin of Indonesian Economic Studies 12, no. 2 (July 1976):106–16.

1038   _____. A Review of Research on the Price, Cost and Value of Children in Indonesia. Jogjakarta: Population Institute, Gadjah Mada University, 1977, 33 pp. Universitas Gadjah Mada, Lembaga Kependudukan. Working Paper Series, no. 12.

1039   _____. Units of Analysis in the Study of Fertility Decision-Making (With Examples Drawn from Research in Java). Jogjakarta: Population Institute, Gadjah Mada University and Demography Department, Australian National University, 1976, 23 pp. Universitas Gadjah Mada, Lembaga Kependudukan. Working Paper Series, no. 6.

1040   HULL, TERENCE H., and HULL, VALERIE J. The Relation of Economic Class and Fertility: An Analysis of Some Indonesian Data. Jogjakarta: Population Institute, Gadjah Mada University, 1976, 39 pp. Universitas Gadjah Mada, Lembaga Kependudukan. Seri laporan. Also published in Population Studies 31, no. 1 (Mar. 1977):43–57.

1041   _____. Social and Economic Support for High Fertility in Indonesia: A Preliminary Review Making Comparisons with African Data. Jogjakarta: Population Institute, Gadjah Mada University, 1976, 51 pp. Universitas Gadjah Mada, Lembaga Kependudukan. Working Paper Series, no. 5.

1042   HULL, TERENCE H., and TUKIRAN. "Regional Variations in the Prevalence of Childlessness in Indonesia." Indonesian Journal of Geography 6, no. 32 (1976):1–25.

1043   HULL, TERENCE H. et al. "Indonesia's Family Planning Story:
        Success and Challenge." Population Bulletin 32 (Nov.
        1977):3-52.

1044   HULL, VALERIE J. "Fertility, Socioeconomic Status and the
        Position of Women in a Javanese Village." Ph.D. disserta-
        tion, Australian National University, 1975, ix, 447 pp.

1045   _____. Fertility, Socioeconomic Status and the Position of
        Women in a Javanese Village. Canberra: Australian National
        University, 1975, ix, 584 pp.

1046   _____. The Positive Relation between Economic Class and Fam-
        ily Size in Java: A Case Study of the Intermediate Varia-
        bles Determining Fertility. Jogjakarta: Population Insti-
        tute, Gadjah Mada University, 1976, viii, 115 pp.
        Universitas Gadjah Mada, Lembaga Kependudukan. Seri
        Monograf, no. 2.

1047   _____. A Study of Birth Interval Dynamics in Rural Java.
        Jogjakarta: Population Institute, Gadjah Mada University
        and Department of Demography, Australian National Univer-
        sity, 1977, 27 pp. Universitas Gadjah Mada, Lembaga
        Kependudukan. Working Paper Series, no. 8.

1048   HULL, VALERIE J.; KODIRAN; and SINGARIMBUN, IRAWATI.
        Pembentukan Keluarga di Kalangan Universitas: Hasil-hasil
        Sementara dari Suatu Studi Kasus. Family Formation in the
        University Community: Preliminary Results of a Case Study.
        Jogjakarta: Lembaga Kependudukan, Universitas Gadjah Mada,
        1976, ii, 150 pp. Universitas Gadjah Mada, Lembaga
        Kependudukan. Seri Laporan, no. 9.

1049   HULL, VALERIE J., and SALADI, RININGSIH. "Peranan Status
        Wanita terhadap Penurunan Fertilitas" [The role of women in
        decreasing fertility]. Warta ZPG: Journal of the Student
        Movement for Zero Population Growth 32, no. 3 (1977):2-5.

1050   IHROMI, T. OMAS et al., comps. Kedudukan Wanita dan Keluarga
        Berencana di Indonesia [The status of women and family
        planning in Indonesia]. Suatu studi yang dilaksanakan deh
        Team Peneliti Tentang Kedudukan Wanita dan Keluarga Beren-
        cana. Jakarta Perkumpulan Keluarga Berencana Indonesia,
        1973, 309 pp.

1051   _____. The Status of Women and Family Planning in Indonesia.
        A study conducted by the Research Team on the Status of
        Women and Family Planning in Indonesia, and the National
        Family Planning Coordinating Board. Jakarta: Indonesian
        Planned Parenthood Association, 1973, 309 pp.

1052   INDONESIA, Biro Pusat Statistik. Keterangan fertilitas
        penduduk Indonesia. Fertility of the Indonesian Popula-
        tion. Jakarta: Biro Pusat Statistik, 1977, 130 pp. Sur-
        vey Penduduk Antar Sensus 1976. Seri Tabulasi, no. 1.

1053   _____. Perkiraan Angka Kelahiran dan Kematian di Indonesia
        Berdasarkan Sensus Penduduk 1971. Estimates of Fertility
        and Mortality in Indonesia Based on the 1971 Population
        Census. Jakarta: Biro Pusat Statistik, 1976, iv, 67 pp.
        Sensus Penduduk 1971, 1971 Population Census. Series,
        SP76-102.

1054   INDONESIA, Biro Pusat Statistik, and WORLD FERTILITY SURVEY.
        Indonesia Fertility Survey, 1976: Principal Report.
        2 vols. Jakarta, 1978, xvii, 158; x, 278 pp.

1055   INTERNATIONAL BANK FOR RECONSTRUCTION AND DEVELOPMENT.
        Doctors and Dukuns, Puppets and Pills: A Look at
        Indonesia's Family Planning Program. Washington, D.C.:
        World Bank, 1972, 143 pp.

1056   IRSAN, IBRAHIM. "Kinderlosigkeit in Nordsumatra: Untersuch-
        ungen über die Eignung verschiedener Methoden zur Klärung
        der Pathogenese der Sterilität" [Childlessness in North
        Sumatra: studies on the suitability of various methods
        for clarifying the pathogenesis of sterility]. Inaugural
        Dissertation, Freie-Universität Berlin, 1969, 81 pp.

1057   ISKANDAR, N. "Sex Preference of Children and Contraceptive
        Use by Women Wanting No More Children in Jakarta, 1968."
        Majalah Demografi Indonesia 1, no. 1 (June 1974):7-20.

1058   _____. When Z.P.G. in Indonesia? Jakarta: Fakultas Ekonomi,
        Lembaga Demografi, Universitas Indonesia, 1974, 27 pp.

1059   ISKANDAR, N., and JONES, GAVIN WALLIS. "Effect of Infant and
        Child Mortality in Subsequent Fertility in Indonesia."
        Majalah Demografi Indonesia 4, no. 7 (1977):1-24.

1060   ISKANDAR, NUR SUTAN. Beberapa Proyeksi Penduduk untuk
        Indonesia Menurut Pulau-pulau Utama, 1971-2001 [Some
        population projections for Indonesia according to major
        islands, 1971-2001]. Jakarta: Lembaga Demografi, Fakul-
        tas Ekonomi, Universitas Indonesia, 1976, 33 pp.

1061   ISMAN, SUNTORO. "Peningkatan Pendidikan dan Partisipasi
        Kerja Wanita dalam Usaha Penurunan Fertilitas: Sebuah
        Tinjauan Peranan Pendidikan dan Peranan Wanita dalam
        Masyarakat yang Sedang Berkembang" [Upgrading educational
        levels and female employment in the effort to reduce fer-
        tility: a survey of the role of education and women in a

developing society]. Jakarta: Fakultas Ekonomi, Universitas Indonesia, 1975, 13 pp.

1062 JONES, GAVIN WALLIS. "Fertility Levels and Trends in
Indonesia." Population Studies 13, no. 1 (Mar. 1977):
29-41.

1063 JUNUS, ETTY; SOETEDJO M.; and CLINTON, J. JARRETT. Indonesian
National Family Planning Service Statistics: The System
and First Year Results. Jakarta: National Family Planning
Coordinating Board, 1972, 21 pp. Technical Report Series,
Monograph, no. 1.

1064 JUNUS, ETTY et al., eds. Growth and Development of the Indonesian National Family Planning Program Data System.
Jakarta: National Family Planning Coordinating Board,
1973, 19 pp. Technical Report Series, Monograph, no. 2.

1065 KIMIN, M. BASIR. "Masalah Kelahiran dalam Hubungannya dengan
Pendidikan Daerah Sumatera Selatan" [The birth problem in
connection with education in the region of South Sumatra].
Ekonomi [Jakarta] 10, no. 1 (1972):109-13.

1066 KOMALIG, ASKE THEO. The Relationship of Socio-Economic Factors with Fertility and Attitudes towards Family Planning
in North Sulawesi. Singapore: Southeast Asia Population
Research Awards Program (SEAPRAP), International Development Research Centre, Asia Regional Office, 1975, 45 pp.

1067 "Kumpulan Keputusan/Instruksi Menteri Dalam Negeri dan
Instansi Pusat Lainnya tentang Pola Operasi Pembinaan
Kesejahteraan Keluarga, Pelaksanaan Keluarga Berencana,
Pembinaan/Bimbingan/Perlindungan Koperasi dan Pelaksanaan
Badan Usaha Unit Desa" [Collected decisions/instructions of
the Minister of Internal Affairs and other centers with regard to the mode of operation, development, implementation,
cooperative development and guidance of family welfare, and
planning of the rural unit]. Dihimpun oleh Pusat Pendidikan, guna kepentingan badan-badan pendidikan, Departemen
Dalam Negeri. Jakarta, 1973, 19, 24 pp.

1068 KOESNOE, MUHAMMAD. Kedudukan Wanita menurut Adat Beberapa
Masyarakat Pedesaan Madura (Dihubungkan dengan Persoalan
Keluarga Berencana [The status of women according to
various customary laws in rural Madura (relating to the
problems of family planning]. Surabaya: BKKBN Pusat,
1975, 109 pp.

1069 _____. Peranan Adat dalam Proses Mengambil Keputusan Menjadi
Perserta dalam Keluarga Berencana dalam Masyarakat Pedesaan
[The role of 'adat' in the process of deciding whether to

participate in family planning in a rural community].
Jakarta: Badan Koordinasi Keluarga Berencana Nasional,
1972, 10 pp.

1070 _____. "Persoalan Keluarga Berencana dan Adat di Jatim"
[Family planning and 'adat' di Jatim]. Surabaya: Pusat
Penelitian, Universitas Airlangga, 1972, 14 pp.

1071 "Law and Population in Indonesia: Country Report." In
SOUTHEAST ASIAN REGIONAL SEMINAR ON LAW AND POPULATION,
Jakarta, 1975. Law and Population. Edited by Teuku
Mohamed Radhie et al. Jakarta: Yayasan Penelitian dan
Pengembangan Hukum, 1976, pp. 106-19. (Includes discussion
of laws on family planning, marriage, and inheritance.)

1072 LEMBAGA KESEHATAN NASIONAL. Identifikasi Acceptor2 Baru
Keluarga Berentjana Kotamadya Surabaja [Identification of
new acceptors of family planning in Kotamadya Surabaja].
Jakarta: Lembaga Keluarga Berentjana Nasional, 1970,
32 pp.

1073 LOKAKARYA NASIONAL UNTUK MENELAAH PENELITIAN MENGENAI KEGIATAN
DUKUN BAYI YANG ADA HUBUNGANNYA DENGAN KESEHATAN IBU DAN
ANAK DAN KELUARGA BERENCANA, Jakarta, 1972. The Role of
the Traditional Midwife in the Family Planning Program.
Report of the National Workshop to Review Researches into
Dukun Activities Related to M.C.H. Care and Family Planning
Program. Organized by the Department of Health, Republic
of Indonesia. Jakarta[?], 1972. 83 pp.

1074 LOKAKARYA PENELITIAN KEPENDUDUKAN, Jogjakarta, 1976. Kertas2
Kerja [Workshop on Population Study, Jogjakarta, 1976.
Working papers]. Disusun oleh Masri Singarimbun, Terence
H. Hull dan Rufin Kedang. Jogjakarta: Lembaga Pendudukan,
Universitas Gadjah Mada, 1976, 114 pp. Universitas Gadjah
Mada, Lembaga Kependudukan. Seri laporan, no. 11.

1075 LOKAKARYA TEKNIK ANALISA STATISTIK KELUARGA BERENCANA DI
INDONESIA, Jogjakarta, 1978. Kumpulan Kertas Kerja [Work-
shop on the Technique of Statistical Analysis for Family
Planning in Indonesia, Jogjakarta, 1978. Collection of
working papers]. Disusun oleh Ignatius Slamet et al.
Jogjakarta: Lembaga Kependudukan, Universitas Gadjah Mada,
1978, xi, 196 pp. Universitas Gadjah Mada, Lembaga
Kependudukan. Seri Kertas Kerja Lokakarya, no. 3.

1076 LUBIS, FIRMAN; NIEHOF, ANKE; and ASTUTI, PUDJI. The Traditional Midwife in the Kecamatan Serpong: The Dukun Bayi
Survey June 1973. Leiden: Institute of Cultural and Social Studies, Leyden State University, 1973, 33, 13 pp.
Family Planning Project Serpong, Indonesia. Serpong Paper,
no. 5.

1077 LUBIS, FIRMAN et al. <u>General Health Services and Mother and</u>
      <u>Child Health Care in the Clinic of the Family Planning</u>
      <u>Project Serpong</u>. Leiden: Institute of Cultural and Social
      Studies, Leyden State University, 1972. Family Planning
      Project Serpong, Indonesia. Serpong Paper, no. 4.

1078 _____. <u>Report of the Course for Traditional Midwives in the</u>
      <u>Kecamatan Serpong</u>. Leiden: Institute of Cultural and So-
      cial Studies, Leyden State University, 1974. v, 32, 5 pp.
      Family Planning Project Serpong, Indonesia. Serpong Paper,
      no. 14.

1079 McDONALD, PETER F.; YASIN, MUHAMMAD; and JONES, GAVIN WALLIS.
      <u>Levels and Trends in Fertility and Childhood Mortality in</u>
      <u>Indonesia</u>. Jakarta: Lembaga Demografi, Fakultas Ekonomi,
      Universitas Indonesia, 1976, ix, 79 pp.

1080 MANDERSON, LENORE. <u>Overpopulation in Java: Problems and Re-</u>
      <u>actions</u>. Canberra: Department of Demography, Australian
      National University, 1974, 131 pp.

1081 MARTIONO, KOEN (Mrs.) "Kesejahteraan Ibu dan Anak dan
      Keluarga Berencana Tak Dapat Dipisahkan Satu Sama Lain"
      [Maternal and child welfare and family planning are inter-
      related]. <u>Kesehatan Masyarakat</u>, 1, no. 3 (1971):30-36.

1082 MARTIONO, KOEN S. <u>Four Years of Contraceptive Service in</u>
      <u>Jakarta, 1968-1971</u>. Jakarta: Bureau of Reporting and
      Documentation, National Family Planning Coordinating
      Board, 1973, 28 pp.

1083 MEIER, GITTA. "Family Planning in the Banjars of Bali."
      <u>International Family Planning Perspectives and Digest</u> 5,
      no. 2 (June 1979):63-66.

1084 MEYER, PAUL A.; SINGARIMBUN, MASRI; and HULL, TERENCE H.
      "Measures of Family Planning Acceptance in West Java and
      Central Java." <u>Majalah Demografi Indonesia</u> 9 (June 1978):
      93-101.

1085 MUDJIMAN, HARIS. <u>Lack of Interest in Family Planning Informa-</u>
      <u>tion among the Urban People of Surakarta</u>. Singapore:
      Southeast Asia Population Research Awards Program (SEAPRAP),
      International Development Research Centre and Ford Founda-
      tion, 1977, 36 pp. SEAPRAP Research Report, no. 12.

1086 MUHARDJONO. "Uraian ka LKB ABRI dalam Rapat Kerdja Terbatas
      PUSKES ABRI: Penjempurnaan Pelaksanaan Keluarga Berentjana
      ABRI" [Statement of the head of the Armed Forces Family
      Planning Program issued by the Workshop on the Armed Forces
      Health Center concerning progress in the practice of family

planning in the Armed Forces]. Majalah Kesehatan ABRI, 3 no. 7 (1971):28–37.

1087 MOELJODIHARDJO, SOETEDJO, and CLINTON J. JARRETT. Contraceptive Trends in Indonesia's Developing Family Planning Program, 1972-1973. Jakarta: National Family Planning Coordinating Board, 1973, 25 pp. Technical Report Series, Monograph, no. 5.

1088 MOELJODIHARDJO, SOETEDJO, and PARSONS, J.S. Trends in Achievements in the Indonesia Family Planning Program. Jakarta: National Family Planning Coordinating Board, 1977, 31 pp.

1089 MUNIR, ROZY. Cermin Mahasiswa-mahasiswa Baru Universitas Indonesia pada Awal Tahun 1974 tentang Pengetahuan dan Sikap terhadap Masalah Kependudukan dan Keluarga Berencana [Views of new students of the University of Indonesia at the beginning of 1974 on knowledge and atttitude towards population problems and family planning]. Jakarta: Lembaga Demografi, Fakultas Ekonomi, Universitas Indonesia, 1975, iv, 20 pp.

1090 NARENDA, NGURAH Ida Bagus. "Bali: Her Population Estimation from 1971 to 2001 and its Implication to Family Planning." Master's thesis, University of Singapore, 1974, 68 pp.

1091 NASUTION, A. HAMZAH. Repelita: Keluarga Berentjana, Keluarga Sedjahtera [Guidance: family planning, a happy family]. Jakarta: Panto Teungku, 1969, 101 pp.

1092 NIEHOF, ANKE. Fertility in Kecamatan Serpong. Leiden: Institute of Cultural and Social Studies, Leyden State University, 1974, ii, 28, 3 pp. Family Planning Project Serpong, Indonesia. Serpong Paper, no. 6.

1093 _____. "Fertility in Serpong, West Java: A Base Line Study." Majalah Demografi Indonesia 1, no. 2 (Dec. 1974):162–87.

1094 NIEHOF, ANKE, and HASYIR, ANIDAL. The Traditional Midwife as a Motivator for Family Planning. Leiden: Institute of Cultural and Social Studies, Leyden State University, 1975, x, 100, xxxi pp. Family Planning Project Serpong, Indonesia. Serpong Paper, no. 25.

1095 NOTOSOEDIRDJO, MOELJONO. "The Attitude of the Pregnant Javanese towards Their Pregnancies: An Approach to the Study of Abortion in Indonesia." Majalah Kesehatan Jiwa 2, no. 1 (1976):3–12.

1096   OEY, MAYLING. "Differential Fertility among Female-Centered
       Social Groups in Indonesia, 1971." Majalah Demografi
       Indonesia 1, no. 2 (Dec. 1974):46-69.

1097   OKA, I. GUSTI AGUNG. Bertentangankah Keluarga Berencana
       menurut Pandangan Agama Hindu [Family planning according to
       the Hindu point of view]. Denpasar: Parisada Hindu Dharma
       Pusat, 1971[?], 25 pp.

1098   PANITYA ADHOC KELUARGA BERENCANA. Pandangan Agama terhadap
       "Keluarga Berentjana" [Religious view of family planning].
       Jakarta: Pertj. Hidajah, 1968[?], 58 pp.

1099   PANOEDJOE. "Keluarga Berentjana dalam Rangka Penbangunan
       Nasional" [Family planning in national development].
       Majalah Kesehatan ABRI 3, no. 7 (1971):14-26.

1100   PAPANEK, HANNA et al. "Wanita di Jakarta: Kehidupan Keluarga
       dan Keluarga Berencana" [Women in Jakarta: family life and
       family planning]. Masyarakat Indonesia 5, no. 2 (Dec.
       1978):217-59.

1101   _____. "Women in Jakarta: Family Life and Family Planning."
       In Cultural Factors and Population in Developing Countries,
       Washington, D.C.: Smithsonian Institution, Interdisci-
       plinary Communications Program, 1976. pp. 129-66.
       Occasional Monograph, no. 6.

1102   PARDOKO, R.H. Factors Influencing the Preference of Family
       Planning Method in East Java. Surabaya: National Insti-
       tute of Public Health and Teachers College Surabaya, 1973,
       26 pp. National Institute of Public Health. Research Re-
       port Series, no. 25.

1103   PARDOKO, R.H.; DWIDJOSEPUTRO, D.; and SOEPARMANTO, P. The
       Behaviour of Women after the Acceptance of Family Planning:
       A Study in East Java. Surabaya: National Institute of
       Public Health, 1973. 76 pp. National Institute of Public
       Health. Research Report Series, no. 30.

1104   PARDOKO, R.H., and SOEMARTONO. The Integration of Family
       Planning within the Maternal and Child Health Services:
       An Operational Study in East Java. Surabaya: Lembaga
       Kesehatan National Surabaya, 1974, 92 pp.

1105   PARDOKO, R.H., and SOEROSO, Z. Fertility of Indonesian Women
       in Surabaja Municipality. Surabaya: BKKBN, 1971, 34,
       8 pp.

1106   PERKUMPULAN KELUARGA BERENCANA INDONESIA. Aspek2 Hukum dalam
        Keluarga Berentjana [Legal aspects of family planning].
        Jakarta: Perkumpulan Keluarga Berentjana Indonesia, 1971,
        ii, 92 pp.

1107   _____. Draft Report of the KAP Survey: Knowledge, Attitudes,
        and Practices of Family Planning. Jakarta: Perkumpulan
        Keluarga Berentjana Indonesia, 1968, 72, 34 pp.

1108   _____. Facts and Figures. Jakarta: Perkumpulan Keluarga
        Berentjana Indonesia, 1972.

1109   _____. Family Law and Fertility in Indonesia. A Study Con-
        ducted by the Indonesian Planned Parenthood Association in
        Cooperation with the Brawijaya University in Malang.
        Jakarta: Perkumpulan Keluarga Berentjana Indonesia, 1978,
        125 pp.

1110   _____. Hasil-hasil Penelitian Pengetahuan--Sikap--Praktek
        Keluarga Berentjana Kabupaten Bekasi, 1967. [Results of
        the survey on knowledge, attitudes, and practice of family
        planning, Kabupaten Bekasi, 1967]. Jakarta: Perkumpulan
        Keluarga Berentjana Indonesia, 1969, iii, 69 pp.

1111   _____. Hasil Survey Evaluasi Mass Media Dibeberapa Wilajah di
        Djakarta-Raya [Results of the mass media evaluative survey
        in several districts in Jakarta-Raya]. Jakarta:
        Perkumpulan Keluarga Berentjana Indonesia, 1970, 1 vol.
        (various pagings).

1112   _____. Legal Aspects of Family Planning in Indonesia.
        Medford, Mass.: Fletcher School of Law and Diplomacy,
        Tufts University, 1971, 35, 12 pp.

1113   _____. Naskah Kongress ke-1, Djakarta, February, 1967 [First
        Congress copy, Jakarta, February, 1967]. Jakarta:
        Perkumpulan Keluarga Berentjana Indonesia, 1970, 275 pp.

1114   _____. Penelitian Pengetahuan, Sikap, Praktek Keluarga
        Berentjana Djakarta, 1968: Laporan Metodologi [A study of
        knowledge, attitude, and practice of family planning,
        Jakarta, 1968: report of methodology]. Jakarta:
        Perkumpulan Keluarga Berentjana Indonesia, 1970, 1 vol.
        (various pagings).

1115   _____. PKBI, 1970-1972. Jakarta: Perkumpulan Keluarga
        Berentjana Indonesia, 1973, 96 pp.

1116 _____. Research on the Attitude of Medical Practitioners in Jakarta Raya towards the Family Planning Program, October 1971. Jakarta: Indonesian Planned Parenthood Association, 1973, 63 pp.

1117 POSTMA, PETRONELLA A. "Djakarta and Family Planning." Review of Southeast Asian Studies 1, pt. 3 (1971):24-44.

1118 PURBANGKORO, MURDIYANTO. Evaluation of Family Planning Program in East Java. Singapore: Southeast Asia Population Research Awards Program (SEAPRAP), International Development Research Centre, Asia Regional Office, and Ford Foundation, 1975, ii, 50 pp. SEAPRAP Research Report, no. 4.

1119 _____. The Special Drive in Java: An Evaluation of an Indonesian Family Planning Program Intensive Campaign. Jember, Indonesia: Jember University, 1978, 73 pp.

1120 POERNOMO, BAMBANG. "Keluarga Berencana Ditinjau dari Aspek Hukum Pidana" [Family planning viewed from the aspect of criminal law]. Hukum Nasional 7, no. 23 (1974):34-52.

1121 PURWODIHARDJO, SUBAGIO. Keluarga Berentjana sebagai Unsur Penting dalam Usaha Kesedjahteraan Ibu dan Anak [Family planning as an important factor in maternal and child health]. Jakarta: Biro Penerangan dan Motivasi, Badan Koordinasi Keluarga Berentjana Nasional, 1971, 22 pp.

1122 RACHIM, ANGGARA A., and SALEA, GERARDUS. Peningkatan Program keluarga Berencana melalui Motivator didalam Masyarakat [Improving the family planning progam through motivating society]. Jakarta: Fakultas Kesehatan Masyarakat, Universitas Indonesia, 1974, 80 pp.

1123 RAHARDJO, PUDJO. "Population and Health: A Study of the Relationship between Health Delivery Activities and Contraceptive Acceptance in Indonesia." Ph.D. dissertation, University of Pittsburgh, 1977, 233 pp. Abstracted in Dissertation Abstracts International 38, no. 6 (Dec. 1977): 3760-A. University Microfilms International, order no. 77-21,207.

1124 RAHARDJO, PUDJO, and REESE, THOMAS H. Indonesian National Family Planning Service Statistics: A Cost-Effectiveness Analysis. Jakarta: National Family Planning Coordinating Board, 1972, 14 pp. Technical Reports Series, Monograph no. 3.

1125   RAMLI, AHMAD. "Abortus Ditinjau dari Segi Agama Islam"
        [Abortion viewed from the Muslim religion]. Majalah
        Kedokteran Indonesia 15, nos. 11/12 (1965):525-31.

1126   REDMANA, HAN ROCHANDI. Beberapa Persoalan Penduduk di
        Indonesia [Population problems in Indonesia]. Jakarta:
        Lembaga Ilmu Pengetahuan Indonesia and Lembaga Ekonomi dan
        Kemasjarakatan Nasional, 1970, 101 pp.

1127   ROGERS, EVERETT M. A Field Study of Family Planning Incen-
        tives and Field Staff in Indonesia. With the assistance of
        a field study committee. Jakarta: Indonesian Planned
        Parenthood Association, 1971, 2, xiii, 95, A23 pp.

1128   RUSHWAN, H. et al. "Contraceptive Practice after Women Have
        Undergone 'Spontaneous' Abortion in Indonesia and Sudan."
        International Journal of Gynaecology and Obstetrics 15
        (1977):241-49.

1129   SALIM, AGUS. Fertilitas dan Pengetahuan Sikap dan Praktek
        Keluarga Berencana di Tiga Desa di Aceh Utara [Fertility
        and knowledge and the attitude and practice of family
        planning in three villages in Aceh Utara]. Banda Aceh,
        Indonesia: Lembaga Demografi, Fakultas Ekonomi, Universi-
        tas Syiah Kuala, 1976, ix, 84 pp.

1130   SASTROAMIDJOJO, ACHMAD SENO. Membina Keluarga Bahagia [Build-
        ing a happy family]. Jakarta: Kinta, 1967[?], 201 pp.

1131   SEMINAR HUKUM DAN KEPENDUDUKAN, Jakarta, 1974. Laporan
        [Seminar on Law and Population, Jakarta, 1974. Report].
        Disusun oleh Nani Soewondo. Sponsored by Perkumpulan
        Keluarga Berencana Indonesia, Fakultas Hukum, Universitas
        Indonesia and United Nations Fund for Population Activities.
        Jakarta: Pusat Latihan dan Penelitian Nasional, Perkumpulan
        Keluarga Berencana Indonesia, 1974, 94 pp.

1132   SEMINAR PEMUDA DAN FAMILY PLANNING, Pasarminggu, Indonesia,
        1969. Sambutan dan Prasaran [Seminar on Youth and Family
        Planning, Pasarminggu, Indonesia, 1969. Proceedings].
        Jakarta: Komite Nasional Madjlis Pemuda Sedunia (WAY) di
        Indonesia, 1969, 112 pp.

1133   SEMINAR PERANAN PEMUDA DALAM KELUARGA BERENCANA, Purwokerto,
        Indonesia, 1976. Laporan dan Kertas2 Kerja [Seminar on the
        Role of Youth in Family Planning, Purwokerto, Indonesia,
        1976. Report and working papers]. Organized by Fakultas
        Ekonomi, Universitas Negeri Jendral Soedirman and BKKBN
        Kapubaten Banyumas, 19-20 March 1976. Purworkerto:
        Fakultas Ekonomi, Universitas Negeri Jendral Soedirman,
        1976, 1 vol. (various pagings).

1134   SEMINAR TENTANG KEDUDKAN WANITA DAN KELUARGA BERENCANA,
       Jakarta, 1973 [Seminar on the Status of Women and Family
       Planning, Jakarta, 1973]. Diselenggarakan oleh Komisi
       Nasional Kedudukan Wanita Indonesia, Kongres Wanita Indo-
       nesia and Koordinasi Wanita Golkar Pusat. Jakarta, 1973,
       1 vol. (various pagings).

1135   SEMINAR UNTUK PEMBERANTASAN BUTAHURUF FUNGSIONIL YANG
       DITERAPKAN PADA PENDIDIKAN KEPENDUDUKAN DAN KELUARGA
       BERENCANA, Lembang, Indonesia, 1973. Laporan [Seminar on
       the Eradication of Functional Illiteracy in Population
       Education and Family Planning, Lembang, Indonesia, 1973.
       Report]. Jakarta: Departemen Pendidikan dan Kebudayaan,
       1973, 1 vol. (various pagings).

1136   SETIADI, BERNADETTE N. Relationship between Several Socio-
       Psychological Variables and the Decision to Follow the
       Family Planning Program. Singapore: Southeast Asia Popu-
       lation Research Awards Program, International Development
       Research Centre and Ford Foundation, 1977, 44, 13 pp.
       SEAPRAP Research Reports, no. 18.

1137   SIGIT, HANANTO. "Demographic Change, Consumption Patterns and
       Planned Income Growth: A Two-sector Study of the Economic
       Consequence of Alternative Fertility Reductions in Indo-
       nesia." Ph.D. dissertation, University of Hawaii, 1975,
       xiv, 266 pp.

1138   SIMPOSIUM ABORTUS, 2d, Surabaya, 1973. Kumpulan Naskah-naskah
       Ilmiah dalam Simposium Abortus di Surabaya, Tanggal
       2 Agustus 1973 [Symposium on Abortion, 2d, Surabaya, 1973.
       Collection of papers from the Symposium on Abortion in
       Surabaya, 2 August 1973]. Jakarta: Bahagian Penerbitan
       dan Perpustakaan Biro V, Departemen Kesehatan, 1974, 128 pp.

1139   SIMPOSIUM KONTRASEPSI, Bandung, Indonesia, 1967. Kontrasepsi
       [Symposium on Contraception, Bandung, Indonesia, 1967.
       Contraception]. Bandung: Madjalah Kedokteran Bandung,
       1976, 150 pp.

1140   SINGARIMBUN, MASRI. "Family Planning in Indonesia." Bulletin
       of Indonesian Economic Studies, no. 10 (June 1968):48-55.

1141   _____. "Status dan Persepsi Wanita terhadap Masalah Kepen-
       dudukan" [Status and perception of women towards population
       problems]. Prisma 4, no. 5 (Oct. 1975):19-24.

1142   _____. "Two Old Contraceptive Practices, Coitus Interruptus
       and Abstinence, and Their Relationship with New Contracep-
       tive Practices in Two Indonesian Societies." Berita Kajian
       Sumatera 3, no. 2 (May 1974):35-38. (On the Karo Batak and
       the Javanese.)

1143   SINGARIMBUN, MASRI; DARROCH, RUSSELL K.; and MEYER, PAUL A.
       Value of Children: A Study in Java; Preliminary Tabula-
       tions from the Indonesian Value of Children Survey. Nilai
       Anak: Hasil Penelitian di Jawa; Tabulasi Pendahuluan dari
       Survey Nilai Anak di Indonesia. Jogjakarta: Population
       Institute, Gadjah Mada University, 1977, xxxvi, 146 pp.
       Universitas Gadjah Mada, Lembaga Kependudukan. Seri
       Laporan, no. 13.

1144   SINGARIMBUN, MASRI, and HULL, TERENCE H. Social Responses to
       High Mortality Which Act to Support High Fertility.
       Jogjakarta: Population Institute, Gadjah Mada University,
       1977, 30 pp. Universitas Gadjah Mada, Lembaga Kependudu-
       kan. Working Paper Series, no. 10.

1145   SINGARIMBUN, MASRI; HULL, TERENCE H.; and MEYER, PAUL A.
       "Measures of Family Planning Acceptance in West Java and
       Central Java: Preliminary Results of the Indonesian Value
       of Children Survey." Majalah Demografi Indonesia 5, no. 9
       (June 1978):93-101.

1146   SINGARIMBUN, MASRI, and MANNING, CHRIS. "Beberapa Catatan
       tentang Pengetahuan, Sikap dan Praktek Keluarga Berencana
       di Mojolama dan Kedungiri" [Some notes on the knowledge,
       attitude, and practice of family planning in Mojolama and
       Kedungiri]. Majalah Demografi Indonesia 1, no. 2 (1974):
       70-88.

1147   _____. Fertility and Family Planning in Mojolama.
       Jogjakarta: Institute of Population Studies, Gadjah
       Mada University, 1974, viii, 171 pp.

1148   _____. "Keluarga Berencana, Motivasi dan Pola Sosial-Ekonomi:
       Kasus Mojolama" [Family planning, motivation, and socio--
       economic pattern: the case of Mojolama]. Prisma 3, no 2
       (1974):31-43.

1149   SINGARIMBUN, MASRI et al. Penelitian Vasektomi [Study on
       Vasectomy]. Jogjakarta: Lembaga Kependudukan, Universi-
       tas Gadjah Mada dan Bethesda Hospital, 1976, vi, 31 pp.
       Universitas Gadjah Mada, Lembaga Kependudukan. Seri
       Laporan, no. 2.

1150   SINGQUEFIELD, JEANNE CAIRNS. "Estimating Fertility from Data
       on Current Pregnancy Status of Women." Majalah Demografi
       Indonesia 5, no. 10 (Dec. 1978):25-39.

1151   SINQUEFIELD, JEANNE CAIRNS, and JONES, GAVIN WALLIS. "The
       Validity of Family Planning Statistics: A Comment."
       Bulletin of Indonesian Economic Studies 12, no. 3 (Nov.
       1976):95-99.

1152   SINQUEFIELD, JEANNE CAIRNS, and SUNGKONO, BAMBANG. "Fertility
        and Family Planning Trends in Java and Bali." Inter-
        national Family Planning Perspectives and Digest 5, no. 2
        (June 1979):43-58.

1153   SISDJIATMO, KUSUMOSUWIDHO; JASIN, MUHAMMAD; and MUNIR, ROZY.
        Beberapa Perubahan Demografis pada Keadaan dan Komposisi
        Penduduk: Wanita Indonesia; selama Dasawarsa antar Sensus
        1961-1971 [Demographic changes regarding the position and
        composition of the population: Indonesian women; 1961-
        1971]. Jakarta: Lembaga Demografi, Fakultas Ekonomi,
        Universitas Indonesia, 1975, 86 pp.

1154   Situation Report. New York: ERIC, 1975, 31 pp. (Family
        planning in Indonesia and Philippines.)

1155   SONTOSUDARMO, ALIP. "Some Estimation of Fertility and Mor-
        tality in Yogyakarta Special Region." Indonesian Journal
        of Geography 6, no. 32 (Dec. 1976):41-48.

1156   SRI DJUARINI, and SUDIBYO. Proyek Akseptor Mantap sebagai
        Motivator di Kecamatan Samigaluh, Kulon Progo, Yogyakarta
        [Acceptor project on motivation at Kecamatan Samigaluh,
        Kulon Progo, Jogjakarta]. Jakarta: Perkumpulan Keluarga
        Berencana Indonesia, Pusat Latihan & Penelitian Nasional,
        1976, 46 pp.

1157   SOEBANDI. Social and Economic Influence on Family Size in the
        District of Malang, East Java. Singapore: Southeast Asia
        Population Research Awards Program (SEAPRAP), International
        Development Research Centre and Ford Foundation, 1977, ii,
        66 pp. SEAPRAP Research Report, no. 15.

1158   SUDIBYO. "Saya Melihat Ibu-ibu Perkebunan Ber-K.B." [Family
        planning used by mothers on plantations]. Keluarga
        Berentjana, no. 29 (1974):29-31.

1159   SUHARSO. "Tingkat Pendidikan dan Kesuburan Ibu" [Educational
        level and fertility]. Dokumentasi LEKNAS 3 (1970):28-33.

1160   SUHARTO, SAM, and CHO, LEE JAY. Preliminary Estimates of
        Indonesian Fertility Based on the 1976 Inter-Censal Popula-
        tion Survey. Honolulu: East-West Center, 1978, vi, 21 pp.
        East-West Population Institute. Papers, no. 52. Paper
        presented at the Conference on Comparative Fertility Tran-
        sition in Asia, Tokyo, March 1978.

1161   SOEJATNI. "Rôle et participation des femmes dans la planifi-
        cation des naissances" [The role and participation of women
        in family planning]. Archipel, no. 13 (1977):295-306.

1162   SOEKARTO, ADI, and HULL, TERENCE H. Perilaku Keluarga Beren-
        cana: Sebuah Studi Perbandingan Kelompok PKAK dan Non PKAK
        di Yogyakarta [Family planning behavior: a comparative
        study between PKAK and non-PKAK groups in Jogjakarta].
        Jogjakarta: Lembaga Kependudukan, Universitas Gadjah Mada,
        1977, v, 59 pp. Universitas Gadjah Mada, Lembaga Kepen-
        dudukan. Seri Laporan, no. 14.

1163   SUKOTO, L., and SOSROSUMARTO, NJ. B. KWARI. Keluarga Beren-
        tjana dalam Dunia Katolik di Indonesia [Family planning
        among Catholics in Indonesia]. Jakarta: Badan Koordinasi
        Keluarga Berentjana Nasional, Biro Penerangan dan Motivasi,
        1972, 39 pp.

1164   SUMAPRAJA, SUDRAJI, and SAIFUDDIN, A. BARI. "Angket Kontra-
        sepsi, Sterilisasi, Abortus, dan Sex Education." [Ques-
        tionnaire on contraception, sterlization, abortion, and
        sex education]. Majalah Obstetri dan Ginekologi Indonesia
        1, no. 2 (1974):142-52.

1165   SUMARDJAN, SELO. "Kedudukan Bidan di dalam Masyarakat
        Indonesia" [The position of midwives in the Indonesian
        community]. Keluarga Sejahtera 1, no. 1 (1969):41-47.

1166   SOEMARTONO, ROEKMIATI. "Persoalan Birth Control untuk
        Masjarakat Indonesia" [The issue of birth control for the
        Indonesian society]. Redjeki Surabaja: n.p., 1960, 48 pp.

1167   SURJANINGRAT, SUWARDJONO. "Indonesia." Studies in Family
        Planning 6, no. 8 (Aug. 1975):222-25. (On family planning
        programs in 1974.)

1168   _____. Latar Belakang Program Nasional Keluarga Berentjana di
        Indonesia [The background of the national family planning
        program in Indonesia]. Jakarta: Biro Penerangan Motivasi,
        Badan Koordinasi Keluarga Berentjana Nasional, 1971, 19 pp.

1169   _____. Masalah Kependudukan dan Pelaksanaan Keluarga Beren-
        cana di Indonesia [Population problems and implementation
        of family planning in Indonesia]. Jakarta: Badan Koordi-
        nasi Keluarga Berencana Nasional, Biro Penerangan dan
        Motivasi, 1972, 24 pp. Seri MD-Badan Koordinasi Keluarga
        Berencana Nasional, Biro Penergangan dan Motivasi, 5/1972.

1170   _____. Peranan Kaum Ibu [The role of women]. Jakarta: Badan
        Koordinasi Keluarga Berencana Nasional, 1972, 11 pp.

1171   SUTADIWIRIA, DJAKA. "Keluarga Berencana Perlu Dilaksanakan
        oleh Keluarga Prajurit" [Family planning should be prac-
        ticed by the soldier's family]. Karya Wira Jati, no. 35
        (1972):48-59.

1172   SOETEDJO, M., and CLINTON, J. JARRETT. <u>Contraceptive Use in</u>
        <u>1974-1975: The Indonesian National Family Planning Pro-</u>
        <u>gram</u>. Jakarta: National Family Planning Coordinating
        Board, 1976, 32 pp. National Family Planning Coordinating
        Board, Indonesia. Technical Report Series, Monograph,
        no. 12.

1173   SOEWONDO, NANI, ed. <u>Law and Population in Indonesia</u>. Com-
        piled by the IPPA Committee on Law and Population. Spon-
        sored by the U.N. Fund for Population Activities. Jakarta:
        National Training and Research Centre for Family Planning,
        IPPA, 1974, v, 155 pp.

1174   SOEWONDO, NANI; DJOEWARI, O.; and RYDER, BROOKS. "Population
        and Family Planning in Indonesia: Preliminary Report."
        Jakarta: 1970, 28 pp.

1175   SUYONO, HARYONO. "The Adoption of an Innovation in a Develop-
        ing Country: The Case of Family Planning in Indonesia."
        Ph.D. dissertation, University of Chicago, 1972, viii,
        112 pp.

1176   _____. <u>Religious Differential Fertility of Jakarta Women: An</u>
        <u>Exploratory Study</u>. Jakarta: Biro Pusat Statistik, 1974,
        38 pp.

1177   TALOGO, R.W. "The Attitude of Pregnant Females on Family
        Planning." <u>Paediatrica Indonesiana</u> (Apr./June 1966):
        101-108.

1178   TAN, MELY GIOK LAN. <u>Causes and Consequences of Population</u>
        <u>Explosion</u>. Jakarta: Lembaga Ekonomi dan Kemasyarakatan
        Nasional, 1973, 18 pp. (On birth control.)

1179   _____. "Hubungan Sosial dan Kebudayaan dengan Keluarga
        Berencana" [The social and cultural context of family
        planning in Indonesia]. <u>Indonesia Magazine</u>, no. 17
        (1973):25-28, 43-50.

1180   _____. <u>The Social and Cultural Context of Family Planning in</u>
        <u>Indonesia</u>. Jakarta: National Institute of Economic and
        Social Research (LEKNAS) Population Studies Center, 1971,
        34 pp.

1181   TANNY, JACQUELINE B., comp. <u>Family Planning Approaches in</u>
        <u>Indonesia, Derived from the Indonesian Periodical Press</u>.
        Honolulu: East-West Center, 1969, 43 pp. Hawaii Univer-
        sity, East-West Center, Institute of Advanced Projects.
        Occasional Papers of Research Publications and Transla-
        tions, Translation Series, no. 34.

1182   TEACHMAN, JAY D., and RAHARDJO, PUDJO. "Contraceptive Deliv-
       ery Systems: An Evaluation of Clinic vs. Village in
       Indonesia." Evaluation Review 4 (Feb. 1980):75-92.

1183   _____. "Contraceptive Use in the Indonesian Village Distribu-
       tion System: Continuation and Effectiveness." Inter-
       national Family Planning Perspectives and Digest 5, no. 2
       (June 1979):66-72.

1184   THOMAS, R. MURRAY. "Attitudes towards Birth Control in
       Bandung, Indonesia." Indonesia [Ithaca, N.Y.], no. 4
       (Oct. 1967):74-87.

1185   TITUS, M.J. Differential Fertility and Mortality in Djakarta
       Raya, Indonesia: A Socio-Spatial Analysis of the 1961
       Census Based on the Demographic Transition Model. Utrecht:
       afd. Sociale Geografie Ontwikkelingslanden, Geografisch
       Instituut, Universiteit Utrecht, 1972, 47 pp. Bulletin
       sociale geografie ontwikkelingslanden. Serie 2, no. 2,
       Dec. 1972.

1186   TRISNAMANSYAH, SUTARYAT. The Effects of Socio-Cultural and
       Socio-Economic Factors on Fertility and Family Planning in
       the Rural District of West Java. Singapore: Southeast
       Asia Population Research Awards Program (SEAPRAP), Inter-
       national Development Research Centre and Ford Foundation,
       1976, iv, 152 pp. SEAPRAP Research Report, no. 7.

1187   UNIVERSITAS DIPONEGORO, Pusat Studi Kependudukan. Laporan
       Penelitian Pengetahuan, Sikap, Praktek Keluarga Berencana
       Tenaga Kerja Wanita Pabrik Rokok Kudus, 1975 [Report of a
       study of women workers in the cigarette industry and their
       knowledge of, attitudes to, and practice of family plan-
       ning in Kudus Regency, 1975]. Kerjasama antara Pusat Studi
       Kependudukan, Pusat Riset dan Pengembangan, Universitas
       Diponegoro, Semarang, dengan Badan Koordinasi Keluarga
       Berencana Nasional, Propinsi Jawa Tengah, Badan Koordinasi
       Keluarga Berencana Nasional Pusat, Jakarta. Semarang:
       Universitas Diponegoro, Pusat Studi Kependudukan, 1978, x,
       97 pp.

1188   UNIVERSITAS INDONESIA, Lembaga Demografi. Beberapa Keuntungan
       Sosial Ekonomis kerana Reduksi Fertilitas [Some socio-
       economic benefits from reducing fertility]. Jakarta:
       Universitas Indonesia, 1972, xv, 309 pp.

1189   _____. Indonesian Fertility-Mortality Survey 1973: Prelimi-
       nary Report. (6 vols. in 1.) Jakarta, 1974.

1190 UNIVERSITAS TANJUNGPURA, Fakultas Ekonomi. Pengetahuan,
      Sikap, dan Praktek Keluarga berencana Golongan Ethnis Cina
      di Kalimantan Barat [Knowledge of, attitude to, and prac-
      tice of family planning of the Chinese in Kalimantan Barat
      Province]. Pontianak: Proyek Penelitian BKKBN bekerja
      sama dengan Fakultas Ekonomi, Universitas Tanjungpura,
      1977, ii, 98 pp.

1191 WARTOMO, YOYOH (Mrs.) "Pegawai Wanita dan Keluarga Berencana"
      [Women workers and family planning]. Keluarga Sejahtera
      1, no. 1 (1969):84-87.

1192 WAURAN, M.H., and SUPIT, E.B. Keluarga Berentjana [Family
      planning]. Bandung: Indonesia Pub. House, 1972, 79 pp.
      (On legal aspects.)

1193 WAY, ANN ADAMS. "Housing Conditions, Levels of Living, and
      Fertility in Indonesia." Ph.D. dissertation, University of
      Chicago, 1978, xiv, 343 pp. Abstracted in Dissertation
      Abstracts International 39, no. 4 (Oct. 1978):2568-A.

1194 WHITE, BENJAMIN N.F. "Production and Reproduction in a Java-
      nese Village." Ph.D. dissertation, Columbia University,
      1977, xii, 494 pp.

1195 WIROMIJOYO, WINARNO. Program Keluarga Berencana di Daerah
      D.I.Y. [Family planning program in D.I.Y. district].
      (2 vols. in 1.) Jogjakarta: D.P.R.D.-D.I.Y., 1974.

1196 WORKSHOP TENTANG PENERANGAN DAN PENDIDIKAN DALAM MASJARAKAT
      UNTUK KELUARGA BERENTJANA, Jakarta, 1971. Hasil [Workshop
      on Educating the Society in Family Planning, Jakarta, 1971.
      Proceedings]. Jakarta: Badan Koordinasi Keluarga Beren-
      tjana Nasional, Daerah Chusus Ibu Kota Jakarta Raya, 1971,
      1 vol. (various pagings).

1197 WORLD FERTILITY SURVEY. The Indonesian Fertility Survey,
      1976: A Summary of Findings. London: World Fertility
      Survey, 1978, 9 pp. World Fertility Survey, no. 11.

1198 ZUIDBERG, LIDA C.L., ed. Family Planning in Rural West Java.
      Leiden: Institute of Cultural and Social Studies, Leyden
      State University; Jakarta: Penerbit Djambatan, 1977, xvi,
      325 pp.

1199 _____. Marriage, Fertility and Family Planning in the
      Kecamatan Serpong: Some Intermediate and Socio-Economic
      Variables. Leiden: Institute of Cultural and Social
      Studies, Leyden State University, 1975, 91 pp. Family
      Planning Project Serpong, Indonesia. Serpong Paper, no. 16.

Malaysia

1200   ABDUL HAMID ARSHAT. "Peranan Wanita dalam Pembiakan" [The
       role of women in fertility]. 11 pp. Paper presented at
       the Seminar 'Wanita Malaysia Masakini', Bangi, Selangor,
       1979, organized by the Faculty of Social Sciences and
       Humanities, Universiti Kebangsaan Malaysia.

1201   ABDUL RAZAK bin HUSSEIN. "Government Policy on Birth Control
       in Malaysia." Kajian Ekonomi Malaysia 3, no. 1 (June 1966):
       3-6.

1202   ABDULLAH bin SAMAN. "Aspek2 Peranchang Keluarga" [Aspects of
       family planning]. B.Econ. academic exercise, University of
       Malaya, 1971, viii, 120 pp.

1203   ABEDIN, SALEHA MAHMOOD. "Islam and Muslim Fertility: Socio-
       logical Dimensions of a Demographic Dilemma." Ph.D. dis-
       sertation, University of Pennsylvania, 1977, 261 pp.
       Abstracted in Dissertation Abstracts International 38,
       no. 8 (Feb. 1978):5066-67-A. University Microfilms Inter-
       national, order no. 7730174. (Includes some information
       relating to Indonesia and Malaysia.)

1204   ABU BAKAR bin HAMZAH. Peranchang Keluarga [Family planning].
       Kota Bharu, Malaysia: Pustaka Aman Press, 1970, 56 pp.

1205   ADAM bin ABDUL KADIR. "Beberapa Persoalan Perancangan
       Keluarga" [Several issues in family planning]. Dewan
       Masyarakat 16, no. 11 (Nov. 1978):20-22.

1206   AHMAD bin MUHAMMAD IBRAHIM. Law and Population in Malaysia.
       Medford, Mass.: Law and Population Programme, Fletcher
       School of Law and Diplomacy, Tufts University, 1977,
       51 pp. Law and Population Monograph Series, no. 45.

1207   ALLADIN HASHIM. "Family Planning Activities in FELDA Land
       Schemes." Kuala Lumpur: Federal Land Development Author-
       ity, 1973, 13, 4 pp.

1208   AMIN AL-JAROMI. "Islam dan Perancangan Keluarga" [Islam and
       family planning]. Suara Majlis Ugama Islam Kedah 5 (1967):
       45-48.

1209   ARIFFIN MARZUKI. "Malaysia: The Family Planning Programme,
       1967." Studies in Family Planning 26 (Jan. 1968):12-15.

1210   AROKIASAMY, JOHN T. "Study of the Knowledge, Attitudes and
       Practices of Family Planning among Married Men Presenting
       Themselves at the Armed Forces Sick Quarters." Master's
       thesis, University of Malaya, 1976, 103 pp.

1211   BADRUD DUZA, M., and BALDWIN, C. STEPHEN. Nuptiality and
        Population Policy: An Investigation in Tunisia, Sri Lanka,
        and Malaysia. New York: Population Council, 1977, viii,
        83 pp.

1212   BUTZ, WILLIAM P., and DaVANZO, JULIE. The Malaysian Family
        Life Survey: Summary Report. Santa Monica, Calif.: Rand
        Corporation for U.S. Agency for International Development,
        1978, vii, 22 pp. Rand Report, no. R-2351-AID.

1213   CALDWELL, JOHN CHARLES. "Fertility Decline and Female Chances
        of Marriage in Malaya." Population Studies 17, no. 1
        (July 1963):20-32.

1214   CHEE, STEPHEN, and FONG, CHAN ONN. A Comparative Study on the
        Administration of Family Planning Programmes in the ESCAP
        Region: Organizational Determinants of Performance in
        Family Planning Services--the Malaysian Case. Bangkok:
        ECAFE, 1975, v, 108 pp.

1215   CHEW, S.Y. "Right of State to Regulate Families." 16 pp.
        Paper presented at the Fourth Malaysian Law Conference,
        Kuala Lumpur, October 1977, organized by the Bar Council
        of Malaya.

1216   CHO, LEE JAY; PALMORE, JAMES A., Jr.; and SAUNDERS, LYLE.
        "Recent Fertility Trends in West Malaysia." Demography 5,
        no. 2 (1968):732-44.

1217   CHO, LEE JAY; TAN, EDWARD KAH JOO; and SHANTAKUMAR, G. Esti-
        mates of Fertility for West Malaysia, 1957-1967. Kuala
        Lumpur: Department of Statistics, 1969, iv, 16 pp.
        Malaysia, Department of Statistics. Research Paper,
        no. 3.

1218   COMBINED CONFERENCE ON EVALUATION OF MALAYSIA NATIONAL FAMILY
        PLANNING PROGRAMME AND EAST ASIA POPULATION PROGRAMMES,
        Kuala Lumpur, 1970. Proceedings. Organized by National
        Family Planning Board, Malaysia. Kuala Lumpur: National
        Family Planning Board, 1970, iv, 470 pp.

1219   DeVANZO, JULIE, and BUTZ, WILLIAM P. Influences on Fertility
        and Infant Mortality in Developing Countries: The Case of
        Malaysia. Santa Monica, Calif.: Rand Corporation for U.S.
        Agency for International Development, 1978, vii, 14 pp.
        Rand Note, N-1166-AID.

1220   FEDERATION OF FAMILY PLANNING ASSOCIATIONS, Malaysia. Lapuran
        Tahunan. Annual Report. Kuala Lumpur, 1974-.

1221   FONG, CHAN ONN. Attitudes of Local Leaders to Family Planning
        in Peninsular Malaysia. Singapore: Southeast Asia Popula-
        tion Research Awards Program (SEAPRAP), International Devel-
        opment Research Centre and Ford Foundation, 1976, 51 pp.
        SEAPRAP Research Report, no. 8.

1222   _____. Socio-Economic Determinants of Fertility in Peninsular
        Malaysia. Singapore: Southeast Asia Population Research
        Awards Program (SEAPRAP), International Development Re-
        search Centre and Ford Foundation, 1978, iv, 43 pp.
        SEAPRAP Research Report, no. 19.

1223   GANAPATHY, SOMASUNDRAM. "Family Planning Movement in Malaya
        and Singapore." B.Econ. academic exercise, University of
        Malaya, 1966, vi, 62 pp.

1224   HAMZAH SENDUT. "Rural-Urban Fertility Differentials in
        Malaysia." Technical Association of Malaysia, Journal 14,
        no. 1, (Jan./Mar. 1966):13-17.

1225   HANNA, WILLARD ANDERSON. "Family Planning in Malaysia: Pro-
        grams and Prospects." American Universities Field Staff,
        Reports on Family Planning Programs, Southeast Asia Series
        19, no. 6 (Jan. 1971). 11 pp.

1226   HEW, WAI SIN; PENG, JUI YUN; and ARIFFIN MARZUKI. "A Field
        Study of Depo-provera; Its Use as a Contraceptive Method
        by Women in a Rural Town in West Malaysia from February
        1968 to December 1969." Medical Journal of Malaysia 27,
        no. 4 (June 1973):299-305.

1227   HUDAWI, MUHAMMAD NUH. Merenchanakan Kelahiran Anak: Berisi
        Sesuatu Yang Bertalian dengan Faedah Perkahwinan dan Faedah
        Anak, Terjadinya Anak didalam Rahim, Malthusianisme,
        Pembatasan, Penjarangan, dan Sebab-sebab Tidak Beranak
        [Planned parenthood: consists of the purpose of marriage
        and the significance of the child, conception, Malthusian-
        ism, birth control, contraception, causes of sterility].
        Kuala Lumpur: Pustaka Melayu Baru, 1969, 79 pp.

1228   JOHNSON, JOHN TIMOTHY. "Evaluation of Family Planning Pro-
        grams: Presentation of a General Model, and Its Applica-
        tion to the National Family Program of Malaysia." Ph.D.
        dissertation, University of Michigan, 1973, 338 pp. Ab-
        stracted in Dissertation Abstracts International 34, no. 3
        (Sept. 1973):1170-71-B. University Microfilms Interna-
        tional, order no. 73-21,527.

1229 _____. "Influences on Family Planning Acceptance: An Analysis of Background and Program Factors in Malaysia." Studies in Family Planning 10, no. 1 (Jan. 1979):15-24.

1230 JOHNSON, JOHN TIMOTHY; TAN BOON ANN; and CORSA, LESLIE.
"Assessment of Family Planning Programme Effects on Births:
Preliminary Results Obtained through Direct Matching of
Birth and Programme Acceptor Records." Population Studies
27, no. 1 (Mar. 1973):86-96.

1231 JOHNSON, JOHN TIMOTHY; TAN, BOON ANN; AND PALAN, V.T.
"Seasonality of Births for West Malaysia's Two Main Racial
Groups." Human Biology 47, no. 3 (Sept. 1975):295-307.

1232 JOHNSON, JOHN TIMOTHY et al. "Impact of the Malaysian Family
Planning Programme on Births: A Comparison of Matched Acceptor and Non-acceptor Birth Rates." Population Studies
32, no. 2 (July 1978):215-30.

1233 KOBLENZER, PETER JOHANN. "The Fertility and Child Loss Rates
of the Rungus Dusun of Maksangkong-Dampirit, with a Study
of the Conditions Responsible for the Latter." Master's
thesis, University of London, 1959, iii, 78 pp.

1234 KOBLENZER, PETER JOHANN, and CARRIER, NORMAN H. "Fertility,
Mortality and Nuptiality of the Rungus Dusun." Population
Studies 13, no. 3 (Mar. 1960):266-77.

1235 LAM, C.K. "Family Planning Knowledge, Attitude and Practice
in the Rural Areas of Sarawak." Journal of Biosocial
Science 11, no. 3 (July 1979):315-23.

1236 LEMBAGA PERANCHANG KELUARGA KEBANGSAAN, Malaysia. Annual Report. Laporan Tahunan. Kuala Lumpur, 1st, 1967-.

1237 LIM, LAY SEAN. "Family Planning in Penang Island (Rural)."
D.P.H. thesis, University of Singapore, 1969, 46 pp.

1238 LOO, PEK TAI. "Significance of a Fertility Reduction on Economic Development in West Malaysia." B.Econ. academic
exercise, University of Malaya, 1969, vi, 104 pp.

1239 McTAGGART, W.D. "A Note on Age-Specific Fertility in Malaya,
1962." Geographica 1 (1964/65):23-30.

1240 MALAYSIA, Jabatan Perangkaan. Laporan Perantaraan ke-atas
Penyiasatan Keluarga. Interim Report on Family Survey:
KAP Study. Kuala Lumpur: Jabatan Perangkaan, 1971, viii,
62 pp.

1241 MALAYSIA, Jabatan Perangkaan, and WORLD FERTILITY SURVEY.
Malaysian Fertility and Family Survey--1974. First Country
Report, by R. Chandler et al. Kuala Lumpur: Department of
Statistics and National Family Planning Board, 1977, xx,
193, 501 pp.

1242 MALAYSIA, Laws, statutes, etc. "Family Planning Act, 1966.
Act No.42 of 1966." In Acts of Parliament Passed during
the Year 1966, pp. 395-402. Kuala Lumpur: Government
Printer, 1966.

1243 "Malaysia: Women Who Enrolled in Family Planning Program Had
30% Fewer Births Than Unenrolled." International Family
Planning Perspectives and Digest 2, no. 4 (1976):13-14.

1244 The Malaysian Fertility and Family Survey 1974: A Summary of
Findings. The Hague: International Statistical Institute,
1978, 12 pp. World Fertility Survey, no. 4, January 1978.

1245 MELDAHL, EDWARD N. "The Incidence and Cost of Pregnancy among
Employees of Industry: Availability of Community Planning
Services to Employees of Industry." 1 vol. Kuala Lumpur:
Edward N. Meldahl, n.d.

1246 MILNE, J.C. "Birth Rates and Race Fertility in Malaya."
Malayan Medical Journal 8 (Dec. 1933):287-89.

1247 NATIONAL FAMILY PLANNING SEMINAR, 1st, Kuala Lumpur, 1968.
Proceedings. Kuala Lumpur: National Family Planning
Board, 1968, 144 pp.

1248 NATIONAL FAMILY PLANNING SEMINAR, 2d, Kuala Lumpur, 1970.
Proceedings. Kuala Lumpur: National Family Planning
Board, 1970, 185 pp.

1249 NATIONAL SEMINAR ON FERTILITY PLANNING TOWARDS ACHIEVING
GREATER SOCIAL AND ECONOMIC PROGRESS, Kuala Lumpur, 1976.
Papers. Kuala Lumpur: National Family Planning Board,
1976, 1 vol. (various pagings).

1250 NATIONAL SEMINAR ON GENERAL CONSEQUENCES OF POPULATION GROWTH,
2d, Kuala Lumpur, 1970. Proceedings of the Second National
Seminar on General Consequences of Population Growth, Dewan
Tunku Abdul Rahman, Kuala Lumpur, 16-17 March 1970. Kuala
Lumpur: National Family Planning Board, Malaysia, 1970[?],
185 pp.

1251 NESS, GAYL DEFORREST, and ANDO, HIROFUMI. "The Politics of
Population Planning in Malaysia and the Philippines."
Journal of Comparative Administration 3, no. 3 (Nov. 1971):
296-329.

1252 NOR LAILY AZIZ, Datin. Impact of Family Planning on Perinatal Mortality. Kuala Lumpur: Lembaga Perancang Keluarga Negara, 1980, 48 pp. Lembaga Perancang Keluarga Negara. Occasional Paper, no. 2.

1253 _____. "The National Family Planning Programme and Its Role in Socioeconomic Development." In Malaysia: Some Contemporary Issues in Socioeconomic Development. Edited by Cheong Kee Cheok et al. Kuala Lumpur: Persatuan Ekonomi Malaysia, 1979, pp. 234-47.

1254 _____. Population and Family Development: The Malaysian Experience. Kuala Lumpur: Lembaga Perancang Keluarga Negara, 1979, 44 pp. Lembaga Perancang Keluarga Negara. Occasional Paper, no. 1. Paper presented at the Seminar on Malaysian Fertility and Family Survey/Population and Development, Penang, June 1979.

1255 NOR LAILY AZIZ, Datin, and HASHIM, RITA RAJ. Penduduk, Perancang Keluarga dan Wanita. Population, Family Planning and Women. Kuala Lumpur: Lembaga Perancang Keluarga Negara, 1978, 107 pp.

1256 NOR LAILY AZIZ, Datin; TAN, BOON ANN; and KUAN, LIN CHEE. The Malaysian National Family Planning Programme. Kuala Lumpur: Lembaga Perancang Keluarga Negara, 1977, vi, 53 pp.

1257 OOI, O.S. "The Demand for Abortion in an Urban Malaysian Population." Medical Journal of Malaysia 25, no. 3 (Mar. 1971):175-81.

1258 PALMORE, JAMES A., Jr. "Malaysia: The West Malaysian Family Survey, 1966-1967." Studies in Family Planning, no. 40 (Apr. 1969):11-20.

1259 PALMORE, JAMES A., Jr., and ARIFFIN MARZUKI. "Marriage Patterns and Cumulative Fertility in West Malaysia, 1966-1967." Demography 6, no. 4 (Nov. 1969):383-401.

1260 PALMORE, JAMES A., Jr.; HIRSCH, PAUL M.; and ARIFFIN MARZUKI. "Interpersonal Communication and the Diffusion of Family Planning in West Malaysia." Demography 8 (Aug. 1971): 411-25. Also published as Working Paper no. 12 of the East-West Population Institute, East-West Center, Honolulu. (1971, 33 pp.)

1261 PALMORE, JAMES A., Jr. et al. Report on the West Malaysia Family Survey, 1966-1967. Kuala Lumpur: National Family Planning Board, 1968, xliv, 534 pp.

126

1262   PENG, JUI YUN; NOR LAILY AZIZ, Datin; and ARIFFIN MARZUKI.
        "Village Midwives in Malaysia." Studies in Family Plan-
        ning 3, no. 2 (Feb. 1972):25-28.

1263   PENG, JUI YUN et al., comps. Malaysia Family Planning Annual
        Statistical Report 1967-1970. Kuala Lumpur: National
        Family Planning Board, 1974, xxii, 352 pp.

1264   PRYOR, ROBIN JOHN, and YOUNG, MEI LING. A Note on Changes in
        Family Size and Fertility Control in Peninsular Malaysia.
        Canberra: Australian National University, 1975, 17 pp.

1265   RAJ KARIM, and NOR LAILY AZIZ, Datin. Panduan Ceramah
        Kesihatan Ibu dan Kanak-kanak dan Perancangan Keluarga
        untuk Pegawai dan Kakitangan Kesihatan [A guide for talks
        on maternal and child health and family planning for health
        officers and staff]. Kuala Lumpur: Yunit Kesihatan Ibu
        dan Kanak-kanak, Kementerian Kesihatan, 1977, 72 pp.

1266   RAMACHANDRAN, K.V., and SHANTAKUMAR, G. Fertility Differen-
        tials in West Malaysia. Bombay: International Institute
        for Population Studies, 1974, 88 pp.

1267   RAMLAH HAJI MUDA. "A Study of the Attitudes of the Local
        Elites of Dungun on Population and Family Planning." B.A.
        academic exercise, University of Malaya, 1976, viii, 69 pp.

1268   RESEARCH CONTRIBUTIONS TO POPULATION STUDIES, Kuala Lumpur,
        1975. Papers. Jointly sponsored by Persatuan Ekonomi
        Malaysia and Lembaga Perancang Keluarga Negara, Malaysia,
        29-30 December 1975. Kuala Lumpur, 1975, 198 pp.

1269   RIDKER, ROLAND G., and MUSCAT, ROBERT J. "Incentives for
        Family Planning and Fertility Reduction: An Illustration
        for Malaysia." Studies in Family Planning 4, no. 1
        (Jan. 1973):1-11.

1270   ROBERTSON, J.F. "Fertility in the Urban Kampongs of Kota
        Kinabulu--Sabah--Malaysia." Brunei Museum Journal 3,
        no. 4 (1976):70-76.

1271   RODRIGUEZ, GERMÁN. "Family Planning Availability and Contra-
        ceptive Practice." Family Planning Perspectives 11
        (Jan./Feb. 1979):51-56. (Analysis of world fertility
        survey data from Colombia, Costa Rica, Korea, Malaysia,
        and Nepal.)

1272   SABAH, Department of Lands and Surveys. Family Structure in
        Some Kampongs of Kota Kinabalu. Kota Kinabalu, 1969, viii,
        82 pp. Town Planning Bulletin, 14. (Includes information
        on marriage and divorce, fertility, and family planning.)

1273   SAW, SWEE HOCK. "Birth Control Use at Eve of National Action
       Programme in West Malaysia." Journal of Family Welfare 16,
       no. 3 (Mar. 1970):15-19.

1274   _____. "Family Planning Attitudes in West Malaysia." South-
       east Asian Journal of Sociology 2 (May 1969):59-61.

1275   _____. "Family Planning Knowledge, Attitudes and Practice in
       Malaya." Demography 5, no. 2 (1968):702-9.

1276   _____. "Female Attitude towards Birth Control." Opinion
       [Malaysia] 2 (1968):206-7.

1277   _____. "Fertility Differentials in Early Postwar Malaya."
       Demography 4, no. 2 (1967):641-56.

1278   _____. "A Note on the Fertility Levels in Malaya during 1947-
       1957." Malayan Economic Review 12, no. 1 (Apr. 1967):
       117-24.

1279   _____. "Patterns of Fertility Decline in Malaysia, 1956-
       1965." Kajian Ekonomi Malaysia 3, no. 1 (June 1966):7-14.

1280   SCHIEFFELIN, OLIVIA, comp. and ed. Muslim Attitudes toward
       Family Planning. New York: Population Council, 1973, vii,
       145 pp.

1281   SEKHON, P.S. "Welfare of Agro-Industrial Workers through
       Family Planning." Economic Bulletin [Kuala Lumpur] 1,
       no. 3 (1975):50-53.

1282   SEMINAR ON POPULATION, Fraser's Hill, Malaysia, 1977. Pro-
       ceedings. Kuala Lumpur: Faculty of Economics and Admin-
       istration, University of Malaya, 1978[?], ix, 79 pp.

1283   SEMINAR WANITA DAN PERTUBUHAN SUKARELA WANITA MENGENAI
       PEMBANGUNAN KELUARGA, Kuala Lumpur, 1979. Lapuran [Seminar
       on Women and Women's Voluntary Organizations concerning
       Family Development, Kuala Lumpur, 1979. Report]. Orga-
       nized by Lembaga Perancang Keluarga Negara, Malaysia.
       Kuala Lumpur, 1980[?], 248 pp.

1284   SHAMSUDDIN bin ABDUL RAHMAN et al. "Malaysia." Studies in
       Family Planning 6, no. 8 (Aug. 1975):230-32. (On family
       planning programs in 1974.)

1285   SINNATHURAY, T.A. et al. Report on Maternal Health and Early
       Pregnancy Wastage in Peninsular Malaysia. Edited by Indra
       Pathmanathan. Under the joint sponsorship of FFPA and the
       International Development Research Centre, Canada. Kuala
       Lumpur, 1977, ix, 166 pp.

1286   TAKESHITA, JOHN YUZURU. "West Malaysia: 1969 Family Planning
       Acceptor Follow-up Survey; Some Preliminary Findings."
       Studies in Family Planning, no. 51 (Mar. 1970):18-23.

1287   TAN, FRANK E.H. "An Appraisal of the Role of the Intra-
       uterine Contraceptive Device for Family Planning in
       Malaysia." Medical Journal of Malaysia 31, no. 2 (Dec.
       1976):123-27.

1288   TEOH, SOONG KEE. "Sexual Offences." 10 pp. Paper presented
       at the Seminar on Health, Food and Nutrition, Penang,
       15-20 September 1979, organized by the Consumers' Associa-
       tion of Penang.

1289   THAMBU, JOHAN A.M. "Abortions--Government Hospitals: Penin-
       sular Malaysia, 1960-1972." Medical Journal of Malaysia
       29, no. 4 (June 1975):258-62.

1290   THAMBYPILLAI, VIMALA. A Study of the Knowledge of and Atti-
       tude towards Family Planning among Rural Malay Women.
       Kuala Lumpur: Department of Social and Preventive Medi-
       cine, University of Malaya, 1979, 118 pp.

1291   UNESCO/KPPK Seminar "Women in Population Education and Lit-
       eracy Programmes" Petaling Jaya, Malaysia, 1976. Report.
       Organized by the National Union of the Teaching Profession
       in cooperation with the National Commission for UNESCO,
       Malaysia. Petaling Jaya: National Union of Teaching Pro-
       fession, 1976, ii, 83 pp.

1292   VERBRUGGE, LOIS M. "Peers as Recruiters: Family Planning
       Communications of West Malaysian Acceptors." Journal of
       Health and Social Behavior 19, no. 1 (Mar. 1978):51-68.

1293   VERON, JACQUES. "Appartenance ethnique et comportement des
       populations de Malasie et de Singapour" [Ethnic origin and
       demographic behavior of the populations of Malaysia and
       Singapore]. Population 33, nos. 4/5 (July/Oct. 1978):
       937-50.

1294   WORKSHOP/SEMINAR ON VOLUNTARY FAMILY PLANNING MOVEMENT IN
       MALAYSIA: PROBLEMS AND PROSPECTS, Kuala Lumpur, 1976.
       Proceedings. Kuala Lumpur: Federation of Family Planning
       Associations, 1976, 127 pp.

1295   YAHYA bin YAACOB. "National Family Planning Board: Some
       Problems of Communication--a Study of Kampong Endah."
       B.Econ. academic exercise, University of Malaya, 1970,
       vii, 84 pp.

1296   YONG, VINCENT. "Perancang Keluarga" [Family planning].
       Aktual, no. 5 (June 1979):20-23.

Philippines

1297   ABELEDA, AMPARO MARIANO. "Cohort Fertility: A Case Study of
       a Philippine Community." Master's thesis, University of
       the Philippines [Quezon City], 1970, 101 pp.

1298   ABENOJA, MACRINA K. "Current Fertility in the Eastern Visayas:
       An Application of the 'Own-Children-Underfive' Method."
       Philippines Quarterly of Culture and Society 4, no. 2
       (June 1976):110-29.

1299   ALBERTO, CYNTHIA S. "How Husband-Wife Relations Affect Fer-
       tility Behavior: A Study of Urban Working Class Filipino
       Couples." Options for Policy and Practice 4, no. 2
       (Mar./Apr. 1978):1-16.

1300   ALCID, AURORA B., and ESTOLAS, JOSEFINA V. Preludes to and
       Family Planning Schemes. Manila: National Book Store,
       1976, ix, 134 pp.

1301   ALLEN, LENOLA BUSBY. "Personal and Family Characteristics:
       Bases for Developing Family Planning Materials for Inter-
       national Audiences." Ph.D. dissertation, Iowa State Uni-
       versity, 1977, 247 pp. Abstracted in Dissertation Abstracts
       International 38, no. 11 (May 1978):6573-74-A. University
       Microfilms International, order no. 7805921. (Subjects
       were from four developing countries including the
       Philippines.)

1302   ANDRES, TOMAS QUINTIN D.; GAERLAN, JOSEFINA E.; and LIMPINGCO,
       DELIA A. Sex Education and Family Planning for Filipinos.
       Quezon City: Ken, 1974, x, 159 pp.

1303   ANGELES, NOLI DE LOS. "Marriage and Fertility Patterns in the
       Philippines." Philippine Sociological Review 13, no. 4
       (Oct. 1965):232-48.

1304   APELO, RUBEN. "Family Planning for Maternal and Child
       Health." Philippine Journal of Pediatrics 17, no. 4
       (Aug. 1968):258-61.

1305   _____. "Practice of Birth Control: A Study of 1,000 Women
       in Manila." Philippine Medical Association, Journal 41,
       no. 10 (Oct. 1965):707-16.

1306   ARCE, WILFREDO FLORENDA, and SILAYAN-GO, AURORA. Family Planning in Tondo: Housewives, Husbands and Clinics. Final report of the IPC/POMCH 1969 Tondo family planning study submitted to the Commission on Population by the Institute of Philippine Culture on 30 June 1972. Quezon City: Institute of Philippine Culture, Ateneo de Manila University, 1972, 154 pp.

1307   BACALA, J.C. "Christian Family Planning." Philippine Journal of Nursing 31, no. 2 (1962):98-100.

1308   BAILEN, JEROME B. "The Reluctant Motivators: Traditional Midwives and Modern Family Planning in Marinduque." In Philippines Popular Research: Papers and Proceedings of an Experts' Meeting. Edited by Rodolfo A. Bulatao. Makati, Rizal: Population Center Foundation, 1976, pp. 377-404.

1309   BALLWEG, JOHN A. "Selection of a Family Planning Method: A Philippine Example." Journal of Biosocial Science 4, no. 4 (Oct. 1972):411-25.

1310   BALLWEG, JOHN A., and MacCORQUODALE, DONALD W. "Family Planning Method Change and Dropout in the Philippines." Family Planning Résumé 1, no. 1 (1977):192-98.

1311   BALLWEG, JOHN A., and WARD, SUSAN S. Assessment of Family Planning Acceptability in the Philippines. Blacksburg, Va.: Virginia Polytechnic Institute and State University, 1973, xiii, 224 pp.

1312   BARRETO, FELISA R. "Family Planning as a Means of Population Control in the Philippines: An Economic Study." Master's thesis, Far Eastern University [Manila], 1969, 98 pp.

1313   _____. "Knowledge, Attitudes, and Practice of Family Planning in the Philippines, 1972." Studies in Family Planning 5, no. 9 (Sept. 1974):294-99.

1314   BETTY, SAMUEL ADAMS. "Some Determinants of Communication Network Structure and Productivity: A Study of Clinic Staff Interaction in Two Philippine Family Planning Organizations." Ph.D. dissertation, Michigan State University, 1974, 209 pp. Abstracted in Dissertation Abstracts International 35, no. 9 (Mar. 1975):7404-B. University Microfilms International, order no. 75-7117.

1315   BRAVO, MARIA CIJUELA. "The Parental Problems on Family Planning in the Municipality of Padada, Davao del Sur, 1970-1974." Master's thesis, International Harvardian University, 1975, vi, 145 pp.

131

1316   BULATAO, RODOLFO A. Attitudes toward Legal Measures for Popu-
        lation Control: Social-Psychological Factors Affecting
        Ethical-Cultural Acceptability. A report submitted to the
        Commission on Population. Quezon City: University of the
        Philippines, 1974, viii, 125 pp.

1317   _____, ed. Philippine Population Research: Papers and Pro-
        ceedings of an Experts' Meeting. Makati, Rizal: Popula-
        tion Center Foundation, 1976, xiv, 577 pp.

1318   BULATAO, RODOLFO A., and LEE, LUKE T. "The Impact of Law on
        Fertility Behavior: Perspectives of Philippine Influen-
        tials." Philippine Law Journal 48, no. 3 (July 1973):
        324-55.

1319   BUSTRILLOS, NENA R. "Pattern of Fertility Behaviour of
        Couples in Rural Laguna, 1966." Philippine Sociological
        Review 14, no. 4 (Oct. 1966).

1320   CANLAS, DANTE B. "Income, Education, Fertility and Labor
        Force Participation: Philippines 1973." 28 pp. Paper
        presented at the Seminar on Labor Supply under the joint
        sponsorship of the Council for Asian Manpower Studies and
        the Organization of Demographic Associates held in Makati,
        Rizal, Philippines, June 1976.

1321   CANLAS, DANTE B., and ENCARNACIÓN, JOSÉ. Income, Education,
        Fertility and Employment: Philippines 1973. Diliman,
        Quezon City: Council for Manpower Studies, University of
        the Philippines, 1977, 48 pp.

1322   CARD, JOSEFINA J. "The Correspondence of Data Gathered from
        Husband and Wife: Implications for Family Planning Stud-
        ies." Social Biology 25, no. 3 (Fall, 1978):196-204.
        (Data gathered from Filipino and Caucasian married couples
        in the San Francisco area.)

1323   _____. "Differences in the Antecedents and Consequences of
        the Motivation for Fertility Control among Filipino Mi-
        grants and Caucasian Controls." Journal of Population 2,
        no. 2 (Summer 1979):140-61.

1324   _____. "The Malleability of Fertility-related Attitudes and
        Behavior in a Filipino Migrant Sample." Demography 15,
        no. 4 (Nov. 1978):459-76.

1325   CASTILLO, GELIA TAGUMPAY. "Some Sociological Considerations
        in Promoting Family Planning Programs." Solidarity 5
        (Mar. 1970):12-16.

1326   CASTRO, NILDA M. <u>Marital Social Mobility in the Philippines</u>.
        Singapore: Southeast Asia Population Research Awards Pro-
        gram, 1976, 100 pp. SEAPRAP Research Report, no. 2.

1327   CHILDREN'S MEDICAL CENTER PHILIPPINES, INC., Institute of
        Maternal and Child Health. <u>The Potential of Traditional
        Birth Attendants of Hilots as Family Planning Motivators in
        Rural Communities of the Philippines</u>. Quezon City: IMCH,
        1974, 50 pp.

1328   CONCEPCIÓN, MERCEDES B. "Female Employment and Fertility in
        the Philippines." <u>Philippine Economic Journal</u> 12, nos. 1/2
        (1973):524-35.

1329   _____. "Female Labour Force Participation and Fertility."
        <u>International Labour Review</u> 109, nos. 5/6 (May/June 1974):
        503-17.

1330   _____. "Fertility Differences among Married Women in the
        Philippines." Ph.D. dissertation, University of Chicago,
        1963, 140 pp.

1331   _____. <u>Fertility Differences among Married Women in the
        Philippines</u>. Quezon City: Population Institute, Univer-
        sity of the Philippines System, 1974, 8 pp.

1332   _____. "On Fertility and Family Planning in the Philippines."
        <u>Economic Research Journal</u> 14, no. 1 (June 1967):41-52.

1333   _____. "110 Millions by the Year 2001." <u>Philippine Socio-
        logical Review</u> 18, nos. 3/4 (July/Oct. 1970):211-25.

1334   _____. "Philippines." <u>Studies in Family Planning</u> 6, no. 8
        (Aug. 1975):232-36. (On family planning programs in 1974).

1335   _____. "Population Policy and Family Planning." In <u>Popula-
        tion of the Philippines</u>, by United Nations Economic and
        Social Commission for Asia and the Pacific. Bangkok:
        ESCAP, 1978, pp. 172-207.

1336   _____. "Problems in Fertility Measurement and Their Implica-
        tions for Future Research." In <u>Philippine Population Re-
        search: Papers and Proceedings of an Experts' Meeting</u>.
        Edited by Rodolfo A. Bulatao. Makati, Rizal: Population
        Center Foundation, 1976, pp. 183-91.

1337   CONCEPCIÓN, MERCEDES B., and FLIEGER, WILHELM. "Family Build-
        ing Patterns of Young Manila Couples." <u>Philippine Socio-
        logical Review</u> 16, nos. 3/4 (July/Oct. 1968):162-83.

1338 _____. "Studies of Fertility and Family Planning in the Philippines." Demography 5, no. 2 (1968):714-31.

1339 _____. Studies of Fertility and Fertility Planning in the Philippines. Quezon City: Population Institute, University of the Philippines System, 1969, 50 pp.

1340 CONCEPCIÓN, MERCEDES B., and HENDERSHOT, GERRY ELLSWORTH. "Factors Associated with Married Women's Ideal Family Size and Approval of Family Planning." Saint Louis University Research Journal [Baguio City, Philippines], 6, nos. 3/4 (Sept./Dec. 1968):355-74.

1341 _____. "Prospects of a Fertility Decline in the Seventies." In Philippine Population in the Seventies. Edited by Mercedes B. Concepción. Manila: Community Publishers, 1969, pp. 367-96.

1342 CONCEPCIÓN, MERCEDES B.; PASCUAL, ELVIRA MENDOZA; and STINNER, WILLIAM F. Differences in Childbearing Patterns of Filipino Women 25-34 Years, National Demographic Survey, 1968. Manila: Population Institute, University of the Philippines, 1972, 25 pp. Report submitted to the United States Agency for International Development pursuant to contract no. 92-154.

1343 CONCEPCIÓN, MERCEDES B. et al. "The Childbearing Patterns of Young Filipino Women." In A Demographic Path to Modernity: Patterns of Early-Transition in the Philippines. Edited by Wilhelm Flieger and Peter Colin Smith. Quezon City: University of the Philippines Press, 1975, pp. 127-52.

1344 COSTELLO, MICHAEL ANTHONY. "Trends and Differentials in Marital Fertility in Misamis Oriental Province, the Philippines." Ph.D. dissertation, University of Chicago, 1977, xii, 344 pp. Abstracted in Dissertation Abstracts International 38, no. 3 (Sept. 1977):1678-79-A.

1345 CRUZ, ERMINDA CORTEZ. "Family Planning Acceptors at the Nicanor Reyes Memorial Foundation Hospital, Maternal and Child Health and Family Planning Center." Master's thesis, Far Eastern University [Manila], 1974, iv, 127 pp.

1346 DACAYANAN, FELICIDAD M., and ISAAC, JOSEFINA DY R. Towards Building the Filipino Family Today. Quezon City: Bustamante Press, 1974, 212 pp. Asian Social Institute, Inc. Social Awareness Series, no. 1.

1347   DEL FIERRO, ALFONSO CHONG, Jr. "Rural-Urban Migration and
        Differential Fertility in the Philippines." Ph.D. disser-
        tation, University of Kentucky, 1974, 138 pp. Abstracted
        in Dissertation Abstracts International 36, no.3 (Sept.
        1975):1838-39-A. University Microfilms International,
        order no. 75-18,472.

1348   DEL MUNDO, FE, and FULGENCIO, QUERUBIN. "Introduction of
        Family Planning to Philippine Communities through Maternal
        and Child Health Clinics (1968-69)." Philippine Medical
        Association, Journal 46, no. 5 (May 1970):263-75.

1349   DEMETRIA, AGNES M. "Folk Methods of Birth Control." Master's
        thesis, University of San Carlos [Cebu City, Philippines],
        1969, 171 pp.

1350   DIZON, JESUS A.N., and MIRALAO, VIRGINIA A. The Hilot in
        Oriental Mindoro. Final report submitted to the Institute
        of Maternal and Child Health by the Institute of Philippine
        Culture, 2 April 1973. Quezon City: Institute of Philip-
        pine Culture, Ateneo de Manila University, 1973, 173 pp.

1351   DOHERTY, JOHN F. "Population Growth and Fertility Control."
        Philippine Studies 12, no. 2 (Apr. 1964):348-51.

1352   ENCARNACIÓN, JOSÉ. Effects of Family Income and Education on
        Fertility: Cross-Section Results, Philippines, 1968.
        Quezon City: Institute of Economic Development and Re-
        search, University of the Philippines, 1972, 15 pp. IEDR
        Discussion Paper, no. 72-9.

1353   _____. "Family Income, Education, Labor Force Participation
        and Fertility." In A Demographic Path to Modernity: Pat-
        terns of Early-Transition in the Philippines. Edited by
        Wilhelm Flieger and Peter Colin Smith. Quezon City:
        University of the Philippines Press, 1975, pp. 190-200.

1354   _____. "Family Income, Educational Level, Labor Force Par-
        ticipation and Fertility." Philippine Economic Journal 12,
        nos. 1/2 (1973):536-49.

1355   _____. Fertility and Labor Force Participation: Philippines,
        1968. Quezon City: Institute of Economic Development and
        Research, University of the Philippines, 1973, 39 pp. IEDR
        Discussion Paper, no. 73-13.

1356   ENGRACIA, LUISA T. et al. Estimates of Fertility in the
        Philippines Derived by the Own-Children Method, 1960-1968:
        UNFPA-NCSO Population Research Project. Manila: National
        Economic and Development Authority, National Census and

135

Statistics Office, 1977, xiii, 37 pp. Philippines (Republic), National Census and Statistics Office. Monograph
no. 9.

1357 ERIC [Educational Resources Information Center]. Situation
Report. New York: ERIC, 1975, 31 pp. (Family planning in
Indonesia and Philippines.)

1358 FAMILY HEALTH CARE, INC., Washington. A Review of the
Philippines' Population Programme. Washington, D.C.:
Family Health Care, Inc., 1977, 1 vol. (various pagings).

1359 FAMILY PLANNING ORGANIZATION OF THE PHILIPPINES, Research and
Evaluation Division. Filipino Viewpoints on Family Plan-
ning. Manila: Research and Evaluation Division, Family
Planning Organization of the Philippines, 1972, vi, 174 pp.

1360 FINDLEY, SALLY E., and ORR, ANN C. Patterns of Urban-Rural
Fertility Differentials in Developing Countries: a Sug-
gested Framework. Washington, D.C.: U.S. Agency for
International Development, 1978, vii, 242 pp. (Framework
is applied to data for Philippines, Peru, Tanzania, and
Egypt.)

1361 FLIEGER, WILHELM. "Fertility Levels and Fertility Trends."
In A Demographic Path to Modernity: Patterns of Early-
Transition in the Philippines. Edited by Wilhelm Flieger
and Peter Colin Smith. Quezon City: University of the
Philippines Press, 1975, pp. 91-124.

1362 _____, ed. "Sociological Dimensions of Population Growth in
the Philippines." Philippine Sociological Review 19,
nos. 3/4 (July/Oct. 1971):151-59.

1363 FLIEGER, WILHELM, and SMITH, PETER COLIN, eds. A Demographic
Path to Modernity: Patterns of Early-Transition in the
Philippines. Quezon City: University of the Philippines
Press, 1975, xxvi, 318 pp.

1364 GALANG, R.T. "Women in Family Planning and Community Living."
Philippine Extension Worker 4, no. 1 (1959):6-7.

1365 GARCIA, Q. Ma. "Notes on Contraception." Philippiniana
Sacra 1, no. 3 (1966):465-95.

1366 GATCHALIAN, JOSE G., and AGANON, MARIE E. The San Pablo Experiment: Educational Strategies in Family Planning for
Rural Workers. Quezon City: Asian Labour Education Center, 1975, 82 pp.

136

1367   GILLON, RAANAN. "Not 'Abortion on Demand.'" <u>MD Journal</u> 20,
        no.5 (1971):256-61.

1368   GONZALES, MYRNA C.; ALEGRE, MARIETTA P.; and CROSS, ANNE R.
        <u>An Analysis of Cumulative Fertility in the Philippines</u>
        <u>Using 1975 Census Data</u>. Manila: National Census and
        Statistics Office, National Economic and Development
        Authority, 1978, 17 pp. UNC/CH-NCSO Population Research
        Project. Occasional Papers, no. 2.

1369   GOROSPE, VITALIANO R. "Catholic Hierarchy and the Population
        Problem." <u>Philippine Studies</u> 17 (1969):806-10.

1370   _____. "Freedom and the Ethnics of Philippine Population Con-
        trol." <u>Philippine Studies</u> 24 (1st Quarter 1976):37-63.

1371   _____. "A Layman on the Development of the Church's Doctrine
        on Contraception." <u>Philippine Studies</u> 14 (Apr. 1966):
        310-25.

1372   _____, ed. <u>Freedom and Philippine Population Control</u>. Quezon
        City: New Day Publishers, 1976, xix, 387 pp.

1373   _____, ed. <u>Responsible Parenthood in the Philippines</u>. Manilla:
        Ateneo Publications Office, 1970, xxiii, 268 pp.

1374   GUTHRIE, GEORGE M. "Psychological Factors and Preferred Fam-
        ily Size." <u>Saint Louis University Research Journal</u> [Baguio
        City, Philippines] 6, nos. 3/4 (1968):391-98.

1375   GUZMAN, E.A. de. "Trends and Differentials in Fertility."
        In <u>Population of the Philippines</u>, by United Nations Eco-
        nomic and Social Commission for Asia and the Pacific.
        Bangkok: ESCAP, 1978, pp. 117-35.

1376   HARMAN, ALVIN J. <u>Fertility and Economic Behaviour of Families</u>
        <u>in the Philippines</u>. Santa Monica, Calif.: Rand, 1970, xv,
        84 pp. Rand Corporation. Research Memorandum, RM-6385-AID.

1377   _____. <u>Interrelationships between Procreation and Other Fam-</u>
        <u>ily Decision Making</u>. Santa Monica, Calif.: Rand Corp.,
        1969, 55 pp. Rand Corporation. Paper, P-4267.

1378   HAUSER, PHILIP MORRIS. "Implications of Fertility Analysis
        for Family Planning in the Philippines." Part of summary
        report under Contract USAID [U.S. Agency for International
        Development] no. 92-154. Manila, 1972, 29 pp.

1379   HAWLEY, AMOS H. "Rural Fertility in Central Luzon. <u>American</u>
        <u>Sociological Review</u> 20, no. 1 (Feb. 1955):21-27.

1380   _____. "Fertility of an Urban Population in the
       Philippines." In Papers in Demography and Public Adminis-
       tration. Quezon City: Institute of Public Administration,
       University of the Philippines, 1954, pp. 27-42. Reprinted
       from Philippine Statistician (Dec. 1953).

1381   HEALY, GERALD W. "After 'Humanae Vitae': Contraception and
       Abortion." Philippine Studies 22 (3d. and 4th quarter
       1974):263-79.

1382   _____. "Moral Aspects of Family Planning in Contemporary
       Christian Society." In The Filipino Christian Family in a
       Changing Society, pp. 10-20. Manila: Christian Family
       Movement, 1965

1383   HENDERSHOT, GERRY ELLSWORTH. "Cityward Migration and Urban
       Fertility in the Philippines." Ph.D. dissertation,
       University of Chicago, 1970, 221 pp.

1384   _____. "Cityward Migration and Urban Fertility in the
       Philippines." Philippine Sociological Review 19, nos. 3/4
       (July/Oct. 1971):183-91.

1385   _____. "Differences in Contraceptive Knowledge, Attitudes,
       and Practice by Rural-Urban Residence History: Currently
       Married Women Aged 15-44, Philippines, 1973." Philippine
       Sociological Review 23, nos. 1/4 (Jan./Oct. 1975):101-25.

1386   HERRIN, ALEJANDRO N. "Rural Electrification and Fertility
       Change in the Southern Philippines." Population and Devel-
       opment Review 5, no. 1 (Mar. 1979):61-86.

1387   HIDAY, VIRGINIA ALDIGÉ. "Agricultural Organization and Fer-
       tility: A Comparison of Two Philippine Frontier Communi-
       ties." Social Biology 25, no. 1 (Spring 1978):69-79.

1388   _____. "Migration, Organization, and Fertility in the
       Philippines." International Migration Review 12 (Aug.
       1978):370-85.

1389   HOLLNSTEINER, MARY RACELIS. "The Filipino Family Confronts
       the Modern World." In Responsible Parenthood in the
       Philippines. Edited by V.R. Gorospe. Quezon City: Ateneo
       de Manila Publication Office, 1970, pp. 19-44.

1390   HUTCHISON, IRA WALTER. "Conjugal Relations and Family Plan-
       ning." Philippine Quarterly of Culture and Society 2,
       nos. 2/3 (June/Sept. 1975):146-58.

1391 _____. "Husband-Wife Interaction and Fertility Patterns in the Philippines." Ph.D. dissertation, University of Notre Dame, 1970, x, 247 pp. Abstracted in Dissertation Abstracts International 31, no. 9 (Mar. 1971):4917-18-B. University Microfilms International, order no. 71-5541.

1392 JAYME, BRIGIDA L. "Family Role and Fertility Behavior of the Upper Class Urban Married Filipina." 30 pp. Paper presented at the Seminar on Labor Supply under the joint sponsorship of the Council for Asian Manpower Studies and the Organization of Demographic Associates held in Makati, Rizal, Philippines, June 1976.

1393 _____. Family Roles and Fertility Patterns of Two Generations of Urban Upper Class Filipina Wives and Mothers. Singapore: Southeast Asia Population Research Awards Program (SEAPRAP), International Development Research Centre, Asia Regional Office and Ford Foundation, 1976, 73 pp. SEAPRAP Research Report, no. 6.

1394 JUNSAY, ALMA T. "The Post-partum Approach to a KAP Survey among Married Women in Davao City." Master's thesis, Silliman University [Dumaguete City, Philippines], 1976[?].

1395 _____. The Post-partum Approach to a KAP Survey among Married Women in Davao City. Singapore: Southeast Asia Population Research Awards Program, 1976, 61 pp. SEAPRAP Research Report, no. 5.

1396 JUPP, KATHLEEN M. "Urban-Rural Differentials in the Fertility of Married Women in the Philippines in 1956." Philippine Statistician 9, no. 2 (June 1960):60-71.

1397 KINTANAR, AGUSTIN et al. Studies in Philippine Economic-Demographic Relationships. Quezon City: Economic Research Associates and Institute of Economic Development and Research of the School of Economics, University of the Philippines, 1974, xvii, 288 pp.

1398 KOEHLER, JOHN E. The Philippine Family Planning Program: Some Suggestions for Dealing with Uncertainties. Santa Monica, Calif.: Rand Corp., 1970, xi, 25 pp. Rand Corporation Memorandum, RM-6149-AID.

1399 LACAR, LUIS Q. "Factors Influencing the Attitudes of Catholic and Protestant Filipino College Students in the Philippines towards Fertility and Fertility Control." Ph.D. dissertation, Western Michigan University, 1974, 253 pp. Abstracted in Dissertation Abstracts International 35, no. 6 (Dec. 1974):3911-12-A. University Microfilms International, order no. 74-28,852.

1400   LAING, JOHN E. "Differentials in Contraceptive Use-
        Effectiveness in the Philippines." Studies in Family
        Planning 5, no. 10 (Oct. 1974):302-13.

1401   _____. "Estimating the Effects of Contraceptive Use on Fer-
        tility: Techniques and Findings from the 1974 Philippine
        National Acceptor Survey." Studies in Family Planning 9,
        no. 6 (June 1978):150-62.

1402   _____. "Use Effectiveness of Family Planning in the
        Philippines, 1970-72." Philippine Sociological Review 21,
        no. 2 (Apr. 1973):137-51.

1403   LAING, JOHN E., and PHILLIPS, JAMES F. "Survey Findings on
        Family Planning Effects in the Philippines, 1968-73."
        Philippine Sociological Review 23, nos. 1/4 (Jan./Oct.
        1975):91-99.

1404   LAING, JOHN E. et al. Final Report on the 1974 National
        Acceptor Survey. Quezon City: Population Institute,
        University of the Philippines, 1977, 258 pp.

1405   Law and Population in the Philippines. Medford, Mass.: Law
        and Population Programme, Fletcher School of Law and
        Diplomacy, Tufts University, 1974, v, 151 pp. Law and
        Population Book Series, no. 9. Published originally in
        the Philippine Law Journal 48, no. 3 (July 1973):356-428
        under the title "Population Law in the Philippines," by
        Carmelo V. Sison.

1406   LEDESMA, DOLORES A. "An Evaluative Survey of the Responsible
        Parenthood Service of the Family Life Advisory Center of
        the Diocese of Ozamis City." Northwestern Mindanao Re-
        search Journal 1, no. 1 (1974/75):8-19.

1407   LEE, HYO CHAI et al. Recent Empirical Findings on Fertility.
        Korea, Nigeria, Tunisia, Venezuela, Philippines. Washing-
        ton, D.C.: Interdisciplinary Communications Program,
        Smithsonian Institution, 1976, 144 pp. Occasional Mono-
        graph Series, no. 7.

1408   LOPEZ, Ma. ELENA. The Hilot in Family Planning: An Evalua-
        tion of the IMCH Program in Oriental Mindoro. Final Report
        Submitted to the Institute of Maternal and Child Health by
        the Institute of Philippine Culture, Ateneo de Manila Uni-
        versity. Quezon City: Institute of Philippine Culture,
        Ateneo de Manila Uniersity, 1974, 410 pp.

1409   LOZARE, BENJAMIN V. "Communication between Couples and
        Decision-Making in Relation to Family Planning." In
        Philippine Population Research: Papers and Proceedings of
        an Experts' Meeting. Edited by Rodolfo A. Bulatao. Makati,
        Rizal: Population Center Foundation, 1976, pp. 307-22.

1410   LYNCH, FRANK. A Family-Planning Acceptor Study: Final Report
        Submitted to USAID and the Commission on Population by the
        Institute of Philippine Culture on 15 February 1974.
        Quezon City: Institute of Philippine Culture, Ateneo de
        Manila University, 1974, 68 pp.

1411   MADIGAN, FRANCIS C. "Decline from High Fertility in Western
        Misamis Oriental: Interpretation of a Philippine Case
        History." In The Economic and Social Supports for High
        Fertility: Proceedings of the Conference Held in Canberra,
        November 1976. Canberra: Department of Demography,
        Australian National University, 1977, pp. 275-85.

1412   _____. "Fertility Rates and Patterns in Misamis Oriental and
        Southern Leyte Provinces, 1971-1976." PSSC Social Science
        Information 5, no. 3 (Oct./Dec. 1977):3-12.

1413   MADIGAN, FRANCIS C., and AVANCEÑA, ROSALIO O. "Philippine
        Fertility and Mortality with Special Reference to the North
        Mindanao Region: A Critique of Recent Estimates. Part 1:
        The Philippines in General. Part 2: The North Mindanao
        Region." Philippine Sociological Review 12 (Jan./Apr.
        1964):35-53.

1414   MALAGA, LORNA B. "The Problem of Growing Too Fast: An
        Empirical Study on the Knowledge, Attitudes and Practice
        Regarding Family Planning with an Introductory Chapter on
        the Interrelationship between Population Growth and Socio-
        Economic Aspects of Development." Saint Louis University
        Research Journal [Baguio City, Philippines] 7, nos. 1/2
        (Mar./June 1976):115-333.

1415   MANAGO-ULGADO, P. "Family Size Preferences of Filipino Ado-
        lescents." 21 pp. Paper presented at the Population
        Socialization Conference, 16-21 December 1974, East-West
        Center Population Institute, Honolulu.

1416   MANALILI, ALFREDO LUIS CURA. "The Family Planning Movement
        and the Protestant's View." Unitas 39, no.3 (Sept. 1966):
        383-99.

1417   MARTÍNEZ-ESQUILLO, N. "Conjugal Interaction and Fertility
        Behavior among the Filipino Urban Working Class." Master's
        thesis, Ateneo de Manila University [Manila], 1978, 301 pp.

1418   MATURAN, EULALIO G. "The Bohol Culture: Implications for
       Health and Family Planning Promotion." Studies in Family
       Planning 10, nos. 6/7 (June/July 1979):189-92.

1419   MIRALAO, VIRGINIA A. An Evaluation of DSW Family-Planning
       Services: Final Report. Prepared for the United States
       Agency for International Development and the Commission of
       Population by the Institute of Philippine Culture. Quezon
       City: Institute of Philippine Culture, Ateneo de Manila
       University, 1973, vii, 236 pp.

1420   MOVIDO, MONINA S. "Comics--Magazine Exposure and Family Plan-
       ning Knowledge, Attitudes and Practices among Murphy Libis
       Housewives." Philippine Journal of Communications Studies
       1, no. 1 (Sept. 1971):44-59.

1421   NACPIL, EMERITO P. "Theologians Response to the BRAC 1967
       Filipino Family Survey." Saint Louis University Research
       Journal [Baguio City, Philippines] 6 (1968):426-27.

1422   NAZARET, FRANCISCO V., and CHAVES, HIDALGO V. "Fertility
       Survey of 1963 in the Philippines." Philippine Sociologi-
       cal Review 12, nos. 1/2 (Jan./Apr. 1964):5-16.

1423   NAZARET, FRANCISCO V.; DIAZ, A.; and RAMACHANDRAN, K.V.
       "Differential Fertility by Occupational Groups in the
       Philippines." Philippine Statistician 11, no. 1 (Mar.
       1962):2-19.

1424   NESS, GAYL DEFORREST, and ANDO, HIROFUMI. "The Politics of
       Population Planning in Malaysia and the Philippines."
       Journal of Comparative Administration 3, no. 3 (Nov. 1971):
       296-329.

1425   OMRAN, ABDEL R., and STANDLEY, C.C. Family Formation Patterns
       and Health: An International Collaborative Study in India,
       Iran, Lebanon, Philippines and Turkey. Geneva: World
       Health Organization, 1976, 562 pp.

1426   OSTERIA, TRINIDAD SARAO. "Family Size Differentials in Five
       Selected Areas in the Philippines." Master's thesis,
       University of the Philippines [Quezon City], 1968, 112 pp.
       (On differences in family size of married women.)

1427   _____. "Variations in Fertility with Breast-Feeding Practice
       and Contraception in Urban Filipino Women: Implications
       for a Nutrition Program." In Nutrition and Human Repro-
       duction. Edited by W. Henry Mosley. London: Plenum
       Press, 1978, pp. 411-32.

1428 PACHECO, ANTONIA ROMULO. "An Analysis of Family Size Preference and Attitudes toward Family Planning in Selected Areas
in the Philippines." Master's thesis, University of the
Philippines [Quezon City], 1968, 110 pp.

1429 PACHECO, ANTONIA ROMULO, and OSTERIA, TRINIDAD SARAO. "Some
Findings on the Attitudes toward Family Size Preferences
and Family Limitation." Statistical Reporter 10, no. 3
(1966):1-8.

1430 PAL, AGATON P. "Family Planning Project at Silliman University: Experiences and Insights." Silliman Journal 15,
no. 3 (1968):371-84.

1431 PAQUEO, VICENTE B. "The Family Planning Evaluation Sub-
Model." In Studies in Philippine Economic-Demographic
Relationships. Edited by Agustin Kintanar. Quezon City:
Institute of Economic Development and Research, University
of the Philippines, 1974, pp. 144-99.

1432 _____. "The Family Planning Program." In Studies in Philippine Economic-Demographic Relationships. Edited by Agustin
Kintanar. Quezon City: Institute of Economic Development
and Research, University of the Philippines, 1974,
pp. 118-43.

1433 PARADO, JAMES P. "Botica sa barangay." Studies in Family
Planning 10, nos. 6/7 (June/July 1979):212-13.

1434 PASCUAL, ELVIRA MENDOZA. "Differential Fertility in the
Philippines." Philippine Sociological Review 19, nos. 3/4
(July/Oct. 1971):209-30.

1435 _____. "Fertility Differentials in the Philippines." Ph.D.
dissertation, University of Chicago, 1971, 164 pp.

1436 PATRON, JOSEFINA S. "Perspective for a Program in Family
Planning." Silliman Journal 20 (1973):357-72.

1437 PERALTA, LOURDES TACUD. "Family Planning in Relation to Family Size and Spacing of Siblings of Married Female Elementary School Teachers of Ilocos Sur." Master's thesis,
Northwestern College [Philippines], 1974, 120 pp.

1438 PHILIPPINES. University, Population Institute, Family Planning Evaluation Office. Philippine Family Planning Knowledge Attitudes and Practices: Baseline Data, 1968. Quezon
City: Population Institute, University of the Philippines,
1973, 103 pp.

1439   PHILIPPINES (REPUBLIC), Bureau of the Census and Statistics.
        Fertility and Labor Force Characteristics. Manila: Bureau
        of the Census and Statistics, 1965, x, 32 pp. Census of
        the Philippines, 1906: Population and Housing: Special
        Report.

1440   _____, Department of Health, Bohol Province Maternal Child
        Health/Family Planning Project. Annual Report. Manila.
        no. 1-, 1975-.

1441   _____, National Commission for UNESCO. Proceedings of the
        UNESCO National Commission of the Philippines Eight Bi-
        ennial Conference ('Population Problems in the Second
        Development Decade') 6-8 September 1973, Manila. Manila:
        The Commission, 197-, v, 120, 25 pp.

1442   "The Philippines: A Country Report." In SOUTHEAST ASIAN
        REGIONAL SEMINAR ON LAW AND POPULATION, Jakarta, 1975.
        Law and Population. Edited by Teuku Mohamed Radhie et al.
        Jakarta: Yayasan Penelitian dan Pengembangan Hukum, 1976,
        pp. 154-84. (Includes discussion on laws of family plan-
        ning, inheritance and maternity benefits.)

1443   PHILLIPS, JAMES F. "Continued Use of Contraception among
        Philippine Family Planning Acceptors: A Multivariate
        Analysis." Studies in Family Planning 9, no. 7 (July
        1978):182-92.

1444   PHILLIPS, JAMES F., and BAYAN, FLORA B. "Paramedical and Lay
        Paramedical Prescriptions of Oral Contraceptive: An Ex-
        periment in the Bicol Region." In Philippine Population
        Research: Papers and Proceedings of an Experts' Meeting.
        Edited by Rodolfo A. Bulatao. Makati, Rizal: Population
        Centre Foundation, 1976, pp. 405-29.

1445   PHILLIPS, JAMES F., and LLORENTE, R.L. Method Preference
        among Philippine Family Planning Acceptors. Quezon City:
        Population Institute, University of the Philippines System,
        1975, 23, 17 pp.

1446   PHILLIPS, JAMES F., and ZABLAN, ZELDA C. Trends in All
        Method Continuation and Pregnancy Rates for Women Who
        Accept over the 1970-1972 Period; 1974 NAS. Quezon City:
        Population Institute, University of the Philippines, 1975,
        15 pp. Research Note, no. 30.

1447   PIDO, ANTONIO J.A. "Differential Fertility Patterns in
        Cagayan de Oro City." Philippine Sociological Review 11
        (Jan./Apr. 1963):91-98.

1448   PINON, ANTONIO T. "How to Think on the 'Humanae Vitae' and
        Its Obligation on Catholics." Philippiniana Sacra 3,
        no. 9 (1968):491-518.

1449   _____. "A Reply to the Questionnaire Submitted by the
        Philippine Social Science Council (December 1969)."
        Philippiniana Sacra 5, no. 13 (1970):1-42. (On religious
        and moral aspects.)

1450   PINON, MANUEL. "The Issues in Birth Control." Philippiniana
        Sacra 1, no. 1 (1966):156-74. (On religious aspects.)

1451   PULLUM, THOMAS W. "A Comparison of Recent Philippine Fertil-
        ity with the Natural Fertility Model." Paper submitted
        persuant to USAID contract no. 92-154. Quezon City:
        University of the Philippines, 1972. 25 pp.

1452   _____. "A Comparison of Recent Philippine Fertility with the
        Natural Fertility Model." In A Demographic Path to Mod-
        ernity: Patterns of Early-Transition in the Philippines.
        Edited by Wilhelm Flieger and Peter Colin Smith. Quezon
        City: University of the Philippines Press, 1975,
        pp. 173-89.

1453   _____. "Differentials in Marital Fertility." In A Demo-
        graphic Path to Modernity: Patterns of Early-Transition
        in the Philippines. Edited by Wilhelm Flieger and Peter
        Colin Smith. Quezon City: University of the Philippines
        Press, 1975, pp. 153-72.

1454   QUIROLGICO-LUGUE, LYDIA, and DE LEON, MARIA FE MANGUERA.
        Textbook on Family Planning: With an Overview of Popula-
        tion Trends, Problems and Policies. Manila: Rex Book
        Store, 1974, xiii, 130 pp.

1455   RAMOS, VIOLETA L. "An Analysis of the Marriage and Fertility
        Patterns in Six Barrios in the Philippines." Master's
        thesis, University of the Philippines [Quezon City], 1961,
        ii, 112 pp.

1456   REANTASO, SUSAN V. "Population Growth: An Economic Dilemma."
        Commerce Journal 26, no. 2 (Mar. 1976):39-46.

1457   REGUDO, ADRIANA CRUZ. "The Effects of Age at Marriage on the
        Fertility of Ever-Married Women in the Ilocos, Central
        Luzon and Bicol Regions, 1960." Philippine Statistician 14
        (Dec. 1965):265-81.

1458 _____. "Fertility Patterns of Ever-Married Women in the Ilocos, Central Luzon and Bicol Regions, 1960." Master's thesis, University of the Philippines [Quezon City], 1965, 100 pp.

1459 REINING, PRISCILLA et al. Village Women: Their Changing Lives and Fertility: Studies in Kenya, Mexico and the Philippines. Washington, D.C.: American Association for the Advancement of Science, 1977, x, 273 pp.

1460 ROBERTO, EDUARDO L. "Management of Family Planning Programs in the Philippines: An Agenda for Research." In Philippine Population Research: Papers and Proceedings of an Experts' Meeting. Edited by Rodolfo A. Bulatao. Makati, Rizal: Population Centre Foundation, 1976, pp. 437-53.

1461 RODIL-MARTIRES, CONCEPCION. "Attitudes and Opinions towards Family Planning." Education Quarterly 14, no. 4 (Apr. 1967):65-69.

1462 ROSALES, VICENTE J.A. "The Catholic Choice of Rhythm." Unitas 49 (Dec. 1976):474-501.

1463 _____. "Control of Population Growth in the Philippines." Unitas 39 (1966):460-67.

1464 ROSENZWEIG, MARK RICHARD. "Female Work Experience, Employment Status, and Birth Expectations: Sequential Decision-making in the Philippines." Demography 13, no. 3 (Aug. 1976): 339-56.

1465 RUPRECHT, THEODORE K. "Fertility Control and Per Capita Income in the Philippines: Some First Approximation." Philippine Economic Journal 6 (1967):21-48.

1466 SANIEL, FELIZA L. "The Bohol IUD Program." Studies in Family Planning 10, nos. 6/7 (June/July 1979):211-12.

1467 SANVICTORES, LOURDES L. "Is There an Economic Need for Family Limitations in the Philippines?" Unitas 38, no. 3 (1965): 439-47.

1468 SEMINAR-WORKSHOP ON THE ROLE OF FPA CLINICS IN RELATION TO COMMUNITY-BASED FAMILY SERVICES, Manila, 1975. Seminar-Workshop on the Role of FPA Clinics in Relation to Community-Based Family Planning Services, Manila, Philippines 6-11 February 1975. Sponsored by Regional Medical Committee, International Planned Parenthood Federation, East and South East Asia and Oceania Region in cooperation with the Family Planning Organization of the Philippines. Kuala Lumpur: Printed by Economy Printers, 1976[?], 112 pp.

1469 SILAYAN-GO, AURORA, and LYNCH, FRANK. IPC/POPCOM 1971 Mass
      Media Study: Final Report. Quezon City: Institute of
      Philippine Culture, Ateneo de Manila University, 1971, 47,
      27 pp.

1470 SISON, C.V., and FELICIANO, M.S. "Law and Population." In
      Population of the Philippines, by United Nations Economic
      and Social Commission for Asia and the Pacific. Bangkok:
      ESCAP, 1978, pp. 298-312. (Includes laws on contraception,
      abortion, sterilization, marriage, legal separation, in-
      heritance, and maternity benefits.)

1471 SMITH, PETER COLIN. "Appendix A: Regional Fertility and
      Nuptiality Indices for 1960." In A Demographic Path to
      Modernity: Patterns of Early-Transition in the Philippines.
      Edited by Wilhelm Flieger and Peter Colin Smith. Quezon
      City: University of the Philippines Press, 1975,
      pp. 249-60.

1472 _____. 'Births Averted' Versus 'Marriages Averted': Some
      Preliminary Results from the Economic-Demographic Model.
      Quezon City: Population Institute, University of the
      Philippines System, 1974, 8, 7 pp.

1473 _____. Demographic Profiles of the Filipina: An Approach to
      the Analysis of Life Cycles." Quezon City: Population
      Institute, University of the Philippines, 1974, 9 pp.

1474 _____. Educational Differentials in Overall and Marital
      Fertility, 1968-1972. Quezon City: Population Institute,
      University of the Philippines System, 1975, 10 pp.

1475 _____. "Fertility and Nuptiality: The Local-Area Mosaic."
      In A Demographic Path to Modernity: Patterns of Early-
      Transition in the Philippines. Edited by Wilhelm Flieger
      and Peter Colin Smith. Quezon City: University of the
      Philippines Press, 1975, pp. 201-33.

1476 _____. "Philippine Regional and Provincial Differentials in
      Marriage and Family Building, 1960." Philippine Socio-
      logical Review 19, nos. 3/4 (July/Oct. 1971):159-82.

1477 _____. "The Turn-of-the-Century Birth-Rate: Estimates from
      Birth Registration and Age Structure." In A Demographic
      Path to Modernity: Patterns of Early-Transition in the
      Philippines. Edited by Wilhelm Flieger and Peter Colin
      Smith. Quezon City: University of the Philippines Press,
      1975, pp. 82-90.

1478   STINNER, WILLIAM F.   "Modernization, Marriage and Childbear-
       ing: A Synthesis of Research Findings." In A Demographic
       Path to Modernity: Patterns of Early-Transition in the
       Philippines. Edited by Wilhelm Flieger and Peter Colin
       Smith. Quezon City: University of the Philippines Press,
       1975, pp. 3-37.

1479   STINNER, WILLIAM F., and MADER, PAUL DOUGLAS. "Government
       Policy and Personal Family Planning Approval in Conflict
       Settings: The Case of the Muslim Minority in the Southern
       Philippines." Population Studies 29, no. 1 (Mar. 1975):
       53-59.

1480   ____. "Sons, Daughters or Both? An Analysis of Family Sex
       Composition Preferences in the Philippines." Demography
       12, no. 1 (Feb. 1975):67-79.

1481   SUAREZ, ANA PILAR. "Knowledge, Attitudes and Practices in
       Family Planning among Public Health Workers in Quezon
       City." Master's thesis, University of the Philippines
       [Quezon City], 1969.

1482   TALLO, VERONICA L. "An Overview of Bohol." Studies in Family
       Planning 10, nos. 6/7 (June/July 1979):188-89.

1483   TAN, D.A. "On Legalization of Abortion." Philippine Medical
       Association, Journal 46, no. 12 (Dec. 1970):715-16.

1484   TIRA, MERCEDES A.B. "Family Planning in the Philippines."
       Fookien Times Philippines Yearbook (1975):340-43.

1485   UBIAS, ROSENDA CAYETANO. "Family Planning as Perceived by
       Third and Fourth Year Female Collegiate Students in
       Cabanatuan City, 1973-1974." Master's thesis, Philippine
       Wesleyan College, 1975, vii, 219 pp.

1486   ULACK, RICHARD. "The Fertility of a Low-Income Urban Popula-
       tion in Southeast Asia." Asian Profile 7, no. 1 (Feb.
       1979):63-74. (On the Philippines.)

1487   VALENCIA, LUZVIMINDA. "Broadway Project, an Exploratory KAP
       Study." General Education Journal 21 (1971):59-72.

1488   VANDEPORTAELE, DAN D., and FLIEGER, WILHELM. "Fertility
       Differentials in Capiz and Negros Oriental, Central
       Philippines." Philippine Quarterly of Culture and Society
       4, no. 4 (Dec. 1976):264-82.

1489   VARELA, AMELIA P.   "Analytical Assessment of the Family Plan-
       ning Program in Philippines."   In Management of Family
       Planning Programs in Asia: Concepts, Issues and Approaches.
       Edited by In-Joung Whang.   Kuala Lumpur: Asian Centre for
       Development Administration, 1976, pp. 270-313.

1490   _____.   "Family Planning in the Philippines: Assessment of
       Program Implementation."   Philippine Journal of Public Ad-
       ministration 20, no. 3 (July 1976):236-60.

1491   WILLIAMSON, NANCY E.   "The Bohol Project and Its Impact."
       Studies in Family Planning 10, nos. 6/7 (June/July 1979):
       195-210.

1492   _____.   The Bohol Project: Progress Report on an Experiment
       to Improve Rural Health and Family Planning in the
       Philippines.   New York: The Population Council, 1979,
       46 pp.   Population Council.   International Programs Work-
       ing Papers, no. 5.

1493   ZABLAN, ZELDA C.   "The Prediction of Adoption and Continued
       Practice of Contraception among Enrollees in Family Plan-
       ning Clinics: 1972."   Philippine Sociological Review 23,
       nos. 1/4 (Jan./Oct. 1975):29-54.

1494   ZABLAN, ZELDA C., and PHILLIPS, JAMES F.   Characteristics of
       Eligible Women.   Quezon City: Population Institute, Uni-
       versity of the Philippines System, 1974, 10 pp.

Singapore

1495   ANDERSON, JOHN E.; CHENG, MARK C.E.; and WAN, FOOK KEE.   "A
       Component Analysis of Recent Fertility Decline in
       Singapore."   Studies in Family Planning 8, no. 11
       (Nov. 1977):282-87.

1496   ANDERSON, MARGARET GRACE.   "Family Planning in a Modernising
       Malay Community in Singapore."   D.P.H. thesis, University
       of Singapore, 1969, 95, 23 pp.

1497   CHANG, CHEN TUNG.   "Female Employment and Fertility Behavior."
       In Public Policy and Population Change in Singapore.   Ed-
       ited by Peter S.J. Chen and James T. Fawcett.   New York:
       The Population Council, 1979, pp. 167-86.

1498   _____.   "Fertility Transition in Singapore."   Ph.D. disserta-
       tion, University of Chicago, 1973, 246 pp.

1499   _____.   Fertility Transition in Singapore.   Singapore:
       Singapore University Press, 1974, xvi, 229 pp.

1500   _____. A Study of Family Planning in Singapore: The First
          Five-Year National Family Planning Program, 1966-70.
          Singapore: Economic Research Centre, University of
          Singapore, 1972, 70 pp. Research Monograph Series, no. 5.

1501   CHANG, CHEN TUNG, and HAUSER, PHILIP MORRIS. "The Impact on
          Fertility of Singapore's Family Planning Program." In
          Measuring the Effect of Family Planning Programs on Fer-
          tility. Edited by C. Chandrasekaran and Albert I.
          Hermalin. Dolhain, Belgium: Ordina Editions, 1975,
          pp. 381-425.

1502   CHANG, CHENG TUNG, and YEH, STEPHEN HUA KUO. "A Study of
          Singapore's National Family Planning Programme." Malayan
          Economic Review 17, no. 1 (Apr. 1972):51-77.

1503   CHEN, AI JU, and PANG, SWEE LAN. "Births Averted in Singapore
          during 1966-1975." Singapore Statistical Bulletin 6 (Dec.
          1977):57-70.

1504   _____. Factors Influencing the Crude Birth Rate in Singapore,
          1966-1973. Singapore: Singapore Family Planning and Pop-
          ulation Board, 1975, 22 pp. FPPB Paper, no. 33.

1505   CHEN, PETER SHOU JEN. A Comparative Study of Husband-Wife
          Communication and Family Planning in Four Asian Countries:
          National Report, Republic of Singapore. Bangkok: Popula-
          tion Division, ECAFE, 1972, 525 pp.

1506   _____. "Development Policies and Fertility Behaviour: The
          Singapore Experience of Social Disincentives." Southeast
          Asian Affairs (1978):245-56.

1507   _____. Ethnicity and Fertility: The Case of Singapore.
          Singapore: Chopmen Enterprises, 1979, 26 pp. University
          of Singapore, Department of Sociology. Sociology Working
          Paper, no. 65.

1508   _____. "Family Planning Programme and Policy in Singapore."
          Review of Southeast Asian Studies 2, no. 4 (1972):33-48.

1509   _____. "Policies Affecting the Family and Fertility Be-
          haviour." In Public Policy and Population Change in
          Singapore. Edited by Peter S.J. Chen and James T.
          Fawcett. New York: The Population Council, 1979,
          pp. 187-202.

1510   _____. Population Policy and Social Science Research on Pop-
          ulation in Singapore. Singapore: Chopmen Enterprises,
          1977, 26 pp. University of Singapore, Department of Soci-
          ology. Working Paper, no. 66.

1511   ____. Social and Psychological Aspects of Fertility: Find-
        ings from Family Planning Research in Singapore. Singapore:
        Department of Sociology, University of Singapore, 1974, 27,
        3 pp. University of Singapore, Department of Sociology.
        Working Paper, no. 23.

1512   ____. "Social and Psychological Aspects of Fertility in
        Singapore." In Social and Psychological Aspects of Fertil-
        ity in Asia. Edited by Henry P. David and Sung Jin Lee.
        Washington, D.C.: Transnational Family Research Institute,
        1974[?], pp. 39-50.

1513   ____. "A Study of Legalised Abortion in Singapore." In
        Psychosocial Aspects of Abortion. Edited by Henry P.
        David. Washington, D.C.: Transnational Family Research
        Institute, 1974, pp. 72-79.

1514   CHEN, PETER SHOU JEN, and FAWCETT, JAMES T., eds. Public
        Policy and Population Change in Singapore. New York: The
        Population Council, 1979, vii, 275 pp. (Includes articles
        on population policies and programs and fertility control
        policies.)

1515   CHEN, PETER SHOU JEN, and TAI, CHING LING. "Social Surveys on
        Population and Family Planning in Singapore." Review of
        Southeast Asian Studies 5 (1975):1-15.

1516   CHENG, MARK C.E. et al. "Sterilization Failures in Singapore:
        An Examination of Ligation Techniques and Failure Rates."
        Studies in Family Planning 8, no. 4 (Apr. 1977):109-15.

1517   "Country Report: Singapore." In SOUTHEAST ASIAN REGIONAL
        SEMINAR ON LAW AND POPULATION, Jakarta, 1975. Law and
        Population. Edited by Teuku Mohamed Radhie et al.
        Jakarta: Yayasan Penelitian dan Pengembangan Hukum, 1976,
        pp. 185-223. (Includes discussion of laws on family plan-
        ning, marriage, inheritance, and maternity benefits.)

1518   FAMILY PLANNING SEMINAR FOR COMMUNITY LEADERS OF BOON TECK,
        KIM KEAT, KHO CHUAN AND TOA PAYOH CONSTITUENCIES/COMMUNITY
        CENTRES, Singapore, 1973. Report. Singapore: Singapore
        Family Planning and Population Board, 1974, 58 pp.

1519   FAMILY PLANNING SEMINAR FOR COMMUNITY LEADERS OF GEYLANG
        SERAI, KAMPONG CHAI CHEE, KAMPONG KEMBANGAN, AND KAMPONG
        UBI CONSTITUENCIES, Singapore, 1974. Report. Jointly
        organized by the Singapore Family Planning and Population
        Board . . . et al. Sponsored by the Asia Foundation.
        Singapore: Singapore Family Planning and Population Board,
        1975, 30 pp. (Malay and Chinese editions also published.)

1520   FAMILY PLANNING SEMINAR FOR COMMUNITY LEADERS OF JALAN KAYU,
        NEE SOON, SEMBAWANG AND THOMSON CONSTITUENCIES, Singapore,
        1975. Report. Sponsored by Asia Foundation. Singapore:
        Singapore Family Planning and Population Board, 1975,
        32 pp.

1521   GANAPATHY, SOMASUNDRAM. "Family Planning Movement in Malaya
        and Singapore." B.Econs. academic exercise, University of
        Malaya, 1966, vi, 62 pp.

1522   HALL, PETER GEOFFREY. Law and Population Growth in Singapore.
        Medford, Mass.: Fletcher School of Law and Diplomacy,
        Tufts University, 1973, 57 pp. Law and Population Mono-
        graph Series, no. 9.

1523   HANNA, WILLARD ANDERSON. Singapore: The Case for Efficiency.
        Hanover, N.H.: American Universities Field Staff, 1971,
        14 pp. (The impact of population problems on society.)

1524   HASSAN, RIAZ. "Perception of Population Policies." In Public
        Policy and Population Change in Singapore. Edited by
        Peter S.J. Chen and James T. Fawcett. New York: The Popu-
        lation Council, 1979, pp. 133-47.

1525   HOOI, SEE CHOON. "Abortion: A Survey of 1,000 Cases."
        Medical Journal of Malaysia 17, no. 4 (June 1963):282-87.

1526   KANAGARATNAM, K. "Singapore: The National Family Planning
        Program." Studies in Family Planning, no. 28 (Apr. 1968):
        1-11.

1527   KANAGARATNAM, K., and KHOO, CHIAN KIM. "Singapore: The Use
        of Oral Contraceptives in the National Program." Studies
        in Family Planning 1, no. 48 (Dec. 1969):1-9.

1528   KHOO, SIEW EAN. Effects of Program Contraception on Fertil-
        ity: A Comparison of Three Asian Countries. Honolulu:
        East-West Center, 1978, ix, 58 pp. East-West Population
        Institute. Papers, no. 54. (On Taiwan, Singapore, and
        Thailand.)

1529   LAM, KEN YIN. "Family Planning in Ten Chinese Families: A
        Study of Some Aspects of the Use of Family Planning Service
        in Singapore." B.A. academic exercise, University of
        Singapore, 1959, 170 pp.

1530   LEAN, TYE HIN; CHI, I CHENG; and McCANN, MARGARET F. "Female
        Sterilization Trends in Singapore, 1970-1974." Chapel
        Hill, N.C.: International Fertility Research Program,
        1975, 8 pp.

1531 LIM, TECK BENG. "Sterilization in the Female: A Preliminary Report of 636 Cases from Singapore." Obstetrical and Gynaecological Society, Proceedings 4, no. 2 (Oct. 1973): 50-58.

1532 LOH, BOON PIAH, and HO, TAK CHEW. "Analytical Assessment of Implementation Systems for Family Planning Programme in Singapore." Singapore: Institute of Humanities and Social Sciences, College of Graduate Studies, Nanyang University, 1976, 38 pp.

1533 LOH, MARGARET. Beyond Family Planning Measures in Singapore. Singapore: Singapore Family Planning and Population Board, 1976, 35 pp. FPPB Paper, no. 40. Country paper submitted for the IGCC Regional Workshop on Reducing Fertility Through Beyond Family Planning Measures, Penang, 1976.

1534 _____. The Population Problem and the Interrelationship between the Status of Women, Development and Population (with Some Reference to Singapore). Singapore: Singapore Family Planning and Population Board, 1975, 15 pp. FPPB Paper, no. 36.

1535 _____. "The Singapore National Family Planning and Population Programme with Special Reference to New Directions and Emphasis, 1973/74." Singapore Public Health Bulletin 13 (Jan. 1974):14-27.

1536 _____. The Singapore National Family Planning Programme, the First Seven Years, 1966-1972: A Paper Presented at a Family Planning Seminar. Singapore: Singapore Family Planning and Population Board, 1973, 16 pp. FPPB Paper, no. 20.

1537 _____. Towards Replacement Level: The Singapore National Family Planning and Population Programme, 1966-1974. Rev. ed. Singapore: Singapore Family Planning and Population Board, 1976, 16 pp. FPPB Paper, no. 34.1.

1538 _____. The Two-Child Family: A Social Norm for Singapore. Singapore: Singapore Family Planning and Population Board, 1975, 13 pp. FPPB Paper, no. 25.3.

1539 _____. "Working Women in Singapore: Some Family Planning and Population Considerations." Singapore Public Health Bulletin 15 (Jan. 1975):7-12.

1540 MILLIS, JEAN. "A Study of the Effect of Nutrition on Fertility and the Outcome of Pregnancy in Singapore in 1947 and 1950." Medical Journal of Malaysia 6 (1952):157-77.

1541   NATIONAL SEMINAR ON LABOUR-MANAGEMENT COOPERATION IN POPULA-
       TION AND FAMILY PLANNING ACTIVITIES, Singapore, 1973.
       Papers. Singapore, 1973, 1 vol. (various pagings).

1542   NEVILLE, WARWICK. "The Birth Rate in Singapore." Population
       Studies 32, no. 1 (Mar. 1978):113-33.

1543   PAKSHONG, DOLLY IRENE. "Family Planning in Singapore."
       D.P.H. thesis, University of Singapore, 1967, 70 pp.

1544   QUAH, SIAM TEE. "Family Planning, Abortion and Sterilization
       Statistics in Singapore." Singapore Statistical Bulletin
       1 (Dec. 1972):69-78.

1545   SALAFF, JANET WEITZNER, and WONG, ALINE K. "Are Disincentives
       Coercive? The View from Singapore." International Family
       Planning Perspectives and Digest 4, no. 2 (1978):50-55.

1546   SAW, SWEE HOCK. "The Development of Population Control in
       Singapore." Contemporary Southeast Asia 1, no. 4 (Mar.
       1980):348-66.

1547   _____. "Singapore: Resumption of Rapid Fertility Decline in
       1973." Studies in Family Planning 6, no. 6 (June 1975):
       166-69.

1548   SCHIEFFELIN, OLIVIA, comp. and ed. Muslim Attitudes toward
       Family Planning. New York: Population Council, 1973, vii,
       145 pp.

1549   SHANTAKUMAR, G. "A Note on the Recent Increase in Fertility
       in Singapore." Malayan Economic Review 18, no. 2 (Oct.
       1973):43-49.

1550   SINGAPORE, Laws, statutes, etc. "The Singapore Family Plan-
       ning and Population Board Act. Chapter 168." In The
       Statutes of the Republic of Singapore. Rev. ed. Singapore:
       Government Printer, 1970, pp. 365-73.

1551   _____. "Voluntary Sterilization Act, 1974. (Act 25 of 1974)."
       In Supplement to the Statutes of Singapore. Singapore:
       Singapore National Printers, 1974, pp. 219-23.

1552   SINGAPORE, Legislative Assembly. White Paper on Family Plan-
       ning. Singapore: Government Printer, 1965, 25 pp. Com-
       mand Paper, Cmd. 22 of 1965.

1553   SINGAPORE, National Statistical Commission. "Statistics
       Related to Family Planning in Singapore, 1966-1974."
       Singapore Statistical Bulletin 4, no. 2 (1975):99-102.

1554   SINGAPORE, Select Committee on the Abortion Bill and the Volun-
        tary Sterilization Bill. Report. P. Coomaraswamy, chair-
        man. Singapore: Government Printer, 1969, 1 vol. (various
        pagings). Singapore Parliament. Papers, 1969. Parl. 6.

1555   SINGAPORE FAMILY PLANNING AND POPULATION BOARD. Annual Report.
        Singapore: Singapore Family Planning and Population Board.
        1st, 1966-.

1556   _____. Family Planning: A Series of 12 Papers on Family
        Planning, from Dec. 1965 to Dec. 1967. Singapore: Public
        Health Division, Ministry of Health, 1968, 68 pp.

1557   _____. Family Planning: A Series of 12 Weekly Talks on Fam-
        ily Planning, Broadcast over Radio Singapura & Rediffusion
        (Singapore) Ltd. from 2nd Oct., 1966 to 18th Dec., 1966.
        Singapore: Public Health Division, Ministry of Health,
        1967, 37 pp.

1558   _____. Family Planning: Why and How. Singapore: Public
        Health Division, n.d., 44 pp.

1559   SINHA, A.C. "A Clinical Trial on the Use of Margulies Spiral
        (I.U.D.) among 200 Women in Singapore." Singapore Medical
        Journal 7, no. 1 (Mar. 1966):42-50.

1560   "Social Change, the Family and Fertility." Obstetrical and
        Gynaecological Society, Proceedings 4 (Oct. 1973):89-96.

1561   TAN, NALLA. "Knowledge and Attitudes of Pre-University Stu-
        dents to Family Planning." Singapore Medical Journal 16
        (1975):19-30.

1562   TAN, SIOK BIE; LEE, JAMES; and RATNAM, S.S. "Effects of Dis-
        incentives on Decisions about Pregnancy and Abortion." In
        Public Policy and Population Change in Singapore. Edited
        by Peter S.J. Chen and James T. Fawcett. New York: The
        Population Council, 1979, pp. 151-66. Also published in
        American Journal of Public Health 68 (Feb. 1978):119-24.

1563   UNITED NATIONS FUND FOR POPULATION ACTIVITIES. Singapore.
        New York: United Nations Fund for Population Activities,
        1977[?], 31 pp.

1564   VAITHILINGAM, D.K., and FUNG, MAUREEN. Family Planning and
        Family Organisation. Edited by Ann Wee. Singapore:
        Department of Social Work, University of Singapore, 1973,
        84 pp. University of Singapore, Department of Social Work.
        Resource Paper Series, no. 3.

1565   VERON, JACQUES. "Appartenance ethnique et comportement des
        populations de Malaisie et de Singapour" [Ethnic origin and
        demographic behavior of the populations of Malaysia and
        Singapore]. Population 33, nos. 4/5 (July/Oct. 1978):
        937-50.

1566   WAN, FOOK KEE. Communications Strategy in the Singapore Fam-
        ily Planning Programme. Singapore: Singapore Family Plan-
        ning and Population Board, National Family Planning Centre,
        1971, 5 pp. FPPB Paper, no. 14.

1567   _____. Contraceptive Service Delivery in the Singapore Na-
        tional Programme. Singapore: Singapore Family Planning
        and Population Board, 1976, 13, 8 pp. FPPB Paper, no. 43.

1568   _____. The Experience of Population Control in Singapore:
        10-Year Review. Singapore: Singapore Family Planning and
        Population Board, 1976, 15, 6 pp. FPPB Paper, no. 39.
        Also published in Singapore Public Health Bulletin, no. 17
        (July 1976):7-28.

1569   _____. The First Five Years of the Singapore Family Planning
        Programme, 1966 to 1970. Singapore: Singapore Family
        Planning and Population Board, 1971, 17 pp. FPPB Paper,
        no. 10.

1570   _____. The Place of Female Sterilization in the Singapore Na-
        tional Family Planning and Population Programme. Singapore:
        Singapore Family Planning and Population Board, 1977,
        14 pp. FPPB Paper, no. 49.

1571   _____. Population Growth and Ecology with reference to
        Singapore. Singapore: Singapore Family Planning and
        Population Board, 1971, 8 pp. FPPB Paper, no. 11.

1572   _____. "Sexual Sterilization in Singapore: Some Epidemio-
        logical Aspects and Demographic Impact." Academy of Medi-
        cine, Singapore, Annals 3, no. 4 (1974):324-30.

1573   WAN, FOOK KEE, and CHEN, AI JU. Singapore: Effects of a Na-
        tional Family Planning Programme. Singapore: Singapore
        Family Planning and Population Board, 1973, 9 pp. FPPB
        Paper, no. 22.

1574   WAN, FOOK KEE; CHEN, AI JU; and TAN, JESSIE. "Oral Contra-
        ceptive Continuation Rates in the Singapore National Pro-
        gram, 1962-1972." Studies in Family Planning 6, no. 1
        (Jan. 1975):17-21.

1575   WAN, FOOK KEE, and LOH, MARGARET. "Fertility Policies and the
       National Family Planning and Population Programme." In
       Public Policy and Population Change in Singapore. Edited
       by Peter S.J. Chen and James T. Fawcett. New York: The
       Population Council, 1979, pp. 97-108.

1576   _____. "Singapore." Studies in Family Planning 6, no. 8
       (Aug. 1975):236-38. (On family planning programs in 1974.)

1577   _____. The Singapore National Family Planning and Population
       Programme, 1966-1976. Singapore: Singapore Family Plan-
       ning and Population Board, 1977, 25 pp. FPPB Paper,
       no. 42.3.

1578   _____. "Target Zero." Singapore Trade and Industry (Aug.
       1974):6-15.

1579   WAN, FOOK KEE, and QUAH, SIAM TEE. "Singapore: A Study of
       Continuation Rates." Studies in Family Planning 2, no. 12
       (Dec. 1971):257-59.

1580   WAN, FOOK KEE, and SAW, SWEE HOCK. "Knowledge, Attitudes and
       Practice of Family Planning in Singapore." Studies in
       Family Planning 6, no. 4 (Apr. 1975):109-12.

1581   _____. Report of the First National Survey on Family Planning
       in Singapore. Singapore: Singapore Family and Population
       Board and National Statistical Commission, 1974, xv,
       141 pp.

1582   WEE, KENNETH KIM SENG. Laws Affecting Population and Family
       Planning in Singapore. Singapore: UNFPA Law and Popula-
       tion Project, 1976, x, 170 pp. United Nations Fund for
       Population Activities, Law and Population Project. Report,
       no. 1.

1583   _____. "Legal Aspects of Population Policies." In Public
       Policy and Population Change in Singapore. Edited by
       Peter S.J. Chen and James T. Fawcett. New York: The
       Population Council, 1979, pp. 29-46.

1584   WILLIAMSON, NANCY E.; LEAN, TYE HIN; and VENGADASALAM, D.
       "Evaluation of an Unsuccessful Sex Pre-Selection Clinic in
       Singapore." Journal of Biosocial Science 10, no. 4 (Oct.
       1978):375-88.

1585   WOLFERS, D., ed. Post-partum Intra-uterine Contraception in
       Singapore. Amsterdam: Excerpta Medica, 1970, ix, 193 pp.

1586   WONG, ALINE K., and SALAFF, JANET WEITZNER. "Planning Births
       for a Better Life: Working Class Response to Population
       Disincentives." In Public Policy and Population Change in
       Singapore. Edited by Peter S.J. Chen and James T. Fawcett.
       New York: The Population Council, 1979, pp. 109-31.

1587   WU, SAU SAN. "Singapore Family Planning Programme 1966-1970
       and Its Impact on Fertility Decline: With Special Refer-
       ence to Ethnic Groups." D.P.H. thesis, University of
       Singapore, 1972, 66 pp.

1588   YEH, STEPHEN HUA KUO. "Some Observations on Fertility Decline
       in Singapore." In Population Problems in the Pacific. Ed-
       ited by Minoru Tachi and Minoru Muramatsu, pp. 96-102.
       Tokyo: Eleventh Pacific Science Congress, 1971.

1589   YEOH, SAW AI. "A Study of Family Planning Acceptors and
       Refusors among Post-partum Contract Service Contacts--
       1st July 1971 to 31st December 1971." D.P.H. thesis,
       University of Singapore, 1973, 55 pp.

1590   YOONG, THERESA AI LEN. "A Review of Home Visiting to Post
       Partum Family Planning Defaulters at a Maternal and Child
       Health Clinic." Master's thesis, University of Singapore,
       1974, 78 pp.

1591   Youth and Population: A Matter of Concern: A Seminar on
       Population and Family Life Education. Singapore: Family
       Planning Association of Singapore, 1976, 1 vol. (various
       pagings).

1592   YUNG, SIEW MAT (FOONG). "The Post-partum Family Planning
       Programme of Singapore: A Study of Refusers at a Family
       Planning Clinic." D.P.H. thesis, University of Singapore,
       1972, 84 pp.

Thailand

1593   APHICHAT CHAMRATRITHIRONG. "Fertility, Nuptiality and Migra-
       tion in Thailand, 1970 Census: The Multiphasic Response
       Theory." Ph.D. dissertation, Brown University, 1976,
       277 pp. Abstracted in Dissertation Abstracts International
       38, no. 1 (July 1977):499-A. University Microfilms Inter-
       national, order no. 77-14,098.

1594   ARNOLD, FRED, and CHINTANA PEJARANONDA. Economic Factors in
       Family Size Decisions in Thailand. Bangkok: Institute of
       Population Studies, Chulalongkorn University and London:
       World Fertility Survey, 1977, iii, 33 pp. World Fertility
       Survey, Survey of Fertility. Thailand Report, no. 2.

1595 BALDWIN, GEORGE B. "The McCormick Family Planning Program in
      Chiang Mai, Thailand." Studies in Family Planning 9,
      no. 12 (Dec. 1978):300-313.

1596 BURNIGHT, ROBERT G., and BOONLERT LEOPRAPAI. Attitudes of
      Rural Thai Women toward Induced Abortion. Bangkok:
      Institute of Population and Social Research, Mahidol Uni-
      versity, 1975, 19 pp. Mahidol University. Institute for
      Population and Social Research. Working Paper, no. 7.
      Also published in Journal of Biosocial Science 9 (Jan.
      1977):61-72.

1597 BURNIGHT, ROBERT G.; VERASING MUANGMUN; and COOK, MICHAEL
      JOHN. Male Sterilization in Thailand: A Follow-up Study.
      Bangkok: Institute for Population and Social Research,
      Mahidol University, 1974, 19, 2 pp. Mahidol University,
      Institute for Population and Social Research. Working
      Paper, no. 5. Also published in Journal of Biosocial
      Science 7, no. 4 (1975):377-91.

1598 CHAIWAT PANJAPHONGSE, and NARONG TIENSONG. Thailand: Popu-
      lation and Population Education. Bangkok: Thai Watana
      Panich Press, 1976, 76 pp.

1599 CHAKRIT NORANITPADUNGKARN. "Family Planning Program in
      Thailand: System, Issues and Problems. In Management of
      Family Planning Programs in Asia: Concepts, Issues and
      Approaches. Edited by In Joung Whang. Kuala Lumpur:
      Asian Centre for Development Administration, 1976,
      pp. 334-67.

1600 CHAMNONG BOONCHOO. A Multi-variate Analysis of Fertility
      Preference in Lampoon. Singapore: SEAPRAP (Southeast
      Asia Population Research Awards Program), 1977, ii, 45 pp.
      SEAPRAP Research Report, no. 11.

1601 CHAVALIT SIRIPIROM. "Fertility Differentials in Chiangmai,
      Thailand: Socio-Economic, Life-style, and KAP Character-
      istics." Ph.D. dissertation, University of Syracuse, 1976,
      187 pp. Abstracted in Dissertation Abstracts International
      38, no. 8 (Feb. 1978):5070-A. University Microfilms Inter-
      national, order no. 7724577.

1602 CHIRA HONGLADAROM. "The Effect of Child Mortality on Fer-
      tility in Thailand." Ph.D. dissertation, University of
      Washington, 1978, 96 pp.

1603 CHULALONGKORN UNIVERSITY, Institute of Population Studies.
      The Survey of Fertility in Thailand: Country Report. A
      joint project of the Institute of Population Studies,
      Chulalongkorn University and Population Survey Division,
      National Statistical Office. Bangkok: Institute of Popu-
      lation Studies, Chulalongkorn University, 1977. 2 vols.
      World Fertility Survey. Report, no. 1.

1604 CLARK, E. CUNNINGHAM. "Thai 'Injection' Doctors." Journal
      of Social Science and Medicine 4 (1970):1-24. (On contra-
      ceptives.)

1605 COOK, MICHAEL JOHN. Female Labour Force Participation and
      Fertility in Rural Thailand: Some Preliminary Findings.
      Bangkok: Institute for Population and Social Research,
      Mahidol University, 1975, 26 pp.

1606 _____. "Female Labor Force Participation, Modernity and Fer-
      tility in Rural Thailand." Ph.D. dissertation, Brown Uni-
      versity, 1977, 299 pp. Abstracted in Dissertation Abstracts
      International 38, no. 12 (June 1978):7586-A. University
      Microfilms International, order no. 7809045.

1607 COOK, MICHAEL JOHN, and BOONLERT LEOPRAPAI. Labor Force Par-
      ticipation, Village Characteristics and Modernism and Their
      Influence on Fertility among Rural Thai Women. Bangkok:
      Institute for Population and Social Research, Mahidol Uni-
      versity, 1977, 164 pp. (Part II published in 1978, 29 pp.)

1608 _____. "Some Observations on Abortion in Thailand." Paper
      presented at the Asian Regional Research Seminar on Psycho-
      social Aspects of Abortion, Kathmandu, Nepal, November
      1974.

1609 "Country Report: Thailand." In SOUTHEAST ASIAN REGIONAL
      SEMINAR ON LAW AND POPULATION, Jakarta, 1975. Law and
      Population. Edited by Teuku Mahamed Radhie et al.
      Jakarta: Yayasan Penelitian dan Pengembangun Hukum, 1976,
      pp. 264-71. (Includes discussion of laws on family plan-
      ning, status of women, and maternity benefits.)

1610 COWGILL, DONALD O. et al. Family Planning in Bangkhen,
      Thailand. Bangkok: Institute for Population and Social
      Research, Mahidol University, 1973, 212 pp.

1611 _____. "Sterilization: A Case of Extensive Practice in a
      Developing Nation." Milbank Memorial Fund Quarterly 49,
      no. 3, pt. 1 (July 1971):363-78.

1612   EBNET, DUANE MICHAEL. "The Influence of Traditional Values
        and Beliefs on Family Planning Decisions in Thailand."
        Ph.D. dissertation, University of Minnesota, 1977, 196 pp.
        Abstracted in <u>Dissertation Abstracts International</u> 38,
        no. 10 (Apr. 1978):6343-A. University Microfilms Inter-
        national, order no. 7802659.

1613   GOLDSTEIN, SIDNEY. "The Influence of Labour Force Participa-
        tion and Education on Fertility in Thailand." <u>Population
        Studies</u> 26, no. 3 (Nov. 1972):419-36. Also published sepa-
        rately as Chulalongkorn University, Institute of Population
        Studies. Research Report, no. 9, 1972, iv, 28 pp.

1614   _____. "Interrelations between Migration and Fertility in
        Thailand." <u>Demography</u> 10, no. 2 (May 1973):225-41. Also
        published separately as Chulalongkorn University, Institute
        of Population Studies. Research Report, no. 5, 1971,
        45 pp.

1615   _____. "Religious Fertility Differentials in Thailand, 1960."
        <u>Population Studies</u> 24, no. 3 (Nov. 1970):325-37.

1616   GOLDSTEIN, SIDNEY; GOLDSTEIN, ALICE; and SAUVALUCK PIAMPITI.
        <u>The Effect of Broken Marriage on Fertility Levels in
        Thailand</u>. Bangkok: Institute of Population Studies,
        Chulalongkorn University, 1973, 30 pp. Chulalongkorn
        University, Institute of Population Studies. Paper,
        no. 4.

1617   GOLDSTEIN, SIDNEY, and PENPORN TIRASAWAT. <u>The Fertility of
        Migrants to Urban Places in Thailand</u>. Honolulu: East-
        West Center, 1977, v, 49 pp. East-West Population Insti-
        tute. Papers, no. 43.

1618   GROSSMAN, RICHARD A.; TERMSRI CHUMNIJARAKIJ; and PRASONGPORN
        CHARUMILIND. "A Study of New Contraceptive Acceptors of
        Pills and IUDs at Three Bangkok Clinics." <u>Contraception</u>
        16, no. 1 (July 1977):67-77.

1619   HASHIMOTO, MASANORI, and CHIRA HONGLADAROM. <u>Effects of Child
        Death on Fertility in Thailand</u>. Bangkok: Thammasat Uni-
        versity, 1978, 25 pp. Thammasat University, Faculty of
        Economics. Discussion Paper Series, no. 68.

1620   HAWLEY, AMOS H., and VISID PRACHUABMOH. "Family Growth and
        Family Planning in a Rural District in Thailand." <u>Pro-
        ceedings: Family Planning and Population Programs</u>, by
        International Conference on Family Planning Programme,
        Geneva, 1965. Chicago: University of Chicago Press,
        1966, pp. 523-44.

1621   _____. "Family Growth and Family Planning: Responses to a
        Family Planning Action Program in a Rural District of
        Thailand." Demography 3, no. 2 (1966):319-31.

1622   HOGAN, DENNIS P. "An Evaluation of the Demographic Impact of
        the National Family Planning Program of Thailand." Report
        prepared for the United States Agency for International
        Development under a contract awarded to the Community and
        Family Study Center, University of Chicago, 1978.

1623   JONES, GAVIN WALLIS, and JAWALAKSANA RACHAPAETAYAKOM. Fer-
        tility and Contraception in the Rural North of Thailand.
        Bangkok: Manpower Planning Division, National Economic
        Development Board, 1970, iv, 22 pp.

1624   JONES, GAVIN WALLIS, and YANEE SOONTHORNTHUM. Fertility and
        Contraception in the Rural South of Thailand. Bangkok:
        Manpower Planning Division, National Economic Development
        Board, 1971, 27 pp.

1625   KAMHAENG CHATURACHINDA, and MALLE THAMLIKITKYE. "The Epi-
        demiology of Illegally Induced Abortion." Paper presented
        at the seminar, Southeast Asia Addresses Its Health Prob-
        lems: Current Research and Education Activities, Bangkok,
        October, 1974.

1626   KHOO, SIEW EAN. Effects of Program Contraception on Fertility:
        A Comparison of Three Asian Countries. Honolulu: East-West
        Center, 1978, ix, 58 pp. East-West Population Institute,
        Papers, no. 54. (On Taiwan, Singapore, and Thailand.)

1627   _____. "Measuring the Thai Family Planning Program's Impact
        on Fertility Rates: A Comparison of Computer Models."
        Studies in Family Planning 10, no. 4 (Apr. 1979):137-45.

1628   KNODEL, JOHN, and NIBHON DEBAVALYA. "Thailand's Reproductive
        Revolution." International Family Planning Perspectives
        and Digest 4, no. 2 (1978):34-49.

1629   KNODEL, JOHN, and PICHIT PITAKTEPSOMBATI. "Fertility and
        Family Planning in Thailand: Results from Two Rounds of a
        National Study." Studies in Family Planning 6, no. 11
        (Nov. 1975):402-13.

1630   _____. Fertility and Family Planning in Thailand: Results of
        the Second Round of a National Survey. Bangkok: Institute
        of Population Studies, Chulalongkorn University, 1975,
        59 pp. Chulalongkorn University. Institute of Population
        Studies. Paper, no. 19.

1631 _____. "Thailand: Fertility and Family Planning among Rural and Urban Women." Studies in Family Planning 4, no. 9 (Sept. 1973):229-55.

1632 KNODEL, JOHN, and VISID PRACHUABMOH. "Demographic Aspects of Fertility in Thailand." Population Studies 28, no. 3 (Nov. 1974):423-48.

1633 _____. "Desired Family Size in Thailand: Are the Responses Meaningful?" Demography 10, no. 4 (Nov. 1973):619-37.

1634 _____. The Fertility of Thai Women. Bangkok: Institute of Population Studies, Chulalongkorn University, 1973, iv, 87 pp. Chulalongkorn University. Institute of Population Studies. Research Report, no. 10.

1635 _____. "Preferences for Sex of Children in Thailand: A Comparison of Husbands' and Wives' Attitudes." Studies in Family Planning 7, no. 5 (May 1976):137-43.

1636 LEWIS, PAUL WHITE. "The Introduction of a Family Planning Program to Akhas in Thailand." Ph.D. dissertation, University of Oregon, 1978, 246 pp. Abstracted in Dissertation Abstracts International 39, no. 2 (Aug. 1978):963-64-A. University Microfilms International, order no. 7814320.

1637 LUECHAI CHULASAI. The Roles of Husbands and Fathers in Family Planning in Rural Chiang Mai. Singapore: Southeast Asia Population Research Awards Program (SEAPRAP), International Development Research Center, Asia Regional Office and Ford Foundation, 1975, iii, 20 pp. SEAPRAP Research Report, no. 3.

1638 McDANIEL, EDWIN B. "Use of a Long-acting Injectable Contraceptive in a Postpartum Family Planning Programme." Asian Journal of Medicine 9 (Apr. 1973):133-35.

1639 McDANIEL, EDWIN B., and TIENG PARDTHAISONG. "Return of Menstruation and Fertility in Thai Women after Contraceptive Injections." Journal of Biosocial Science 3, no. 2 (Apr. 1971):209-22.

1640 MATHANA T. PHANANIRAMAI. "A Micro-Economic Analysis of the Determinants of Fertility in Thailand." Ph.D. dissertation, University of Hawaii, 1979, viii, 155 pp.

1641 MAURER, KENNETH; RATAJCZAK, ROSALINDA; and SCHULTZ, T. PAUL. Marriage, Fertility and Labor Force Participation of Thai Women: An Econometric Study. Santa Monica, Calif.: Rand Corporation, 1973, xiv, 54 pp. Rand Report, R-829.

1642   MUECKE, MARJORIE ANN. "'Reproductive Success' among the
        Urban Poor: A Micro-level Study of Infant Survival and
        Child Growth in Northern Thailand." Ph.D. dissertation,
        University of Washington, Seattle, 1976, 435 pp. Ab-
        stracted in Dissertation Abstracts International 38, no. 3
        (Sept. 1977):1506-A. University Microfilms International,
        order no. 77-18,394.

1643   NATIONAL SEMINAR ON POPULATION PROBLEMS IN THAILAND, Bangkok,
        1963. Papers. Bangkok: National Research Council, 1963,
        510 pp.

1644   NG, RONALD C.Y. "Early Warning for Fertile Thailand." Geo-
        graphical Magazine 47, no. 4 (Jan. 1975):239-42.

1645   NIBHON DEBAVALYA. Female Employment and Fertility: Cross-
        sectional and Longitudinal Relationships from a National
        Sample of Married Thai Women. Bangkok: Institute of
        Population Studies, Chulalongkorn University, 1977, 88 pp.
        Chulalongkorn University, Institute of Population Studies.
        Working Paper, no. 24.

1646   _____. "A Study of Female Labor Force Participation and Fer-
        tility in Thailand." Ph.D. dissertation, University of
        Pennsylvania, 1975, 271 pp. Abstracted in Dissertation
        Abstracts International 36, no. 12 (June 1976):8328-A.
        University Microfilms International, order no. 76-12,267.

1647   _____. "A Study of Female Labor Force Participation and Fer-
        tility in Thailand." 65 pp. Paper presented at the Sem-
        inar on Labour Supply, under the joint sponsorship of the
        Council for Asian Manpower Studies and the Organization of
        Demographic Associates held in Makati, Rizal, Philippines,
        June 1976.

1648   NIBHON DEBAVALYA, and KNODEL, JOHN. Fertility Transition in
        Thailand: A Comparative Analysis of Survey Data. Bangkok:
        Institute of Population Studies, Chulalongkorn University
        and Population Survey Division, National Statistical Of-
        fice, 1978, 34 pp. World Fertility Survey, Survey of Fer-
        tility in Thailand. Report, no. 3.

1649   ORRAWIN TROCKI. Attitudes toward Family Planning and Popula-
        tion Education among Teachers and Students. Singapore:
        Southeast Asia Population Research Awards Program
        (SEAPRAP), International Development Research Centre and
        Ford Foundation, 1977, 128 pp. SEAPRAP Research Report,
        no. 21.

1650   PEERASIT KAMNUANSILPA. "The Relationship between Family
        Structure and Fertility in Thailand." Ph.D. dissertation,
        University of Missouri, 1975, 112 pp. Abstracted in <u>Dis-
        sertation Abstracts International</u> 36, no. 10 (Apr. 1976):
        6992-A. University Microfilms International, order no.
        76-7512.

1651   PISUTE UTAMOTE. "An Overall EIC Programme of the Planned
        Parenthood Association of Thailand." 18 pp. Paper pre-
        sented at the Seminar Workshop on EIC, Philippines,
        10-14 June 1974.

1652   "Population and Family Planning in Thailand." <u>Bangkok Bank
        Monthly Review</u> 19, no. 6 (June 1978):241-47.

1653   PORNCHAI BOODSAYASAKUL. "Determinants of Family Planning
        Practice in Rural Thailand." Ph.D. dissertation, Univer-
        sity of North Carolina, 1977, 82 pp. Abstracted in <u>Disser-
        tation Abstracts International</u> 38, no. 6 (Dec. 1977):
        3753-A. University Microfilms International, order no.
        77-27,229.

1654   PRAPAPEN SUWAN. <u>A Study of the Development of Thai Children's
        Opinion Concerning Family Size Preference</u>. Singapore:
        Southeast Asia Population Research Awards Program, 1977,
        ii, 63 pp. SEAPRAP Research Report, no. 17.

1655   RADOM SETTEETON. "The Problem of Population Growth in
        Thailand: With Emphasis on Food Production and Family
        Planning." Ph.D. dissertation, Michigan State University,
        1967, 217 pp. Abstracted in <u>Dissertation Abstracts Inter-
        national</u> 28, no. 12 (June 1968):5158-A. University Micro-
        films International, order no. 68-7962.

1656   RILEY, JAMES NELSON. "Cohabitation, Natality, and Mortality
        in Rural Thailand and Burma." In <u>Culture, Natality, and
        Family Planning</u>. Edited by John F. Marshall and Steven
        Polgar. Chapel Hill, N.C.: Carolina Population Center,
        University of North Carolina, 1976, pp. 24-49.

1657   RILEY, JAMES NELSON, and SANTHAT SERMSRI. <u>The Variegated Thai
        Medical System as a Context for Birth Control Services</u>.
        Bangkok: Institute for Population and Social Research,
        Mahidol University, 1974, 71 pp. Mahidol University,
        Institute for Population and Social Research. Working
        Paper, no. 6.

1658   ROBINSON, WARREN C.; NOPMANEE SOMBOONSUB; and SUCHA
        SUWANNAPIROM. "Changing Thai Attitudes towards Fertility
        and Family Size." <u>Southeast Asian Journal of Social Sci-
        ence</u> 4, no. 1 (1975):19-28.

1659   RODGERS, G.B. "Fertility and Desired Fertility: Longitudi-
        nal Evidence from Thailand." Population Studies 30, no. 3
        (Nov. 1976):511-26.

1660   ROSENFIELD, ALLAN G., and SOMSAK VARAKAMIN. "The Postpartum
        Approach to Family Planning: Experiences in Thailand from
        1966 to 1971." American Journal of Obstetrics and Gynae-
        cology, no. 113 (May 1972):1-13.

1661   ROSENFIELD, ALLAN G. et al. "Thailand: Family Planning
        Activities 1968 to 1970." Studies in Family Planning 2,
        no. 9 (Sept. 1971):181-92.

1662   SATIT NIYOMYAHT. "Differential Fertility in Thailand: An
        Analysis of Social and Economic Factors Affecting Fertil-
        ity." Ph.D. dissertation, Washington University, St. Louis,
        1974, 222 pp. Abstracted in Dissertation Abstracts Inter-
        national 35, no. 4 (Oct. 1974):2409-10-A. University
        Microfilms International, order no. 74-22,539.

1663   SMYTHE, HUGH H., and NIBONDH SASIDHORN. "Population Control
        in Thailand through Family Sterilization." American Jour-
        nal of Economics and Sociology 24, no. 3 (July 1965):
        301-306.

1664   SOMJIT SUPANNATAS. Birth Control among Postpartum Thai Women.
        Bangkok: Faculty of Public Health, Mahidol University,
        1977, x, 128 pp.

1665   _____. "Some Factors Affecting the Non-acceptance of a Birth
        Control Method in the Postpartum Period among Thai Married
        Women Who Already Have Two Children." Dr.P.H. dissertation,
        University of California, Berkeley, 1975, 182 pp. Ab-
        stracted in Dissertation Abstracts International 37, no. 1
        (July 1976):165-B. University Microfilms International,
        order no. 76-15,082.

1666   SOMPHONG SHEVASUNT; HOGAN, DENNIS P.; and KWANCHAI THAITHONG.
        "Fertility and Family Planning in Rural Northern Thailand."
        Studies in Family Planning 9, no. 8 (Aug. 1978):212-21.

1667   SOMSAK, VARAKAMIN et al. "Attitudes toward Abortion in
        Thailand: A Survey of Senior Medical Students." Studies
        in Family Planning 8, no. 11 (Nov. 1977):288-93.

1668   SOOMBOONSUK, A. et al. "A Comparative Controlled Trial in
        Rural Thailand of Three Intrauterine Devices." Contra-
        ception 18, no. 2 (Aug. 1978):137-50.

166

1669   SOONTAREE SUVIPAKIT, and FAWCETT, JAMES T. "Attitudes and
        Behaviour Affecting Fertility in Two Thai-Muslim Communi-
        ties." Journal of Social Sciences [Bangkok] 7, no. 1
        (1970):186-96.

1670   SUCHART PRASITHRATHSIN. "Economic and Fertility Behavior of
        the Rural People in Thailand." Ph.D. dissertation, Brown
        University, 1971, xlii, 521 pp. Abstracted in Dissertation
        Abstracts International 32, no. 9 (Mar. 1972):5370-A. Uni-
        versity Microfilms International, order no. 72-8162.

1671   _____. "Female Labor Force Participation and Fertility Be-
        havior in Rural Thailand." Journal of Social Sciences
        [Bangkok] 8, no. 4 (Oct. 1971):34-48.

1672   _____. "A Pilot Survey of Religious Beliefs and Practices
        as Affecting Population Change in Thailand." 17 pp.
        Paper prepared for SEADAG Population Panel Seminar, Bali,
        August 1974.

1673   _____. Some Factors Affecting Fertility and Knowledge, Atti-
        tude and Practice of Family Planning among Rural Thai
        Women. Bangkok: Institute of Population Studies,
        Chulalongkorn University, 1973, 109 pp. Chulalongkorn
        University, Institute of Population Studies. Working
        Paper, no. 2.

1674   SUPALAK PURNASIRI, and KUMAREE KOMARAKUL. Report on Pre-
        testing of the Motivation Kit for Use in the Project
        Family Planning Communication Development and Integrated
        Campaigns (THA/72/P07). Bangkok: United Nations Develop-
        ment Programme Support Communication Service, 1976, 13 pp.

1675   The Survey of Fertility in Thailand: Country Report. 2 vols.
        Bangkok: Institute of Population Studies, Chulalongkorn
        University and National Statistical Office; London:
        World Fertility Survey, 1977, xvi, 188 pp.; xviii, 524 pp.

1676   The Survey of Fertility in Thailand, 1975: A Summary of Find-
        ings. The Hague: International Statistical Institute,
        1978, 11 pp. World Fertility Survey, no. 6, 1978.

1677   THAILAND, Ministry of Public Health, National Family Planning
        Program. Family Planning in Thailand, 1965-1970. Bangkok:
        National Family Planning Program, Ministry of Public Health,
        1971, 28 pp.

1678   _____. Family Planning in Thailand, 1965-1971. Bangkok:
        National Family Planning Program, Ministry of Public Health,
        1972, 33 pp.

1679   THAILAND, National Economic and Social Development Board,
       Population and Manpower Planning Division. Report on the
       Survey of Fertility Behaviour in the Context of Demographic
       and Socio-Economic Development of Muslim Societies in
       Thailand. Bangkok: National Economic and Social Develop-
       ment Board, Population and Manpower Planning Division,
       1978, 58 pp.

1680   _____ et al. Population Growth in Thailand, by Manpower
       Planning Division, National Economic Development Board,
       National Family Planning Program, Ministry of Public
       Health, and Institute of Population Studies, Chulalongkorn
       University. 2d ed. Bangkok, 1972, 41 pp.

1681   THANAVADEE TANIA BOONLUE. "A Study of Media, Husband-Wife
       Communication for Family Planning and Social Development in
       Rural Northern Thailand." Ph.D. dissertation, University
       of Chicago, 1979, 350 pp. Abstracted in Dissertation Ab-
       stracts International 40, no. 1 (July 1979):478-A.

1682   THIENCHAY KIRANANDANA. "An Economic Study of Fertility De-
       termination among Rural and Urban Thais." Ph.D. disserta-
       tion, Duke University, 1978, 163 pp. Abstracted in Dis-
       sertation Abstracts International 39, no. 9 (Mar. 1979):
       5642-A. University Microfilms International, order no.
       7905361.

1683   _____ . An Economic Analysis of Fertility Determination among
       Rural and Urban Thai Women. Bangkok: Institute of Popu-
       lation Studies, Chulalongkorn University, 1977, 17 pp.
       Chulalongkorn University, Institute of Population Studies.
       Working Paper, no. 20.

1684   TIENG PARDTHAISONG. The Recent Fertility Decline in the
       Chiang Mai Area of Thailand. Honolulu: East-West Center,
       1978, vii, 36 pp. East-West Population Institute. Paper,
       no. 47.

1685   TONGPLAEW NARKAVONNAKIT. "Abortion in Rural Thailand: A
       Survey of Practitioners." Studies in Family Planning 10,
       nos. 8/9 (Aug./Sept. 1979):223-29.

1686   _____ . Rural Abortion in Thailand: A National Survey of
       Practitioners. Bangkok: National Family Planning Program,
       1979, 31 pp.

1687   VICHAI RUNGPITARANGSI. Fertility in Thailand 1960-1970.
       Bangkok: Institute of Population Studies, Chulalongkorn
       University, 1977, 79 pp. Chulalongkorn University, Insti-
       tute of Population Studies. Working Paper, no. 22.

1688   VISID PRACHUABMOH, and KNODEL, JOHN. Preferences for Sex of
        Children in Thailand: Results from the Second Round of a
        National Survey. Bangkok: Institute of Population Stud-
        ies, Chulalongkorn University, 1975, 17 pp. Chulalongkorn
        University, Institute of Population Studies. Working
        paper, no. 23.

1689   VISID PRACHUABMOH; KNODEL, JOHN; and ALERS, J. OSCAR. "Pref-
        erence for Sons, Desire for Additional Children, and Family
        Planning in Thailand." Journal of Marriage and the Family
        36, no. 3 (Aug. 1974):601-14.

1690   VORAVIDH CHAROENLOET, and BOONLERT LEOPRAPAI. Report on
        Contraceptive Continuation Rates and Use-Effectiveness in
        Bangkok Metropolis: 1975. Bangkok: Institute for Popula-
        tion and Social Research, Mahidol University, 1976, iii,
        36 pp.

1691   WICHID YAMBOONRUANG. "The Influence of Some Aspects of Mod-
        ernization on Fertility: A Time-Series and Cross-sectional
        Analysis of the Thai Data." Ph.D. dissertation, University
        of Pittsburgh, 1977, 190 pp. Abstracted in Dissertation
        Abstracts International 38, no. 5 (Nov. 1977):3079-A.
        University Microfilms International, order no. 77-23,564.

1692   Youth Consultation on Role of Students in Family Planning,
        Samut Prakan, Thailand, 1975, Report. Bangkok: Youth
        Project, Field Operation Division, Planned Parenthood
        Association of Thailand, 1976, ii, 162 pp.

FEMINISM AND WOMEN'S RIGHTS

Southeast Asia

1693   DAW, ROWENA. "Political Rights of Women: A Study of the
        International Protection of Human Rights." Malaya Law
        Review 12 (Dec. 1970):308-36.

1694   "Feminism in Asia." Feminist Japan 1, no. 4 (Feb. 1978):34-59.

1695   INTERNATIONAL WORKSHOP ON FEMINIST IDEOLOGY AND STRUCTURES IN
        THE FIRST HALF OF THE DECADE FOR WOMEN, Bangkok, 1979.
        Work in Progress: Report. Bangkok: Asian and Pacific
        Centre for Women and Development, 1979[?], iii, 17 pp.

1696   REGIONAL SEMINAR ON THE STATUS OF WOMEN AND FAMILY PLANNING
       FOR COUNTRIES WITHIN THE ECONOMIC COMMISSION FOR ASIA AND
       THE FAR EAST REGION, Jogjakarta, Indonesia, 1973. Papers.
       Organized by the United Nations in cooperation with the
       Government of Indonesia. New York: United Nations, 1974,
       i, 31 pp. United Nations Document ST/ESA/Ser.B2.

1697   SANTILLAN-CASTRENCE, PURA. "Some Thoughts on the Feminist
       Movement in Southeast Asia." Philippine Sociological Re-
       view 5 (Apr. 1957):61-66.

1698   SCHENK, M.G., and MUNAR, SUNDARI. Gerakan Wanita Dunia
       [International women's movement]. Jakarta: Djambatan,
       1950, 140 pp. Meneropong Dunia, no. 1.

1699   SEMINAR ON MEASURES REQUIRED FOR THE ADVANCEMENT OF WOMEN WITH
       SPECIAL REFERENCE TO THE ESTABLISHMENT OF A LONG-TERM PRO-
       GRAMME, Manila, 1966. Report. Organized by the United
       Nations, Division of Human Rights, in cooperation with the
       Government of the Philippines. New York, 1967, iii, 44 pp.
       United Nations Document ST/TAO/HR/28.

1700   SHAPLEN, JUNE H. "Women's Lib in Asia: An Assessment." Asia
       Magazine (Feb. 1975):3-8. (Covers Hong Kong, Japan,
       Thailand, Malaysia, and Singapore.)

1701   SHREERANGARAJAN, M. "Status of Women and Women's Movement in
       Asia." United Asia 1 (May 1949):129-33.

1702   THARPAR, ROMILA. "The History of Female Emancipation in
       Southern Asia." In Women in the New Asia. Edited by
       Barbara E. Ward. Paris: Unesco, 1963, pp. 473-94.

Burma

1703   COOPER, ELIZABETH. "Emancipated Women of Burma." Asia [New
       York] 19 (1919):771-74.

1704   MacMAHON, ALEXANDER R. "Woman's Rights in Burma." Gentle-
       man's Magazine 262 (1887):475-82.

Indochina

1705   BERGMAN, ARLENE EISEN. "Glimpses of Women's Liberation in
       Vietnam." Majority Report 6 (Mar. 1977):1.

1706   _____. Women of Viet Nam. 2d ed. Edited and produced col-
       lectively by Susan Adelman et al. San Francisco: Peoples
       Press, 1975, 255 pp.

1707   Frauen in Vietnam [Women in Vietnam]. Prepared under the di-
        rection of Margret Peters. 2 aufl. Cologne: Initiativ-
        komitee für Deutsch-Vietnamesische Kulturbeziehungen, 1976,
        107 pp.

1708   GINSBURGS, GEORGE. "The Role of Law in the Emancipation of
        Women in the Democratic Republic of Vietnam." American
        Journal of Comparative Law 23, no. 4 (Fall 1975):613-52.

1709   MARR, DAVID GEORGE. "The 1920s Women's Rights Debates in
        Vietnam." Journal of Asian Studies 35, no. 3 (May 1976):
        371-89.

1710   MOLANDER, CECILIA. Kvinna i Vietnam [Women in Vietnam].
        Uppsala: Nordiska Afrikainst, 1978, 144 pp.

1711   PHAM THI QUE. "Le contact avec l'Occident et le mouvement
        féministe à travers la littérature vietnamienne dans la
        première moitié du vingtième siècle" [Contact with the
        West and the feminist movement as seen through Vietnamese
        literature during the first half of the twentieth century].
        Ph.D. dissertation (Doctorat de 3e cycle), Université de
        Paris IV, 1973, 260, xxv pp.

1712   "The Social Revolution towards Sex Equality in Vietnam."
        Horizons (1956):25.

Indonesia

1713   ABDULGANI, RUSLAN, Hadji. Bersama-sama Wanita Menyelesaikan
        Revolusi [Together women will complete the revolution].
        Jakarta: Departemen Penerangan, 1964, 55 pp.

1714   AMIN, MARIA. "Menindjau Kongress Wanita seluruh Indonesia"
        [A review of "Kongress Wanita" throughout Indonesia].
        Pudjangga Baru 11, no. 2 (Aug. 1949):51-55.

1715   BARIED, BAROROH. "Un mouvement de femmes musulmanes:
        'Aisyiyah'" [Muslim women's movement: 'Aisyiyah'].
        Archipel, no. 13 (1977):129-36.

1716   Buku Tahunan Wanita 1953 [Women's yearbook, 1953]. Medan:
        Dunia Wanita, 1953, 448 pp.

1717   Congresnummer: Congress Perempoean Indonesia Jang Kedoea atau
        PPII, 28-31 Des. 1929 di Jacatra [The Second Indonesian
        Women's Congress or PPII 28-31 December 1929 in Jakarta].
        Weltevreden, 1930, 81 pp.

1718   Di Tangan Wanita [In women's hands]. Jakarta: Yayasan Idayu,
        1975, 40 pp.

1719   Gerakan Wanita Indonesia. Lebih Giat Meluaskan Gerakan untuk
       Terlaksananya Piagam Hak-hak Wanita Indonesia [More efforts
       towards the expansion of the movement for the achievement
       of women's rights in Indonesia]. Jakarta, 1958, 144 pp.

1720   _____. Meluaskan Aksi-aksi untuk Memperkuat Tuntutan Hak-hak
       Wanita, Anak-anak dan Perdamaian [The expansion of actions
       towards the strenthening of demands for the rights of
       women, children, and peace]. Jakarta, 1956, 36 pp.

1721   _____. Peraturan Dasar Gerwani dan Resolusi-resolusi Kongres
       Gerwani Ke2 [Regulations of the policy of Gerwani and its
       resolutions at the second congress of Gerwani]. Surabaya:
       Gerwani, 1954, 41 pp.

1722   HUDAWI, MUHAMMAD NUH. Penuntun Hak-hak dan Kewajiban Kaum
       Wanita [A guide to the rights and responsibilities of
       women]. Medan: Amka, 1957, 59 pp.

1723   INDONESIA, Departemen Penerangan. Buku Peringatan 30 (i.e.
       tiga puluh) Tahun Kesatuan Pergerakan Wanita Indonesia,
       22 Desember 1928-22 Desember 1958 [Commemorative book of
       thirty years of the Indonesian Women's Movement Associa-
       tion, 22 December 1928-22 December 1958]. Jakarta:
       Departemen Penerangan, 1958, 397, 8 pp.

1724   _____. The Indonesian Women's Movement: A Chronological Sur-
       vey of the Women's Movement in Indonesia. Jakarta:
       Departemen Penerangan, 1958, 82 pp.

1725   JACKSON, MOLLY. "East Timor." ISIS International Bulletin
       (Apr. 1977):15-16.

1726   "Kartini-kartini Kampus" [Women emancipators on campus].
       Economica 6, no. 10 (1976):14-19.

1727   KARTOWIJONO, SUJATIN. "Kebangkitan Gerakan Wanita Indonesia"
       [The rise of the Indonesian women's movement]. Suara Guru
       25, no. 4 (1975):35-38; 25, no. 5 (1975):42-46; 25, no. 6
       (1975):48-50.

1728   _____. Perkembangan Pergerakan Wanita Indonesia: Ceramah
       pada Tanggal 27 Maret 1975 di Gedung Kebangkitan Nasional
       Jakarta [The development of the Indonesian women's move-
       ment: speech given on 27 March 1975 at Gedung Kebangkitan
       Nasional, Jakarta]. Jakarta: Yayasan Idayu, 1975, 32 pp.

1729   Kenang-kenangan Congres Gerwani Ke2 Diselenggarakan pada
       Tanggal 25-31 Maart 1954 [Reminiscences of the Second
       Gerwani Congress held on 25-31 March 1954]. Jakarta:
       Pustaka Rakjat, 1954, 66 pp.

1730 Kenang-kenangan Kongres Gerwani Ke3 di Solo, 22-28 Desember
      1957 [Reminiscences of the Third Gerwani Congress in Solo,
      22-27 December 1957]. Jakarta: Gerwani, 1955, 144 pp.

1731 "Kesimpulan-kesimpulan Seminar Wanita di Djakarta, 9 Maret
      1958" [Summary of Seminar on Women in Jakarta, 9 March
      1958]. Pusara 20, nos. 1/2 (1958):36-39.

1732 KOMISI NASIONAL KEDUDUKAN WANITA INDONESIA. Perlaksanaan Per-
      nyataan tentang Penghapusan Diskriminasi terhadap Wanita di
      Indonesia: Sebuah Laporan [The implementation of the
      declaration to abolish discrimination against women in
      Indonesia: a report]. Jakarta: Komisi Nasional Kedudukan
      Wanita Indonesia, 1973, 38 pp.

1733 KONGRES WANITA INDONESIA. Buku Kenang Kenangan Kongres Kowani
      Ke13 [Souvenir book of the 13th Congress of Kowani].
      Jakarta: Kowani, 1974, 208 pp.

1734 _____. Himpunan Tjermah-tjermah mengenai Hak-hak Azasi
      Manusia Didepan KOWANI [A collection of lectures on human
      rights presented before KOWANI]. Diselenggarakan oleh
      KOWANI dan BPOW Djaya (Badan Pusat Organisasi Wanita
      Djaya). Jakarta: Biro Penerangan Dewan Pimpinan KOWANI,
      1966.

1735 _____. Kongres Wanita Indonesia [Indonesian Women's Con-
      gress]. Jakarta: Kowani, 1975, 2, 19 pp.

1736 _____, Majelis Permusyawaratan. Hasil2 Majelis Permusya-
      waratan Kowani [Proceedings of Conference Council, Kowani].
      Jakarta: Majelis Permusyawaratan Kowani, 1975.

1737 _____. Sejarah Setengah Abad Pergerakan Wanita Indonesia [A
      history of half a century of the Indonesian women's move-
      ment]. Jakarta: Balai Pustaka, 1978, xxxii, 531 pp.

1738 LASMINDER, S.R., and SUBIYANTO, P. URIP, comps. Kesatuan
      Pergerakan Wanita Indonesia [The unity of the Indonesian
      women's movement]. Jakarta: Kongres Wanita Indonesia,
      1974, 208 pp.

1739 LEAGUE OF WOMEN VOTERS OF THE UNITED STATES, Overseas Educa-
      tion Fund. "Women in Indonesia." Washington, D.C.:
      League of Women Voters, n.d.

1740 LEGOWO, S.A. "Nasib Kaum Wanita Ada Ditangan Kaum Wanita Sendiri" [The fate of women is in their own hands]. Jakarta: Sekretariat Koordinator Urusan Irian Barat, 1965, 12 pp.

1741 MASDANI, J. "Beberapa Konsekwensi Psikologik Emansipasi Wanita Indonesia" [Some psychological consequences of the emancipation of Indonesian women]. Jiwa 2, no. 1 (Jan. 1969):34-45.

1742 MUDIGDIO; SURASTO, SETATI; and SJARIFUDIN, AMIR. Hak-hak Politik Wanita [Political rights of women]. Jakarta: Pembaruan, 1960, 40 pp.

1743 OEY, MAYLING. "Closing the Gap: The Achieving Indonesian Women." Jurnal Penelitian Sosial 2, no. 5 (May 1977): 49-63.

1744 Peranan Wanita Indonesia Dalam Pembangunan [The role of Indonesian women in development]. Jakarta: Norindo Pratama, 1975, 973 pp.

1745 POEDJOBUNTORO, SOEPENI. Wanita dan Pemilihan Umum [Women and the general elections]. Jakarta: Widjaja, 1954, 152 pp.

1746 SCHUT, JOH A.F. "Het feminisme op Boeroe" [Feminism in Boeroe]. Mededelingen vanwege het Nederlandsche Zendeling-genootschap 1887:113-22.

1747 "Soal Wanita" [Women's issues]. Basis 1 (May 1952):266-70.

1748 SUBANDRIO, HURUSTIATI. "De Indonesische vrouw in de wereld van vandaag" [The Indonesian woman in the world of today]. Stiousa jaarboek (1950):33-47.

1749 SOEDJATMOKO. "Gerakan Wanita di Indonesia, Langkah Berikut-nya?" [Women's movement in Indonesia, what is the next step?]. Basis 22 (June 1973):302-09.

1750 _____. "Les mouvements féministes indonésiens à l'heure du 'développement'" [Indonesian women's movements at the time of development]. Présenté par Bénédicte Milcent. Archipel, no. 13 (1977):307-14.

1751 SUHARTI, SUWARTO. "Menghidupkan Grup Wanita dan Meluaskan Keanggotaan Partai Dikalangan Wanita" [The revival and expansion of the membership of the party among women]. Bintang Merah (June 1958):252-60.

1752   SIMPOSIUM TENTANG RE-EVALUASI PERGERAKAN WANITA INDONESIA,
        Jakarta, 1969. Kertas-kertas Kerja [Symposium on the Re-
        evaluation of the Indonesian Women's Movement, Jakarta,
        1969. Working papers]. Diselenggarakan oleh Dewan
        Kongres Wanita Indonesia. Jakarta: Kongres Wanita
        Indonesia, 1969, 60 pp.

1753   VREEDE-DE STUERS, CORA. "L'émancipation de la femme indo-
        nésienne" [The emancipation of the Indonesian women].
        Ph.D. dissertation, Université de Paris, 1957, 313 pp.

1754   _____. L'émancipation de la femme indonésienne [The emancipa-
        tion of the Indonesian women]. Paris: Mouton, 1959, xvi,
        175 pp. Le monde d'outre-mer passé et présent. 1. Série:
        Etudes, no. 6.

1755   _____. The Indonesian Woman: Struggles and Achievements.
        The Hague: Mouton, 1960, 204 pp.

Malaysia

1756   ADAM bin ABDUL KADIR. "Wanita dan Perjuangan" [Women and
        their struggle]. Dewan Masyarakat 14, no. 7 (July 1976):
        20-21.

1757   ADIBAH AMIN. "Where Women's Lib is Nothing New." New
        Straits Times Annual (1978):44-49.

1758   AISHAH GHANI. "Men Must Learn to Live with Less Privilege and
        Power. . . ." Malaysian Business (Oct. 1973):70-71.

1759   ASIAH binti ABU SAMAH. "Emancipation of Malay Women (1945-
        1957)." B.A. academic exercise, University of Singapore,
        1960, v, 87 pp.

1760   AZIZAH KASSIM. "Wanita Kebebasan dan Persamaan Hak" [Women's
        liberation and equal rights]. Wanita [Kuala Lumpur],
        no. 110 (Sept. 1978):40-41.

1761   GONG, CHIN KEEN. "Women's Rights and the Equality Provision
        of Article 8 of the Constitution." 5 pp. Paper presented
        at the Fifth Malaysian Law Conference, Kuala Lumpur, 1979,
        organized by the Bar Council of Malaysia.

1762   HAN, SUYIN. "The Women of Malaya." African Women 2 (June
        1957):63-65.

1763   _____. "The Woman of Malaya and Her Independence after
        Merdeka." Eastern World 11, no. 8 (Aug. 1957):46-48.

1763a   "Kebebasan perempuan Melayu" [The emancipation of Malay
        women]. Mastika 35, no. 4 (Apr. 1975):114-19.

1764   LIEW, ELIZABETH C.H. "An Interview with Elizabeth C.H. Liew,
       President of the South Malaya Federation of Women Lawyers.
       On Why Absolute Equality Can Never Be Achieved." Malaysian
       Business (Apr. 1974):22-24, 27.

1765   MASHKURAH binti HAJI YASSIN. "Hak-hak dan Kewajipan Wanita
       di dalam Islam (Kajian Perbandingan)" [The rights and re-
       sponsibilities of women in Islam: a comparative study].
       B.A. academic exercise, Universiti Kebangsaan Malaysia,
       1974.

1766   RAHMAH SAAD. "Kearah Mana Perjuangan Pergerakan Wanita.
       Malaysia dan Woman's Lib" [Towards the fight for a women's
       movement. Malaysia and woman's lib]. Wanita [Kuala
       Lumpur], no. 79 (Feb. 1976):54-55.

1767   SIVARETNAM, JOSEPHINE PREMLA. "Women's Rights and the Law:
       A Comparative Study on Sex Discrimination." LL.B. academic
       exercise, University of Malaya, 1977, vii, 96 pp.

1768   YASSIN, A.F. "Hak Wanita dalam Muktamar 7 Mac" [Women's
       rights in the 7th March convention]. Dewan Masyarakat 13,
       no. 2 (Feb. 1975):34-35.

1769   ZAHARAH NAWAWI. "Wanita Menuntut Hak" [Women demand their
       rights]. Mastika 35, no. 11 (Dec. 1975):65-71.

1770   ZAINON JAAFAR. "Benarkan Gerakan Pembebasan Wanita Benar-
       benar Dapat Membebaskan Wanita?" [Can the women's libera-
       tion movement really free women?]. Dewan Masyarakat 13,
       no. 9 (Sept. 1975):35-40.

Philippines

1771   AGUILING, MILAGROS HULAR. "Woman Suffrage in the Philippines:
       An Interpretative Study." Master's thesis, Far Eastern
       University [Manila], 1955, iv, 177 pp.

1772   ALANO, C.M. "A Forum on Women's Rights and Divorce Filipino
       Style." Expressweek 4 (14 Oct. 1976):22-23.

1773   _____. "How Liberated is the Filipino Woman?" Expressweek 3
       (25 Sept. 1975):20-21.

1774   ANONAS, GREGORIO. Woman Suffrage. Manila: Bureau of
       Printing, 1932, 32 pp.

1775   BABST, A.P. "Portraits of Mother and Father by a Feminist
       Daughter." Focus 3 (1 Mar. 1975):8-9.

1776   BAILON, S.C. "Women's Right and the Nurse." Philippine
        Journal of Nursing 44 (Jan./Mar. 1975):23-31.

1777   BAYANI-ARCILLA, SOCORRO. "The Development of Political Rights
        of Filipino Women." Master's thesis, University of Manila
        [Manila], 1953, v, 188 pp.

1778   BLANCO, CONSUELO S. "Enlightened Feminism for National Sur-
        vival." Philippine Historical Association, Historical
        Bulletin 19, nos. 1/4 (Jan./Dec. 1975):45-51.

1779   CASTAÑEDA, MAURA C. "Civil and Political Rights of Women in
        the Philippines." Master's thesis, University of Manila
        [Manila], 1949, 87 pp.

1780   CASTILLO, GELIA TAGUMPAY. "On Liberating Filipino Women:
        Which Women?" n.p., 11 pp.

1781   CHRISTITCH, ANNIE. "Position of Women in the Philippine
        Islands: A Woman Suffrage Bill; Serbian Women's Advance."
        International Woman Suffrage News 14 (Feb. 1920):71-72.

1782   CORTES, IRENE R. Women's Rights under the 1973 Constitution.
        Quezon City: University of the Philippines Press, 1975,
        81 pp. Professorial Chair Lectures, Monograph no. 10.

1783   _____. "Women's Rights under the 1973 Constitution."
        Philippine Law Journal 50, no. 1 (Feb. 1975):1-24.

1784   "Decree Ensures Filipino Women Equal Opportunities in Area of
        Employment." New Philippines 36, no. 1 (Dec. 1975):46-50.

1785   FELICES, GUADALUPE. "Advantages and Disadvantages of Woman
        Suffrage in the Philippines." Master's thesis, Far Eastern
        University [Manila], 1952, xi, 105 pp.

1786   FERNANDO, ENRIQUE M. "The Movement for Equal Rights: The
        Validity of Legislation Beneficial to Women." Philippine
        Law Journal 51 (1976):441-54.

1787   GOZUN, SYLVIA CABANEZ. "The History of Women Suffrage in the
        Philippines." Master's thesis, Far Eastern University
        [Manila], 1951.

1788   JAVELLANA, YOLANDA Q., ed. Woman and the Law. Conference
        jointly sponsored by the Federacion Internacional de Abo-
        gados and the University of the Philippines Law Center.
        Quezon City: University of the Philippines Law Center,
        1975, viii, 120 pp. (Reprinted from the Philippine Law
        Journal 50, no. 1 [Feb. 1975]. Round Table Conference:
        Achieving for Women Full Equality Before the Law, Quezon
        City, 1975.)

1789 KALAW, PURA VILLANUEVA. Filipino Women: The Challenge They Meet. Manila: Crown Printing, 1951, 15 pp.

1790 _____. How the Filipina Got the Vote. Manila: Crown Printing, 1952, 58 pp.

1791 LEGARDA, TRINIDAD F. "Philippine Women and the Vote." Philippine Magazine 28, no. 4 (Sept. 1931):163-65, 196-200.

1792 LIM, PILAR H. "Women's Suffrage since 1937." Unitas 40, no. 3 (Sept. 1967):414-22.

1793 LUCIANO, LEONOR INES. "The Legal and Christian Perspectives of Women's Role." Unitas 48, no. 2 (June 1975):251-58.

1794 MARQUEZ, N.R. "The Filipino Women and the Equality of the Sexes." Focus 4 (13 Dec. 1975):10-11.

1795 NAVARRO, AGUSTINA ROSITA. "A Comparative Analysis of the Rights of Women under the Old and the New Civil Code." Master's thesis, University of Manila [Manila], 1950, 126 pp.

1796 OSIAS, CAMILO. "Women and Freedom." Philippine Economy Review 5, nos. 11/12 (June/July 1959):24-25, 36-37.

1797 PALMA, RAFAEL. The Woman and the Right to Vote. Manila: Bureau of Printing, 1919, 28 pp. Address delivered in support of Bill no. 23 of the Senate in the sessions held on 22 November and 25 November 1919.

1798 _____. "Woman Suffrage in the Philippines." Philippine Review 5, no. 7 (July 1920):462-69; 5, no. 8 (Aug. 1920):488-; 5, no. 9 (Sept. 1920):619-.

1799 PARAS, EDGARDO. "The Civil Rights of Women in the Philippines." Centro Escolar University, Manila, Graduate and Faculty Studies 1 (1950):176-200.

1800 PECSON, GERONIMA T. "Fifty Years of Feminist Movement in the Philippines." Fookien Times Philippine Yearbook (1955):42-44, 78-80.

1801 PERRIN, PACIENCIA M. "A Comparative Study of the Political Rights of the Filipino Women and Those of United States." Master's thesis, Centro Escolar University [Manila], 1951, vi, 124 pp.

1802 ROMERO, FLERIDA RUTH P. "Economic Equality of Working Women under Our Laws." Integrated Bar of the Philippines, Journal 3 (3d quarter 1975):197-204.

1803 _____. Women's Status in Philippine Society. Diliman, Q.C.: University of the Philippines Law Center, 1979, 23 pp.

1804 SANTIAGO, ALEJANDRINA. "Pioneers of Woman's Movement in the Philippines." Philippine Review 5, no. 3 (March 1920): 223-24.

1805 SHAHANI, LETICIA RAMOS. "Liberating the Filipino Woman." Philippines Quarterly 7, no. 4 (Dec. 1975):35-40.

1806 SONGALIA, DOMINGO A. Women's Rights. Manila: Atlantic Publications, 1958, xxxvi, 237 pp.

1807 SUAREZ, D. TORREVILLAS. "Bridging the Equality Gap." Philippine Panorama 5 (25 July 1976):14-15; 5 (1 Aug. 1976):30.

1808 _____. "It's Not Liberating Women, but Extending Rights to All." Philippine Panorama 4 (4 May 1975):10-11.

1809 _____. "The Law: What's Good for Men Should Be Good for Women." Philippine Panorama 4 (2 Feb. 1975):6-7.

1810 SUBIDO, TRINIDAD (TARROSA). The Feminist Movement in the Philippines, 1905-1955. A golden book to commemorate the golden jubilee of the feminist movement in the Philippines. Manila: National Federation of Women's Clubs, 1955, 76 pp.

1811 TABADA-PILAPIL, BERNARDINA. "An Analytical Study of Women's Rights under the New Civil Code." LL.M. thesis, Philippine Law School [Pasay City, Philippines], 1951, iii, iv, 159 pp.

1812 URIATE, TRIFINA G. "A Study of the Moral and Legal Rights of the Filipino Wife in Relation to Family Living." Thesis, University of the Visayas [Cebu City, Philippines], 1970, 122 pp.

1813 VELILIA, AMANDO L. "Woman Suffrage is a Failure." LL.M. thesis, University of Santo Tomas [Manila], 1937, 23 pp.

1814 WOODHAM, A. "Women's Lib: and What It Reveals about Ourselves." Expressweek 3 (5 June 1975):18-19.

1815 WYNNE, ALISON. No Time for Crying: Stories of Philippine Women Who Care for Their Country and Its People. Kowloon: Resource Centre for Philippine Concerns, 1979, 120 pp.

1816   ZAPANTA, E.G. "Women's Lib in the Philippines." UST Journal
        of Education (Oct./Nov. 1971):60-61.

Singapore

1817   WONG, ALINE K. "Exorcising the Double Standard (Sex Discrimi-
        nation in Singapore)." New Directions 1, no. 3 (Sept.
        1974):18-19.

1818   _____. Women in Modern Singapore. With the assistance of
        Chew Oon Ai, Tan Mei Ling, and Phay Ai Lien. Singapore:
        University Education Press, 1975, 137, 7 pp.

Thailand

1819   SIREE AMATAYAKUL. "A Critical Study of the Development of
        Political and Civil Rights of Women in Thailand." Master's
        thesis, University of Manila [Manila], 1965, 163 pp.

                    GENERAL WORKS; HISTORY

            (See also Social Conditions and Status)

Southeast Asia

1820   ALDABA-LIM, ESTEFANIA J. "The Role and Status of Young Asian
        Women Today." Unesco Philippines 5, nos. 5/6 (May/June
        1965):156-63.

1821   AMERICAN ASSOCIATION OF UNIVERSITY WOMEN. East Meets West:
        Culturally Conditioned Views of the Role of Women. Pacific
        Basin Conference. Honolulu: East-West Center, 1977,
        183 pp.

1822   APPADORAI, ANGADIPURAM, ed. The Status of Women in South
        Asia. Bombay: Orient Longmans, 1954, v, 171 pp.

1823   ASEAN WOMEN LEADERS AND INTERNATIONAL WOMEN'S YEAR POST CON-
        FERENCE MEETING, Jakarta, 1975. Report. Organized under
        the auspices of the ASEAN Sub-Committee on Women of the
        ASEAN Permanent Committee on Socio-Cultural Activities.
        Jakarta, 1975, 1 vol. (various pagings).

1824   ASIAN REGIONAL CONFERENCE OF THE ASSOCIATED COUNTRY WOMEN OF
        THE WORLD, Kuala Lumpur, 1979. Papers. Theme of confer-
        ence: Today's Child Tomorrow's Citizen. Host society, the
        National Association of Women's Institutes, Peninsular
        Malaysia. Kuala Lumpur, 1979, 1 vol. (various pagings).

                           180

1825   "Asian Women." Impact 10, no. 4 (Apr. 1975):entire issue.

1826   BALBOA, FORMANDA S. "Progress of Asian Women." Fookien Times
        Philippines Yearbook (1959):186-90.

1827   BENITEZ, HELENA Z. "The Challenge of Change to Women in Asia
        and in the Far East." Fookien Times Philippines Yearbook
        27, (1967):302, 304-6, 310.

1828   BOULDING, ELISE; NUSS, SHIRLEY A.; and LEE, DOROTHY. Handbook
        of International Data on Women. Beverly Hills, Calif.:
        Sage Publications, 1976, 468 pp.

1829   CHIPP, SYLVIA A., and GREEN, JUSTIN JAY, eds. Asian Women in
        Transition. University Park, Pa.: Pennsylvania State
        University Press, 1980[?], 274 pp. (Among countries dis-
        cussed are the Philippines, Malaysia, and Indonesia.)

1830   CHUNG, BETTY JAMIE. "Some Thoughts on the Status of Women in
        Southeast Asia: 1975, the International Women's Year."
        Southeast Asian Affairs (1976):130-45.

1831   DANIEL, KIRAN, and LEE, SOO JIN. Asian Women Confront, Chal-
        lenge, Change. Asian Focus. Singapore: Christian Con-
        ference of Asia, 1977, 60 pp.

1832   EXPERT GROUP MEETING ON THE IDENTIFICATION OF THE BASIC NEEDS
        OF WOMEN OF ASIA AND THE PACIFIC AND ON THE FORMULATION OF
        A PROGRAMME OF WORK, Tehran, 1977. Report. Bangkok:
        Asian and Pacific Centre for Women and Development,
        1980[?], iv, 67 pp.

1833   FEDERATION OF ASIAN WOMEN'S ASSOCIATIONS. Women of Asia and
        World Peace: Proceedings of the Fourth Convention,
        June 25-27, 1967. Edited by Geronima T. Pecson. Held at
        Centro Escolar University Auditorium, Mendiola, Manila,
        Philippines. Manila, 1968, vii, 86 pp.

1834   GORDON, ELIZABETH. "Women of Asia." Contemporary Review
        299, no. 1330 (Nov. 1976):266-68.

1835   GOSWAMI, U.S. "War Emancipates Women in Southeast Asia."
        Modern Review 138, no. 3 (Sept. 1975):266-69.

1836   IGLITZEN, LYNNE B., and ROSS, RUTH, eds. Women in the World:
        A Comparative Study. Santa Barbara, Calif.: Clio Books,
        1976, xviii, 427 pp. Studies in Comparative Politics,
        no. 6.

1837 INTERNATIONAL WOMEN'S DAY, Hong Kong, 1978. Papers. Hong
      Kong: Hong Kong Council of Women, 1978, 20 pp.

1838 "Leadership Roles of Women in S.E. Asia." In Contemporary
      South-east Asia: An Emerging Center of World Influence.
      A symposium organized by Ohio University, Southeast Asia
      Program, May 1976.

1839 LEBRA, JOYCE CHAPMAN, and PAULSON, JOY. Chinese Women in
      Southeast Asia. Singapore: Times Books International,
      1980, 250 pp.

1840 LEGASPI, LEONARDO Z., ed. The Role of Women in Development:
      Seminar Papers and Statements. Manila: University of
      Santo Tomas Press, 1976.

1841 MANALO, ROSARIO G. "Women and World Peace." ASEAN Journal 2,
      no. 1 (Oct. 1975):3-9.

1842 MARCOS, IMELDA ROMUALDEZ. "The Role of Asian Women."
      Philippine Historical Association, Historical Bulletin 19,
      nos. 1/4 (Jan./Dec. 1975):40-44.

1843 O'BARR, JEAN F. Women in Developing Societies: A Packet of
      Resource Materials for Use at the College Level. Durham,
      N.C.: Comparative Area Studies Program, Center for Inter-
      national Studies, Duke University, 1975, 105 pp.

1844 _____. Third World Women: Factors in Their Changing Status.
      Durham, N.C.: Center for International Studies, Duke
      University, 1976, vii, 94 pp.

1845 PAN-PACIFIC WOMEN'S CONFERENCE. Women of the Pacific: Being
      a Record of the Proceedings. Honolulu: Pan-Pacific Union,
      1st, 1928-. (First conference was held in 1928.)

1846 PAPANEK, HANNA. "Women in South and Southeast Asia: Issues
      and Research." Signs 1, no. 1 (Autumn 1975):193-214.

1847 SEMINAR ON THE ROLE OF WOMEN IN THE PRESERVATION AND DEVELOP-
      MENT OF CULTURES IN THE COMMUNITY, Karachi, 1958. Pro-
      ceedings. Convened by the All Pakistan Women's Association
      in cooperation with UNESCO. Karachi, 1958, 180 pp.

1848 TINKER, IRENE. "Pengaruh Pembangunan Yang Merugikan Kaum
      Wanita" [Development which is detrimental to women].
      Prisma 4, no. 5 (Oct. 1975):33-43.

1849 UNESCO. Unesco and International Women's Year, 1975. Paris:
      UNESCO, 1974[?], 35 pp.

1850   UNITED NATIONS, Asian and Pacific Centre for Women and Devel-
        opment. Environmental Issues Affecting Women with Particu-
        lar Reference to Housing and Human Settlements. Papers
        prepared for APCWD workshops held in collaboration with
        National Buildings Organisation (NBO), New Delhi, April-
        June 1980, New Delhi. Bangkok: APCWD, 1980, 164 pp.

1851   _____. Manual on Project Development. Preparation of mate-
        rials, design, and graphs by Sunira Chaturvedi-Heyn.
        Bangkok: APCWD, 1979, 78 pp.

1852   _____. Participation of Women in Decision-making . . . Some
        Guidelines. Bangkok: Asian and Pacific Centre for Women
        and Development, 1980, v, 50 pp.

1853   _____. Report of the Training Course on Research Methodolo-
        gies and the Administration of Research, Bogor, Indonesia,
        Nov.-Dec., 1979. Bangkok: APCWD, 1980, 55 pp.

1854   _____. Report of the Training Course on the Techniques of
        Participation for Women. Bangkok: APCWD, 1978, 33 pp.

1855   _____. Techniques of Participation for Women. Regional
        Training Course, Bangkok, 13 June-14 July, 1978. Bangkok:
        1978, 1 vol. (various pagings).

1856   WARD, BARBARA E. "Women and Technology in Developing Coun-
        tries." Impact of Science on Society 20, no. 1 (Jan./Mar.
        1970):93-101.

1857   _____. "Women in the New Asia: Excerpts." Unesco Courier
        17 (Sept. 1964):4-27.

1858   _____, ed. Women in the New Asia: The Changing Social Roles
        of Men and Women in South and South-East Asia. Paris:
        UNESCO, 1963, 529 pp.

1859   WHYTE, ROBERT ORR, and WHYTE, PAULINE. Rural Asian Women:
        Status and Environment. Singapore: Institute of South-
        east Asian Studies, 1978, 34 pp. Institute of Southeast
        Asian Studies, Singapore. Research Notes and Discussion
        Paper, no. 9.

1860   WOMEN'S INTERNATIONAL DEMOCRATIC FEDERATION. Les femmes
        d'Asie et d'Afrique: documents [The women of Asia and
        Africa: documents]. Budapest, 1948, 173 pp.

1861 _____. The Women of Asia and Africa: Documents. Budapest, 1948, 170 pp. (Report of the Commission of The Women's International Democratic Federation which visited the countries in South East Asia, and additions presented in the course of the discussion of this report by the Preparatory Committee for the Conference of the Women of Asia, at Budapest, 23 November to 2 December 1948.)

1862 WONG, ALINE K. "The Changing Roles and Status of Women in ASEAN." Contemporary Southeast Asia 1, no. 2 (Sept. 1979): 179-93.

1863 WORLD CONFERENCE OF THE INTERNATIONAL WOMEN'S YEAR, Mexico City, 1975. Papers. New York: United Nations, 1975, 696 pp. United Nations Document E/CONF.66/1-E/CON.66/NGO/5.

1864 _____. Report. New York: United Nations, 1976, vi, 199 pp. United Nations Document E/CONF.66/34.

1865 ZAI MOKHSIN, Siti. "Wanita ASEAN" [ASEAN women]. Sarina 1, no. 10 (Jan. 1977):40-43.

Burma

1866 BIXLER, NORMA. "Social Organization." In Burma: A Profile. London: Pall Mall Press, 1971, pp. 150-83. (Includes a description of women's clothing, family, marriage, divorce, and status of women in Burma.)

1867 BROWN, GRANT R. "Burma." In Women of All Nations. Edited by Thomas Athol Joyce and Northcote W. Thomas. New York: Funk & Wagnalls, 1915, Vol. 3, pp. 559-74.

1868 MYA SEIN, Daw. "Towards Independence in Burma: The Role of Women." Asian Affairs 59, pt. 3 (Oct. 1972):288-99.

1869 _____. "The Women of Burma: A Tradition of Hard Work and Independence." Atlantic Monthly, Supplement (Perspective of Burma) 201, no. 2 (Feb. 1958):122-25.

1870 PE MAUNG TIN. "Women in the Inscriptions of Pagan." In Burma Research Society, Fiftieth Anniversary Publications 1 (1960):411-21. Reprinted from Burma Research Society, Journal 25 (1935):149-59.

1871 SCHERMAN, LUCIAN, and SCHERMAN, CHRISTINO. Im Stromgebiet des Irrawaddy: Birma und Seine Frauenwelt [In the Irrawaddy River basin: Burma and its world of women]. Munich: Oskar Schloss, 1922, 132 pp.

1872 THAN KHIN MYO. "Burmese Girl's Notebook." Unesco Courier 28 (Mar. 1975):26-27, 32-33.

1873 UNITED NATIONS. Asian and Pacific Centre for Women and Devel-
       opment. Selected Country Papers Presented at the ACPWD
       Expert Group Meeting on the Identification of the Basic
       Needs of Women of Asia and the Pacific and Formulation of
       a Programme of Work, Tehran, Iran, December 1977. Bangkok:
       APCWD, 1980, 89 pp. (Studies on the position of women in
       six countries--Burma, Sri Lanka, India, Pakistan, Japan,
       and Singapore.)

1874 YARHAM, E.R. "Women of Burma." Eastern World 9, no. 6
       (June 1957):35-36.

Indochina

1875 ARANETA, G.C. "Vietnamese Women: Their Forgotten Traditions."
       Mirror Magazine (2 Nov. 1967):6-7.

1876 L'Asie nouvelle illustrée, 28 Feb.-31 Mar. 1937 6th year,
       no. 48. (This issue of the magazine is devoted to Viet-
       namese women.)

1877 BENESA, LEONIDAS. "The Woman of Laos." Philippines Herald
       Magazine (Mar. 1962):6-7.

1878 BERGMAN, ARLENE EISEN. Femmes du Vietnam [Women of Vietnam].
       Paris: des Femmes, 1975, 296 pp.

1879 _____. Women of Viet Nam. 2d ed. Edited and produced col-
       lectively by Susan Adelman et al. San Francisco: Peoples
       Press, 1975, 255 pp.

1880 BEURDELEY, CECILE. "La mode féminine: clé de l'art khmer"
       [The feminine mode: key to Khmer art]. Connaissance des
       arts, no. 133 (Mar. 1963):104-11.

1881 BORTON, Lady. "Voices from Vietnam." Ms 2, no. 1 (July
       1973):66-69, 114.

1882 BUCHANAN, KEITH. "The Women of Angkor." Eastern Horizon 2,
       no. 12 (Oct. 1963):13-15. (On depictions of women at
       Angkor Wat.)

1883 CHANDOLA, HARISH. "Vietnam Journal: New Position of Women."
       Economic and Political Weekly 8, no. 16 (Apr. 1973):744-46.

1884 COUGHLIN, RICHARD JAMES. The Position of Women in Vietnam.
       New Haven, Conn.: Southeast Asia Studies, Yale University,
       1950, i, 45 pp. Cultural Report Series.

1885   _____. "The Position of Women in Vietnam." In Status of
            Women in South Asia. Edited by Angadipuram Appadorai.
            Bombay: Orient Longmans, 1954, pp. 133-52.

1886   CULHANE, CLAIRE. "Women and Vietnam." Canadian Dimension
            10, no. 8 (June 1975):4-8.

1887   GRACE, PAUL et al., eds. Vietnamese Women in Society and
            Revolution. Vol. 1. The French Colonial Period. Trans-
            lated by Ngo Vinh Long. Cambridge, Mass.: Vietnam Re-
            source Centre, 1974, 207 pp.

1888   GRANT, ZALIN. "Mobilization of Women in Vietnam." New Repub-
            lic 158, no. 22 (1 June 1968):11-13.

1889   HAUER, DOROTHEA. "Feen mit golden Glöckchen: Frauen im Delta
            des Roten Flusses" [The fairies with the little golden
            bells: women in the Red River Delta]. Westermanns Monat-
            shefte 157 (Sept. 1934):77-84.

1890   HEALY, PATRICIA; KHAMPHENG BOUPHA; and NANG TENG. "Laos:
            Women in the Revolution." Refractory Girl, no. 12
            (Sept. 1976):36-37.

1891   HERRING, FRANCES W. "Appointment in Djakarta: Women from
            U.S. and South and North Vietnam Meet in Indonesia." New
            World Review 33 (Aug./Sept. 1965):17-20.

1892   HO CHI MINH. "Annamese Women and French Domination." In On
            Revolution: Selected Writings, 1920-66. New York: F.A.
            Praeger, 1969, pp. 13-14. (On torture and rape of Viet-
            namese women by French soldiers.)

1893   HOANG DAO. Mu'o'i dien tam niem. Saigon: Khai-Tri, 1964,
            65 pp.

1894   HOI LIEN HIEP PHU NU' VIET NAM. Glorious Daughters of Viet
            Nam. Hanoi: Viet Nam Women's Union, 197-, 149 pp.
            (Contents: 1. Phuong Vu, "Mother Diem." 2. Han An, "The
            Fifth President." 3. Minh Lan, "One Thousand Days in the
            Fighting." 4. Van Lam, "The 609 Brigade." 5. Thanh
            Phuong, "Girls of the Coastal Region." 5. To Minh Nguyet,
            "The Story of a Paper-making Engineer." 6. Xuan Thu,
            "Doctor Thai Lan Thu." 7. To Minh Nguyet, "The Hand of
            the Schoolmistress." 8. Trung Dong, "Sea Flowers."
            9. Quoc Vuong, "Our ICBM." 10. Quoc Vuong, "The Young
            Village Policewoman." 11. Ngoc Due, "The Girl Who Destroys
            Bombs." 12. Nguyen Thanh, "The Young Women Gunners and the
            7th Fleet." 13. Hoang Tuan Nha, "The Courageous Sampan
            Woman." 14. Kien Lian Son, "The Mother of Huong Bac.")

1895   HOANG VAN CO. La femme vietnamienne et son evolution [The
        Vietnamese woman and her evolution]. Saigon: Son Hai,
        1955, 136 pp.

1896   KILGORE, MARGARET. "The Female War Correspondent in Vietnam."
        The Quill [Chicago] 60 (May 1972):9-12.

1897   LE KWANG KIM. "Viet-Nam: Twenty Years of Change and Turmoil."
        Unesco Courier 17 (Sept. 1964):22-27. (On women in Vietnam
        since 1940.)

1898   LECLERE, ADHEMARD. Cambodge: le roi, la famille royale et
        les femmes du palais [Cambodia: the king, the royal family,
        and the women of the palace]. Saigon: Impr. Libraire
        Claude, 1905, 26 pp.

1899   LIANG, GORDON S.Y. "The Women of Vietnam." Asia Magazine 9,
        no. 52 (Dec. 1969):4-6, 8-9.

1900   MAI THI TU, and LE THI NHAM TUYET. Women in Viet Nam. Hanoi:
        Foreign Languages Publishing House, 1978, 326 pp.

1901   Mot so hinh anh Bac Ho voi phu nu. Hanoi: Phu Nu, 1972,
        57 pp. (Chiefly a pictorial work.)

1902   NATIONAL WOMEN'S CONGRESS OF VIET NAM, 4th. "Glorieuses
        filles du Viet Nam: rapport des deleguees au 4e Congress
        des Femmes du Viet Nam" [Glorious daughters of Vietnam:
        report of delegates at the 4th Women's Congress of Vietnam].
        2 vols. Hanoi: Union des Femmes du Viet Nam, 1975.

1903   _____. Viet Nam Women's Progress through Figures from the 3rd
        National Women's Congress, March 1961 to the 4th National
        Women's Congress, March 1974. Hanoi: Union des Femmes du
        Viet Nam[?], 1975, 26 pp.

1904   PETER, M. Frauen in Vietnam [Women in Vietnam]. Cologne:
        Initiativkomitee für Deutsch-Vietnamesische Kulturbezie-
        hungen, 1976, 107 pp.

1905   Phu nu mien Nam, anh hung bat khuat trung hau dam dang. n.p.:
        Hoi Lien hiep Phu nu giai phong mien Nam, 1974[?], 34 pp.
        (Pictorial work which includes studies of women.)

1906   "Present Day Trung Sisters Celebrate Women's Day. Trung Sis-
        ters--Past and Legend." News from Vietnam 4, no. 11
        (Apr. 1958):6-11.

1907   RANDALL, MARGARET. Spirit of the People. Vancouver, B.C.:
        New Star Books, 1975, 95 pp. (On Vietnamese women.)

1908 SKEAT, WALTER W. "Siam and Cambodia." In Women of All Nations. Vol. 3. Edited by Thomas Athol Joyce and Northcote W. Thomas. New York: Funk & Wagnalls, 1915, pp. 550-58.

1909 STAFFORD, ANN [pseud.]. Saigon Journey. London: Campion Press, 1960, 188 pp.

1910 TAN PHU'O'NG. Khao-luan ve phu-nu Viet-Nam. Saigon: Huynh-Van, 1951, 124 pp.

1911 Vietnamese Women. Hanoi: Xunhasaba, 1966, 306 pp. Vietnamese Studies, no. 10. (Contents: Mai Thi Tu, "The Vietnamese Woman, Yesterday and Today"; "The Struggle of South Vietnamese Women"; Viet Ching, "The Hoang Ngan Women Partisans"; Mai Anh, "North Vietnamese Women in Face of American Aggression"; Le Mai Huong, "Up from the Mind"; Vu Can, "With the Namdinh Weavers.")

1912 WINDSCHUTTLE, ELIZABETH. "Women in the Vietnam War." Refractory Girl, no. 12 (Sept. 1976):4-10; Australian Left Review, no. 53 (1976):17-24.

1913 Women in Viet Nam. Hanoi: Foreign Languages Publishing House, 1978, 324 pp.

1914 "Women in Vietnam." In We the Vietnamese: Voices from Vietnam. Edited by François Sully. New York: Praeger, 1971, pp. 69-80.

1915 Women in Vietnam: Selected Articles from Vietnamese Periodicals, Saigon, Hanoi, 1957-1966. Translated by Chiem T. Keim. Honolulu: Institute of Advanced Projects, East-West Center, 1967, 76 pp. Occasional Papers of Research Publications and Translation, Translation Series, no. 25.

Indonesia

1916 Archipel. "Numéro spécial: regards sur les Indonésiennes," no. 13 (1977). (Entire issue is devoted to Indonesian women.)

1917 ASMARA, DJAJA. Wanita di Medan Pertempuran [Women at war]. Padang Pandjang, Indonesia: Poestaka Merdeka, 1948, 61 pp.

1918 BAKRY, MUHAMMAD KASSIM, Hadji. Siapa Itu Perempuan? [What is a woman?]. Jakarta: Mega Bookstore, 1964[?], 136 pp.

1919 BETHUNE, MARY McLEOD. Wanita Pelopor Kemadjuan [Women as pioneers of development]. Jakarta: Immajority, 1957, 208 pp.

1920 BONEFF, MARCEL. "Préceptes et conseils pour les femmes de Java" [Precepts and advice for Javanese women]. Archipel, no. 13 (1977):211–34.

1921 CAYRAC, FRANÇOISE. "En relisant Sarinah" [Reading 'Sarinah' again]. Archipel, no. 13 (1977):235–62.

1922 DEWANTARA, KI HADJAR. "La question féminine" [The feminine question]. Presenté et traduit par Monique Zaini-Lajoubert. Archipel, no. 13 (1977):247–66.

1923 DUMADI, SAGIMUN MULUS. Wanita Indonesia dan Pantja Sila [Indonesian women and Pantja sila]. Jogjakarta: Pantja sila, 1953, 144 pp.

1924 GRAAFLAND, N. "De vrouwen in de Minahassa" [The women in the Minahassa]. Mededeelingen vanwege het Nederlandsche Zendelinggenootschap 25 (1881):316–38.

1925 HERING, B.B., ed. Indonesian Women: Some Past and Current Perspectives. Proceedings of a seminar at James Cook University of North Queensland. Brussels: Centre d'Etude du Sud-Est Asiatique et de l'Extrême-Orient, 1976, 163 pp.

1926 HUEVEN, G.B.J. VAN. "Oostindische dames van Tempo-Doeloe" [East Indies ladies from the old times]. De Indische gids 56 (1934):1074–1100.

1927 HOOYKAAS-VAN LEEUWEN BOOMKAMP, JACOBA HINDRIKA. Vrouwenkamp op Java, met tekeningen van Kick Hofer [Women prison camps in Java, with illustrations from Kick Hofer]. Uitg. ten bate van de Stichting "Nederland Helpt Indie". Amsterdam: G. Kolff, 1946, 61 pp.

1928 IHROMI, T. OMAS et al., comps. Kedudukan Wanita dan Keluarga Berencana di Indonesia [The status of women and family planning in Indonesia]. Suatu studi yang dilaksanakan deh Team Peneliti Tentang Kedudukan Wanita dan Keluarga Berencana. Jakarta Perkumpulan Keluarga Berencana Indonesia, 1973, 309 pp.

1929 _____. The Status of Women and Family Planning in Indonesia. A study conducted by the Research Team on the Status of Women and Family Planning in Indonesia, and the Family Coordination Board. Jakarta: Indonesian Planned Parenthood Association, 1973, 309 pp.

1930 INDONESIA, Kementerian Penergangan. "Alam Pikiran Wanita sedjak Kartini--1952" [The thoughts of women since Kartini --1952]. Sumbangsih Djapendro Djabar Bg. Perwartaan guna menjambut hari Kartini. Bandung: Djawatan Penerangan Propinsi Djawa-Barat Bagian Pewartaan, 1952[?], 24 pp.

1931 INDONESIA (REPUBLIC, 1945-1949), Departemen van Opvoeding, Kunsten en Wetenschappen. De Indonesische vrouw, 1898-1948 [The Indonesian women, 1898-1948]. Jakarta, 1948, 31 pp.

1932 KATHIRITHAMBY-WELLS, R.J. "The Role of Women in Javanese History with Special Reference to Early Nineteenth Century Jogjakarta." Paper presented at the Seventh Conference of the International Association of Historians of Asia, August 1977, held in Bangkok, Thailand.

1933 "Kesimpulan-kesimpulan Seminar Wanita di Djakarta 9 Maret 1958" [Summary of Seminar on Women in Jakarta, 9 March 1958]. Pusara 20, nos. 1/2 (1958):36-39.

1934 KRIEG, ELFRIEDE. Die javanische Frau [The Javanese woman]. Aus dem indischen Frauenleben, der deutschen Frauenwelt gedwidmet. Neukirchen, Kreis Mors: Missionsbuchhandlung Stursberg, 1926, 96 pp.

1935 LANS, B.H. "De Soendaneesche vrouw in het licht van het heden, het verleden en de toekomst" [The Sudanese woman in the light of the present, the past, and the future]. Verslagen der Algemeene vergaderingen van het Indische genootschap (1920):29-58.

1936 MANGKOEDIMEDJO, Raden Ajoe. "Kemadjoen Bangsa Perempoean" [Progress of women]. Poetri Hindia (July 1909):162-66.

1937 _____. "Les progrès de la gent féminine (1909)" [The progress of women, 1909]. Présenté et traduit par Claudine Salmon. Archipel, no. 13 (1977):119-28.

1938 NEFERTITI [pseud.]. Between You and Me. Jakarta: Gunung Agung, 1960, 120 pp. (Articles on women in Indonesia and on Indonesian society taken from the author's regular column in the Indonesian Herald.)

1939 NITISASTRO, WIDJOJO. Beberapa Data Kwantitatif tentang Penduduk Wanita Indonesia [Some quantitative data regarding Indonesian women]. Jakarta: Departemen Urusan Research Nasional, 1965, ii, 55 pp.

1940 NOTOPURO, HARDJITO. Masalah Wanita: Kedudukan dan Peranannya [Problems of women: status and role]. Jakarta, 1973, 22, 6 pp.

1941 OVINK-SOER, M.C.E. Vrouwenleven in de desa [Women's life in the village]. Amsterdam: L.J. Veen, 1901, 296 pp.

1942   "Présentation du dossier. Introduction to This Issue. Kata
        Penghantar." Archipel, no. 13 (1977):3-20. (Numéro spé-
        cial: regards sur les Indonésiennes.)

1943   "Race and Color in Colonial Society: Biographical Sketches by
        a Eurasian Woman concerning Pre-World War II Indonesia."
        Translated and edited by Paul W. van der Veur. Indonesia
        [Ithaca, N.Y.] no. 8 (Oct. 1969):69-79. (By an anonymous
        woman. Deals extensively with women.)

1944   SAJOGYO, PUDJIWATI et al. The Role of Women in Different Per-
        spectives. Bogor: Rural Dynamics Studies, Agro-Economic
        Survey and Center for Rural Sociological Research, Bogor
        Agricultural University, 1980, 1 vol. (various pagings).

1945   _____. "Studying Rural Women in West Java." Studies in Fam-
        ily Planning 10, nos. 11/12 (Nov./Dec. 1979):364-70.

1946   SALMON, CLAUDINE. "Le role des femmes dans l'émigration
        Chinoise en Insulinde" [The role of women in Chinese emi-
        gration in the Archipelago]. Archipel, no. 16 (1978):
        161-74.

1947   SCHRIJVERS, JOKE, and POSTEL-COSTER, ELS. "Minangkabau Women:
        Change in a Matrilineal Society." Archipel, no. 13 (1977):
        79-104.

1948   SIWINTO, R.S. "Les femmes dans la société indonésienne
        d'aujourd'hui" [Women in Indonesian society today].
        Archipel, no. 13 (1977):315-20.

1949   SRIMAYA, N.A. Primbon Wanita [Women's manual]. Tjet. 7.
        Surabaya: Marfiah, n.d., 32 pp.

1950   SUBADIO, MARIA ULFAH, and IHROMI, T. OMAS. Peranan dan
        Kedudukan Wanita Indonesia: Bunga Rampai Tulisan-tulisan
        [Role and status of Indonesian women: anthology of writ-
        ings]. Jakarta: Gadjah Mada University Press, 1978, xx,
        346 pp.

1951   SUDJOKO. "Wanita Kota: Sebuah Sketsa" [Urban women: a
        sketch]. Prisma 4, no. 5 (Oct. 1975):62-70.

1952   SOEKARNO, President of Indonesia. Djadikan Indonesia Poros
        The New Emerging Forces! Amanat pada Resepsi Penutupan
        Kongres Persatuan Wanita Kristen Indonesia pada Tanggal
        28 Februari 1964 di Istana Olahraga Gelora Bung Karno,
        Senajan, Djakarta [Let women be the pivot of the new
        emerging forces. Message at the closing reception of the
        Congress of the Indonesian Christian Women's Association on
        28 February 1964 at Istana Olahraga Gelora Bung Karno,

Senajan, Jakarta]. Jakarta: Departemen Penerangan R.I., 1964, 14 pp. Penerbitan Chusus, 304.

1953 _____. Djangan Masuk Perangkap Kontra Revolusi. Amanat pada Kongres 'Wanita Indonesia' di Istana Olahraga Gelora Bung Karno, Senajan, Djakarta, pada Tanggal 19 Mei 1963 [Do not fall into the trap of the contra revolution. Message to the Congress "Indonesian Women" at Istana Olahraga Gelora Bung Karno, Senajan, Jakarta on 19 May 1963]. Jakarta: Departemen Penerangan R.I., 1963, 18 pp. Penerbitan Chusus, 262.

1954 _____. Peranan Wanita Indonesia dalam Pembangunan Semesta Berentjana. Amanat pada Peringatan Hal Ibu di Istana Negara, Tanggal 22 Desember 1960 [The role of women in the overall development plan. Message on Women's Day at Istana Negara, 22 December 1960]. Jakarta: Departemen Penerangan R.I., 1961, 16 pp. Penerbitan Chusus, 157.

1955 _____. Persatuan Total dengan Poros Nasakom. Amanat pada Kongres Gerwani Ke-IV di Gedung Wanita, Djakarta, 14 Desember 1961 [Total association is the pivot of Nasakom. Message to the Fourth Gerwani Congress at Gedung Wanita, Jakarta, 14 December 1961]. Jakarta: Departemen Penerangan R.I., 1962, 22 pp. Penerbitan Chusus, 207.

1956 _____. Revolusi Indonesia Tidak Dapat Berdjalan tanpa Wanita! Amanat pada Resepsi Pembukaan Kongres Ke-V Wanita Demokrat Indonesia pada Tanggal 16 Djuli 1964 di Istana Gelora Bung Karno, Senajan, Djakarta [The Indonesian revolution cannot progress without women's support. Message at the opening reception of the Fifth Congress of the Democratic Women of Indonesia on 16 July 1964 at Istana Gelora Bung Karno, Senajan, Jakarta]. Jakarta: Departemen Penerangan R.I., 1964, 22 pp. Penerbitan Chusus, 329.

1957 _____. Sarinah Kewadjiban Wanita dalam Perdjuangan Republik Indonesia [Sarinah, the responsibilities of women in the struggle of the Republic of Indonesia]. Jakarta: Jajasan Pembangunan, 1953, 329 pp.

1958 _____. Tidak Ada Bangsa Jang Besar tanpa Perbuatan. Amanat pada Hari Ibu Tanggal 22 Desember 1961 di Istana Negara [There can be no powerful nation without efforts made. Message on Women's Day, 22 December 1961 at Istana Negara]. Jakarta: Departemen Penerangan R.I., 1962, 15 pp. Penerbitan Chusus, 193.

1959   _____ . Tidak Ada Kompromi dengan Nekilim! Amanat pada
Peringatan Hari Wanita Internasional pada Tanggal 8 Maret
1965 di Istana Negara, Djakarta [There is no compromise
with nekilim! Message on International Women's Day on
8 March 1965 at Istana Negara, Jakarta]. Jakarta:
Departemen Penerangan, 1965, 14 pp.

1960   _____ . Wanita Indonesia Selalu Ikut Bergerak dalam Barisan
Revolusioner! Amanat pada Upatjara Pembukaan Kongres Ke-10
Kongres Wanita Indonesia di Istana Gelora Bung Karno,
Senajan, Djakarta, pada Tanggal 24 Djuli 1964 [Indonesian
women are always active in the revolutionary movement.
Message at the opening ceremony of the Tenth Congress,
Indonesian Women's Congress at Istana Gelora Bung Karno,
Senajan, Jakarta on 24 July 1964]. Jakarta: Departemen
Penerangan, 1964, 24 pp.

1961 SUKMADYANI. "Ibu Pertiwi dan Wanita" [The fatherland and
women]. Mawas Diri 4, no. 6 (1975):33-44.

1962 SURYOCHONDRO, SUKANTI. "The Status, Role and Achievements of
Women in Indonesia." In The Role of Women in Development:
Seminar Papers and Statements. Edited by Leonardo Z.
Legaspi. Manila: University of Santo Tomas Press, 1976,
pp. 82-96.

1963 SUTARDJO, NOERDJANA. Bunga Rampai Wanita [An anthology on
women]. Medan: Tagore, 1949, 104 pp.

1964 SWAAN-KOOPMAN, C. Vrouwen in Indië [Women in the Indies].
Amsterdam: H.J. Paris, 1932, 152 pp.

1965 TAN, MELY GIOK LAN. "Wanita Indonesia: Menuju Cakrawala
Baru?" [Indonesian women: towards a new era?]. Prisma 4,
no. 5 (Oct. 1975):3-9.

1966 TEMENGGUNG, ARSUL. Wanita di Indonesia [Women in Indonesia].
Jakarta: Chailan Sjamsoe, 1953, 120 pp.

1967 VAN LITH-VAN SCHREVEN, M.A.E., and HOOYKAAS-VAN LEEUWEN
BOOMKAMP, JACOBA HINDRIKA, eds. Indisch vrouwen jaarboek
[Indies women yearbook]. Jogjakarta: Kalff-Buning, 1948,
31 pp.

1968 VREEDE-DE STUERS, CORA. "L'émancipation de la femme indonésienne" [The emancipation of the Indonesian woman].
Ph.D. dissertation, Université de Paris, 1957, 313 pp.

1969   _____ . L'émancipation de la femme indonésienne [The emancipation of the Indonesian woman]. Paris: Mouton, 1959,
xvi, 175 pp.

1970 _____ . The Indonesian Women: Struggles and Achievements.
The Hague: Mouton, 1960, 204 pp.

1971 WALL, V.I. van de. Vrouwen uit de Compagnie's tijd [Women
from the Company's time]. Weltevreden and Amersfoort,
1923. (Indonesia during the colonial times.)

1972 WIDER, JOAN (Schutzman). "Indonesian Women in New York: A
Study of Culture Contact." Master's thesis, New York
University, 1964.

1973 _____ . "Indonesian Women in the Hague: Colonial Immigrants
in the Metropolis." Ph.D. dissertation, New York University, 1967, iv, 274 pp. Abstracted in Dissertation Abstracts 29, no. 1 (July 1968):29-30-B. University Microfilms International, order no. 68-10,103.

1974 "Women in Indonesia Applying Natural Role to Many Areas."
Report on Indonesia 11, no. 2 (1961):14-15.

1975 WOODSMALL, RUTH FRANCES. Women and the New East.
Washington, D.C.: Middle East Institute, 1960, Part 5,
pp. 195-241.

1976 ZAINUDDIN, H.M. Srikandi Atjeh [The brave women of Acheh].
Medan: Pustaka Iskandar Muda, 1966, 139 pp.

Malaysia

1977 ALATAS, SAROJINI ZAHARAH. "Prominent Women in Malaysia."
Archipel, no. 13 (1977):327-35.

1978 "An American Looks at Malay Women." Orient 6 (June 1964):
26-28.

1979 BROWNFOOT, JANICE N. "Community Relations and Women's
Organisations--European Women and the Asian Communities in
Colonial Malaysia c. 1900-1957." 40 pp. Paper presented
at the Eighth Conference of the International Association
of Historians of Asia, Kuala Lumpur, August 1980.

1980 CHIN, YOON FONG. "Chinese Female Immigration to Malaya in
the 19th and 20th Centuries." 23 pp. Paper presented at
the Eighth Conference of the International Association of
Historians of Asia, Kuala Lumpur, August 1980.

1981 FATIMAH HAMID-DON. "The Status, Roles and Achievements of
Women in Malaysia." In The Role of Women in Development:
Seminar Papers and Statements. Edited by Leonardo Z.
Legaspi. Manila: University of Santo Tomas Press, 1976,
pp. 23-38.

1982   HAMIMA DONA MUSTAFA. "Sumbangan Wanita Malaysia kepada Tahun
        Wanita Antarabangsa" [The contribution of Malaysian women
        to the International Women's Year]. Wanita [Kuala Lumpur]
        no. 78 (Jan. 1976):36-38.

1983   ISMAIL bin ABAS. "Wanita dalam Persejarahan Melayu" [Women
        in Malay history]. Dewan Masyarakat 12, no. 10 (Oct.
        1975):40-41.

1984   KHADIJAH MUHAMMAD. "Malay Women: A Historical Perspective."
        Paper presented at the Seventh Conference of the Interna-
        tional Association of Historians, August 1977, held in
        Bangkok, Thailand.

1985   LIM, JOO HOCK. "Chinese Female Immigration into the Straits
        Settlements, 1860-1901." South Seas Society, Journal 22,
        pts. 1/2 (1967):58-110.

1986   MANDERSON, LENORE. "Malay Women and Development in Peninsular
        Malaysia. Some Preliminary Notes." Kabar Seberang, no. 2
        (June 1977):61-84.

1987   _____. "A Woman's Place: Malay Women and Development in
        Peninsular Malaysia." In Issues in Malaysian Development.
        Edited by James C. Jackson and Martin Rudner. Singapore:
        Published for the Asian Studies Association of Australia
        by Heinemann Educational Books (Asia), 1979, pp. 233-71.

1988   MERICAN, MARINA. "Sayed Shaikh al-Hadi dan Pendapat2-nya
        mengenai Kemajuan Kaum Perempuan (sebagai Tersiar di-dalam
        Majallah al-Ikhwan)" [Sayed Shaikh al-Hadi and his views on
        the progress of women, as reported in the journal al-
        Ikhwan]. B.A. academic exercise, University of Malaya,
        1960, 82 pp.

1989   NATIONAL COUNCIL OF WOMEN'S ORGANISATIONS. Laporan Hari
        Wanita Persekutuan Tanah Melayu, 25 Ogos 1962 [Report on
        Women's Day, Federation of Malaya, 25 August 1962]. Kuala
        Lumpur: Economy Printers, 1963.

1990   SAFIAH KARIM, Nik. "Wanita Malaysia Masakini" [Malaysian
        women today]. Mastika 40, no. 2 (Feb. 1980):141-49.

1991   SEMINAR GPW, Serdang, Malaysia, 1979. Kertaskerja-kertaskerja
        [Working papers]. Organized by Federal Land Development
        Authority GPW (Gerakan Persatuan Wanita--Women's Associa-
        tion). Serdang, Malaysia, 1979. 1 vol. (various pagings).

1992   SEMINAR LATIHAN KEPIMPINAN BAGI WANITA SABAH, Kota Kinabalu,
        1973. Kertaskerja-kertaskerja [Training Seminar on Leader-
        ship for Women in Sabah, Kota Kinabalu, 1973. Working Pa-
        pers]. Kota Kinabalu: Pusat Pembangunan Masyarakat, 1973,
        1 vol. (various pagings).

1993   SEMINAR TAHUN WANITA ANTARABANGSA, Kuala Lumpur, 1975. Work-
        ing Papers [Seminar on International Women's Year, Kuala
        Lumpur, 1975]. Kuala Lumpur: Wanita MCA Selangor, 1975,
        1 vol. (various pagings).

1994   SEMINAR 'WANITA MALAYSIA MASAKINI,' Bangi, Selangor, 1979.
        Papers [Seminar 'Malaysian Women Today,' Bangi, Selangor,
        1979]. Organized by the Faculty of Social Sciences and
        Humanities, Universiti Kebangsaan Malaysia, Bangi, Selangor,
        1979, 1 vol. (various pagings).

1995   SKEAT, WALTER W. "The Malay Peninsula." In Women of All Na-
        tions. Vol. 1. Edited by Thomas Athol Joyce and Northcote
        W. Thomas. New York: Funk & Wagnalls, 1915, pp. 186-201.

1996   WEE, ANN E. "Some Aspects of the Status of Chinese Women in
        Malaya." In Status of Women in South Asia. Edited by
        Angadipuram Appadorai. Bombay: Orient Longmans, 1954,
        pp. 153-65.

1997   WEEKES-VAGLIANI, WINIFRED. "Malaysia (Based on the Family
        Life Survey of the Rand Corporation)--Case Studies." In
        Women in Development at the Right Time for the Right Rea-
        sons. Paris: Development Centre, Organisation for Eco-
        nomic Co-operation and Development, 1980, pp. 58-149.

Philippines

1998   ABAYA, CONSUELO. "The Filipino Woman Is Sitting Pretty."
        Philippines Yearbook (1950/1951):68-71.

1999   AGUILA, CONCEPCION A. "Women in a Challenging World." Centro
        Escolar University, Manila, Graduate and Faculty Studies 7
        (1956):1-6.

2000   ALZONA, ENCARNACIÓN. "The Filipino Woman: A Backward Glance,
        1925-1950." Fookien Times Philippines Yearbook, Silver
        Jubilee Edition (1926/1951):95-96.

2001   _____. The Filipino Woman: Her Social, Economic and Politi-
        cal Status 1565-1933. Manila: University of the Philip-
        pines Press, 1934, 94 pp.

2002   _____. "Rizal's Legacy to the Filipino Woman." Fookien Times
        Philippines Yearbook (1954):103-4, 125-30.

2003 _____. "The Role of the Filipino Women in the Republic."
Fookien Times Philippines Yearbook 16 (1953):99-100,
121-22, 141.

2004 _____. "What of the Filipino Women?" Philippine Review 1,
no. 1 (Mar. 1943):33-38.

2005 ASUNCION, GENOVEVA C. "Portrait of the Filipina." Philippine
Journal of Philately 14, no. 5 (May/June 1964):8-12.

2006 BASS, FLORA (Gardner). Philippine Women and Dolls. Laguna
Beach, Calif.: Mermaid Books, 1955, 111 pp.

2007 BENAVIDES, ENRIQUETA R. "The Filipino Woman's Role."
Fookien Times Philippines Yearbook (1961):239-41, 260.

2008 _____. The Filipino Woman's Social, Economic and Political
Status. Manila: Cultural Foundation of the Philippines,
1958, 17 pp.

2009 BLEY, NINA (VALMONTE). "The Urban Filipino Woman." Master's
thesis, Ateneo de Manila University [Manila], 1972, 97 pp.

2010 BULATAO, RODOLFO A. "National Survey on the Status and Roles
of Women in the Philippines. Preliminary Report." Manila:
University of the Philippines, 1977.

2011 CORTES, IRENE R. "Status of Women." In Population of the
Philippines, by United Nations Economic and Social Commission for Asia and the Pacific. Bangkok: ESCAP, 1978,
pp. 313-21.

2012 CUE, MAGDALENA ALONSO-VILLABA. The Mission of Women: A
Return to Their Original Role. Manila: University of
Santo Tomas, 1975, iii, 67 pp.

2013 FLORES, ANGELITA L. "A Study of the Role of the Filipino
Women in the National Movement." Master's thesis, University of Santo Tomas [Manila], 1960, viii, 212 pp.

2014 GREEN, JUSTIN JAY. "The High Status of Filipinas: Myth or
Reality? Or the Problem of Finding a Chameleon in a Rain
Forest with Only a Microscope or Telescope for Tools."
Paper presented at the 27th Annual Meeting of the Associa-
tion for Asian Studies, San Francisco, California, March
1975.

2015 GUERRERO NAKPIL, CARMEN. "The Filipino Woman." Orient 3
(Aug. 1952):29-32, 61-63.

2016   _____. "The Filipino Woman." Asian & Pacific Quarterly of
        Cultural and Social Affairs 12, no. 2 (Summer 1980):10-18.

2017   _____. "The Filipino Woman." Philippines Quarterly 7, no. 4
        (Dec. 1975):18-25.

2018   _____. "The Filipino Woman in Legend and History."
        Philippines Quarterly 7, no. 3 (Sept. 1975):2-6.

2019   _____. Woman Enough; and Other Essays. Quezon City: Vibal,
        1963, vii, 149 pp.

2020   JACINTO, AMADO. Womanhood: A Modern Interpretation. Manila:
        Ilagan & Sañga Press, 1940, xvii, 170 pp.

2021   KALAW, PURA VILLANUEVA. Filipino Women: The Challenge They
        Meet. Manila: Crown Printers, 1951, 15 pp.

2022   LIZANO, LOLITA R. The Wonderful New World of Women: A Mini-
        Encyclopedia. Quezon City: New Day Publishers, 1976,
        viii, 285 pp.

2023   MENDOZA-GUAZÓN, MARÍA PAZ. The Development and Progress of
        the Filipino Women. 2d ed. Manila: Kiko Printing Press,
        1951, 72 pp.

2024   _____. My Ideal Filipino Girl. n.p., 1931, 189 pp.

2025   _____. "Woman's Status under Independence: A Discerning
        Glimpse into the Future of Fair Sex." Philippines Yearbook
        1 (1933/1934):17, 24.

2026   MONTIEL, CRISTINA, and HOLLNSTEINER, MARY RACELIS. The
        Filipino Woman: Her Role and Status in Philippine Society.
        Final report submitted to the Local Water Utilities Admin-
        istration by the Institute of Philippine Culture on
        30 March 1976. Manila: Ateneo de Manila University,
        Institute of Philippines Culture, 1976, vii, 52 pp.

2027   OCAMPO, ESTEBAN de. "Rizal on the Filipina Woman." Filipina
        1 (Nov./Dec. 1944):4-5.

2028   OROSA, SEVERINA (LUNA). Rizal and the Filipino Woman.
        Rizal's Liga Filipina. Manila, 1961, 47 pp.

2029   PHILIPPINES (REPUBLIC), National Commission on the Role of
        Filipino Women. Annual Report. Manila: National Commis-
        sion on the Role of Filipino Women, 1976.

2030   _____. "In the Mainstream of National History." In The Role of Women in Development: Seminar Papers and Statements. Edited by Leonardo Z. Legaspi. Manila: University of Santo Tomas Press, 1976, pp. 188-96.

2031   _____. Review and Appraisal of Progress Made in Attaining the Objectives of the United Nations Decade for Women: Philippines. Prepared by the National Commission on the Role of Filipino Women for the UN ESCAP Regional and Preparatory Conference for the World Conference of the United Nations Decade for Women 5-9 November 1979, New Delhi, India. Manila[?] 1979, 69 pp.

2032   PHILIPPINES (REPUBLIC), National Media Production Center. The Filipina: A Humanizing Force in Philippine Development. Manila: National Media Production Center, 1975, 56 pp.

2033   POLICARPIO, PAZ T. "Filipino Women in History." B.Sc. thesis, University of the Philippines [Quezon City], 1924, 126 pp.

2034   PROSIA-PEÑA, CASILDA SY. "The Rise of the Filipino Women in the Social, Economic and Political Fields Since the End of the Spanish Regime up to the Present Time." Master's thesis, University of San Carlos [Cebu City, Philippines], 1953, viii, 119 pp.

2035   QUESADA, JUAN, Jr. "The Filipino Woman." Philippines Quarterly 7, no. 3 (Sept. 1975):7-16.

2036   RAUSA-GOMEZ, LOURDES, and TUBANGUI, HELEN R. "Reflections on the Filipino Woman's Past." Philippine Studies (1st and 2d quarter 1978):125-41.

2037   REYES, FELINA. "Filipino Women, Their Role in the Progress of Their Nation." Washington, D.C.: Women's Bureau, Department of Labor, 1951, 9 pp.

2038   RIZAL Y ALONSO, JOSÉ. A Letter to the Young Women of Malolos. Manila: Bureau of Printing, 1932, 35 pp. Biblioteca Nacional de Felipinas. Documento, no. 8. (In Tagalog, Spanish, and English.)

2039   ROJAS-ALETA, ISABEL; SILVA, TERESITA L.; and ELEAZAR, CHRISTINE. A Profile of Filipino Women: Their Status and Role. Prepared for the United States Agency for International Development. Manila: Philippine Business for Social Progress, 1977, xxvii, 400 pp.

2040 ROMERO, FLERIDA RUTH P. "Women's Status in Philippine Society." Fookien Times Philippines Yearbook (1978):324-29,
337, 359.

2041 SANTOS, ALFONSO P. Heroic Virgins and Woman Patriots: Female
Patriotism during the Japanese Occupation. Retold and edited by Alfonso P. Santos. Manila: National Book Store,
1977, x, 158 pp.

2042 SHAHANI, LETICIA RAMOS. "Challenge of Modernization to the
Filipino Woman." Bureau of Women and Minors, Digest 1,
no. 3 (Mar. 1972):1-10.

2043 _____. "Issues Facing the Filipino Woman during International
Women's Year--1975." Manila: Institute of Philippine Culture, 1974.

2044 SONZA, DEMY P. "The Filipino Woman in History." Southeast
Asia Journal [Iloilo City, Philippines] 11, no. 1 (1979):
35-39.

2045 "A Special Supplement on Women." Times Journal (5 July 1975).
(Contents: 1. Teresa Reyes Tunay, "The True Measure of
Liberalism." 2. "A Special UN Report--Women Today: Their
Situation and Status." 3. Demographic Trends: Women Con-
tinue to Have Higher Life Expectancy than Men." 4. "Legal
Situation: The Principle of Equal Rights of Men and Women
Has Now Been Recognised." 5. "Rural Electrification: The
Filipino Woman Has Found Her Place in Cooperative Electri-
fication." 6. "Education: Economic Factors Play Vital
Role." 7. "Economic Activity and Employment." 8. "Par-
ticipation in Public Life." 9. Margaret Mead, "Liberation
Liberates." 10. "Quotations from Rizal: Duties of the
Filipino Woman." 11. "The Gutsy Dozen: Filipinas."
12. Dorothea E. Woods, "The Teen-age Girl in the Third
World: Her Problems and Prospects." 13. Alice C.
Villadolid, "Liberated Filipina: Redefining a Difficult
Role." 14. Vic Bumatay, "The Filipino Woman Isn't Truly
Liberated (Yet)." 15. "Young Blood Needed in Women's
Associations." 16. "Fighting Sexism in Language."
17. Amado de los Reyet, "Men's Lib.")

2046 THOMAS, NORTHCOTE WHITRIDGE. "The Philippine Islands." In
Women of All Nations. vol. 1. Edited by Thomas Athol
Joyce and Northcote W. Thomas. New York: Funk & Wagnalls,
1915, pp. 202-8.

2047 WYNNE, ALISON. No Time for Crying: Stories of Philippine
Women Who Care for Their Country and Its People. Kowloon:
Resource Centre for Philippine Concerns, 1979, 120 pp.

Singapore

2048   BROWNFOOT, JANICE N.   "Community Relations and Women's Orga-
         nisations--European Women and the Asian Communities in
         Colonial Malaysia c. 1900-1957."   40 pp.   Paper presented
         at the Eighth Conference of the International Association
         of Historians of Asia, Kuala Lumpur, August 1980.

2049   CHENG, SIOK HWA.   "Singapore Women: Legal Status, Educational
         Attainment, and Employment Patterns."   Asian Survey 17,
         no. 4 (Apr. 1977):358-74.

2050   _____.   "The Status, Roles and Achievements of Women in
         Singapore."   In The Role of Women in Development: Seminar
         Papers and Statements.   Edited by Leonardo Z. Legaspi.
         Manila: University of Santo Tomas Press, 1976, pp. 57-77.

2051   _____.   Women in Singapore: Legal, Educational and Economic
         Aspects.   Singapore: Nanyang University, 1976, 32 pp.
         Nanyang University, College of Graduate Studies, Institute
         of Humanities and Social Science.   Occasional Paper Series.

2052   CHEW, JOY OON AI, and TAN, MEY LING.   "The Present Status of
         Singaporean Women: Self-Image."   B.A. academic exercise,
         University of Singapore, 1973, 77 pp.

2053   PHAY, AI LIEN.   "The Present Status of Singaporean Women."
         B.A. academic exercise, University of Singapore, 1973,
         65 pp.

2054   SALMON, CLAUDINE.   "Être femme à Singapour" [Women in
         Singapore].   Archipel, no. 19 (1980):161-68.

2055   TAN, NALLA.   "The Role of Women in Nation Building."   National
         Youth Leadership Training Institute, Singapore, Journal
         (Sept. 1972):61-66.

2056   _____.   "Singapore Women and International Women's Year--
         1975."   National Youth Leadership Training Institute,
         Singapore, Journal (Dec. 1974):107-12.

2057   UNITED NATIONS, Asian and Pacific Centre for Women and Devel-
         opment.   Selected Country Papers Presented at the ACPWD
         Expert Group Meeting on the Identification of the Basic
         Needs of Women of Asia and the Pacific and Formulation of
         a Programme of Work, Tehran, Iran, December 1977.   Bangkok:
         APCWD, 1980, 89 pp.   (Studies on the position of women in
         six countries--Burma, Sri Lanka, India, Pakistan, Japan,
         and Singapore.)

2058   WONG, ALINE K. Women in Modern Singapore. With the assis-
        tance of Chew Oon Ai, Tan Mey Ling, and Phay Ai Lien.
        Singapore: University Education Press, 1975, 137, 7 pp.

Thailand

2059   BACHFELD, AUGUST. "Die Frau in Siam" [The woman in Siam].
        Umschau 32 (1968):215-18.

2060   DUANGDUEN BISALPUTRA. "The Status, Roles and Achievements of
        Women in Thailand." In The Role of Women in Development:
        Seminar Papers and Statements. Edited by Leonard Z.
        Legaspi. Manila: University of Santo Tomas Press, 1976,
        pp. 15-22.

2061   DUPLATRE, LOUIS. Essai sur la condition de la femme au Siam
        [Essay on the condition of women in Siam]. Lyon: Société
        Anonyme de l'Imprimerie A. Rey, 1922, 107 pp. (Ph.D. dis-
        sertation, Université de Grenoble.)

2062   LA LOUBÈRE, SIMON de. "Of the Women of the Palace, and of
        the Officers of the Wardrobe." In The Kingdom of Siam.
        Reprint ed. Kuala Lumpur: Oxford University Press, 1969,
        pp. 100-102.

2063   NANTANEE JAYASUT et al. Status of Thai Women in Two Rural
        Areas: Survey Report. Bangkok: National Council of
        Women of Thailand, 1977, 34 pp.

2064   PRAJUB TIRABUTANA. A Simple One: The Story of a Siamese
        Girlhood. Ithaca, N.Y.: Department of Far Eastern Stud-
        ies, Southeast Asia Program, Cornell University, 1958,
        51 pp. Cornell University, Southeast Asia Program. Data
        Paper, no. 30.

2065   REYNOLDS, CRAIG JAMES. "A Nineteenth Century Thai Buddhist
        Defense of Polygamy and Some Remarks on the Social History
        of Women in Thailand." Paper presented at the Seventh
        Conference of the International Association of Historians
        of Asia, August 1977, held in Bangkok, Thailand.

2066   SAISUREE CHUTIKUL. "Women in Rural Northeast Society in
        Thailand." Khon Kaen, Thailand: Khon Kaen University,
        n.d.

2067   SKEAT, WALTER W. "Siam and Cambodia." In Women of All Na-
        tions. Vol. 3. Edited by Thomas Athol Joyce and Northcote
        W. Thomas. New York: Funk & Wagnalls, 1915, pp. 550-58.

2068   SUMALEE VIRAVAIDYA. "A Woman's Place in Thailand: 3 Impres-
        sions." UNICEF News (July 1973):23-25.

2069   THAMMASAT UNIVERSITY, Faculty of Social Administration, De-
        partment of Social Work. Study of the Status and Role of
        Women in 21 Villages of Lampang Province, Thailand.
        Bangkok: Department of Social Work, Faculty of Social
        Administration, Thammasat University, 1975, 69 pp.

2070   WAN WAITHAYAKORN. "The Status and Activities of Thai Women."
        Foreign Affairs Bulletin [Bangkok] 6, no. 3 (Dec. 1966/
        Jan. 1967):239-42.

HEALTH AND WELFARE

(See also Family Planning and Fertility, Psychology and Psychiatry)

Southeast Asia

2071   PASTRANA, GAGRIEL. "Abortions in the Religions of Southeast
        Asia." Unitas 48, no. 4 (Dec. 1975):639-54.

2072   PENG, JUI YUN; SRISOMANG KEOVICHIT; and MacINTYRE, REGINALD,
        eds. Role of Traditional Birth Attendants in Family Plan-
        ning: Proceedings of an International Seminar Held in
        Bangkok and Kuala Lumpur, 19-26 July 1974. Ottawa:
        International Development Research Centre, 1974, 107 pp.

2073   WORLD HEALTH ORGANIZATION. Women in Health and Development in
        South East Asia. Report Prepared by World Health Organiza-
        tion, South East Asia Regional Office, New Delhi, India.
        New Delhi[?], 197-, 21 pp.

Burma

2074   THYNN THYNN. "Central Women Hospital." Forward [Rangoon] 9,
        no. 1 (Aug. 1970: 12-17. (Based on data collected by
        Myint Myint Than.)

Indochina

2075   BROWNMILLER, SUSAN. "The Real Spoils of War." Ms 4, no. 6
        (Dec. 1977):82-85. (Excerpt from Against Our Will: Men,
        Women and Rape. On women in the Vietnamese war.)

2076   DINH THI CAN. "Mother and Child Welfare." Vietnamese Studies,
        no. 25 (1970):41-45.

2077   DINH VAN THANG. "The Hanoi Institute for the Protection of
        Mother and Newborn Child." Women of Vietnam, nos. 3/4
        (1971):39-43.

2078   MIGOZZI, JACQUES. "Caractères de la mortalité féminine et de
        la mortalité des enfants au Cambodge" [Characteristics of
        female and child mortality in Cambodia]. In Etudes de géo-
        graphie tropicale offertes, by Pierre Gourou. Paris:
        Mouton, 1972, pp. 209-22. Le monde d'outre-mer passé et
        présent. Première série: études, 38.

Indonesia

2079   CRITCHFIELD, RICHARD. "Discovering Indonesia's Women." Asia
        [New Jersey] 2, no. 4 (Nov./Dec. 1979):8-17.

2080   GAMBIRO. "Services Rendered by the Mother and Child Health
        Activities in Indonesia." Paediatrica Indonesiana 4,
        nos. 1/2 (1964):135-62.

2081   "Health and Education Favoured over Rights by Women of
        Indonesia." Asia 3 (Nov. 1976):2-3.

2082   HULL, VALERIE J. "Women, Doctors, and Family Health Care:
        Some Lessons from Rural Java." Studies in Family Planning
        10, nos. 11/12 (Nov./Dec. 1979):315-25.

2083   INDONESIA, Departemen Kesehatan. "Laporan Workshop Kesedjah-
        teraan Ibu dan Anak 13 Maret s/d 18 Maret" [Report on the
        Workshop on Maternal and Child Health 13-18 March].
        Jakarta, 1971.

2084   JOESOEF, E. "Maternal Mortality." Majalah Kesehatan Angkatan
        Perang 8, nos. 5/6 (1958):127-36.

2085   KARIMUDIN, T. "Beberapa Tjatatan tentang Perawatan dan
        Perlindungan Kesehatan Tenaga Kerdja Wanita dalam Proses
        Produksi" [Some notes on the health services and protection
        of women workers in the production process]. Dokumentasi
        Tenaga Kerdja 5, no. 1 (1972):4-8.

2086   LUBIS, FIRMAN et al. General Health Services and Mother and
        Child Health Care in the Clinic of the Family Planning
        Project Serpong. Leiden: Institute of Cultural and Spe-
        cial Studies, Leyden State University, 1972. Family Plan-
        ning Project Serpong, Indonesia. Serpong Paper, no. 4.

2087   MARTIONO, KOEN (Mrs.). "Kesejahteraan Ibu dan Anak dan
        Keluarga Berancana Tak Dapat Dipisahkan Satu Sama Lain"
        [Maternal and child welfare and family planning are inter-
        related]. Kesehatan Masyarakat 1, no. 3 (1971):30-36.

2088   MARTOATMODJO et al. "Masalah Anemi Gizi pada Wanita Hamil
        dalam Hubungannya dengan Pola Konsumi Makanan" [The problem
        of nutritional anemia during pregnancy and its relationship
        to food consumption patterns]. Penelitian Gizi dan Makanan,
        no. 3 (1973):22-24.

2089   NOTOSOEDIRDJO, MOELJONO. "The Attitude of the Pregnant
        Javanese Women towards Their Pregnancies: An Approach to
        the Study of Abortion in Indonesia." Majalah Kesehatan
        Jiwa 2, no. 1 (1976):3-12.

2090   PRAWIROHARDJO, SOEBAGJO. "Kesejahteraan Ibu dan Anak:
        Peranan Penting Untuk Kesejahteraan Keluarga" [Mother and
        child welfare: the important role in family welfare].
        Majalah Administrasi Negara 3, no. 3 (1961):85-87.

2091   POERNOMO, SONJA. "Sedjarah Perkembangan Kesedjahteraan Ibu &
        Anak" [The history of the development of maternal and child
        welfare services]. Majalah Kesehatan 4, no. 27 (1971):
        13-15.

2092   PURWODIHARDJO, SUBAGIO. Keluarga Berentjana sebagai Unsur
        Penting dalam Usaha Kesedjahteraan Ibu dan Anak [Family
        planning as an important factor in maternal and child
        health]. Jakarta: Biro Penerangan dan Motivasi, Badan
        Koordinasi Keluarga Berentjana Nasional, 1971, 22 pp.

2093   RAHARDJO, PUDJO. "Population and Health: A Study of the
        Relationship between Health Delivery Activities and Contra-
        ceptive Acceptance in Indonesia." Ph.D. dissertation,
        University of Pittsburgh, 1977, 233 pp. Abstracted in
        Dissertation Abstracts International 38, no. 6 (Dec. 1977):
        3760-A. University Microfilms International, order no.
        77-21,207.

2094   RAMLI, AHMAD. "Abortus Ditinjau dari Segi Agama Islam"
        [Abortion viewed from the Muslim religion]. Majalah
        Kedokteran Indonesia 15, nos. 11/12 (1965):525-31.

2095   REMMELTS, R. "Maternal Mortality in Batavia in 1935."
        Geneeskundig tijdschrift voor Nederlandsch-Indie 76 (1936).

2096   SEMINAR PENGGUGURAN KANDUNGAN BERDASARKAN PERTIMBANGAN
        KESEHATAN, Jakarta, 1979. Hasil Seminar [Seminar on
        Abortion for Health Reasons, Jakarta, 1969. Proceedings].
        1 vol. Jakarta, Departemen Kesehatan R.I., 1979.

2097   SOEDIGDOMARTO, S. HARJONO.   "Pengguguran Kehamilan atas
       Indikasi Sosio Medik" [Termination of pregnancy for socio-
       medical reasons].   Majalah Obstetri dan Ginekologi
       Indonesia 1, no. 2 (1974):77-87.

2098   SOEGIANO, MOH.   "Peranan Balai Kesejahteraan Ibu dan Anak
       dalam Masyarakat" [Role of the Mother and Child Welfare
       Center in the community].   Pedoman dan Berita Departemen
       Kesehatan, no. 1 (1965):53-56.

2099   SUHASIM, R., and DIPOLEGO, ACHMAD.   "Social Pediatrics in the
       Framework of Mother and Child Welfare Activities in the
       Public Health Scheme of Indonesia."   Paediatrica Indonesiana
       4, no. 4 (1964):266-75.

2100   SULIANTI.   "Mempertinggi Pendidikan Kaum Ibu menuju Kesejah-
       teraan Keluarga" [Raising the education of women in family
       welfare].   Majalah Administrasi Negara 3, no. 3 (1961):
       89-92.

2101   SUMANPOUW, HANNY.   "Beberapa Pengalaman Abortus Provocatus di
       Surabaya" [Some experiences regarding induced abortion in
       Surabaya].   Majalah Obstetri dan Ginekologi Indonesia 1,
       no. 2 (1974):110-13.

2102   SOERJANINGSIH; JOEDOSEPOETRO, SOETOMO; and SOEWONDO,
       HOEPOEDINO.   "Some Aspects of Unwanted Pregnancy: A Pre-
       liminary Report on a Survey at the Dr. Soetomo Hospital,
       Surabaya, Indonesia."   Majalah Kedokteran Surabaya 12,
       no. 2 (1975):41-45.

2103   SUTEDJO, P.   "Organization of Mother and Infant Care Services
       (Urban) in Indonesia."   Paediatrica Indonesiana 14,
       nos. 9/10 (1974):143-47.

2104   TOHA, MOH.   "Meninjau ke Kesejahteraan Ibu dan Anak" [Survey
       of maternal and child welfare].   Majalah Kedokteran
       Indonesia 6, no. 7 (1956):249-56.

2105   ZWAAN, J.P. KLEIWEG de.   "Abortus Provocatus in den Indischen
       Archipel" [Abortus provocatus in the Indies Archipelago].
       Mens en maatschappij 4 (1928):33-50, 127-44.

Malaysia

2106   ABDUL AZIZ bin ABDUL HAMID, Ungku.   "HAWA, 'Haul Wanita'.
       Suatu Perbadanan untuk Membantu Wanita Bergerak" [HAWA,
       'Haul Wanita'. An organization to help (rural) women
       (working in towns)].   Wanita [Kuala Lumpur], no. 82 (May
       1976):14-15, 82.

2107 _____. "Menubuhkan HAWA demi Pekerja Wanita Melayu Baru"
[Setting up HAWA to help new Malay women workers]. Paper
presented at Muktamar Kedua Pertubuhan-Pertubuhan Perempuan
Islam Malaysia, Kuala Lumpur, 1977, organized by the Muslim
Women's Welfare Board.

2108 AFSARI. "Pusat Membantu Mangsa Rogol" [Center to help rape
victims]. Saripati, no. 1 (Feb. 1977):58-60.

2109 AINON MUHAMMAD. "Rogol dari Kacamata Wanita" [Rape from
women's viewpoint]. Dewan Masyarakat 14, no. 5 (May 1976):
25-26.

2110 _____. "Wanita Kampung Mangsa Kota" [Rural women, urban vic-
tims]. Dewan Masyarakat 13, no. 6 (June 1975):28-29.

2111 ARIFFIN MARZUKI, and THAMBU, JOHAN A.M. "Maternal Mortality
in the Government Hospitals, West Malaysia, 1967-1969."
Medical Journal of Malaysia 27, no. 3 (Mar. 1973):203-6.

2112 BRODIE, M. "The Health of Women and Children in Malaya."
Royal Sanitary Institute, London, Journal 58 (1937):305-24.

2113 CHEN, PAUL CHIEH YEE. "An Assessment of the Training of the
Traditional Birth Attendant of Rural Malaysia." Medical
Journal of Malaysia 31, no. 2 (Dec. 1976):93-99.

2114 _____. "Developing World: Incorporating the Traditional
Birth Attendant into the Health Team, the Malaysian Example." Tropical and Geographical Medicine 29 (1977):192-96.

2115 _____. "Effects of the Trained Midwife on Traditional Domiciliary Midwifery in a Rural Malay Community." Southeast
Asian Journal of Tropical Medicine and Public Health 1
(1970):212-14.

2116 _____. "Midwifery Services in a Rural Malay Community."
M.D. thesis, University of Malaya, 1975, xxv, 427 pp.

2117 _____. "Providing Maternal and Child Care in Rural Malaysia."
Tropical and Geographical Medicine 29 (1977):441-48.

2118 _____. "Reasons Underlying the Maternal Choice of Midwives in
Rural Malaysia." Medical Journal of Malaysia 32, no. 3
(Mar. 1978):200-205.

2119 JAGJIT SINGH. "Midwifery Services in Negri Sembilan (with
Particular Reference to Domiciliary Midwifery Services)."
D.P.H. thesis, University of Singapore, 1966, 33 pp.

2120 JAHARAH ISKANDAR. "Bila Berlaku Rogol Kenapa Wanita Disa-
lahkan" [When rape occurs, why is the woman blamed].
Mastika 36, no. 8 (Aug. 1976):78-83.

2121 KARIM, WAZIR-JAHAN B.A. "Bringing out the Green in Women and
Children: A View of Health Development in Malaysia."
34 pp. Paper presented at the International Symposium on
Local Level Development Alternatives, Universiti Sains
Malaysia, Penang, 1979.

2122 KARUNAIVELL, ARUMUGAM. "Deaths in Kuala Trengganu District--
1977: Being an Exploratory Study into the Death Registration System Currently Operating and the Factors Influencing
the Occurrence of Deaths." Master's thesis, University of
Malaya, 1979, vii, 120 pp. (Includes maternal mortality.)

2123 KHAIRUDDIN YUSOF. "Maternal Mortality amongst the Rural
Malays." Medical Journal of Malaysia 28, no. 3 (Mar.
1974):149-53.

2124 KONG, H.; NG, K.H.; and SINNATHURAY, T.A. "Maternal Mortality
in University Hospital, Kuala Lumpur, Malaysia." Medical
Journal of Malaysia 28, no. 4 (June 1974):226-28.

2125 LIM, EWE SENG. "The Provision of Maternal and Child Health
Services in an Estate in South Kedah." D.P.H. thesis,
University of Singapore, 1971, 30 pp.

2126 LLEWELLYN-JONES, DEREK. "Maternal Deaths." Medical Journal
of Malaysia 13, no. 1 (Sept. 1958):103-8.

2127 _____. "The Prevention of Maternal Deaths." Medical Journal
of Malaysia 11, no. 4 (June 1957):291-99.

2128 LOURDENADIN, S. "Maternity Services in Federation of Malaya."
Medical Journal of Malaysia 17, no. 4 (June 1963):269-73.

2129 MAIMUNAH YUSOFF. "HAWA, Disokong oleh Pemimpin Masyarakat dan
Gadis Kilang" [HAWA, (an organization) accepted by com-
munity leaders and female factory workers]. Wanita [Kuala
Lumpur], no. 83 (June 1976):34-35.

2130 _____. "Rafidah (Aziz) Terangkan Maksudnya: Syor Tubuhkan
Sebuah Pusat Membantu Mangsa-mangsa Rogol Dibidas" [Rafidah
Aziz explains the reasons for the suggestion to set up a
center to assist rape victims to recover]. Wanita [Kuala
Lumpur], no. 91 (Feb. 1977):36-37.

2131 MAIZATUN ATAMADINI. "Menyelamat Gadis Desa Hanyut di Kota" [Safeguarding the rural girls in towns]. Santajiwa 27 (July/Aug. 1976):26-28.

2132 MALAYSIA, National Health Council, Maternal and Child Health Committee. "A Study of the Maternal and Child Health Services in the States of Malaya." Kuala Lumpur: Maternal and Child Health Committee, National Health Council, 197-[?], ii, 22 pp.

2133 NORMADIAH GHANI. "Rogol: Suatu Jenayah Yang Dahsyat" [Rape: an abhorrent crime]. Mastika 36, no. 1 (Jan. 1976):110-13.

2134 OOI, O.S. "The Demand for Abortion in an Urban Malaysian Population." Medical Journal of Malaysia 25, no. 3 (Mar. 1971):175-81.

2135 PHANG, KOOI YOONG. "The Rehabilitation Centre for Women and Girls: A Study." LL.B. academic exercise, University of Malaya, 1979, v, 114 pp.

2136 RAJ KARIM, and NOR LAILY AZIZ, Datin. Panduan Ceramah Kesihatan Ibu dan Kanak-kanak dan Perancangan Keluarga untuk Pegawai dan Kakitangan [A guide for talks on maternal and child health and family planning for health officers and staff]. Kuala Lumpur: Yunit Khsihatan Ibu dan Kanak-Kanak, Kementerian Kesihatan, 1977, 72 pp.

2137 REED, J.G. "Maternal Mortality among Indian Estate Women." British Medical Association, Malayan Branch, Journal 4 (1940):13-32.

2138 SAMBHI, JAGJIT SINGH. "The Changing Pattern of Maternal Mortality in Developing Countries." Far East Medical Journal 5 (May 1969):160-62. (Case study of Kuching General Hospital, Sarawak, Malaysia.)

2139 _____. "Danger of Improved Antenatal Care in Rural Areas without Adequate Hospital Facilities." In Malaysia-Singapore Congress of Medicine, 5th, Proceedings 5 (1970): 17-19. Kuala Lumpur: Academy of Medicine of Malaysia, 1970. (Pertains to Sarawak.)

2140 _____. "Severe Complications of Pregnancy and Labour following Bomoh's Abdomen." In Singapore-Malaysia Congress of Medicine, 4th, Proceedings 4 (1969):406-9. Singapore: Academy of Medicine, 1969.

2141 SANDOSHAM, ARTHUR ANANTHARAJ. "Effective Methods of Maternal Care in Rural Areas--Prenatal, Delivery and Post-natal." Berita MMA 4, no. 1 (1972):10-12.

2142   SEMINAR KEBANGSAAN MENGENAI PERANAN PAKAR-PAKAR DALAM
        MENINGGIKAN TARAF KESIHATAN KELUARGA, Penang, 1973.
        Laporan [National Seminar on the Role of Specialists in
        Promoting Family Health, Penang, 1973. Report]. Kuala
        Lumpur: Percetakan Kerajaan, 1977, vii, 221 pp.

2143   SEMINAR WANITA DAN PERTUBUHAN SUKARELA WANITA MENGENAI
        PEMBANGUNAN KELUARGA, Kuala Lumpur, 1979. Lapuran
        [Seminar on Women and Women's Voluntary Organizations
        concerning Family Development, Kuala Lumpur, 1979.
        Report]. Organized by Lembaga Perancang Keluarga Negara,
        Malaysia. Kuala Lumpur, 1980[?], 248 pp.

2144   SINGH, JESWANT. "A Study of the Generation, Flow and Utiliza-
        tion of Data in Maternal and Child Health Programme."
        Master's thesis, University of Malaya, 1977, iii, 90 pp.

2145   SINNATHURAY, T.A. et al. Report on Maternal Health and Early
        Pregnancy Wastage in Peninsular Malaysia. Edited by Indra
        Pathmanathan. Under the joint sponsorship of FFPA and the
        International Development Research Centre, Canada. Kuala
        Lumpur: Federation of Family Planning Associations, 1977,
        ix, 166 pp.

2146   SOTHIRAJAH, VIMALA. "Maternal Mortality in Temerloh District,
        from 1970 to 1978." Master's thesis, University of Malaya,
        1979, iii, 46 pp.

2147   THAMBU, JOHAN A.M. "Abortions--Government Hospitals: Penin-
        sular Malaysia, 1960-1972." Medical Journal of Malaysia
        29, no. 4 (June 1975):258-62.

Philippines

2148   ACHACOSO-ANGALA, SALUD. "Skinfold Thickness as an Indicator
        of Leanness-Fatness of Female College Students." Master's
        thesis, Philippine Women's University [Manila], 1962, vii,
        55 pp.

2149   BACTAT, JEAN L. "Health Problems of Mother and Children
        (under Five Years) in Vinzons, Camarines Norte." Master's
        thesis, University of the Philippines [Quezon City], 1965,
        xxiv, 177 pp.

2150   BORROMEO, MARIA ASUNCION E. "Dietary and Nursing Practices of
        Filipino Mothers in a Selected Economy." Master's thesis,
        University of the Philippines [Quezon City], 1966, vii,
        97 pp.

2151   CAUSING, AURORA FERIA. "The Physical Health Problems of High
        School Students with Special Reference to the Girls' High
        School of the University of San Carlos." Master's thesis,
        University of San Carlos [Cebu City, Philippines], 1955,
        xi, 192 pp.

2152   CHENG, JACINTO. "Unwed Mothers Project." Philippines Free
        Press 54 (2 Sept. 1961):68-69.

2153   DAUZ, P.A. "Some Observations on the Second Regional Seminar
        on Maternal and Child Health: Paediatric Education, Held
        Feb. 13-18, 1967 at W.H.O. Headquarters, Manila." Pulse
        12, no. 3 (1968):7-9.

2154   DEL MUNDO, FE et al. "Cooperative Efforts between Private
        Medical and Government Health Sectors in the Philippines
        through Maternal and Child Health Services." Philippine
        Medical Association, Journal 14, no. 4 (Apr. 1968):173-83.

2155   DIMITRI, M.C. "The Contribution of Women to Community
        Health." Philippine Medical Women's Association, Journal
        13 (July/Sept. 1975):113-16.

2156   DIZON, F.C. "State of Health of Women in the Philippines:
        Access to Health Services." Philippine Medical Women's
        Association, Journal 13 (Apr./June 1975):66-74.

2157   DOMANTAY, J.P. "The Socio-Economic Problems of Unwed Mothers."
        Social Work [Manila] 6, no.3 (Mar. 1961):551, 556, 561-62.

2158   DOMANTAY, NEMESIO. "Maternal Care in Quezon City, Philippines,
        for the Three Years 1947-1949." Master's thesis, Yale Uni-
        versity, 1951.

2159   ENCARNACION-FUENTEBELLA, CARIDAD. "A Dietary Survey of
        Filipino Pregnant and Lactating Mothers in Victorias,
        Negros Occidental as a Basis for a Nutrition Program."
        Master's thesis, Philippines Women's University [Manila],
        1956, viii, 101 pp.

2160   FERNANDEZ, PURITA MEDALLE. "The Integrated Maternal and Child
        Health Services in Zamboanga City, Philippines, and a Study
        of a Health Center Rio Hondo--Sta. Barbara Health Centre."
        D.P.H. thesis, University of Singapore, 1973, 68 pp.

2161   GALLEN, MOIRA. "Abortion Choices in the Philippines." Journal
        of Biosocial Science 11, no. 3 (July 1979):281-88.

2162   GAWAT, ASUNCION R.   "A Study of the Correctional Institution
       for Women: Needs of Inmates and Services Rendered by the
       Socio-Civic and Religious Organization." Master's thesis,
       Centro Escolar University [Manila], 1968, 156 pp.

2163   _____. "A Study of the Correctional Institution for Women:
       Needs of Inmates and Services Rendered by the Socio-Civic
       and Religious Organization." Centro Escolar University,
       Manila, Graduate and Faculty Studies 19 (1967):222-32.

2164   GILLON, RAANAN. "Not 'Abortion on Demand'." MD Journal
       [Rizal, Philippines] 20, no. 5 (May 1971):256-61.

2165   GUTHRIE, HELEN A.   "Infant and Maternal Nutrition in Four
       Tagalog Communities." In Modernization and Its Impact in
       the Philippines. Vol. 4. Edited by Walden F. Bello and
       Alfonso de Guzman. Quezon City: Ateneo de Manila Univer-
       sity Press, 1969, pp. 60-92.

2166   HEALY, GERALD W.   "After 'Humanae Vitae': Contraception and
       Abortion." Philippine Studies 22 (3d and 4th quarter
       1974):263-79.

2167   JESUS, MERCEDES de, Sister. "The Determination of the Calorie
       Intake of Young Adult Filipino Women (Twenty-one to
       Twenty-nine Years Old) Maintaining Desirable Body Weight."
       Master's thesis, Centro Escolar University [Manila], 1968,
       94 pp.

2168   JOCANO, F. LANDA. "Maternal and Child Care among the
       Tagalogs in Bay, Laguna, Philippines." Asian Studies 8,
       no. 3 (Dec. 1970):277-300.

2169   JOROLAN-DE los REYES, LOURDES.   "The Relation of an Adequate
       Diet in Pregnancy to the Length of Parturition and the
       Quality of Milk Produced." Master's thesis, Philippine
       Women's University [Manila], 1957, 64 pp.

2170   KINTANAR, PRISCILLA S.   "An Educational Approach to the Study
       of Nutritional Deficiencies and Cures of the Filipino
       Nursing Mother." Master's thesis, Adamson University
       [Manila], 1955, 83 pp.

2171   LARA, MELISSA A. de.   "Food Classification among Some Mothers
       in a Suburban Community and Its Implications to Nutrition
       Education." Master's thesis, University of the Philippines
       [Quezon City], 1969, 97 pp.

2172   LAXAMANA, FELICITAS A. "Some Factors That Affect Patients'
       Care in an Obstetrical Department of a Selective Hospital."
       Master's thesis, Philippine Women's University [Manila],
       1968, 30 pp.

2173   MENDOÑEZ, BELEN C. "An Appraisal of the Services Rendered to
       the Wards of the Philippine Training School for Girls from
       June 1959 to May 1961." Master's thesis, Philippine
       Women's University [Manila], 1962, v, 103 pp.

2174   MERCADO, AGUSTIN. "On the Maternity Benefits Bill."
       Philippine Social Security Bulletin 4, nos. 9/10 (1962):
       151-56.

2175   MONDOÑEDO, MARY VERONICA. "A Study to Determine the Effects
       of Residential Care and Treatment on the Attitudes of Fifty
       Unmarried Mothers." Master's thesis, Ateneo de Manila Uni-
       versity [Manila], 1974, ix, 154 pp.

2176   ORDONEZ, M.R. "The Unmarried Mothers and the Public Health
       Nurses." Philippine Journal of Nursing 34, no. 1 (1964):
       28-32.

2177   PASCUAL, LEONORA RAMOS. "Patient Reactions to the Quality of
       Obstetrical Nursing Service in the Philippine General
       Hospital." Master's thesis, Philippine Women's University
       [Manila], 1968, 138 pp.

2178   PEREZ, ALFREDO Y., Jr. "A Study of the Maternal Health Ser-
       vices of the Rural Health Unit, Salcedo, Eastern Samar."
       Master's thesis, University of the Philippines [Quezon
       City], 1968, 104 pp.

2179   PHILIPPINES (REPUBLIC), Department of Health, Bohol Province
       Maternal Child Health/Family Planning Project. Annual
       Report. Manila, no. 1-, 1975-.

2180   _____, Laws, statutes, etc. Philippine Medical Care and
       Woman and Child Labor Law. Compiled and edited by CBSI
       Editorial Staff. Manila: Central Book Supply, 1971,
       111 pp.

2181   POLONIA, MARY STANILAUS P. de. "A Study of Some Factors Per-
       tinent to the Emotional Stability of Marriage of Counselees
       at Two Centers Run by the Good Shepherd Sisters." Master's
       thesis, Ateneo de Davao [Davao City, Philippines], 1975,
       91 pp.

2182 RAQUEÑO, RESURRECCION O. "A Survey of the Dietary Intake of
      First-year Girls in Public Secondary Schools in Manila."
      Master's thesis, Far Eastern University [Manila], 1962,
      vi, 136 pp.

2183 RECIO, D.M. "One Concept of Maternal and Child Care."
      Pulse 8, no. 1 (1963):10-11, 21.

2184 REIS, A.D. "Maternal and Child Health Problems Encountered
      in Family Planning." Santo Tomas Journal of Medicine 25,
      no. 4 (July/Aug. 1970):218-34.

2185 ROMUALDEZ, VICTORIA A. "The Role of Homemaking Course at
      High School Level in the Moral Rehabilitation of Women in
      Postwar Philippines." Master's thesis, University of
      Manila [Manila], 1948, 87 pp.

2186 SAMONTE, MARY PIERRE, Sister. "A Study of Some Characteris-
      tics of Unmarried Mothers Served in an Accredited Agency."
      Thesis, Centro Escolar University, 1969, vii, 130 pp.

2187 SANTOS, DOMINADORA L. "Euthenics 3 and Its Relation to the
      Knowledge in Nutrition of Some Women Students in the Uni-
      versity of Philippines." Master's thesis, University of
      the Philippines [Quezon City], 1961, ix, 61 pp.

2188 SHOTWELL, MONICA. "Weary of Life--at Fifteen." Philippine
      Sociological Review 25, nos. 3/4 (July/Oct. 1977):113-17.
      (On female patients at the National Mental Hospital in the
      Philippines.)

2189 TAN, D.A. "On Legalization of Abortion." Philippine Medical
      Association, Journal 46, no. 12 (Dec. 1970):715-16.

2190 UNITED NATIONS, Social Welfare and Development Centre for
      Asia and the Pacific. Applied Nutrition Rural Prototype
      in a Philippine Village: A Case Study on Rural Women's
      Role in Community Life. Prepared by the Philippine Busi-
      ness for Social Progress, n.p., 1978, 50 pp.

2191 VALENZUELA, A.V. "Abortion in Filipino Women." Philippine
      Medical Association, Journal 46, no. 11 (Nov. 1970):655-67.

2192 VILLARAMA, ANTONIA. "Maternal Mortality in the Philippines."
      In American Congress on Obstetrics and Gynaecology,
      Evanston, 1941. Evanston, Ill.: Mumm Print Shop, 1942,
      pp. 348-50.

2193   YUTUC-MUTYA, VARGAS. "A Survey of the Food Habits of the
       Senior Girl Students of a Public High School in an Urban
       Community of the Philippines." Master's thesis, Centro
       Escolar University [Manila], 1952, ix, 159 pp.

2194   ZABLAN, ANTONIETA E. "Maternal and Child Health Practices."
       Studies in Family Planning 10, nos. 6/7 (Jun./July 1979):
       192-94.

Singapore

2195   CHAI, FOOK SEE. "A Study of the Blind Women in Singapore:
       Their Problems and Their Ways of Life and the Social Ser-
       vices Which Contribute to Their Needs." B.A. academic
       exercise, University of Singapore, 1961, 170 pp.

2196   CHIANG, LYNDA SHIH CHEN. "Development Assessment in Toa Payoh
       Maternal and Child Health Clinic." Master's thesis, Uni-
       versity of Singapore, 1975, 56 pp.

2197   DAVIES, T.A. LLOYD, and MILLS, ROSEMARY. "Young Mothers in
       Singapore." Medical Journal of Malaysia 12, no. 4 (June
       1958):585-601.

2198   HENG, VIRGINIA, and LAILY IBRAHIM. Two Studies of Social Work
       in the Field of Abortion. Edited by Ann Wee. Singapore:
       Department of Social Work, University of Singapore, 1973,
       vi, 165 pp. Singapore. University, Department of Social
       Work. Resource Paper Series, no. 2.

2199   HOOI, SEE CHOON. "Abortion: A Survey of 1,000 Cases."
       Medical Journal of Malaysia 17, no. 4 (June 1963):282-87.

2200   JAYAKUMAR, LALITHA (RAJAHRAM). "A Study and Appraisal of the
       Domiciliary After-care Service, Singapore, 1965-1969."
       D.P.H. thesis, University of Singapore, 1971, 55 pp.

2201   LAM, SIAN LIAN. "A Study of Syphilis in Pregnancy in Women
       Attending the Maternal and Child Health Clinics,
       Singapore." Master's thesis, University of Singapore,
       1974, 61 pp.

2202   LEAN, TYE HIN. "Maternal Mortality in Singapore, 1955-1959."
       Singapore Medical Journal 1, no. 3 (Sept. 1960):87-95.

2203   _____. "Maternal Mortality in Singapore, Recent Survey 1960-
       1962." Singapore Medical Journal 6, no. 3 (Sept. 1965):
       133-41.

2204 _____. "Prenatal Health and Maternity Services in the Republic of Singapore." Obstetrical and Gynaecological Society,
Proceedings 4 (Mar. 1973):1-7.

2205 LEE, ANN SARAH TSE AI. "Congenital Abnormalities in the Maternal and Child Health Service, Singapore, 1970." D.P.H.
thesis, University of Singapore, 1972, 50 pp.

2206 LEE, YONG KIAT. "The Non-clinical Aspects of Induced Abortion
in Singapore." Master's thesis, University of Singapore,
1966, 155 pp.

2207 LEONG, WAN KAI. "Public Assistance and the Women with Depen-
dent Children: A Study of a Group of Cantonese Lone Women
Drawing Public Assistance and Having Young Children Depen-
dent on Them." B.A. academic exercise, University of
Singapore, 1959, 178 pp.

2208 LIM, CONNIE KIM LOAN. "Maternity Mortality in Singapore."
D.P.H. thesis, University of Singapore, 1958, 50 pp.

2209 LIM, MAGGIE. "History of Maternal and Child Welfare Services,
Singapore City." D.P.H. thesis, University of Singapore,
1956, 101 pp.

2210 _____. "The Maternal and Child Health Services in Singapore."
Singapore Paediatric Society, Journal 8 (1966):29-41.

2211 LOH, MARGARET CHENG SIM (TEO). "A Study of the Domiciliary
Delivery Service in Singapore, 1955-1969." D.P.H. thesis,
University of Singapore, 1971, 85 pp.

2212 LOW, SAW LEAN. "A Study of the Sabin Immunization Programme
in Maternal and Child Health Clinics, Singapore (1964-
1970)." D.P.H. thesis, University of Singapore, 1972,
72 pp.

2213 MARIS STELLA GIRLS' SCHOOL, SINGAPORE, Child Welfare and Social Work Section. Teen-age Girls' Family Problems,
Singapore: Survey on Sixteen to Seventeen Year-old Girls
of Chinese Descent from Queenstown and the Farrer Road
Kampong--Their Attitudes towards Life and Patterns of Behaviour, with Special Emphasis on Their Family Relationship Values. Singapore: D. Moore, 1965, x, 158 pp.

2214 MILLIS, JEAN. "The Influence of Maternal Age and Birth Order
on the Outcome of Pregnancy in Poor Chinese Women." Annals
of Human Genetics 22, pt. 4 (July 1958):362-69. (On Chinese women in Singapore.)

2215 _____. "A Study of the Effect of Nutrition on Fertility and
the Outcome of Pregnancy in Singapore in 1947 and 1950."
Medical Journal of Malaysia 6 (1952):152-77.

2216 NG, ALLAN Y.H. "The Pattern of Rape in Singapore." Singapore
Medical Journal 15 (1974):49-50.

2217 PUNNA CHERUVARI, SUSHAMA. "Pregnancy and Infant-Care, Beliefs
and Practices among Some Singapore Malays." B.A. academic
exercise, University of Singapore, 1955, 79 pp.

2218 SIM, LEE WAH. "Unwed Mothers in Singapore: An Exploratory
Study." B.A. academic exercise, University of Singapore,
1976, 104 pp.

2219 SIMMONS, IDA MABEL MURRAY. "Pioneer Maternity and Child Welfare Work in Rural Singapore from 1927 to 1938." Malaya
[London] (Feb. 1958):20-21.

2220 _____. "Pioneering Maternity and Child Welfare in Rural
Singapore, 1927-1934." Public Health Nursing 27 (1935):
370-74.

2221 SINGAPORE, Ministry of Health, Maternal and Child Health
Services. Annual Report, 1974-.

2222 TEOH, H.K., and ONG, C.S. "A Study of Unmarried Mothers
Seeking Legal Abortions." In Singapore-Malaysia Congress
of Medicine, 6th. Proceedings 6 (1971):282-84. Singapore:
Academy of Medicine, 1971.

2223 VENGADASALAM, D. "A Follow-up Study of Applicants for Legalised Abortions Whose Pregnancies Were Not Terminated." In
Singapore-Malaysia Congress of Medicine, 6th. Proccedings
6:276-81. Singapore: Academy of Medicine, 1971.

Thailand

2224 BOONCHUAN HONGSKRAI. "Assessment of Day Care Centers for the
Working Women." 3 pp. Paper presented at the Seminar on
Women Wage Earners in Thailand, Pattaya, 18-20 April 1975.

2225 HANKS, JANE RICHARDSON. Maternity and Its Rituals in Bang
Chan. Ithaca, N.Y.: Department of Asian Studies, South-
east Asia Program, Cornell University, 1963, x, 128 pp.
Data Paper, no. 51, 1963.

2226 HAUCK, HAZEL MARIE. Maternal and Child Health in a Siamese
Rice Village: Nutritional Aspects; Studies in Bang Chan,
1952-1954. Ithaca, N.Y.: Department of Far Eastern Studies, Southeast Asia Program, Cornell University, 1959, xii,
70 pp. Data Paper, no. 39, 1959.

2227   PRAMOTE RATTAKUL. "Septic Abortion: The Scourge of Modern
       Obstetrics." Medical Association of Thailand, Journal 54
       (1971):312-17.

2228   STAHLIE, T.D. "Pregnancy and Childbirth in Thailand."
       Tropical and Geographical Medicine 2 (1960):127-37.

2229   TONGPLAEW NARKAVONNAKIT. "Abortion in Rural Thailand: A
       Survey of Practitioners." Studies in Family Planning 10,
       nos. 8/9 (Aug./Sept. 1979):223-29.

2230   _____. Rural Abortion in Thailand: A National Survey of
       Practitioners. Bangkok: National Family Planning Program,
       1979, 31 pp.

LEGAL STATUS; LAWS, ETC.

(On laws on family planning see
Family Planning and Fertility)

Southeast Asia

2231   CHUNG, BETTY JAMIE, and NG, SHUI MENG. The Status of Women in
       Law: A Comparison of Four Asian Countries. Singapore:
       Institute of Southeast Asian Studies, 1977, 63 pp. Insti-
       tute of Southeast Asian Studies. Occasional Papers Series,
       no. 49. (Countries are Malaysia, the Philippines, Republic
       of China, and Thailand.)

2232   RICAFRENTE, CHERRY-LYNN S. "International Labor Standards for
       Working Women." Philippine Law Journal 50, no. 1 (Feb.
       1975):55--79.

2233   SIHOMBING, JUDITH E., and FINLAY, H.A., eds. Lawasia Family
       Law Series. Singapore: Published by Singapore University
       Press for the Law Association for Asia and the Western
       Pacific, 1980. (Vol. 1: Afghanistan, Iran, South Korea,
       Sri Lanka, and Thailand. 230 pp. Six volumes forthcoming.
       Among subjects covered are marriage, divorce, maintenance
       of spouses and children.)

Brunei

2234   AHMAD bin MUHAMMAD IBRAHIM. "The Status of Muslim Women in
       Family Law in Malaysia and Brunei." Malaya Law Review 5,
       no. 2 (Dec. 1963):313-37; 6, no. 1 (July 1964):40-82; 6,
       no. 2 (Dec. 1964):353-86.

2235   _____. The Status of Muslim Women in Family Law in Malaysia, Singapore and Brunei. Singapore: Malayan Law Journal, 1965, xviii, 121 pp.

2236   _____. "The Status of Women in Family Law in Malaysia, Singapore and Brunei." Malaya Law Review 7, no. 1 (July 1965):54-94; 7, no. 2 (Dec. 1965):299-313; 8, no. 1 (July 1966):46-85; 8, no. 2 (Dec. 1966):233-69.

Burma

2237   BURMA, Legislative Council. "The Buddhist Women's Special Marriage and Succession Act. Burma Act XXIV, 1939. 30th December, 1939." Rangoon, 1940, 10 pp.

2238   GAUNG, U. Translation of a Digest of the Burmese Buddhist Law concerning Inheritance and Marriage: Being a Collection of Texts from Thirty-six Dhammathats. 2 vols. Compared and arranged under the supervision of U Gaung. Rangoon: Superintendent of Government Printing, 1902-1909.

2239   GLEDHILL, ALAN. "Burmese Law in Nineteenth Century, with Special Reference to the Position of Women." Cahiers d'histoire mondiale 7, no. 1 (1962):172-94.

2240   _____. "Community of Property in the Marriage Law of Burma." In Family Law in Asia and Africa. Edited by James N.D. Anderson. London: G. Allen and Unwin, 1968, pp. 205-17.

2241   _____. "The Status of Women in Burmese Law." Société Jean Bodin pour l'histoire comparative des institutions, Recueils 11 (1959):269-73.

2242   HLA AUNG, U. "Some Aspects of Marriage under Burmese Buddhist Law and Malayan Muslim Law." Burma Research Society, Journal 48, pt. 2 (Dec. 1965):1-15.

2243   KHETARPAL, SURAJ PARKASH. "Marriage and Inheritance in Burmese Buddhist Law." Ph.D. dissertation, University of London, 1959, xvi, 880, xxxvi pp.

2244   _____. "Property of the Marriage: Burmese Law." American Journal of Comparative Law 15, no. 4 (1966/67):754-71.

2245   MAUNG MAUNG, U. "Law and Custom in Burma and the Burmese Family." J.S.D. dissertation, Law School, Yale University, 1962, 291 pp.

2246   _____. Law and Custom in Burma and the Burmese Family. The Hague: Martinus Nijhoff, 1963, xii, 155 pp.

2247   MAUNG THEIN. "Customary Law of Burmese Marriages in British
       Burma." Ph.D. dissertation, University of London, 1941.

2248   SING KHO KHAO. "Customs Denies Women to Inherit." Guardian
       [Rangoon] 12, no. 2 (Feb. 1965):43-44.

Indochina

2249   BARRIERE, A. "La femme en droit annamite moderne" [The woman
       in modern Annamite law]. Thèse, Toulouse, 1920, 87 pp.

2250   BUI THI CAM. Etude sur la condition privée de la femme en
       droit annamite [Study on the private statute of the woman
       in Annamite law]. Thèse. Paris: Loviton, 1940, 110 pp.

2251   BUI TUONG CHIEU. "La polygamie dans le droit annamite: con-
       tribution à l'étude du droit comparé" [Polygamy in Annamite
       law: contribution to the study of comparative law]. Thèse
       pour le Doctorat en Droit, Université de Paris, 1933,
       xiii, 130 pp.

2252   _____. La polygamie dans la droit annamite [Polygamy in
       Annamite law]. Paris: Rousseau, 1933, xiii, 130 pp.

2253   DANG THI TAM. "Le divorce en droit vietnamien" [Divorce in
       Vietnamese law]. Thèse pour le Doctorat d'Etat, Université
       de Paris, 1967, 310 pp.

2254   _____. "Le divorce en le droit vietnamien" [Divorce in Viet-
       namese law]. Vocation asiatique, no. 4 (1968):70-74.

2255   DUONG KIEN. Giai thich luat Gia thu tu he va tai san cong
       dong [Law on marriage, filiation, and community property].
       Saigon: Khai Tri, 1964, 240 pp. (A detailed study of
       Law no. 15/64 governing marriage, filiation, and community
       property.)

2256   GENTILE-DUQUESNE, PIERRE de. La situation juridique de la
       femme annamite [The legal status of the Annamite woman].
       Thèse. Paris: Jouvre, 1925, 158 pp.

2257   GINSBURGS, GEORGE. "The Role of Law in the Emancipation of
       Women in the Democratic Republic of Vietnam." American
       Journal of Comparative Law 23, no. 4 (Fall 1975):613-52.

2258   HA NHU VINH. Che-do hon-san phap-dinh trong luat Viet-nam;
       khao-cuu doi-chieu luat Viet-nam va luat ngoai-quoc de
       gop phan vao cong-cuoc cai-cach che-do hon-san. Saigon,
       1967, 710 pp. (Includes marriage law.)

2259   HO CHI MINH. "Excerpt from a Talk at a Cadres' Meeting Debat-
       ing the Draft Law on Marriage and the Family (October
       1950)." In On Revolution: Selected Writings, 1920-66.
       New York: F.A. Praeger, 1969, pp. 336-37.

2260   HUY UU. "Application of Marriage and Family Laws." U.S. JPRS
       Translations from Hoc Tap (Studies) North Vietnam (Sept.
       1964):18-32.

2261   KIM CHIN. "The Marriage and Family Law of North Vietnam."
       International Lawyer 7, no. 2 (Apr. 1973):440-50.

2262   le GADEC, YVES. "A Propos de la situation de la femme en
       droit laotien" [Regarding the position of women in Laotian
       law]. Moniteur d'Indochine, no. 575 (5 Apr. 1930).

2263   LE PHONG THUAN, EMMANUEL. La polygamie en droit vietnamien
       [Polygamy in Vietnamese law]. Rome: Pontifica Universitas
       Urbaniana, 1967.

2264   Le VAN HO. La mère de famille annamite [The mother of the
       Annamite family]. Paris: Les éditions Domat-Montchrestien,
       1932, 121 pp. Institut de Droit Comparé, Etudes de socio-
       logie et d'ethnologie juridiques, vol. 16.

2265   . La mère de famille en droit annamite [The mother of
       the family in Annamite law]. Thèse. Paris: Loviton et
       Domat-Montchrestien, 1932, 94 pp.

2266   "League of Women Needs to Play Active Role in Application of
       Marriage and Family Law." U.S. JPRS. Translations of Po-
       litical and Sociological Information on North Vietnam,
       no. 32, 19,171 (14 May 1963).

2267   LINGAT, ROBERT. Les régimes matrimoniaux de sud-est de
       l'Asie: essai de droit comparé indochinois [Marriage
       statutes of Southeast Asia: essay on Indochinese compara-
       tive law]. 1 vol. Paris: E. de Boccard, 1952. Publica-
       tions de l'Ecole française d'Extrême-Orient, vol. 34.

2268   Luat gia dinh [Family law]. Saigon: Bo Tu Phap, 1960, 47 pp.
       (Text and annotation of the Family Law of 1959.)

2269   LUSTÉGUY, PIERRE. La femme annamite du Tonkin dans l'institu-
       tion des biens cultuels (huong-hoa). Etude sur une enquête
       récente [The role of women in Tonkinese religion and prop-
       erty. Study based on a recent investigation]. Paris:
       Nizet et Bastard, 1935, 126 pp.

2270 _____. The Role of Women in Tonkinese Religion and Property. Translated by Charles A. Messner. New Haven: Human Relations Area Files Press, 1954, vii, 149 pp.

2271 NGUYEN HUU DUONG. "Van de ly di cua ngoai kieu" [Divorce between aliens in Vietnam]. Phap-Ly Tap-San 16, no. 1 (1963): 169-80.

2272 NGUYEN HUY DAU. "Quelques questions relatives au droit familial du Viet-Nam" [Several questions pertaining to family law in Vietnam]. Phap-Ly Tap-San 16, no. 1 (1963):238-72.

2273 _____. "Thuyet tieu huy gia thu trong dan luat Viet-Nam" [Nullity of marriage in Vietnamese civil law]. Phap-Ly Tap-San 16, no. 3 (1963):209-30.

2274 NGUYEN HUY LAI. Les régimes matrimoniaux en droit annamite [Marriage statutes in Annamite law]. Paris: F. Loviton, 1934, 226 pp.

2275 NGUYEN LUONG. "Vai nhan xet ve dao luat hon nhan va gia dinh cua mien Bac" [Observations on the marriage and family laws of the Democratic Republic of Vietnam]. Que Huong, no. 8 (1960):159-75.

2276 NGUYEN PHU DUC. La veuve en droit viêtnamien: contribution à l'étude du patrimoine familial en droit viêtnamien [The widow in Vietnamese law: contribution to the study of the family property in Vietnamese law]. Saigon: Ministère de l'Education Nationale, 1964, 291 pp. Publication Tu sach vien khao co. So 7.

2277 NGUYEN QUANG TAO. Giai thich luat gia dinh [Explanation of family law]. Saigon: Cao-Dam Anh An-Quan, 1959, 67 pp.

2278 NGUYEN TAN THANH. "La condition de la femme mariée au Viet-Nam" [The condition of the married woman in Vietnam]. Thèse pour le Doctorat en Droit, Université de Paris, 1953, 148 pp.

2279 _____. "Tinh cach gia thu bat doan tieu trong giao luat va luat Viet-Nam" [The indissolubility of marriage in canon law and Vietnamese law]. Luat Hoc Kinh-Te 4, nos. 3/4 (1959):389-402.

2280 NGUYEN VAN HUONG. "The Democratic Republic of Vietnam." Review of Contemporary Law 7 (1960):210-23. (On the status of women in the world today.)

2281   NGUYEN VAN SI. Nguoi dan ba Viet Nam [Saigon: Long Giang,
       1953, 142 pp.

2282   NGUYEN XUAN CHANH. "Duyen co ly hon trong luat hien hanh"
       [Causes for divorce in the current law]. Phap-Ly Tap-San
       18, no. 3 (1965):169-85.

2283   _____. "Gia thu trong luat Viet-Nam" [Marriage in Vietnamese
       law]. Luat Hoc Kinh-Te 5, no. 3 (1960):137-228.

2284   _____. Luat gia dinh gian yeu [Family law]. Saigon, 1963,
       287 pp. (Includes discussions on the legal relationship
       between husband and wife, parent and child.)

2285   _____. "Nghia vu cap duong" [Alimony obligation]. Phap-Ly
       Tap-San 18, no. 1 (1965):169-90; no. 2:182-96.

2286   _____. Précis du droit familial vietnamien [A summary of
       Vietnamese family law]. Saigon: Departemen de la Justice,
       1963, 228 pp.

2287   _____. "Van de ly hon cua ngoai kieu truoc phap dinh Viet-Nam"
       [Divorce of aliens before Vietnamese courts]. Phap-Ly
       Tap-San 16, no. 2 (1963):173-87.

2288   _____. "The Widow's Right in Vietnamese Customary Law."
       Phap-Ly Tap-San 17, no. 2 (1964):195-210.

2289   _____. "The Widow's Statute in Vietnamese Customary Law."
       In CONFERENCE ON FAMILY LAW AND CUSTOMARY LAW IN ASIA,
       Singapore, 1964. Family Law and Customary Law in Asia:
       A Contemporary Perspective. Edited by David C. Buxhaum.
       The Hague: Martinus Nijhoff, 1968, pp. 252-61.

2290   NGUYEN XUAN DUONG. "Can phat huy vai tro cua phu nu trong
       viec thi hanh luat hon nhan va gia dinh" [Develop the role
       of women in implementing the law on marriage and the fam-
       ily]. Phu-nu Viet-Nam, no. 225 (1 Dec. 1968):19-20.

2291   PHAN NGHIA. "Tinh trang phap ly cua nguoi phu nu Viet-Nam"
       [Legal status of the Vietnamese woman]. Phap-Ly Tap-San
       27, no. 2 (1974):185-213.

2292   PHAN VAN THIET. Phu nu Viet-Nam truoc phap luat [Vietnamese
       women and the law]. Saigon: Vo Van Van, 1955, 159 pp.

2293   PHOUK CHHAY. "La femme khmère et sa situation juridique à
       l'époque des temps modernes, de la prise de Lovek (1593)
       au Protectorat (1863)" [The Khmer woman and her legal
       status in modern times, from the capture of Lovek (1593)
       to the Protectorate (1863)]. Bulletin de liaison des
       étudiants en droit, no. 2 (1962):31-38.

2294   THIERRY, JEAN. "L'évolution de la condition de la femme en
        droit privé cambodgien" [The evolution of the condition of
        the woman in Cambodian private law]. Thèse pour le Docto-
        rat en Droit, Université de Paris, 1954, 268 pp.

2295   _____. L'évolution de la condition de la femme en droit
        privé cambodgien [The evolution of the condition of the
        woman in Cambodian private law]. Phnom-Penh: Institut
        National d'Etudes Juridiques, Politiques et Economiques,
        1955, 178 pp. Phnom-Penh, Cambodia, Institut National
        d'Etudes Juridiques, Politiques et Economiques. Etudes
        Khmeres et Asiatiques, 1.

2296   TRAN VAN TRAI. La famille patriarcale annamite [The Annamite
        patriarchal family]. Paris: P. Lapagesse, 1942, xv,
        360 pp. (Includes marriage law and customs.)

2297   TRINH DINH TIEU. La femme mariée en droit vietnamien: étude
        comparée des droits vietnamien et français [Married women
        in Vietnamese law: a comparative study of Vietnamese and
        French laws]. Toulouse: Soubiron, 1958, 442 pp. Mémoires
        de l'Académie de Législation, 4.

2298   VIETNAM, Laws, statutes, etc. "Code of the Family." Saigon:
        n.p., 1959, 25 pp. (Text of the Family Law of 2 January
        1959.)

2299   _____. "Sac-luat so 15/64 ngay 23-7-1964 qui dinh gia thu tu
        he va tai san cong dong" [Decree-law no. 15/64 of 23 July
        1964, regulating marriage, filiation, and community prop-
        erty]. Phap-Ly Tap-San 17, no. 2 (1964):222-58.

2300   Vu Van Mau. "Pham vi ap dung cua luat Gia dinh trong thoi
        gian" [Application of the Family Law with respect to time].
        Luat Hoc Kinh-Te 6, no. 3 (1961):17-44. (Deals in part
        with cases involving concubinage, common law marriage, and
        filiation.)

Indonesia

2301   AMIN, DJAMARI. Seminar Hukum Perkahwinan [Seminar on marriage
        law]. Jakarta: Panitnya Seminar PPGPII Puteri, 1958,
        112 pp.

2302   AMIR, DJA'FAR. Jojodoan (Nikah-Talak-Rujuk) [Matrimony:
        marriage, divorce, and reconciliation]. Solo: Pembina,
        1966, 94 pp.

2303   _____. Seluk Beluk Perkahwinan dalam Islam: Ilmu Feqih;
        bagi Nikah [The details of marriage in Islam: Islamic
        law; the marriage ceremony]. Sala: Ab. Sitti Sjamsiah,
        1965, 55 pp.

2304   ARTODIBYO, NOROYONO. "Beberapa Problem atas Asas Monogami
        pada Undang-undang tentang Perkahwinan dalam Hubungannya
        dengan Pasal 279 KUHP" [Some problems of monogamy princi-
        ples in marriage law in relation to Article 279 of the
        Indonesian Code of Law]. Publico 4, nos. 14/15 (1976):
        32-41.

2305   ASHSHIDDIQY, MUHAMMAD HASBI. Lapangan Perdjuangan Wanita
        Islam [The struggle of Muslim women]. Medan: Pustaka
        Timur, 1950, 51 pp.

2306   _____. Polygami Menurut Hukum Islam [Polygamy according to
        Islam]. Jakarta: Bulan-Bintang, 1955, 20 pp.

2307   ASMARAMAN. Usia Dewasa Lelaki dan Wanita [The age of maturity
        for males and females]. Semarang: Asmaraman, 1951, 92 pp.

2308   al-ATTAR, 'ABD al-NASIR TAWFIQ. Poligami: Ditinjau dari Segi
        Agama, Sosial dan Perundang-Undangan [Polygamy: studied
        from the religious, social, and legal aspects]. Alih
        bahasa: Chadidjah Nasution. Jakarta: Bulan Bintang,
        1976, 344 pp.

2309   BADAN PENASEHAT PERKAHWINAN DAN PENYELESAIAN PERCERAIAN PUSAT.
        Diskusi Badan Penasehat Perkahwinan dan Penyelesaian
        Perceraian (B.P.4) Pusat, Tanggal 9 s/d 10 Mei 1974 di
        Wisma Sejahtera, Jakarta [Discussions of the Central Ad-
        visory Board on Marriage and Divorce 9-10 May 1974 in
        Wisma Sejahtera, Jakarta]. Diselenggarkan oleh Bahagian
        Pendidikan B.P.4 Pusat. Jakarta: B.P.4 Pusat, 144 pp.

2310   BAKKER, H. "Voldoet de wetgeving betreffende huwelijken
        tusschen personen behoorende tot de beide staatkundige
        categoriën der indische bevolking . . ." [The law regard-
        ing marriage between persons belonging to both legal clas-
        sifications of the Netherlands Indies population . . .].
        Nederlandsch-Indische Juristen-Vereeniging, Handelingen 3,
        no. 1 (1887):65-83.

2311   BAKRY, HASBULLAH. Pengaturan Undang2 Perkahwinan Ummat Islam
        [Compilation of Muslim marriage laws]. Jakarta: Bulan
        Bintang, 1970, 126 pp.

2312   BISRI, CIK HASAN. "Undang-undang Perkahwinan dan Masalah
        Kependudukan di Indonesia" [The marriage laws and popula-
        tion problems in Indonesia]. Bulletin Forum Studi 2,
        no. 2 (1976):9-15.

2313   BOERENBEKER, EGBERT ADRIAAN. De vrouw in het Indonesisch
        adatrecht [Women in Indonesian customary law]. The Hague:
        J.C.V. Langen, 1931, 219 pp.

2314   BOOMGAARD, SIPKO RITZO. De rechstoestand van de getrouwde
        vrouw volgens het adatrecht van Nederlandsch-Indië [The
        legal status of married women according to the customary
        law of the Netherlands Indies]. Leiden: E. Ijdo, 1926,
        viii, 132 pp.

2315   DISKUSI HUKUM ADAT WARIS DI BALI, Denpasar, Indonesia, 1971.
        Hasil-hasil Diskusi Hukum Adat Waris di Bali dengan Thema
        Pokok Kedudukan Wanita dalam Hukum Waris Menurut Hukum Adat
        Bali [Proceedings of the Discussion on Law of Inheritance
        in Bali with the theme of the status of women in inheri-
        tance law according to Balinese customary law]. 1 vol.
        Jakarta: Lembaga Pembinaan Hukum Nasional, 1973.

2316   "Diskusi Hukum Waris mengenai Hak Mewaris bagi Janda dan Anak-
        anak Angkat" [Discussion on the law of inheritance for
        widows and adopted children]. Hukum Nasional 7, no. 23
        (1974):53-54.

2317   DISKUSI MENGENAI BEBERAPA MASALAH DALAM HUKUM PERKAHWINAN DAN
        HUKUM WARIS DI KALIMANTAN SELATAN, Banjarmasin, Indonesia,
        1972. Hasil-hasil Diskusi mengenai Beberapa Masalah dalam
        Hukum Perkahwinan dan Hukum Waris di Kalimantan Selatan
        [Proceedings of the Discussion on Several Problems in Mar-
        riage and Inheritance Laws in South Kalimantan]. Cet. 2.
        Jakarta: Lembaga Pembinaan Hukum Nasional, 1972.

2318   "Diskusi mengenai Beberapa Masalah dalam Hukum Perkahwinan dan
        Hukum Waris di Kalimantan Selatan" [Discussion of several
        problems in marriage and inheritance laws in South
        Kalimantan]. Hukum Nasional 5, no. 17 (1972):69-77.

2319   DISKUSI TENTANG HUKUM WARIS, Jakarta, 1974. Hasil-hasil
        Diskusi tentang Hukum Waris dengan Topic: Hak Mewaris bagi
        Janda dan Anak/Anak Angkat [Proceedings of the Discussion
        on Law of Inheritance with the topic: rights of inheri-
        tance for widows, children, and adopted children]. 1 vol.
        Jakarta: Lembaga Pembinaan Hukum Nasional, 1974.

2320   DJINDANG, MOCH. SALEH. Hukum Harta Benda Perkahwinan dalam
        Hukum Adat Sulawesi Selatan [Law of marriage property in
        the customary law of South Sulawesi]. Makasar, 1964,
        90 pp.

2321   DJOJODIGOENO, MAS MUKMIN. "Pencatatan Perkahwinan" [Registra-
        tion of marriage]. Hukum dan Masyarakat, nos. 1/2 (1964):
        4-8.

2322   _____. "Perjodohan" [Wedlock]. Hukum dan Masyarakat 2,
        nos. 3/4 (1957):26-35.

2323   _____. Perjodohan: Azas2 Hukum Nasional dalam Bidang Hukum Perkahwinan [Wedlock: basic national laws on marriage]. Jakarta: Lembaga Pembinaan Hukum Nasional, 1963, 21 pp.

2324   FAJAR, A. MUKTI. "Beberapa Catatan atas Paper Saudara Noroyono Artodibyo, SH: Beberapa Problema atas Asas Monogami pada Undang-undang tentang Perkawinan dalam Hubungannya dengan Pasal 279 KUHP" [Some notes on Noroyono Artodibyo's paper: some problems of monogamy principles in marriage law in relation to Article 279 of the Indonesian Code of Law]. Publico 4, nos. 14/15 (1976):42-43.

2325   _____. "Beberapa Catatan tentang Hukum Harta Perkawinan dalam Undang-undang No. 1 Tahun 1974" [Some notes on the marriage property law in Law no. 1/1974]. Publico 2, no. 8 (1974): 5-10.

2326   _____. Undnag-undang No. 1 Tahun 1974 dan Perkawinan campuran" [Law no. 1/1974 and mixed marriages]. Publico 2, no. 7 (1974):21-27.

2327   GAZALBA, SIDI. Menghadapi Soal2 Perkahwinan dengan Lampiran Undang2 Perkahwinan, 1974, Penjelasan dan Peraturan Pelaksanaan [The problems of marriage with appendices on the marriage law of 1974 and their implementation]. Jakarta: Pustaka Antara, 1975, 168 pp.

2328   GOUW, GIOK SIONG. "Segi-segi Hukum Peraturan Perkawinan Tjampuran [Staatsblad 1898 no. 158)" oleh Sudargo Gautama. [The legal aspects of mixed marriages]. Disertasi, Universitas Indonesia, 1955, 285 pp.

2329   _____. Segi-segi Hukum Peraturan Perkahwinan Tjampuran (Staatsblad 1898, No. 158) [The legal aspects of mixed marriages]. 3d ed. Jakarta: Djambatan, 1961, xii, 219 pp.

2330   HADIKUSUMA, HILMAN. Hukum Perkahwinan Adat [Customary law of marriage]. Bandung: Alumni, 1977, 214 pp.

2331   HAKIM, S.H. Hukum Islam (Perkawinan, Pewarisan, Wakaf) [Islamic law: marriage, inheritance, 'wakaf' property]. Jakarta: Lambang, 1968, 50 pp.

2332   _____. Hukum Perkawinan: Menurut Undang-undang tentang Perkawinan, Undang-undang No. 1 Tahun 1974, L.N. 1974, beserta Undang-undang Perkawinan tsb. sebagai Lampiran [Marriage law: according to Marriage Law No. 1, 1974 L.N. 1974]. Bandung: Eleman, 1974, 51 pp.

2333   HAMID, ZAHRI. Pokok-pokok Hukum Perkahwinan Islam dan Undang-
        undang Perkawinan di Indonesia [Fundamental Muslim marriage
        law and Indonesian marriage law]. Jakarta[?]: Binacipta,
        1978, iv, 148 pp.

2334   HAMZAH, AMIR. "Asas Monogami dan Poligami dalam UU Nomor 1
        Tahun 1974 Ditinjau dari Segi Hukum Islam" [Monogamy and
        polygamy principles of Law no. 1, 1974, as seen from
        Islamic law]. Publico 4, nos. 14/15 (1976):48-60.

2335   HARAHAP, M. YAHYA. Pembahasan Hukum Perkawinan Nasional
        Berdasarkan Undang-Undang No. 1 Tahun 1974 Peraturan
        Pemerintah No. 9 Tahun 1975 [A discussion of the national
        marriage law based on Law no. 1 1974 regulation no. 9,
        1975]. Medan: Zakir Trading, 1975, 288 pp.

2336   HASSAN, ABBAS. Hukum Perkawinan dan Rumahtangga [Marriage
        law and the home]. Medan: Saiful, 1953, 68 pp.

2337   HASSELT, JOHAN PHILIP van. De botsingsbepalingen van de
        Huwelijksordonnantie voor Christen-Indonesiers, Artt. 72
        t/m 76 I. St. 1933 nr. 74 [The conflicting rules of the
        Marriage Act for Christian Indonesians, Artt. 72 t/m 76 I.
        St. 1933 nr. 74]. Leiden: De Jong, 1952, 198 pp.

2338   HAZAIRIN. De Redjang: de volksordening, het verwantschaps-,
        huwelijks- en erfrecht [The Rejang: their social organiza-
        tion, kinship, marriage, and inheritance laws]. Bandung:
        A.C. Nix, 1936, 242 pp.

2339   _____. Tinjauan mengenai Undang-undang Perkawinan, Nomor
        1/1974 dan Lampiran U.U. Nomor 1/1974 tentang Perkawinan
        [A study of the Marriage Law, number 1/1974 and its supple-
        ment number 1/1974 on marriage]. Jakarta: Tintamas,
        1975, 68 pp.

2340   HOLLEMAN, FREDERIK DAVID. De privaatrechtelijke positie van
        de Indonesische vrouw [The position of Indonesian women in
        private law]. Melbourne: Netherlands Indies Government
        Printing Works, 1944, 78 pp.

2341   _____. Kedudukan Hukum Wanita Indonesia dan Perkembangannya
        di Hindia Belanda [The legal status of the Indonesian
        woman and her development in the Netherlands-Indies].
        Diterdjemahkan dengan pengawasan dewan redaksi oleh
        Soegarda Poerbakawatja dan Mastini H. Prakoso. Dengan
        kata pengantar oleh Soetan Mohamad Sjah. Jakarta:
        Bhratara, 1971, 95 pp.

2342 _____. "De rechtspositie van de inheemsche vrouw en haar ont-
wikkeling in Nederlandsch-Indië" [The legal position of the
native woman and her development in the Netherlands Indies].
Koloniaal tijdschrift 30 (1941):50-80, 172-214.

2343 Hukum Adat Perkawinan Batak Karo, Hukum Waris Adat di Tapanuli
Selatan dan Tengah, Beberapa Catatan mengenai Hukum
Kekeluargaan Adat Masyarakat Batak di Tapanuli dan di
Perantauan [Customary marriage law of Batak Karo, customary
law of inheritance in South and Middle Tapanuli, and notes
on customary family law of the Bataks in Tapanuli and else-
where]. Dihimpun dibawah redaksi dan bimbingan Sumarsono
Mestoko. Bandung: Jurusan Pendidikan Kewargaan Negara dan
Hukum, Institut Keguruan dan Ilmu Pendidikan, 1975, 151 pp.

2344 HUTAURUK, A.M. Hukum Perkahwinan Adat Batak [Batak customary
marriage law]. Medan: Mitra, 1960, 87 pp.

2345 IHROMI, T. OMAS. "Beberapa Catatan mengenai Kedudukan Wanita
dalam Hukum Adat Waris dalam Susunan Keluarga Yang Parental"
[Several notes on the rights of women in customary inheritance law according to parental family structures].
Majalah Fakultas Hukum [Universitas Indonesia], no. 1
(1975):15-29.

2346 INDONESIA, Departemen Pendidikan Pengajaran dan Kebudayaan.
Perkahwinan di Tanah Gayo [Marriage in Tanah Gayo].
Jakarta: Bagian Bahasa, Jawatan Kebudayaan, 1960, 36 pp.

2347 INDONESIA, Laws, statutes, etc. Himpunan Peraturan dan Undang-
undang R.I. tentang Perkawinan serta Peraturan Pelaksanaanya
[Collection of marriage law and regulations together with
the rules for implementation]. Dihimpun oleh Moch.
Asnawi. Kudus: Menara, 1975, iii, 536 pp.

2348 _____. Himpunan Peraturan tentang Perkawinan [Collection of
marriage regulations]. Dihimpun oleh K. Wantjik Saleh.
3d ed. Jakarta: Ichtiar Baru-Van Hoeve, 1976, 161 pp.

2349 _____. Hukum Perkawinan Indonesia [Indonesian marriage laws].
Oleh K. Wantjik Saleh. Jakarta: Ghalia, 1976, 228 pp.

2350 _____. Peraturan Pemerintah Republik Indonesia Nomor 9,
Tahun 1975 tentang Pelaksanaan Undang-Undang Nomor 1 Tahun
1974 tentang Perkawinan [Regulation of the Government of
the Republic of Indonesia, number 9, 1975, on the implementation of Law number 1, 1974 on marriage]. Jakarta:
Departemen Penerangan, 1975, 27 pp.

2351 _____ . Sekitar Pembentukan Undang-undang Perkawinan Beserta
Peraturan Pelaksanaannya [The formation of marriage laws
together with the rules for their implementation].
Jakarta: Departemen Kehakiman, 1974, 318 pp.

2352 _____ . Undang-undang Republik Indonesia, Nomor 1 tahun 1974
tentang Perkawinan [Law of Indonesia, no. 1, 1974 concerning marriage]. Jakarta: Departemen Penerangan, 1974,
31 pp.

2353 _____ . Undang-undang R.I. No. 1 Tahun 1974 tentang Perkawinan,
Diundangkan di Jakarta pada Tgl.2 Januari 1974 [R.I. Law
no. 1, 1974 on marriage, enacted in Jakarta on 2 January
1974]. Jogjakarta: U.P. Indonesia, 1974, 72 pp.

2354 JAFIZHAM, T., comp. Himpunan Undang-undang Perkawinan,
Pendaftaran dan Peradilan Agama/Umum [Collection of marriage laws, registration and the administration of justice,
religious and general]. Cet.3. Medan: Percetakan
Mastika, 1976, 165 pp.

2355 JAHJA, MOECHTAR. Kedudukan Wanita dalam Hukum Islam [The
status of women in Muslim law]. Kuliah umum diutjapkan
dalam rapat senat terbuka Institut Agama Islam Negeri.
Jakarta: Djajamurni, 1961, 36 pp.

2356 JAYLANI, TEDJANINGSIH. "Islamic Marriage Law in Indonesia."
Master's thesis, McGill University, 1959, iv, 170 pp.

2357 JUNUS, MAHMUD. Hukum Perkawinan dalam Islam . . . menurut
Mazhab Sjafi'i, Hanafi, Maliki dan Hanbali, serta Diberi
Dalil2 dan Keterangan Jang Memuaskan [Marriage law in
Islam . . . according to the Shafi'i, Hanafi, Maliki, and
Hanbali schools of thought]. Tjet. ke-2. Jakarta:
Mahmudiah, 1960, xi, 182 pp.

2358 KARTAHADIMADJA, AOH. Poligami [Polygamy]. Jakarta: Pustaka
Jaya, 1975, 126 pp.

2359 Kasus Nikah Megawati Sukarnoputri dengan Hassan Gamal [The
marriage case of Megawati Sukarnoputri and Hassan Gamal].
Medan: Percetakan Mestika, 1973, 133 pp.

2360 KATZ, JUNE S., and KATZ, RONALD S. "Legislating Social
Change in a Developing Country: The New Indonesian Marriage Law Revisited." American Journal of Comparative Law
26, no. 2 (Spring 1978):309-20.

2361   _____. "The New Indonesian Marriage Law: A Mirror of
        Indonesia's Political, Cultural and Legal Systems."
        American Journal of Comparative Law 23, no. 4 (Fall 1975):
        653-81.

2362   Kearah Keluarga Bahagia, Tulisan Uraian Ibu S. Kartowijono,
        Lie Pok Liem, Tan Hoo Nio dan T.O. Simatupang dalam Panel
        Discussion 'Undang-undang Perkawinan' Tanggal 26 Apr. 1959
        di Djakarta [Towards a happy family: the writings of Ibu
        S. Kartowijono, Lie Pok Liem, Tan Hoo Nio, and T.O.
        Simatupang in the panel discussion on 'Marriage Laws'
        26 April 1959 in Jakarta]. Jakarta: Bahagian Keputrian
        Dewan Mahasiswa, Universitas Indonesia, 1959, 44 pp.

2363   KEUNING, JOHANNES. Verwantschapsrecht en volksordening,
        huwelijksrecht en erfrecht in het Koeriagebeid van
        Tapanoeli [Kinship and social order: marriage and in-
        heritance laws in Koeria region of Tapanoeli]. Leiden:
        E. Ijdo, 1948, 155 pp.

2364   KOESNOE, MUHAMMAD. "Beberapa Catatan mengenai Rancangan
        Undang-undang tentang Perkawinan Campuran" [Several notes
        on the law regarding mixed marriages]. Hukum Nasional 2,
        no. 5 (1969):3-13.

2365   _____. Kedudukan Wanita menurut Adat Beberapa Masyarakat
        Pedesaan Madura (Dihubungkan dengan Persoalan Keluarga
        Berencana) [The status of women according to various cus-
        tomary laws in rural Madura (relating to the problems of
        family planning)]. Surabaya, 1975, 109 pp.

2366   _____. "Saat Jadinya Perkawinan menurut Adat 'Ngerorod' di
        Bali" [Time for 'ngerorod' marriage in Bali]. Hukum
        Nasional 5, no. 17 (1972):51-68.

2367   KOESWADJI, HERMIEN HADIATI. "Law and Development: The Legal
        Status of Women in Indonesia; Their Role and Challenge in
        Creating a New National Law." Malaya Law Review 18, no. 2
        (1976):339-60.

2368   KWEE, OEN GOAN. Dasar2 Perceraian [The principles of
        divorce]. Jakarta: Permatan, 1959, 68 pp.

2369   LATIF, H.S.M. NASARUDDIN. Kasus Jodoh dan Perkawinan:
        Kumpulan Tulisan [Cases on marriage: collected writings].
        Jakarta: B.P.4 Pusat, 1973, 197 pp.

2370   "Law and Population in Indonesia: Country Report." In SOUTH-
        EAST ASIAN REGIONAL SEMINAR ON LAW AND POPULATION, Jakarta,
        1975. Law and Population. Edited by Teuku Mohamed Radhie
        et al. Jakarta: Yayasan Penelitian dan Pengembangan
        Hukum, 1976, pp. 106-19. (Includes discussion of laws on
        family planning, marriage, and inheritance.)

2371   LEV, DANIEL S. "Islamic Courts and Divorce: Function and
        Change. Islamic Courts and Inheritance Problems." In
        Islamic Courts in Indonesia: A Study of the Political
        Bases of Legal Institutions. Berkeley: University of
        California Press, 1972, pp. 135-222.

2372   LOEBIS, ALI BASJA. Hukum Perkawinan Islam di Indonesia
        [Muslim marriage law in Indonesia]. Jakarta, 1969, 200 pp.

2373   _____. Hukum Perkahwinan Islam dan Hubungannya dengan
        Peradilan Agama di Indonesia [Muslim marriage law and its
        relation to the religious court in Indonesia]. Jakarta:
        Permata, 197-[?], 35 pp.

2374   LUBIS, JUSUF A. Undang2 Perkawinan [Marriage law]. Medan:
        Damai, 1956, 48 pp.

2375   MAHADI. "Pengaruh Piagam Jakarta terhadap Pelaksanaan
        Perkawinan" [The influence of the Jakarta Charter on the
        implementation of marriage]. Hukum Nasional 2, no. 3
        (1969):27-44.

2376   MAHYIDDIN, SYAHABUDDIN. "Beberapa Kebiasaan dalam Perkawinan
        dan Pembagian Pustaka menurut Adat Gayo" [Some practices
        relating to marriage and division of property in Gayo
        custom]. Sinar Darussalam 8, no. 62 (1975):14-22.

2377   MARZUKI, T. "Menyambut Berlakunya Undang-undang Perkawinan
        No. 1 Tahun 1974" [To welcome the introduction of Marriage
        Law no. 1, 1974]. Sriwijaya 12, no. 5 (1975):35-39.

2378   MEETER, P. "De rechstoestand der Chineesche vrouw in Ned.
        Indië" [The legal status of the Chinese woman in the
        Netherlands Indies]. Het recht in Nederlandsch-Indië 32
        (1879):345-73.

2379   MOYER, DAVID S. The Logic of the Laws: A Structural Analysis
        of Malay Language Legal Codes from Bengkulu. The Hague:
        Nijhoff, 1975, ix, 304 pp. Instituut voor Taal- Land- en
        Volkenkunde. Verhandelingen, 75. (Based on the author's
        Ph.D. thesis, Leiden University. Includes customary laws
        of marriage.)

2380   MUHAEMIN. "Sejarah dan Perkembangan UU (Undang Undang)
        Perkawinan di Indonesia" [The history and development of
        marriage law in Indonesia]. Bulletin Forum Studi 1, no. 3
        (1975):3-14; 1, nos. 4/5 (1975):3-12.

2381   MOELIONO, C.S. "The Role of Women in Law, Women in Society."
        Hukum 2, no.3 (1975):114-19.

2382   MU'THI, ABDUL. "Sedikit tentang Hukum Perzinaan" [Notes on
        the law of adultery in Islam]. Gema Islam 4, nos. 79/80
        (1965):13, 15, 16.

2383   NIWAN, LELY M. Perkawinan Menurut K.U.H. Perdata [Marriage
        according to civil law]. Ujungpandang: Lembaga Penelitian
        Hukum F.H., Universitas Hasanuddin, 1964[?], 33 pp.

2384   NOTOPURO, HARDJITO. "Beberapa Catatan tentang Hukum
        Perkawinan dan Pewarisan di Daerah Karo (Sumetera Utara)"
        [Some notes on the laws of marriage and inheritance in
        Karo district, North Sumatra]. Hukum Nasional 4, no. 11
        (1971):95-105.

2385   _____. Beberapa Tjatatan tentang Pokok-pokok Hukum Perkawinan
        dan Pewarisan Bali [Some notes on the fundamental marriage
        and inheritance laws of Bali]. Jakarta: Lembaga Pembinaan
        Hukum Nasional, 1972, 59 pp.

2386   _____. "Masalah Zinah dalam Rangkaian Delik Kesusilaan:
        Ungkapan Berdasar Hukum Adat" [Adultery as a moral of-
        fense: some comments from the viewpoint of customary law].
        Hukum Nasional 1, no. 1 (1968):56-78.

2387   _____. Peranan Wanita dalam Masa Pembangunan di Indonesia
        [The role of women in Indonesia's development]. Jakarta
        Timur: Ghalia Indonesia, 1979, 144 pp. (On Indonesian
        laws relating to women and their rights.)

2388   _____. "Perkawinan: Pengertian dan Maksud Tujuannya"
        [Marriage: its meaning and objectives]. Hukum Nasional
        3, no. 7 (1970):57-85.

2389   _____. "Tentang Barang Gono-Gini dan Barang Asal serta Hak
        Mewarisi bagi Janda, Anak/Anak Angkat" [Regarding 'gono-
        gini' goods and 'original goods' and the right of inheri-
        tance of widows, children, and adopted children]. Hukum
        Nasional 1, no. 2 (1968):48-59.

2390   OBENG, HERMAN SOESANG. "Harta Perkawinan dalam Masyarakat
        Madura" [Marriage property in the Madura community].
        Publico 2, nos. 5/6 (1974):6-19.

2391 _____. "Harta Perkawinan dalam Masyarakat Madura di Sumenep"
     [Marriage property in the Madura community of Sumenep].
     Hukum Nasional 7, no. 24 (1974):85-95.

2392 PAPANEK, HANNA. "Marriage, Divorce and Marriage Law Reform in
     Indonesia." Paper presented at the Workshop on the Role
     and Status of Women in Contemporary Muslim Societies, Cen-
     ter for the Study of World Religions, Harvard University,
     April 1975.

2393 PELLO, M.J. "Masalah Kedudukan Anak Wanita terhadap Harta
     Kekayaan Orang Tua" [The position of the daughter with re-
     gard to her parents' wealth]. Hukum Nasional 4, no. 11
     (1971):106-10.

2394 PRINS, JAN. De Indonesische huwelijkswet van 1974 [The Indo-
     nesian Marriage Law of 1974]. Met een Nederlandse vert.
     van de wettekst door K.L. Tan. Nijmegen: Katholieke
     Universteit, 1977, 144 pp. Publikaties over volksrecht, 3.

2395 _____. "Le statut de la femme indonésienne" [The status of
     the Indonesian woman]. Société Jean Bodin pour l'histoire
     comparative des institutions, Recueils 12 (1959):329-34.

2396 PRODJODIKORO, WIRJONO, Raden. Hukum Perkawinan di Indonesia
     [Marriage law in Indonesia]. Tjet. 5. Bandung: Sumur
     Bandung, 1966, 135 pp.

2397 _____. "Kedudukan Hukum Wanita di Indonesia" [The legal
     status of Indonesian women]. Hukum, nos. 5/6 (1957):5-13.

2398 _____. "Usaha Memperbaiki Hukum Perkawinan di Indonesia"
     [Attempts to improve the marriage law in Indonesia].
     Hukum dan Masyarakat 2, nos. 3/4 (1957):15-25.

2399 RASJIDI, LILI. "Satu Tinjauan atas Undang-Undang Republic
     Indonesia Nombor 1, Tahun 1974 tentang Perkahwinan" [A
     study of the Law of the Republic of Indonesia, number 1,
     1974 regarding marriage]. Journal of Malaysian and Com-
     parative Law 3, pt. 1 (June 1976):81-100.

2400 _____. "Undang-undang Perkawinan dan Penceraian di Malaysia
     dan Indonesia" [Marriage and divorce laws in Malaysia and
     Indonesia]. LL.M. thesis, University of Malaya, 1978,
     xvii, 401 pp.

2401 RASYIDI, M. Kasus R.U.U. Perkawinan dalam Hubungan Islam dan
     Kristen [The case of the law of marriage in relation to
     Islam and Christianity]. Jakarta: Bulan Bintang, 1974,
     68 pp.

2402　ROEM, MOHAMAD. <u>Poligami, Monogami dan Praktek Peredilan Agama</u> [Polygamy, monogamy, and the practice of the religious court]. Jakarta: H. Ghazali Ismail, 1973, 28 pp.

2403　SAKETAPY, J.E. "Sekitar Problema Perzinahan" [The problem of adultery]. <u>Hukum dan Keadilan</u> 4, no. 3 (1973):17-29.

2404　SALAYAN, ABDUL WAHID. <u>Hak Wanita: Perbandingan Hukum Islam dengan Hukum Perdata (B.W.) dalam Soal2 Wanita</u> [Women's rights: a comparison of Islamic and civil laws on issues concerning women]. Medan: Bintang, 1959, 176 pp.

2405　SALEH, K. WANTJIK. <u>Uraian Peraturan Pelaksanaan Undang-undang Perkawinan</u> [Explanation on the rules of implementing the marriage law]. Jakarta: Ichtiar Baru, 1975, 64 pp.

2406　SALIJ, H. JATHAR. "Polygamy and Divorce in Indonesia: The New Marriage Law." <u>Akademika</u>, no. 12 (Jan. 1978):65-75.

2407　SARDJONO, R. "Berbagai-bagai Masalah Hukum dalam Undang-undang Perkawinan No. 1, Tahun 1974" [Various problems of law in the Marriage Law no. 1, 1974]. <u>Trisakti</u> 1, no. 1 (1976):21-68.

2408　SARI, N.E. RATNA. <u>Kedudukan Wanita dalam Hukum Islam</u> [The status of women in Islamic law]. 2d ed. Medan: Islamiyah, 1950, 55 pp.

2409　SEMBIRING, BUDI. "Inventarisasi Hukum Benda Perkawinan Adat" [Inventory of legacies in customary marriages]. <u>Berkala Pembangunan</u> 2, no. 1 (1960):12-14; 2, no. 2 (1961):34-37; 2, no. 3 (1961):17-20; 2, no. 4 (1961):34-37.

2410　SEMINAR HUKUM PERKAWINAN, Jakarta, 1958. <u>Seminar Hukum Perkawinan: Prasaran dan Kesimpulan</u> [Seminar on Marriage Law: proceedings]. Organized by Gerakan Peminda Islam Indonesia Puteri. Jakarta: Panitya Seminar P.P.G.P.I.I. Puteri, 1958[?], 112 pp.

2411　SERIE, MUSTOPA HUSIN. "Kawin Bergubalan/Lari dari Sumatra Selatan" [Marriage by elopement or abduction in South Sumatra]. <u>Hukum Nasional</u> 4, no. 13 (1971):70-77.

2412　SHIDDIEQY, T.M. HASBI ASH. "Masalah Mahar (Mas Kawin) Ditinjau dari Segi Hukum Islam" [The problem of dowry seen from the viewpoint of Islamic law]. <u>Sinar Darussalam</u> 4, no. 32 (1971):6-13.

2413　SIDIK, ABDULLAH. "Pasah dan Chuluk bagi Wanita" ['Pasah' and 'chuluk' divorces for women]. <u>al-Jami'ah</u> 4, no. 2 (1965): 7-11.

2414 _____ . Hukum Perkawinan Islam [Islamic marriage law].
Jakarta: Tintamas, 1968, vii, 100 pp.

2415 SINAGA, B. "Hukum Adat Perkawinan di Simalungun" [Customary
marriage law in Simalungun]. Berkala Pembangunan 3, no. 2
(1962):14-15; 3, nos. 3/4 (1962):4-5; 3, no. 5 (1962):
20-21; 3, no. 6 (1962):24-26; 3, nos. 7/8 (1962):14-15; 3,
no. 10 (1962):24-25; 3, nos. 11/12 (1962):14-16.

2416 SJAH, ISMAIL MOHAMAD. Pancaharian bersama Suami-Istri (Adat
Gonogini) Ditinjau dari Sudut Hukum Islam [Joint income of
husband and wife according to the Gonogini custom as seen
from the point of view of Islamic law]. Jakarta: Bulan
Bintang, 1965, 76 pp.

2417 SOFWAN, SRI SOEDEWI MASJCHUN (Mrs.). "Hak Mewaris bagi Janda
dan Anak/Anak Angkat" [The right of inheritance for widows,
children, and adopted children]. Hukum Nasional 7, no. 24
(1974):72-83.

2418 SOSROATMODJO, H. ARSO, and AULAWI, H.A. WASIT, comps. Hukum
Perkawinan di Indonesia [Marriage law in Indonesia].
Jakarta: Bulan Bintang, 1975, 212 pp.

2419 SUBANDRIO, HURUSTIATI. "The Legal and Social Position of
Women in Indonesia." Civilisations 1, no. 4 (1951):31-39.

2420 SUDARSONO, SIDDIK. Masalah Administrasi dalam Masalah
Perkahwinan Umat Islam Indonesia Menyongsong Lahirnya
Undang2 Perkawinan Indonesia [The administrative problems
in the marriages of the Muslims in Indonesia and the new
marriage law of Indonesia]. Jakarta: Dara, 1964, 294 pp.

2421 SOEDIJANA, F.X. "Beberapa Masalah Pelaksanaan Perkawinan
Berdasarkan UU No. 1/1974 & PP No. 9/1975" [Some problems
regarding the execution of marriage based on Law no. 1/
1974 and Government Regulation no. 9/1975]. Mimbar Hukum,
no. 4 (1975):5-10.

2422 SOEDJATI, R. "Abortus Provocatus Criminalis Dikerjakan oleh
Seorang Doktor dari Segi Hukum" [Abortus provocatus
criminalis carried out by a doctor and its legal implica-
tions]. Majalah Kedokteran Diponegoro 9, no. 2 (1974):
66-72.

2423 SUHARTI. Undang-undang Perkawinan [Marriage laws]. Jakarta:
Pembaruan, 1960, 132 pp.

2424   SUKANDAR, SRI SUMARWANI (Mrs.) "Beristeri Lebih dari Seorang:
        Tinjauan U.U. Perkawinan dan Peraturan Pelaksanaannya"
        [More than one wife: review of the Marriage Law and the
        implementation of its regulations]. Oriza 1, no. 1 (1976):
        30-43.

2425   SOEKANTO, SOERJONO. "Garis-garis Besar Hukum Perkawinan Adat
        Kebudayaan Suay Umpu Mego-Pak Lampung Papadon" [Principles
        of the customary marriage law of Kebuayaan Suay Umpu Mego-
        Pak Lampung Papadon]. Hukum Nasional 2, no. 5 (1969):
        13-42.

2426   _____. "Hak Mewaris bagi Janda dan Anak/Anak Angkat" [The
        right of inheritance for widows, children, and adopted
        children]. Hukum Nasional 7, no. 23 (1974):73-96.

2427   SUTANTOI, R. Wanita dan Hukum [Women and the law]. Bandung:
        Alumni, 1979, 114 pp.

2428   SOETOMO, R. Perkahwinan dan Perkahwinan Anak-anak [Marriage
        and child marriages]. Weltevreden: Balai Poestaka, 1928,
        58 pp.

2429   SUWARNO, L.S.H. "Perkawinan antara Agama: Tanggapan atas
        Tulisan Prof. S.A. Hakim" [Marriages of mixed religions:
        reply to Prof. S.A. Hakim's article]. Hukum dan Keadilan
        3, nos. 5/6 (1972):20-26.

2430   SOEWONDO, NANI. "Aspek-aspek Medis Hukum mengenai Abortus di
        luar Negeri dan di Indonesia" [Legal and medical aspects
        of abortion abroad and in Indonesia]. Hukum Nasional 4,
        no. 13 (1971):3-13.

2431   _____. "The Indonesian Marriage Law and Its Implementation
        Regulation." Archipel, no. 13 (1977):283-94.

2432   _____. Kedudukan Wanita Indonesia dalam Hukum dan Masjarakat
        [The status of women in Indonesia in law and society].
        Tjet 2. Jakarta: Timur Emas, 1968, 221 pp.

2433   _____. "Law and the Status of Women in Indonesia." In Law
        and the Status of Women: An International Symposium.
        Edited by the Columbia Human Rights Law Review, Columbia
        University School of Law. New York: Centre for Social
        Development and Humanitarian Affairs, United Nations, 1977,
        pp. 123-40. Originally published in the Columbia Human
        Rights Law Review 8, no. 1 (Spring/Summer 1976).

2434   _____. "Masalah Undang-undang Perkawinan" [Problems in mar-
        riage law]. Hukum Nasional 1, no. 1 (1968):18-31.

2435   _____. "Soal Undang-undang Perkawinan" [Problems in marriage
        law]. Hukum dan Masyarakat 2, no. 1 (1957):32-39.

2436   SYAHRANI, RIDUAN, and ABDURRAHMAN. "Masalah-masalah Hukum
        Perkahwinan di Indonesia" [Problems of marriage law in
        Indonesia]. Cet. 2. Banjarmasin: Lembaga Perpustakaan/
        Penerbitan, Fakultas Hukum, Universitas Lambung Mangkurat,
        1978, iii, 89 pp.

2437   THAHA, NASHRUDDIN. Pedoman Perkawinan Islam: Nikah, Talak,
        Rudju [Manual on Muslim marriage: wedding, repudiation,
        reconciliation]. Tjet. 4. Jakarta: Bulan Bintang, 1967,
        180 pp.

2438   THAHAR, KAMARISAH. Jaminan Islam tentang Hak-hak Wanita
        sebagai Manusia Yang Sempurna [Islam's guarantee of the
        rights of women]. Medan: Universitas Islam Sumatera
        Utara, 1968, 151 pp.

2439   THALIB, SAJUTI. "Harta Bersama Suami Isteri dalam Hukum
        Islam" [Common property of husband and wife in Islamic
        law]. Hukum dan Keadilan 2, no. 1 (1970):30-42.

2440   _____. Hukum Kekeluargaan Indonesia: Berlaku bagi Umat
        Islam [Indonesian family law for Muslims]. Jakarta:
        Yayasan Penerbit Universitas Indonesia, 1974, xv, 187 pp.

2441   TRANGGONO, HARTONO. "The Role of Women in Law." Hukum 2,
        no. 3 (1975):103-13.

2442   UNIVERSITAS AIRLANGGA, Seksi Hukum Islam. Beberapa Segi Hukum
        Islam Yang Diresipiir Secara Konkrit dalam Masyarakat Sasak
        di Lombok [Reception of several aspects of Muslim law by
        the Sasak community in Lombok]. Surabaya: Seksi Hukum
        Islam, Universitas Airlangga, 1974, 100 pp.

2443   UNIVERSITAS UDAYANA. "Kedudukan Wanita Bali di dalam
        Perwarisan Menurut Hukum Adat Bali (Suatu hasil penelitian
        lapangan)" [The status of Balinese women in inheritance
        according to the customary law of Bali]. Den Pasar:
        Fakultas Hukum Pengetahuan Masyarakat, Universitas Udayana,
        1973, 16 pp.

2444   VREEDE-DE STUERS, CORA. "A propos du R.U.U. histoire d'une
        législation matrimoniale" [Regarding R.U.U. history of
        legislation on marriage]. Archipel, no. 8 (1974):12-30.

2445 WILKEN, GEORGE ALEXANDER. <u>Over de verwantschap en het huwelijks- en erfrecht bij de volken van den Indischen archipel, beschouwd uit het oogpunt van de nieuwere leerstellingen op het gebied der maatschappelijke ontwikkelingsgeschiedenis</u> [On kinship and the marriage and inheritance laws among the peoples of the Indonesian archipelago, considered in connection with recent concepts regarding the history of the development of society]. Leiden: E.J. Brill, 1883, 40 pp.

2446 _____. "Over de verwantschap en het huwelijks--en erfrecht bij de volken van het Maleische ras" [On kinship and the marriage and inheritance laws among the peoples of the Malay race]. <u>De Indische gids</u> 5 (1883):656-746.

2447 _____. "Over huwelijks- en erfrecht bej de volken van Zuid-Sumatra" [On marriage and inheritance laws among the peoples of South Sumatra]. <u>Bijdragen tot de taal-, land- en volkenkunde</u> 6, no. 6 (1891):149-235.

Malaysia

2448 ABDUL JALIL bin HAJI HASSAN. "The Influence of the Shāfi'i School of Muslim Law on Marriage and Divorce in the Malay Peninsula, with Special Reference to the State of Trengganu." Ph.D. dissertation, University of St. Andrews, 1969, 358 pp.

2449 ABDUL KADIR bin YUSOF. "Woman and the Law." <u>Malayan Law Journal</u> (Aug./Sept. 1975)xxi-xxviii.

2450 ABDUL RASHID, Nik. "Women's Rights and the Equality Provision of Article 8 of the Constitution." 33 pp. Paper presented at the Fifth Malaysian Law Conference, Kuala Lumpur, October 1979, organized by the Bar Council (States of Malaya).

2451 ABU CHIK MAT SAROM; ABU HASSAN bin AHMAD; and SULAIMAN bin IDRIS. <u>Asal Usul Adat Perpateh Negri Sembilan</u> [The origins of 'adat perpateh' in Negri Sembilan]. Perenchana: Mohammad Idris bin Haji Abdullah. Kuala Pilah: Malay Press, 1962, 94 pp.

2452 ADAM, FRANCIS JOHEN. "Customary Law relating to Marriage, Divorce and Inheritance among the Land Dayaks in Sarawak." LL.B. academic exercise, University of Malaya, 1977, viii, 94 pp.

2453   AHAMAD bin MUHAMMAD IBRAHIM. "Administration of Muslim Law
        in Sabah." Journal of Malaysian and Comparative Law 2,
        pt. 2 (1975):309-40. (Includes discussion on laws of mar-
        riage, divorce, inheritance, etc.)

2454   _____. "Developments in the Marriage Laws in Malaysia and
        Singapore." Malaya Law Review 12, no. 2 (Dec. 1970):
        257-76.

2455   _____. Family Law in Malaysia and Singapore. Kuala Lumpur:
        Faculty of Law, University of Malaya, 1973, xv, 345 pp.

2456   _____. Family Law in Malaysia and Singapore. Singapore:
        Malayan Law Journal. 1978, xvi, 313 pp.

2457   _____. "Islam and Customary Law in the Malaysian Legal Con-
        text." In CONFERENCE ON FAMILY LAW AND CUSTOMARY LAW IN
        ASIA, Singapore, 1964. Family Law and Customary Law in
        Asia: A Contemporary Perspective. Edited by David C.
        Buxbaum. The Hague: Martinus Nijhoff, 1968, pp. 89-105.
        (Includes discussion on marriage, divorce, adoption, prop-
        erty, and inheritance laws.)

2458   _____. "The Law Reform (Marriage and Divorce) Bill, 1972."
        Malayan Law Journal (Jan. 1973):vii-ix.

2459   _____. "The Law Reform (Marriage and Divorce) Bill, 1975."
        Journal of Malaysian and Comparative Law 2, no. 2 (Dec.
        1975):354-63.

2460   _____. "Marriage of Muslims with Non-Muslims." Malayan Law
        Journal 31, no. 3 (Mar. 1965):xvi-xvii.

2461   _____. "Muslim Family Law in Selangor." al-Islam 3, no. 3
        (July/Sept. 1972):17-29.

2462   _____. "Muslims in Malaysia and Singapore: The Law of Matri-
        monial Property." In Family Law in Asia and Africa. Ed-
        ited by James N.D. Anderson. London: G. Allen and Unwin,
        1968, pp. 182-209.

2463   _____. "Recent Proposed Changes in the Family Law in
        Malaysia." Journal of Malaysian and Comparative Law 5,
        pt. 2 (1978):199-224. (Includes discussion on laws of
        marriage, divorce, property, etc.)

2464   _____. "The Status of Muslim Women in Family Law in Malaysia
        and Brunei." Malaya Law Review 5, no. 2 (Dec. 1963):
        313-37; 6, no. 1 (July 1964):40-82; 6, no. 2 (Dec. 1964):
        353-86.

2465 _____. The Status of Muslim Women in Family Law in Malaysia, Singapore and Brunei. Singapore: Malayan Law Journal, 1965, xviii, 121 pp.

2466 _____. "The Status of Women Family Law in Malaysia, Singapore and Brunei." Malaya Law Review 7, no. 1 (July 1965):54-94; 7, no. 2 (Dec. 1965):299-313; 8, no. 1 (July 1966):46-85; 8, no. 2 (Dec. 1966):233-69.

2467 AMRAN KASIMIN. "Filsafah Pembahagian Harta Waris Perempuan" [Philosophy regarding the division of property among female heirs]. Menara, no. 8 (1978):33-35.

2468 AZIZAH ABDUL RAZAK, and MUHAMMAD AKHIR YAAKUB. "Undang-undang Keluarga Islam di Malaysia" [Muslim family law in Malaysia]. Dakwah, no. 25 (Mar. 1979):36-43.

2469 BALIA YUSOFF bin MUHAMMAD WAHI. "The Malay Customary Law in Perak on Marriage, Divorce and Inheritance." LL.B. academic exercise, University of Malaya, 1976, viii, 92 pp.

2470 BRADDELL, ROLAND. "Chinese Marriages as Regarded by the Supreme Court of the Straits Settlements." Royal Asiatic Society of Great Britain and Ireland, Straits Branch, Journal 83 (Apr. 1921):153-65.

2471 BUXBAUM, DAVID CHARLES, ed. "Chinese Family Law in a Common Law Setting. A Note on the Institutional Environment and the Substantive Family Law of the Chinese in Singapore and Malaysia." In CONFERENCE ON FAMILY LAW AND CUSTOMARY LAW IN ASIA, Singapore, 1964. Family Law and Customary Law in Asia: A Contemporary Perspective. The Hague: Martinus Nijhoff, 1968, pp. 146-77. (Includes discussion on status of secondary wives.)

2472 DAW, ROWENA. "Some Problems of Conflict of Law in West Malaysia and Singapore Family Law." Malaya Law Review 14, no. 2 (Dec. 1972):179-208. (Includes legal aspects of marriage and divorce.)

2473 DEVASER, K.L. "Current Legislation in Peninsular Malaysia: Some Thoughts for International Women's Year, 1975." Malayan Law Journal (Dec. 1975):lxxxix-xcii.

2474 DICKSTEIN, H.L. "Radwan v. Radwan and the 1972 Malaysian Law Reform (Marriage and Divorce) Bill, 1972." Malayan Law Journal (Sept. 1973):xv-xvii.

2475 EBIN, EWON. "Suatu Kajian Undang-undang Adat Dusun Ranau di
       Sabah mengenai Perkahwinan, Perceraian dan Warisan" [A
       study of the customary laws of the Dusun Ranau in Sabah
       regarding marriage, divorce, and inheritance]. LL.B.
       academic exercise, University of Malaya, 1978, xii, 162 pp.

2476 FARIDDAH binti HAJI ISMAIL. "Marital Rights of a Muslim Woman
       in the Federal Territory." LL.B. academic exercise, Uni-
       versity of Malaya, 1977, ix, 127 pp.

2477 FEDERATION OF WOMEN LAWYERS, Malaysia. "Current Legislation
       in Peninsular Malaysia: Some Thoughts for International
       Women's Year, 1975." Malayan Law Journal (Dec. 1975):
       lxxv-lxxxix.

2478 _____. "Current Legislation in Peninsular Malaysia: Some
       Thoughts for International Women's Year, 1975." ii, 26 pp.
       Paper presented at the Third Malaysian Law Conference,
       Kuala Lumpur, October 1975, organized by the Bar Council
       (States of Malaya).

2479 GAZALBA, SIDI. Di Ambang Pintu Perkawinan [On the threshold
       of marriage]. Kuala Lumpur: Pustaka Antara, 1976, 118 pp.

2480 GONG, CHIN KEEN. "Women's Rights and the Equality Provision
       of Article 8 of the Constitution." 5 pp. Paper presented
       at the Fifth Malaysian Law Conference, Kuala Lumpur,
       October 1979, organized by the Bar Council (States of
       Malaya).

2481 GREAT BRITAIN, Committee . . . to Examine and Report on S.S.
       Ordinance no. 15 of 1927 (Women and Girls Protection
       Amendment Ordinance) and F.M.S. Enactment No. 18 of 1927
       (Women and Girls Protection Amendment Enactment). Report.
       Lord Balfour of Burleigh, Chairman. London: H.M.S.O.,
       1929, 19 pp. House of Commons. Command paper, Cmd.3294.

2482 HLA AUNG, U. "Some Aspects of Marriage under Burmese Buddhist
       Law and Malayan Muslim Law." Burma Research Society, Jour-
       nal 48, no. 2 (Dec. 1965):1-15.

2483 HOOKER, M.B. The Personal Laws of Malaysia: An Introduction.
       Kuala Lumpur: Oxford University Press, 1976, xxxiv,
       276 pp. (Includes sections on adultery, divorce, inheri-
       tance, and marriage.)

2484 HUE, SIEW KHENG. "A Critical Study of the Existing Law Relat-
       ing to Marriage and the Proposed Reforms." LL.B. academic
       exercise, University of Malaya, 1975, vii, 51 pp.

2485 JACKSON, DAVID. "The Invalidity of a Marriage by the Law of
      Its Place of Celebration." Malaya Law Review 5, no. 2
      (Dec. 1963):388-92.

2486 _____. "A Wife's Right to Occupy the Matrimonial Home: A
      Comparative Study." Malaya Law Review 5, no. 2 (Dec.
      1963):213-44.

2487 JUNAIDAH binti MUHAMMAD SAID. "A Study of the Control of
      Polygamy among Muslims, Selangor and the Federal Terri-
      tory." LL.B. academic exercise, University of Malaya,
      1977, vii, 48 pp.

2488 KHUMBAT, A. "The Medical Practitioner and the Abortion Law in
      Malaysia." Berita MMA 7 (1975):10-11, 16.

2489 LEE, SIOW MONG. "Chinese Customary Marriage and Divorce."
      Malaya Law Journal 2 (July 1972):iii-vi.

2490 LEONG, MAGGIE MEI KAY. "Evidence in Rape Cases." LL.B. aca-
      demic exercise, University of Malaya, 1979, viii, 107 pp.

2491 LIAW, YOCK FANG. Undang-undang Melaka. The Laws of Malacca.
      The Hague: Martinus Nijhoff, 1976, 211, 20 pp. Biblio-
      theca Indonesica, 13. (Includes sections on laws relating
      to women.)

2492 LIEW, ELIZABETH C.H. "Ethics of Abortion." 14 pp. Paper
      presented at the Fourth Malaysian Law Conference, Kuala
      Lumpur, October 1977, organized by the Bar Council (States
      of Malaya).

2493 MALAYA, Laws, statutes, etc. The Divorce Ordinance, 1952.
      Ordinance No. 74 of 1952. Kuala Lumpur: Government
      Printer, 1953, 20 pp.

2494 _____. "The Married Women Ordinance, 1957, No. 36 of 1957."
      In Federal Ordinances and State and Settlement Enactments
      Passed during the Year 1957. Kuala Lumpur: Government
      Printer, 1959, pp. 271-77.

2495 MALAYSIA, Laws, statutes, etc. Civil Marriage Ordinance,
      1952. (F.M.44 of 1952) together with the Subsidiary Legis-
      lation Made Thereunder. Kuala Lumpur: Government Printer,
      1970, 47 pp.

2496 _____. Civil Marriage Ordinance, 1952, together with the
      Subsidiary Legislation. The Divorce Ordinance, 1952; The
      Christian Marriage Ordinance, 1956 and The Married Women
      Ordinance, 1957. 4 vols in 1. Kuala Lumpur: Jabatan
      Chetak Kerajaan, 1953-70.

2497   _____. Employment Ordinance, 1955 . . . together with . . .
Employment (Employment of Women) (Female Conductors) Regulations 1958 (L.N.150 of 1958) and Employment (Employment
of Women) (Shift Workers) Regulations, 1970 (P.U.(A) 319 of
1970). Kuala Lumpur: Jabatan Cetak Kerajaan, 1975, 91 pp.

2498   _____. Law Reform (Marriage and Divorce) Act, 1976 (Act 164).
Kuala Lumpur: Government Printer, 1976, 52 pp.

2499   _____. Married Women and Children (Enforcement of Maintenance)
Act, No. 8 of 1968. Kuala Lumpur: Government Printer,
1968, 9 pp.

2500   _____. Registration of Marriage Ordinance, 1952 (F.M.53 of
1952). Together with the Subsidiary Legislation Made
Thereunder. Kuala Lumpur: Jabatan Cetak Kerajaan, 1970,
12 pp.

2501   _____. Women and Girls Protection Act, 1973. Kuala Lumpur:
Government Printer, 1973, 28 pp.

2502   MALAYSIA, Parlimen, Jawatankuasa Pilihan bagi Mengkaji Rang
Undang-undang Membaharui Undang-undang Perkahwinan and
Perceraian, 1972. Lapuran Permulaan. Preliminary Report.
Kuala Lumpur: Pengarah Percetakan, 1974, x, 247 pp. (The
Joint Select Committee comprises the Select Committee of
the Dewan Rakyat appointed to study the Law Reform (Mar-
riage and Divorce) Bill, 1972 and the Select Committee of
the Dewan Negara appointed to study the Report of the Royal
Commission on Non-Muslim Marriage and Divorce Laws.)

2503   MALAYSIA, Royal Commission on Non-Muslim Marriage and Divorce
Laws. Report. Chairman: Tan Sri Ong Hock Thye. Kuala
Lumpur: Government Printer, 1972, iii, 68 pp.

2504   MAZNAH binti HAJI HARON. "Muslim Marriage and Divorce in the
Federal Territory." LL.B. academic exercise, University
of Malaya, 1975, vi, 105 pp.

2505   MUHAMMAD bin MUHAMMAD SAHED, Shaikh. "Pelacuran: Kawalan
Sosial dan Undang-undang di Malaysia (dengan Rujukan di
Pulau Pinang)" [Prostitution: social control and law in
Malaysia--with reference to Penang]. LL.B. academic exer-
cise, University of Malaya, 1976, iv, 117 pp.

2506   MUHAMMAD DIN bin ALI. "Malay Customary Law and the Family."
In CONFERENCE ON FAMILY LAW AND CUSTOMARY LAW IN ASIA,
Singapore, 1964. Family Law and Customary Law in Asia: A
Contemporary Perspective. Edited by David C. Buxbaum.
The Hague: Martinus Nijhoff, 1968, pp. 179-201. (In-
cludes discussion on marriage property, role of the woman,

marriage system, prohibition of marriage relationship, and succession of property.)

2507 NORDIN SELAT. "Hukum Perkahwinan dan Hukum Perceraian" [Marriage and divorce laws]. Mastika 36, no. 12 (1976):20-24.

2508 PARR, C.W.C. "Marriage in Negri Sembilan." In Readings in Malay Adat Law. Edited by M.B. Hooker. Singapore: Singapore University Press, 1970, pp. 399-406.

2509 PHANG, KOOI YOONG. "The Rehabilitation Centre for Women and Girls: A Study." LL.B. academic exercise, University of Malaya, 1979, v, 114 pp.

2510 RAFIAH SALIM. "Wanita dan Undang-undang" [Woman and the law]. Wanita [Kuala Lumpur], no. 101 (Dec. 1977):27, 56.

2511 RAMLAH NIK MAHMOOD, Nik. "Muslim Divorce in Kelantan: A Socio-Legal Study." LL.B. academic exercise, University of Malaya, 1979, vii, 191 pp.

2512 RAMLY bin ALI. "Undang-undang mengenai Khalwat di Malaysia (dengan Tinjauan Khas di Wilayah Persekutuan, Selangor dan Melaka)" [Laws on 'khalwat' (close proximity) in Malaysia: with a special study of the Federal Territory, Selangor, and Malacca]. LL.B. academic exercise, University of Malaya, 1978, vii, 96 pp.

2513 RASJIDI, LILI. "Undang-undang Perkahwinan dan Penceraian di Malaysia dan Indonesia" [Marriage and divorce laws in Malaysia and Indonesia]. LL.M. thesis, University of Malaya, 1978, xvii, 401 pp.

2514 RATNAM, ISAAC PAUL. "Effect of Apostacy and Conversion on Marriage." LL.M. thesis, University of Singapore, 1969, 164 pp.

2515 SANDIN, BENEDICT. "Some Iban (Sea Dyak) Customary Law in Sarawak. Customs regarding Engagement, Marriage, and Widowhood." In CONFERENCE ON FAMILY LAW AND CUSTOMARY LAW IN ASIA, Singapore, 1964. Family Law and Customary Law in Asia: A Contemporary Perspective. Edited by David C. Bauxbaum. The Hague: Martinus Nijhoff, 1968, pp. 41-44.

2516 SARIF bin WAN AHMAD, Wan. "Taraf Wanita dalam Islam" [The status of women in Islam]. LL.B. academic exercise, University of Malaya, 1977, vi, 165 pp.

2517   SHAMSUDDIN bin ABDUL RAHMAN et al. "Country Report: Malaysia
       Law and Population in Malaysia." In SOUTHEAST ASIAN RE-
       GIONAL SEMINAR ON LAW AND POPULATION, Jakarta, 1975. Law
       and Population. Edited by Teuku Mohamed Radhie et al.
       Jakarta: Yayasan Penelitian dan Pengembangan Hukum, 1976,
       pp. 120-25. (Includes discussion on laws on family plan-
       ning, marriage and divorce, inheritance, and employment of
       women.)

2518   SHERIDAN, LIONEL ASTOR. "Malay Marriages." In Studies in
       Law: An Anthology of Essays in Municipal and International
       Law. Bombay: Patna Law College, 1961, pp. 492-508.

2519   SIRAJ, MEHRUN. "Conciliation Procedures in Divorce Proceed-
       ings." Malaya Law Review 7, no. 2 (Dec. 1965):314-25.

2520   _____. "The Control of Polygamy." Malaya Law Review 6, no. 2
       (Dec. 1964):387-405.

2521   _____. "Current Legislation in Peninsular Malaysia: Some
       Thoughts for International Women's Year, 1975." Malayan
       Law Journal (Dec. 1975):xciii-xcvi.

2522   _____. "Recent Changes in the Administration of Muslim Family
       Law in Malaysia and Singapore." International Comparative
       Law Quarterly 17 (Jan. 1968):221-32.

2523   SIVARETNAM, JOSEPHINE PREMLA. "Women's Rights and the Law:
       A Comparative Study on Sex Discrimination." LL.B. academic
       exercise, University of Malaya, 1977, vii, 96 pp.

2524   TAYLOR, EVAN NUTALL. "Customary Law of Rembau." Royal
       Asiatic Society of Great Britain and Ireland, Malayan
       Branch, Journal 7, pt. 1 (Aug. 1929):1-289. (Includes
       discussion on laws relating to matriarchy, marriage, and
       divorce.)

2525   _____. "Malay Family Law: An Essay on the Law and Custom
       relating to the Distribution of Property on Dissolution of
       Marriage among Peninsular Malays." Royal Asiatic Society
       of Great Britain and Ireland, Malayan Branch, Journal 15,
       pt. 1 (May 1937):i-ix, 1-78.

2526   _____. "Mohammedan Divorce by Khula. Inheritance in Negri
       Sembilan: Two Papers." Royal Asiatic Society of Great
       Britain and Ireland, Malayan Branch, Journal 21, pt. 2
       (1948):1-130.

2527   TEOH, JIN INN. "The Legislation of Abortion: A Psychia-
       trist's View." Berita MMA 6 (1975):3, 7.

2528   THIVY, JOHN A. "Comments on the Proposed Straits Settlements 'Monogamus Marriage Bill' and the 'Marriage Registration Bill.'" n.p., n.d., 1 vol. (various pagings).

2529   TOH, FLORENCE HUAT NEO. "The Abortion Law: A Reform." LL.B. academic exercise, University of Malaya, 1975, iii, 74 pp.

2530   "Woman and the Family." Intisari 2, no. 2 (1964[?]):9-73. (Contents: 1. M. Siraj, "Status Muslim Woman/Family Law Singapore." 2. M. Siraj, "Effective Administration/Social Change." 3. Shirle Gordon, "Marriage/Divorce in the Eleven States of Malaya and Singapore." 4. Mohd. Din bin Ali, "Malay Customary Law/Family." 5. Ahmad bin Muhammad Ibrahim, "Islam Customary Law/Malaysia.")

2531   WONG, SIONG YONG, and KOH, K.L. "The Chinese Christian and the Law of Marriage in West Malaysia." Malaya Law Review 9, no. 1 (July 1976):147-52.

2532   ZAKARIA, SHAIKHA. "Muslim Women and the Law of Islam in West Malaysia." Master's thesis, University of Kent at Canterbury, 1973, 156 pp.

2533   ZALEHA YUSOF. "Sumbangan Undang-undang dalam Gunatenaga Wanita di Malaysia" [Laws governing female employment in Malaysia]. LL.B. academic exercise, University of Malaya, 1979, v, 72 pp.

2534   ZALIKHAH binte MD. NOR, Siti. "Perkahwinan dan Perceraian di Kalangan Masharakat Islam di Malaysia Semenanjung" [Marriage and divorce in Muslim Society in Peninsular Malaysia]. LL.M. thesis, University of Malaya, 1978, xv, 371 pp.

2535   _____. "Status dan Hak Wanita di dalam Undang-undang Keluarga Islam" [The status and rights of women under Islamic family law]. 11 pp. Paper presented at the Seminar 'Wanita Malaysia Masakini,' Bangi, Selangor, 1979, organized by the Faculty of Social Sciences and Humanities, Universiti Kebangsaan Malaysia.

Philippines

2536   ABAYA, ROSALIA M. "Female Criminality in the Philippines." LL.M. thesis, University of Manila [Manila], 1952, 178 pp.

2537   AGUILAR, JESUS R. "The Validity of Foreign Divorce Decrees." Philippine Law Journal 42, no. 4 (Sept. 1967):526-43.

2538   ALMEYDA, HECTOR B.; AMORES, FELIPE C.; and MAGPANTAY, ENRIQUETO I. "Civil Law." Philippine Law Journal 40, no. 2 (Apr. 1965):203-29. (Includes a survey on the laws of marriage and property relations between the spouses.)

2539   ANTONIO, F.G. "Comments on the Lex Loci Celebrationis Rule in
        Relation to the Nationality Theory as to Marriage." Uni-
        versity of the East Law Journal 4, no. 2 (Oct. 1961):
        196-204.

2540   AZCUNA, A.S. "The Legal Effects of Pregnancy as Illness or
        Disability." Ateneo Law Journal 11, no. 3 (Jan. 1962):
        247-54.

2541   BORROMEO, FEDERICO O. "The Adverse Effects of the New Woman
        and Child Labour Law." Bureau of Women and Minors, Digest,
        no. 1 (Dec. 1971):15-18.

2542   CABANILLA, W.T. "A Critical Analysis of the Lex Loci Cele-
        brationis Rule in Determining the Validity of Foreign Mar-
        riages." University of the East Law Journal 3, no. 2
        (Oct. 1960):268-79.

2543   CARALE, BARTOLOME S. "Criminal Adultery and Fornication in
        the Philippines: A Re-examination." Philippine Law Jour-
        nal 45 (1970):344-52.

2544   CHANCO, MARIA ANA C.; FUNK, RICHARD V.; and HUGO, VICTOR C.
        "Civil Law." Philippine Law Journal 39, no. 1 (Feb. 1964):
        87-92. (Includes a discussion on property relations be-
        tween husband and wife, property, paternity, and filia-
        tion.)

2545   "Changes in Philippine Marriage Legislation: A Proposal.
        Catholic Bishops Conference of the Philippines." Unitas
        49 (Mar. 1976):66-107.

2546   CIPRIANO, J.A. "Legal Separation: A Remedy or a Penalty."
        University of the East Law Journal 6, no. 1 (Aug. 1963):
        47-72.

2547   COLOSO, MANUEL Y. "Analytical and Critical Study of Act 3513
        of the Philippine Legislature Known as the Marriage Law."
        LL.M. thesis, University of the Philippines [Quezon City],
        1932.

2548   CORTES, IRENE R. "Philippine Law and the Status of Women."
        In Law and the Status of Women: An International Sym-
        posium. Edited by the Columbia Human Rights Law Review,
        Columbia University School of Law. New York: Centre for
        Social Development and Humanitarian Affairs, United
        Nations, 1977, pp. 229-61.

2549   _____. "Status of Women." In Population of the Philippines,
        by United Nations Economic and Social Commission for Asia
        and the Pacific. Bangkok: ESCAP, 1978, pp. 313-21.

2550 _____. "Status of Women in Philippine Law." Fookien Times
Philippines Yearbook (1975):334-37.

2551 _____. "Women's Rights under the 1973 Constitution."
Philippine Law Journal 50, no. 1 (Feb. 1975):1-24.

2552 _____. Women's Rights under the 1973 Constitution. Quezon
City: University of the Philippines Press, 1975, 81 pp.
Professorial Chair Lectures, Monograph, no. 10.

2553 CRUZ, LUIS de la. "Physical Examination of the Body of the
Complaining Women in Seduction Cases." Philippines Law
Journal 10, no. 3 (Sept. 1960):91-123.

2554 CUEVA, FELICISIMA A. de la. "The Effect of the Paraphernal
Law upon the Capacity of the Married Woman to Contract
Insurance." Philippine Law Journal 19, no. 7 (Jan. 1940):
302-15.

2555 DASALLE, PURIFICACION F. "An Analytical Study of Marriage
and Divorce." LL.M. thesis, Philippine Law School [Pasay
City, Philippines], 1951, 152 pp.

2556 "Documents." Philippine Law Journal 50, no. 1 (Feb. 1975):
103-47. (Contents: 1. "Constitution of the Republic of
the Philippines." 2. "Presidential Decree No. 148--Amend-
ing Further Certain Sections of Republic Act Numbered Six
Hundred Seventy-nine as Amended, Commonly Known as the
Woman and Child Labor Law." 3. "Presidential Decree No.
633--Creating a National Commission on the Role of
Filipino Women." 4. "Resolutions of the International
Labour Conference--the Employment of Women." 5. "Standards
Approved by Technical Advisory Bodies--the Employment of
Women." 6. "The United Nations Declaration on the Elimi-
nation of Discrimination against Women.")

2557 "Employment of Women and Minors in the Philippines." Labor
Review [Quezon City] 1, no. 4 (Apr. 1965):33-50.

2558 EZEQUIEL, JUSTINIANO R. "Comparative Study of Divorce and
Legal Separation." LL.M. thesis, Southern Luzon College
[Naga City, Philippines], 1950.

2559 FERNANDO, ENRIQUE M. "The Movement for Equal Rights: The
Validity of Legislation Beneficial to Women." Philippine
Law Journal 51 (1976):441-54.

2560 FLORENDO, GERARDO. "Humanizing the Family Law." Philippine
Law Journal 20, no. 4 (Oct. 1940):171-78.

2561   FLORENDO, JUAN C. "Is the Property of a Married Woman Liable
       for the Obligations Incurred by the Husband?" Philippine
       Law Journal 13, no. 3 (Sept. 1933):83-95.

2562   GALLEGO, MANUEL V. "Proposed Amendments to Our Marriage
       Law." LL.M. thesis, University of the Philippines [Quezon
       City], 1919.

2563   GAMBOA, MELQUIADES J. "The Filipino Woman and the Law."
       Philippine Social Sciences and Humanities Review 6, no. 4
       (Oct. 1934):299-305.

2564   GARCIA, EXCELSO. "Nature of Marriage as Reflected in Canon
       and Civil Laws." Unitas 33, no. 4 (1960):857-77; 34, no. 1
       (1961):97-134.

2565   HILARIO, E.A., and DAVID, G.S. "Factors Guiding the Popula-
       tion Growth in the Philippines." Unitas 49, no. 3 (1966):
       341-49. (Includes discussion on marriage law.)

2566   JAVELLANA, YOLANDA Q., ed. Woman and the Law. Conference
       jointly sponsored by the Federacion Internacional de
       Abogados and the University of the Philippines Law Center.
       Quezon City: University of the Philippines Law Center,
       1975, viii, 120 pp. (Reprinted from the Philippine Law
       Journal 50, no. 1 (Feb. 1975). Round Table Conference:
       Achieving for Women Full Equality before the Law, Quezon
       City, 1975.)

2567   JUCO, JORGE M. "Fault, Consent and Breakdown: The Sociology
       of Divorce Legislation in the Philippines." Philippine
       Sociological Review 14, no. 2 (Apr. 1966):67-76.

2568   _____. "Some Legal Aspects of Chinese Marriages in the
       Philippines." Philippine Sociological Review 14, no. 1
       (Jan. 1966):57-59.

2569   LOBINGIER, CHARLES SUMMER. "The Primitive Malay Marriage
       Law." American Anthropologist 12, no. 2 (Apr./June 1910):
       250-56.

2570   LUCIANO, LEONOR INES. "The Legal and Christian Perspectives
       of Women's Role." Unitas 48, no. 2 (June 1975):251-58.

2571   MAGPANTAY, ENRIQUETO I.; GARCIA, E. VOLTAIRE II; and
       FACTORAN, FULGENCIO, Jr. "Civil Law." Philippine Law
       Journal 41 (1966):66-77. (Includes a survey on the laws
       of maintenance, marriage, divorce, and property.)

2572   MALOLOS, NAPOLEON R. "Salient Information in the Proposed
        Civil Code of the Philippines relative to Marriage and
        Divorce." LL.M. thesis, University of Manila [Manila],
        1949, 79, 5 pp.

2573   "Man Was Born Polygamous." Orient 1 (July 1959):135-57.

2574   MARQUEZ, LAZARO A. "Conviction for Adultery as Evidence in
        Divorce Proceedings." Philippine Law Journal 10, no. 7
        (Jan. 1931):279-97.

2575   MARTINEZ, AMANDO. "The Need for Absolute Divorce." Univer-
        sity of the East Law Journal 3, no. 1 (July 1960):52-56.

2576   MAYUGA, P.R. "Woman and Child Labor Law." Philippines Today
        10, no. 2 (1963):22-24.

2577   MEDINA, PRISCILLA (Argonza). "Protection of Women Workers
        under the Workmen's Compensation Law." Social Work
        [Manila] 7 (July 1962):880-83.

2578   MORALDE, J.J. "The Law of Legal Separation Revisited." Far
        Eastern Law Review 10, no. 2 (Nov. 1962):180-93.

2579   MOSQUEDA, ROMAN P. Marriage and Its Dissolution: Handbook.
        Manila: Quis, 1977, 695 pp.

2580   NAVARRO, AGUSTINA ROSITA. "A Comparative Analysis of the
        Rights of Women under the Old and the New Civil Code."
        Master's thesis, University of Manila [Manila], 1950,
        126 pp.

2581   ORTEGA, MANUEL L. "Abortion and the Right of Privacy."
        Philippine Law Journal 48, no. 4 (1973):652-95.

2582   PALMA, CECILIA MUÑOZ. "The Status of Filipino Women under the
        Law." In The Role of Women in Development: Seminar Papers
        and Statements. Edited by Leonardo Z. Legaspi. Manila:
        University of Santo Tomas Press, 1976, pp. 41-56.

2583   _____. "Suggested Reforms in Our Marriage and Divorce Laws."
        LL.M. thesis, University of Manila [Manila], 1947, 63 pp.

2584   PAÑGATO, HUSSAIN S. "Muslim Divorce Customs and Practices as
        Recognized by Law." Far Eastern Law Review 8 (Dec. 1960):
        481-505. (On Mindanao and Sulu.)

2585   PANILIO, LUIS D. "Nationality of Married Women." Ph.D. dis-
        sertation, University of Santo Tomas [Manila], 1938, 94 pp.

2586   PARAS, GLORIA C. "A Critical Study of Woman Labor Laws in
        the Philippines and Some Proposed Reforms Therein." LL.M.
        thesis, Far Eastern University [Manila], 1959, iii, 101 pp.

2587   PAREDES, LOURDES P. "A Critical Study of Section 9 of the
        Philippine Divorce Law." Philippine Law Journal 13, no. 2
        (Aug. 1933):41-71.

2588   "The Philippines: A Country Report." In SOUTHEAST ASIAN
        REGIONAL SEMINAR ON LAW AND POPULATION, Jakarta, 1975.
        Law and Population. Edited by Teuku Mohamed Radhie et al.
        Jakarta: Yayasan Penelitian dan Pengembangan Hukum, 1976,
        pp. 154-84. (Includes discussion on laws of family plan-
        ning, inheritance, and maternity benefits.)

2589   PHILIPPINES (REPUBLIC), Bureau of Women and Minors. The Woman
        and Child Labor Law (Presidential Decree No. 148). Dept.
        of Labor Order No. 7, Series of 1973. Manila: Bureau of
        Women and Minors, 1975, 8 pp.

2590   PHILIPPINES (REPUBLIC), Laws, statutes, etc. Philippine
        Medical Care and Woman and Child Labor Law. Compiled and
        edited by CBSI Editorial Staff. Manila: Central Book
        Supply, 1971, 111 pp.

2591   PIMENTEL, M. "What Every Bride Should Know before She Leaps."
        Sunburst 4 (July 1976):14-18.

2592   PURANGTHIP KAWMANO. "Marriage and Divorce Laws of the
        Philippines and of Thailand: A Comparative Study."
        Master's thesis, University of Manila [Manila], 1970,
        195 pp.

2593   QUISUMBING, P.V. "Working Women: Opportunities and Prob-
        lems." National Security Review 3 (June 1975):7-11.

2594   "Republic Act No. 6237: An Act Further Amending Republic Act
        Numbered Seventy-nine as Amended by Republic Act Numbered
        Eleven Hundred Thirty-One (re Woman and Child Labor Law)."
        University of the East Law Journal 14, no. 2 (Nov. 1971):
        234-37.

2595   "Republic Act No. 2714: An Act to Establish in the Department
        of Labour a Bureau to Be Known as Women and Minors Bureau."
        Law Review [Cebu City, Philippines] 11 (Nov./Dec. 1960):
        328-30.

2596   REYES, DEOGRACIA T. "History of Divorce Legislation in the
        Philippines since 1900." Philippine Studies 1 (June 1953):
        42-58.

2597   REYNOLDS, HARRIET R. "Reply to Professor Juco's Article
       (January 1966 Issue of the PSR) on 'Legal Aspects of
       Chinese Marriages in the Philippines.'" Philippine Socio-
       logical Review 14, no. 3 (July 1966):167-68.

2598   RIVAS, CONSOLACION L. "Married Women under the Philippine
       Laws." LL.M. thesis, University of Manila [Manila], 1948,
       83 pp.

2599   RODRIGUEZ, ANDRELINA V. "The Historical Right of Filipino
       Women to Engage in Business with Special Reference to the
       New Civil Code." Quezon City: College of Business Admin-
       istration, University of the Philippines, 1957.

2600   ROMERO, FLERIDA RUTH P. "Civil Law. Part One: Persons and
       Family Relations." Philippine Law Journal 43, no. 1
       (Feb. 1968):22-37; 44, no. 1 (Feb. 1969):61-73. (Includes
       laws relating to marriage and conjugal partnership.)

2601   _____. "Civil Law. Part One: Persons and Family Relations
       and Obligations and Contracts." Philippine Law Journal
       45, no. 1 (Feb. 1970):31-50; 46, no. 1 (Feb. 1971):52-72;
       47, no. 1 (Feb. 1972):186-212. (Includes laws relating to
       marriage, conjugal partnership, property relationships be-
       tween husband and wife, and paternity and filiation.)

2602   _____. "Economic Equality of Working Women under Our Laws."
       Integrated Bar of the Philippines, Journal 3 (3d quarter
       1975):197-204.

2603   _____. "Historical Background of the Legal Status of Women in
       the Philippines." Philippine Historical Association, His-
       torical Bulletin 19, nos. 1/4 (Jan./Dec. 1975):52-61.

2604   _____. "Philippine Family Law." Philippine Law Journal 51
       (1976):511-20.

2605   _____. "Women and Labor: Is the Economic Emancipation of the
       Filipino Working Woman at Hand?" Philippine Law Journal
       50, no. 1 (Feb. 1975):44-54.

2606   _____. Women's Status in Philippine Society. Diliman, Quezon
       City: University of the Philippines Law Center, 1979,
       viii, 23 pp.

2607   ROMUALDEZ, ESTELA ZIALCITA. "The Woman Delinquent." LL.M.
       thesis, University of the Philippines [Quezon City], 1925.

2608   ROSALES, J.B. "Comments on the Effects of Article 89 of the
       Civil Code of the Philippines (Marriage Law)." University
       of the East Law Journal 4, no. 2 (Oct. 1961):186-95.

2609 ROXAS, VENUSTIANO S.; FERRO, LUALHATI V.; and PEREZ, AMADOR R. "Civil Law." Philippine Law Journal 38, no. 2 (1963): 223-44. (Includes a survey on marriage, property relations between husband and wife, paternity and filiation).

2610 SALONGA, Q.R.A. "Bigamy: Court Decree for Void Marriages?" Ateneo Law Journal 5, no. 3 (Jan. 1956):370-82.

2611 SAN DIEGO, LOURDES P. "Women in Family Law." Philippine Law Journal 50, no. 1 (Feb. 1975):25-35.

2612 SANTA RITA, EMILIO. Church and Civil Law on Marriage Separation in the Philippines. Manila: P. Noval, 1963, viii, 109 pp.

2612a _____. A Proposed Form of Civil Marriage for Catholics and Other Religious Denominations in the Philippines. Manila: Printed by Novel Publishing Co., 1964, vii, 210 pp.

2613 SANVICTORES, LOURDES L. "Women and Business." Philippine Law Journal 50, no. 1 (Feb. 1975):80-87.

2614 SIBULO, EMILY A. "Islamic Laws of Marriage and Divorce as Affected by Philippine Legislation." Philippine Law Journal 49 (1974):406-20.

2615 SISON, C.V., and FELICIANO, M.S. "Law and Population." In Population of the Philippines, by United Nations Economic and Social Commission for Asia and the Pacific. Bangkok: ESCAP, 1978, pp. 298-312. (Includes laws on contraception, abortion, sterilization, marriage, legal separation, inheritance, and maternity benefits.)

2616 SOLOMON, JOSE A. "Validity of Foreign Divorces under Philippine Law." Philippine Law Journal 22, no. 5 (Oct. 1947): 293-98.

2617 SUAREZ, D. TORREVILLAS. "The Law: What's Good for Men Should Be Good for Women." Philippine Panorama 4 (2 Feb. 1975): 6-7.

2618 TABADA-PILAPIL, BERNARDINA. "An Analytical Study of Women's Rights under the New Civil Code." LL.M. thesis, Philippine Law School [Pasay City, Philippines], 1951, iii, iv, 159 pp.

2619 TANADRA, E.Q. "On Discriminatory Laws against Women." MLQU Graduate Journal 4 (Summer 1975):37-40.

2620   TANJANGCO, MIGUEL. "Can a Married Woman in the Philippines
       Engage in Commerce without the Consent of Her Husband."
       Philippine Law Journal 14, no. 3 (Sept. 1934):134-60.

2621   TORRES, JUSTO P., Jr. "The Philosophy of Our Marriage Law."
       Master's thesis, University of Manila [Manila], 1955.

2622   VELILIA, AMANDO L. "Woman Suffrage Is a Failure." LL.M.
       thesis, University of Santo Tomas [Manila], 1937, 23 pp.

2623   VELOSO, C.T. "Divorce, Annulment, Remarriage and Catholics."
       Philippine Panorama 4 (13 Apr. 1975):4-5.

2624   WILEY, SAMUEL R. "The Proposed Decree of Civil Divorce in
       the Philippines." Philippine Priests' Forum 7 (Dec. 1975):
       35-41.

2625   _____. "Some Conflicts between the Canon Law and the Civil
       Code in the Law of Marriage." Philippine Law Journal 49
       (1974):387-420.

2626   YLLA, JUAN. The Civil Marriage Act in the Philippine Islands:
       Commentary on the New Civil Marriage Act in the Philippines,
       No. 3613, in Force on the 5th of June, 1930. Manila:
       University of Santo Tomas Press, 1931, 59, ii pp.

2627   YSAAC, W.Y. "Civil Divorce, Liberation and Culture: Reflec-
       tions of a Filipino." Philippine Priests' Forum 7 (Dec.
       1975):47-55.

Singapore

2628   AHMAD bin MUHAMMAD IBRAHIM. "Developments in the Marriage
       Laws in Singapore since 1959." Malayan Law Journal (June
       1979):cl-clxxiii.

2629   _____. "Developments in the Marriage Laws in Malaysia and
       Singapore." Malaya Law Review 12, no. 2 (Dec. 1970):
       257-76.

2630   _____. Family Law in Malaysia and Singapore. Kuala Lumpur:
       Faculty of Law, University of Malaya, 1973, xv, 345 pp.

2631   _____. Family Law in Malaysia and Singapore. Singapore:
       Malayan Law Journal, 1978, xvi, 313 pp.

2632   _____. "Muslim Marriage and Divorce in Singapore." Malayan
       Law Journal 28, no. 2 (Feb. 1962):xi-xviii.

2633   _____. "Muslims in Malaysia and Singapore: The Law of Matri-
       monial Property." In Family Law in Asia and Africa. Ed-
       ited by James N.D. Anderson. London: G. Allen and Unwin,
       1968, pp. 182-209.

2634   _____. The Status of Muslim Women in Family Law in Malaysia,
        Singapore and Brunei. Singapore: Malayan Law Journal,
        1965, xviii, 121 pp.

2635   _____. "The Status of Women in Family Law in Malaysia,
        Singapore and Brunei." Malaya Law Review 7, no. 1 (July
        1965):54-94; 7, no. 2 (Dec. 1965):299-313; 8, no. 1 (July
        1966):46-85; 8, no. 2 (Dec. 1966):233-69.

2636   ATHULATHMUDALI, L.W., and BARTHOLOMEW, G.W. "The Women's
        Charter." Malaya Law Review 3, no. 2 (Dec. 1961):316-30.

2637   BUXBAUM, DAVID CHARLES, ed. "Chinese Family Law in Common Law
        Setting. A Note on the Institutional Environment and the
        Substantive Family Law of the Chinese in Singapore and
        Malaysia." In CONFERENCE ON FAMILY LAW AND CUSTOMARY LAW
        IN ASIA, Singapore, 1964. Family Law and Customary Law in
        Asia: A Contemporary Perspective. The Hague: Martinus
        Nijhoff, 1968, pp. 146-77. (Includes discussion on status
        of secondary wives.)

2638   CHANDRA MOHAN, S. "Maintenance Proceedings in Singapore and
        the Report of the Committee on Crime and Delinquency: Some
        Observations." Malaya Law Review 16, no. 2 (Dec. 1974):
        230-47.

2639   CHELVAN, CHARMIAN JACQUELINE. "The Women's Charter." B.A.
        academic exercise, University of Singapore, 1973, 51 pp.

2640   CHENG, SIOK HWA. "Singapore Women: Legal Status, Educational
        Attainment, and Employment Patterns." Asian Survey 17,
        no. 4 (Apr. 1977):358-74.

2641   _____. Women in Singapore: Legal, Educational and Economic
        Aspects. Singapore: Nanyang University, 1976, 32 pp.
        Nanyang University, College of Graduate Studies, Institute
        of Humanities and Social Science. Occasional Paper
        Studies.

2642   "Country Report: Singapore." In SOUTHEAST ASIAN REGIONAL
        SEMINAR ON LAW AND POPULATION, Jakarta, 1975. Law and
        Population. Edited by Teuku Mohamed Radhie et al.
        Jakarta: Yayasan Penelitian dan Pengembangan Hukum, 1976,
        pp. 185-223. (Includes discussion on laws on family plan-
        ning, marriage, inheritance, and maternity benefits.)

2643   DAW, ROWENA. "Some Problems of Conflict of Laws in West
        Malaysia and Singapore Family Law." Malaya Law Review 14,
        no. 2 (Dec. 1972):179-208. (Includes legal aspects of
        marriage and divorce.)

2644 de CRUZ, JUDITH; CHEE, MEE DING; and FAWCETT, WELCOME. Apa
      Wanita2 Singapura Perlu Ketahui tentang Undang2 [What
      Singaporean women should know about law]. Singapore:
      Persatuan Peguam2 Wanita Singapura, 1975, 8 pp.

2645 _____. What Singapore Women Should Know about Law.
      Singapore: Singapore Association of Women Lawyers, 1975,
      12 pp.

2646 DJAMOUR, JUDITH. The Muslim Matrimonial Court in Singapore.
      London: Athlone Press, 1966, 191 pp. London School of
      Economics and Political Science. Monographs on Social
      Anthropology, no. 31.

2647 FREEDMAN, MAURICE. "Chinese Family Law in Singapore: The
      Rout of Custom." In Family Law in Asia and Africa. Ed-
      ited by James N.D. Anderson. London: G. Allen and Unwin,
      1968, pp. 49-72. (Includes discussion of laws relating to
      marriage and divorce and the Women's Charter.)

2648 _____. "The Penhas Case: Mixed and Unmixed Marriage in
      Singapore." Modern Law Review 16, no. 3 (July 1953):
      366-68.

2649 GIAM, CHIN TOO. "Maintenance under the Women's Charter."
      LL.M. thesis, University of Singapore, 1971, 135 pp.

2650 HABIBI, SYED AHMAD MOINUDDIN. "Islamic Divorce as a Socio-
      Legal Institution." Ph.D. dissertation, University of
      Singapore, 1970, viii, 267 pp.

2651 HO, THELMA YIN KHAM. "The Present Status of Singaporean
      Women: Legal and Political Aspects." B.A. academic exer-
      cise, University of Singapore, 1973, 60 pp.

2652 JOETHY, RAMALINGAM. "Modern Developments on the Concept of
      Cruelty." LL.M. thesis, Univesity of Singapore, 1970,
      155 pp.

2653 KUMAR, V. "Medico-Legal Aspects of Abortion." Malaya Law
      Review 6, no. 1 (July 1964):17-39.

2654 KWA, S.B.; QUAH, SIAM TEE; and CHENG, MARK C.E. "The Abortion
      Act, 1969: A Review of the First Year's Experience."
      Singapore Medical Journal 12, no. 5 (Oct. 1971):250-55.

2655 McBRIDE, JOHN DOUGLAS. "Law in the Pluralistic State: Malay
      and Chinese Family Law in the Pluralistic State of
      Singapore." Ph.D. dissertation, Southern Illinois Uni-
      versity, 1971, 134 pp. (Includes marriage laws.)

2656   MARSHALL, DAVID, Datuk. "Injuries and Medical Reports in
       Sexual Offences." Singapore: Malayan Law Journal, 1977,
       6 pp.

2657   MILLS, J.V. "Marriage and Kindred Subjects in England,
       Singapore and China." Journal of Comparative Legislation
       and International Law, 3d ser. 31 (1949):25-36.

2658   NORSHIDAH MUHAMMAD AMIN. "The Woman Criminal." B.A. academic
       exercise, University of Singapore, 1960, 107 pp.

2659   PEGG, LEONARD. "The Seven-year Hitch: A Comparative Study of
       Singapore's New Divorce Ground." Malaya Law Review 11,
       no. 2 (Dec. 1969):181-219.

2660   RAJAH, K.S. "The Women's Charter and Customary Marriages."
       Malayan Law Journal 2 (Dec. 1974):xlvi-lv.

2661   RATNAM, ISAAC PAUL. "Effect of Apostacy and Conversion on
       Marriage." LL.M. thesis, University of Singapore, 1969,
       114 pp.

2662   RAWLINGS, R.W. "Jurisdiction under Part IX of the Women's
       Charter." Malaya Law Review 19 (1977):348-54.

2663   SINGAPORE, Laws, statutes, etc. Abortion Act. Chapter 150.
       Singapore: Government Printing Office, 1970, 14 pp.

2664   _____. "Abortion Act 1974 (Act. No. 24 of 1974)." In Supple-
       ment to the Statutes of Singapore. Singapore: Singapore
       National Printers, 1974, pp. 213-17.

2665   _____. The Women's Charter, 1961. Singapore: Government
       Printer, 1961, vi, 69 pp.

2666   _____. The Women's Charter (Registration of Marriage) Rules,
       1961. Singapore: Government Printer, 1961, 11 pp.

2667   SINGAPORE, Legislative Assembly. Report of the Select Com-
       mittee on the Women's Charter Bill. Singapore: Government
       Printer, 1961, 104 pp.

2668   SIRAJ, MEHRUN. "Ancillary Orders on Muslim Divorce: The
       Practice of the Shariah Court in Singapore." Malaya Law
       Review 8, no. 1 (July 1966):86-94.

2669   _____. "The Control of Polygamy." Malaya Law Review 6,
       no. 2 (Dec. 1964):387-405.

2670   _____. "Enticement of [a] Minor and the Validity of Her Mar-
        riage under Muslim Law." Malaya Law Review 5, no. 2
        (Dec. 1963):392-97.

2671   _____. "Recent Changes in the Administration of Muslim Family
        Law in Malaysia and Singapore." International Comparative
        Law Quarterly 17 (Jan. 1968):221-32.

2672   _____. "The Shariah Court of Singapore and Its Control of
        Divorce." Malaya Law Review 5, no. 1 (July 1963):148-59.

2673   _____. "Status Muslim Woman/Family Law Singapore."
        Intisari 2, no. 2 (1964[?]):9-17.

2674   _____. "The Status of Muslim Women in Family Law in
        Singapore." World Muslim League Monthly Magazine 1, no. 2
        (Dec. 1963):40-52.

2675   TAN, NALLA. "Laws and Practice on Status of Working Women and
        Protection of Motherhood in Singapore." 13 pp. Paper pre-
        sented at the TWARO ASEAN and Oceanic Women Seminar,
        Singapore, 1978.

2676   WEE, KENNETH KIM SENG. "Customary Marriages and the Women's
        Charter: Lingering Doubts." Malaya Law Review 14, no. 1
        (July 1972):93-102.

2677   _____. "English Law and Chinese Family Custom in Singapore:
        The Problem of Fairness in Adjudication." Malaya Law Re-
        view 16, no. 1 (July 1974):52-82.

2678   _____. Family Law. Singapore: University of Singapore,
        Malaya Law Review, 1976, 52 pp. Singapore Law Series,
        no. 2.

2679   _____. "The Recognition of Foreign Divorce Decrees: Creativ-
        ity and Orthodoxy." Malaya Law Review 16, no. 1 (July
        1974):142-51.

2680   _____. "The Women's Charter (Amendment) Act 1975." Malayan
        Law Journal 2 (Oct. 1975):xliv-xlvi.

Thailand

2681   ADUL WICHIENCHAROEN, and LUANG CHAMROON NETISASTRA. "Some
        Main Features of Modernization of Ancient Family Law in
        Thailand." In CONFERENCE ON FAMILY LAW AND CUSTOMARY LAW
        IN ASIA, Singapore, 1964. Family Law and Customary Law in
        Asia: A Contemporary Perspective. Edited by David C.
        Buxbaum. The Hague: Martinus Nijhoff, 1968, pp. 89-105.
        (Includes discussion on polygamy, conjugal power of the
        husband, marriage, status of the spouses, matrimonial
        property, and divorce.)

2682 CHARUVASTRA CHUNE NAI. La formation du mariage et la puis-
sance maritale en droit siamois [The establishment of marriage and the powers of a husband in Siamese law]. Paris:
M. Giard, 1922, 260 pp. Thèse pour le Doctorat en Droit,
Université de Paris.

2683 "Country Report: Thailand." In SOUTHEAST ASIAN REGIONAL
SEMINAR ON LAW AND POPULATION, Jakarta, 1975. Law and
Population. Edited by Teuku Mohamed Radhie et al.
Jakarta: Yayasan Penelitian dan Pengembangan Hukum, 1976,
pp. 264-71. (Includes discussion of laws on family plan-
ning, status of women, and maternity benefits.)

2684 NATIONAL INSTITUTE OF CULTURE, Bangkok. Questionnaire on the
Legal Status of Women and Answers of the Government of
Thailand. Bangkok, 1954, 139 pp.

2685 PURANGTHIP KAWMANO. "Marriage and Divorce Laws of the
Philippines and of Thailand: A Comparative Study."
Master's thesis, University of Manila [Manila], 1970,
195 pp.

2686 SANYA DHARMASAKTI, and WIMOLSIRI JAMNARNWEJ. Status of Women
in Thailand. Bangkok: Women Lawyers Association of
Thailand, 1972, 40 pp.

2687 SIREE AMATAYAKUL. "A Critical Study of the Development of
Political and Civil Rights of Women in Thailand." Master's
thesis, University of Manila [Manila], 1965, 163 pp.

2688 THAMRONG PINTARUCHI. "A Critical Study of the Marriage and
Family Laws of Thailand." LL.M. thesis, University of
Manila [Manila], 1964, viii, 170 pp.

2689 THIRA SRITHAMARAKS. "Mariage traditionnel et mariage légal
en droit thailandais actuel" [Traditional marriages and
statutory marriages in present day Thai law]. Ph.D. dissertation (Doctorat d'Université) Université de Caen,
1972, 243 pp.

2690 UKRIT MANGKOLNAVIN. "La situation juridique de la femme
mariée en droit thailandais" [The legal status of married
women in Thai law]. Thèse pour le Doctorat en Droit,
Université de Paris, 1966, 248 pp.

2691 UNITED NATIONS, Economic and Social Council, Committee on the
Status of Women. Status of Women in Family Law. Report of
the Secretary-General based on replies from governments to
part 3 of the questionnaire on the legal status and treatment of women. New York: Economic and Social Council,

United Nations, 1955, 22 pp. United Nations Document
E/CN.6/185/Add. 14. (Federal Republic of Germany, Peru,
and Thailand.)

LITERARY ASPECTS; LITERARY COLLECTIONS; WOMEN IN LITERATURE

2692   ADIBAH AMIN. "This Pretty Girl Is Also One of Malaysia's
Finest Writers." Straits Times Annual (1973):117-20. (On
Khadijah Hashim.)

2693   AIMY, B.D. "Une grande poetesse: Ho-Xuan-Huang" [A great
poetess: Ho-Xuan-Huang]. France-Asie 8 (Nov. 1952):
941-50.

2694   ALISJAHBANA, SUTAN TAKDIR. "Kaoem Poeteri dan Pembangoenan
Kesoesatraan Baroe" [Women and the development of modern
literature]. Pudjangga Baru 3 (1935/36):131-38.

2695   _____. "Kedudukan Perempuan dalam Kesusasteraan Timur Baru"
[The position of women in literature in the New East].
Pudjangga Baru 8 (Nov. 1940):154-64.

2696   BRAND, MONA. Daughters of Vietnam. Hanoi: Foreign Languages
Publishing House, 1958, 183 pp.

2697   CHAMBERT-LOIR, HENRI. "Les femmes et l'écriture. La litté-
rature féminine indonésienne" [Women and their writings.
Literature by Indonesian women]. Archipel no. 13 (1977):
267-82.

2698   CHIVAS-BARON, CLOTILDE. Three Women of Annam. Authorized
translation by Faith Chipperfield. New York: Frank-
Maurice, 1925, 267 pp.

2699   _____. Trois femmes annamites [Three women of Annam].
Paris: E. Fasquelle, 1922, 287 pp.

2700   CONDA, ADELFA F. "The Women Characters in Selected Novels of
Gonzalez, Santos, Joaquin, and Polotan." Master's thesis,
University of Nueva Caceres, [Naga City, Philippines],
1969, ci, 95 pp.

2701   CONG, HUYEN TOH NU THI, NHATRANG. "The Traditional Roles of
Women as Reflected in Oral and Written Vietnamese Litera-
ture." Ph.D. dissertation, University of California,
Berkeley, 1973, iv, 273 pp.

2702   CRUZ, SIXTO D. VERA. "Five Major Filipino Women Essayists in English: An Appreciative Study." Master's thesis, National Teachers College [Manila], 1956, viii, 280 pp.

2703   CUESTA, MILAGROS L. "A Study of Maria Paz Mendoza-Guanzon's [sic] on Filipino Womenhood." Master's thesis, Far Eastern University [Manila], 1951, 91 pp.

2704   DANG JIJAH. "Beberapa Hal dalam Penulisan dan Penulis Wanita Sabah" [Some aspects of women writers of Sabah and their writings]. 14 pp. Paper presented at the Seminar Penulis dan Penulisan di Sabah held in Kota Kinabalu, 1978. Sponsored by Persatuan-Persatuan Penulis Yayasan Sabah, Dewan Bahasa dan Pustaka and Kementerian Kebudayaan, Belia dan Sukan Negeri.

2705   DAROY, ESTER VALLADO. "The Characteristic Trends in the Prose Fiction Writing in English by Some Filipino Women Writers." Master's thesis, Philippine Women's University [Manila], 1961, vi, 107 pp.

2706   DURAND, MAURICE M. L'oeuvre de la poétesse viêtnamienne Hô-Xuan-Huong [The work of the Vietnamese poetess, Hô-Xuan-Huong]. Paris: Adrien-Maisonneuve, 1968, 192 pp. Ecole Française d'Extrême-Orient, Collection de textes et documents sur l'Indochine, 9. Textes Nôm, no. 2.

2707   DUY LAM. Ngay nao con dan ba; tap van vui. Saigon: Nguyen Dinh Vuong, 1967, 11 pp.

2708   ESCASINAS, FILOMENA RIVERA. "The Women in Philippine Plays Written in English." Master's thesis, University of San Carlos [Cebu City, Philippines], 1966, 225 pp.

2709   GARCIA, AURORA TORRES. "A Study of Selected Women Characters in the Short Stories of N.V.M. Gonzalez." Master's thesis, Immaculate Concepcion College [Philippines], 1974, 6, 120 pp.

2710   GIL, A. "The Farmer's Wife: Portraits by Gonzales, Arguilla and Villa." Philippine Quarterly of Culture and Society 1, no. 2 (1973):86-91.

2711   GREGORIO, CLEO Z. "A Critical Analysis of the Representative Short Stories of the Two Well Known Pre-war and Two Outstanding Post-war Women Writers." Master's thesis, Far Eastern University [Manila], 1960, 235 pp.

2712 GREGORIO, MINERVA B. "Character Traits of Filipino Women in
      Rizal's Time as Revealed by the Characters in His Novels."
      Master's thesis, Philippine Women's University [Manila],
      1961, 158 pp.

2713 GUERRERO NAKPIL, CARMEN. Women Enough: And Other Essays.
      Quezon City: Vibal Publishing Co., 1963, vii, 149 pp.

2714 HAJAR binti IBRAHIM, Siti. "Perwatakan Tokoh Wanita dalam
      Roman Belenggu, Layar Terkembang dan Salah Asuhan" [The
      characterization of women in the novels, "Belenggu,"
      Layar Terkembang," and "Salah Asuhan"]. B.A. academic
      exercise, Universiti Kebangsaan Malaysia, 1975.

2715 HENG, GERALDINE, ed. The Sun in Her Eyes: Stories by
      Singapore Women. Singapore: Woodrose Publications, 1976,
      101 pp.

2716 "How 'Three Responsibility' Women Appear through Vietnamese
      Films." Women of Vietnam, nos. 3/4 (1970):25-27.

2717 HUFANA, ALEJANDRINO G. Imelda Romualdez Marcos: A Tonal
      Epic. Manila: Konsensus, 1975, 219 pp.

2718 ILIAS ZAIDI. "Sajak-sajak Wanita: Ditangannya Bunga
      Dimatanya Cinta" [Women poets: flower in her hand, love
      in her eyes]. Dewan Sastera 5, no. 10 (1975):27-29.
      (Malaysian poetesses.)

2719 JASMA OTHMAN, Siti. "Kedudukan Wanita Melayu Tradisional
      seperti Digambarkan dalam Cerita-cerita 'Jenaka' dan
      Cerita-cerita Penglipor Lara Melayu" [The status of tradi-
      tional Malay women as portrayed in Malay "jenaka" stories
      and folk-tales]. B.A. academic exercise, University of
      Malaya, 1977.

2720 JOYOSUPADMO, SRI MULYONO. Wayang dan Karakter Wanita [Plays
      and female characters]. Jakarta: Gunung Agung, 1977,
      144 pp.

2721 KARTINI, ANITA. "Tokoh-tokoh Wanita dalam Roman Indonesia
      Modern" [Women characters in modern Indonesian novels].
      Master's thesis, Universitas Indonesia, 1965.

2722 KATZ, NAOMI, and MILTON, NANCY, comps. Fragment from a Lost
      Diary and Other Stories: Women of Asia, Africa and Latin
      America. Boston: Beacon Press, 1973, xviii, 317 pp.

2723 KHIN MYA KYU. "Les femmes de lettres birmanes" [Burmese
      women writers]. Ph.D. dissertation (Doctorat d'Univer-
      sité), Université de Paris IV, 1970, ii, 241 pp.

2724   MAIMONAH binti A. MAJID. "Gambaran Imej Wanita Melayu dalam
        Cerpen-cerpen Majallah 'Wanita' (1969-1975)" [Images of
        Malay women in the short stories of the magazine 'Wanita'
        1969-1975]. B.A. academic exercise, University of Malaya,
        1976, v, 80 pp.

2725   MALAG MANLICLIC, CELIA. "The Literary Aspects of the Short
        Stories of Estrella D. Alfon." Centro Escolar University,
        Manila, Graduate and Faculty Studies, no. 6 (1955):95-116.

2726   MATTANI RUTNIN. "The Change in the Role of Women in Contempo-
        rary Thai Literature." In Modern Thai Literature: The
        Process of Modernization and the Transformation of Values,
        pp. 101-9. Published in East Asian Cultural Studies, 17,
        nos. 1/4 (Mar. 1978).

2727   MELLA, CESAR T. Poems for Imelda. Makati, Rizal: Printed
        by Buendia Commercial Press, 1969, 64 pp.

2728   MOC, NAM OW, ed. Only a While, the Mountain Sleeps: The
        Story of Woman and a Look at the Singapore Girl.
        Singapore: Single Spark Creation Corner, 1977, 78 pp.

2729   MOYE, CORAZON C. "A Study of the Women Characters in Eighteen
        Zarzuelas of Iluminado Lucente." Master's thesis, Divine
        Word University [Tacloban City, Philippines], 1968.

2730   MUHAMMAD MANSUR ABDULLAH. "Novel-novel Khadijah Hashim
        Bercorak Didaktik" [Khadijah Hashim's didactic novels].
        Dewan Sastera 7, no. 1 (Jan. 1977):46-49.

2731   NAVARRO-LIM, PURIFICACION. "A Critical Study of the Educa-
        tional Value of the Writings of Maria A. Kabigon."
        Master's thesis, University of San Carlos [Cebu City,
        Philippines], 1964, 124 pp.

2732   NGUYEN HUU TAN. "La femme viêtnamieene d'autrefois à travers
        les chansons populaires" [Vietnamese women of yesterday as
        seen through popular songs]. Société des études indo-
        chinoises de Saigon, Bulletin 45, no. 1 (1 Trimestre 1970):
        1-113.

2733   NGUYEN PHAN LONG. "Deux héroines viêtnamiennes" [Two Viet-
        namese heroines]. France-Asie 3, no. 22 (1948):175-82;
        no. 23 (1948):284-91.

2734   NURAZMI bin KUMTUM. "Sumbangan Salma Manja di Bidang Prosa"
        [The contribution of Salma Manja to prose literature].
        Mastika 39, no. 7 (1979):80-87. (Malaysian writer.)

2735   OHN MAUNG, KYAIKLAT U. "A Famous Poetess and Her Famous
        Song." Guardian [Rangoon] 10 (Sept. 1963):37. (On
        Princess Hlaing Hteik Khaung Tin.)

2736   PALMA, RAFAEL. "In Defense of the Modern Filipino Woman."
        In Philippine Prose and Poetry, by Bureau of Public
        Schools, Manila. Manila: Bureau of Printing, 1951,
        pp. 79-80.

2737   PAREJA, LENA STRAIT. "Estrella D. Alfon: A Bibliography."
        General Educational Journal 29 (1st Sem. 1975/1976):203-19.
        (Filipino writer.)

2738   PHAM THI QUE. "Le contact avec l'Occident et le mouvement
        féministe à travers la littérature vietnamienne dans la
        première moitié du vingtième siècle" [Contact with the
        West and the feminist movement as seen through Vietnamese
        literature during the first half of the twentieth century].
        Ph.D. dissertation (Doctorat de 3e cycle), Université de
        Paris IV, 1973, 260, xxv pp.

2739   POLOTAN, KERIMA. "The Woman as Writer." Focus 4 (22 Nov.
        1975):8.

2740   PRIHATMI, TH. SRI RAHAYU. Pengarang-Pengarang Wanita
        Indonesia: Seulas Pembicaraan [Indonesian women writers:
        a discussion]. Jakarta: Pustaka Jaya, 1977, 93 pp.

2741   _____. Pengarang Wanita Indonesia dalam Prosa [Indonesian
        women prose writers]. Jakarta: Lembaga Bahasa Nasional,
        1974, 61 pp.

2742   POERBATJARAKA. "Wanita, Priya dan Perempuan" [Explanation of
        the words 'wanita,' 'priya,' and 'perempuan']. Bahasa dan
        Sastra 5, no. 1 (1956):30-36.

2743   QUEMADA, DAVID V. "Major Influences on Seven Leading
        Philippine Poets in English (Jose Garcia Villa, R. Zulueta
        da Costa, Trinidad Tarrosa Subido, Angela Manalang Gloria,
        Bienvenido N. Santos, Homero Ch. Veloso, and Edith L.
        Tiempo) since 1930." Master's thesis, Silliman University
        [Dumaguete City, Philippines], 1953, viii, 320 pp.

2744   RAHMAH SAAD. "Ke Mana Hilangnya Sasterawan Wanita?" [Where
        have the women writers gone to?]. Wanita [Kuala Lumpur],
        no. 102 (Jan. 1978):16, 21.

2745   RELAMPAGOS, ESPERANZA L. "The Contributions of English-
        writing Filipino Women Authors to Modern Philippine Liter-
        ature." Master's thesis, University of San Carlos
        [Manila], 1957, vi, 113 pp.

2746   RODIL, CARMEN F. "The Characters in the Short Stories of
        Estrella Alfon-Rivera." Master's thesis, University of
        San Carlos [Manila], 1953, 148 pp.

2747   ROSIDI, AJIP. "Asmara Hadi: Mawar Segar atas Luka Cinta"
        [Asmara Hadi: a fresh rose on a wounded heart]. Basis 12,
        no. 4 (1963):107-14.

2748   SAFIAH KARIM, Nik. "Kegiatan Wanita Melayu dalam Kesu-
        sasteraan" [The involvement of Malay women in literature].
        Dewan Masyarakat 7, no. 12 (1969):42-43.

2749   SALMON, CLAUDINE. "Presse féminine ou féministe?" [Feminine
        or feminist press?]. Archipel, no. 13 (1977):157-92.

2750   SANTILLAN-CASTRENCE, PURA. The Women Characters in Rizal's
        Novels. Manila: Regal Publishing Co., 1960, viii, 155 pp.

2751   SARBINI bin YATIN. "Gambaran Wanita Melayu Mengikut Novel-
        novel Melayu Tahun Enampuluhan" [Malay women as portrayed
        in Malay novels in the 1960s]. B.A. academic exercise,
        University of Malaya, 1976, iv, 67 pp.

2752   SEBSOW, H.D. "New Directions for Women Writers." Focus 4
        (22 Nov. 1975):12-13.

2753   SEGOVIA, SELONNA BORROMEO. "A Study of the Attitudes of
        Kerima Polotan's Female Characters and Their Moral Impli-
        cations." Master's thesis, University of Negros Occidental-
        Recoletos [Philippines], 1975, 5, 125 pp.

2754   Seserpih Pinang Sepucuk Sirih: Bunga Rampai Puisi Wanita
        [A taste of betel and lime: an anthology of poetry by
        women]. Disprakarsai oleh Nelly Adam Malik. Disunting
        oleh Toeti Heraty. Diterjemahkan oleh John M. McGlynn.
        Jakarta: Pustaka Jaya, 1979, 232 pp.

2755   SHAMSUDDIN bin OTHMAN. "Adibah Amin: Kreativiti, Jernalisme
        Kerinduan dan Cinta" [Adibah Amin: creativity, journalism,
        and love]. Wawancara oleh Dinsman dengan Adibah Amin.
        Dewan Sastera 9, no. 9 (1979):22-28. (Malaysian writer.)

2756   SUDJIMAN, PANUTI. "Dua Cerpen Adibah Amin" [Two short stories
        of Adibah Amin]. Dewan Sastera 4, no. 8 (1975):42-43.

2757   SUTLIVE, VINSON H. "The Many Faces of Kumang: Iban Women in
        Fiction and Fact." Sarawak Museum Journal 25, no. 46
        (1977):157-64.

2758   TAYLOR, JEAN STEWART. "The World of Women in the Colonial
        Dutch Novel." Kabar Seberang 2 (June 1977):26-41.

2759   TEEUW, A. "Some Post-war Women Authors." In Modern Indo-
        nesian Literature. Vol. 1. 2d ed. The Hague: Martinus
        Nijhoff, 1979, pp. 212-14. Koninklijk Instituut voor
        Taal-, Land- en Volkenkunde. Translation Series 10, 1.

2760   TERRENAL, QUINTIN C. "Maria Clara and the Three Men in Her
        Life: An Interpretation of Rizal's 'Noli me tangere.'"
        Philippine Quarterly of Culture and Society 4, no. 1
        (Mar. 1976):1-18.

2761   TRAN CUU CHAN. Les grandes poètesses du Viêt-nam: études
        littéraires: Doan Thi-Diem, Ba Huyen Thanh-Quan, Ho-Xuan-
        Huong, Suong Nguyet-Anh [The great poetesses of Vietnam:
        literary studies: Doan Thi Diem, Ba Huyen Thanh-Quan, Ho-
        Xuan-Huong, Suong Nguyet Anh]. Saigon: Imprimerie de
        l'Union Nguyen Van-Cua, 1950, vii, 110 pp.

2762   TRIPAT, KAUR SANTOKH. "Shhh . . . Mum is Writing." New
        Straits Times Annual (1980):112-14, 116-17. (On Malaysian
        women writers.)

2763   UMAR JUNUS. "Dunia Lelaki dan Perempuan: Permasalahan dalam
        Novel-novel Indonesia. A: Manifestasi dalam Novel-novel
        Indonesia. B: Latar Belakang Sosio-Budaya" [Man's and
        woman's world: problems in Indonesian novels. A: Mani-
        festation in Indonesian novels. B: Socio-Cultural back-
        ground]. Dewan Bahasa 20, no. 7 (1976):407-23; 20, no. 8
        (1976):479-505.

2764   VALENZUELA, FLORITA A. "A Sociological Analysis of the Women
        Characters of Kerima Polotan." Master's thesis, Guagua
        National College [Philippines], 1978, 154 pp.

2765   VARELA, LOURDES Y. "Magdalena G. Jalandoni: Hiligaynon
        Writer." Philippine Quarterly of Culture and Society 4,
        no. 1 (Mar. 1976):37-45.

2766   VELASCO-TOMELDAN, YOLANDA. "A Critical Study of Magdalena
        Jalandoni as a Novelist with Special Reference to Ang
        Bangay Sang Patyo." Master's thesis, University of the
        Philippines [Quezon City], 1952, 384 pp.

2767   _____. "Magdalena Jalandoni and the Hiligaynon Novel."
        Diliman Review 1 (Apr. 1953):185-99.

2768   Wanita, Antoloji Cherpen2 Wanita [Women, an anthology of
        women's short stories]. Kuala Lumpur: Pustaka Antara,
        1964, 147 pp.

2769   WOODCROFT-LEE, CARLIEN PATRICIA. "The Woman behind the Mask:
        Techniques Employed in Characterisation of Women in Indo-
        nesian Prose Writing 1921-1965." Master's thesis,
        Australian National University, 1975, vi, 393 pp.

2770   "The Writer is a Woman." Sunday Times Magazine [Manila] 10
        (26 June 1955):16-19. (On Estrella D. Alfon.)

2771   YAHAYA bin ISMAIL. Ulasan dan Kajian Novel 'Badai Semalam'
        (Karya Khadijah Hashim) [Commentary and study of the novel
        'Badai semalam': work of Khadijah Hashim]. Singapore:
        Pustaka Nasional, 1970, 28 pp. (Malaysian authoress.)

2772   ZAKARIA AHMAD. "Penyaer Wanita" [Women poets]. Dewan
        Masyarakat 5, no. 10 (1967):50-53.

2773   ZAPANTA, ARACELI G. "A Comparative Study of the Women Charac-
        ters in the Works of Fiction of Nick Joaquin and N.V.M.
        Gonzalez." Master's thesis, University of San Carlos
        [Manila], 1966, ii, 123 pp.

MARRIAGE AND DIVORCE

(For legal aspects see
Legal Status, Laws, etc.)

Southeast Asia

2774   BLAYO, YVES. "Les premiers mariages féminins en Asie" [First
        marriages of women in Asia]. Population 33, nos. 4/5
        (July/Oct. 1978):951-88. (Includes Southeast Asia.)

2775   CHONG, KWONG TEK et al. Lovers for Life. Singapore: The Way
        Press, 1971, 163 pp.

2776   RISHI, W.R. PADMA SHRI. Marriages of the Orient. Singapore:
        Chopmen Enterprises, 1970, 140 pp.

2777   SHAPIRO, WANEN. "Asymmetric Marriage in Australia and South-
        east Asia." Bijdragen tot de taal-, land- en volkenkunde
        125, no. 1 (1969):71-79.

Brunei

2778   ROBERTSON, J.F. "Very Young Brides." Brunei Museum Journal
        2, no. 3 (1971):31-38.

2779   ROKIAH binti MUHAMMAD SALLEH. "Adat Perkahwinan Orang Melayu
       Brunei" [Marriage customs of Malays in Brunei]. Bahana 11,
       no. 24 (1976):18-27.

2780   SHARIFFUDIN, P.M. "The Royal Wedding." Brunei Museum Journal
       1, no. 1 (1969):1-4.

Burma

2781   AUNG THAN TUN. "Burmese Marriage." Guardian [Rangoon] 9
       (Sept. 1962):11-15.

2782   BAUGH, TIMOTHY GENE. "Du Kak Si. The Structural Implications
       of Matrilateral Cross Cousin Marriage: The Tlingit Case."
       Ph.D. dissertation, University of Oklahoma, 1978, 161 pp.
       Abstracted in Dissertation Abstracts International 39,
       no. 4 (Oct. 1978):2381-A. University Microfilms Inter-
       national, order no. 7817891.

2783   BLACKMORE, THAUNG. "Old-Style Marriages in Modern Burma."
       Eastern Horizon 1, no. 10 (Apr. 1961):26-29.

2784   FIFE, D. MacD. "A Shan Marriage and Divorce." Eastern World
       3 (Nov. 1949):28-29.

2785   KHIN KHIN U, Daw. "Marriage in the Burmese Muslim Community."
       Burma Research Society, Journal 37 (1954):24-34.

2786   LEACH, EDMUND RONALD. "Aspects of Bridewealth and Marriage
       Stability among the Kachin and Lakher." Man 57 (Apr.
       1957):50-55.

2787   LEHMAN, FREDERIC K. "On Chin and Kachin Marriage Regula-
       tions." Man 5, no. 1 (Mar. 1970):118-25.

2788   MYINT, M. PHONE. "Burmese Marriage Customs." Guardian
       [Rangoon] 3 (Apr. 1956):13-14.

2789   NASH, JUNE, and NASH, MANNING. "Marriage, Family, and Popu-
       lation Growth in Upper Burma." Southwestern Journal of
       Anthropology 19, no. 3 (Autumn 1963):251-66.

2780   RILEY, JAMES NELSON. "Cohabitation, Natality, and Mortality
       in Rural Thailand and Burma." In Culture, Natality, and
       Family Planning. Edited by John F. Marshall and Steven
       Polgar. Chapel Hill: Carolina Population Center, Univer-
       sity of North Carolina, 1976, pp. 24-49.

2791   SPIRO, MELFORD ELLIOT. Kinship and Marriage in Burma: A
       Cultural and Psychodynamic Analysis. Berkeley: University
       of Calfornia Press, 1977, xix, 313 pp.

2792 _____. "Marriage Payments: A Paradigm from the Burmese Per-
      spective." Journal of Anthropological Research 31, no. 2
      (Summer 1975):89-115.

2793 TAUNG, PALINE. "The Kachin Marriage System." Guardian
      [Rangoon] 21, no. 9 (Sept. 1974):18-20; no. 10 (Oct. 1974):
      17-20; no. 12 (Dec. 1974):13-17; 22, no. 3 (Mar. 1975):
      26-29; no. 4 (Apr. 1975):19-22; no. 5 (May 1975):14-17;
      no. 7 (July 1975):16-20; no. 8 (Aug. 1975):23-24; no. 9
      (Sept. 1975):32-37; no. 10 (Oct. 1975):25-33.

2794 TE, BA. "A Marriage Custom among the Ahkas and Myinchas."
      Burma Research Society, Journal 16 (1926):43-45.

2795 THEODORSON, GEORGE A. "Romanticism and Motivation to Marry in
      the United States, Singapore, Burma, and India." Social
      Forces 44, no. 1 (Sept. 1965):17-27.

2796 WHITE, WALTER GRAINGE. "Births and Marriages." In The Sea
      Gypsies of Malaya, by Walter Grainge White. London:
      Seeley, Service & Co., 1922, pp. 199-208.

Indochina

2797 CHEVALLIER, GEORGES. "Les motifs de divorce chez les
      Annamites" [Divorce grounds for the Annamite people].
      Revue indochinoise (Oct. 1904):539-50.

2798 COURTOIS, E. "La famille annamite: mariages, naissances,
      décès, cérémonies auxquelles ils donnent lieu" [The
      Annamite family: marriages, births, deaths, and the cere-
      monies arising from them]. Revue indochinoise (1900):
      509-11.

2799 DAGUIN, ARTHUR, and DUBREVIL, ALPHONSE. Le mariage cambodgien
      [Cambodian marriage]. Paris: Lucien Dorbon, 1906, 89 pp.

2800 ESNAMBUG, B. d'. "Rites du mariage au Cambodge" [Marriage
      rites of Cambodia]. Indochine, sud-est asiatique (Oct.
      1953):26.

2801 FOURNIER, CHRISTIANE. "Mariages et enterrements annamites"
      [Annamite weddings and funerals]. La géographie 57 (1932):
      456-65.

2802 HICKEY, GERALD CANNON. "The Family as a Social Group." In
      Village in Vietnam, by Gerald Cannon Hickey. New Haven
      and London: Yale University Press, 1964, pp. 99-133.
      (Includes sections on marriage, pregnancy, polygyny and
      concubinage, and divorce.)

2803 KER NOU, and NHIEUK NOU. "Kpuon Abah-bibah ou le livre de
      mariage der khmers" [Kpuon Abah-bibah or the Khmer book of
      marriage]. Ecole Française d'Extrême-Orient, Bulletin 60
      (1973):243-328.

2804 "Le mariage annamite" [Annamite marriage]. France-Asie,
      no. 5 (Aug. 1946):222-25.

2805 NGUYEN KIM CHI. "Etude sur le problème de la perception ré-
      ciproque et de le communication dans le mariage franco-
      vietnamien" [Study of the problem of mutual perception and
      of communication in marriages between French and Vietnamese
      people]. Ph.D. dissertation (Doctorat de 3e cycle), Uni-
      versité de Paris VII, 1973, vi, 342, 24 pp.

2806 NGUYEN PHU DOC. "Les rites du mariage lao et du mariage
      vietnamien" [Lao and Vietnamese marriage rites]. Bulletin
      des Amis du Royaume Lao, no. 1 (Apr./June 1970):51-70.

2807 NGUYEN VAN HUYEN, ed. Recueil des chants de mariage tho de
      Langso'n et Cao-bang [Collection of Tho wedding songs in
      Langso'n and Cao-bang]. Hanoi: Impr. d'Extrême-Orient,
      1941, xxviii, 181 (i.e 279) pp. Ecole française d'Extrême-
      Orient. Collection de textes et documents sur l'Indochine,
      5.

2808 PHAM VAN LUU. "Le mariage annamite" [Annamite marriage].
      Société de géographie et d'études coloniales de Marseille,
      Bulletin (1906):265-74.

2809 PICH SAL. "Le mariage cambodgien" [Cambodian marriage].
      Revue et complétée par Chan Seng et Charles Meyer. Phnom
      Penh: Université Buddhique, Preah Sihanouk Raj, 1962[?],
      20 pp.

2810 "The Rights of Freedom in Matrimony." U.S. JPRS. Selected
      Translations from Nhan Dan (the People) North Vietnam,
      no. 6 (Aug. 1961):44-47.

2811 SARIN CHHAK. "Faut-il supprimer la polygamie?" [Is it neces-
      sary to suppress polygamy?]. Bulletin de liaison des
      étudiants en droit, no. 4 (1963):43-45.

2812 SICÉ, EUGÈNE. Le mariage en pays d'Annam, selon la tradition
      ancestrale et les coutumes religieuses et d'après la légis-
      lation et la jurisprudence [Marriage in Annam according to
      ancestral tradition, religious customs, legislation, and
      jurisprudence]. Dijon: Bernigaud et Privat, 1929, 203 pp.

2813 STENTON, JEAN E. "Royal Wedding of Cambodia." Canadian Geo-
      graphical Journal (Dec. 1964):206-11.

2814   TRAN VAN TRAI. La famille patriarcale annamite [The Annamite
        patriarchal family]. Paris: P. Lapagesse, 1942, xv,
        360 pp. (Includes marriage laws and customs.)

Indonesia

2815   "Adat Pertunangan dan Perkawinan Daya" [Customs relating to
        Daya engagement and marriage]. Mimbar Indonesia 16, no. 11
        (1962):14-15.

2816   ADELANTE. "Concubinaat bij de Ambtenaren van het Binnen-
        landsch bestuur in Nederlandsch-Indië" [Concubinage among
        the civil servants of the government in the Netherlands
        Indies]. Tijdschrift voor Nederlandsch-Indië. 2d n.s.
        2 (1898):304-14.

2817   AHMADY, MUHAMMAD ALI. Islam dan Perkawinan [Islam and mar-
        riage]. Jakarta: Alma'arif, 1951, 106 pp.

2818   ANOM, I GUSTI NGURAH. "Perkawinan di Bali" [Marriage in
        Bali]. Basis 18, no. 2 (1968):58-61.

2819   ANTON PAIN, Ratu. "An Adoption of the Adat Marriage Rites of
        the Dawanese People of Timor, Indonesia, as a Proposed
        Marriage Rite for Dawanese Catholics." Master's thesis,
        Ateneo de Manila University [Manila], 1972, 122 pp.

2820   al-ATTAR, 'ABD al-NASIR TAWFIQ. Poligami: Ditinjau dari Segi
        Agama, Sosial dan Perundangan-undangan [Polygamy: studied
        from the religious, social, and legal aspects]. Alih
        bahasa: Chadidjah Nasution. Jakarta: Bulan Bintang,
        1976, 344 pp.

2821   BACHTIAR, MUCHONO. "Penganten Remaja dan Problemnya" [The
        young bride and her problems]. Pusara 44, no. 9 (1976):
        345-52.

2822   BAIHAQI, A.K. "Masalah Perceraian di Acheh: Kasus Studi di
        Dua Kecamatan" [The problem of divorce in Acheh: a case
        study of two districts]. Sinar Darussalam 8, no. 64
        (1975):45-54.

2823   BAKRI, SARMAN. "Tentang Perkawinan di Daerah Kalimantan"
        [Marriage in Kalimantan]. Mimbar Indonesia 14, no. 27
        (1960):13-15, 31.

2824   BALANG SIRAN, PENGHULU, and SANDIN, BENEDICT. "Murut Wedding
        in Kalimantan." Sarawak Museum Journal 11 (1963):88-93.

2825   BASRI, ASRUL. "Tata Cara Perkawinan di Bekasi" [Marriage cus-
        toms in Bekasi]. Manusia Indonesia 4, nos. 5/6 (1970):
        169-71.

2826   BERTHE, LOUIS. "Cara Perkawinan dan Susunan Masyarakat pada
        Orang Buna' di Timor Tengah" [Marriage customs and social
        structure of the Buna' people in Central Timor]. Majalah
        Ilmu-ilmu Sastra Indonesia 3, nos. 2/3 (1966):91-128.

2827   _____. "Le mariage par achat et la captation des gendres dans
        une société semi-féodale: les Buna' de Timor central"
        [Arranged marriages with dowry and the captation of sons-
        in-law in a semifeudal society: the Buna' of Central
        Timor]. L'Homme 1, no. 3 (Sept./Dec. 1961):5-31.

2828   BOON, JAMES A. "The Balinese Marriage Predicament:
        Individual, Strategical, Cultural." American Ethnologist
        3, no. 2 (May 1976):191-214.

2829   BORAHIMA, RIDWAN; WAJONG, P.; and DEJENEN. Adat dan Upacara
        Perkawinan Sukubangsa Bugis dan Makasar di Desa Baju Bodoa,
        Sulawesi Selatan ['Adat' and the wedding ceremony of the
        Bugis and Makasar ethnic groups in the village of Baju
        Bodoa, Southern Sulawesi]. Jakarta: Lembaga Sejarah dan
        Antropologi, Departemen Pendidikan dan Kebudayaan, 1974,
        iv, 61 pp.

2830   BRACONIER, A. de. "Het kazerne-concubinaat in Ned.-Indië"
        [The concubinage in the military of the Netherlands
        Indies]. Vragen van de dag 28 (1913):974-95.

2831   BRANDEWIE, ERNEST, and ASTEN, SIMON. "Northern Balunese
        (Timor) Marriage and Kinship: A Study of Symbols."
        Philippines Quarterly of Culture and Society 4, no. 1
        (Mar. 1976):19-30.

2832   BROUWER, M.A.W. "Pelembagaan Sexualitas: Tinjauan Psiko-
        Sosial tentang Perkawinan" [The institution of sexuality:
        a socio-psychological view of marriage]. Prisma 5, no. 5
        (1976):3-12.

2833   BURN, PETER. "Women in Rejang Society: Hazairin's Defence of
        Jujur Marriage." RIMA; Review of Indonesian and Malayan
        Affairs 10, no. 2 (July/Dec. 1976):85-102.

2834   CHAPON, DIANA. Divorce and Fertility: A Study in Rural Java.
        Jogjakarta: Population Institute, Gadjah Mada University,
        1976, x, 115 pp.

2835   ECKLUND, JUDITH LOUISE. "Marriage, Seaworms and Song:
        Ritualized Responses to Cultural Change in Sasak Life."
        Ph.D. dissertation, Cornell University, 1977, 216 pp.
        Abstracted in Dissertation Abstracts International 38,
        no. 7 (Jan. 1978):4239-A. University Microfilms Inter-
        national, order no. 77-28, 710.

2836 ERICKSON, CAROL J. "Isirawa Kinship and Exchange Marriage."
      Irian 5, no. 1 (Feb. 1976):22-44.

2837 FOORE, ANNIE [pseud.]. Indische huwelijken [Marriage in the
      Netherlands Indies]. 2d ed. Rotterdam: n.p.

2838 GALESTIN, A.A. "Huwelijksrecht en huwelijksgebruiken in de
      Timoreschen Archipel" [The marriage rights and rituals in
      the Timor archipelago]. De Indische gids 30 (1908):594-613.

2839 GARTIWA, SUWATI. "Beberapa Macam Perkawinan di Indonesia"
      [Various types of marriages in Indonesia]. Manusia
      Indonesia 2, no. 1 (1968):2-15.

2840 GAZALBA, H.S. "Poligami dan Masalah Sosial" [Polygamy and
      social problems]. Daya Sosial 3, nos. 5/6 (1960):42-64.

2841 GINARSA, KLUT. "Sedikit tentang Adat Upacara Perkawinan,
      Mengandung dan Bersalin bagi Umat Hindu Bali" [Brief notes
      on the customs of marriage, pregnancy, and confinement
      ceremonies of the Hindu Balinese]. Bahasa dan Budaya 6,
      no. 6 (1958):3-9; 7, no. 1 (1958):9-18.

2842 GOETHALS, PETER RANDALL. "Kinship and Marriage in West
      Sumbawa." Ph.D. dissertation, Yale University, 1961,
      169 pp.

2843 _____. "Task Groups and Marriage in West Sumbawa. Inter-
      mediate Societies, Social Mobility and Communication."
      In AMERICAN ETHNOLOGICAL SOCIETY ANNUAL MEETING, 1959.
      Proceedings. Seattle: University of Washington Press,
      1959, pp. 45-59.

2844 GONDOWARSITO, SIDIK. "Sekelumit tentang Tata Cara Adat dan
      Upacara Pengantin Jawa" [Brief notes on the 'adat' system
      and the Javanese wedding ceremony]. Dian 13, no. 3 (1965):
      16-24.

2845 GURITNO, PANDAM. "Beberapa Data mengenai Perkawinan di Desa
      Marangan" [Some data on marriage in the Marangan district].
      Sosiografi Indonesia 1, no. 1 (1959):59-74.

2846 _____. "Beberapa Hasil Penyelidikan tentang Kehidupan
      Perkawinan" [Some research findings on married life].
      Medan Ilmu Pengetahuan 1, no. 3 (1960):230-44.

2847 _____. "A Cross-cultural Study of Divorce: With Special
      Reference to a Javanese Village in Jogjakarta, Central
      Java." Master's thesis, Cornell University, 1964, ix,
      119 pp.

2848 al-HADAR, YASMINE S. Perkawinan dan Perceraian di Indonesia:
      Sebuah Studi Antara Kebudayaan [Marriage and divorce in
      Indonesia: a cross-cultural study]. Jakarta: Lembaga
      Demografi, Fakultas Ekonomi, Universitas Indonesia, 1977,
      iv, 105 pp. Survey Fertilatas Mortalitas Indonesia, 1973.
      Seri Monografi, no. 4.

2849 HAMZAH, A. "'Marola' sebagai Bagian dari Pelaksanaan Adat
      Bugis" ['Marola' (bride follows bridegroom) as a part of
      Buginese marriage custom]. Majalah Universitas Hasanuddin,
      nos. 12/13 (1963):483-85.

2850 HAZAIRIN. De Redjang: de volksordening, het verwantschaps-,
      huwelijks- en erfrecht [The Redjang: their social orga-
      nization, kinship, marriage, and inheritance law]. Bandung:
      A.C. Nix, 1936, 242 pp.

2851 HULL, TERENCE H., and SALADI, RININGSIH. "The Application of
      Hutterite Fertility-weighted Indexes to Studies of Changing
      Marriage Patterns." Jogjakarta: Lembaga Kependudukan,
      Universitas Gadjah Mada, 1977, 14 pp.

2852 "Huwelijk en concubinaat" [Marriage and concubinage]. De
      Indische gids 33 (1911):410-32.

2853 INDONESIA, Angkatan Darat, Dinas Administrasi Personil Militer.
      "Buku Petundjuk tentang Nikah, Talak, Rudjuk (NTR) dan
      Penundjukan Isteri" [Guide to marriage, divorce and recon-
      ciliation, and exposure of wife]. Bandung, 1967, 34 pp.

2854 JAFIZHAM, T. "Persoalan Wanita Muslim Kawin dengan Pria Non
      Muslim" [Problems of Muslim women married to non-Muslim
      men]. Sinar Darussalam 6, no. 49 (1973):11-12; 6, no. 50
      (1973):25-26; 6, no. 51 (1973/74):15-16, 17; 7, no. 52
      (1974):14-16; 7, no. 53 (1974):20-21.

2855 JAYAWARDENA, CHANDRA. "Achenese Marriage Customs."
      Indonesia [Jakarta], no. 23 (Apr. 1977):157-73.

2856 JUNUS, ANDI M. "Adat Perkawinan di Sulawesi Selatan" [Mar-
      riage customs in South Sulawesi]. Dian 13, nos. 5/6
      (1965):16-24.

2857 K.H.D. "Adat Perkawinan sebagai Usaha Kebudayaan" [Marriage
      custom as a cultural effort]. Pusara 18, no. 12 (1957):
      2-3.

2858 KLOOS, P. "Duolinearie afstamming en het matrilaterale cross-
      cousin huwelijk" [Two lineal descent and the matrilineal
      cross-cousin marriage]. Bijdragen tot de taal-, land- en
      volkenkunde 119 (1963):287-99. "Repliek" [Rejoinder].

Bijdragen tot de taal-, land- en volkenkunde 120, no. 3
(1964):368-75.

2859   KOOT, W.D.   _Het concubinaat_ [The concubinage].   Surabaya,
       1905.

2860   KUSUMA, SUTARSIH MULIA.   _Beberapa Aspek Perbedaan Pola_
       Perkawinan di Indonesia Dewasa Ini [Some aspects of the
       differences in marriage patterns in Indonesia today].
       Jakarta: Lembaga Demografi, Fakultas Ekonomi, Universitas
       Indonesia, 1976, ix, 117 pp.

2861   LATIF, H.S.M. NASARUDDIN.   "Kepentingan Nasihat Perkawinan
       bagi Kesejahteraan Keluarga" [The importance of marriage
       counseling for family welfare].   _Majalah Administrasi_
       Negara 3, no. 2 (1961):51-53, 56.

2862   _____.   "Kepentingan Nasihat Perkawinan di Indonesia" [The
       importance of marriage counseling in Indonesia].   _Keluarga_
       Sejahtera 1, no. 2 (1969):33-38.

2863   _____.   _Masalah Perkawinan dan Keluarga_ [Marriage problems and
       the family].   Jakarta: Kiblet, 1970, 176 pp.

2864   _____.   "Nasihat Perkawinan: Proses dan Metodenya" [Marriage
       counseling procedures and methods].   _Keluarga Sejahtera_ 1,
       no. 4 (1969):55-61.

2865   LOEBIS, H.A.A.   "Perkawinan menurut Agama Islam" [Marriage
       according to Islam].   _Lembaran Ilmu Pengetahuan IKIP_
       Semarang 4, no. 5 (1975):11-15.

2866   McDONALD, P., and DURAHMAN, E.H.   "Marriage and Divorce in
       West Java: An Example of the Effective Use of Marital
       Histories." Jakarta: Faculty of Economics, Universitas
       Indonesia, 1974, 34 pp.

2867   MANAFE, D.   "Adat Lembaga dalam Perkawinan di Roti-Lelunuk"
       [Marriage customs on Roti island-Lelunuk].   _Bahasa dan_
       Budaya 9, nos. 1/2 (1961):45-57.

2868   MARETIN, J.V.   "Disappearance of Matriclan Survivals in
       Minangkabau Family and Marriage Relations."   _Bijdragen tot_
       de taal-, land- en volkenkunde 117, no. 1 (1961):168-95,
       304.

2869   "Marriage in Indonesia."   _Asian Review_ 56 (Apr. 1960):140-45.

2870   "Masalah Perkawinan di Bawah Umur" [Child marriages].   _Suara_
       Guru 16, no. 6 (1962):16-20.

2871   MEULEMAN, LUCIE ESTHER. "The Relation of Menarche, Marriage
       and Pregnancy among Native Women of the Netherlands Indies."
       Geneeskundig tijdschrift voor Nederlandsch-Indie (Oct.
       1937):2413-25.

2872   MIDDLEKOOP, P. "Adat Marriage for Christians on the Island of
       Timor." Majalah Ilmu Bahasa, Ilmu Bumi dan Kebudayaan
       Indonesia 536 (1958):538-57.

2873   MOLENAERE, ADRIAAN. Huwelijken onder en zonder de wet in
       Neerlandsch Oost-Indië [Legal and illegal marriages in the
       Netherlands Indies]. Leiden, 1876.

2874   MUNAWARDI. "Pokok-pokok Dasar Perkawinan" [Marriage funda-
       mentals]. Daya Sosial 1, no. 3 (1958):12-16.

2875   NAZIR, M., and AMINULLAH, H. Pedoman Bersuami [Marriage
       manual]. Diterbitkan buku ini untuk mendjundjung tinggi
       putusan Kongress Muhammadijah ke-26 di Djokjakarta.
       Tjet 8. Medan: Saiful, 1950, 80 pp.

2876   NEEDHAM, RODNEY. "Endeh: Terminology, Alliance, and Analy-
       sis." Bijdragen tot de taal-, land- en volkenkunde 124,
       no. 3 (1968):305-35.

2877   _____. "Endeh II, Test and Confirmation" Bijdragen tot de
       taal-, land- en volkenkunde 126, no. 2 (1970):246-58.

2878   _____. "A Note on Kinship and Marriage on Pantara." Bijdragen
       tot de taal-, land- en volkenkunde 112 (1956):285-90.

2879   P.S. "Cinta dalam Pertunangan" [Love and engagement]. Basis
       12, no. 11 (1963):335-39; 12, no. 12 (1963):371-75.

2880   PAPANEK, HANNA. "Marriage, Divorce and Marriage Law Reform in
       Indonesia." Paper presented at the Workshop on the Role
       and Status of Women in Contemporary Muslim Societies,
       Center for the Study of World Religions, Harvard University,
       April 1975.

2881   PRAAG, SEMUEL van. Sexualiteit en huwelijk bij de volkeren der
       aarde: Indonesië [Sexuality and marriage among the peoples
       of the world: Indonesia]. Amsterdam: de Gulden Ster,
       1934, 537 pp.

2882   PRAPANTJA, DJAKARTA. Wedding Ceremonials. Jakarta: Govern-
       ment Printing Office, 196-, 90 pp.

2883   PRASASTABUSANA, D.S. "Pertunangan di Daerah Besuki" [An En-
       gagement in Besuki region]. Indonesia [Jakarta] 5, no. 10
       (1954):560-66.

277

2884 POERBA, SURALEN. "Upacara Adat Perkawinan di Simalungan" [Traditional marriage ceremony in Simalungun]. Bahasa den Budaya 6, no. 5 (1958):36-41.

2885 RAHAJOE, Sri (Mrs.) "Beberapa Bentuk Perkawinan di Daerah Kejawen" [Several types of marriage in the Kajawen region]. Lembaran Ilmu Pengetahuan IKIP Semarang 4, no. 2 (1974):18-21.

2886 SALAM, SOLICHIN. Menindjau Masalah Polygami: Menghidangkan Pendapat 200 Sardjana dan Tjerdik Pandai Indonesia [A study of the problems of polygamy: views of 200 Indonesian graduates and experts]. Jakarta: Tintamas, 1959, 16, 248 pp.

2887 SASTROAMIDJOJO, ACHMAD SENO. Perkahwinan dan Kesehatan [Marriage and health]. Tjet. ke-3. Jakarta: Gunung Agung, 1965, 339 pp.

2888 SETYAWATI, M.R.; LIENTJE; and PRAWIROHARDJO, SOEJONO. "Motivasi Perkawinan di Kalangan Mahasiswa di Yogyakarta" [Marriage motivation among university students in Jogjakarta]. Profil Saraf Jiwa 4, nos. 3/4 (1973):1-6.

2889 SETYONEGORO, KUSUMANTO. "Beberapa Aspek dalam Praktek Marriage Counseling" [Some aspects of marriage counseling in practice]. Jiwa 3, no. 2 (1970):57-64.

2890 SIDARTO (Mrs.) "Adat-Istiadat Perkawinan di Yogyakarta" [Marriage customs in Jogjakarta]. Sana Budaya, no. 13 (1963):29-32.

2891 SINGARIMBUN, MASRI. "Marriage." In Kinship, Descent and Alliance among the Karo Batak. Los Angeles: University of California Press, 1975, pp. 146-88.

2892 SINGARIMBUN, MASRI, and MANNING, CHRIS. "Marriage and Divorce in Mojolama." Indonesia, no. 17 (Apr. 1974):67-82.

2893 STRATIN, L.B. van. De Indonesische bruidschat" [Indonesian dowry]. Ph.D. dissertation, Leiden University, 1927, 116 pp.

2894 SUHADI, KUNTJORO, and AMITABA, I.G.B. "Perkawinan antara Saudara Kembar" [Marriage between twin brother and sister]. Majalah Kedokteran Surabaya 11, no. 1 (1974):26-28.

2895 SOEMARDI. "Liku-liku dan Pengaruh Poligami" [Deviance and the influence of polygamy]. Stannia 3, no. 3 (1972):30-31, 33.

2896   SURYAHADI, I.S. <u>Wanita Pro dan Kontra Poligami</u> [Women for and
       against polygamy]. Semarang: Jajasan Gedung Wanita, 1959,
       vi, 98 pp.

2897   SOETOMO, R. <u>Perkawinan dan Perkawinan Anak-anak</u> [Marriage and
       child marriages]. Weltevreden: Balai Poestakan, 1928,
       58 pp.

2898   SYAH, ISMAIL MUHAMAD. "Adat Perkawinan di Acheh Utara"
       [Marriage customs in North Acheh]. <u>Sinar Darussalam</u> 7,
       no. 58 (1974):25-32.

2899   TANDJUNG, NADIMAH. <u>Islam dan Perkahwinan</u> [Islam and marriage].
       Tjet 4. Jakarta: Bulan Bintang, 1971[?], 167 pp. 1st to
       3d eds. published under title, <u>Perkawinan dan Masjarakat</u>.

2900   TANDOW, O.P. "Pernikahan: Krisis dalam Kehidupan Manusia"
       [Marriage: a crisis in man's life]. <u>Jiwa</u> 2, no. 1 (1969):
       66-70.

2901   TARIGAN, HENRI GUNTUR. "Perkawinan Simbolis pada Masyarakat
       Karo" [Symbolic marriage among the Karo]. <u>Budaya Jaya</u> 4,
       no. 40 (1971):574-76.

2902   _____. "Symbolic Marriage among the Karo." <u>Berita Kajian
       Sumatera</u> 3, no. 2 (May 1974):32-34.

2903   TAULU, H.M. "Perkawinan Bangsa Malesung Zaman Dulu" [Marriage
       of the Malesung community in early times]. <u>Bulletin
       YAPERNA</u> 3, no. 16 (1976):27-49.

2904   TRAJONO. "Dua Upacara, Waktu Ada Perayaan Perkawinan di
       Cilacap" [Two wedding ceremonies in Cilacap]. <u>Bahasa dan
       Budaya</u> 7, no. 5 (1959):189-98.

2905   TUGBY, DONALD J. "The Social Function of Mahr in Upper
       Mandailing, Sumatra." <u>American Anthropologist</u> 61, no. 4
       (Aug. 1959):631-40. ("Mahr" is the payment made by a man
       to any woman he marries.)

2906   TUMENGGUNG, ARSUL. <u>Persiapan sebelum Berumah Tangga</u> [Prepara-
       tions before marriage]. Tjet 2. Medan: Madju, 1959,
       92 pp.

2907   <u>Tuntunan Tjara Memperbaiki Perkawinan: Hasil dari Keputusan
       Mu'tamar Muhamadijah Ke 24 di Bandjarmasin</u> [Ways to improve
       marriage: resolutions of the 24th Muhammadijah Confer-
       ence]. Jogjakarta: Pusat Pimpinan Muhammadijah, 1936[?],
       37 pp.

2908   UNIVERSITAS TANJUNGPURA. Adat Perkawinan Suku Bangsa Melayu
       di Sambas [Marriage customs of the Malays in Sambas
       Regency]. Pontianak: Universitas Tanjungpura, 1979, ii,
       62 pp.

2909   VALERI, VALERIO. "Alliances et échanges matrimoniaux à Seram
       Central (Moluques)" [Marriages and matrimonial exchanges
       in Seram Central (Moluccas)]. L'Homme 15, nos. 3/4
       (July/Dec. 1975):83-107; 16, no. 1 (Jan./Mar. 1976):125-49.

2910   van der KROEF, JUSTUS MARIA. "Women and the Changing Marriage
       Pattern of Indonesia." American Catholic Sociological Re-
       view 18 (1957):113-27. Abstracted in Marriage & Family
       Living 20 (Feb. 1958):87.

2911   WAJONG, P., ed. Adat dan Upacara Perkawinan Jawa di
       Yogyakarta [Javanese marriage customs and ceremonies in
       Jogjakarta]. Jakarta: Lembaga Sejarah dan Antropologi,
       1974, v, 49 pp.

2912   WATI, NGURAH. "Adat Perkawinan di Bali" [Marriage customs in
       Bali]. Dian 13, no. 4 (1965):19-24.

2913   WIDIYATMIKA, MUNANDJAR; SURATHA, I. GEDE; and FRANS, J.A.
       Adat Istiadat dan Upacara Perkawinan Suku Dawan, Sumba dan
       Lamaholot, Daerah Nusa Tenggara Timur [Marriage customs of
       Dawan, Sumba and Lamaholot sub-ethnic groups in Nusa
       Tenggara Timur Province]. Kupang: Biro Penelitian,
       Universitas Nusa Cendana, 1978, vii, 147 pp.

2914   WILKEN, GEORGE ALEXANDER. "Huwelijken tusschen bloedver-
       wanten" [Marriage between relatives]. De gids 54, no. 2
       (1890):478-521.

2915   _____. Over de verwantschap en het huwelijks- en erfrecht
       bij de volken van den Indischen archipel, beschouwd uit het
       oogpunt van de nieuwere leerstellingen op het gebied der
       maatschappelijke ontwikkelingsgeschiedenis [On kinship and
       the marriage and inheritance law among the peoples of the
       Indonesian archipelago, considered in connection with
       recent concepts regarding the history of the development
       of society]. Leiden: E.J. Brill, 1883, 40 pp.

2916   _____. "Plechtigheden en gebruiken bij verlovingen en
       huwelijken bij de volken van den Indischen archipel"
       [Rituals and customs at betrothals and marriages among the
       peoples of the Indonesian archipelago]. Bijdragen tot de
       taal-, land- en volkenkunde 35 (1886):140-219; 38 (1889):
       380-462.

2917 _____. The Sociology of Malayan Peoples. Being Three Essays on Kinship, Marriage, and Inheritance in Indonesia. Translated by G. Hunt. Kuala Lumpur: Committee for Malay Studies, 1921, x, 172 pp. Papers on Malay Subjects, 2d series, 5.

2918 _____. "De verbreiding van het matriarchaat op Sumatra" [The spread of the matriarchate in Sumatra]. Bijdragen tot de taal-, land- en volkenkunde 37 (1888):163-215.

2919 _____. "Verkrachting in kinderhuwelijk" [Rape in child-marriage]. Tijdschrift voor strafrecht 5 (1891):412-28.

2920 YUNUS, KAHRUDIN. Hidup Ber-keluarga Menurut Islam [Family life according to Islam]. Jakarta: Fikiran-Baru, 1968, 115 pp.

2921 ZUIDBERG, LIDA C.L. "Marriage, Fertility and Family Planning in the Kecamatan Serpong: Some Intermediate and Socio-Economic Variables." Leiden: Institute of Cultural and Social Studies, Leyden State University, 1975, 91 pp. Family Planning Project, Serpong, Indonesia. Serpong Paper, no. 16.

2922 ZUIDBERG, LIDA C.L., and HASYIR, ANIDAL. "Family, Marriage and Fertility in Serpong." In Family Planning in Rural West Java. Edited by Lida C.L. Zuidberg. Leiden: Institute of Cultural and Social Studies, Leyden State University; Jakarta: Penerbit Djambatan, 1977, pp. 73-104.

Malaysia

2923 ABANG YUSUF bin ABANG PUTEH. Beberapa Segi Adat Perkahwinan Orang2 Melayu Sarawak Teristimewa di Kuching [Some aspects of the marriage customs among the Sarawak Malays with special reference to Kuching]. Kuala Lumpur: Dewan Bahasa dan Pustaka, 1964, xvii, 113 pp. Dewan Bahasa dan Pustaka, Kuala Lumpur. Siri Pengetahuan Umum, bil. 4.

2924 _____. Some Aspects of the Marriage Customs among the Sarawak Malays with Special Reference to Kuching. Kuala Lumpur: Dewan Bahasa dan Pustaka, 1966, xvii, 98 pp. Dewan Bahasa dan Pustaka, Kuala Lumpur. Siri Pengetahuan Umum, bil. 7.

2925 ABDUL KAHAR bin BADOR. "Kinship and Marriage among the Negri Sembilan Malays." Master's thesis, University of London, 1963, 224 pp.

2926   ABDUL RAHMAN bin MUSTAFA. "Penceraian dalam Islam dan
        Perbandingannya dengan Undang-undang Keluarga Malaysia
        Barat" [Divorce in Islam and its comparison with the family
        law of West Malaysia]. B.A. academic exercise, Universiti
        Kebangsaan Malaysia, 1976.

2927   ABDUL SAMAD HADI, and MUHAMMAD SHAM SANI. "A Note on the
        Geographical Aspect of Marriages: Marriage among the
        Malays in the Kelang District as an Illustration."
        Akademika, no. 5 (July 1974):1-10.

2928   ABU HUSNY [pseud.]. Falsafah Rumah Tangga [Philosophy of
        marriage]. Kuala Lumpur: Pustaka Antara, 1967, 116 pp.

2929   AINON MUHAMMAD. "Tinjauan Kembali Masalah Penceraian dan
        Poligami" [Review of the problems of divorce and polygamy].
        Dewan Masyarakat 13, no. 4 (Apr. 1975):38-39.

2930   ALI bin KARIM. "Pandangan Islam terhadap Adat Perkahwinan di
        Alor Gajah Melaka" [Islamic view on marriage customs in
        Alor Gajah Malacca]. B.A. academic exercise, Universiti
        Kebangsaan Malaysia, 1977.

2931   AMINAH HAJI ZAKARIA. "Hikmat dan Rahsia Kahwin" [The wisdom
        and secrets of marriage]. Wahida 1, no. 5 (June 1979):
        40-47.

2932   AMPALAVANAR RAJESWARY. "Family and Marriage." In "Social
        and Political Developments in the Indian Community of
        Malaya 1920-41." Master's thesis, University of Malaya,
        1969, pp. 162-91.

2933   AMRAN KASIMIN. Konflik Poligami di Malaysia [The conflict of
        polygamy in Malaysia]. Petaling Jaya: Karya Publishing
        House, 1978, 141 pp.

2934   ASMAH AHMAD. "Pola Perkahwinan Pertama Orang-orang Melayu di
        Kuala Lumpur dan Petaling Jaya, Tahun-tahun 70an, Satu
        Analisa Awal" [The pattern of first marriage among the
        Malays in Kuala Lumpur and Petaling Jaya in the 1970s, a
        preliminary analysis]. Ilmu Alam, no. 8 (May 1979):1-7.

2935   AWANG SABTU bin AMPUAN SAPIUDDIN. "Perkahwinan: Upacara dan
        Pandangan Yang Berbeza-beza" [Marriage: varying ceremonies
        and views]. Bahana 3, nos. 9/12 (1968):438-41.

2936   BAARTMANS, FRANCIS. "Marriage among "the Lepo' Tau" Kenyah
        Long Moh, Baram, Sarawak." Related by Tama Kalang Taja.
        Brunei Museum Journal 2, no. 3 (1971):17-30.

2937   BADRUD DUZA M., and BALDWIN, C. STEPHEN. "Non-familial Female
        Roles as Determinants of Female Age at Marriage: Compara-
        tive Perspectives of Tunisia, Sri Lanka, and Malaysia."
        Paper presented at the Annual Meeting of the Population
        Association of America, Seattle, Washington, April 1975.

2938   _____. Nuptiality and Population Policy: An Investigation in
        Tunisia, Sri Lanka, and Malaysia. New York: Population
        Council, 1977, viii, 83 pp.

2939   BORHAN MOHAMMAD ZAIN. "Perceraian Dikalangan Orang-orang
        Melayu" [Divorce among Malays]. Saripati 3, no. 27 (June
        1979):68-70.

2940   CALDWELL, JOHN CHARLES. "Fertility Decline and Female Chances
        of Marriage in Malaya." Population Studies 17, no. 1
        (July 1963):20-32.

2941   CRAIN, JAY BOUTON. "The Lun Dayeh of Sabah, East Malaysia:
        Aspects of Marriage and Social Exchange." Ph.D. disserta-
        tion, Cornell University, 1970, xiii, 410 pp. Abstracted
        in Dissertation Abstracts International 31, no. 12 (June
        1971):7055-56B. University Microfilms International,
        order no. 71-14,618.

2942   EDMONDS, JULIET. "Religion, Intermarriage and Assimilation:
        The Chinese in Malaya." Race 10 (July 1968):57-67.

2943   FAUZI HAJI AWANG al-FATIMY. "Poligami: Beberapa Peraturan
        Yang Asasi" [Polygamy: several basic rules]. Roh Islam
        2, no. 8 (Mar. 1976):25-30.

2944   GORDON, SHIRLE. "Marriage/Divorce in the Eleven States of
        Malaya and Singapore." Intisari 2, no. 2 (1964[?]):23-32.

2945   HABIBAH binti ABDULLAH. "Pandangan Umum tentang Perkahwinan
        di dalam Syariat Islam dan Masyarakat Melayu" [Public
        opinion on marriage in Islam and in Malay society]. B.A.
        academic exercise, Universiti Kebangsaan Malaysia, 1974.

2946   al-HADI, ALWI, Syed. "Marriage Customs. Rules Governing
        Marriage." In Malay Customs and Traditions. Edited by
        Alwi bin Sheikh Alhady. Singapore: Published by Donald
        Moore for Eastern Universities Press, 1962, pp. 22-51;
        87-93.

2947   HEADLY, D. "Some Illanun and Bajau Marriage Customs in the
        Kota Belud District, North Borneo." Royal Asiatic Society
        of Great Britain and Ireland, Malaysian Branch, Journal 24,
        pt. 3 (Oct. 1951):159-62.

2948 HUMPHREYS, J.L. "A Naning Wedding-Speech." Royal Asiatic
Society of Great Britain and Ireland, Straits Branch,
Journal 72 (1916):25-33.

2949 JOACHIM ULOK LAENG. "Why Matched Marriages Should Be
Abolished." Sarawak Gazette, no. 1398 (Aug. 1974):170-71.

2950 KOBLENZER, PETER JOHANN, and CARRIER, NORMAN H. "Fertility,
Mortality and Nuptiality of the Rungus Dusun." Population
Studies 13, no. 3 (Mar. 1960):266-77.

2951 KUCHIBA, MASUO; TSUBOUCHI, YOSHIHIRO; and MAEDA, NARIFUMI,
eds. "Marriage, Divorce and the Family." In Three Malay
Villages: A Sociology of Paddy Growers in West Malaysia.
Honolulu: University Press of Hawaii, 1979, pp. 157-75.

2952 MAEDA, NARIFUMI. "The Malay Family as a Social Circle." Includes comments by Mohd. Dahlan Hj. Aman. Southeast Asian
Studies 16, no. 2 (Sept. 1978):40-72. (Includes discussion
on marriage and divorce.)

2953 MAIMUNAH ARSHAD. "Upacara-upacara dalam Pekahwinan (Adat
Perpatih dan Perbilangan Adat Yang Mengikutnya)" [Wedding
ceremonies: 'adat perpatih' and the 'adat' sayings that
accompany them].

2954 MARZUKI bin HAMID. "Pengaruh Adat Perpatih dalam Pemikiran
Masyarakat Jelebu, Negeri Sembilan dengan Penekanan Khusus
kepada Perkahwinan dan Warisan" [The influence of 'adat
perpatih' on the thinking of the society in Jelebu, Negeri
Sembilan with special emphasis on marriage and inheri-
tance]. B.A. academic exercise, Universiti Kebangsaan
Malaysia, 1975.

2955 MAXWELL, Sir WILLIAM EDWARD. "Test of Virginity amongst the
Malays." Indian Antiquary 17 (1889):61-62.

2956 "Mereka Tak Tentang Poligami" [Those for polygamy]. Wahida
1, no. 3 (Apr. 1979):27-33.

2957 MILLER, HARRY. "Royal Wedding." Straits Times Annual (1957):
33-37.

2958 MINCHIN, GEO. "Marriage Customs of Chinese Residents in the
Straits of Malacca." Notes and Queries on China and Japan
[Hong Kong] (Aug. 1870):81-86.

2959 MOKHTAR bin HAJI MUHAMMAD DOM. Malay Wedding Customs. Kuala
Lumpur: Federal Publications, 1979, viii, 80 pp.

2960   MUHAMMAD ALI MUHAMMAD. "Perkahwinan dan Pencheraian Dika-
        langan Masharakat Melayu (Khususnya bagi Mukim Kelebang
        Besar and Mukim Bukit Rambai, Melaka)" [Marriage and di-
        vorce among the Malays of Mukim Kelebang Besar and Mukim
        Bukit Rambai, Malacca]. B.A. academic exercise, University
        of Malaya, 1965, ii, 58 pp.

2961   MUHAMMED bin SYED HASSAN SHAHABUDDIN, Syed. "The Three Million
        Dollar Wedding." Malaysia in History 4, no. 2 (1958):10-12.

2962   MUHAMMAD ISA FARHY YASSIN. "Poligami: Melihat Paradok dan
        Keanihannya" [Polygamy: Paradox and Peculiarities]. Dewan
        Masyarakat 2 (1975):32-33.

2963   MUHAMMAD ZAIN bin ARIFFIN. "Adat Perkahwinan Dikalangan
        Masyarakat Melayu di Negeri Kedah Dipandang dari Kacamata
        Islam" [Marriage customs among the Malays in Kedah seen
        from the Muslim viewpoint]. B.A. academic exercise,
        Universiti Kebangsaan Malaysia, 1975.

2964   NG, KIM LEONG. "Perkahwinan Champuran Melayu-Tionghua: Satu
        Studi Kes terhadap Lima Keluarga di Kuala Lumpur [Mixed
        marriages: Malay-Chinese; a case study of five families
        in Kuala Lumpur]. B.A. academic exercise, University of
        Malaya, 1972, 95 pp.

2965   NG, LUM SONG. "The Position of Chinese Women in Marriage and
        in the Family: A Comparison of Two Residential Areas in
        Penang." Master's thesis, Universiti Sains Malaysia, 1977,
        xii, 278 pp.

2966   PALMORE, JAMES A., Jr., and ARIFFIN MARZUKI. "Marriage Pat-
        terns and Culmulative Fertility in West Malaysia, 1966-
        1967." Demography 6, no. 4 (Nov. 1969):383-401.

2967   RABUSHKA, ALVIN. "Intermarriage in Malaya: Some Notes on the
        Persistence of the Race Factor." Asia Quarterly 1 (1971):
        103-8.

2968   ROSS, ERUTHEANATHAN JOSEPH. "A Research Made on Some Aspects
        of Marital Breakdowns among the Tamils in Malaya." B.A.
        academic exercise, University of Singapore, 1957, 97 pp.

2969   SABAH, Department of Lands and Surveys. Family Structure in
        Some Kampongs of Kota Kinabalu. Kota Kinabalu, 1969, viii,
        82 pp. Town Planning Bulletin, 14. (Includes information
        on marriage and divorce, fertility, and family planning.)

2970   SABDIN GHANI. "Malay Wedding Customs." Sabah College Borneo
        Society, Journal 4, no. 12 (1962):37-40.

2971   SATHER, CLIFFORD. "Social Rank and Marriage Payments in an
       Immigrant Moro Community in Malaysia." Ethnology 6, no. 1
       (Jan. 1967):97-102.

2972   SHAHAR BANUN JAAFAR. "Sebab dan Akibat Perceraian Dikalangan
       Wanita Melayu" [Causes and effects of divorce among Malay
       women]. B.A. academic exercise, University of Malaya,
       1969, ix, 211 pp.

2973   SHARIPAH binti MOHAMAD. "Fungsi dan Kuasa Wali (Perkahwinan)
       dalam Islam dan serta Perlaksanaannya Menurut Undang-undang
       Pentadbiran" [The function and powers of the 'wali' (mar-
       riage) in Islam as well as its implementation in accordance
       with the laws of the administration]. B.A. academic exer-
       cise, Universiti Kebangsaan Malaysia, 1976.

2974   SHEPPARD, MUBIN. "Bujam Epok Bertundan: A Wedding Ceremony
       Recalled." Federation Museums Journal 9 (1964):32-36.

2975   _____. "The King's Daughter Weds." Straits Times Annual
       (1963):12-16.

2976   SIA, WEE TENG. "Adat Istiadat Perkahwinan Orang-Orang Melayu
       Kelantan" [Marriage customs of Kelantanese Malays]. B.A.
       academic exercise, Universiti Kebangsaan Malaysia, 1977.

2977   SIN, FONG HAN. "Inter-group Marriages among Chinese Speech
       Groups in Sabah, East Malaysia: Continuity and Change."
       Southeast Asian Journal of Social Science 6, nos. 1/2
       (1978):1-16.

2978   SMITH, THOMAS EDWARD. "Marriage, Widowhood and Divorce in
       the Federation of Malaya." In INTERNATIONAL POPULATION
       CONFERENCE, New York, 1961. Proceedings. Vol. 2. London,
       1963, pp. 302-10.

2979   STRAITS SETTLEMENTS, Chinese Marriage Committee. Proceedings
       of the Committee Appointed by His Excellency the Governor
       to Report on Matters Concerning Chinese Marriages.
       Singapore: Government Printing Office, 1926, 155 pp.

2980   _____. Report. Chairman: D. Beatty. Singapore: Government
       Printing Office, 1926, 26 pp. Straits Settlements Legis-
       lative Council. Command Paper, no. 51 of 1926.

2981   STRANGE, HEATHER. "Continuity and Change: Patterns of Mate
       Selection and Marriage Ritual in a Malay Village." Journal
       of Marriage and the Family 38, no. 3 (Aug. 1976):561-71.

2982   SWIFT, MICHAEL GODFREY. "A Note on the Durability of Malay
       Marriages." Man 58, no. 208 (Oct. 1958):155-59.

2983   TAHA ABDUL KADIR. "Kekeluargaan Perkahwinan di Kampong Pandan Baru" [Family and marriage in Kampong Baru]. B.A. academic exercise, University of Malaya, 1970, xiv, 185 pp.

2984   TAN, SENG TEE. "Marriage Customs of Malacca Chinese." *Malacca Guardian Wankang Memento* (Nov. 1933):16-17.

2985   TEOH, JIN INN. "Marriage, Family and Education in Malaysia." 25 pp. Paper presented at the Seminar on Planning for a Better Family Life organized by YWCA and the Federation of Family Planning Associations, Malaysia, held in Genting Highlands, Malaysia, May 1974.

2986   TSUBOUCHI, YOSHIHIRO. "Islam and Divorce among Malay Peasants." In *Southeast Asia: Nature, Society and Development*. Edited by Shinichi Ichimura. Honolulu: University Press of Hawaii, 1976, pp. 24-43.

2987   _____. "Marriage and Divorce among Malay Peasants in Kelantan." *Journal of Southeast Asian Studies* 6, no. 2 (Sept. 1975):135-50.

2988   VON ELM, BARBARA R., and HIRSCHMAN, CHARLES. "Age at First Marriage in Peninsular Malaysia." *Journal of Marriage and the Family* 41, no. 4 (Nov. 1979):877-91.

2989   WINSTEDT, Sir RICHARD OLOF. "The Hindu Element in Malay Marriage Ceremony." *Royal Asiatic Society of Great Britain and Ireland, Straits Branch, Journal* 79 (1918):105.

2990   _____. "Upper Perak Marriage Ceremonies." *Federation Museums Journal* 9, no. 1 (1920):88-92.

2991   YAHAYA bin MAT PIAH. "Peresapan Adat dalam Perkahwinan, Penceraian dan Pembahagian Harta Dikalangan Masyarakat Melayu Larut Utara, Perak" [The influence of 'adat' on marriage, divorce and division of property among the Malay community in Larut Utama, Perak]. B.A. academic exercise, Universiti Kebangsaan Malaysia, 1976, vii, 55 pp.

2992   YONG, SIEW PENG. "Ethnic Intermarriages: A Study in Social Integration." B.Econs. academic exercise, University of Malaya, 1972, vii, 70 pp.

2993   ZAINON JAAFAR. "Penentangan terhadap Poligami" [Opposition to polygamy]. *Dewan Masyarakat* 14, no. 5 (1976):21-24.

2994   ZAITON AJAMAIN. "Satu Tinjauan Am Adat Perkahwinan Suku Kaum Berunai di Sabah" [A general study of the marriage customs of the Berunai clan in Sabah]. *Malaysia in History* 16, no. 2 (1973):23-28.

Philippines

2995   AHERN, HILARY. "The Primacy of Justice in Marriage: A Com-
        parative Study of Marriage and Love." Master's thesis,
        University of Santo Tomas [Manila], 1960.

2996   ALANO, C.M. "A Forum on Women's Rights and Divorce Filipino
        Style." Expressweek 4 (14 Oct. 1976):23-23.

2997   ALCANTARA, RUBEN R. "The Filipino Wedding in Waialua,
        Hawaii: Ritual Retention and Ethnic Subculture in a New
        Setting." Amerasia Journal 1, no. 4 (Feb. 1972):1-12.

2998   ALIP, EUFRONIO M. "Marriage Customs and Ceremonies in the
        Pre-Spanish Philippines." Unitas 10, no. 8 (Feb. 1932):
        440-46.

2999   ALUYEN, RODOLFO M. "Negrito Wedding." Panorama 13 (July
        1961):48-51.

3000   ANGELES, NOLI de LOS. "Marriage and Fertility Patterns in the
        Philippines." Philippine Sociological Review 13, no. 4
        (Oct. 1965):232-48.

3001   ANIMA, NID. Courtship and Marriage Practices among Philippine
        Tribes. Quezon City: Omar Publications, 1975, 146 pp.

3002   _____. "From the Philippines: The Filipino Bride Price."
        Sarawak Gazette, no. 1392 (Feb. 1974):33-34.

3003   _____. "Maguindanao(w) Courtship and Marriage Practices."
        Sarawak Gazette, no. 1395 (May 1974):97-98.

3004   _____. "Marriage Practices in Ilacandia." Sarawak Gazette
        no. 1389 (Nov. 1973):253-54.

3005   BARTON, ROY FRANKLIN. "How Marriage-Prohibitions Arose."
        Philippine Magazine 35, no. 8 (Aug. 1938):380-81, 394.
        (On the Ifugao of the Philippines.)

3006   BATIL, AMOR. "Courtship and Marriage in Apayao." Journal of
        East Asiatic Studies 8, nos. 1/2 (Jan./Apr. 1959):202-6.
        Reprinted from Philippine Magazine 32, no. 5 (May 1935):
        241, 252; 32, no. 6 (June 1935):285, 306.

3007   BELLO, FORTUNATO L. "Marriage Customs among the Maguindanao
        Moslems." Mindanao Historical Journal 11, nos. 2/3/4
        (Apr./Dec. 1962):11-13.

3008   BIELOUSS, EVA GABRIELLE. "The Marriage Ceremonies of the
        Philippine Peoples." Master's thesis, Catholic University,
        1937, 95 pp.

3009   ____. "The Marriage Ceremonies of the Philippine Peoples."
        Primitive Man 11, nos. 3/4 (July/Oct. 1938):37-58.

3010   BILLIET, FRANCIS. "Kalingga Marriage Prohibitions." Primi-
        tive Man 8, no. 3 (July 1935):71-72.

3011   BOVET, THEODORE. "Mixed Marriages and Their Problems."
        Philippine Federation of Private Medical Practitioners,
        Journal 15, no. 1 (Jan. 1966):31-37.

3012   CAINGLET, EMETERIO B. "The Marriage Customs among the Muslims
        in Bongao, Sulu and Their Educational Significance."
        Master's thesis, University of San Carlos [Cebu City,
        Philippines], 1966, 96 pp.

3013   CALHOUN, JOHN W. "American-Filipino Marriages: A Descriptive
        Study of Twenty Inter-racial Problem Marriages Involving
        United States Military Personnel and Filipinos." Master's
        thesis, University of the Philippines [Quezon City], 1955,
        153 pp.

3014   CASTILLO, CARMEN ROBLES. "A Study of the Marriage Customs
        and Practices in the Rural Areas of Bohol." Master's
        thesis, Rafael Palma College [Tagbilaran, Bohol,
        Philippines], 1965.

3015   CASTRO, NILDA M. Marital Social Mobility in the Philippines.
        Singapore: Southeast Asia Population Research Awards Pro-
        gram, International Development Research Centre, Asia Re-
        gional Office and the Ford Foundation, 1976, 100 pp.

3016   CATANGUI-MONCADA, PILAR S. "An Analytical Study of the Mar-
        riage Customs of the Bicol Province (Albay, Camarines
        Norte, Camarines Sur, Catanduanes, Masbate and Sorsogon)."
        Ph.D. dissertation, University of Santo Tomas [Manila],
        1959, 194 pp.

3017   CAVANERO, BENJAMIN G. "The Tribal Marriage." Contemporary
        Review 224, no. 1279 (Feb. 1974):101-4. (On the Badjao,
        Yakan, and Samal.)

3018   COQUIA, JORGE R. "FIDA Resolution." Philippine Studies 8
        (1960):837-40. (On divorce.)

3019   DELANEY, JOHN P. Marriage is Forever. Manila: Manor Press,
        1956, xvi, 106 pp.

3020   DEMING, MARY. "The Influence of Marriage on Occupational Mo-
        bility in the Philippines: A Reformulation of the 'Social
        Mobility Hypothesis.'" Philippine Sociological Review 23,
        nos. 1/4 (Jan./Oct. 1975):55-74.

3021   De TORRE, JOSEPH M., ed. The Church Speaks on Marriage and
       Celibacy. Rizal, Philippines: Sinag-Tala, 1976, 388 pp.

3022   DIA, MATILDE A. "The Problem of Mixed Marriage." Philippine
       Christian Advance 15 (Dec. 1963):17-19.

3023   DUMLAO, ALEJANDRO. "Ancient Marriage Customs among the
       Ilocanos." The College Folio 1, no. 3 (Feb. 1911):135-41.

3024   EGGAN, FRED, and SCOTT, WILLIAM HENRY. "Ritual Life of the
       Igorots of Sagada: Courtship and Marriage." Ethnology 4,
       no. 1 (Jan. 1965):77-111.

3025   ENEREZ, JUAN AREÑO. "A Study of the Courtship and Marriage
       Customs in Leyte." Master's thesis, St. Paul's College
       [Tacloban City, Philippines], 1964, 153 pp.

3026   ESCIO, CARLOS A., Jr. "The Taosug Concept of Marriage in the
       Light of Catholic Principles." Master's thesis, University
       of Santo Tomas [Manila], 1959, vii, 76 pp.

3027   _____. "The Taosug Concept of Marriage in the Light of
       Catholic Principles." Unitas 32 (Jan./Mar. 1959):230-32.

3028   FACULO, A. "Wedding and Other Rites in Apayao." Philippine
       Magazine 32, no. 6 (June 1935):285, 302, 304, 306.

3029   GALANG, RICARDO C. "Bukidnon Marriage." Philippine Magazine
       31, no. 5 (May 1934):195, 209-12. Reprinted in Journal of
       East Asiatic Studies 4 (Apr. 1955):260-64.

3030   GARCIA, EXCELSO. "The Celebration of Mixed Marriages."
       Philippiniana Sacra 2, no. 4 (Jan./Apr. 1967):141-74.

3031   _____. "Particular Discipline on Marriage in the Philippines
       during the Spanish Regime." Philippiniana Sacra 7, no. 22
       (Jan./Apr. 1973):7-85.

3032   GONZALES-MANALO, ROSARIO. "The 'No-Fault' Divorce Decree for
       the Philippines." Fookien Times Philippines Yearbook
       (1976):330-31, 375.

3033   GUTIERREZ-GONZALEZ, ELIZABETH. "Duration of Marriage and
       Perceptual Behaviour of Spouses." Philippine Journal of
       Psychology 1, no. 1 (Nov. 1968):53-61.

3034   HART, DONN V. "The Seventh Sacrament: Tale of a Village Wed-
       ding." Solidarity 10, nos. 5/6 (Sept./Dec. 1976):54-63.

3035 HUNT, CHESTER L., and COLLER, RICHARD W. "Intermarriage and
      Cultural Change: A Study of Philippine-American Marriages."
      Social Forces 35/36, no. 3 (Mar. 1957):223-30.

3036 INDAH, ANNURA. "Didactic Ballad on Marriage as Sung by Indah
      Annura." Sulu Studies 3 (1974):131-50.

3037 JUBAIRA, IBRAHIM A. "Marriage and Morals among Moslem
      Filipinos." Liwayway 36 (2 May 1960):104-5.

3038 JUCO, JORGE M. "Fault, Consent and Breakdown--the Sociology
      of Divorce Legislation in the Philippines." Philippine
      Sociological Review 14, no. 2 (Apr. 1966):67-76.

3039 KIEFER, THOMAS F. "Bride Theft and Abduction of Women among
      the Tausug of Jolo: Some Cultural and Psychological Fac-
      tors." Philippine Quarterly of Culture and Society 2,
      no. 3 (Sept. 1974):123-31.

3040 LACAR, LUIS Q. "Sociological Dynamics in Muslim-Christian
      Marriages in Midsayap and Pikit, North Cotabato." Master's
      thesis, Silliman University [Dumaguete City, Philippines],
      159 pp.

3041 LAPUZ, LOURDES. Filipino Marriages in Crisis. Quezon City:
      New Day Publisher, 1977, 136 pp.

3042 LIQUETE, L. GONZALES. "Old Marriage Customs in the
      Philippines." Philippine Magazine 28, no. 1 (June 1931):
      17-18, 48-51; 28, no. 2 (July 1931):83-84, 92-93; 28,
      no. 5 (Oct. 1931):227-29, 232-34; 28, no. 8 (Jan. 1932):
      402-4, 429-30.

3043 LUMAUIG, G.B. "Wedding Customs of the Gaddangs." Orient 3
      (May 1961):106-8.

3044 LYNCH, FRANK. "The Conjugal Bond Where the Philippines
      Changes." Philippine Sociological Review 8 (July/Oct.
      1960):48-51.

3045 MACALINAO-SOLIS, MIGUELA. "Marital Conflicts: A Study of the
      Causes, Nature, and Extent of Conflicts among 685 Couples
      in the Philippines." Master's thesis, University of
      Philippines [Quezon City], 1939.

3046 MacDONALD, CHARLES. "Une discussion de mariage Palawan:
      texte traduit et commenté" [A discussion on Palawan mar-
      riages]. Asie du Sud-est et monde insulindien 5, no. 4
      (1974):81-139.

3047   McELROY, BARTON L.   "The Ideal and the Practical in Manobo
       Marriage." University of the Philippines Anthropology
       Bulletin 3, no. 1 (1967/1968):3-5.

3048   MAGLANGIT, VIRGINIA R.   "The Maranao Woman: Growing up, Edu-
       cation, Courtship and Marriage." Solidarity 9, no. 7
       (Sept./Oct. 1975):36-42.

3049   MANAWIS, MARIANO D.   "Courtship and Marriage among the Peas-
       ants of Cagayan." Journal of East Asiatic Studies 7
       (1958):224-26; and Philippine Magazine 32, no. 3 (Mar.
       1935):146-47, 150-51.

3050   MANUEL, E. ARSENIO. "Manuvu Marriage." University of the
       Philippines Anthropology Bulletin 1, no. 1 (Sept. 1963):
       8-9, 12.

3051   MARTIN, CARIDAD. "Filipino Wedding: A Comparison of the
       Past and the Present." Social Process in Hawaii 21 (1957):
       50-53.

3052   MARTÍNEZ-ESQUILLO, N. "Conjugal Interaction and Fertility Be-
       haviour among the Filipino Urban Working Class." Master's
       thesis, Ateneo de Manila University [Manila], 1978, 301 pp.

3053   MOSQUEDA, ROMAN P. Marriage and Its Dissolution: Handbook.
       Manila: Quis, 1977, 695 pp.

3054   MURRAY, FRANCIS, Jr. "Increasing Population Pressure and
       Changing Marriage Modes in Central Luzon." Anthropological
       Forum 3, no. 2 (1972):180-88.

3055   NURGE, ETHEL. "Factors Operative in Mate Selection in a
       Philippine Village." Eugenics Quarterly 5, no. 3 (Sept.
       1958):162-68.

3056   OLIZON, N. "A Sikh Wedding in Manila." Sunburst 3 (June
       1975):38-41.

3057   ORACION, TIMOTEO S. "Magahat Marriage Practices." Philippine
       Sociological Review 12, nos. 1/2 (Jan./Apr. 1964):101-9.

3058   PACYAYA, ALFREDO G. "Changing Customs of Marriage, Death,
       and Burial among the Sagada." Practical Anthropology 8,
       no. 3 (May/June 1961):125-33.

3059   PALLESEN, KEMP. "Reciprocity in Samal Marriage." Sulu
       Studies 1 (1972):123-42.

3060   PANGILINAN, LIBERATO G. "Marriage: Time for a Second Look."
       Contemporary Studies 4 (Dec. 1967):208-23.

3061   PAREDES, AMANTE F. "Strange Marriage Customs of the
        Philippines." Orient 6 (Jan. 1964):44-46.

3062   PEREZ, LOURDES C. "Filipino-American Intermarriage: A Study
        of Cross-cultural Role Expectations." Master's thesis,
        Ateneo de Manila University [Manila], 1965, xi, 143 pp.

3063   "Philippine Marriage Ritual Celebration of Matrimony without
        Mass." Boletín eclesiástico de Filipínas 43 (Aug. 1968):
        536-47.

3064   "Philippine Marriage Ritual within the Mass." Boletín ecle-
        siástico de Filipínas 42 (May/June 1968):360-71.

3065   PHILIPPINES. University, Population Institute. Provincial
        and Urban-Rural Differences in Marriage Pattern: The Evi-
        dence for the 1960's. Manila: Population Institute,
        University of the Philippines, 1975, 13 pp.

3066   PINARD, LEO WILLIAM (II). "Courtship in an Urban Visayan
        Setting." Philippine Quarterly of Culture and Society 3,
        nos. 2/3 (June/Sept. 1975):98-113.

3067   QUISUMBING, LOURDES REYNES. Marriage Customs in Rural Cebu.
        Cebu City: University of San Carlos, 1965, viii, 7 pp.
        San Carlos Publications. Series A, Humanities, no. 3.

3068   _____. "A Study of the Marriage Customs of the Rural Popula-
        tion of the Province of Cebu." Master's thesis, University
        of San Carlos [Cebu City, Philippines], 1956, x, 177 pp.

3069   RAFEL, S. STEPHEN. "Intermarriage: A Critical Evaluation of
        Twenty Post World War II Intermarriages between Filipina
        and Americans on the Island of Luzon." Master's thesis,
        University of the Philippines [Quezon City], 1954, 189 pp.

3070   RAMOS, VIOLETA L. "An Analysis of the Marriage and Fertility
        Patterns in Six Barrios in the Philippines." Master's
        thesis, University of the Philippines [Quezon City], 1961,
        ii, 112 pp.

3071   REID, LAWRENCE A. "Ritual and Ceremony in Mountain Province:
        A Guinaang Wedding Ceremony." Philippine Sociological Re-
        view 9, nos. 3/4 (1961):1-53.

3072   REYNO, RODOLFO U. "Customary Wedding among the Ilocanos."
        Philippine Magazine 35, no. 7 (July 1938):336, 346, 348.

3073   REYNOLDS, HARRIET R. "Evaluation and Expectations towards
        Mate Selection and Marriage of Filipino College Students."
        Philippine Sociological Review 14, no. 4 (Oct. 1966):212-26.

3074 _____. "Marriage as a Focal Point in Cultural Orientation of Chinese Adults and Children in Ilocos." Philippine Sociological Review 13, no. 4 (Oct. 1965):249-59.

3075 _____. "Modern Marriage and Courtship among the Isneg, Apayao (Abstract)." Philippine Sociological Review 16, nos. 3/4 (July/Oct. 1968):191-92.

3076 ROSS, C.B. "The Price of a Moro Bride." Asia 30 (1930): 838-41.

3077 ROSS, DANIEL GERALD, S.J. "Manila Family Study: A Cognitive Study of Conjugal Power in the Chinese Family Influenced by Cultural Change." Ph.D. dissertation, University of Notre Dame, 1976, 172 pp. Abstracted in Dissertation Abstracts International 37, no. 3 (Sept. 1976):1829-30-A. University Microfilms International, order no. 76-19,475.

3078 "A Sample of Courtship and Marriage Attitudes Held by U.P. [University of the Philippines] Students." Philippine Sociological Review 2, no. 3 (Oct. 1954):31-45.

3079 SANTA RITA, EMILIO. A Proposed Form of Civil Marriage for Catholics and Other Religious Denominations in the Philippines. Manila: Printed by Novel Publishing Co., 1964, vii, 210 pp.

3080 SAQUING, CHRISTINA. "Marriage Customs of the Ifugaos." Sound and Sense 2, nos. 3/4 (1971):269-73.

3081 SARREAL, ROBERTO A. "Patterns of Age at Marriage in Manila, 1952." Philippine Sociological Review 2, no. 3 (Oct. 1954): 27-30.

3082 SCHEANS, DANIEL J. "The Ilocano: Marriage and the Land." Philippine Sociological Review 13, no. 1 (Jan. 1965):57-62.

3083 SHAHANI, LETICIA RAMOS. "Are the Family and Marriage Still Relevant?" Fookien Times Philippines Yearbook (1978): 330-31.

3084 SMITH, PETER COLIN. "Age at Marriage in the Philippines." Master's thesis, University of the Philippines [Quezon City], 1966, 96 pp.

3085 _____. "Age at Marriage: Recent Trends and Prospects." Philippine Sociological Review 16, nos. 1/2 (Jan./Apr. 1968):1-16.

3086 _____. "Appendix A: Regional Fertility and Nuptiality Indices for 1960." In A Demographic Path to Modernity: Patterns of Early-Transition in the Philippines. Edited by Wilhelm Flieger and Peter Colin Smith. Quezon City: University of the Philippines Press, 1975, pp. 249-60.

3087 _____. "Changing Patterns of Nuptiality." In A Demographic Path to Modernity: Patterns of Early-Transition in the Philippines. Edited by Wilhelm Flieger and Peter Colin Smith. Quezon City: University of the Philippines Press, 1975, pp. 41-81.

3088 _____. "Educational Attainment and Choice of Spouse: An Introductory Note on Assortative Mating." Philippine Sociological Review 23, nos. 1/4 (Jan./Oct. 1975):106-18.

3089 _____. Evidence of Continuing Nuptiality Change: New National Data on Marital Status from the 1970 Census and the 1973 NDS. Manila: Population Institute, University of the Philippines System, 1974, 6 pp.

3090 _____. "Fertility and Nuptiality: The Local-Area Mosaic." In A Demographic Path to Modernity: Patterns of Early-Transition in the Philippines. Edited by Wilhelm Flieger and Peter Colin Smith. Quezon City: University of the Philippines Press, 1975, pp. 201-33.

3091 _____. "The New Nuptiality: Recent Evidence of Delayed Marriage and a Projection to 2000." Philippine Sociological Review 23, nos. 1/4 (Jan./Oct. 1975):7-19.

3092 _____. "Philippine Nuptiality in the Twentieth Century." In Population and Development in Southeast Asia. Edited by John F. Kantner and Lee McCaffrey. Lexington, Mass.: D.C. Heath, 1975, pp. 31-56.

3093 _____. "Philippine Regional and Provincial Differentials in Marriage and Family Building: 1960." Philippine Sociological Review 19, nos. 3/4 (July/Oct. 1971):159-82.

3094 _____. "Trends and Differentials in Nuptiality." In Population of the Philippines, by United Nations Economic and Social Commission for Asia and the Pacific. Bangkok: ESCAP, 1978, pp. 136-59.

3095 SODUSTA, JESUCITA. "A Study of the Marriage Customs and Family Practices of the Inhabitants of Siargao Island." Master's thesis, University of San Carlos [Cebu City, Philippines], 1964, viii, 98 pp.

3096   STINNER, WILLIAM F. "Modernization, Marriage and Childbear-
        ing: A Synthesis of Research Findings." In A Demographic
        Path to Modernity: Patterns of Early-Transition in the
        Philippines. Edited by Wilhelm Flieger and Peter Colin
        Smith. Quezon City: University of the Philippines Press,
        1975, pp. 3-37.

3097   _____. "Urbanization and Household Structure in the
        Philippines." Journal of Marriage and the Family 39, no. 2
        (May 1977):377-86.

3098   STOKES, W.R. "The Physician's Role in Improving Marital Com-
        munication." Philippine Federation of Private Medical
        Practitioners, Journal 15, no. 1 (1966):15-21.

3099   SUGUITAN, LAURA A. "A Study of the Factors on Successful Mar-
        riage among Teachers." Master's thesis, Union College of
        Manila, 1949. vii, 103 pp.

3100   TAN, BELEN, and MEDINA, GATUE. "Changing Marriage Patterns
        among Slum Dwellers." General Education Journal 21 (1971):
        31-58.

3101   TOLENTINO, ARTURO M. "Do We Have Easy Divorce Now?"
        Philippine Review 1 (May 1943):1-8.

3102   VALDELLON, RENATO. "The New Marriage Rite of the Philippines."
        Contemporary Studies 5, no. 3 (1968):168-76.

3103   VANOVERBERGH, MORICE. "The Isneg Life Cycle: II. Marriage,
        Death and Burial." Catholic Anthropological Conference,
        Publications 3, no. 3 (Dec. 1938):187-280.

3104   WIDEMAN, BERNARD. "The Woman's Case for Divorce." Far East-
        ern Economic Review 90, no. 47 (Nov. 1975):30, 35.

3105   YABYABIN, ANACLETO P. "Courtship and Marriage among the
        Mangyans." Panorama 10 (Jan. 1958):5-9.

3106   ZAIDE, CEFERINO A., Jr., and FABELLA, GABRIEL, Jr. Family
        Relationship: A Sociological Interpretation. Manila:
        College Professors Publishing Corp., 1967, 169 pp. (In-
        cludes marriage.)

Singapore

3107   APPLIED RESEARCH CORPORATION. A Study in Non-Muslim Divorce
        in Singapore, by Applied Research Corporation for Ministry
        of Social Affairs. Singapore: Applied Research Corpora-
        tion, 1979, ix, 164 pp.

3108   CHEW, SOCK FOON, and MacDOUGALL, JOHN ARTHUR. <u>Forever Plural:</u>
        <u>The Perception and Practice of Inter-communal Marriage in</u>
        <u>Singapore</u>. Athens: Ohio University, 1977, 61 pp. Ohio
        University, Center for International Studies. Southeast
        Asia Series, no. 45.

3109   DJAMOUR, JUDITH. <u>Kekeluargaan dan Perkahwinan Orang Melayu</u>
        <u>Singapura</u> [Malay kinship and marriage in Singapore].
        Kuala Lumpur: Dewan Bahasa dan Pustaka, 1979, x, 209 pp.
        Siri Pelajaran Tinggi DBP, no. 122.

3110   _____. <u>Malay Kinship and Marriage in Singapore</u>. London:
        University of London, 1959, 151 pp. London School of Eco-
        nomics and Political Science. Monographs on Social Anthro-
        pology, no. 21.

3111   _____. <u>The Muslim Matrimonial Court in Singapore</u>. London:
        Athlone Press, 1966, 191 pp. London School of Economics
        and Political Science. Monographs on Social Anthropology,
        no. 31.

3112   FREEDMAN, MAURICE. <u>Chinese Family and Marriage in Singapore</u>.
        New York: Johnson Reprint Corp., 1970, 249 pp. First pub-
        lished in London in 1957.

3113   _____. "Chinese Kinship and Marriage in Singapore." <u>Journal</u>
        <u>of Southeast Asian Studies</u> 3, no. 2 (Sept. 1962):65-73.

3114   GORDON, SHIRLE. "Marriage/Divorce in the Eleven States of
        Malaya and Singapore." <u>Intisari</u> 2, no. 2 (1964[?]):23-32.

3115   HASSAN, RIAZ. "Interethnic Marriage in Singapore: A Socio-
        logical Analysis." <u>Sociology and Social Research</u> 55, no. 3
        (Apr. 1971):305-23.

3116   _____. <u>Interethnic Marriage in Singapore: A Study in Inter-</u>
        <u>ethnic Relations</u>. Singapore: Institute of Southeast Asian
        Studies, 1974, vii, 85 pp. Institute of Southeast Asian
        Studies, Singapore. Occasional Paper, no. 21.

3117   _____. "The Religious Factor in Inter-ethnic Marriage in
        Singapore." <u>Sedar</u> (1969/70):47-52.

3118   HASSAN, RIAZ, and BENJAMIN, GEOFFREY. <u>Ethnic Outmarriage</u>
        <u>Rates in Singapore: The Influence of Traditional Socio-</u>
        <u>Cultural Organisation</u>. Singapore: University of
        Singapore, 1972, 20 pp. University of Singapore,
        Department of Sociology. Working Paper, no. 1.

3119 _____ . "Ethnic Outmarriage Rates in Singapore: The Influence
of Traditional Socio-Cultural Organization." Journal of
Marriage and the Family 35, no. 4 (Nov. 1973):731-38.

3120 _____ . "Ethnic Outmarriage Rates in Singapore: The Influence
of Traditional Socio-Cultural Organization." In INTER-
NATIONAL CONGRESS OF ANTHROPOLOGICAL AND ETHNOLOGICAL
SCIENCES, 9th, Chicago, 1973. Changing Identities in
Modern Southeast Asia. Edited by David J. Banks. The
Hague: Mouton, 1976, pp. 111-26.

3121 HO, YAM PENG. "Baba Wedding." Straits Times Annual (1969):
58-60.

3122 KAYE, BARRINGTON. "Marital Status." In Upper Nankin Street
Singapore: A Sociological Study of Chinese Households Liv-
ing in a Densely Populated Area. Singapore: University of
Malaya Press, 1960, pp. 167-89.

3123 KUO, EDDIE CHEN YU, and HASSAN, RIAZ. Some Social Concomitants of Interethnic Marriage in Singapore. Singapore:
Department of Sociology, University of Singapore, 1974,
28 pp. Singapore. University, Department of Sociology.
Working Paper, no. 32.

3124 _____ . "Some Social Concomitants of Interethnic Marriage in
Singapore." Journal of Marriage and the Family 38, no. 3
(Aug. 1976):549-60.

3125 KUO, EDDIE CHEN YU; HASSAN, RIAZ; and WONG, ALINE K. The Contemporary Family in Singapore: Structure and Change.
Singapore: Singapore University Press, 1979, x, 306 pp.
(Includes chapters on women's status, working mothers, marriage, and divorce.)

3126 LEE, CHE FU; POTVIN, RAYMOND H.; and VERDIECK, MARY J.
"Interethnic Marriage as an Index of Assimilation: The
Case of Singapore." Social Forces 53, no. 1 (Sept. 1974):
112-19.

3127 LEE, GEOK BEE. "Inter-ethnic Marriage in the Islamic Religion." B.A. academic exercise, University of Singapore,
1978, iii, 67 pp.

3128 LEON, JOSEPH J., and SAKIHARA, G. KAZUO. "Further Analysis,
the Case of Singapore: Marriage Patterns as an Indicator
of Assimilation." International Journal of Sociology of the
Family 6, no. 2 (Autumn 1976):291-97.

3129 LIM, JANET YUEN KHENG. "Interethnic Marriage in Singapore: A
Study of 15 Cases." B.A. academic exercise, University of
Singapore, 1975, 91 pp.

3130   MATHEW, MARY. "Marriage Patterns and Community Identity
        among the Syrian Christians in Singapore." B.A. academic
        exercise, University of Singapore, 1975, 74 pp.

3131   MUHAMMAD KHALIL bin MUHAMMAD NASIR. "Divorce and the Muslim
        Husband." B.A. academic exercise, University of Singapore,
        1969, 114 pp.

3132   "Muslim Marriage and Divorce in Singapore." World Muslim
        League Monthly Magazine 3 (Oct./Nov. 1966):18-26.

3133   NUR AINI binti MUBARAK. "Marriage Relationships in the Malay
        Community." B.A. academic exercise, University of
        Singapore, 1967, 113 pp.

3134   SAW, SWEE HOCK. "The Changing Married Population in
        Singapore during 1947-1957." South-east Asian Journal of
        Sociology 3 (1970):62-63.

3135   SEMINAR/FORUM ON SEX, LOVE AND MARRIAGE, Singapore, 1970.
        Sex, Love and Marriage: Proceedings. Organized by the
        Beatty Secondary School Singapore. Singapore: Chopmen
        Enterprises, 1971, 80 pp.

3136   SEMINAR ON MARRIAGE IN GENERAL, Singapore, 1978. Papers and
        Programme. Organized by the Singapore Association of
        Women Lawyers. Singapore, 1978, 100 pp.

3137   SINGAPORE, Registry of Muslim Marriages and the Shariah
        Court. Annual Report, 1960-. Singapore: Government
        Printing Office.

3138   SIRAJ, MEHRUN. "Muslim Marriages in Singapore." World Muslim
        League Monthly Magazine 1 (Jan. 1964):41-50.

3139   STIRLING, WILLIAM GEORGE. "A Chinese Wedding in the Reform
        Style." Royal Asiatic Society of Great Britain and
        Ireland, Malaysian Branch, Journal 3, pt. 3 (Dec. 1925):
        1-5.

3140   STRAITS SETTLEMENTS, Chinese Marriage Committee. Proceedings
        of the Committee Appointed by His Excellency the Governor
        to Report on Matters concerning Chinese Marriages, 1926.
        Singapore: Government Printing Office, 1926, 155 pp.

3141   _____. Report. Chairman: D. Beatty. Singapore: Government
        Printing Office, 1926, 26 pp. Straits Settlements Legis-
        lative Council. Command Paper, no. 51 of 1926.

3142   TAI, CHING LING. "A Sociological Analysis of Divorce in
        Singapore." Southeast Asian Journal of Social Science 3,
        no. 1 (1975):61-84.

3143   TEO, SERENE LEE HOON. "Marital Conflict and Divorces in
        Singapore." B.Soc.Sc. academic exercise, University of
        Singapore, 1976, v, 118 pp.

3144   THEODORSON, GEORGE A. "Romanticism and Motivation to Marry in
        the United States, Singapore, Burma, and India." Social
        Forces 44, no. 1 (Sept. 1965):17-27.

3145   TOPLEY, MARJORIE DOREEN. "Ghost Marriages among the Singapore
        Chinese." Man 55 (1955):29-30. "A Further Note." Man 56
        (1956):71-72.

3146   WEE, ANN E. "Chinese Women of Singapore: Their Present
        Status in the Family and in Marriage." In Women in the New
        Asia. Edited by Barbara E. Ward. Paris: Unesco, 1963,
        pp. 376-408.

3147   WONG, SZE TAI. "Effects of Marital Crisis and Marital Break-
        down on Children: A Review." Academy of Medicine,
        Singapore, Annals (Jan. 1974):60-66.

3148   YEH, STEPHEN HUA KUO. "Chinese Marriage Patterns in
        Singapore." Ph.D. dissertation, New York University, 1969,
        301 pp. Abstracted in Dissertation Abstracts International
        31, no. 3 (Sept. 1970):1398-A. University Microfilms
        International, order no. 70-16,119.

3149   _____. "Chinese Marriage Patterns in Singapore." Malayan
        Economic Review 4, no. 1 (1964):102-12.

3150   _____. "Love and Courtship among Singapore Chinese: A Study
        in Social Change." South-east Asian Journal of Sociology
        1, no. 1 (May 1968):25-38.

Thailand

3151   ANUMAN RAJATHON, Phrayā. The Story of Thai Marriage Custom.
        Bangkok: National Culture Institute, 1954, 15 pp. Thai
        Culture Series, no. 13.

3152   _____. "The Story of Thai Marriage Custom." Asian Culture
        Quarterly 1, no. 1 (Autumn 1973):55-62.

3153   APHICHAT CHAMRATRITHIRONG. "Fertility, Nuptiality and Migra-
        tion in Thailand, 1970 Census: The Multiphasic Response
        Theory." Ph.D. dissertation, Brown University, 1976,
        277 pp. Abstracted in Dissertation Abstracts International
        38, no. 1 (July 1977):499-A. University Microfilms Inter-
        national, order no. 77-14,098.

3154   _____. Thai Marriage Pattern: An Analysis of the 1970 Census Data. Bangkok: Institute for Population and Social Research, 1978, 38 pp.

3155   CHAMRIENG BHAVICHITRA. "Thai Marriage and Family." Master's thesis, Indiana University, 1962, v, 76 pp.

3156   "Courtship and Marriage." Siam Repository 5 (1873):46-50.

3157   GARDINER, HARRY W.; SINGH, U.P.; and D'ORAZIO, DONALD E. "The Liberated Woman in Three Cultures: Marital-Role Preferences in Thailand, India, and the United States." Human Organization 33, no. 4 (Winter 1974):413-15.

3158   KAMBHU, LEIGH R. Thailand Is Our Home: A Study of Some American Wives of Thais. Cambridge, Mass.: Center for International Studies, Massachusetts Institute of Technology, 1963, i, 113 pp.

3159   KEMP, JEREMY H. "Initial Marriage Residence in Rural Thailand." In In Memoriam, Phya Anuman Rajathon: Contribution in Memory of the Late President of the Siam Society. Edited by Tej Bunnag and Michael Smithies. Bangkok: Siam Society, 1970, pp. 73-85.

3160   la LOUBERE, SIMON de. "Concerning the Marriage and Divorce of the Siameses [sic]." In The Kingdom of Siam. Reprint ed. Kuala Lumpur: Oxford University Press, 1969, pp. 51-53.

3161   MAURER, KENNETH; RATAJCZAK, ROSALINDA; and SCHULTZ, T. PAUL. Marriage, Fertility, and Labor Force Participation of Thai Women: An Econometric Study. Santa Monica: Rand Corporation, 1973, xiv, 54 pp. Rand Report, R-829.

3162   MILES, DOUGLAS JAMES. "Marriage, Agriculture and Ancestor Worship among the Pulangka Yao." Ph.D. dissertation, University of Sydney, 1976, xi, 466 pp.

3163   _____. "Yao Bride-Exchange Matrifiliation and Adoption." Bijdragen tot de taal-, land- en volkenkunde 128, no. 1 (1972):99-117. (Study based principally on the Chiengrai Province, North Thailand.)

3164   REYNOLDS, CRAIG JAMES. "A Nineteenth Century Thai Buddhist Defense of Polygamy and Some Remarks on the Social History of Women in Thailand." Paper presented at the Seventh Conference of the International Association of Historians of Asia, August 1977, held in Bangkok, Thailand.

3165   RILEY, JAMES NELSON. "Cohabitation, Natality, and Mortality
       in Rural Thailand and Burma." In Culture, Natality and
       Family Planning. Edited by John F. Marshall and Steven
       Polgar. Chapel Hill: Carolina Population Center, Univer-
       sity of North Carolina, 1976, pp. 24-49.

3166   SEIDENFADEN, ERIK. "Mon Influence on Thai Institutions."
       Siam Society, Journal 36, no. 1 (1945):41-66. (On customs
       of settling third of property on wife upon divorce.)

3167   SMITH, HAROLD E. "Polygamy and Marriage Registration in
       Thailand." Southeast Asia 2, no. 3 (1973):291-300.

3168   _____. "The Thai Family: Nuclear or Extended." Journal of
       Marriage and the Family 35, no. 1 (Feb. 1973):136-41. (In-
       cludes the subject of marriage.)

3169   SUTHEP SOONTORNPASUCH. "The Thai Family: A Study of Kinship
       and Marriage among the Central Thai Peasantry." Master's
       thesis, University of London, School of Oriental and Afri-
       can Studies, 1963, vi, 206 pp.

MARRIED WOMEN AND MOTHERS

(On maternal welfare and health
services see Health and Welfare)

3170   ABELGAS, M.G. "The Working Mother and Women's Lib." Focus 3
       (8 Nov. 1975):32-33. (Philippines.)

3171   ALBERTO, CYNTHIA S. "How Husband-Wife Relations Affect Fer-
       tility Behavior: A Study of Urban Working Class Filipino
       Couples." Options for Policy and Practice 4, no. 2
       (Mar./Apr. 1978):1-16.

3172   ALILING, RACHEL YAMBAO. "Food and Nutrition Attitudes of
       Rural Mothers in Eight Barrios of Cavite: Implications for
       a National Nutrition Education Program." Ph.D. disserta-
       tion, University of the Philippines [Quezon City], 1976,
       vii, 134 pp.

3173   ANOS, NORA B. "A Study of the Problems That Affect the Mari-
       tal Adjustment of the Husbands and Wives of Eulogio
       Rodriguez Memorial School of Arts and Trades, 1969-71."
       Master's thesis, Arellano University [Manila], 1974, viii,
       130 pp.

3174 ANTERO, LINA B. "The Home and Family Backgrounds of Selected
Married Women Teachers in the Public Elementary Schools of
Naga City." Ed.D. dissertation, Centro Escolar University
[Manila], 1974, xvii, 406 pp.

3175 ARAULLO, SOCORRO R. "The Culture of the Urban Dual-Career
Families of Barrio Balong-Bato, San Juna, Rizal." Ph.D.
dissertation, Centro Escolar University [Manila], 1975, 13,
529 pp.

3176 ARCEO-ORTEGA, ANGELINA. "A Career-Housewife in the Philippines." In Women in the New Asia. Edited by Barbara E.
Ward. Paris: Unesco, 1963, pp. 365-73.

3177 BRUSELAS, E.D. "Working Housewife or Working Career Wife?"
Focus 3 (8 Nov. 1975):36-37. (Philippines.)

3178 CANLAS, DANTE B., and MUHAMMAD RAZAK. "Education and Labor
Force Participation of Married Women: West Malaysia 1970."
Quezon City: School of Economics, University of the
Philippines, 1979, 22 pp. Philippines. University, School
of Economics. Discussion Paper, 7910.

3179 CASTRO, JUDY, and REYNES-SALAZAR, CELIA. The Labor Force Participation Rate of Married Women in Pasig. Quezon City:
Institute of Economic Development and Research, University
of the Philippines, 1976, 28 pp. IEDR Discussion Paper,
no. 76-6.

3180 CHANDRA, L.S. "Peranan Ibu dalam Pendidikan Anak dalam
Masyarakat Urban" [The role of the mother in a child's
education in urban society]. Jiwa 10, no. 1 (1977):77-82.
(Indonesia.)

3181 CONCEPCIÓN, MERCEDES B. "Fertility Differences among Married
Women in the Philippines." Ph.D. dissertation, University
of Chicago, 1963, 140 pp.

3182 CURABO, YOLINDA DIAO. "A Study of the Gainfully Employed
Mothers Who Are Teachers in Dipolog, Zamboanga del Norte."
Master's thesis, Silliman University [Dumaguete City,
Philippines], 1965, xi, 101 pp.

3183 _____. "A Study of the Gainfully Employed Mothers Who Are
Teachers in Dipolog, Zamboanga del Norte." Silliman Journal 17, no. 2 (1970):227-28.

3184 DURAN, MAGDALENA. "Employment Discrimination against Married
Women." Philippine Labor 1 (Oct. 1962):23-24.

3185 ENCARNACIÓN, JOSÉ. <u>A Note on Labor Force Participation of Married Women: Philippines, 1968</u>. Quezon City: Institute of Economic Development and Research, University of the Philippines, 1972, 6 pp. IEDR Discussion Paper, no. 72-21.

3186 FATIMAH HAMID-DON. "Wanita sebagai Suri Rumahtangga dan Pembangunan Negara" [Women as housewives and national development]. <u>Wanita</u>, no. 79 (Feb. 1976):76-77. (Malaysia.)

3187 FLORES, PURA M. "Career Women and Motherhood in a Changing Society." <u>Philippine Educational Forum</u> 14, no. 1 (Mar. 1965):50-56.

3188 FLORES, PURA M., and GOMEZ, ILUMINADA. "Maternal Attitudes toward Child Rearing." <u>Philippine Educational Forum</u> 13, no. 3 (Nov. 1964):27-40.

3189 GABE, N.D. "The Joys and Woes of a Working Mother." <u>Focus</u> 3 (25 Jan. 1975):36-37. (Philippines.)

3190 GARCIA, MIGUEL. "The Working Mother." Ph.D. dissertation, University of Santo Tomas [Manila], 1967, 60 pp.

3191 _____. "Working Mother." <u>Philippiniana Sacra</u> 2 (Jan./Apr. 1967):58-100.

3192 GOH, SIONG HWEE. "Some Singapore Mothers with Large Families. A Study of Some Aspects of Life of Twenty-Six Mothers Who Have Recently Given Birth to Their Tenth or Higher Child in Kandang Kerbau Maternity Hospital." Thesis for the Diploma in Soc.Sc., University of Singapore, 1959, 208 pp.

3193 GORDON, SHIRLE. "The Condition of Our Plantation Workers: The Mothers and Fathers of the Children." <u>Intisari</u> 3, no. 4 (1970):49-55. (Malaysia.)

3194 GURITNO, PANDAM. "Beberapa Hasil Penyelidikan tentang Kehidupan Perkawinan" [Some research findings on married life]. <u>Medan Ilmu Pengetahuan</u> 1, no. 3 (1960):230-44.

3195 HACKENBERG, BEVERLY H., and HACKENBERG, ROBERT A. "Social Indicators of Premarital and Postmarital Labor Force Participation among Women in Region XI: Southeast Mindanao." Manila: WID Special Studies Program, Institute of Philippine Culture, Ateneo de Manila University, 1979, 15 pp.

3196 HAMIDJOJO-MUNAR, SUNDARI. <u>Ibu dan Pendidikan</u> [Mother and education]. 5th ed. Medan: Pustaka Andalas, 1955, 68 pp.

3197   HILOMEN-GUERRERO, SYLVIA. "An Analysis of Husband-Wife Roles
        among Filipino Professionals at U.P. Los Banos Campus."
        Philippine Sociological Review 13, no. 4 (Oct. 1965):
        275-81.

3198   IBAÑEZ-LUCIANO, JOSEFA. "Some Problems of Children as Related
        to Mother-Child Relationship: Its Implication for School
        Social Work." Master's thesis, Philippine Women's Univer-
        sity [Manila], 1967.

3199   INDRAKILA, SONTRANG. "Fungsi Kaum Wanita sebagai Isteri, Ibu
        Produsen dan Konsumen" [The functions of women as wives,
        mothers, producers, and consumers]. Mawas Diri 4, no. 4
        (1975):51-56. (Indonesia.)

3200   JAAFAR bin ABDUL RAHIM. "Hak untuk Bekas-Bekas Isteri
        Peneroka LKTP" [The rights of ex-wives of FELDA settlers].
        Dewan Masyarakat 13, no. 3 (Mar. 1975):9-10. (Malaysia.)

3201   JACOB, FLORANIE. "Personality Need Patterns and Satisfactory
        Marital Interaction among Filipino Couples." Master's
        thesis, Ateneo de Manila University [Manila], 1974, viii,
        106 pp.

3202   JAYME, BRIGIDA L. "Family Role and Fertility Behaviour of the
        Upper Class Urban Married Filipina." 30 pp. Paper pre-
        sented at the Seminar on Labor Supply under the joint
        sponsorship of the Council for Asian Manpower Studies and
        the Organization of Demographic Associates held in Makati,
        Rizal, Philippines, June 1976.

3203   _____. Family Roles and Fertility Patterns of Two Generations
        of Urban Upper Class Filipino Wives and Mothers.
        Singapore: Southeast Asia Population Research Awards
        Program (SEAPRAP), International Development Research
        Centre, Asia Regional Office and the Ford Foundation,
        1976, 75 pp. SEAPRAP Research Report, no. 6.

3204   JAYME-HO, TERESA. Time Allocation, Home Production and Labor
        Force Participation of Married Women: An Exploratory
        Study. Quezon City: Institute of Economic Development
        and Research, 1976, 38 pp. IEDR Discussion Paper, no.
        76-8.

3205   JIMENEZ, RAMON T. "The Filipino Working Mother and the
        Children She Sends to School." Contemporary Studies 2,
        nos. 2/3 (June/Sept. 1965):126-35.

3206   KAYE, BARRINGTON. "Marital Status." In Upper Nankin Street
        Singapore: A Sociological Study of Chinese Households
        Living in a Densely Populated Area. Singapore: University
        of Malaya Press, 1960, pp. 167-89.

3207   KIM, BOK LIM C. "Asian Wives of U.S. Servicemen: Women in
       Shadows." Amerasia Journal 4 (1977):91-117. (On women
       from Japan, Korea, the Philippines, Thailand, and Vietnam.)

3208   KUO, EDDIE CHEN YU, and WONG, ALINE K. The Contemporary Fam-
       ily in Singapore: Structure and Change. Singapore:
       Singapore University Press, 1979, x, 306 pp. (Includes
       chapters on women's status, working mothers, etc.)

3209   LEE, GUAT CHYE. "Children with Working Mothers." B.A. aca-
       demic exercise, University of Singapore, 1972, 86 pp.

3210   LIM, PILAR H. "The Role of Mothers Today." Centro Escolar
       University, Manila, Graduate and Faculty Studies, no. 20
       (1969):9-12.

3211   MACEDA, DELFINA SALVADOR. "Use of Time by Married Homemakers
       in the Teaching Force, Manila, Philippines." Ph.D. disser-
       tation, Cornell University, 1958, 183 pp. Abstracted in
       Dissertation Abstracts 19, no. 10 (Apr. 1959):2597. Uni-
       versity Microfilms International, order no. 59-686.

3212   MONTAGU, ASHLEY. "Emotional Etiquette for Working Wives."
       Orient 4 (June 1962):103-18. (Philippines.)

3213   NEGADO, AURORA SEBASTIAN. "Causes of Marital Conflict among a
       Hundred and Nineteen Cases under Study." Master's thesis,
       Centro Escolar University [Manila], 1953, vi, 215 pp.

3214   ORRATHAI SRITHONGS. "A Comparative Study of Attitudes towards
       Child Rearing Practices between Mothers of Juvenile Delin-
       quents and Mothers of Normal Adolescents." Master's thesis,
       Chulalongkorn University, 1968, vi, 76 pp.

3215   PABLO, PATRICIA O. "A Comparative Analysis of Selected Socio-
       logical Variables Affecting Working and Non-working Mothers,
       and School Achievement of Pre-adolescent Children in the
       Division of City Schools." Master's thesis, St. Louis
       University [Baguio City, Philippines], 1972, 107 pp.

3216   PAGSIBIGAN, GLORIA M. "Attitudes towards Working Mothers of
       Children in Six Selected Public Elementary Schools in
       Manila." Master's thesis, Centro Escolar University
       [Manila], 1968, 115 pp.

3217   _____. "Attitudes towards Working Mothers of Children in Six
       Selected Public Elementary Schools in Manila." Centro
       Escolar University, Manila, Graduate and Faculty Studies,
       no. 19 (1968):71-85.

3218   PALABRICA, MARILOU B. "A Study of Attitudes and Motives of
        Married Women That Underlie the Large Family in Modern
        Urban Cagayan de Oro." Master's thesis, Xavier University
        [Cagayan de Oro City, Philippines], 1969, 68 pp.

3219   PAQUEO, VICENTE B., and ANGELES, EDNA. An Analysis of Wife's
        Labor Force Participation in the Philippines and the
        Threshold Hypothesis. Quezon City: Institute of Economic
        Development and Research, School of Economics, University
        of the Philippines, 1979, 41, 3 pp. University of the
        Philippines. Discussion Paper, 79-13.

3220   POPKIN, BARRY MICHAEL. "The Production of Child Welfare in
        Rural Filipino Households: The Impact of Changes in the
        Role of the Mother." 33 pp. Paper presented at the
        Seminar on Labor Supply, under the joint sponsorship of the
        Council for Asian Manpower Studies and the Organization of
        Demographic Associates held in Makati, Rizal, Philippines,
        June 1976.

3221   POPKIN, BARRY MICHAEL, and SOLON, F. Income, Time, the Work-
        ing Mother and Child Nurtiture. Quezon City: Institute
        of Economic Development and Research, 1975, 40 pp. IEDR
        Discussion Paper, no. 75-9.

3222   PRIBADI, SUHUD. "Peranan Ibu dalam Pembentukan Kepribadian"
        [The role of the mother in personality development]. Daya
        Sosial 3, nos. 1/2 (1960):78-72. (Indonesia.)

3223   PRIJONO, ONNY S. "Suatu Dilemma untuk Ibu-ibu Yang Bekerja:
        Dengan Fokus terhadap Ibu-ibu Rumah Tangga di Kota Yang
        Bekerja di Luar Rumahnya" [A dilemma for working mothers:
        with a focus on urban wives who work outside their homes].
        Analisa 7, no. 5 (May 1978):391-406.

3224   RAMOS, MAXIMO. "Secrets of the Barrio Housewife." Philippine
        Magazine 35, no. 9 (Sept. 1938):426, 430, 435.

3325   REINOSO, JUVENAL. "The Working Mother." Philippine Labor 2,
        no. 2 (Feb. 1963):24-25.

3226   RIVERA, EFREN. "Wives, Be Subject to Your Husbands."
        Philippiniana Sacra 3, no. 8 (1968):231-47.

3227   SCHIJFSMA, J.H. "De kolonistenvrouw in Ned. Indië" [The
        colonial wife in the Netherlands Indies]. Indisch vrouwen
        jaarboek (1936).

3228   SINGAPORE EMPLOYERS FEDERATION. Survey Report on Part-time
        Employment of Housewives. Singapore: Research Section,
        Singapore Employers Federation, 1979, 50 pp.

3229   SIPOEH, R.H. Firasat Wanita: Untuk Penjesuaian Kebaikan dan
       Kebahagian Suami-Isteri [A manual for women: for the ad-
       justment/suitability, goodness and happiness of husband
       and wife]. Surabaja: Marfiah, 1962, 35 pp.

3230   SUJUD, ASWARNI. "Tugas Ibu Sebagai Pendidik Yang Affectional"
       [Mother's duty as an affectional educator]. Jiwa Baru 17,
       no. 39 (1969):13-16.

3231   SULEIMAN, IBU. Tugas Wanita sebagai Istri [The duties of a
       woman as a wife]. Jakarta: Mahabhrata, n.d., 36 pp.

3232   SULIANTI. "Mempertinggi Pendidikan Kaum Ibu menuju Kese-
       jahteraan Keluarga" [Upgrading the education of mothers for
       family well-being]. Majalah Administrasi Negera 3, no. 3
       (1961):89-92. (Indonesia.)

3233   TEMPOROSA, J.L. "Mother: Our Unsung Heroine." Philippine
       Journal of Education 55 (Aug. 1976):126-27.

3234   TEOH, JIN INN. "The Working Mother and Child Development."
       44 pp. Paper presented at MTUC (Malaysian Trade Union
       Congress) Second Women's Convention, Petaling Jaya,
       Malaysia, held in November 1976.

3235   _____. "The Working Mother and Child Development." 31 pp.
       Paper presented at the Seminar 'Wanita Malaysia Masakini',
       Bangi, Selangor, 1979, organized by the Faculty of Social
       Sciences and Humanities, Universiti Kebangsaan Malaysia.

3236   THANH, Y. "Exemption of Labor Duties for Women with Children
       (Vietnam)." U.S. JPRS Translations of Political and Socio-
       logical Information on North Vietnam 141 (11 Feb. 1965):
       7-8.

3237   THOMAS, R. MURRAY, and SURACHMAD, WINARNO. "Social-class
       Differences in Mothers' Expectations for Children in
       Indonesia." Journal of Social Psychology 57 (1962):303-7.

3238   UMALI, SALUD O. "A Study of the Methods in Homemaking with
       Emphasis on Housekeeping as Practised by a Group of House-
       wives in the District of Galas, Quezon City." Master's
       thesis, Centro Escolar University [Manila], 1956, v,
       259 pp.

3239   UNIVERSITI PERTANIAN MALAYSIA, Faculty of Educational Services,
       Research Committee (UNICEF). The Needs of Children and
       Mothers in Malaysia. Kuala Lumpur: Faculty of Educational
       Services, Universiti Pertanian Malaysia, 1977, viii,
       362 pp.

3240   URIATE, TRIFINA G. "A Study of the Moral and Legal Rights of
        the Filipino Wife in Relation to Family Living." Thesis,
        University of Visayas [Cebu City, Philippines], 1970,
        122 pp.

3241   WONG, ALINE K. "Maternal Employment, Education and Changing
        Family Values in Singapore." Journal of Economic Develop-
        ment and Social Change in Asia and Pacific 1, no. 1 (1976):
        23-40.

MUSLIM WOMEN

        (On laws regarding Muslim women see Legal
        Status, Laws, etc. On marital aspects see
        Marriage and Divorce. On Indonesian and
        Malay women see Indonesia and Malaysia
        under relevant subject headings)

3242   ABDUL RAHMAN HAJI ABDULLAH. "Kerja untuk Wanita Islam:
        Sejauh Mana Hak Mereka?" [Employment for Muslim women: to
        what extent do they have rights?]. Dewan Masyarakat 14,
        no. 7 (July 1976):17-19.

3243   ACHMAD, AFTABUDDIN. Wanita dalam Islam dan Kristen [Women in
        Islam and Christianity]. Di Indonesiakan oleh O. Hashem.
        Surabaja: Japi, 1963, 16 pp.

3244   ADIBAH AMIN. "Ahmad Luthfi on the Education and Freedom of
        Women: A Critical Examination of His Views on the Educa-
        tion and Freedom of Muslim Women in Malaya as Stated and
        Implied in His Novels," by Khalidah Adibah binti Haji Amin.
        B.A. academic exercise, University of Singapore, 1957, iv,
        39 pp.

3245   AFZA, NAZHAT. Posisi Wanita dalam Islam [The position of
        women in Islam]. Jakarta: Sinar Hudaya, 1971, 78 pp.

3246   AHMAD NAJIB OSMAN. "Peranan Wanita Islam" [The Role of Muslim
        women]. Fajar Islam 1, no. 1 (1974):5-9.

3247   AMINAH TENGKU ALI, TENGKU. "Lapangan Pergerakan Wanita Islam
        Khususnya di Malaysia" [Muslim women's movement with spe-
        cial reference to Malaysia]. B.A. academic exercise,
        Universiti Kebangsaan Malaysia, 1977.

3248   ANWAR IBRAHIM. "Konsep Perjuangan Wanita Islam" [Concept of
        freedom for Muslim women]. Panji Masyarakat 1, no. 5
        (Oct. 1976):32-33.

3249   _____. "Peranan Wanita Islam dalam Masyarakat" [The role of
        Muslim women in society]. Suara Taqwa, no. 13 (Nov. 1977):
        30-33.

3250   ASHSHIDDIQY, MUHAMMAD HASBI. Lapangan Perdjuangan Wanita
        Islam [The struggle of Muslim women]. Medan: Pustaka
        Timur, 1950, 51 pp.

3251   AZIZ, MUCHTAR. "Perkembangan Madrasah Muslimat di Indonesia,
        1908-1942" [The development of women's religious schools in
        Indonesia]. B.A. academic exercise, Universitas Gadjah
        Mada [Jogjakarta], 1966, 34 pp.

3252   AZIZAH A. RAHMAN. "Peranan Wanita dalam Politik dan Agama di
        Kubang Pasu" [The role of women in politics and religion
        in Kubang Pasu]. B.A. academic exercise, University of
        Malaya, 1975, 90 pp.

3253   BIDAYAH, Siti. "Muslim Women's Long Way in the Fight for
        Equality." Asian and Pacific Quarterly of Cultural and
        Social Affairs 5, no. 2 (Autumn 1973):82-83. (On the Mus-
        lim Women's Welfare Board in Malaysia.)

3254   BUDIMAN RADZI. Kedudokan Perempuan dalam Islam [The position
        of women in Islam]. Penang: H. Abdullah L.M. Noordin
        Arrawi, 1956[?], 56 pp.

3255   CHALIL, MUNAWWAR, Hadji. Nilai Wanita [The value of women].
        Bandung: Alma'arif, 1969, 245 pp.

3256   CIK HUSNAYANIE, Tengku. "Wanita Muslimah: Hak dan
        Kewajibannya" [Muslim women: their rights and responsi-
        bilities]. al-Islam 6, no. 5 (May 1979):9-10.

3257   CUISINIER, JEANNE. "Les madrasah féminines de Minangkabau"
        [Koranic schools for Minangkabau women]. Revue des études
        islamiques (1955):107-19.

3258   DRADJAT, ZAKIAH. "Peranan Wanita Islam dalam Kehidupan
        Masyarakat" [The role of Muslim women in community life].
        Sinar Darussalam 2, no. 10 (1969):21-31.

3259   FATHIYAH HAK. "Pembebasan Wanita Siapa Pelopornya?" [Freedom
        of women: who is the pioneer?]. Fajar Islam 12 (1973):
        20-24.

3260 FATHYIYAH HAJI KADIR. "Peranan Wanita Islam dalam Pembangunan Masharakat Malaysia" [The role of Muslim women in the development of Malaysian society]. Dewan Masyarakat 3 (Aug. 1965):10-13.

3261 al-HADI, SHAIKH, Syed. Kitab alam perempuan, bahath dan huraian kegunaan dan kebiasaan perempuan bagi faedah dirinya dan perhimpunan kaum bangsa dan watan-nya, dengan dalil 'akhli dan Nakli Shari'at Islam [The book on the world of women, debates and discussions on the use and habits of women for personal advantages, for her race and people, with explanations from those knowledgeable in Islam]. Penang: Jelutong Press, 194-? 153 pp.

3262 HAMIDAH NOOR, Ibu Hajjah. "Wanita Islam Dapat Hak Sama" [Muslim women have equal rights]. Dakwah 1, no. 1 (Mar. 1977):20-21.

3263 HAMKA [pseud.]. Kedudukan Perempuan dalam Islam [The position of women in Islam]. Oleh Abdul Malik Karim Amrullah. Kuala Lumpur: Penerbitan Utusan Melayu, 1974, 86 pp.

3264 HASSAN, A. Perempoean Islam Didewan dan Podium [Muslim women in the council and the 'podium']. 2d ed. Bangil: Persatoean Islam, 1949, 33 pp.

3265 _____. Wadjibkah Perempuan Berdjuma'ah? [Is it obligatory for women to congregate for the Friday prayers?]. Bangil: Persatuan Islam, 1955, 27 pp.

3266 IBNU SHAMS. "Wanita dan Masalahnya" [Women and their problems]. al-Islam 6, no. 5 (May 1979):6-8.

3267 JAAFAR SIDDIQ YASIN, Haji. "Peranan Wanita di Bidang Dakwah" [The role of women in the missionary movement]. Wanita [Kuala Lumpur], no. 96 (July 1977):36-37.

3268 al-JUFRI, ABDILLAH, Syed. "Kewajipan dan Tanggong-jawab Wanita Islam" [The responsibilities of Muslim women]. Fajar Islam 13 (1973):26-28.

3269 KERNKAMP, W.J.A. "De Islam en de vrouw in Indië" [Islam and women in the Indies]. Vox theologica 16 (1945):10-13.

3270 LEMBAGA KEBAJIKAN PEREMPUAN ISLAM PERSEKUTUAN TANAH MELAYU. Cenderamata 15 Tahun: 1961-1975 [Muslim Women's Welfare Board, Federation of Malaya. Souvenir 15 years: 1961-1975]. Kuala Lumpur: L.K.P.I. Persekutuan Tanah Melayu, 1976, xi, 96 pp.

3271   MAGLANGIT, VIRGINIA R. The Role of the Educated Maranaw Mus-
       lim Women in a Contemporary Maranaw Society. Manila:
       Philippine Women's University, 1971, 210 pp.

3272   MAIMUNAH JUNID. "Wanita, Islam dan Perjuangan-nya" [Women,
       Islam and their struggle]. Fajar Islam (1 Sept. 1970):
       27-28.

3273   MARYAM JAMEELAH. "Pergerakan Pembebasan Wanita Ala Barat
       Mengharcunkan" [Women's liberation movement according to
       West ruins--rather than consolidates]. Diterjemahkan oleh
       Abdul Majid Hj. Khatib. Roh Islam 2, no. 8 (Mar. 1976):
       31-41.

3274   MASHKURAH binti HAJI YASSIN. "Hak-hak dan Kewajipan Wanita
       didalam Islam (Kajian Perbandingan)" [The rights and re-
       sponsibilities of women in Islam: a comparative study].
       B.A. academic exercise, Universiti Kebangsaan Malaysia,
       1974.

3275   Mengundjingi Majtamar Wanita Islam di Pakistan: Verslag
       Lembaga Wanita Badan Kongres Muslimin Indonesia [The Muslim
       Women's Conference in Pakistan: report of the Women's
       Board, Indonesian Muslim Congress]. Jakarta: Badan
       Kongres Muslimin Indonesia, 1952, 101 pp.

3276   Modernisasa Wanita Menurut Islam [Modernization of women ac-
       cording to Islam]. Padang, Indonesia: Projek Penerangan
       Bimbingan dan Dakwah Agama Islam Propinsi Sumatra Barat,
       1973.

3277   "Moral Rumahtangga di Tangan Wanita" [The morals of the family
       lie in the hands of women]. al-Islam 3, no. 4 (Apr. 1976):
       18-21.

3278   "Moral Wanita Mesti Dilindung" [The morals of women must be
       protected]. al-Islam 4, no. 4 (Apr. 1977):25, 28, 37.
       (Report of the Second Convention of Muslim Women's Orga-
       nisations, Kuala Lumpur, 1977.)

3279   MUHAMMAD bin WAN MUHAMMAD ALI, Wan. "Wanita dalam Islam
       [Women in Islam]. Roh Islam 2, no. 11 (June 1976):33-36;
       2, no. 12 (July 1976):27-32; 2, no. 13 (Aug. 1976):38-42.

3280   MUHAMMAD HATTA YASIN. "Kedudukan Wanita dalam Islam" [The
       position of women in Islam]. al-Islam 6, no. 5 (May
       1979):3-5, 24.

3281   MUHAMMAD NAWAWI MUHAMMAD. "Aurat Wanita Islam dan Akibatnya"
       [Exposure of the body of Muslim women and its consequences].
       Hikmah, no. 9 (Apr. 1979):12-15.

3282 MUHAMMADIJAH, Madjlis 'Aisjijah. "Tuntutan Nasjiatul
      'Aisjijah" [Guidance of the Nasjiatul 'Aisjijah religious
      group]. Jakarta: P.P. Muhammadijah Madjlis 'Aisjijah,
      Seksi Pendidikan dan Pengadjaran, 1962[?], 16 pp.

3283 MUKTAMAR PERTUBUHAN-PERTUBUHAN PEREMPUAN ISLAM MALAYSIA, 1st,
      Kuala Lumpur, 1975. Kertas2 Kerja [Convention of Muslim
      Women's Organisations, 1st, Kuala Lumpur, 1975, Working
      Papers]. Organized by Lembaga Kebajikan Perempuan Islam.
      Kuala Lumpur, 1975, 1 vol. (various pagings).

3284 MUKTAMAR PERTUBUHAN-PERTUBUHAN PEREMPUAN ISLAM MALAYSIA, 2nd,
      Kuala Lumpur, 1977. Kertaskerja [Convention of Muslim
      Women's Organizations, 2nd, Kuala Lumpur, 1977. Working
      Papers]. Organized by Lembaga Kebajikan Perempuan Islam,
      Kuala Lumpur, 1977, 1 vol. (various pagings).

3285 NAWAWI HAJI AHMAD. "Sejuah Mana Wanita Islam Boleh Bergerak
      dalam Politik?" [How far can Muslim women advance in poli-
      tics?]. Keluarga, no. 39 (June 1979):30-31, 64-65.

3286 _____. "Wanita dalam Sistem Islam" [Women in the Islamic
      sytem]. al-Islam 6, no. 6 (June 1979):16-21.

3287 PIJPER, G.F. "De vrouw en de moskee" [The woman and the
      mosque]. In Fragmenta Islamica: studiën over het
      Islamisme in Nederlandsch-Indië. Leiden: E.J. Brill,
      1934, pp. 1-58.

3288 RAFIDAH OSMAN. "Kaum Wanita sebelum dan sesudah Islam"
      [Women before and after Islam]. Mimbar Islam (Nov./Dec.
      1973):16-20, 34-35.

3289 RAMDZAN HAJI CHALI. "Kedudukan dan Peranan Wanita di dalam
      Islam dan Adat Perpatih serta Realitinya di dalam Kontek
      Masyarakat Melayu Beradat Perpatih di Nerasau, Remban,
      Negeri Sembilan" [The status and role of women in Islam
      and 'adat perpatih' in the context of an 'adat perpatih'
      community in Nerasau, Rembau, Negri Sembilan]. B.A. aca-
      demic exercise, University of Malaya, 1976, 109 pp.

3290 RANI, A.N. Wanita dalam Islam [Women in Islam]. Surabaya:
      Radja-Pena, 1967, 16 pp.

3291 RUSMIATI HARUN. "Hak-hak dan Tanggungjawab Wanita dari Kaca
      Mata Islam" [Rights and responsibilities of women from the
      Islamic viewpoint]. 11 pp. Paper presented at the Seminar
      GPW (Gerakan Persatuan Wanita), Serdang, Malaysia, January,
      1979.

3292 _____. "Perjuangan Wanita Menekam Diri?" [Are women's struggles self-repressive?]. al-Islam 2, no. 10 (Oct. 1975):
17-19.

3293 SAFIAH KARIM, Nik. "Peranan Wanita Islam dalam Masyarakat"
[The role of Muslim women in society]. Keluarga, no. 38
(May 1979):18-20.

3294 SAID, M. al-Quran tentang Wanita [The Koran on women].
Bandung: Peladjar, 1960[?], 153 pp.

3295 SALAYAN, ABDUL WAHID. Fungsi Wanita dalam Islam [The function
of women in Islam]. Jakarta: Direktorat Djenderal Bimbingan Masjarakat Islam Projek Penerangan, Bimbingan Da'awah
Chutbah Agama Islam Pusat, 1971, 32 pp.

3296 SALEHAH OSMAN. "Peranan Wanita Islam dalam Pembangunan"
[The role of Muslim women in development]. al-Islam 4,
no. 3 (Mar. 1977):32-34.

3297 SEMINAR WANITA, Singapore, 1977. Kertas2 Kerja [Women's
Seminar Singapore, 1977. Working Papers]. Sponsored by
Persatuan Mahasiswa Islam, University of Singapore,
Singapore, 1977, 35 pp.

3298 SEMINAR WANITA MEMAHAMI ISLAM, Kuala Lumpur, 1978. Kertas
Kerja [Women's Seminar on Understanding Islam, Kuala
Lumpur, 1978, Papers]. Organized by Bahagian Wanita
PERKIM, Kuala Lumpur, 1978, 1 vol. (various pagings).

3299 SUBANDRIO, HURUSTIATI. "The Position of Women in a Muslim
Family in Indonesia." Islamic Review 37, no. 9 (Sept.
1949):35-39.

3300 SUBHI AS SALEH. "Islam Muliakan Wanita" [Islam respects
women]. al-Islam 3, no. 3 (Mar. 1976):38-40.

3301 SUHAILA MUHAMMAD NOAH, Datin. "Kemajuan Kebendaan tanpa
Agama Membawa Kemusnahan" [Maternal progress without religion brings disaster]. al-Islam 6, no. 5 (May 1979):
14-15. (Speech delivered at the Seminar Wanita Islam,
7 April 1979.)

3302 "Woman and the Family." Intisari 2, no. 2 (1964[?]):9-73.
(Contents: 1. M. Siraj, "Status Muslim Woman/Family Law
Singapore." 2. M. Siraj, "Effective Administration/Social
Change." 3. Shirle Gordon, "Marriage/Divorce in the Eleven
States of Malaya and Singapore." 4. Mohd. Din bin Ali,
"Malay Customary Law/Family." 5. Ahmad bin Muhammad
Ibrahim, "Islam Customary Law/Malaysia.")

3303   YASIN bin KU IBRAHIM, Ku. "Tutup Muka Wanita menurut Pan-
        dangan Islam" [Covering the face of women according to
        Islam]. Sarina 1, no. 12 (Mar. 1977):103-11.

3304   ZUHRI SAIFUDDIN, KIAI, Hadji. "Wanita Tiang Agama dan
        Masjarakat" [Woman is the pillar of religion and society].
        Memuat pidato sambutan Menteri Agama dan Kania Sumentapura
        pada peringatan Hari Kartini. Jakarta: Departemen Agama,
        1962, 16 pp.

POLITICAL ACTIVITIES

3305   ABDUL MAJID bin AHMAD KHAN. "An Analysis of the UMNO Kaum Ibu
        as a Women's Political Organisation." B.A. academic exer-
        cise, University of Malaya, 1970, vi, 70 pp.

3306   ABDULGANI, RUSLAN, Hadji. Bersama-sama Wanita Menjelesaikan
        Revolusi [Together women will complete the revolution].
        Jakarta: Departemen Penergangan, 1964, 55 pp.

3307   'ALAM, SYAMSUL. "Opu Daeng Risadju, Wanita Alim Yang Jadi
        Kaum Pergerakan" [Opu Daeng Risadju, a female Muslim
        scholar who became an activist]. Mimbar Ulama 1, no. 4
        (1976):76-80.

3308   "All the Women Struggle to Maintain the Traditions of the
        Revolution." U.S. JPRS. Translations of Political and
        Sociological Information on North Vietnam, no. 123
        (23 Nov. 1964):20-21.

3309   AMARA RAKSASTAYA. "The Political Role of Southeast Asia
        Women." American Academy of Political and Social Science,
        Annals, 375 (Jan. 1968):86-90.

3310   ANIS binti SABIRIN. "Wanita dan Politik" [Women and Politics].
        Dewan Masyarakat 4, no. 2 (Feb. 1962):18-23. (On Malaysia.)

3311   ANNIE ZAKIAH MERICAN. "Seragam dan Sekata di Perhimpunan
        Wanita MCA" [Together at the meeting of Malaysian Chinese
        Association, Women's Section]. Wanita [Kuala Lumpur],
        no. 99 (Oct. 1977):70-71.

3312   ASEAN WOMEN LEADERS AND INTERNATIONAL WOMEN'S YEAR POST CON-
        FERENCE MEETING, Jakarta, 1975. Report. Organized under
        the auspices of the ASEAN Sub-Committee on Women of the
        ASEAN Permanent Committee on Socio-Cultural Activities.
        Jakarta, 1975, 1 vol. (various pagings).

3313   AVENA, M.R. "The Ziga Story." Examiner (Feb. 1964):5, 24-25,
        28. (On Philippines.)

3314   AZIZAH A. RAHMAN. "Peranan Wanita dalam Politik dan Agama di
        Kubang Pasu" [The role of women in politics and religion
        in Kubang Pasu]. B.A. academic exercise, University of
        Malaya, 1975, 90 pp.

3315   BAYANI-ARCILLA, SOCORRO. "The Development of Political Rights
        of Filipino Women." Master's thesis, University of Manila
        [Manila], 1953, v, 188 pp.

3316   BUI HIEN. Mot cuoc do'i truyen ky. Hanoi: Phu Nu, 1976,
        148 pp.

3317   BUNCH-WEEKS, CHARLOTTE. "Asian Women in Revolution." Women:
        A Journal of Liberation 1, no. 4 (1970):2-9. (On Vietnam.)

3318   CHAN, HENG CHEE. "Notes on the Mobilization of Women into the
        Economy and Politics of Singapore." In Political and So-
        cial Change in Singapore. Edited by Wu Teh-yao. Singapore:
        Institute of Southeast Asian Studies, 1975, pp. 13-35.
        Southeast Asian Perspectives no. 3.

3319   CLERMONT, ANDRE. "La femme Vietminh" [The Vietminh woman].
        Indochine, sud-est asiatique, no. 20 (Aug. 1953):30-34.

3320   "Cooperation of Chinese Women Living in North Vietnam in War
        against U.S. Stressed." U.S. JPRS. Translations on North
        Vietnam, no. 146 (13 Apr. 1967):40, 620.

3321   DE LEON, BELEN ATIENZA. "Selection of Women as Senatorial
        Candidates." Master's thesis, University of the Philip-
        pines [Quezon City], 1973, 201 pp.

3322   FARIDAH IDRIS. "Para Perwakilan Tambah Matang dan Bijak.
        Perhimpunan Agung Pergerakan Wanita UMNO Malaysia Yang
        Ke 25" [The delegates are more mature and intelligent.
        25th Annual General Meeting of the United Malays National
        Organization Women's Section]. Wanita [Kuala Lumpur],
        no. 85 (Aug. 1976):38-39.

3323   _____. "Perjuangan Mereka belum Tamat" [Their struggle is
        not yet over]. Wanita [Kuala Lumpur], no. 107 (June 1978):
        34-35.

3324   _____. "Wanita Harus Menjadi Hero Bukan Heroine" [Women
        should be heroes not heroines]. Wanita [Kuala Lumpur],
        no. 109 (Aug. 1978):14-15, 72.

3325   GREEN, JUSTIN JAY. "Women leaders of the Philippines: Social Backgrounds and Political Attitudes." Ph.D. dissertation, Syracuse University, 1970, xiv, 368 pp. Abstracted in Dissertation Abstracts International 31, no. 11 (May 1971): 6122-23-A. University Microfilms International, order no. 71-10,921.

3326   GUERRERO NAKPIL, CARMEN. "Party Politics." Philippines Free Press 54, no. 34 (Aug. 1961):3, 49-52.

3327   HASROM, HARON, and YASSIN, A.F. "Lima Tokoh Wanita di Parlimen" [Five women leaders in Parliament]. Dewan Masyarakat 13, no. 1 (Jan. 1975):12-16. (On Malaysia.)

3328   "A Heroic Daughter of a Heroic Land." Women of Vietnam, no. 1 (1970):31-33.

3329   HINDLEY, DONALD. "Women." In The Communist Party of Indonesia 1951-1963. Berkeley: University of California Press, 1966, pp. 200-211. (Contents: 1. "The Work of the Party." 2. "Gerwani." 3. "The Work of SOBSI and Its Trade Unions." 4. "The Work of BTI.")

3330   HO, THELMA YIN KHAM. "The Present Status of Singaporean Women: Legal and Political Aspects." B.A. academic exercise, University of Singapore, 1973, 60 pp.

3331   "De I.E.V.V.O. en politiek" [The I.E.V.V.O. (Indo Europees(ch) Verbond Vrouwen Organisatie) and politics]. Onze stem 21 (1940):169-70. (On the Netherlands Indies.)

3332   KARIMAH ZAINAB. "Wanita Melayu dalam Konteks Perubahan Ekonomi dan Politik: Satu Kes Studi di Kota Bharu" [Malay women in the context of economic and political change: a case study in Kota Bharu]. Master's thesis, University of Malaya, 1975, ix, 279 pp.

3333   KHADIJAH binti MOHAMED SIDEK. "Riwayat hidup saya: My Life," by Ardjasani [pseud.]. Eastern Horizon 2, no. 1 (Jan. 1962):11-17; 2, no. 2 (Feb. 1962):16-23; 2, no. 3 (Mar. 1962):39-50; 2, no. 4 (Apr. 1962):37-46; 2, no. 5 (May 1962):47-52; 2, no. 6 (June 1962):39-47; 2, no. 7 (July 1962):49-57; 2, no. 8 (Aug. 1962):47-51; 3, no. 1 (Jan. 1964):55-61; 3, no. 2 (Feb. 1964):54-60; 3, no. 3 (Mar. 1964):58-63; 3, no. 4 (Apr. 1964):53-58; 3, no. 5 (May 1964):56-58. (Malaysian female politician.)

3334   KONG, Y.S. "The Participation of Women in Public Life in Sarawak." African Women 3 (Dec. 1958):16-19.

3335   LAILA SHUKRY el HAMAMSY. "The Political Role of Women in
       Tropical and Sub-tropical Countries." In Women's Rôle in
       the Development of Tropical and Subtropical Countries, by
       International Institute of Differing Civilizations.
       Brussels: International Institute of Differing Civiliza-
       tions, 1959, pp. 470-87.

3336   LE CHAN PHUONG. "Strengthening the Role of Women." U.S.
       JPRS. Translations of Political and Sociological Informa-
       tion on North Vietnam, no. 123 (23 Nov. 1964):15-19.

3337   MAHAZIR KU IDRUS, Ku. "Penyertaan Wanita didalam Politik di
       Kawasan Tunjang, Kedah" [The participation of women in
       politics in Tunjang, Kedah]. B.A. academic exercise,
       University of Malaya, 1976, iv, 74 pp.

3338   MAHZOM AHMAD SHAH, Wan. "Penyertaan Wanita Melayu dalam
       Pergerakan Wanita UMNO di Kg. Bharu, Pulau Pinang" [The
       participation of Malay women in the UMNO Women's Section
       in Kg. Bharu, Penang]. B.A. academic exercise, University
       of Malaya, 1974, vi, 91 pp.

3339   MALAYSIAN CHINESE ASSOCIATION, National Wanita Section, Gen-
       eral Assembly. Report of the Secretary-General. Kuala
       Lumpur, 1st, 1975-.

3340   MANDERSON, LENORE. "Aspects of the Leadership of the
       Pergerakan Kaum Ibu UMNO Malaysia: The Sumatran Connec-
       tion." RIMA; Review of Indonesian and Malayan Affairs 12,
       no. 2 (Dec. 1978):17-42.

3341   _____. "The Development of the Pergerakan Kaum Ibu UMNO,
       1945-1972." Ph.D. dissertation, Australian National
       University, 1977, xvii, 351 pp.

3342   _____. "Going Through the Motions: Aspects of the Organiza-
       tional Activities of the Pergerakan Kaum Ibu UMNO Malaysia,
       1949-1972." International Journal of Women's Studies 2,
       no. 1 (Jan./Feb. 1979):1-26.

3343   _____. "Peranan Wanita dalam Politik" [The role of women in
       politics]. Kancil (Aug. 1977):52-55, 90.

3344   _____. "The Shaping of the Kaum Ibu (Women's Section) of the
       United Malays National Organization." In Women and Na-
       tional Development: The Complexities of Change. Edited
       by Wellesley Editorial Committee. Chicago: University of
       Chicago Press, 1977, pp. 210-28. Also in Signs 3, no. 1
       (Autumn 1977):210-28.

3345 _____. "Women in Politics: Change or Continuum. The Case of Malay Women in West Malaysia." Paper presented at the Seventh Conference of the International Association of Historians, August 1977, held in Bangkok, Thailand.

3346 _____. "Women in Public Life: Theoretical and Critical Implications." 23 pp. Paper presented at the Seminar "Wanita Malaysia Masakini," Bangi, Selangor, 1979, organized by the Faculty of Social Sciences and Humanities, Universiti Kebangsaan Malaysia.

3347 _____. Women, Politics and Change: The Kaum Ibu UMNO, Malaysia, 1945-1972. Kuala Lumpur: Oxford University Press, 1980, xiv, 294 pp.

3348 MARYAM IBRAHIM, Siti. "Wanita UMNO Kurang Pemimpin" [UMNO Women's Section lacks leaders]. Komentar, no. 6 (Apr./May 1977):38-40.

3349 MAUNG MAUNG. "Women Officers of the Burma Army." Guardian [Rangoon] 2, no. 5 (May 1953):23-27.

3350 MORRIS, SAM. "South Vietnam's Only Lady Mayor." Nation [Manila] 2 (3 July 1967):40-41.

3351 MUHAMMAD ALIAS. "Kursus Politik Wanita UMNO: Satu Kesepian Yang Menakutkan?" [UMNO Women's Section political course: the lack of support is cause for worry]. Mastika 37, no. 6 (June 1977):12-16.

3352 NAWAWI HAJI AHMAD. "Sejauh Mana Wanita Islam Boleh Bergerak dalam Politik?" [How far can Muslim women go in politics?]. Keluarga, no. 39 (June 1979):30-31, 64-65.

3353 "New Woman in the Socialist Society: Excerpts of Speech Given by Le Duan, March 4-7, 1974." Journal of Contemporary Asia 5, no. 3 (1975):387-92.

3354 NGUYEN THI THAP. "Develop Women's Potentialities to Build Socialism." U.S. JPRS. Translations from Hoc Tap (Studies) North Vietnam (7 Jan. 1965):53-67.

3355 _____. "We Pledge to Unite around the Party." Women of Vietnam, no. 1 (1970):9-10. (Speech made by the President of the Vietnam Women's Union at the meeting commemorating the 40th anniversary of the Vietnam Workers' Party, 3 February 1970.)

3356 NIERRAS, LETICIA CANEJA. "Political and Social Status of Women in Java." Master's thesis, Cornell University, 1958, iv, 99 pp.

3357   NISWATY binti Haji DIMYATI. "Penglibatan Wanita dalam Politik
        (Satu Kajian Kes Pergerakan Wanita UMNO, Bahagian Kapat)"
        [The participation of women in politics: a case study of
        the Kapat Division, Women's Section of UMNO]. B.A. aca-
        demic exercise, Universiti Kebangsaan Malaysia, 1976, vi,
        92 pp.

3358   NYUN-HAN, EMMA. "The Socio-Political Roles of Women in
        Japan and Burma." Ph.D. dissertation, University of
        Colorado, 1972, x, 623 pp. Abstracted in Dissertation
        Abstracts International 33, no. 8 (Feb. 1973):4499-A.
        University Microfilms International, order no. 73-1810.

3359   PHAM VAN DONG. "Heighten Our Determination to Struggle and
        Step up Socialist Revolution and Women's Movement in the
        North." U.S. JPRS. Translations of Political and Socio-
        logical Information on North Vietnam, no. 61 (5 Feb. 1964):
        1-3.

3360   PHAN CANH. "A Woman District Chief on the Highland."
        Vietnam 148 (1970):24-25.

3361   PHAN THI MAI. "The Last Words of One Who Loves Vietnam."
        Women: A Journal of Liberation 1, no. 4 (1970):27. (Poem
        by a female student leader who immolated herself as a pro-
        test against the war in Vietnam.)

3362   PHUONG HUY. "A Young Lady Candidate--Doctor." Women of
        Vietnam, nos. 3/4 (1970):17-18.

3363   POLOTAN, KERIMA. "The Women." Philippines Free Press 54,
        no. 44 (Nov. 1961):20-24.

3364   _____. "The Women (and Some of the Men) in the Convention."
        Philippines Free Press 57, no. 48 (Nov. 1964):4, 48-49, 52,
        54.

3365   POEDJOBUNTORO, SOEPENI. Wanita dan Pemilihan Umum [Women and
        the general elections]. Jakarta: Widjaja, 1954, 152 pp.

3366   RAMLAH ADAM. "Pergerakan Wanita Umno Malaysia 1945-1972:
        Satu Analisa" [Umno Women's Section movement 1945-1972:
        an analysis]. Malaysia dari Segi Sejarah, no. 9 (1980):
        26-54.

3367   _____. "Sejarah Awal Pergerakan Kaum Ibu UMNO" [The early
        history of the UMNO Women's Section]. Jernal Sejarah 15
        (1977/78):117-21.

3368   RED, ISAGANI V. "Mass Media Exposure and Attitude towards the Socio-Political Leadership of Women." B.A. academic exercise, University of the Philippines [Quezon City], 1974, 25 pp.

3369   SAN ANDRES-ZIGA, TECLA. "Women in Politics and Government." Philippine Law Journal 50, no. 1 (Feb. 1975):36-43.

3370   "South Vietnamese Prisoners Speak." Women: A Journal of Liberation 3, no. 3 (1972):40-43. (Women political prisoners.)

3371   STAUDT, KATHY. "Politics and Philippine Women: An Exploratory Study." Philippine Journal of Public Administration 17, no. 4 (Oct. 1973):466-84.

3372   STENTON, JEAN E. "Cambodia's Women Forge Ahead." Examiner (9 Aug. 1964):8, 28.

3373   "Sum-up of Work among Women: Important Contributions to the Great Victories of the People." Women of Vietnam, no. 2 (1971):1-6.

3374   TAN, HELEN. "Women and Politics in Malaysia." Paper presented at the Leadership and Training Seminar, Petaling Jaya, 5-6 February 1977, organized by Malaysian Ceylonese Congress.

3375   "Thirteen Years of the Communist Women Movement: Indochina." U.S. JPRS. Translations on South and East Asia, no. 27 20,596 (8 Aug. 1963).

3376   TIEU BAN NGHIEN CUU LICH SU PHONG TRAO PHU NU. Con duong giai phong: hoi ky. Hanoi: Phu Nu, 1976, 162 pp.

3377   TORRENTO, JESUS-MANUEL. "Political Facts on Filipino Females." Weekly Graphic 32 (4 Aug. 1965):20-27.

3378   TURLEY, WILLIAM S. "Women in the Communist Revolution in Vietnam." Asian Survey 12, no. 9 (Sept. 1972):793-805.

3379   UNION OF VIET-NAM WOMEN IN FRANCE. Women of Viet-Nam in the Struggle for National Liberation. Paris: Imprimere Centrale Commercial, 1948, 16 pp.

3380   UNITED MALAYS NATIONAL ORGANISATION, Pergerakan Kaum Ibu. Penyata Tahunan [Annual report]. Kuala Lumpur, 1947-.

3381   _____. Pergerakan Kaum Ibu UMNO: Sejarah dan Kejayaan2nya [UMNO Women's Movement: its history and success]. Kuala Lumpur, 1968.

3382   "Vietnamese Women Exercise Their Rights as Masters of the
        Country." Women of Vietnam, no. 2 (1971):7-8.

3383   Vrouwen en politieke internering in Indonesië [Women and po-
        litical detention in Indonesia]. Amsterdam: Amnesty
        International, 1975, 14 pp.

3384   "With Eternal Gratitude to the Great Lenin, the Vietnamese
        Women Are Resolved to Fight along with Our Entire People
        to Defeat the U.S. Aggressors and to Successfully Build
        Socialism." Women of Vietnam, no. 1 (1970):1-8, 36.
        (Speech made by the Vietnamese women's delegation at a
        symposium held in Moscow, 17-21 February 1970.)

3385   ZAINAB HAJI ABDUL KARIM, Nik. "Sumbangan Wanita Melayu
        Kelantan dalam Bidang Pelajaran, Ekonomi dan Politik ke
        Arah Pembangunan Negara" [The contribution of Malay women
        from Kelantan in the fields of education, economics, and
        politics to national development]. 13 pp. Paper presented
        at the Seminar "Wanita Malaysia Masakini," Bangi, Selangor,
        1979, organized by the Faculty of Social Sciences and
        Humanities, Universiti Kebangsaan Malaysia.

PSYCHOLOGY AND PSYCHIATRY

3386   ABEAR, CARMENCITA M. "Survey of the Career Aspirations of
        Senior College Women in Selected Schools in Davao City."
        Master's thesis, Ateneo de Davao [Philippines], 1973,
        100 pp.

3387   ACKERMAN, SUSAN ELLEN. "Industrial Conflict in Malaysia: A
        Case Study of Rural Malay Female Workers." 20 pp. Paper
        presented at the Seminar "Wanita Malaysia Masakini," Bangi,
        Selangor, 1979, organized by the Faculty of Social Sciences
        and Humanities, Universiti Kebangsaan Malaysia. (On mass
        hysteria among Malay female workers.)

3388   ACKERMAN, SUSAN ELLEN, and LEE, RAYMOND LAI MING. "Mass
        Hysteria and Spirit Possession in Urban Malaysia: A Case
        Study." Journal of Sociology and Psychology 1 (1978):
        24-35. (Study on Malay women.)

3389   ADIKUSOMO, ARMAN. "Isteri Kedua, Tinjauan 13 Kasus dari
        Sudut Kesehatan Jiwa" [The second wife: a psychiatric
        observation of thirteen cases]. Jiwa 7, no. 4 (1974):
        49-61.

3390   AINADO, WASIMAN. Pengetahuan tentang Djiwa Wanita [Under-
            standing the psychology of women]. Semarang: Astanabuku
            Abede, 196-[?], 96 pp.

3391   AINON MUHAMMAD. "Konflik Sosial dan Kejiwaan Dikalangan
            Wanita Pendidikan Tinggi [Social and psychological conflict
            among women with higher education]. Dewan Masyarakat 13,
            no. 10 (Oct. 1975):42-44.

3392   AROM TANPRAPHAT. "A Study of the Relationship between Crea-
            tivity, Academic Achievement, Scholastic Aptitude, Sex, and
            Vocational Interests of Tenth Grade Thai Students." Ed.D.
            dissertation, University of Northern Colorado, 1976,
            100 pp. Abstracted in Dissertation Abstracts International
            37, no. 1 (July 1976):119-20-A. University Microfilms
            International, order no. 76-16,300.

3393   BACABAC, CONSUELO M. "Personality Adjustment of Career
            Women." Master's thesis, University of San Agustin [Iloilo
            City, Philippines], 1970, 395 pp.

3394   BANAAG, Mary of the Holy Spirit, Sister. "A Study of the
            Academic Achievements of the Girls Enrolled in the Fourth
            Year High School at St. Bridget's College during the Aca-
            demic Year 1961-1962." Master's thesis, St. Bridget's
            College [Batangas, Philippines], 1962, vii, 116 pp.

3395   CHENG, CONCEPCION MOLINA. "A Comparative Study of Two Groups
            of High School Girls on Fundamental Attitudes in Love,
            Courtship and Marriage." Master's thesis, Ateneo de Manila
            University [Manila], 1963, v, 80 pp.

3396   CHIAM, HENG KENG. "A Study of the Self Concept of Form Four
            Students in an Urban Area and Some of Its Correlates."
            Ph.D. dissertation, University of Malaya, 1976, ii,
            155 pp. (Study based on two boys' schools and two girls'
            schools.)

3397   CHUA YAU, VICTORIA D. "An Analytic Interpretation of the
            Personality Factors of 628 BSEED Women Students of the
            University of Visayas as Compared to Those of 600 BSEED
            Women Students of the Divine Word College, Tagbilaran,
            Bohol." Master's thesis, University of San Carlos [Cebu
            City, Philippines], 1965, ix, 91 pp.

3398   COLLER, RICHARD W. "A Sample of Courtship and Marriage Atti-
            tudes held by U.P. Students." Philippine Sociological Re-
            view 2, no. 3 (Oct. 1954):31-45.

3399   CRUZ, SOFIA STA. ROMANA. "Adjustment Problems of the Girls
        in Torres High School: A Survey." Master's thesis,
        University of San Carlos [Cebu City, Philippines], 1963,
        xi, 141 pp.

3400   DAYAO, ENRIQUETA CAPIRAL. "Characteristics of a Select Group
        of Adolescents as Revealed by Standardized Tests Filipino
        Youth Study No. 3." Master's thesis, Ateneo de Manila
        University [Manila], 1960, iv, iii, 119 pp. (On Filipino
        adolescent girls.)

3401   DELFINO, CUSTODIO. "A Comparative Study of School Achievement
        of Sixth Grade Boys and Girls." Master's thesis, Central
        Philippine University [Iloilo City, Philippines], 1962,
        127 pp.

3402   DONAHUE, ELIZABETH ANN. "A Study of the Psychological Charac-
        teristics of 3 Sub-groups in a Religious Congregation of
        Women as Revealed by a Battery of Standardised Tests."
        Master's thesis, Ateneo de Manila University [Manila],
        1963, viii, 177 pp.

3403   ENRIQUEZ, OFELIA A. "A Comparative Study of the Temperaments
        of Some American and Filipino Female Adolescents as Re-
        vealed by the Thurstone Temperament Schedule." Master's
        thesis, University of San Carlos [Cebu City, Philippines],
        1966, vi, 58 pp.

3404   EUFEMIO, FLORA. "Foster Mothers: Their Responses on the
        Parent Attitude Research Instrument (PARI) in Relation to
        Their Role Performance." Philippine Sociological Review
        15, nos. 3/4 (July/Oct. 1967):94-105.

3405   FABELLA, VIRGINIA P. "Relationship between the Vocational
        Interests and Aptitudes of One Hundred Freshmen in a Col-
        lege for Women." Master's thesis, Ateneo de Manila Univer-
        sity [Manila], 1963, v, 122 pp.

3406   FLORES, PURA M., and GOMEZ, ILUMINADA. "Maternal Attitudes
        toward Child Bearing." Philippine Educational Forum 13,
        no. 3 (Nov. 1964):27-40.

3407   FLORO, TEODORA L. "The Boy-Girl Relation Problems of Ado-
        lescence: Its Implications to the Proposed Guidance Pro-
        gram of St. Mary's Academy (Meycavayan)." Master's thesis,
        De la Salle College [Manila], 1967.

3408   GARCIA, ELMA B. "A Statistical Study of the Personality Pro-
        files of College Women of the Cebu Normal School on the
        IPAT 16 Personality Factor Questionnaire 1964-1965."

Master's thesis, University of San Carlos [Cebu City, Philippines], 1966, xi, 122 pp.

3409 GARDINER, HARRY W. "Attitudes of Thai Students toward Marriage Roles." Journal of Social Psychology 75 (June 1968): 61-65.

3410 GARY, JOSEPH R. "A Rorschach Study of the Personality Structure of Selected Contemporary Filipina Manila College Students." Ph.D. dissertation, University of Santo Tomas [Manila], 1973, 343 pp.

3411 GHOZALI, ENDANG (Mrs.), and PRASADIO, TRIMAN. "Aspek Psikiatri Kehamilan di Luar Pernikahan: Suatu Survey di Surabaya" [The psychiatric aspects of unmarried mothers: a survey in Surabaya]. Majalah Kesehatan Jiwa 2, no. 1 (1976):13-16.

3412 GUTHRIE, GEORGE M. "Structure of Maternal Attitudes in Two Cultures." Journal of Psychology 62, no. 2 (Mar. 1966): 155-65. (Includes the Philippines.)

3413 GUTIERREZ-GONZALEZ, ELIZABETH. "Duration of Marriage and Perceptual Behaviour of Spouses." Philippine Journal of Psychology 1, no. 1 (Nov. 1968):53-61.

3414 JACOB, FLORANIE. "Personality Need Patterns and Satisfactory Marital Interaction among Filipino Couples." Master's thesis, Ateneo de Manila University [Manila], 1974, viii, 106 pp.

3415 KLOSS, JOSEPHINE B. "A Survey of the Personality Adjustment Problems of the University of San Carlos Girls High School Using the Minnesota Problem Check List and the California Test of Personality." Master's thesis, University of San Carlos [Cebu City, Philippines], 1971, 126, 4 pp.

3416 LEE, RAYMOND LAI MING. "The Social Meaning of Mass Hysteria in West Malaysia and Singapore." Ph.D. dissertation, University of Massachusetts, 1979, 292 pp. Abstracted in Dissertation Abstracts International 40, no. 3 (Sept. 1979):1689-A. University Microfilms International, order no. 7920862. (Focuses on mass hysteria involving Malay women.)

3417 LEE, RAYMOND LAI MING, and ACKERMAN, SUSAN ELLEN. "The Sociocultural Dynamics of Mass Hysteria: A Case Study of Social Conflict in West Malaysia." Psychiatry 43, no. 1 (Feb. 1980):78-88. (Focuses on Malay women.)

3418   LUZ, CELERINA S. SP. S. "A Survey of the Attitudes of Pre-
        adolescent Girls in a Catholic Grade School in the Greater
        Manila Area." Master's thesis, Ateneo de Manila University
        [Manila], 1976, 117 pp.

3419   MAGLEO, RICARDO GALECIA. "A Comparative Study of the Academic
        Achievement of Fourth Grade Boys and Girls in San Carlos
        Pangasinan." Master's thesis, University of the Philip-
        pines [Quezon City], 1935.

3420   MANIQUIS, FE CONSOLATA, Sister. "Characteristics of a Select
        Group of Adolescents as Represented by Standardized Tests:
        Filipino Youth Study No. 11." Master's thesis, Ateneo de
        Manila University [Manila], 1964, vii, 126 pp. (On
        Filipino adolescent girls.)

3421   MASDANI, J. "Beberapa Konsekwensi Psikologik Emansipasi
        Wanita Indonesia" [Some psychological consequences of the
        emancipation of Indonesian women]. *Jiwa* 2, no. 1 (Jan.
        1969):34-45.

3422   _____. "Peranan Wanita dalam Pembangunan Sosial dan Mental
        Health" [The role of women in social development and mental
        health]. *Jiwa* 5, no. 4 (1972):1-7.

3423   MONDOÑEDO, MARY VERONICA. "A Study to Determine the Effects
        of Residential Care and Treatments on the Attitudes of
        Fifty Unmarried Mothers." Master's thesis, Ateneo de
        Manila University [Manila], 1974, ix, 154 pp.

3424   MUHAMMAD ZIN bin ABD. AZIZ. "Kajian mengenai Sikap terhadap
        Pekerjaan, Nilai, Aspirasi, Alientation dan Relative De-
        privation Pekerja-pekerja Wanita Kilang Letronik" [A Study
        of the attitude of women workers in electronic factories
        towards work, values, aspirations, alienation, and relative
        deprivation]. B.A. academic exercise, University of Malaya,
        1976, v, 80 pp.

3425   ONG, TERESITA A. "A Cross-cultural Study of the Social Ex-
        pectations by Men and Women in Two Branches of an Inter-
        national Bank in Manila and Tokyo." Master's thesis,
        University of the Philippines [Quezon City], 1975, xvii,
        180 pp.

3426   ORRATHAI SRITHONGS. "A Comparative Study of Attitudes toward
        Child Rearing Practices between Mothers of Juvenile Delin-
        quents and Mothers of Normal Adolescents." Master's
        thesis, Chulalongkorn University, 1968, vi, 76 pp.

3427   PABLO, PATRICIA O. "A Comparative Analysis of Selected Socio-
        logical Variables Affecting Working and Non-working
        Mothers, and School Achievement of Pre-adolescent Children
        in the Division of City Schools." Master's thesis, St.
        Louis University [Baguio City, Philippines] 1972, 107 pp.

3428   PALABRICA, MARILOU B. "A Study of Attitudes and Motives of
        Married Women that Underlie the Large Family in Modern
        Urban Cagayan de Oro." Master's thesis, Xavier University
        [Cagayan de Oro City, Philippines], 1969, 68 pp.

3429   PALANCA, ERIKA V. "A Comparative Study of Personality Pro-
        files of Some Filipino Female Students of Divine World
        College, Laoag City and the University of San Carlos, Cebu
        City, 1964-1969, Using the IPAT 16 Personality Factor
        Questionnaire." Master's thesis, University of San Carlos
        [Cebu City, Philippines], 1969, vii, 74, 13 pp.

3430   PICZON, CONSUELO P. "A Study of the Personality Traits of
        Popular Girls of the Philippine Normal School." Master's
        thesis, Cosmopolitan College [Manila], 1950, 94 pp.

3431   PRASADIO, TRIMAN; ISKANDAR, O.; and SUKADANA, A. ADI. "Sex-
        Role Inversion pada Pemadin Ludruk Wanita" [Sex role in-
        version in 'ludruk' actresses]. _Jiwa_ 5, no. 1 (1972):7-20.

3432   PRAWIROHARDJO, SOEJONO. "Lesbianism (Case Report). Profil
        Saraf." _Jiwa_ 2, no. 3 (1971):1-5.

3433   PREEJA DHUNMA. "A Study of Moral Values of Two Age Groups of
        Farm and Nonfarm Adolescent Boys and Girls in Three Geo-
        graphical Regions of Thailand." Ed.D. dissertation, Uni-
        versity of Maryland, 1966, 191 pp. Abstracted in _Disser-
        tation Abstracts International_ 27, no. 9 (Mar. 1967):
        2872-73-A. University Microfilms International, order no.
        67-2001.

3434   RAMOS, JULIETA M. "Interpersonal Values of Senior High School
        Boys and Girls in a Certain Manila Secondary School."
        Master's thesis, Philippine Women's University [Manila],
        1964, viii, 128 pp.

3435   SAMANO, ALMA. "A Study of the Expressed Occupational Choices
        of Third and Fourth Year Girls in a Rural Parochial High
        School in Relation to Their Occupational Interests and
        Scholastic Aptitudes." Master's thesis, Ateneo de Manila
        University [Manila], 1974, ix, 117 pp.

3436   SAYON, POMPOSA C. "Some Personal Problems of Female College
        Freshmen from Rural Areas Studying in Two Davao City
        Catholic Schools." Master's thesis, University of Santo
        Tomas [Manila], 1974, x, 147 pp.

3437   SHAHAJARATUDDUR SHEIKH ABDUL HALIM. "Sikap Wanita-wanita
        Melayu didalam Bidang Pekerjaan" [Attitude of Malay women
        towards work]. B.A. academic exercise, University of
        Malaya, 1969, v, 139 pp.

3438   _____. "Sikap Wanita2 Melayu terhadap Perkembangan Hari Ini"
        [The attitude of Malay women towards development today].
        Mastika 28, no. 7 (July 1968):27-30.

3439   SISON, ASUNCION ORDONEZ. "Marital Communication and Its Rela-
        tions to Marital Adjustment among Marriage Encounter Couples
        in the Greater Manila Area." Master's thesis, Ateneo de
        Manila University [Manila], 1976, 116 pp.

3440   SUSARA, LILY Z. "A Study of the Intelligence and Scholastic
        Achievement of First Year Students of the Girls' High
        School, Far Eastern University, Manila, 1960-1961."
        Master's thesis, Far Eastern University [Manila], 1963,
        xii, 123 pp.

3441   TEOH, JIN INN. "Epidemic Hysteria and Social Change: An Out-
        break in a Lower Secondary School in Malaysia." Singapore
        Medical Journal 16, no. 4 (Dec. 1975):301-6. (A rural
        Malay girls' school.)

3442   TEOH, JIN INN; SOEWONDO, SAESMALIJAH; and SIDHARTA, MYRA.
        "Epidemic Hysteria in Malaysian Schools: An Illustrative
        Episode." Psychiatry 38, no. 3 (Aug. 1975):258-68.
        (Focuses mainly on rural Malay girls' schools.)

3443   THEODORSON, GEORGE A. "Attitudes of Burmese Men and Women to
        Male Dominance in the Family." Burma Research Society,
        Journal 51, no. 1 (June 1968):17-21.

3444   THOMAS, AMMINI. "A Study of Attempted Suicide among Young
        South Indian Women in Singapore." Thesis for the Diploma
        in Soc.Sc., University of Singapore, 1959, 168 pp.

3445   THOMAS, R. MURRAY, and SURACHMAD, WINARNO. "Social-class Dif-
        ferences in Mothers' Expectations for Children in
        Indonesia." Journal of Social Psychology 57 (1962):303-7.

3446   TORREFRANCA, LOURDES HORDISTA. "An Analysis of the Personality
        Profiles of Some BSEED Women Students in Divine Word Col-
        lege, Bohol, as Revealed on the IPAT 16 Personality Factor
        Questionnaire 1964-1965." Master's thesis, University of
        San Carlos [Cebu City, Philippines], 1965, 117 pp.

3447   TSOI, W.F. et al. "Psychological Effects of Abortion: A
        Study of 1,739 Cases." Singapore Medical Journal 17 (1976):
        68-73.

3448   VACHHER, MANJU, and KHAIRUDDIN YUSOF. "A Psychosexual Study
        of Abortion Seeking Behaviour." Medical Journal of
        Malaysia 33, no. 1 (Sept. 1978):50-56.

3449   VERA, A.M. de, and BELENA, D.M. "A Survey on the Attitudes of
        the Husbands towards the Gainful Employment of Their Wives."
        CLSU Scientific Journal 3 (Oct./Dec. 1967):89-95.

3450   VERORA, REBECCA P. "Stressful Situations in Clinical Prac-
        tice Met by Nursing Students of Quezon Memorial Hospital
        School of Nursing during the School Year 1973-1974."
        Master's thesis, Luzonian University [Lucena City,
        Philippines], 1974, xi, 115 pp.

3451   VIDAL, CHARITO. "A Comparative Analysis of the Personality
        Traits of BSEED College Women of the University of San
        Carlos and of Three Other Teacher-Training Institutions of
        Cebu and Bohol Based on the IPAT 16 Personality Factor
        Questionnaire." Master's thesis, University of San Carlos
        [Cebu City, Philippines], 1966, 98 pp.

3452   YOUNGBLOOD, ROBERT LINLEY. "Female Dominance and Adolescent
        Filipino Attitude Orientations and School Achievement."
        Journal of Asian and African Studies 13, nos. 1/2 (Jan./Apr.
        1978):63-79.

3453   _____. "Self-Esteem and Academic Achievement of Filipino High
        School Students." Educational Research Quarterly 1, no. 2
        (Summer 1976):27-36.

                              RELIGION

                     (See also Muslim Women)

3454   ACHMAD, AFTABUDDIN. Wanita dalam Islam dan Kristen [Women in
        Islam and Christianity]. Di Indonesiakan oleh O. Hashem.
        Surabaja: Japi, 1963, 16 pp.

3455   BILLOTE, C. "On Women in Liturgical Functions." Philippine
        Priests' Forum 7 (June 1975):68-69.

3456   BINNEY, JOHN G. Christianity and the Karen Women. American
        Baptist Union, 18--[?].

3457   CAHILL, ANNE PATRICE, Sister. "The Educational and Social
        Works of the Sisters of St. Paul de Chatres in the
        Philippines." Master's thesis, University of Santo Tomas
        [Manila], 1938.

3458   CASUSO, ANDREN. "Religious Vocational Concepts of Filipino Girls." Master's thesis, Ateneo de Manila University [Manila], 1971, 139 pp.

3459   CLAPANO, ESPERANZA. "A Study of the Expected Qualities of Modern Religious Women." Master's thesis, Ateneo de Manila University [Manila], 1974, iv, 88 pp.

3460   DINH-THUC IOACHIM. "Les soeurs amantes de la croix au Viet Nam." Thesis (Dissertation ad Lauream, Pontificia Università Gregoriana, Rome), 1960.

3461   EAST ASIA SEMINAR OF THE WORLD FEDERATION OF METHODIST WOMEN, Singapore, 1968. Christ's Challenge to Asian Women. Report of the East Asia Seminar held 28 June-2 July 1968. Singapore: World Federation of Methodist Women, 1968, 106 pp.

3462   FERRARIS, MARIA RITA, Sister. "Mother Ignacia del Espiritu Santo and the Retreat Movement for Women in the Philippines." Master's thesis, Ateneo de Manila University [Manila], 1964, 103 pp.

3463   GOEMAAT, LOUISE. Onder Javaanse vrouwen [Among Javanese women]. Kampen: J.H. Kok, 1949, 40 pp.

3464   GRENVILLE, VIOLET. "Women and Worship in Burmah." Nineteenth Century and After 31 (1892):1001-7.

3465   JOAQUIN, N. "Beatas: The Intrepid God-Seekers of 17th Century Manila." Archipelago 3, no. A-25 (1976):8-18.

3466   KHIN MYO CHIT. "Women in Buddhism." Guardian [Rangoon] 21, no. 8 (Aug. 1974):8-12.

3467   LACUESTA, MARIA MACARIUS, Sister. "Religious Knowledge and Attitudes of Girls in Catholic High Schools." Master's thesis, St. Paul's College [Dumaguete City, Philippines], 1957, xi, 181 pp.

3468   LANSANG, MARY BERNARD. "Difficulties Encountered by Junior Sisters: Some Implications for Religious Formation." Master's thesis, Ateneo de Manila University [Manila], 1974, 117 pp.

3469   LICHNUCO, LUISA R. "A History of the Maryknoll Sisters in the Philippines." Master's thesis, Ateneo de Manila University [Manila], 1961, 196 pp.

3470   LUCIANO, LEONOR INES. "The Legal and Christian Perspectives of Women's Role." Unitas 48, no. 2 (June 1975):251-58.

3471 LUSTÉGUY, PIERRE. La femme annamite du Tonkin dans l'institutions des biens cultuels (huong-hoa). Etude sur une en-
quête récente [The role of women in Tonkinese religion and
property. Study based on a recent investigation]. Paris:
Nizet et Bastard, 1935, 126 pp.

3472 _____. The Role of Women in Tonkinese Religion and Property.
Translated by Charles A. Messner. New Haven: Human Relations Area Files Press, 1954, vii, 149 pp.

3473 OGILVIE, AMPARO R., Sister. "A Study of the Missionary Work
of the Sisters of Charity in the Philippines." Master's
thesis, University of Santo Tomas [Manila], 1952, ii,
96 pp.

3474 "On Women in the Sacred Ministry." Philippine Priests' Forum
7 (Sept. 1975):8-9.

3475 OSMEÑA, SERGIO. "The Moral and Spiritual Influence of
Filipino Women. Speech before the Catholic Women's
League, Feb 25, 1940." Manila: Bureau of Printing,
1941, 11 pp.

3476 OUNG, M.M. Hla. "The Women of Burma." Buddhism 1 (1903):
61-82.

3477 PHILIPPINE FEDERATION OF CHRISTIAN CHURCHES, Women's Work
Committee. The Joy of Sharing: 1957 Program Guide for
Women's Societies. Manila: Philippine Federation of
Christian Churches, 1957[?], 109, ii, 39 pp.

3478 _____. Women's Societies . . . Living the Faith: 1959 Program Guide for Women's Societies. Manila: Philippine
Federation of Christian Churches, 1959[?], vi, 23b, 38,
17 pp.

3479 "The Role of Religious Women." Boletín eclesiástica de
Filipinas [Manila] 39 (Jan./Feb. 1965):262-72.

3480 ROSIN-REUSSER, B.F. Indonesische Frauen in der Kirche von
heute [Indonesian women in the present-day church]. Basel:
Basler Missionsbuchhandlung G.m.b.H., 1954, 31 pp. Die
Sammlung der Gemeinde, 9.

3481 Wanita Pendjiwa Masjarakat, Renungan-renungan Kemasjarakatan
dari Indjil [Women are the soul of the society: reflections of the Christian community]. Jogjakarta: Jajasan
Kanisuis, 1970, 74 pp.

3482   YOUNG WOMEN'S CHRISTIAN ASSOCIATION, Singapore. Annual Report, 1967/68-. Singapore: Young Women's Christian Association, 1968-.

3483   YOUNG WOMEN'S CHRISTIAN ASSOCIATION OF MALAYSIA BIENNIAL CONFERENCE, 10th, Kuala Lumpur, 1976. Papers. Kuala Lumpur: YWCA of Malaysia, 1976, 1 vol. (various pagings).

SOCIAL CONDITIONS AND STATUS

(See also General Works; History; Marriage and Divorce; Married Women and Mothers)

Southeast Asia

3484   ALDABA-LIM, ESTEFANIA J. "The Role and Status of Young Asian Women Today." Unesco Philippines 5, nos. 5/6 (May/June 1965):156-63.

3485   ASEAN WOMEN LEADERS AND INTERNATIONAL WOMEN'S YEAR POST CONFERENCE MEETING, Jakarta, 1975. Report. Organized under the auspices of the ASEAN Sub-Committee on Women of the ASEAN Permanent Committee on Socio-Cultural Activities. Jakarta, 1975, 1 vol. (various pagings).

3486   BLOODWORTH, DENNIS. "Ladies Only." In An Eye for the Dragon. Edited by Dennis Bloodworth. London: Secker & Warburg, 1970, pp. 161-69.

3487   "The Changing Role of S.E. Asian Women." Special joint issue of Southeast Asia Chronicle no. 66 (Jan./Feb. 1979) and Pacific Research Bulletin, nos. 5/6 (July/Oct. 1978), 27 pp.

3488   EXPERT GROUP MEETING ON THE DEVELOPMENT OF WOMEN'S ORGANIZATIONS IN RURAL AREAS, Bangkok, 1978. Papers. Bangkok: United Nations Economic and Social Commission for Asia and the Pacific, 1978, 1 vol. (various pagings).

3489   FISHER, MARGUERITE J. "The Women of Asia Examine Their Responsibilites." Social Studies 46, no. 8 (Dec. 1955): 283-86.

3490   HOLLNSTEINER, MARY RACELIS. "Anti-poverty Strategies and Research in Asia, Extracts from an Interview." Community Development Journal 9, no. 3 (Oct. 1974):187-90.

3491   HUNTER, PENELOPE. "The Status of Chinese Women in Southeast
       Asia." Master's thesis, University of London, 1964,
       178 pp.

3492   INTERNATIONAL CONGRESS OF ANTHROPOLOGICAL AND ETHNOLOGICAL
       SCIENCES, 9th, Chicago, 1973. Women Cross-culturally:
       Change and Challenge. Edited by Ruby Rohrlich-Leavitt.
       The Hague: Mouton, 1975, xiv, 669 pp.

3493   LEBRA, JOYCE CHAPMAN, and PAULSON, JOY. Chinese Women in
       Southeast Asia. Singapore: Times Books International,
       1980, 250 pp.

3494   MATTHIASSON, CAROLYN J. Many Sisters: Women in Cross-
       cultural Perspective. New York: Free Press, 1974, xxii,
       443 pp.

3495   REGIONAL SEMINAR ON THE STATUS OF WOMEN AND FAMILY PLANNING
       FOR COUNTRIES WITHIN THE ECONOMIC COMMISSION FOR ASIA AND
       THE FAR EAST REGION, Jogjakarta, Indonesia, 1973. Papers.
       Organized by the United Nations in co-operation with the
       Government of Indonesia. New York: United Nations, 1974,
       i, 31 pp. United Nations Document ST/ESA/Ser.B2.

3496   The Role of Non-governmental Organizations in Planning for
       Children and Youth in National Development. Report of a
       seminar sponsored by the International Council of Women
       in co-operation with the United Nations Children's Fund in
       Bangkok, January 1964. New York[?]: United Nations[?],
       1964. 1 vol. (various pagings). United Nations Document,
       E/ICEF/NGO/86.

3497   SHAHANI, LETICIA RAMOS. "The Status of Women in Asia and
       National Development Programs." Asian & Pacific Quarterly
       of Cultural and Social Affairs 5, no. 2 (Autumn 1973):
       60-67.

3498   SOUTH AND SOUTH EAST ASIAN WORKSHOP, New York, 1956. South
       and South East Asian Workshop, April 19th-May 14th, 1956.
       Theme: The responsibilities of freedom; purpose, the
       interchange of ideas and experiences among a group of
       women leaders working towards citizen responsibility in a
       free society. New York: 1956. 1 vol. (various pagings).

3499   UNITED NATIONS, Asian and Pacific Centre for Women and Devel-
       opment. Environmental Issues Affecting Women with Par-
       ticular Reference to Housing and Human Settlements. Papers
       prepared for APCWD workshops held in collaboration with
       National Buildings Organisation (NBO), New Delhi, April-
       June 1980, New Delhi. Bangkok: APCWD, 1980, 164 pp.

3500   WARD, BARBARA E.   "Men, Women and Change: An Essay in Under-
       standing Social Roles in South and South-East Asia."   In
       Women in the New Asia.   Paris: Unesco, 1963, pp. 25-99.

3501   _____, ed.   Women in the New Asia: The Changing Social Roles
       of Men and Women in South and South-East Asia.   Paris:
       Unesco, 1963, 529 pp.

3502   WINZELER, ROBERT L.   "Sex Role Equality, Wet Rice Cultivation,
       and the State in Southeast Asia."   American Anthropologist
       76, no. 3 (Sept. 1974):563-66.

Burma

3503   AUNG THAN TUN.   "Burmese Women."   Guardian [Rangoon] 12, no. 4
       (Apr. 1965):40-45; no. 5 (May 1965):33-41.

3504   BROWNE, EDMOND CHARLES.   "The Burmese Women."   In The Coming
       of the Great Queen: A Narrative of the Acquisition of
       Burma.   London: Harrison, 1888, pp. 287-99.

3505   FIELDING-HALL, HAROLD.   "Burmese Women."   Blackwood's Magazine
       157 (1895):776-88.

3506   FURNIVALL, JOHN SYDENHAM.   "Dr. Ross and Mother Kin."   Burma
       Research Society, Journal 1, pt. 1 (1911):46-511.   (Answer
       to G.R.T. Ross's criticism of his notes on the Burmese
       matriarchy.)

3507   _____.   "Matriarchal Vestiges in Burma."   Burma Research So-
       ciety, Journal 1, pt. 1 (1911):15-30.

3508   _____.   "Matriarchy in Burma."   Burma Research Society, Jour-
       nal, 2 (1912):230-33.

3509   KHIN MYO THAM.   "From a Young Burmese Girl's Notebook."
       Unesco Courier 28 (Mar. 1975):26-27.

3510   MAUNG MAUNG.   "Women on the Wing."   Guardian [Rangoon] 3
       (Sept. 1956):30-34.

3511   MI MI KHAING, Daw.   "Burma: Balance and Harmony."   In Women
       in the New Asia.   Edited by Barbara E. Ward.   Paris:
       Unesco, 1963, pp. 104-37.

3512   _____.   Burmese Family.   Bombay: Orient Longmans, 1956,
       140 pp.   (Autobiographical account by a Burmese woman.)

3513   MYA SEIN, Daw.   "Towards Independence in Burma: The Role of
       Women."   Asian Affairs 59, pt. 3 (Oct. 1972):288-99.

3514   _____. "The Women of Burma: A Tradition of Hard Work and
        Independence." Atlantic Monthly Supplement (Perspective
        of Burma) 201, no. 2 (Feb. 1958):122-25.

3515   NI NI GYI. "Family in Transition." Unesco Courier 17 (Sept.
        1964):13-16. (On women in Burma.)

3516   _____. "Patterns of Social Change in a Burmese Family." In
        Women in the New Asia. Edited by Barbara E. Ward. Paris:
        Unesco, 1963, pp. 138-48.

3517   _____. "Patterns of Social Change in a Burmese Family."
        Guardian [Rangoon] 12, no. 2 (Feb. 1965):20-21.

3518   NYUN-HAN, EMMA. "The Socio-Political Roles of Women in Japan
        and Burma." Ph.D. dissertation, University of Colorado,
        1972, 634 pp. Abstracted in Dissertation Abstracts Inter-
        national 33, no. 8 (Feb. 1973):4499-A. University Micro-
        films International, order no. 73-1810.

3519   ROSS, G.R.T. "Critical Notes on Mr. Furnivall's Paper on
        Matriarchal Vestiges in Burma." Burma Research Society,
        Journal 1, pt. 1 (1911):103-7.

3520   SEIN, SEIN MA. "The Position of Women in Hinaya Buddhist
        Countries (Burma, Ceylon, and Thailand)." Master's thesis,
        University of London, 1958, iv, 177 pp.

3521   THEODORSON, GEORGE A. "Attitudes of Burmese Men and Women to
        Male Dominance in the Family." Burma Research Society,
        Journal 51, no. 1 (June 1968):17-21.

3522   WHITE, WALTER GRAINGE. "How the Women Live." In The Sea
        Gypsies of Malaya. London: Seeley, Service & Co., 1922.
        pp. 249-560.

Indochina

3523   BEURDELEY, CÉCILE. "Dating the Dancing Girls of Cambodia."
        Réalités, no. 153 (Aug. 1963):66-69.

3524   BLOOD, DORIS. "Women's Speech Characteristics in Cham."
        Asian Culture 3, nos. 3/4 (1961):139-43.

3525   BUCHANAN, KEITH. "The Women of Angkor." Eastern Horizon 2,
        no. 12 (Oct. 1963):13-15.

3526   CHANDOLA, HARISH. "Vietnam Journal: New Position of Women."
        Economic and Political Weekly 8, no. 16 (Apr. 1973):744-46.

3527 COUGHLIN, RICHARD JAMES. "Pregnancy and Birth in Vietnam."
In Southeast Asian Birth Customs: Three Studies in Human
Reproduction. Edited by Donn V. Hart, Phya Anuman Rajadhon,
and Richard J. Coughlin. New Haven, Conn.: Human Relations Area Files Press, 1965, pp. 209-73.

3528 COURTOIS, E. "La famille annamite: mariages, naissances,
décès, cérémonies auxquelles ils donnent lieu" [The
Annamite family: marriages, births, deaths, and the ceremonies arising from them]. Revue indochinoise (1900):
509-11.

3529 DANG PHUC THONG. La femme dans la société annamite [The woman
in Annamite society]. Hanoi: Imprimerie Tan-Dan, 1931,
39 pp.

3530 D'ENJOY, PAUL. "Le rôle de la femme dans la société annamite"
[The role of the woman in the Annamite society]. Société
d'Anthropologie de Paris, Bulletin et mémoires. 5th ser.
4 (1903):305-17.

3531 EBIHARA, MAY. "Khmer Village Women in Cambodia: A Happy
Balance." In Many Sisters: Women in Cross-cultural Per-
spective. Edited by Carolyn J. Matthiason. New York:
Free Press, 1974, pp. 305-48.

3532 Frauen in Vietnam [Women in Vietnam]. Prepared under the direction of Margret Peters. 2. aufl. Cologne: Initiativ-
komitee für Deutsch- Vietnamesische Kulturbeziehungen,
1976, 107 pp.

3533 GRACE, PAUL et al. Vietnamese Women in Society and Revolution. Vol. 1. The French Colonial Period. Translated by
Ngo Vinh Long. Cambridge, Mass.: Vietnam Resource Centre,
1974-, 207 pp.

3534 HOSKINS, MARILYN W. "Vietnamese Women: Their Roles and Their
Options." In INTERNATIONAL CONGRESS OF ANTHROPOLOGICAL AND
ETHNOLOGICAL SCIENCES, 9th, Chicago, 1973. Changing Iden-
tities in Modern Southeast Asia. Edited by David J. Banks.
The Hague: Mouton, 1976, pp. 127-46.

3535 LE HONG CHUONG. "Students and Girls of Viet-Nam Seen Through
Popular Songs." Asia [Saigon] 2, no. 6 (Sept. 1952):
243-49.

3536 LE KWANG KIM. "Viet-nam: Twenty Years of Change and Turmoil." Unesco Courier 17 (Sept. 1964):22-27. (Women of
Vietnam.)

3537   _____. "A Woman of Viet-Nam in a Changing World." In Women
         in the New Asia. Edited by Barbara E. Ward. Paris:
         Unesco, 1963, pp. 462-70.

3538   LÉVY, BANYEN PHIMMASONE. "Yesterday and Today in Laos: A
         Girl's Autobiographical Notes." In Women in the New Asia.
         Edited by Barbara E. Ward. Paris: Unesco, 1963,
         pp. 244-65.

3539   LIFTON, B.J. "Young Women of Indochina." Mlle, 41 (July
         1955):50-55.

3540   MAI THI TU, and LE THI NHAM TUYET. Women in Viet Nam. Hanoi:
         Foreign Languages Publishing House, 1978, 326 pp.

3541   MOLANDER, CECILIA. Kvinna i Vietnam [Women in Vietnam].
         Uppsala: Nordiska Afrikainst, 1978, 144 pp.

3542   NGO DINH NHU. "Vietnamese Women in the Course of History:
         An Address . . . before the International Women's Associa-
         tion at the Presidential Palace." Vietnamese-American
         Association, Journal 2, no. 1 (Mar. 1957):16-36.

3543   NGUYEN TRAI. Gia-huan ca Thi-Nam Dinh-gia-Thuyet dinh-chinh
         va chu-thich. In lan 3. Saigon: Tan Viet, 1953, 50 pp.

3544   NGUYEN VAN HUYEN. Les chants alternés des garçons et des
         filles en Annam [Alternating songs of boys and girls in
         Annam]. Paris: P. Geuthner, 1934, 224 pp.

3345   OLSEN, NEIL H. "Matrilineal Societies in Southeast Asia:
         Examples from Highland Vietnam." In INTERNATIONAL CONGRESS
         OF ANTHROPOLOGICAL AND ETHNOLOGICAL SCIENCES, 9th, Chicago,
         1973. Changing Identities in Modern Southeast Asia. Ed-
         ited by David J. Banks. The Hague: Mouton, 1976,
         pp. 249-55.

3546   WERMINE, WILLIAM R. "650 Women and Children: No Man's Land."
         Vietnam Magazine 7, no. 4 (1974):14-16.

Indonesia

3547   ADELANTE. "Concubinaat bij de Ambtenaren van het Binnen-
         landsch bestuur in Nederlandsch-Indië" [Concubinage among
         the civil servants of the government in the Netherlands
         Indies]. Tijdschrift voor Nederlandsch-Indië. 2d n.s. 2
         (1898):304-14.

3548   ADLIN RINA. Penuntuan Wanita (dan) Prija Modern [A guide for
         the modern woman and man]. Medan: Madju, 1960, 136 pp.

3549   ALISJAHBANA, SUTAN TAKDIR, ed. "The Place of Women." In
       Indonesia: Social and Cultural Revolution. Kuala Lumpur:
       Oxford University Press, 1966, pp. 105-15.

3350   ARSONTMODJO, S. SOEDIBIO. Wanita dan Rumah Tangga [Women and
       the home]. 3d ed. Jakarta: BPK Gunung Malia, 1974, 77 pp.

3351   _____. Wanita Rumah Tangga dan Anak-anak [Housewives and
       children]. Jakarta: Gunung Mulia, 1970, 80 pp.

3552   BRACONIER, A. de. "Het kazerne-concubinaat in Ned. Indië"
       [The concubinage in the military of the Netherlands Indies].
       Vragen van de dag 28 (1913):974-95.

3553   "The Century's Changed Women." Indonesian Affairs 1,
       nos. 4/5 (1951):40-44.

3554   CHABOT, HENDRIK Th. "Jonge vrouwen in conflict" [Young women
       in conflict]. Indonesië 8 (1955):40-47.

3555   _____. Verwantschap, stand en sexe in Zuid-Celebes [Kinship,
       class, and sex in South Sulawesi]. Groningen: J.B.
       Wolters, 1950, 277 pp.

3556   CHRISTANAND. Wanita: Bahan Renungan dan Bimbingan Penggalan
       Mental bagi Para Gadis Remaja [Women: reflections on men-
       tal guidance for girls]. Jogjakarta: Yayasan Konisius,
       1977, 39 pp.

3557   CRITCHFIELD, RICHARD. "Discovering Indonesia's Women." Asia
       [New Jersey] 2, no. 4 (Nov./Dec. 1979):8-17.

3558   CUISINIER, JEANNE. "L'action sociale des femmes en Indonésie"
       [The social action of Indonesian women]. Revue socialiste
       92 (1955):489-96.

3559   _____. "Islam et matriarcat à Minangkabau" [Islam and
       matriarchy in Minangkabau]. L'Institut de Science Econo-
       mique Appliquée, Cahiers. Serie V. Humanités: économie,
       ethnologie, sociologie, no. 6 (July 1963):47-62.

3560   DAHLAN, AISYAH. "Peranan Wanita dalam Keluarga" [The role of
       women in the family]. Mimbar Kekarya ABRI 5, nos. 52/53
       (195):83-90, 99.

3561   DUMADI, SAGIMUN MULUS. Wanita Indonesia dan Pantja Sila
       (Indonesian women and Panja sila]. Jogjakarta: Pantjasila,
       1953, 144 pp.

338

3562 FISCHER, LOUIS. "All Women Are Created Equal." In The Story
of Indonesia. Westport, Conn.: Greenwood Press, 1973,
pp. 192-98.

3563 FRANCILLON, GERARD. "Some Matriarchic Aspects of the Social
Structure of the Southern Tetun of Middle Timor." Ph.D.
dissertation, Australian National University, 1967, xxiii,
478 pp.

3564 FRIEDBERG, CLAUDINE. "La femme et le féminin chez les Bunaq
du centre de Timor" [The women and feminity of the Buna'
Central Timor]. Archipel, no. 13 (1977):37-52.

3565 GEERTZ, HILDRED. The Javanese Family: A Study of Kinship and
Socialization. New York: Free Press of Glencoe, 1961,
xii, 176 pp. (Includes chapters on women, property division at divorce and at death, marriage and divorce, pregnancy and childbirth customs, and the husband and wife
relationship.)

3566 GOEMAAT, LOUISE. Onder Javaanse vrouwen [Among Javanese
women]. Kampen: J.H. Kok, 1949, 40 pp.

3567 HADISUTIRTO, S.M. Wanita Adalah Ibu Keluarga, Ibu Rumah
Tangga, Ibu Masjarakat, Ibu Bangsa [The woman is the
mother of the family, household, society, and nation].
Jakarta: Djawatan Pendidikan Masjarakat, 1951, 24 pp.

3568 HAMIDJOJO-MUNAR, SUNDARI. Renungan Wanita [Reflections on
women]. Medan: Islamijah, 1951, 203 pp.

3569 HAZAIRIN. De Redjang: de volksordening, het verwantschaps-,
huwelijks- en erfrecht [The Redjang: their social organization, kinship, marriage, and inheritance law].
Bandung: A.C. Nix, 1936, 242 pp.

3570 HULL, VALERIE J. "Fertility, Socioeconomic Status and the
Position of Women in a Javanese Village." Ph.D. dissertation, Australian National University, 1975, ix, 447 pp.

3571 _____. Fertility, Socioeconomic Status and the Position of
Women in a Javenese Village. Canberra: Australian National University, 1975, ix, 584 pp.

3572 _____. "Women in Java's Rural Middle Class: Progress or
Regress?" Jogjakarta: Population Institute, Gadjah Mada
University, 1976, 26 pp. Paper prepared for the Fourth
World Congress for Rural Sociology, August 1976, Torun,
Poland.

339

3573 "Huwelijk en concubinaat" [Marriage and concubinage]. De
Indische gids 33 (1911):410-32.

3574 IHROMI, T. OMAS. "Wanita sebagai Penerus Nilai-nilai kepada
Generasi Muda" [Women as transmitters of values to the
young generation]. Prisma 4, no. 5 (Oct. 1975):71-78.

3575 JASPAN, MERVYN AUBREY. "From Patriliny to Matriliny: Structural Change among the Redjang of Southwest Sumatra."
Ph.D. dissertation, Australian National University, 1964,
204 pp.

3576 JAYAWARDENA, CHANDRA. "Women and Kinship in Acheh Besar,
Northern Sumatra." Ethnology 16, no. 1 (Jan. 1977):21-38.

3577 KAHN, J.S. "'Tradition,' Matriliny and Change among the
Minangkabau of Indonesia." Bijdragen tot de taal-, land-
en volkenkunde 132, no. 1 (1976):64-95.

3578 KHATIJAH, PUTEH, Raja. Kemajuan Kaum Ibu di Sumatra, atau,
Melawat ke Sumatra Timur [The advancement of women in
Sumatra, or, visiting East Sumatra]. Ipoh: Warta Kinta
Press, 1938[?], 56 pp. (In Jawi language.)

3579 KOOT, W.D. Het Concubinaat [The concubinage]. Surabaya,
1905.

3580 KORN, VICTOR EMANUEL. "De vrouwelijke mamas in de
Minangkabausche familie" [The female 'mama' in the
Minangkabau family]. Bijdragen tot de taal-, land- en
volkenkunde 100 (1941):301-38.

3581 KRAANEN, J. "De vrouw in de Kereesche maatschappij" [The
woman in the Kereesche society]. Onze missiën 5 (1921/22):
84-104.

3582 KRUIJT, ALBERTUS CHRISTIAAN. "De plaats die de Javaansche
vrouw inneemt in de samenleving en in de christengemeente"
[The position occupied by the Javanese woman in her society
and Christian society]. Mededeelingen vanwege het
Nederlandsche Zendelinggenootschap 52 (1908):318-35.

3583 KOENTJARANINGRAT. "Bride-Price and Adoption in the Kinship
Relations of the Bgu of West Irian." Ethnology 5, no. 3
(July 1966):233-44.

3584 LIEM, SIANG HOK. "Peranan Kaum Wanita dalam Masalah
Perumahan" [The role of women in housing problems].
Masalah Bangunan 3, no. 1 (1958):3-19, 28.

3585　MARETIN, J.V.　"Disappearance of Matriclan Survivals in Minangkabau Family and Marriage Relations."　<u>Bijdragen tot de taal-, land- en volkenkunde</u> 117, no. 1 (1961):168-95; "Errata" 117, no. 2 (1961):304.

3586　MASDANI, J.　"Peranan Wanita dalam Pembangunan Sosial dan Mental Health" [The role of women in social development and mental health].　<u>Jiwa</u> 5, no. 4 (1972):1-7.

3587　MINATTUR, JOSEPH.　"Matriliny in Minangkabau."　<u>Modern Review</u> 123 (Dec. 1968):874-76.

3588　NASOETION, MASDOELHAK HAMONANGAN.　<u>De plaats van de vrouw in de Bataksche maatschappij</u> [The place of women in Batak society].　Utrecht: Kemink, 1943, 118 pp.

3589　NIERRAS, LETICIA CANEJA.　"Political and Social Status of Women in Java."　Master's thesis, Cornell University, 1958, iv, 99 pp.

3590　NILAKUSUMA, S.　<u>Wanita didalam dan diluar Rumah Tangga</u> [Women in and outside the home].　Tjet. 3.　Bukittingi: Nusantara, 1960, 205 pp.

3591　NOOR, YETTY RIZALI.　"Wanita dan Masyarakat" [Women and society].　<u>Mimbar Indonesia</u> 14, no. 26 (1960):23-24, 30.

3592　_____.　"Women's role in Society and Development in Indonesia."　<u>Impact</u> 10, no. 4 (Apr. 1975):130-32.

3593　NOTOPURO HARDJITO.　"Masalah Wanita Kedudukan dan Peranannya" [Women's problems, their status, and role].　Jakarta:　The Author, 1973, 27 pp.

3594　PAPANEK, HANNA.　"Jakarta Middle Class Women:　Modernization, Employment and Family Life."　In <u>What is Modern Indonesian Culture</u>?　Edited by Gloria Davis.　Athens:　Ohio University Press, 1979.

3595　_____.　"Research on Women by Women:　Interview Selection and Training in Indonesia."　<u>Studies in Family Planning</u> 10, nos. 11/12 (Nov./Dec. 1979):412-15.

3596　PAPANEK, HANNA; IHROMI, T. OMAS; and RAHARDJO, YULFITA.　"Changes in the Status of Women and Their Significance in the Process of Social Change:　Indonesian Case Studies."　47 pp.　Paper presented at the Sixth International Conference on Asian History, sponsored by the International Association of Historians of Asia, Jogjakarta 1974.

3597   PAPANEK, HANNA et al. "Wanita di Jakarta: Kehidupan Keluarga
        dan Keluarga Berencana" [Women in Jakarta: Family Life and
        Family Planning]. Masyarakat Indonesia 5, no. 2 (Dec.
        1978):217-59.

3598   _____. "Women in Jakarta: Family Life and Family Planning."
        In Cultural Factors and Population in Developing Countries.
        Washington, D.C.: Smithsonian Institution, Interdisciplin-
        ary Communications Program, 1976, pp. 129-66. Occasional
        Monograph, no. 6.

3599   POENSEN, M.C. "Iets over het Javaansche gezin" [Something
        about the Javanese Family]. Mededeelingan vanwege het
        Nederlandsche Zendelinggenootschap 31 (1887):112-50,
        220-61.

3600   RADJO PENGHULU, IDROES HAKIMI DT. Buku Pegangan Bundo Kan-
        duang di Minangkabau [Status and duties of a Minangkabau
        woman]. Bandung: Rosda, 1978, x, 54 pp.

3601   RODENWALDT, ERNST. "Invloed van de tropen op het geslachts-
        leven van de vrouw" [Influence of the tropics on the sex
        life of the woman]. Ons nageslacht 4 (1931):146-64.

3602   ROEDER, O.G. "The Maidens of Java." Far Eastern Economic Re-
        view 53, no. 8 (Aug. 1966):347-48.

3603   ROŻNOWSKI, FRANCISZEK. "Badania antropologiczne młodzieży
        męskiej i żeńzkiejz wyspy Palue (Mate Wyspy Sun-
        dajskie . . . Indonezja)" [Anthropological studies of
        male and female youth from the island of Paloe (Lesser
        Sunda Islands . . . Indonesia]. Ph.D. dissertation
        (Rozprawa doktorska), Uniwersytet im. A. Mickiewicza w
        Poznaniu (Poland), 1973.

3604   SACHLAN, PAR (Mrs.). "Benarkah Wanita Tidak Suka Dijadikan
        Obyek Seksuil?" [Is it true that women dislike being sexual
        objects?]. Mawas Diri 4, no. 6 (1975):5-8.

3605   SADLI, SAPARINAH, and BIRAN, ZAINAL. "Permissive Attitudes in
        Sexual Relations." Prisma, no. 4 (Nov. 1976):65-71.

3606   SISWORAHARDJO, S. "Case Study on Social Welfare Strategies to
        Enhance Women's Roles in Socio-Economic Development and
        Leadership in the Rural Areas, Suradita, Subdistrict of
        Serpong, Tangerang." Jakarta, 1979, viii, 35 pp. Paper
        presented at the Workshop on Social Welfare Strategies to
        Enhance Women's Roles in Economic Development Activities
        and Leadership, Jakarta, 1979.

3607 "Social Position of Women." <u>Report on Indonesia</u> 6, no. 1
       (Aug./Sept. 1954):35-36.

3608 SRY UMYATY. <u>Wanita dalam Tingkatan Masjarakat</u> [Women in the
       social structure]. Tjet. 2. Surabaya: Pustaka Baru,
       1950, 53 pp.

3609 STOLER, ANN. "Class Structure and Female Autonomy in Rural
       Java." In <u>Women and National Development</u>. Edited by
       Wellesley Editorial Committee. Chicago: University of
       Chicago Press, 1977, pp. 74-89.

3610 SUBANDRIO, HURUSTIATI. "The Legal and Social Position of
       Women in Indonesia." <u>Civilisations</u> 4 (1951):31-40.

3611 _____. "The Position of Women in a Muslim Family in
       Indonesia." <u>Islamic Review</u> 37, no. 9 (Sept. 1949):35-39.

3612 _____. "The Respective Roles of Men and Women in Indonesia."
       In <u>Women in the New Asia</u>. Edited by Barbara E. Ward.
       Paris: Unesco, 1963, pp. 230-42.

3613 _____. "The Social Life of Women in Indonesia." <u>Islamic Re-
       view</u> 40, no. 8 (Aug. 1952):16-19.

3614 SOELAIMAN, H. "Adat Bujang Berkenalan dengan Gadis di Daerah
       Sumatera Selatan" [The tradition of boys getting acquainted
       with girls in south Sumatra]. <u>Medan Bahasa</u> 5, no. 6
       (1955):19-23; 5, no. 7 (1955):16-19.

3615 SULEIMAN, SATYAVATI. "Indonesian Women Today." <u>International
       Relations Quarterly</u> 2 (Nov. 1959):6-10.

3616 SUPARNO HS. "Transfer Isteri" [Wife swapping]. <u>Mawas Diri</u>
       4, no. 11 (1975):56-59.

3617 SOERATMAN, DARSITI. "Tiga Perempat Abad Melaksanakan Cita-
       cita Kartini" [Three quarters of a century for developing
       the ideology of Kartini]. <u>Pusara</u> 44, no. 4 (1976):125-31.

3618 SOERIOKOESOEMO, N.S.A. GANI. "Sekitar Perbaikan Kedudukan
       Wanita Indonesia" [On the improvement of the status of the
       Indonesian Woman]. <u>Daya Sosial</u> 1, no. 4 (1958):28-32.

3619 SUTJIPTO. "Irian Barat: Peranan dan Kedudukan Wanita dari
       Masa Kemasa, Uraian Disampaikan kepada Para Anggota Perwib,
       pada Tanggal 14 Djanuari, 1965, di Wisma Koreri, Djakarta"
       [West Irian: the role and status of women from time to
       time, a briefing given to the members of Perwib on
       14 January 1965, in Wisma Koreri, Jakarta]. Jakarta:
       Projek Penerbitan Sekretariat Koordinator Urursan Irian
       Barat, 1965, 14 pp.

3620   SOEWONDO, NANI. Kedudukan Wanita Indonesia dalam Hukum dan
        Masjarakat [The status of Indonesian women in law and so-
        ciety]. Tjet. 2. Jakarta: Timur Emas, 1968, 221 pp.

3621   TANNER, NANCY. "Matrifocality in Indonesia and Africa and
        among Black Americans." In Women, Culture, and Society.
        Edited by Michelle Zimbalist Rosaldo and Louise Lamphere.
        Stanford, Calif.: Stanford University Press, 1974,
        pp. 129-56.

3622   VALERIE, RENEE. "La position sociale de la femme dans la
        société traditionnelle des Moluques centrales" [The social
        position of women in the traditional society of Central
        Moluccas]. Archipel, no. 13 (1977):53-78.

3623   WAHAB, M. WAHIB. Fungsi Wanita dalam Masjarakat [Function of
        women in society]. Jakarta: Djawatan Penerangan Agama,
        1960, 12 pp.

3624   WIDER, JOAN (Schutzman). "Indonesian Women in New York: A
        Study of Culture Contact." Master's thesis, New York
        University, 1964.

3625   _____. "Indonesian Women in the Hague: Colonial Immigrants
        in the Metropolis." Ph.D. dissertation, New York Univer-
        sity, 1967, iv, 274 pp.

Malaysia

3626   ABDUL GHANI ROKAMBOL, and AZIZAH KASSIM. "Kedudukan Wanita
        Adat Perpateh di Negeri Sembilan dalam Konteks Masyarakat
        Hari Ini" [The status of women in 'adat perpateh' in
        Negeri Sembilan in today's social context]. Manusia dan
        Masyarakat 3 (1974):73-81.

3627   ABDUL KAHAR bin BADOR. "Kinship and Social Change among the
        Matrilineal Malays in Negri Sembilan." In Southeast Asia
        in the Modern World. Edited by Berhard Grossmann.
        Wiesbaden: Otto Harrassowitz, 1972, pp. 180-91.

3628   ABDULLAH MALIM BAGINDA. "A Case Study on the Role of
        Malaysian Rural Women in Community Life." 38 pp. Paper
        presented at the Expert Group Meeting on the Development of
        Women's Organizations in Rural Areas, Bangkok, April/May
        1978, organized by the Economic and Social Commission for
        Asia and the Pacific.

3629   ABU BAKAR bin WAN TEH IBRAHIM, Wan. "The Pemaju Kampong: A
        Woman Community Development Working in Action. Kuala
        Lumpur: Community Development Division, Ministry of Agri-
        culture and Rural Development, 1975, 6 pp. Risalah KEMAS,
        no. 2.

3630   ACKERMAN, SUSAN ELLEN. "Cultural Process in Malaysian Indus-
       trialization: A Study of Malay Women Factory Workers."
       Ph.D. dissertation, University of California, San Diego,
       1980, xiv, 292 pp.

3631   ADNAN KAMIS. "Imej Wanita Sekadar Jadi Simbol Berahi [Image
       of women as being a sex symbol]. Mastika 33, no. 10
       (Oct. 1973):106-9.

3632   AHMAD HAJI YUSUF. "Kedudukan dan Peranan Wanita dalam
       Masyarakat Adat Perpateh" [The status and role of women in
       the 'adat perpateh' society]. Wanita [Kuala Lumpur],
       no. 69 (Apr. 1975):65, 76.

3633   AHMADI ASMARA [pseud.]. Gadis Hari Ini [Girls today]. Kuala
       Pilah, Malaysia: Sentosa Store, 1959, 66 pp.

3634   _____. Falsafah Cara mengenai Perempuan [The philosophical
       way of women]. 4th ed. Marang, Trengganu, Malaysia:
       Penerbit HMBA, 1972, 111 pp.

3635   AINON MUHAMMAD. "Modenisasi dan Implikasinya terhadap Peranan
       serta Fungsi Kaum Wanita" [Modernization and its implica-
       tions for the role and function of women]. Dewan Masyarakat
       13, no. 3 (Mar. 1975):6-8.

3636   AISAH MURAD, Siti. "Aneka Majalah untuk Wanita" [Various
       journals for women]. Dewan Sastera 9, no. 3 (Mar. 1979):
       59-60.

3637   ANIS binti SABIRIN. Peranan Wanita Baru [The role of the new
       woman]. Kuala Lumpur: Penerbitan Utasan Melayu, 1969,
       136 pp.

3638   _____. "Wanita dalam Zaman Perolehan" [Women in a changing
       society]. Dewan Masyarakat 4 (Aug. 1966):26-29.

3639   ASIS UJANG. "Penyesuaian Adat dan Syara' bagi Kedudukan
       Wanita Beradat Perpatih di Kampung Terusan" [The synthesis
       of adat and Islamic laws for the status of 'adat perpatih'
       women in Kampong Terusan]. B.A. academic exercise, Univer-
       sity of Malaya, 1976, 79 pp.

3640   AZIZAH KASSIM. "Kedudukan Wanita Adat Perpateh di Negeri
       Sembilan dalam Konteks Masyarakat Hari Ini" [The position
       of women in 'adat perpateh' in Negri Sembilan in today's
       social context]. Manusia dan Masyarakat 13 (1974):73-81.

3641 _____. "Kedudukan Wanita di-dalam Masharakat Melayu Beradat Perpateh di-Negeri Sembilan" [The position of women in Malay 'adat perpateh' society in Negri Sembilan]. Master's thesis, University of Malaya, 1969, 260 pp.

3642 _____. "A Matrilineal Society in the Context of Development: The Adat Perpatih Case." Federation Museums Journal. n.s. 21 (1976):41-52.

3643 BHUPALAN, F. RASAMAH, and FATIMAH HAMID-DON. "Hari Wanita, Federation of Malaya: Report of Women's Day, 25th August, 1962." Kuala Lumpur: Hari Wanita Committee, 1962, 42 pp.

3644 CHEN, PAUL CHIEH YEE; AHMAD NOORDIN, Raja; and LEE, Y.N. "Food Beliefs of Rural Malay Women of Trengganu." Medical Journal of Malaysia 34, no. 2 (Dec. 1979):100-107.

3645 DE MOUBRAY, GEORGE ALEXANDER de CHAZAL. Matriarchy in the Malay Peninsula and Neighbouring Countries. London: G. Routledge, 1931, ix, 292 pp.

3646 FATIMAH ARIFFIN, Siti. "Peranan dan Kedudokan Wanita di Masyarakat Kampong Kerdau" [The role and status of women in the Kampong Kerdau community]. B.A. academic exercise, University of Malaya, 1965, iv, 53 pp.

3647 FATIMAH HAMID-DON. "Wanita sebagai Suri Rumahtangga dan Pembangunan Negara" [Women as housewives and their role in national development]. Wanita [Kuala Lumpur], no. 79 (Feb. 1976):76-77.

3648 FIRTH, ROSEMARY. "House-keeping among Malay Peasant Women." Man 42, no. 33 (May/June 1942):67-68.

3649 _____. "The Position of Women." In Housekeeping among Malay Peasants. London: Athlone Press, 1966, pp. 26-34.

3650 GORDON, SHIRLE. "The Condition of Our Plantation Workers: The Mothers and Fathers of the Children." Intisari 3, no. 4 (1970):49-55.

3651 GUPTA, ANIMA SEU, and LYNN, D.B. "A Study of Sexual Behaviour in Females." Journal of Sex Research 8, no. 3 (Aug. 1972): 208-18.

3652 HASAN HAJI HAMZAH. "Wanita: Tidak Ada Lagi Kewanitaannya?" [Women: no longer feminine?]. Sarina 3, no. 35 (Feb. 1979):92-95.

3653   HIRSCHMAN, CHARLES, and AGHAJANIAN, AKHBAR. "Women's Labour
       Force Participation and Socioeconomic Development in
       Peninsular Malaysia, 1957-70." Journal of Southeast Asian
       Studies 11, no. 1 (Mar. 1980):30-49.

3654   ISMAIL MUHAMMAD. "Wanita Melayu didalam Masharakat Moden"
       [Malay women in the modern society]. Dewan Masyarakat 3
       (Apr. 1965):38-41.

3655   JAAFAR bin ABDUL RAHIM. "Hak untuk Bekas-bekas Isteri
       Peneroka LKTP" [The rights of the ex-wives of FELDA
       settlers]. Dewan Masyarakat 13, no. 3 (Mar. 1975):9-10.

3656   JAAFAR bin HARUN. "Keadaan Sosial dan Ekonomi Pelajar-pelajar
       Perempuan Alor Setar, Kedah" [The socioeconomic status of
       female students in Alor Setar, Kedah]. B.A. academic exer-
       cise, University of Malaya, 1978, xii, 205 pp.

3657   JASMA OTHMAN, Siti. "Kedudukan Wanita Melayu Tradisional
       seperti Digambarkan dalam Cerita-cerita Jenaka dan Cerita-
       cerita Penglipor Lara Melayu" [The status of traditional
       Malay women as portrayed in Malay 'jenaka' stories and
       folk-tales]. B.A. academic exercise, University of Malaya,
       1977.

3658   KAMAL HASSAN. "Delimma Wanita Golongan Menengah Melayu"
       [Dilemma of Malay middle-class women]. Panji Masyarakat 2,
       no. 9 (May 1977):10-12, 52.

3659   KHADIJAH MUHAMMAD. "Migration and the Matrilineal System of
       Negeri Sembilan, Malaysia." Ph.D. dissertation, University
       of Pittsburgh, 1978, 394 pp. Abstracted in Dissertation
       Abstracts International 39, no. 9 (Mar. 1979):5598-A.
       University Microfilms International, order no. 7902773.

3660   _____. "Penjejasan Maruah Wanita dalam Penulisan" [Defamation
       of women's image in writings]. Mastika 37, no. 8 (Aug.
       1977):42-47.

3661   _____. "Sikap Masyarakat terhadap Wanita" [The attitude of
       society towards women]. Wanita [Kuala Lumpur], no. 93
       (Apr. 1977):14-15.

3662   KOMANYI, MARGIT ILONA. "The Iban Woman's Role: A Brief Sum-
       mary of Observations at Samu on the Paku River." Sarawak
       Museum Journal 19, no. 38 (1971):253-56.

3663 _____. "The Real and Ideal Participation in Decision-making of Iban Women: A Study of a Longhouse Community in Sarawak, East Malaysia." Ph.D. dissertation, New York University, 1973, vii, 143 pp. Abstracted in Dissertation Abstracts International 33, no. 10 (Apr. 1973):4631-B. University Microfilms International, order no. 73-8177.

3664 LIM, JOO HOCK. "Chinese Female Immigration into the Straits Settlements, 1860-1901." South Seas Society, Journal 22, pts. 1/2 (1967):58-110.

3665 MAIMONAH binti A. Majid. "Gambaran Imej Wanita Melayu dalam Cerpen-cerpen Majallah 'Wanita' (1969-1975)" [Images of Malay women in short stories of the magazine 'Wanita' 1969-1975]. B.A. academic exercise, University of Malaya, 1976, v, 80 pp.

3666 MUHAMMAD KAMAL HASSAN. "Dilema Wanita Melayu Masakini" [Dilemma of Malay women today]. Wanita [Kuala Lumpur], no. 94 (May 1977):22-23, 64, 76.

3667 NAGATA, JUDITH A. "Kinship and Social Mobility among the Malays." Man 11, no. 3 (Sept. 1976):400-409.

3668 NAMIRI JAMIL. "Siapa Kata Wanita Setia?] [Who says women are loyal?]. Mastika 34, no. 7 (July 1974):17-22.

3669 NARAYANAN, P.P. "The Integration of Women in the Economic and Social Life: General Situation, Difficulties, Obstacles to Be Overcome." Union Herald 55, no. 208 (Oct. 1975): 6-15.

3670 NG, LUM SONG. "Position of Chinese Women in Marriage and in the Family: A Comparison of Two Residential Areas in Penang." Master's thesis, Science University of Malaysia, 1977, xii, 278 pp.

3671 NORDIN SELAT. "Some Facts and Fallacies with Regard to the Position of Men in Adat Perpatih." Federation Museums Journal 15 (1970):101-20.

3672 O'BRIEN, LESLIE NOLA. "Class, Sex and Ethnic Stratification in West Malaysia, with Particular Reference to Women in the Professions." 2 vols. Ph.D. dissertation, Monash University, 1979, xix, 743 pp.

3673 _____. "Sex, Ethnicity and the Professions in West Malaysia: Some Preliminary Considerations." Akademika, no. 14 (Jan. 1979):31-42.

3674 PEJIĆ, MAYA. Vrouw in Azië: vrouwen in Maleisië, Thailand en
      Sri Lanka [Women in Asia: Women in Malaysia, Thailand and
      Sri Lanka]. The Hague: Voorlichtingsdienst Ontwikkelings-
      samenwerking van het Ministerie van Buitenlandse Zaken,
      1976, 64 pp.

3675 RAMDZAN HAJI CHALI. "Kedudukan dan Peranan Wanita di dalam
      Islam dan Adat Perpatih serta Realitinya di dalam Kontek
      Masyarakat Melayu Beradat Perpatih di Nerasau, Rembau,
      Negeri Sembilan" [The status and role of women in Islam and
      'adat perpatih' in the context of an 'adat perpatih' com-
      munity in Nerasau, Rembau, Negri Sembilan]. B.A. academic
      exercise, University of Malaya, 1976, 109 pp.

3676 RAMLAH binti JANTAN. "Perubahan Sosio-Ekonomi Yang Dialami
      oleh Gadis-gadis Yang Bekerja di Kilang Letronik" [The
      socioeconomic changes experienced by female workers in
      electronics factories]. B.A. academic exerise, University
      of Malaya, 1976, iv, 74 pp.

3677 ROHANA ARIFFIN. "Exploitation of Women." 20 pp. Paper pre-
      sented at the Seminar 'Wanita Malaysia Masakini,' Bangi,
      Selangor, 1979, organized by the Faculty of Social Sciences
      and Humanities, Universiti Kebangsaan Malaysia.

3678 ROOSE, HASHIMAH. "Changes in the Position of Malay Women."
      In Women in the New Asia. Edited by Barbara E. Ward.
      Paris: Unesco, 1963, pp. 287-94.

3679 RUSMIATI HARUN. "Peranan Wanita Selamatkan Masyarakat
      Pincang" [The role of women in saving a threatened so-
      ciety]. Hikmah, no. 18 (Mar. 1979):23-27.

3680 SABRI HAJI HUSSIN. "Wanita dan Perhambaan ke Atasnya" [Women
      and their servitude]. Sarina 3, no. 35 (Feb. 1979):86-91.

3681 SAFIAH KARIM, Nik. "Kegiatan Wanita Melayu Kelantan di Ibu
      Kota [The activities of the Kelantanese Malay women in the
      city]. Majalah Kelantan 3 (1971):14-15.

3682 _____. "Penjejasan Maruah Kaum Wanita oleh Sebaran Am" [The
      defamation of women's image in the mass media]. Suara
      Taqwa, no. 12 (Oct. 1977):27-31.

3683 SALMON, CLAUDINE. "Le rôle des femmes dans la société
      malaysienne selon Anis Sabirin" [The role of women in
      Malaysian society according to Anis Sabirin]. Archipel,
      no. 13 (1977):321-26.

3684   SAROJINI DEVI APPUTHURAI. "Socio-Economic Aspects of Women
        Plantation Workers: A Case Study of the Indian Women
        Workers of Ladang Tengah." B.A. academic exercise, Uni-
        versity of Malaya, 1971, viii, 102 pp.

3685   SEMINAR ON THE STUDY OF A WOMEN'S BUREAU, Kuala Lumpur, 1965.
        Report. Kuala Lumpur: National Council of Women's Orga-
        nizations, 1965, 68 pp.

3686   SEMINAR WANITA DALAM ZAMAN PERUBAHAN DUNIA HARI INI, Kuala
        Lumpur, 1975. Kertas-kertas Kerja [Seminar on Women in the
        Age of Change, Kuala Lumpur, 1975. Working Papers].
        Organized by the National Council of Women's Organizations.
        Kuala Lumpur, 1975. 1 vol. (various pagings).

3687   SHAJARATUDDUR SHEIKH ABDUL HALIM. "Sikap Wanita2 Melayu
        terhadap Perkembangan Hari Ini" [The attitude of Malay
        women towards development today]. Mastika 28, no. 7
        (July 1968):27-30.

3688   SIRAJ, MEHRUN et al. Wanita Hari Ini di Semenanjung Malaysia
        [Women today in Peninsular Malaysia]. Kuala Lumpur:
        Federation of Family Planning Associations, 1978, 43 pp.

3689   _____. Women Today in Peninsular Malaysia. Kuala Lumpur:
        Federation of Family Planning Associations, 1976, x, 47 pp.

3690   SOH, POH THONG. "Concerning Our Girls." Straits Chinese
        Magazine 11, no. 4 (1907):139-43.

3691   SONG, ONG SIANG. "The Position of Chinese Women." Straits
        Chinese Magazine 1, no. 1 (1897):16-23.

3692   STRANGE, HEATHER. "Village Paths and City Routes: Rural
        Malay Women's Perceptions on Urban Alternatives." Paper
        presented at the Conference on Women and Development,
        Wellesley College, Mass., June 1976.

3693   _____. "The Weavers of Rusila: Working Women in a Malay Vil-
        lage." Ph.D. dissertation, New York University, 1971,
        xxii, 501 pp. Abstracted in Dissertation Abstracts Inter-
        national 32, no. 10 (Apr. 1972):5590-91-B. University
        Microfilms International, order no. 72-13,410.

3694   SURINDER SOIN. "Some Aspects of the Malayan Sikh Community
        with Particular Reference to Women and the Young." B.A.
        academic exercise, University of Singapore, 1956, 111 pp.

3695   SUTLIVE, VINSON H. "The Many Faces of Kumang: Iban Women in
        Fiction and Fact." Sarawak Museum Journal 25, no. 46
        (1977):157-64.

3696   SWIFT, MICHAEL GODFREY. "Men and Women in Malay Society."
       In Women in the New Asia. Edited by Barbara E. Ward.
       Paris: Unesco, 1963, pp. 268-86.

3697   TANG, YANG MOY. "The Position of Women and Their Contribution
       to Rural Productive Efforts: A Case Study in Kedah,
       Malaysia." Master's thesis, Asian Institute of Technology
       [Bangkok], 1976, 86 pp.

3698   THOMAS, SHARON. "Women's Tattoos of the Upper Rajang."
       Sarawak Museum Journal 16, nos. 32/33 (July/Dec. 1968):
       209-34.

3699   WHITE, E. "Dusun Bamboo Fertility Rites." Sarawak Museum
       Journal 9 (July/Dec. 1959):118-20.

3700   WHITEHOUSE, JEANNE. "Of Dusun Women Entertaining."
       Frontiers, no. 3 (1978):28-30.

3701   WINSTEDT, Sir RICHARD OLOF. "Mother-Right among Khasis and
       Malays." Royal Asiatic Society of Great Britain and
       Ireland, Malaysian Branch, Journal 10, pt. 1 (1932):9-13.

3702   ZAIBEDAH ZULKIFLI. "The Place of Women in Malaysia."
       Malaysia [London] (July 1970):8-10.

3703   ZAINON JAAFAR. "Memperdagangkan Kewanitaan Salah Siapa?"
       [Exploiting womanhood--whose fault is it?]. Dewan
       Masyarakat 14, no. 11 (Nov. 1976):32-33.

3704   _____. "Wanita Hari Ini Berada di Persimpangan Jalan" [To-
       day's woman is at the crossroads]. Dewan Masyarakat 14,
       no. 1 (Jan. 1976):32-35.

3705   ZALIKHAH MUHAMMAD NOOR, Siti. "Betapa Peranan Para Siswi?"
       [What is the role of women undergraduates?]. Panji
       Masyarakat 2, no. 8 (Mar. 1977):33-35.

3706   ZULKURNAIN HAJI AWANG. "Peranan Wanita Melayu didalam
       Masyarakat Petani: Satu Kajian mengenai Peranan Sosio-
       Ekonomi Wanita didalam Masyarakat Penanam Padi Kampong Gong
       Kalar, Pasir Puteh, Kelantan" [The role of Malay women in
       agricultural society: a study of the socioeconomic role of
       women in the rice-growing community in Kampong Gong Kalar,
       Pasir Puteh, Kelantan]. B.A. academic exercise, University
       of Malaya, 1974, xi, 85 pp.

Philippines

3707   ABELLO, ELISA G. "The Filipino Woman 25 Years Ago and Now."
       Fookien Times Philippines Yearbook (1973):284-89, 298-99.

3708   ALDABA-LIM, ESTEFANIA J. "The Social Role of Women." Unitas
       46, no. 2 (June 1975):245-50.

3709   _____. "Women in the Philippines." Les Carnets de l'enfance
       28 (1974):67-77.

3710   ALZONA, ENCARNACIÓN. The Social and Economic Status of
       Filipino Women, 1565-1932. Manila: University of
       Philippines Press, 1933, 33 pp. Institute of Pacific
       Relations, 5th Biennial Conference, Banff, 1933. Data
       Papers.

3711   AYUYAO, MARIA LIM. "The Physical Conditions of Twenty Dormi-
       tories Where Centro Escolar University Female Students
       Live." Centro Escolar University, Manila, Graduate and
       Faculty Studies 20 (1969):124-33.

3712   BRANDEWIE, ERNEST. "Maids in Cebuano Society." Philippine
       Quarterly of Culture and Society 1, no. 3 (1973):209-19.

3713   CASTILLO, GELIA TAGUMPAY. "Occupational Sex Roles as Per-
       ceived by Filipino Adolescents." Philippine Sociological
       Review 9, nos. 1/2 (Jan./Apr. 1961):2-11.

3714   CASTILLO, GELIA TAGUMPAY, and HILOMEN-GUERRERO, SYLVIA. "The
       Filipino Woman: A Study in Multiple Roles." Journal of
       Asian and African Studies 4, no. 1 (1969):18-29.

3715   CONKLIN, HAROLD C. "Maling, a Manunoo Girl from the
       Philippines: A Day in Pariwa." In The Company of Man.
       Edited by Joseph Casagrande. New York: Harper & Row,
       1960, pp. 101-19.

3716   CUE, MAGDALENA ALONZO-VILLABA. The Mission of Women: A Re-
       turn to Their Original Role. Manila: University of Santo
       Tomas [Manila], 1975, iii, 67 pp.

3717   EINSIEDEL, LUZ A. The Impact of the Community Development
       Women and Youth and Lay Leadership Institutes of the PACD.
       Quezon City: Community Development Research Council Pub-
       lications, University of the Philippines, (PACD-NEC-AID-UP
       Project) 1966, xviii, 106 pp.

3718   FOX, ROBERT. "Men and Women in the Philippines." In Women in
       the New Asia. Edited by Barbara E. Ward. Paris: Unesco,
       1963, pp. 342-64.

3719   GILANDAS, ALEX; GASTARDO-CONACO, CECILIA; and SEVILLA, JUDY.
       "Sex and the Single Filipina: A Holistic Approach."
       PSSC Social Science Information 6, no. 1 (Apr./June 1978):
       6-10, 14.

3720   GONZALEZ, ANNA MIREN, and HOLLNSTEINER, MARY RACELIS.
       Filipino Women as Partners of Men in Progress and Develop-
       ment: A Survey of Empirical Data and a Statement of Goals
       Fostering Male-Female Partnership. Quezon City: Institute
       of Philippine Culture, Ateneo de Manila University, 1976,
       v, 156 pp.

3721   GREEN, JUSTIN JAY. "The Filipina Elite: Her Social Back-
       grounds and Their Relationships to Development." Philippine
       Educational Forum 19, no. 3 (Nov. 1970):5-40.

3722   _____. "Philippine Women: Towards a Social Structural Theory
       of Female Status." Paper presented at the Southwest Con-
       ference of the Association for Asian Studies, Denton, Texas,
       1973.

3723   _____. "Women Leaders of the Philippines: Social Backgrounds
       and Political Attitudes." Ph.D. dissertation, Syracuse
       University, 1970, xiv, 368 pp. Abstracted in Dissertation
       Abstracts International 31, no. 11 (May 1971):6122-A.
       University Microfilms International, order no. 71-10,921.

3724   GUERRERO TOLDAYA DE GARCÍA, LÍA. "Evolución del estado social
       de la mujer filipina" [Evolution of the social rank of the
       Filipino woman]. Ph.D. dissertation, Universidad de
       Madrid, 1956.

3725   GUTHRIE, GEORGE M., and JACOBS, PEPITA JIMENEZ. "Curiosities
       and the Learning of Sex Roles." In Child Rearing and Per-
       sonality Development in the Philippines. University Park
       and London: Pennsylvania State University, 1966,
       pp. 134-47.

3726   HART, DONN V. "From Pregnancy through Birth in a Bisayan
       Filipino Village." In Southeast Asian Birth Customs:
       Three Studies in Human Reproduction, by Donn V. Hart,
       Phya Anuman Rajadhon, and Richard J. Coughlin. New Haven,
       Conn.: Human Relations Area Files Press, 1965, pp. 1-113.

3727   HUNT, CHESTER L. "Female Occupational Roles and Urban Sex
       Ratios in the United States, Japan and the Philippines."
       Social Forces 43, no. 3 (Mar. 1865):405-17.

3728   INFANTE, TERESITA R. The Woman in Early Philippines and among
       the Cultural Minorities. Manila: Unitas Publications,
       University of Santo Tomas, 1975, 205 pp.

3729   _____. "The Woman in Early Philippines and among the Cultural
       Minorities." Unitas 42, no. 3 (Sept. 1969):1-196.

3730   JACOBSON, HELGA EILEEN. "Women in Philippine Society: More
       Equal than Many." In Many Sisters, Women in Cross-Cultural
       Perspective. Edited by Carolyn J. Matthiasson. New York:
       Free Press, 1974, pp. 349-77.

3731   JAYME, BRIGIDA L. Family Roles and Fertility Patterns of Two
       Generations of Urban Upper Class Filipina Wives and Mothers.
       Singapore: Southeast Asia Population Research Awards Pro-
       gram (SEAPRAP), International Development Research Centre,
       Asia Regional Office and the Ford Foundation, 1976, 73 pp.
       SEAPRAP Research Report, no. 6.

3732   JULIANDA, L. "The Effective Involvement of Women in Cultural
       Advancement." Graduate Forum 6 (Nov. 1976):52-59.

3733   MAGLANGIT, VIRGINIA R. "The Maranao Woman: Growing Up, Edu-
       cation, Courtship and Marriage." Solidarity 9, no. 7
       (Sept./Oct. 1975):36-42.

3734   MENDEZ, PAZ A. "The Progress of the Filipino Woman during the
       Last Sixty Years." Centro Escolar University, Manila,
       Graduate and Faculty Studies 16 (1965):1-29.

3735   MONTIEL, CRISTINA, and HOLLNSTEINER, MARY RACELIS. The
       Filipino Woman: Her Role and Status in Philippine Society.
       Queson City: Institute of Philippine Culture, Ateneo de
       Manila University, 1976, vii, 52 pp.

3736   NAKPIL, C.G. "Letter to the Women of Malolos." Archipelago
       3, no. A-26 (1976):30-33.

3737   OBLEPIAS-RAMOS, LILIA, and SUAREZ, D. TORREVILLAS. Hanap-
       Buhay. Manila: Manila Community Services, Inc., 1978,
       82 pp. (On the Filipino woman's role in family and work.)

3738   ORACION, TIMOTEO S. "Magahat Pregnancy and Birth Practices."
       Philippine Sociological Review 13 (Oct. 1965):268-74.

3739   OSMEÑA, SERGIO. The Moral and Spiritual Influence of Filipino
       Women. Manila: Bureau of Printing, 1941, 11 pp.

3740   PACIS, CONSTANCE M., Sister. "Pre-marriage Adolescent Rela-
       tionship: A Study from a Selected Group of Girls."
       Master's thesis, University of Santo Tomas [Manila], 1967,
       xxii, 443 pp.

3741   PECSON, GERONIMA T. "The Role of Women in Preserving Cultural
       Heritage." Unesco Philippines 3, no. 7 (July 1964):144-47.

3742   PHILIPPINES. University, Social Research Laboratory.
        "Stereotype, Status and Satisfactions: The Filipina among
        Filipinos." PSSC Social Science Information 5, no. 2
        (July/Sept. 1977):7-13.

3743   PHILIPPINES (REPUBLIC), Bureau of Women and Minors. Annual
        Report, 1962[?]-. Manila, 1963[?]-.

3744   PINARD, LEO WILLIAM (II). "Heterosexual Relations in the
        Central Visayas." Ph.D. dissertation, University of Notre
        Dame, 1972, 246 pp. Abstracted in Dissertation Abstracts
        International 32, no. 11 (May 1972):6571-A. University
        Microfilms International, order no. 72-16,271.

3745   POLOTAN, KERIMA. "Between Myth and Malice: To Begin to
        Understand the Bicolanos Look to Their Women." Archipelago
        1, no. 5 (May 1974):16-20.

3746   QUISUMBING, LOURDES REYNES. "An Investigation into Rizal's
        Philosophy of Filipino Womanhood." Master's thesis,
        University of Santo Tomas [Manila], 1963, viii, 241 pp.

3747   RED, ISAGANI V. "Mass Media Exposure and Attitude towards the
        Socio-Political Leadership of Women." B.A. academic exer-
        cise, University of the Philippines [Quezon City], 1974,
        25 pp.

3748   REINING, PRISCILLA et al. Village Women, Their Changing Lives
        and Fertility: Studies in Kenya, Mexico and the Philip-
        pines. Washington, D.C.: American Association for the
        Advancement of Science, 1977, x, 273 pp.

3749   REYES, TEOFILO. "The Role of Women in Socio-Economic Develop-
        ment." Philippine Educational Forum 14, no. 1 (Mar. 1965):
        45-49.

3750   RIMONDO, JEANETTE. "Disposition of Female Adolescents towards
        Premarital Sex." Ph.D. dissertation, St. Louis University
        [Baguio, Philippines], 1977[?].

3751   RODRIGUEZ, FILEMON C. "Women and the Socio-Economic Develop-
        ment." Power and Industry 10, no. 4 (Apr. 1963):8-10, 12,
        26.

3752   ROSALDO, MICHELLE ZIMBALIST, and ATKINSON, JANE MONNIG. "Man
        the Hunter and Women: Metaphors for the Sexes in Ilongot
        Magical Spell." In The Interpretation of Symbolism. Ed-
        ited by Roy Willis. London: Malaby Press, 1975, pp. 43-75.

3753   SAN ANDRES-ZIGA, TECLA. "The Role of the Filipino Woman in
        the Community." Philippine Journal of Nursing 33, no. 4
        (July/Aug. 1964):194-96, 198.

3754   SANTILLAN-CASTRENCE, PURA, ed. Talking Things over with the
        Growing Filipina. A project of the Philippine Association
        of the University Women. Manila: Bordavon Book Co., 1961,
        115 pp.

3755   SARSFIELD, NANCY ANN CHIAVACCI. "An Acculturative Study of
        the Filipino Nurse in New Jersey Hospitals." Ph.D. disser-
        tation, New York University, 1973, 193 pp.

3756   SHAHANI, LETICIA RAMOS. "The Changing Roles of Philipino
        Women and Men." Impact 10, no. 4 (Apr. 1975):136-39.

3757   SHELFORD, R. "Women of the Non-Malay Tribes of the Sunda
        Islands and Celebes." In Women of All Nations. Edited by
        Thomas Athol Joyce and Northcote W. Thomas. Vol. 1. New
        York: Funk & Wagnalls, 1915, pp. 161-85.

3758   SMITH, ROBERT J.; RAMSEY, CHARLES E.; and CASTILLO, GELIA
        TAGUMPAY. "Parental Authority and Job Choices: Sex Dif-
        ferences in Three Cultures." American Journal of Sociology
        64, no. 2 (Sept. 1963):143-49. (Includes the Philippines.)

3759   UMPA, SAIRA R. "Factors Related to the Participation of
        Moranaw Women in Family Decision-making." Master's thesis,
        University of the Philippines [Quezon City], 1972, 94 pp.

3760   UNESCO, Office of the Regional Adviser for Social Sciences in
        Asia and Oceania. Project on Rural Women: Rural Families
        with Dislocated Males. Effects of Urban Male Migration on
        the Female Members Back Home in the Village, Meeting of
        Researchers, Seoul, 19-22 June 1979, Final Report. Bangkok:
        Office of the Regional Adviser for Social Sciences in Asia
        and Oceania, UNESCO, 1979, 45 pp. (Includes the Philippines
        and Thailand.)

3761   UNITED NATIONS, Social Welfare and Development Centre for Asia
        and the Pacific. City Camp/Rock Quarry Handicraft Associa-
        tion: A Case Study on Rural Women's Role in Socio-Economic
        Activities and Community Leadership within a Poverty Con-
        text. Prepared by Philippines Business for Social Progress,
        1978. Bangkok[?]: United Nations Social Welfare and Devel-
        opment Centre for Asia and the Pacific, 1978, 50 pp.

3762   YOUNG, RUTH C. "The Role of Chinese Women in Community Wel-
        fare in the Philippines." Fookien Times Philippines Year-
        book (1949):57-58.

Singapore

3763 BOEY, CHEE KIEW. "A Sociological Study of the San Shui Women Construction Workers." B.A. academic exercise, University of Singapore, 1975, 89 pp.

3764 CHAI, FOOK SEE. "A Study of the Blind Women in Singapore: Their Problems and Their Ways of Life and the Social Services Which Contribute to Their Needs." B.A. academic exercise, University of Singapore, 1961, 170 pp.

3765 CHEE, YOK CHIN. "Young Women Car Park Attendants in Singapore." Thesis for the Diploma in Soc.Sc., University of Singapore, 1968, 99 pp.

3766 CHEW, JOY OON AI, and TAN, MEY LING. "The Present Status of Singaporean Women: Self-Image." B.A. academic exercise, University of Singapore, 1973, 77 pp.

3767 CHIANG, ING LING. "Young Women without Families: A Study of Girls Staying on Their Own without Parental Support." B.A. academic exercise, University of Singapore, 1974, 141 pp.

3768 CHUA, AH MOY. "A Study of Twenty Factory Girls." B.A. academic exercise, University of Singapore, 1974, 116 pp.

3769 FOONG, WONG. "A Chinese Family in Singapore." In Women in the New Asia. Edited by Barbara E. Ward. Paris: Unesco, 1963, pp. 410-21.

3770 GOH, SOON PHING. "A Research Paper on Some Aspects of Women's Life in a Singapore Chinese Fishing Village: With Special Reference to Childcare and Pregnancy Beliefs and Practices in the Village." B.A. academic exercise, University of Singapore, 1955, 137 pp.

3771 HO, IT CHONG. "The Cantonese Domestic Amahs: A Study of a Small Occupational Group of Chinese Women." B.A. academic exercise, University of Singapore, 1959, 162 pp.

3772 KUO, EDDIE CHEN YU, and WONG, ALINE K. The Contemporary Family in Singapore: Structure and Change. Singapore: Singapore University Press, 1979, x, 306 pp. (Includes chapters on women's status, working mothers, etc.)

3773 LAU, WAI HAR. "Impact of Modernization on Women." In Modernization in Singapore: Impact on the Individual. Edited by Tham Seong Chee. Singapore: University Education Press, 1972, pp. 86-87.

3774   LIM, GUEK POH. "Factory Girls in Jurong: An Ethnographic
        Study." B.A. academic exercise, University of Singapore,
        1974, 54 pp.

3775   MARIS STELLA GIRLS' SCHOOL, Singapore, Child Welfare and So-
        cial Work Section. Teen-age Girls' Family Problems,
        Singapore: Survey on Sixteen to Seventeen Year-Old Girls
        of Chinese Descent from Queenstown and the Farrer Road
        Kampong--Their Attitudes towards Life and Patterns of Be-
        haviour, with Special Emphasis on Their Family Relationship
        Values. Singapore, 1965, x, 158 pp.

3776   NATIONAL SEMINAR ON WOMEN IN A TECHNOLOGICAL SOCIETY,
        Singapore, 1973. Women in a Technological Society.
        Sponsored by Unesco in conjunction with WCOTP. Singapore:
        Singapore Teachers Union, 1974, 40 pp.

3777   PHAY, AI LIEN. "The Present Status of Singaporean Women."
        B.A. academic exercise, University of Singapore, 1973,
        65 pp.

3778   SAW, SWEE HOCK. "The Changing Married Population in Singapore
        during 1947-1957." South-east Asian Journal of Sociology
        3 (1970):62-63.

3779   SELVANAYAGAM, JOY SUGUNAM. "Indian Working Women of Low In-
        come Group: A Study of Some Aspects of the Indian Working
        Women and Their Families." B.A. academic exercise, Univer-
        sity of Singapore, 1969, 93 pp.

3780   SIM, LEE WAH. "Unwed Mothers in Singapore: An Exploratory
        Study." B.A. academic exercise, University of Singapore,
        1976, 104 pp.

3781   TAN, NALLA. "The Impact of Modernisation on Women." In
        Modernization in Singapore: Impact on the Individual.
        Edited by Tham Seong Chee. Singapore: University Educa-
        tion Press, 1972, pp. 63-67.

3782   TAN, SALLY HONG CHOO. "A Study of Thirty English-educated
        Chinese Adolescent Girls in Singapore." B.A. academic ex-
        ercise, University of Singapore, 1956, 153 pp.

3783   TANG, CHEE HONG. "The Cantonese Women Building Labourers: A
        Study of a Group of San-Sui Women in the Building Trade."
        B.A. academic exercise, University of Singapore, 1961,
        110 pp.

3784   THOMAS, AMMINI. "A Study of Attempted Suicide among Young
        South Indian Women in Singapore." Thesis for the Diploma
        in Soc.Sc., University of Singapore, 1959, 168 pp.

3785   TOPLEY, MARJORIE DOREEN. "Immigrant Chinese Female Servants and Their Hostels in Singapore." Man 59 (Dec. 1959): 213-15.

3786   _____. "The Organisation and Social Function of Chinese Women's Chai t'ang in Singapore." Ph.D. dissertation, University of London, 1958, xv, 415 pp.

3787   _____. "Chinese Women's Vegetarian Houses in Singapore." Royal Asiatic Society of Great Britain and Ireland, Malayian Branch, Journal 27, pt. 1 (May 1954):51-67.

3788   WEE, ANN E. "Chinese Women of Singapore: Their Present Status in the Family and in Marriage." In Women in the New Asia. Edited by Barbara E. Ward. Paris: Unesco, 1963, pp. 376-408.

3789   WONG, ALINE K. "Maternal Employment, Education and Changing Family Values in Singapore." Journal of Economic Development and Social Change in Asia and Pacific 1, no. 1 (1976): 23-40.

3790   _____. "Women as Minority Group." In Singapore: Society in Transition. Edited by Hassan Riaz. Kuala Lumpur: Oxford University Press, 1976, pp. 291-314.

3791   _____. Women as a Minority Group in Singapore. Singapore: Chopmen Enterprises, 1974, 46 pp. Singapore University, Department of Sociology. Working Paper, no. 29.

3792   _____. "Women in Singapore: A Report." Signs 2, no. 1 (Autumn 1976):213-18.

3793   World in Woman Exhibition, Victoria Memorial Hall, 26-29 April 1975, Souvenir Magazine. Singapore: Singapore Association of Women Lawyers, 1975, 52 pp.

3794   YU, YEE SHOON. "The Singapore Woman." In Socialism That Works . . . the Singapore Way. Edited by C.V. Devan Nair. Singapore: Federal Publications, 1976, pp. 114-22.

Thailand

3795   ANUMAN RAJATHON, Phraya. "Customs Connected with Birth and the Rearing of Children." In Southeast Asian Birth Customs: Three Studies in Human Reproduction. By Donn V. Hart, Phya Anuman Rajadhon, and Richard J. Coughlin. New Haven, Conn.: Human Relations Area Files Press, 1965, pp. 117-204.

3796   BLOFELD, JOHN. "Some Siamese Women." Eastern Horizon 1, no. 3 (Sept. 1960):18-28.

3797   CHAMRIENG BHAVICHITRA. "A Study of Family Life in Thailand."
        Master's thesis, University of the Philippines, 1958,
        233 pp. (Includes an appendix on the convention on the
        political rights of women.)

3798   CHIRAPHAN KANCHANACHITRA. "Some Factors related to Leadership
        Participation of Men and Women in a New York State Com-
        munity and Their Implications for Community Development in
        Thailand." Ph.D. dissertation, Cornell University, 1976,
        257 pp. Abstracted in Dissertation Abstracts International
        37, no. 10 (Apr. 1977):6226-A. University Microfilms
        International, order no. 77-8440.

3799   DAVIS, RICHARD BERNARD. "Muang Matrifocality." Siam Society,
        Journal 61, pt. 2 (July 1973):53-62.

3800   DICKINSON, PRAMUAN. "My Life History in Thailand." In Women
        in the New Asia. Edited by Barbara E. Ward. Paris:
        Unesco, 1963, pp. 452-59.

3801   _____. "Thailand: 'I Am No Longer the Hind Legs of an
        Elephant.'" Unesco Courier 17 (Sept. 1964):17, 21. (On
        women in Thailand.)

3802   "The Fair Sex of Siam." Standard [Bangkok] (28 May 1949):
        18-19, 23, 28-30.

3803   FOOD AND AGRICULTURE ORGANIZATION OF THE UNITED NATIONS.
        Report to the Government of Thailand on Community Develop-
        ment Programs for Women and Youth. Based on the work of
        Joan Acton Smith. Rome: FAO, 1968, iv, 13 pp. FAO no.
        TA.2528. Nu.TA/68/16.

3804   HANKS, LUCIEN M., and HANKS, JANE RICHARDSON. "Thailand:
        Equality between the Sexes." In Women in the New Asia.
        Edited by Barbara E. Ward. Paris: Unesco, 1963,
        pp. 424-45.

3805   KAMBHU, LEIGH R. Thailand is Our Home; A Study of Some Ameri-
        can Wives of Thais. Cambridge, Mass.: Center for Inter-
        national Studies, Massachusetts Institute of Technology,
        1963, 113 pp.

3806   LANDON, KENNETH PERRY. "Ladies Wear Skirts." Asia [New York]
        42 (1942):25-26. (Discussion on changes in female dress
        decreed by the government in 1941.)

3807   LEONOWENS, ANNA HARRIETTE. Siamese Harem Life. With an
        introduction by Freya Stark. London: Arthur Barker,
        1952; New York: Dutton, 1953. (First published in 1873
        under the title, The Romance of the Harem.)

3808   MILES, DOUGLAS JAMES. "Yao Bride-Exchange, Matrifiliation and
        Adoption." Bijdragen tot de taal-, land- en volkenkunde
        128, no. 1 (1972):99-117. (Based on research in Chiengrai
        province, north Thailand.)

3809   MUECKE, MARJORIE ANN. "A Cultural View of Thai Conjugal Fam-
        ily Relationships." Paper presented at the American
        Anthropological Association Annual Meeting, Mexico City,
        1974.

3810   PEJIĆ, MAYA. Vrouw in Azië: vrouwen in Maleisië, Thailand en
        Sri Lanka [Women in Asia: women in Malaysia, Thailand, and
        Sri Lanka]. The Hague: Voorlichtingsdienst Ontwikkelings-
        samenwerking van het Ministerie van Buitenlandse Zaken,
        1976, 64 pp.

3811   POTTER, SULAMITH HEINS. Family Life in a Northern Thai Vil-
        lage: A Study in the Structural Significance of Women.
        Berkeley: University of California Press, 1977, xv, 137 pp.

3812   PRAKAI NONTAWASSEE. "Towards Identity and Self-respect among
        Thai Women." Ecumenical Review 28, no. 1 (Jan. 1976):39-41.

3813   SAISUREE CHUTIKUL. "Women in Rural Northeast Society in
        Thailand." Prepared at Khon Kaen University, Khon Kaen,
        Thailand, n.d., 12 pp.

3814   SEIN, SEIN Ma. "The Position of Women in Hinanaya Buddhist
        Countries (Burma, Ceylon and Thailand)." Master's thesis,
        University of London, 1958, iv, 177 pp.

3815   SRISURANG POOLTHUPYA. "The Changing Roles of Thai Women."
        Paper presented at the Seventh Conference of the Inter-
        national Association of Historians, August 1977, held in
        Bangkok, Thailand.

3816   THAMMASAT UNIVERSITY, Faculty of Social Administration, De-
        partment of Social Work. "Study of the Status and Role of
        Women in the 21 Villages of Lampang Province, Thailand."
        Bangkok: Faculty of Social Administration, Thammasat Uni-
        versity, 1975, 69 pp.

3817   TURTON, ANDREW. "Matrilineal Descent Groups and Spirit Cults
        of the Thai-Yuan in Northern Thailand." Siam Society,
        Journal 60 (1972):217-56.

3818   UNESCO, Office of the Regional Adviser for Social Sciences in
        Asia and Oceania. Project on Rural Women: Rural Families
        with Dislocated Males. Effects of Urban Male Migration on
        the Female Members Back Home in the Village. Meeting of
        Researchers, Seoul, 19-22 June 1979, Final Report.

Bangkok: Office of the Regional Adviser for Social Sources in Asia and Oceania, UNESCO, 1979, 45 pp. (Includes the Philippines and Thailand.)

3819   WARD, VIRGINIA. Women and Youth (CD Way) Pilot Project. Amphur Raman-Changwad Yala. Bangkok: Community Development Bureau, Ministry of the Interior, 1966.

SOCIETIES AND CLUBS

3820   ASIAN REGIONAL CONFERENCE OF THE ASSOCIATED COUNTRY WOMEN OF THE WORLD, 7th, Kuala Lumpur, 1979. Papers. Theme of Conference: Today's Child Tomorrow's Citizen. Host society, National Association of Women's Institutes, Peninsular Malaysia. Kuala Lumpur, 1979, 1 vol. (various pagings).

3821   BROWNFOOT, JANICE N. "Community Relations and Women's Organizations--European Women and the Asian Communities in Colonial Malaysia c. 1900-1957." 40 pp. Paper presented at the Eighth Conference of the International Association of Historians of Asia, Kuala Lumpur, August 1980.

3822   BRUCE, JUDITH. "Women's Organizations: A Resource for Family Planning and Development." Family Planning Perspectives 8, no. 6 (Nov./Dec. 1976):291-97. (Includes Thai organizations.)

3823   "Concept algemeen reglement voor de I.E.V.-Vrouwenorganisatie" [Draft of the general rules for the I.E.V--women's organization]. Onze stem 20 (1939):627. (Netherlands Indies.)

3284   DIAMOND JUBILEE SEMINAR ON TODAY'S GUIDE FOR TOMORROW'S WORLD, Singapore, 1977. Intersem '77, 3rd-8th June 1977: Singapore Girl Guides Diamond Jubilee, 1917-1977. Singapore: SEAMEO Regional Language Centre, 1977, 56 pp.

3825   EXPERT GROUP MEETING ON THE DEVELOPMENT OF WOMEN'S ORGANIZATIONS IN RURAL AREAS, Bangkok, 1978. Papers. Bangkok: United Nations Economic and Social Commission for Asia and the Pacific, 1978, 1 vol. (various pagings).

3826   GRAVE-TERWOGT, A. de. "Richt I.E.V.V.A.'s op, ook op de kleinste plaatsen" [The set-up of the I.E.V.V.A (Indo-European League Women's Organization)--even in the smallest places]. Onze stem 20 (1939):1109-4. (Netherlands Indies.)

3827   HERBERTSON, M.G. "Women's Institutes in Malaya." Colonial Review (Sept. 1953):82-83.

3828 HOLLNSTEINER, MARY RACELIS. "Enhancing the Participation of
      Indonesian Women in Development." A consultant's report to
      the United Nations Children's Fund, 1975. Bangkok: United
      Nations Children's Fund, East Asia and Pakistan Regional
      Office, 1975, 10 pp.

3829 "IEV-VO (De I.E.V. Vrouwen-Organisatie)" [I.E.V--women's orga-
      nization]. Onze stem 12 (1931):1114-15, 1247-49, 1345-46.
      (Netherlands Indies.)

3830 "I.E.V.V.O. contra I.E.V." [I.E.V.V.O (Indo Europees(ch) Ver-
      bond Vrouwen Organisatie) versus I.E.V. (Indo Europees(ch)
      Verbond)]. Onze stem 20 (1939):521. (Netherlands Indies.)

3831 INDO EUROPEES(CH) VERBOND, Vrouwen Organisatie. "Statuten der
      I.E.V.-Vrouwenorganisatie" [Constitution of the I.E.V.-
      women's organization]. Onze stem 13 (1932):1405-07.
      (Netherlands Indies.)

3832 ISMAIL, Mrs. "Women's Organisations in Indonesia." Asian
      Review 55 (1959):303-8.

3833 KONGRES WANITA INDONESIA. Kongres Wanita Indonesia [Indo-
      nesian Women's Congress]. Jakarta: Kowani, 1975, 2,
      19 pp.

3834 _____, Majelis Permusyawaratan. Hasil2 Majelis Permusyawaratan
      Kowani [Proceedings of Conference Council, Kowani].
      Jakarta: Majelis Permusyawaratan Kowani, 1975.

3835 LEGARDA, BENITO. "The Role of Women's Organizations in Devel-
      oping Economy." Philippine Economy and Industrial Journal
      11, nos. 7/8 (July/Aug. 1964):58-59.

3836 LEMBAGA KEBAJIKAN PEREMPUAN ISLAM PERSEKUTUAN TANAH MELAYU.
      Cenderamata 15 Tahun: 1961-1975 [Muslim Women's Welfare
      Board, Federation of Malaya. Souvenir 15 years:
      1961:1975]. Kuala Lumpur: L.K.P.I. Persekutuan Tanah
      Melayu, 1976, xi, 96 pp.

3837 LOMBARD, DENYS. "Aperçu sur les associations féminines
      d'Indonésie" [A look at the women's associations of
      Indonesia]. Archipel, no. 13 (1977):193-210.

3838 "Een misplaatst royement & IEVVO-IEV" [A wrong explusion--the
      Indo-European League Women's Organization and the Indo-
      European League]. Onze stem 20 (1939):441-42. (Nether-
      lands Indies.)

3839 NATIONAL ASSOCIATION OF WOMEN'S INSTITUTES OF MALAYA. Annual
      Report. Petaling Jaya.

3840   NATIONAL COUNCIL OF WOMEN'S ORGANISATIONS. Buku Panduan:
        Handbook. Kuala Lumpur, 1974, 51 pp.

3841   _____. Laporan Hari Wanita Persekutuan Tanah Melayu 25 Ogos
        1962 [Report of Women's Day, Federation of Malaya,
        25 August 1962]. Kuala Lumpur: Economy Printers, 1963.

3842   O'KELLY, ELIZABETH. "Women's Institutes in Sarawak." Women
        Today [London] 6, no. 1 (Dec. 1960):14-16.

3843   PAN-PACIFIC WOMEN'S CONFERENCE. Women of the Pacific: Being
        a Record of the Proceedings. Honolulu: Pan-Pacific Union,
        1st, 1928-.

3844   PARKER, MAUD N. "Report on Women's Club Work in the
        Philippines for the Wood-Forbes Commission." n.p., 1921.

3845   PERSATUAN PEMANDU PEREMPUAN MALAYSIA. Golden Jubilee 1917-
        1967. Kuala Lumpur, 1967, 59 pp. (Girl Guides Associa-
        tion of Malaysia.)

3846   PERSATUAN WANITA DEPARTEMEN AGAMA. Anggaran Dasar-Rumah
        Tangga Persatuan Wanita Departemen Agama (Perwanida):
        Hasil Mubes III di Bandung [Estimates/Housekeeping of
        Women's Association, Department of Religion (Perwanida):
        Proceedings of Mubes III in Bandung]. Jakarta: Pimpinan
        Pusat Perwanida, 1974, 39 pp.

3847   PERSEKUTUAN PERKUMPULAN WANITA SARAWAK. Ulangtahun Kelimabelas
        1962-1977 [Sarawak Federation of Women's Institutes, Fif-
        teenth anniversary, 1962-1977]. Kuching: Persekutuan
        Perkumpulan Wanita Sarawak, 1977, 38 pp.

3848   _____. Ulangtahun Kesepuluh (1962-1972). Sarawak Federation
        of Women's Institutes Tenth Anniversary (1962-1972).
        Kuching: Persekutuan Perkumpulan Wanita Sarawak, 1972,
        32 pp.

3849   POEDJOBUNTORO, SOEPENI. "Kowani: Badan Kongress Wanita
        Indonesia" [Kowani: Indonesian Women's Congress].
        Jogjakarta, 1949, 19 pp.

3850   RANGERS AND SENIOR GIRL SCOUTS SEMINAR ASIA-PACIFIC REGION,
        Kuala Lumpur, 1974. Report of the Rangers and Senior Girl
        Scouts Seminar Asia Pacific Region/Girl Guides Association,
        Malaysia. Kuala Lumpur: Persatuan Pandu Putri Malaysia,
        1975, 131 pp.

3851   Ruby Jubilee Yearbook, 1921-1961. Manila: National Federa-
        tion of Women's Clubs of the Philippines, 1961, 122 pp.

3852 SAFIAH KARIM, Nik. "Beberapa Masalah Yang Dihadapi oleh Pertubuhan-Pertubuhan Wanita di Negeri Ini" [Problems faced by women's organizations in this country]. Bingkisan Pertiwi 3 (1972):16-20. (On Malaysia.)

3853 SEMINAR PESURUHJAYA-PESURUHJAYA PANDU PUTRI MALAYSIA, Kuala Lumpur, 1975. Lapuran/Report on the Seminar for Commissioners of Girl Guides Malaysia, 6th-10th April, 1975. Kuala Lumpur: Persatuan Pandu Putri Malaysia, 1975, 88 pp.

3854 SEMINAR RANCANGAN MALAYSIA KEDUA: GERAKAN PEMBAHARUAN DAN PERANAN-PERANAN PERTUBOHAN-PERTUBOHAN WANITA, Kuala Lumpur, 1972. Kertaskerja-kertaskerja [Seminar on the Second Malaysia Plan: Movement for Change and the Roles of Women's Associations, Kuala Lumpur, 1972. Working Papers]. Kuala Lumpur: Majlis Kebangsaan Pertubohan-Pertubohan Wanita Malaysia, 1972, 1 vol. (various pagings).

3855 SEMINAR WANITA DAN PERTUBUHAN SUKARELA WANITA MENGENAI PEMBANGUNAN KELUARGA, Kuala Lumpur, 1979. Lapuran [Seminar on Women and Women's Voluntary Organizations concerning Family Development, Kuala Lumpur, 1979, Report]. Organized by Lembaga Perancang Keluarga Negara, Malaysia. Kuala Lumpur, 1980[?], 248 pp.

3856 SINGAPORE WOMEN'S ASSOCIATION. "International Women's Year Souvenir, March 9, 1975/Singapore Women's Association." Singapore: Singapore Women's Association, 1975, 12 pp.

3857 SIRAJ, ZAIBUN NISSA. "The Role of a Voluntary Women's Organization in Adult Education." Jurnal pendidikan 6 (Oct. 1976): 113-22.

3858 UNITED NATIONS, Asian and Pacific Centre for Women and Development. APCWD Women's Resource Book, 1979. Produced by International Women's Tribune Centre, New York, for Asian & Pacific Centre for Women and Development, Kuala Lumpur. New York: International Women's Tribune Centre, 1980, 1 vol. (various pagings).

3859 "De verhouding IEV-IEVVO" [The relationship between the Indo-European League and the Indo-European League Women's Organization]. Onze stem 20 (1939):413-16. (Netherlands Indies.)

3860 YOUNG WOMEN'S CHRISTIAN ASSOCIATION, Singapore. Annual Report, 1967/68-. Singapore: Young Women's Christian Association, 1968-.

3861 YOUNG WOMEN'S CHRISTIAN ASSOCIATION OF MALAYSIA. YWCA. 100 Years. Kuala Lumpur: Young Women's Christian Association of Malaysia, 1975, 35 pp.

3862   YUSON, BONIFACIA F.   "History, Organization and Status of the
        Philippine Association of University Women, Far Eastern
        University Chapter." Master's thesis, Far Eastern Univer-
        sity [Manila], 1974, xiv, 136 pp.

3863   ZAHARAH SULAIMAN, Siti. "Perkembangan Perhubungan Wanita dan
        Sumbangannya terhadap Penglibatan Wanita" [The development
        of women's organizations and their contribution towards
        women's involvement]. 11 pp. Paper presented at the
        Seminar 'Wanita Malaysia Masakini', Bangi, Selangor, 1979,
        organized by the Faculty of Social Sciences, Universiti
        Kebangsaan Malaysia.

3864   ZALEHA ISMAIL. "Kegiatan dan Usaha Pertubuhan Wanita untuk
        Pembangunan Negara" [Activities and efforts of women's
        associations for national development]. 8 pp. Paper pre-
        sented at the Seminar GPW (Gerakan Persatuan Wanita),
        Serdang, Malaysia, 1979, organized by GPW, Federal Land
        Development Authority.

3865   ZAWIYAH HAJI NAWAWI. "Kegiatan-kegiatan GPW di Rancangan-
        rancangan Wilayah Johor Tengah" [Activities of GPW in the
        Johor Tengah Scheme]. 11 pp. Paper presented at the
        Seminar GPW (Gerakan Persatuan Wanita), Serdang, Malaysia,
        1979, organized by GPW, Federal Land Development Authority.

Author Index

Index

Index

Index

Index

Hull, Valerie J., 311, 364, 365, 935, 1040, 1041, 1044-1049, 2082, 3570-3572
Humphreys, J.L., 2948
Hunt, Chester L., 553, 3035, 3727
Hoepoedino Soewondo. See Soewondo, Hoepoedino
Hunter, Penelope, 3491
Hurustiati Subandrio. See Subandrio, Hurustiati
Husnayanie, Tengku Cik. See Cik Husnayanie, Tengku
Husnul Akib Suminto. See Suminto, Husnul Akib
Husny, Abu [pseud.]. See Abu Husny [pseud.]
Hussain, Hamidah binti. See Hamidah binti Hussain
Hussain S. Pañgato. See Pañgato, Hussain S.
Hussein, S. Ahmad. See Ahmad Hussein S.
Hussein Onn, Datuk, 442
Hussein, Abdul Razak bin. See Abdul Razak bin Hussein
Hussin, Sabri Haji. See Sabri Haji Hussin
Hutauruk, A.M., 2344
Hutchison, Ira Walter, 1390, 1391
Huy Uu, 2260

Ibañez-Luciano, Josefa, 3198
Ibnu Shams, 3266
Ibrahim A. Jubaira. See Jubaira, Ibrahim A.
Ibrahim, Abdul Latif Haji. See Abdul Latif Haji Ibrahim
Ibrahim, Ahmad bin Muhammad. See Ahmad bin Muhammad Ibrahim
Ibrahim, Anwar. See Anwar Ibrahim
Ibrahim, Khadijah binti. See Khadijah binti Ibrahim
Ibrahim, Ku Yasin bin Ku. See Yasin bin Ku Ibrahim, Ku
Ibrahim, Laily. See Laily Ibrahim
Ibrahim, Muchtaruddin, 50

Ibrahim, Siti Hajar binti. See Hajar binti Ibrahim, Siti
Ibrahim, Siti Maryam. See Maryam Ibrahim, Siti
Ibrahim, Wan Abu Bakar bin Wan Teh. See Abu Bakar bin Wan Teh Ibrahim, Wan
Ibrahim Irsan. See Irsan, Ibrahim
Ida Bagus Astawa. See Astawa, Ida Bagus
Idris, Sulaiman bin. See Sulaiman bin Idris
Idris, Faridah. See Faridah Idris
Idrus, Ku Mahazir Ku. See Mahazir Ku Idrus, Ku
Idroes Rakimi Dt. Radjo Penghulu. See Radjo Penghulu, Idroes Rakimi Dt.
IFFTU-Unesco Asean Seminar on Equal Opportunities for Women in Education and Employment, Kuala Lumpur, 1977, 312, 696
Iglitzen, Lynne B., 1836
Ihromi, T. Omas, 1050, 1051, 1928, 1929, 1950, 2345, 3574, 3596
Ijzerman-Junius, Fr. J.J.A. See Foore, Annie, pseud.
Ilias Zaidi, 2718
Illo, Jeanne Francis I., 554
ILO Regional Seminar on Women Participation in Trade Union Activities, Kuala Lumpur, 1979, 313
Ilustre, M.L., 555
Inciong, E.M., 829
Indah, Annura, 3036
Indo Europees(ch) Verbond, Vrouwen Organisatie, 3831
Indonesia, Angkatan Darat, Dinas Administrasi Personil Militer, 2853
Indonesia, Biro Pusat Statistik, 1052-1054
Indonesia, Central Bureau of Statistics. See Indonesia, Biro Pusat Statistik

Index

International Planned Parenthood
Federation, South East Asia
and Oceania Region, 955-957
International Seminar on Long-
Term Educational and
Training Programmes for the
Advancement of Women in Asia,
Bombay, 1967, 697
International Women's Day, Hong
Kong, 1978, 1837
International Women's Year World
Conference. See World
Conference of the Inter-
national Women's Year,
Mexico City, 1975
International Workshop on
Feminist Ideology and
Structures in the First Half
of the Decade for Women,
Bangkok, 1979, 1695
Irawati, Singarimbun. See
Singarimbun, Irawati
Irsan, Ibrahim, 1056
Isaac, Josefina Dy R., 1346
Ishiwata, Thelma F., 830
Isidro, Julita Alarcon, 205
Iskandar, Jaharah. See Jaharah
Iskandar
Iskandar, N., 1057-1059
Iskandar, Nur Sutan, 1060
Iskandar, O., 3431
Ismail, Fariddah binti Haji.
See Fariddah binti Haji
Ismail
Ismail, Mrs., 3832
Ismail, Yahya bin. See Yahya
bin Ismail
Ismail, Zakaria. See Zakaria
Ismail
Ismail, Zaleha. See Zaleha
Ismail
Ismail bin Abas, 1983
Ismail Mohamad Sjah. See Sjah,
Ismail Mohamad
Ismail Muhamad Syah. See Syah,
Ismail Muhamad
Ismail Muhammad, 3654
Isman, Suntoro, 370, 715, 1061
Ijerman-Junius, Fr. J.J.A. See
Foore, Annie [pseud.]

Jaafar, Shahar Banun. See
Shahar Banun Jaafar
Jaafar, Zainon. See Zainon
Jaafar
Jaafar bin Abdul Rahim, 3200,
3655
Jaafar bin Harun, 444, 3656
Jaafar Siddiq Yasin, Haji, 3267
Jacinto, Amado, 2020
Jackson, Barbara (Ward). See
Ward, Barbara E.
Jackson, David, 2485, 2486
Jackson, Molly, 1725
Jacob, Floranie, 3201, 3414
Jacobs, Pepita Jimenez, 3725
Jacobs, Sue-Ellen, 8
Jacobson, Helga Eileen, 3730
Jafizham, T., 2354, 2854
Jagjit Singh, 2119
Jahan, Rounaq, 320
Jaharah Iskandar, 2120
Jahja Moechtar, 2355
Jameelah, Maryam. See Maryam
Jameelah
Jamil, Namiri. See Namiri Jamil
Jamilah Ariffin, 445-448
Jamnarnwej, Wimolsiri. See
Wimolsiri Jamnarnwej
Jantan, Ramlah binti. See Ramlah
binti Jantan
Jardin, Ma. Rufita, R.V.M., 831
al-Jaromi, Amin. See Amin
al-Jaromi
Jasin, Muhammad, 1153
Jasma Othman, Siti, 2719, 3657
Jaspan, Mervyn Aubrey, 3575
Javellana, Yolanda Q., 1788, 2566
Javier, Mercedes S., 832
Jawalaksana Rachapaetayakom, 1623
Jayakumar, Lalitha (Rajahram),
2200
Jayasut, Nantanee. See Nantanee
Jayasut
Jayawardena, Chandra, 2855, 3576
Jaylani, Tedjaningsih, 2356
Jayme, Brigida L., 1392, 1393,
3202, 3203, 3731
Jayme-Ho, Teresa, 326, 568, 3204
Jesus, Anita V. de. See
de Jesus, Anita V.
Jesus, Mercedes de, Sister, 2167

Index

Phanairamai, Mathana. See
Mathana Phananiramai
Phang Kooi Yoong, 2135, 2509
Phay, Ai Lien, 2053, 3777
Philippine Association of
University Women, 869
Philippine Federation of
Christian Churches, Women's
Work Committee, 3477, 3478
Philippines. University, College
of Education, Dept. of Home
Economics, 870
Philippines. University,
Population Institute, 3065
Philippines. University,
Population Institute, Family
Planning Evaluation Office,
1438
Philippines. University, Social
Research Laboratory, 3742
Philippines (Republic), Bureau
of Public Libraries, 66
Philippines (Republic), Bureau
of the Census and Statistics,
1439
Philippines (Republic), Bureau
of Women and Minors, 586-590,
2589, 3743
Philippines (Republic), Dept. of
Education, 871
Philippines (Republic), Dept. of
Health, Bohol Province
Maternal Child Health/Family
Planning Project, 1440, 2179
Philippines (Republic), Laws,
statutes, etc., 2180, 2590
Philippines (Republic), National
Census and Statistics Office,
591
Philippines (Republic), National
Commission for Unesco, 592,
1441
Philippines (Republic), National
Commission on the Role of
Filipino Women, 2029-2031
Philippines (Republic), National
Media Production Center, 178,
593, 2032
Philippines (Republic), Office
of the First Lady, 179

Phillips, James F., 1403, 1443-
1446, 1494
Phouk Chhay, 2293
Phung Thi Hanh, 355
Phuong Huy, 3362
Phuong Lan, 67
Piah, Yahaya bin Mat. See
Yahaya bin Mat Piah
Piampiti, Sauvaluck. See
Sauvaluck Piampiti
Pich Sal, 2809
Pichit Pitaktepsombati, 1629-1631
Piczon, Consuelo P., 3430
Pido, Antonio J.A., 1447
Piet, Nancy, 386
Pijper, G.F., 3287
Pilapil, Bernardina Tabada-. See
Tabada-Pilapil, Bernardina
Pillay, Manon Mani, 646
Pimental, M., 2591
Pinard, Leo William (II), 3066,
3744
Pindip Boriboonsack, 914
Pineda, L.P., 517
Pinon, Antonio T., 1448, 1449
Pinon, Manuel, 1450
Pintaruchi, Thamrong. See
Thamrong Pintaruchi
Pisute Utamote, 1651
Pitaktepsombati, Pichit. See
Pichit Pitaktepsombati
Pitman, Emma Raymond, 68
Poensen, M.C., 3599
Policarpio, Alfonso P., 180
Policarpio, Paz T., 2033
Polonia, Mary Stanislaus P. de,
2181
Polotan, Kerima, 181, 182, 872,
2739, 3363, 3364, 3745
Pongsapich, Amara. See Amara
Pongsapich
Ponniah, Vivien Joy, 475
Poolthupya, Srisurang. See
Srisurang Poolthupya
Popkin, Barry Michael, 3220, 3221
Pornchai Boodsayasakul, 1653
Posadas, Salud Viduya, 873
Postel-Coster, Els, 1947
Postma, Petronella A., 1117
Potter, Sulamith Heins, 3811

Seminar tentang Penyusunan
Kebijaksanaan Kearah
Peningkatan Partisipasi
Wanita dalam Pekerjaan yang
Berupah, Jakarta, 1976, 403
Seminar untuk Pemberantasan
Butahuruf Fungsional yang
Diterapkan pada Pendidekan
Kependudukan dan Keluarga
Berencana, Lembang,
Indonesia, 1973, 1135
Seminar Wanita, Singapore, 1977,
3297
Seminar Wanita dalam Pers Yang
Membangun, Jakarta, 1974, 404
Seminar Wanita dalam Zaman
Perubahan Dunia Hari ini,
Kuala Lumpur, 1975, 3686
Seminar Wanita dan Pertubuhan
Sukarela Wanita mengenai
Pembangunan Keluarga, Kuala
Lumpur, 1979, 1283, 2143,
3855
Seminar 'Wanita Malaysia
Masakini' Bangi, Selangor,
1979, 1994
Seminar Wanita Memahami Islam,
Kuala Lumpur, 1978, 3298
Seminar Wanita tentang Tenaga
Kerdja Wanita Indonesia dalam
Pembangunan, Tjiloto,
Indonesia, 1971, 405
Seminar-Workshop on the Role of
FPA Clinics in Relation to
Community-Based Family
Planning Services, Manila,
1975, 969, 1468
Semler, Vicki Jane, 970
Sendut, Hamzah. See Hamzah
Sendut
Serie, Mustopa Husin, 2411
Sermsri, Santhat. See Santhat
Sermsri
Sese, Luz B., 606
Setati Surasto. See Surasto,
Setati
Setiadi, Bernadette N., 1136
Setteeton, Radom. See Radom
Setteeton
Setyawati, M.R., 2888
Setynegoro, Kusumanto, 2889

Sevilla, Consuelo G., 890
Sevilla, Judy, 3719
Shah, Wan Mahzom Ahmad. See
Mahzom Ahmad Shah, Wan
Shahabuddin, Syed Mohamed bin
Syed Hassan. See Muhammad
bin Syed Hassan Sahahbuddin,
Syed
Shahajaratuddur Sheikh Abdul
Halim, 3437, 3438, 3687
Shahani, Leticia Ramos, 334,
1805, 2042, 2043, 3083,
3497, 3756
Shahar Banun Jaafar, 2972
Shams, Ibnu. See Ibnu Shams
Shamsiah Abdullah, 277
Shamsuddin bin Abdul Rahman,
1284, 2517
Shamsuddin bin Othman, 2755
Shantakumar, G., 1217, 1266, 1549
Shapiro, Wanen, 2777
Shaplen, June H., 1700
Sharifah binti Hamid, 489
Sharifah Maria Malek, 490
Shariffudin, P.M., 2780
Sharipah binti Mohamed, 2973
Sharma, Prakash C., 15
Sharp, Ilsa, 651
Sheehan, J.J., 74
Shelford, R., 3757
Sheppard, Mubin, 2974, 2975
Sheridan, Lionel Astor, 2518
Shevasunt, Somphong. See
Somphong Shevasunt
Shiddieqy, T.M. Hasbi Ash, 2412
Shotwell, Monica, 2188
Showell, Shirlene, 582
Shreerangarajan, M., 1701
Shu, Chen Lin, 652
Shunk, Caroline Saxe (Merill), 75
Sia, Wee Teng, 2976
Siaco, E.E., 191
Sianu [psued.], 76
Sibulo, Emily A., 2614
Sicé, Eugène, 2812
Sidarto (Mrs.), 2890
Siddik Sudarsono. See Sudarsono,
Siddik
Sidek, Khadijah binti Mohamed.
See Khadijah binti Mohamed
Sidek

Index